COLLECTIVE WAGE DETERMINATION

PROBLEMS AND PRINCIPLES IN
BARGAINING, ARBITRATION, AND LEGISLATION

By

Z. CLARK DICKINSON

PROFESSOR OF ECONOMICS, UNIVERSITY OF MICHIGAN
AUTHOR OF "COMPENSATING INDUSTRIAL EFFORT"

THE RONALD PRESS COMPANY ⚲ NEW YORK

PREFACE

Any consideration of the remuneration of groups of workers, any constructive advice or formulation of policy or decision, must take into account numerous economic and social relationships which are part and parcel of the practical questions involved. These relationships and their bearings upon wage problems constitute the subject matter of this book.

The book is the culmination of a study of the subject which has extended over many years, and it is hoped that its contribution will be of lasting character. While many aspects of collective wages which happen to be of current popular interest are touched upon, the great issues involved are not new ones, and attempts to deal with them as novel phenomena without consideration of experience and history are, to say the least, unfortunate.

The obvious trend toward fewer and larger wage decisions tends to substitute representative group judgments (and powers) for the smaller-scale bargains of individual employers and employees which are assumed in the older economics of wages. Although most people approve of such fundamental objectives as more effective civil rights for labor, besides increasing and better-distributed real wages and leisure, the more thoughtful leaders of labor as well as of industry are frequently disturbed almost as much by fallacious arguments in their own ranks as by the distorted claims of opponents. One dangerous type of fallacy is undue generalization of a proposition which is quite valid—within proper limits. So long as "other things are equal," for instance, lowering of wage rates and prices may stimulate sales and employment; whereas under other conditions raising wage rates, shortening hours, and even certain "make-work" practices may be practicable means (for a time, anyhow) of increasing both employment and total national income. Everyone knows, too, that innumerable sorts of monopolistic practices enable insiders to benefit by sustained prices or wage rates or both; also that, if everyone seeks simultaneously to benefit by restrictive methods, all of us tend to become poorer. Even the seemingly equitable principle that prospering employers should share prosperity with their own workers—as shown in Chapter 9 and elsewhere herein—may become a barrier on the road toward fuller employment.

How can labor's rightful demands for greater job security and freedom-through-organization be met, with a minimum of cost inflation and anti-social restriction?

Keeping these objectives in mind, I have endeavored in the following pages to assist the user of the book in his effort to form a sound judgment on his particular case. Emphasis is placed upon principles and agencies which are of perennial, not transient, significance; though the final chapter discusses the acceleration of previous trends which is attributable to the second World War. The treatment is intended to be sufficiently realistic and concrete to be useful to leaders in labor circles and among employers who are realizing the need of perspective, of seeing their own problems as part of an immensely larger process, as well as to all thoughtful people with a public interest in the great field of labor. It will also, I hope, assist those interested in economic science, in the endless task of analyzing wage causation.

A great many persons and organizations have extended help toward preparation of the book. Among my outstanding obligations, mention should first be made of several grants of funds made by the Horace H. Rackham School of Graduate Studies of the University of Michigan. One of these grants enabled me to do more extensive field work in the United States and in Europe. For able digests of materials, preparation of drafts, and criticism of my own drafts, I am indebted to Gardner Ackley, Robert Rosa, Erich Schiff, and Philip Trezise. Capable services of several undergraduates were made available by the National Youth Administration.

As indicated by specific acknowledgments below, I have drawn especially upon publications of the National Industrial Conference Board, the U. S. Bureau of Labor Statistics, the Brookings Institution, and the International Labor Office. Their staffs, moreover, have responded generously to my numerous requests. My work has benefited particularly from criticism, commentaries, and other materials supplied by E. J. Riches, of the International Labor Office. Dr. R. P. Falkner read an earlier draft of about half the chapters, and contributed a great many valuable suggestions. I have secured advice on many points from various colleagues, notably Professors Margaret Elliott Tracy and William Haber. Finally, I have been assisted in innumerable ways by the University of Michigan's Bureau of Industrial Relations, whose Director, Professor John W. Riegel, has kindly criticized the whole script.

My earlier work, *Compensating Industrial Effort,* which deals particularly with incentives, also treats various other problems of work and pay. Though trade union activities receive some attention, the emphasis in that book is upon individual differences among personnel within the employing organization. In the present volume, social-economic problems connected with collective or large-scale wage handling are given primary consideration. Each of these approaches needs to be supplemented by the other; and these two books explore many of the avenues by which the objectives and methods of labor organizations and of public and private managements are being reconciled.

Z. C. DICKINSON

Ann Arbor, Michigan
September, 1941

CONTENTS

PART I

SURVEY OF THE FIELD

vii

PART IV

WAGE POLICIES AND PRACTICES IN PRIVATE COLLECTIVE BARGAINING

ILLUSTRATIONS

xviii

PART I

SURVEY OF THE FIELD

CHAPTER 1

THE GROUND TO BE COVERED

A majority of the civilized world's population above the most tender years work, or seek work, for hire—for wages, salaries, fees, and other rewards for personal services. The influences tending to raise or lower these hires of labor are of the greatest importance to all others, as well as to the employed people themselves.[1] These employees contend constantly for higher and more secure pay; employers strive to meet payrolls and to keep wage and salary costs within bounds; while citizens and students confusedly search for causes and cures of the poverty connected with such factors as low wages, unemployment, and the waste and sufferings incident to labor disputes.

It is easily possible, to be sure, to exaggerate the rôle played by wages in labor problems. The attractions and repellents of each job include many other elements beside its immediate wages—such as prospects for a career, the hours and other living conditions involved, the job's social standing, its intrinsic interest and ease, and the personal relations with fellow workers and bosses. Many of these elements enter, consciously or otherwise, into both individual and collective labor dealings and disputes, as do also such factors as the political and other ambitions and the pride and temper of leaders concerned. Nevertheless, we need not scratch very far beneath the surface of any labor problem to find some issues of material gain.

---

[1] The "gainful workers" (including the unemployed) constitute something like 40% of the total population of men, women, and children (housewives make up the largest class of adults not considered "gainfully employed"). Of these gainful workers in the United States, over 50% are wage earners, commonly employed at hourly or piece rates and at more or less manual work; and somewhat over 20% are salaried employees and officials. In highly industrialized nations like Great Britain, wage earners make up a larger fraction—perhaps 80%—of the gainfully occupied, chiefly because their classes of employing and self-employed farmers are very much smaller percentages than in America.

3

Spread of Collective Bargaining.—Granting the outstanding importance of wage determination, what is the significance of *collective* wage determination? In what ways is it bound up with other trends toward larger-scale arrangements in economic and social life? How and why has voluntary collective bargaining through trade unions developed, particularly in the United States? What other forces, if any, have tended to replace individual or retail wage bargains by collective and wholesale wage determination?

Like other large social trends, that toward collective wage setting is made up of innumerable contributory changes, and new strains are created at least as fast as old ones are eased. "Individual bargaining" concerning wages and other elements of the labor contract still holds sway where the employing units are small and where other conditions are unfavorable to development of group feeling and organization on the side of employed workers. Small farm and domestic labor supply examples.

As the employer's staff grows, however, the area for individual labor bargains tends to shrink; for instance, all workers must be in the shop approximately the same days and hours. An approach to uniform remuneration for each class of labor is also inevitable in the large establishment and within each district of each industry. Organization of labor unions pushes the collective elements further. Such organization is based largely on the claims that, by presenting a united front, workers can (1) combat discriminatory tactics among bosses and straw-bosses—such as job selling, nepotism and favoritism in work assignments, wages, layoffs, and discharges—and (2) raise the whole wage structure. Such unions often argue that they do not seek entirely to close the door to individual bargaining; that employers who make and abide by collective agreements, and thus pay union rates as minima, can and do pay as much higher wages as are mutually acceptable to superior workers. Although this latter policy and practice has hitherto been overshadowed (in America, at least) by others tending to produce uniformity of output and remuneration among all workers in unionized occupations, such overshadowing is by no means

essential to trade unionism which in numerous ways is outgrow-
ing its cruder forms of collectivism. Nevertheless, it is essential to the existence of unions, and thus to the long-run welfare of labor, that they should at times require some members
to sacrifice opportunities for higher earnings (if any)—for
example, by strike breaking, acting unreasonably as pace setters, or otherwise giving assistance to anti-union employers.

The total results of collective bargaining at its worst naturally compare very unfavorably with "individual bargaining"
at its best, even in the operations of large, more or less monopolistic, industries; and the average actual practices in both organized and unorganized plants leave a great deal to be desired.
In any case, however, the sphere of voluntary collective wage
determination has tended strongly to grow—despite numerous
temporary setbacks—for more than a century in all lands, and
the end of such growth is not yet in sight.

Other Sorts and Sources of Wage Collectivism.—The few
years which immediately followed the first World War were
thought by many people at that particular time to be the
threshold of still greater things in trade union and governmental control of economic life. Many disillusionments quickly
followed. Vast dislocations of employment and of incomes
were part of Europe's heritage from the war; while the
American boom of the 1920's led a great many observers to
think that here "the secret of high wages" had been found, and
that an important part of this secret was our industry's comparative freedom from trade union and legal regulation of
labor conditions. Our companies and plants, to be sure, were
continuing the trend toward larger units, and the company
union movement was swiftly encroaching on that of the trade
unions. Hence, American wages were not, in the Harding-to-
Hoover days, characterized by "individual bargaining" in a
literal sense, but rather by the one-sided collectivism of the
large employer and the employers' organization.

In many other ways, too, that era of "rugged individualism"
was really nursing a movement toward further governmental
and organized-capital collectivism. Unprecedentedly large pub-

lic expenditures, for example, were made through the Farm
Board and the Reconstruction Finance Corporation under the
Coolidge and Hoover administrations, which also saw a great
development of trade associations. In Britain, though trade
union membership tended to decline rather than advance, social
legislation, including minimum-wage boards, went forward.

Since 1929 the movement toward economic and social collectivism has been greatly accelerated throughout the world.
Several forces appear to be mainly responsible, of which the
catastrophic world-wide economic depression, reaching its low
point in 1932-33, is doubtless preeminent. But even if the
severity and duration of this depression had been less, it is
probable that Americans would have seen a revival of trade
unionism and labor legislation on the scale portended by the
decade 1910-20, in which the accelerating factor was the World
War. In many indirect ways we were also influenced by European socialism, notably through propaganda as to its economic
results (particularly on unemployment) in Soviet Russia and
in the apparently anti-socialist regime of Fascist Italy. Meanwhile, the fascist National Socialism of Hitler was preparing
much bigger things than any one realized.

Attention to such matters shows that the great development
of trade union power and social legislation under the Roosevelt
New Deal was part of a world-wide social movement; and that
1939 brought to a head the military programs of the Communist and Fascist collectivisms, reaction to which obliges other
nations to accept further collectivism for the sake of national
defense. Thus the outlook appears to be for considerable further extension of the influence of collective bargaining and legislation over wages before an opposite reaction occurs.

Aspects Studied in This Book.—What are the outstanding
varieties of collective wage determinations (or "adjustments"
or "settlements")? What aspects or phases are selected for
this study? As intimated above, organization has gone a great
way within each of the three parties to any collective wage
arrangement—trade unions on the employee side, large companies and trade associations on the employing side, and various

governmental agencies or public authorities representing consumer and other public interest. (Not infrequently, more than
one organization within one, or more, of these interests will
appear in, or attempt to influence, a particular wage proceeding.)

Another important trend which also spells increasing collectivism in wage affairs is the growing importance of governmental agencies as employers of labor. The wages of soldiers,
sailors, and other members of the armed forces are not so
directly relevant as the constantly growing rolls of civilian public employees. Part of this increase is due to newer types of
state-controlled economic activity, as in the Tennessee Valley
Authority and the state highway departments; furthermore,
the advancing complexity of social life, added to the normal
tendency of politicians to pad public payrolls, results also in
enlargement of the staffs of the older government departments
more than proportional to the growth in population.

A third source of collective wage procedures is seen in
regulation of private wages by public authority, as by laws providing for wage and hour controls and for investigation and
settlement of industrial disputes. State control over wages and
other labor conditions in "private" employment goes much
further in the totalitarian than in the capitalistic regimes, of
course; though in both cases there are many indirect as well
as direct political influences on the wages of workers not
actually employed by public agencies. Organized employees and
employers, moreover, as a matter of course seek to gain economic advantage through political activity as well as through
direct and private economic bargaining.

In those nations, to be sure, in which government has very
sweeping powers over industry and labor—either temporarily
during war, or on the permanent basis of the totalitarian states
—many other means, such as conscription and "social wages,"
are employed toward getting workers into suitable jobs, keeping
them effectively at work, and assisting their families. Such
developments tend to restrict the significance of bargaining over
wage rates. One question which we shall have to raise in the
pages which follow is, Does the progress of authoritarian labor

controls make the older wage methods and principles increasingly obsolescent?

Organization and Objectives of This Book.—Our attention will usually be focused, however, on contemporary American conditions. I have not tried to give many details of totalitarian methods of dealing with wages and other labor conditions, though these methods do form the theme of a major section of Chapter 18. More space is devoted herein to such usages in foreign democratic countries as seem useful by way of showing how various wage problems have been handled abroad, and with what apparent results. The emphasis in this book, moreover, is on private wages throughout—particularly as to how they are affected by both collective bargaining and the operations of governmental agencies. The other sort of wage collectivism mentioned above—in public employment of civilian labor—also supplies material for many illustrations and comments in the following pages.

The route we are to follow is mapped in some detail in the table of contents, and a shorter summary will be useful to conclude this chapter. The remainder of Part I continues an airplane reconnaissance—first, of the types of wage affairs with which we shall be concerned, then of American labor markets and their quotations or statistics. In Parts II and III we proceed to our major analytical problems. After a summary of modern economic theory of wages, most of the fundamental factors in wage problems are explored, such as living costs, production, profits and losses, prevailing wages—and, above all, unemployment. Unemployment is obviously the outstanding economic problem of our time; and throughout this volume we shall be dealing with such questions as these: How far (if at all) is unemployment caused by too high wages? How can it be reduced by wage policies in association with other methods?

Parts IV and V utilize these factor-materials for critical surveys of private and public wage-hour policies and controls. Here we take up (first) the features of union-management agreements and practices—including voluntary arbitration—which have most significance for wages. Then various influences of public policy are considered, such as: laws regulating wages and hours, directly or through public purchases; compulsory settlements of labor disputes; and public wage and salary scales. This Part closes with a chapter on economic effects of the chief types of public wage controls.

In our final chapter we discuss wage problems in wartimes, with an eye on post-war probabilities. Here the implications of our more elementary principles, factors, and other data are interwoven; and interactions of private and public wage policies are brought into somewhat sharper focus.

Use of Economic Research in Collective Wage Determination.—Does careful study of data and arguments pertaining to wages tend materially to affect the practical course of wage fixing? It is true, as we shall have to emphasize frequently later, that there is much psychological "rationalization" in wage arguments; and one must have somewhat confidential communication with many practical people to learn to recognize the more and the less important issues and forces in particular cases. All parties to wage problems, however, have been rapidly developing specialized personnel and investigations of late. More lawyers than ever participate in various ways; but, nowadays, their briefs, arguments, and awards are increasingly permeated by the work of economists, statisticians, and other researchers. The older forms of persuasion—including emotional oratory and journalism—are by no means displaced; and, of course, ponderous "scientific" exhibits can be used ignorantly and/or misleadingly. "Figures won't lie, but liars will figure." Nevertheless, resort to quantitative and other evidence which requires much digging and digesting constitutes an obvious trend in modern labor relations. In the following pages we shall study many of its manifestations.

CHAPTER 2

VARIETIES OF COLLECTIVE WAGE DETERMINATION

The hints contained in the first chapter will now be developed so that the reader will be clearer as to the senses in which this author uses somewhat technical terms, and so that some important matters of general background are in no danger of being overlooked or underestimated. The first section, A, of the present chapter will seek to clear up some common ambiguities of our many-sided subject "wages," and will outline somewhat further the principal types of comprehensive action thereon. Section B will call attention to some further features of voluntary collective bargaining and arbitration; and section C will sketch outlines of public wage controls. Finally, in section D, we shall reflect on these questions: How far do wholesale wage fixers wear their hearts on their sleeves? What considerations and forces can we read between the lines of their documents and other utterances for mass consumption?

A. Wage Terms and Their Meaning

How Wages Are Related to Salaries.—The first ambiguity which needs clarification is the term "wages" itself. When we use this word (as well as derived expressions like "wage earners") literally, and without qualification, we should use it as in business, statistical, and legal parlance—meaning the lower and most numerous payments by employers to hired workers, most of whom do manual work and are paid hourly, piece, or bonus rates, and are subject to layoffs on short notice—and now usually receive higher rates of pay for overtime. We shall also use "salaries" in the practical sense of the higher rates of payment to hired workers, most of whom do "white-collar" or non-manual work of some sort (some of it supervisory), and receive longer notice of layoff or discharge than do wage earners. In many cases such longer notice, and other prerogatives of salaried people (such as more pleasant working conditions, holidays or vacations and odd times off without loss of pay) are associated with only nominal extra pay, if any, for occasional overtime work, outside the normal work day.[1] Usage on these matters, however, is not uniform among employers. The remunerations of certain types of assistant foremen, salespeople, and office workers, for instance, are called wages (usually hourly or piece calculations) by some managements, but designated salaries (weekly or monthly basis) by others. Thus, wages shade into salaries; and it is rather common to refer to the earnings of shop, office, and sales girls as wages, even when they are calculated on a weekly basis.

The foregoing observations are trite enough; but they are necessary here because economic writings on "wage" matters bristle with other usages of this basic term. Adam Smith, for instance, pointed out:

Apothecaries' profit is become a bye-word, denoting something uncommonly extravagant. This great apparent profit, however, is frequently no more than the reasonable wages of labour. The skill of an apothecary is a much nicer and more delicate matter than that of any artificer whatever; and the trust which is reposed in him is of much greater importance. . . . But the whole drugs which the best employed apothecary, in a large market town, will sell in a year, may not perhaps cost him above thirty or forty pounds. Though he should sell them, therefore, for three or four hundred, or at a thousand per cent profit, this may frequently be no more than the reasonable wages of his labour charged, in the only way in which he can charge them, upon the price of his drugs. The greater part of the apparent profit is real wages disguised in the garb of profit.[2]

This sort of reasoning (valid and important, in such a context) has led most economists to define wages, for purposes of their theories, as any and all incomes derived from personal services,

---

[1] The U. S. Fair Labor Standards (Wages and Hours) Act now requires 50% penalty overtime rates of pay for many in the lower-salaried ranks, as well as for wage earners.

[2] *Wealth of Nations,* Bk. I, Ch. 10.

apart from saving and risk-bearing; considering the economic or implicit "wage" of the working proprietor or part-proprietor to be the wage or salary which he could obtain by similar work in the service of another entrepeneur. Economists have also tended to hold the distinction between wages and salaries to be unimportant for general economic analysis.

For realistic and thoroughgoing treatments, however, these distinctions are very significant in several ways—the greater security and reputability, for instance, of salaries by contrast with wages; and the greater stability of salaries by contrast with work-plus-investment-earned profits. Hence, in the present volume the usage of "wages" and "salaries" is restricted to remunerations of *hired* persons, for personal services only. In other contexts, "implicit wage" or "implicit salary" are legitimate terms, with reference to profits or bonuses which are reasonably attributable to "investment of work" rather than mere investment of capital.[3] And, when we consider arguments about "labor's share" of the total product of all industry, we shall not overlook the labors and worries of the millions of active proprietors, including farmers and shopkeepers—employers and self-employed.

Wages as Labor Incomes.—Another cluster of ambiguities, of growing importance with reference to the organized industrial workers whose affairs loom so large in our succeeding chapters, is the complex of relations between wages and other elements of real income of wage earners. These other real-income elements may include not merely (a) garden produce and the use of the owner-occupier's home, (b) still other returns from the worker's labor and property (apart from his wage job, and the "welfare" services provided by his employer),

---

[3] At one point, H. J. Davenport (*Economics of Enterprise*, pp. 66, 67) formally defined wages as "the share of hired labor," but otherwise his discussions of wage theory were in the classic tradition. The distinctions emphasized in my text above and immediately below are well handled in J. Marschak's article on wage theory, in the *Encyclopedia of the Social Sciences*, Vol. 15 (1934). For a brief statistical analysis of numbers of wage earners, in relation to salaried persons and proprietors in the chief industrial groups, see Spurgeon Bell, *Productivity, Wages, and National Income*, Ch. 1 (Washington: Brookings, 1940).

but also (c) the value of whatever uses his household makes of public and philanthropic agencies, over and above what the household pays for these services in fees or taxes. Schools, parks, medical centers, food and other supplies at schools— are further illustrations of what has been called "the social wage." Labor has tended progressively to raise its total real income, in part by using political power to increase social services out of taxation.

Still other sorts of labor incomes are provided by the family allowance schemes which will be noticed later—deductions from wages properly so called, to form pools from which payments are made to the workers' families in accordance with the de· pendents in each.

In view of such considerations, it seems that the terms "wages" and "salaries" should, for purposes of most of the discussions in this book, apply to whatever funds are legally so called—subject though they may be to compulsory withholdings for social insurance, income taxes, trade union dues, or family allowances; and in some contexts we must take cognizance of wages in kind and still other elements in wage earners' real incomes.

Wages as Labor Costs.—In any broad economic study of wages we must alternate between two points of view—the wage earner's income, and the employer's labor cost of production. In the foregoing paragraph we have emphasized wages as labor incomes; in this one we are to underline wages as employer's costs.[4]

Fluctuation in labor costs is a function of two principal variables, the wage and the total personal service for which the wage is paid. In piece or commission methods of wage payment, the *direct* (or "variable") labor cost is relatively constant per piece, affected but little or not at all by rising or falling

---

[4] Both topics are treated further in later chapters, e.g., Ch. 4. Most of the matters discussed in the present chapter, especially in sections B and C, are further developed in greater detail later. These more detailed examinations can readily be located through the table of contents and the index. In this chapter we are viewing the forest, deferring closer inspection of the trees until later.

hourly *earnings*.[5] When the wage is paid on the basis merely of time worked, on the other hand, much more variation is likely to occur in direct labor cost. If hourly rates of pay of "day workers" are materially changed, the presumption is that the cost of such work per unit of production changes in the same direction—though in the same degree only if the average efficiency of this labor remains unchanged.

The "direct labor" above referred to is that whose quantity varies in fairly close relation to output. The total cost of *indirect labor,* on the other hand, like sweepers and other maintenance workers, varies less closely with the rate of production;[6] hence, as a plant approaches its optimum or most efficient rate of operation, output per (direct plus indirect) man-hour normally rises, and total labor cost per unit of product declines in almost equal measure. The number of physical units of output per wage-earner man-hour is often taken as an index of "productivity of labor"; but this usage is liable to be misleading. The production cost in man-hours is affected by factors like mechanization, changes in equipment, methods, styles and quality of materials and products, as well as by the skill and exertions of labor. All such matters, as well as the respective weightings for skill and experience in the various occupations in the labor forces, must be allowed for before we can confidently correlate average hourly wage rates and earnings of labor with labor efficiency and labor cost.

Agencies and Types of Action in Collective Wage Determinations.—In Chapter 1 we indicated some chief varieties of collective or large-scale wage fixing. It will be convenient now to elaborate somewhat upon this theme, in order that the common factors and the peculiarities of each type may be more adequately realized.

---

[5] The employer, however, obtains savings of *overhead* costs by the work of high-efficiency employees, as was emphasized by F. W. Taylor. The high earnings by these workers, therefore, tend toward high profit for the entrepreneur.

[6] Overhead costs include indirect wages, as well as salaries; and the total overhead of any firm includes its literally "fixed charges," such as rent, interest, minimum depreciation and obsolescence, as well as many of its taxes.

VARIABLES AND PATTERNS IN COLLECTIVE WAGE DETERMINATIONS

A. VOLUNTARY
    1. According to (immediate) source of wage funds
        a. Private "profit-making" business
        b. Private non-profit employers, e.g., hospitals, colleges
        c. Governmental agencies as employers

    2. According to relation to labor disputes
        a. Actions
            1. Bargaining, leading to collective or labor agreement
            2. Interpretation and enforcement of agreement
        b. Agencies—notably voluntary arbitration

B. STATE INTERVENTION IN WAGE CONTRACTS
    1. Explicit or direct normal regulation of private wages by a state agency
        a. Legal minimum wages, in relation to hours and other conditions
        b. "Extension of collective agreements"—i.e., State enforcement of trade union rates on both organized and unorganized sections of industry

    2. Regulation incidental to maintaining industrial peace
        a. Authoritative interpretation and enforcement of voluntarily made wage agreements
        b. Compulsory publicity, delay, mediation, arbitration, other adjudications—of other disputes

    3. Indirect control of private wages by State, e.g., via "prevailing" or "fair" wage clauses in public contracts and in import and export regulations

It will be observed that, although the primary analysis in this outline distinguishes between private or voluntary and governmental or compulsory agencies, even this line is actually somewhat blurred and shifting. The State as an employer and wage payer, for example, shades into the State as a regulator of payrolls other than its own. The government units, and their owned or controlled agencies, are voluntary employers, yet their labor affairs are not usually subject to the same types of influence by trade unions and labor boards as are the labor affairs of private employers. As was intimated above, in the present volume rather scanty attention is given to wage fixing by public agencies with reference to their own employees—which, indeed, is not fully collective wage determination unless the public employees are voluntarily represented through their own unions. Although governmental and other non-profit employers signify collective action on the employing side of the wage bargain, in many cases their employees are neither organized nor subject to any adequate protection from arbitrary action by their non-profit employers. In Chapter 19 and elsewhere, however, we shall deal briefly with the topic suggested under B-3 of the preceding outline—indirect influence, by State activities, upon private wages.

Another illustration of the point that voluntary action and State compulsion overlap is afforded by comparison of parts A-2 and B-2 of the outline just given. Arbitration in wage affairs may be, and in America usually is, entirely voluntary; whereas the Arbitration Courts of New Zealand and Australia are armed with sovereign compulsion. In our own country, however, the parties to any sizable labor dispute soon receive attentions from public officials, perhaps acting under one or more of the many Federal and state statutes providing for conciliation, mediation, investigation of such interruptions of work, or perhaps utilizing for this purpose any of the numerous other powers of public officials. As yet, we have almost no machinery in the United States for actual compulsory final settlement of any wage or other labor dispute; but in the course of the conciliation and compulsory delay of stoppage of operations required by law in many cases, government officers have opportunities to exercise many indirect governmental powers and pressures to induce a settlement of the dispute.

B. Voluntary Collective Wage Determinations

The two principal families of collective wage arrangements which are significant for the United States may now be delineated with another degree of detail: first (in this section) the family of voluntary dealings (including arbitration), then (in the next section) the main varieties of public intervention.

Collective Bargaining.—This is the familiar designation of dickerings between representatives of a group of workers and the spokesmen for their employer or employers. In conventional usage it is not material whether there is group concert on the employing side. In practice there usually is, if only in the sense that a corporate legal entity, like the United States Steel Corporation or General Motors or the TVA, is a device whereby a number of owners delegate their employing powers to the active managements. But even when the manager is also the sole owner of the employing enterprise, his dealings with organized labor are called collective bargaining. Not uncommonly, of course, the unit on the employing side is an association, as in various branches of the building, railway, mining, printing, and clothing industries. There are many variations in the types of organization involved, as well as in the territorial units; moreover, with the passage of time, there are many shifts of alliances on both sides.[7]

Collective bargaining tends to result in a written *collective agreement or "contract,"* running for a specified term or until due notice is given by either party that it demands new terms. The first written agreement which it obtains from an employer gives a union enhanced security and prestige; and so hostile employers have demurred at signing such agreements. The National Labor Relations Board has interpreted the "Wagner Act" to require collective agreements to be reduced to writing,

---

[7] Labor unions, for example, may be classified, first, as (a) "company" or "independent" unions, membership in each being restricted to workers in the service of a single employer, and (b) "outside," or intercompany unions, for which the conventional generic title is simply "trade unions." (Since company unions are now of little importance in wage bargaining, my discussions of "unions" hereafter, unless otherwise specified, will refer to "outside" "trade union" wage negotiations.) These are of various sorts, notably craft and industrial. The trade or craft body in the narrower sense, like the Typographical Union in printing, generally was originally a single skilled craft; but in many cases such unions have combined with allied crafts, and/or admitted less skilled workers, and so have become in effect semi-industrial or industrial unions. An industrial union in the fullest sense attempts to organize and represent all workers, whatever their occupations (at least all *manual* wage earners), in its "industry." Few industries, if any, however, can be rigorously defined or demarcated; and most, if not all, industrial unions in practice do not press their jurisdictional claims over some occupations, such as office workers.

and this interpretation has been upheld by the Supreme Court. A well-established union, however, may be content with only verbal understandings.

These labor agreements are legally similar to other business contracts in important respects; and not infrequently one party or the other sues in the courts for alleged breach, asking for compulsory specific performance or pecuniary damages or both. There are important peculiarities of the collective labor contract, however—e.g., involuntary servitude is legally permissible only as punishment for crime, unions and members may have insignificant property resources, and *agents provocateurs* and racketeers sometimes usurp union offices. Such factors have hitherto restrained modern governments from attempting more than exceptionally to enforce collective labor agreements in exactly the same manner as other business contracts. Dissatisfaction over alleged breach of agreement is an important source of labor disputes, which is mitigated by both private and governmental machinery for adjudication or conciliation and arbitration.

Conciliation, Mediation, Arbitration.—These constitute the chief members of a family of arrangements for comprehensive determination of wages and other conditions of employment. The terms imply legally private and voluntary action by the employers and workers, as opposed to authoritative determination of wages and other labor conditions by public agencies; and so logically these activities are phases of collective *bargaining*. Mediation and arbitration often refer, of course, to actual or imminent stoppage of work, in which case the workmen's organization may be hastily improvised and perhaps independent of preexisting trade unions. In American labor disputes, moreover, the leading issue has often been a demand for union recognition and systematic collective bargaining.

As collective bargaining matures, however, its agreements tend to include procedures intended to settle the differences of opinion which inevitably will arise on questions of fact and of interpretation of such agreements. A classical arrangement for this purpose is the joint board of conciliation (or of conciliation and arbitration), composed of representatives of managements and of workers. This device—long and successfully used in many British industries, as well as in some American industries (e.g., coal mining)—provides means for settling individual disputes by committees of employer and employee representatives within the whole industry. Nowadays, however, to Americans "conciliation" and "mediation" commonly mean intercession by outsiders, as from the conciliation branch of the U. S. Department of Labor or from the National Mediation Board (the latter's field has heretofore been railway labor disputes).

A joint and bi-partisan conciliation or grievance board, of course, may become deadlocked; then what happens? Perhaps a strike; but this possibility is apt to be foreseen, and the agreement may provide for arbitration or addition to the board of a neutral referee or umpire, with reference to any altercation which cannot be settled through the joint conciliation processes. Such arbitration naturally implies a chairman who must bear the brunt and who, to be acceptable to both sides, must be in an important sense impartial.

Such impartiality is apt to be accompanied by ignorance of the circumstances and problems of the industry, and so a number of collective agreements have provided for "impartial chairmen" or umpires who are steadily on call to settle disputes arising under these agreements.[8] Most of the organized American clothing and needle trades (including hosiery manufacture) have used this expedient, apparently beginning in the New York and Chicago garment trades about 1911.

Although voluntary labor arbitration is fundamentally a form or implement of collective bargaining, it is of less importance than appears on the surface for discussions of the fundamentals of collective wage determination. Arbitrating personnel, whether employed continuously or engaged independently for each occasion, is usually a really independent factor only for the comparatively minor disputes which arise during the

---

[8] Such chairmen, like other voluntary arbitrators, are paid jointly by employers and union.

lifetime of an agreement. Determination whether the time has come for a general change in wages of the plant or industry, and if so, how much change in which direction, is a task which an arbitrator can determine only within rather narrow limits. More than a few controversies, to be sure, over wage levels have been carried through peaceably by means of arbitration, but in general only to the extent that the arbitrator manages to negotiate what amounts to a new voluntary agreement between the employers and workers. The arbitrator takes the onus of dissatisfaction on both sides; but before he makes his decision, he has reason to believe that the leaders of each side will recognize it as a workable solution. Arbitration, therefore —especially of the impartial chairman sort—is a most valuable means of making a collective agreement work. It is not otherwise an important factor in concluding new agreements or otherwise changing significantly the wage structure.

C. Public Intervention in Labor Incomes

Arbitration is often voluntarily accepted by the two parties as a means of averting or concluding industrial warfare. Formally, and to a large extent practically, voluntary arbitration supplements, not only collective bargaining but also authoritative use of the State's power for the avowed and direct purpose of preventing or settling strikes and lockouts. Both become extremely important in wartimes. We may disregard, for the present, sporadic assertions of the latter power (as in the Adamson Act, one of whose effects was to raise average earnings of train service employees), and concentrate attention on the more continuous and systematic methods of authoritative regulation of wage bargains. Attempting to see the woods in spite of the trees, we may discern outlines of two principal types, and a few sub-types within each. The two may be viewed as: (1) basic minimum-wage laws and (2) other actions by public authorities which undertake to influence wages both at and above such minimum levels. The family allowance schemes of various foreign nations blur somewhat the logic of the foregoing classification, however, and suggest an alternative scheme which is more comprehensive, viz.: public control of wages, (1) based directly on the income needs of workers and their dependents (some legal basic minimum wages, and family allowances), and (2) incidental to the State's efforts to improve labor conditions in other ways (particularly as one means of maintaining industrial peace). For brevity we may refer to the first as public control of the basic wage of unskilled workers, the latter as public regulation of wages in general, including those of skilled workers.

The latter regulation becomes important in any scheme for making strikes and lockouts illegal. If the State is to prevent or settle labor disputes, it must incidentally determine the wages of the skilled workers who are (or have been) most likely to go out on strike. Partly on this account the trade unions of Britain and America, long dominated by skilled craftsmen, have opposed compulsory settlement of strikes; while in recent years they have supported legal minimum-wage boards for occupations and industries in which (a) wages are exceptionally low, and/or (b) there is little, if any, union organization. Anglo-American legal traditions, moreover, have until lately given our governments much more latitude in regulating labor conditions of all sorts with reference to women and young people than on behalf of adult men. Since specifications (a) and (b) above in this paragraph point strongly to industries largely manned, so to speak, by women, the net result has been that Anglo-American legal minimum wages in the past have been applied much more widely to women and young persons than to men. This tide is now turning, however, in both countries.

Family Allowances.—As was intimated above, one form in which the impulse to guarantee "living wages" (i.e., family incomes) to all has manifested itself in numerous countries since (and to some extent before) the war of 1914-18 is family allowances. In effect, schemes of this sort amount to pooling part of the employers' total wage payments to provide funds for distribution in proportion to dependents of the employees. Plans of this sort have been urged by some students of child welfare in place of the older types of minimum wages which theoretically were based upon some "standard" size of family, such as husband, wife, and three dependent children. The latter principle, it was said, attempted to "overpay" workers with fewer than the standard set of dependents, and to "underpay" those with big families. A family allowance system, it should be observed, tends to affect not merely the employed workers of lowest skill, as do the ordinary minimum-wage regulations, but also more highly paid workers, provided they have many dependents. These allowances, moreover, are not literally *wages* from the standpoint of the recipients; the movement is rather a form of social security or prevention of destitution, financed largely by payroll taxes or voluntary contributions from wages, or both.[9]

Authoritative Determination of Wages Incidental to Maintenance of Industrial Peace.—From public controls designed especially to increase the "wage" incomes of the more necessitous workers and dependents of workers, let us turn to other types of wage regulation by public authorities. As a matter of course, all wages, as well as other incomes, are objects of conscious political policy in totalitarian States. In other

---

[9] New Zealand's and New South Wales's "family endowment" schemes, however, are financed in part, at least, by other forms of taxation, as would be the one proposed by J. M. Keynes, in his *How to Pay for the War*.

In the Soviet Union, where one might expect *a priori* that the family-allowance principle would be favorably received, actually it has been rebuffed. At various times individuals with special zeal for reaching the "to each according to his needs" goal have promoted voluntary pooling of wages; but they have been sharply reprimanded as "counter-revolutionists" by Stalin. The explanation of this anomaly appears to be simple. In the first place, the dominant Soviet policy, since the first few years of "War Communism," has been to maintain rather widely differentiated earnings as incentive to effort and efficiency of labor—"to each according to his contribution," until, at some hoped-for future time, "to each according to his need" becomes practicable. Secondly, the Soviet system of social services (e.g., care and maintenance in ill health, old age pensions, and free education and child welfare) theoretically prevents destitution. This system, since 1930, has not included unemployment benefits. Jobs have apparently been available for nearly all able to work (except political offenders); yet this lack of unemployment benefits (which in some other countries are payable when no "*suitable*" employment" is to be had) may perhaps be interpreted as part of the incentive toward effort and political reliability of the worker, in Russia.

nations, regulation of above-minimum wages has usually been incidental to the main objective of minimizing strikes and lockouts. Other strands and patterns in political influences on wages must, however, be recognized at various points of our discussion, notably: (a) "bumping-up"—the automatic tendency of increased minimum rates to exert pressure upward on all other wages in the industry; and (b) the tendency of labor movements, like employers' and other "pressure groups," to use political action to reinforce their economic power. The main phases of the latter trend, in turn, are: (1) "extension of collective agreements" (i.e., enforcement by the State of collective labor bargains on all employers and employees, whether voluntary parties to such bargains or not); and (2) requirement of "prevailing wages" in public contracts and in work-relief payments.

An important tendency became manifest in New Zealand and Australia, in the 1890's, toward public intervention in wage bargains as a means toward preventing and settling strikes and lockouts. These precedents are of special importance for other English-speaking peoples, because of common language and democratic traditions. Elsewhere, too, there has been a development of arbitration, in commercial as well as labor affairs—the essence of which is substitution of voluntary settlements for resort to adjudication by State authority. Here is another reminder that collective labor agreements have many special characteristics, yet are really business contracts. The resort by various governments to "compulsory arbitration" in some types of labor warfare appears to be based, in part, on these two considerations (in addition to the estimates of various lobbyists as to how such legislation can be manipulated in the interests desired by their principals): (1) one side or both may persist in refusal to arbitrate; and so, in attempting to reduce such strife, the legislature may set up agencies not merely of conciliation, but also of adjudication, armed with more or less sovereign powers; and (2) even after agreeing to arbitrate, one party or both may flout the award, and resort to strike, lockout, or boycott tactics. Hence, compulsory arbitration means compulsion to refrain from such economic warfare, whether or not a voluntary labor agreement is alleged to be violated. A more modest program is that exemplified by the Swedish Labor Court, which outlaws industrial stoppages in defiance of collective agreements, but does not make illegal strikes incident to the making of new agreements.

The Australasian Dominions (New Zealand, first) also supply prominent examples of "extension of collective agreements," i.e., enforcement of such agreements, when approved by an arbitration court or other competent authority, by the State on the whole industry concerned, both the organized and unorganized portions. Similar tendencies have appeared in various other countries, and in the labor provisions of our own NRA. Such action by public authority to make the terms of collective agreements binding on non-signatories in their respective industries differs only in a slight degree from compulsory arbitration; public officials in each case must shoulder much responsibility toward capital, labor, and consumers for the equity and effect on public interests of the terms thus set down and widely enforced. And, obviously, the employers and trade unionists who work out such voluntary agreements play for higher stakes than in ordinary collective bargaining, since, if the public agency will accept their terms, they will not then have to face competition from unorganized sections of their own industry, giving less favorable conditions to labor.

Another type of authoritative wage fixing was provided by the short-lived Kansas Court of Industrial Relations, which virtually took cognizance of labor organizations only when they defied its orders. A very small group of interested persons could apply for a fair and compulsory wage determination within any of the four industries (fuel, clothing, food, transport) thus subjected to regulation; and all strikes and lockouts in these industries were made illegal.

D. What Lies Behind Wage Disputes

Factors Influencing Labor Incomes.—One more part of our general background, also sketched very broadly in Chapter 1, calls for some elaboration before we shift our focus to particu-

lars in the "foreground." In the present section let us consider
some circumstances which tend spontaneously and automatically
—perhaps unconsciously—to influence wage rates by supplementing the latter to make up the "net advantage," from the
worker's point of view, of a given job; and in the sections
which follow, let us inquire into the relative importance and
measurability of various factors which are consciously recognized in wage proceedings.

Any actual bargain or award on wages, in which trade
unions or arbitrators have a hand, is apt to include specifications of several, if not numerous, other controversial matters
of labor relations—notably hours and working conditions; pay
for overtime; methods and eligibility in hiring, laying off, dismissal; union recognition, closed shop, "check-off"; and working rules. In railway labor disputes, for example, the rules and
customs as to seniority rights have long been vital issues; the
men would fight not merely for as much immediate employment as was available, at the best wages to be obtained, but
also for maintenance and extension of their long-standing
structure of seniority ranking, which has determined many
important matters such as order of layoff, choice of runs, and
pension expectations.

Any condition of employment which the workers want or
oppose may become a matter for bargain and sale, in that the
wage rate finally, and to some extent, reflects the concessions
which are made by each side on these other matters. Attempts
to keep these issues wholly distinct are apt to lead to confusions
and fallacies.

In a certain arbitration of wages in a printing trade, for
instance, about 1921, the closed-shop employers argued that
they were handicapped by a previous agreement granting a 44-
hour week, because their "open-shop" competitors were operating under a 48-hour week. The arbitrator refused to consider
this argument, on the ground that the employers had voluntarily
granted the 44-hour week, and that it was not germane to the
current wage controversy. Arbitrators must, indeed, keep the
arguments within manageable bounds, but this particular exclu-
sion is open to question. No change of hours was at issue, to

be sure; yet surely the comparative labor costs of the union and non-union shops was an important matter for the wage fixing; and, since wages in both cases were expressed in weekly terms, the respective weekly hours needed to be taken into account.[10]

We might indefinitely pursue the search for factors which contribute to wage determination, and notice many considerations recognized by all parties as relevant to wages, as well as others which have gained less general recognition. Industrial scientists, for instance, are constantly discovering improved methods of illumination, ventilation, and other means of reducing fatigue and increasing comfort; personnel managers are finding means of making work more congenial to the worker; these innumerable circumstances affect output per man and in the long run tend to make higher real wages possible, though few wage earners are conscious of such causation. Economists, too, continuously explore causes impinging on wages, from directions like interest rates and capital and price movements. In the following discussion we shall doubtless slight some factors which the reader may consider important, but at least the effort will be made to present wages as parts of a complex and interdependent and unstable economic equilibrium—not as isolated phenomena.

Ostensible and Real Aims, Achievements.—The foregoing remarks about factors and issues in wage determination, and the great varieties in phraseology and patterns of the arguments offered us, call also for a word of caution on the need of trying to select and/or infer, from among all the claims which are put forward openly by each side and from other evidence, the issues which the various parties really consider to be fundamental. This sort of discrimination should be attempted, not merely with reference to the tendency of labor bargainers, like other bargainers, to ask more at first than they expect finally to get —in order to have a margin for trading and to allow room for a possible arbitrator to "split the difference." It is equally important, though extremely difficult, to perceive the senses in

---

[10] See *Mo. Lab. Rev.*, May 1922, p. 125 (Chicago press feeders' case).

which the initiated leaders of all sorts (in unions and in other groups, as of employers, journalists, politicians) believe and interpret the simple slogans which they use in their addresses to their respective publics. (The briefs and press releases and speeches by representatives of the parties, as well as the language of awards or decisions of arbitrators and other tribunals, are almost necessarily "for public consumption.")

Leaders of groups, the members of which are not highly selected as to education and intelligence, inevitably must make free use of "words of one syllable" and rather simple arguments with most of their constituents, even when communicating privately. And since in their public utterances they are usually attempting to win such support as they can among the rank and file of opposing as well as more sympathetic groups, all such leaders tend to speak considerably in what the "non-party intellectual" is apt to consider shallow platitudes and sophistries. It is a grave error, however, to suppose that most of these practical leaders endeavor *merely* to tell their constituents what the latter want to hear. Devotion to principle is probably as common—indeed, much more common—among labor and business and political chieftains, than among the general population from which they are drawn. But, having determined what strategy and tactics he thinks desirable and feasible for his group, the leader spontaneously and in good faith clothes his policies in euphemisms and in the most plausible *simple* formulations. Conscious deception, even of one's opponents, is probably exceptional; at any rate, wishful thinking in all quarters is, to me, a more plausible hypothesis for the majority of our social disagreements.

A few illustrations of these propositions, with reference to wage controversies, will suffice for the present. We ought not to be surprised that the wage earner's advocates emphasize cost of living as a wage factor, more or less according as it suits their case; nor should we conclude, from this circumstance alone, that they are irresponsible opportunists. In the first place, such a spokesman's position is usually recognized to be somewhat similar to that of any lawyer advocate, so that all realistic people expect him to stress the stronger, not the weaker, features of his principal's case. In the second place, nearly every wage earner and salaried person believes, in some sense and within limits, that his employer should pay a living wage or go out of business; also that this employer should strain himself to the end that the hireling's real wage should tend gradually to advance, and only exceptionally to recede.

Favorite employer arguments, too, are perhaps equally vulnerable, though they too are usually valid within limits. Nearly always the employer's advocate can cite an impressive array of lower wages among his competitors, if only those in foreign lands; and he can argue with conviction that his own section of industry needs relief in labor costs in order to survive competition of the low-wage payers. Penetrating below this surface, we may attempt to ascertain not merely whether the statistical evidence offered is reliable as to samples of occupations and earnings, but whether the higher-wage payers get their money's worth in higher skill, effort, and efficiency, or are compensated by selling at higher prices. Sometimes, when the issue is nominally one of wage rates, the men may gain their point, say in resisting a proposal for reduction; yet the settlement may contain a quiet understanding which gives the employers assurance that their net labor costs will be reduced, by change in "extra" wage costs and/or in the numerous varieties of working rules and practices.[11]

---

11 In a recent arbitration of the employers' demand for a wage cut, the chief union officials were privately convinced beforehand that the economic position of that branch of their industry demanded some reduction in wages as well as in other costs. Through intermediaries a considerable measure of agreement was reached with the employers that such relief could be afforded by the mode indicated in my text above—mainly by reduction in some special wage charges rather than by cutting the normal standard rates. To this extent, therefore, the arbitration proceedings were formalities, enabling the leaders of the parties to avoid suspicions that they had "sold out" their constituencies. The neutral arbitrator well understood the position when he accepted; he knew that he would be the most unpopular individual with the rank and file of both sides after the decision; and his decision in the main followed the informal understanding reached before arbitration.

When this decision was handed down, the union officers adopted and published, to the membership, a resolution strongly condemning the arbitration award (which doubtless was somewhat more unfavorable to the workers than they had expected)—but insisting that the union should maintain its good reputation of abiding by its agreements, one of which had been to accept the result of this arbitration.

As a final illustration, let us notice a family of arguments which purport to apply to a specific industry or establishment some broad social tendency or doctrine. Indexes of production and of distribution of national income have been frequently invoked in wage disputes, but in recent years the favorite of this class has been "maintenance of labor purchasing power." Obviously, these references to broad social problems of wage causation are usually nominal and superficial issues, intended mainly for popular consumption. Though they make such arguments in good faith, none of the labor and industrial leaders is likely to attempt seriously to show just *how much* the wages immediately in question are affected by such large sociological factors.

When we are discussing wages with reference to political and social policies, on the other hand, in our capacities as social scientists, politicians, journalists, writers to editors, or speakers to audiences of one or more, then issues like the division of national income among social classes and wages as purchasing power become real and vital. On this larger stage we must simplify matters even more than on the smaller ones of particular wage disputes, in order to discuss them at all; and all of us then become (in some degree) beggars riding bravely on wish-horses in a joust of slogans. In attempting to assess the quality of any "politician's" leadership, then, we should beware of contenting ourselves with mere cross-examination of his slogans and speeches regardless of their contexts; his quality is much more adequately reflected by the total import of what he gets his following to do. *And whenever a leader in a group normally opposed to our own gets to talking and acting in ways which we can almost wholly approve, the probability is very strong that he will soon be repudiated by his own constituency.*

E. Summary

We are concerned in this book with wages—primarily in the ordinary sense of remuneration of "hourly-rated," usually manual, employees, and secondarily with that of lower-salaried, mostly routine, workers. We study these wages and salaries from the two standpoints of labor incomes and labor costs. The collective wage determination processes which further delimit our field are mainly of two sorts: (a) voluntary collective bargaining, including arbitration; and (b) regulation of private wages by public authorities—notably by way of legal minimum wages and governmental machinery of industrial peace. It is helpful, toward discriminating nominal from real issues in wage controversies, to recall that every leader must address simplified arguments to his own rank and file, and often to those behind other leaders as well; also that what factors are practically germane to any wage controversy will depend in part on how many firms and workers are likely to be affected by the settlement.

CHAPTER 3

THE LABOR MARKET AND THE WAGE-HOUR STRUCTURE

The present chapter develops further the vocabulary of present-day discussion of wage-hour problems, and adds certain needed particulars to the background sketched in Chapters 1 and 2. Four main stages may be herein discerned: in section A, an outline of significant features of labor markets, as compared with other markets of theory and practice; in section B, some highlights of existing wage statistics; in section C, a sketch of the American wage-hour structure, with special attention to annual earnings and wage-hour differentials; and in section D, a brief survey of characteristics of the agencies now collecting wage data and of the prospects for more and better wage information.

A. Labor Markets and Others

The prices of various types of work are established in more or less interconnected labor markets. The reader who holds, with the authors of the Clayton Act, that "the labor of human beings is not a commodity or article of commerce" may be quickly assured that his point of view is not denied, but rather emphasized in the present volume as a whole. The hiring of labor, however, has some important points in common with the buying of commodities and the hiring of land and capital; and so an economic analysis of wages must utilize, so far as applicable, the economic concepts of market and exchange value.[1]

Among the *contrasts* between labor markets and others which might be cited, two will serve our present purposes—

---

[1] See, e.g., Don D. Lescohier, *The Labor Market* (1919); Sumner H. Slichter, "Orderly Marketing of Labor," *New Republic,* Vol. 63, pp. 342-344 (Aug. 6, 1930).

those connected with "non-economic" behavior, and those implied by the "perfect markets" of economic theory.

The first of these was cited by John Stuart Mill when he remarked that "wages, like other things, may be regulated either by competition or by custom."[2] "Custom" in this context includes all the various motivations which cause many "wages" to differ from what the services are worth on a purely commercial basis.

The other contrast involves reference to the abstract economic concept "perfect market." Such a market is defined, not fundamentally in terms of any particular spatial location, but rather in terms of full communication among actual and potential buyers and sellers as to offers, bids, and transactions—all with reference to an entirely standardized good. The bargainer in this perfect market may stand in any of numerous degrees of competitive to monopolistic relations with other bargainers.[3] The fundamentals of the perfect market, to repeat, are: (1) two-way communication of each party in the market with every other party, especially with reference to (2) bids, offers, and transactions concerning (3) a standardized commodity or service (or more than one). The principal grain and other produce exchanges are perhaps the closest existing approximations to perfect commodity markets; the securities exchanges with reference to financial goods, which enjoy some advantages in practicability of standardization. (One share of General Motors, for example, is practically identical with any other such share.)

Obviously, the market in which any person endeavors to buy or sell labor falls very far short of perfection in all these particulars. No completely standard specifications or identifications exist; in a literal sense, every person's labor is in a class by itself. The individual differences among persons who are actually employable in a given "occupation" at a given time and place, however, may easily be exaggerated; and in this book

---

[2] *Political Economy*, Bk. 2, Ch. 11, Sec. 1 (1848).

[3] Formerly, most economists considered perfect competition among sellers as essential to a perfect market; but the newer economics of imperfect competition shows that the market characteristics cited in the text above may vary to a great extent independently of degrees of competition among buyers and among sellers.

we are obliged to speak in terms of carpenters, laborers, machine operators, and so on, of average ability and industry— except where it is both important and practicable to give attention to individual or group differences. We shall presently notice, moreover, the well-marked trend toward more accurate specifications of jobs and workers.[4] We shall see, too, that there are many means whereby information is interchanged among buyers and sellers of labor as to bids, offers, and transactions. Many of these reports, of course, are by word of mouth, personal letters, and advertisements. The labor market reports to which we shall devote most attention in the present volume are statistical reports.

The plural form "labor markets" was used above to emphasize the diversity of labor hiring arrangements in the various industries, occupations, and regions, and the looseness of connection among them all. We may, however, on occasion find it convenient to abstract from these variations and adopt the cliché *"the* labor market" in a sense somewhat analogous to *"the* wheat market." The latter also is rather a loose term, referring to the aggregate of all local, regional, national, and international wheat markets.

B. Some Fundamentals of Wage-Hour Statistics

Quotations: Money Wage Statistics and Indexes.[5]—Most markets for commodities and markets for services, such as those of land and capital, give rise to current quotations, which are instruments of communication among actual and potential buyers and sellers in those markets. Such quotations are commonly of most interest and use while fresh—when they refer to transactions or opportunities of only a few days or hours or minutes before they are received. Labor markets are usually characterized by few, crude, and stale quotations. It may plausibly be argued, in fact, that it is purely metaphorical to speak of quotations at all, with reference to labor. Probably

---

[4] See esp. Ch. 10 below.

[5] For exhibits and discussion pertaining to *real wages,* see esp. Ch. 6 below; also index.

but few of the rather small number of persons who pay any attention to wage statistics think of them in the light of quotations; and no doubt up to the present time they have been much more accurately viewed as historical documents—useful to leisurely economic research on causes and policies affecting wages, but utilizable only to a slight extent directly by employers and hired persons.

Several forces are now at work, however, tending to speed up the processes of collecting and publishing reports on employment and earnings and to make such reports more widely useful in practice. Several avenues of improvement will be discussed in a moment. Such increase of speed and utility, of course, does not necessarily mean any impairment of the value of wage statistics for historical and other research purposes. Whenever we refer to wage and hour statistics, therefore, as we shall frequently in this and remaining chapters, let the reader bear in mind that such statistics do not necessarily report only events of months or years ago, but tend also to give more and more recent information on terms of employment.

In a word, the quotation and the historical research aspects of wage-hour statistics are both emphasized herein.

Types of Wage-Hour Measures.—The principal types of reports on wages and hours may now be passed quickly in review, with some indications of the strong and weak points in each. The terms "wages" and "hours" statistically are not in and of themselves definitive. Statistics of hours may refer to the *nominal* or *normal full-time hours* per work period (as the 8-hour day or the 40-hour week), or to the *actual* number of hours worked per day or week or other period of time. Nominal hours are usually those set by the employer, by employer-employee agreement, or by the State as the normal maximum length of a work period, beyond which penalty overtime wage rates must be paid if such overtime is permissible at all. Actual hours worked, on the other hand, reflect the prevalence of overtime and other complications, in the period to which the actual-hour reports refer. In this connection certain occupations give rise to special difficulties, as in mining, for example, where it may be necessary to pay for the time spent in going from the mine gate to the place of work.

"Average hours (actually) worked per week," which are likely to be computed by dividing total man-hours worked by the total number of persons who worked at any time during this week, tend to be lower than the nominal hours, for two main reasons: (1) some individuals start, some quit, some are absent on account of sickness, etc.; and (2) some workers have less than full-time work opportunity during the week in question because they are laid off for certain days or hours. On the other hand, low labor turnover and much overtime may drive "average hours worked" above the nominal work-week.

The term "wages" denotes any of several related concepts. The *wage rate* is the amount of compensation agreed to be paid per unit of time or per unit of product, and may be listed as a time rate, piece rate, standard rate, basic rate, etc. *Earnings* or *earned rates* are the amounts actually received by wage earners, and are usually expressed in terms of a time unit—as earnings per hour, per day, per week, or per year. Both earnings and rates may include items other than money wages, such as payments in kind, board, lodging, or other allowances. Strictly, such additional items should always be included in estimates of earnings; but in the United States they are important for rather few occupations other than agricultural laborer.[6] "Different ways of figuring" all such items account for many of the apparent prevarications and contradictions in statements about wages.

Those official statistics of wages and hours which are most regularly compiled are published or republished monthly, by the United States Bureau of Labor Statistics (USBLS) under

---

[6] Still other forms of the variables hours and output, in relation to wage rates and earnings, are suggested by the following column headings under "Compensation" in the railway *Wage Statistics,* published monthly and annually by the Interstate Commerce Commission: "Straight time actually worked," "Time paid for but not worked," "Overtime paid for at pro rata rates," "Overtime paid for at punitive rates," and "Constructive allowances." These intricacies, to be sure, apply chiefly to train service men, for whom an extraordinarily complex tangle of rules on payment has grown up over many decades, based on time worked, miles run, and minimum hours which must be paid for in any "day" or part-day in which a man is put to work.

the title Employment and Payrolls.[7] These two latter terms, often referred to in the following pages, may here be briefly explained. "Employment" in this connection means number of people employed at any time during the week or other payroll period to which reference is made.[8] "Payrolls" means total wages earned by all the people counted under "Employment." Hence "average weekly earnings" are very simply computed by dividing the total (dollar) payroll for the week by the number of people "employed."

In recent years, moreover, "average *hourly* earnings" have been published monthly for many industries. This figure requires further data from the employers—namely, total number of man-hours worked during the week. All man-hours thus reported are totaled for each industrial group, and divided into the corresponding total (dollar) payrolls: the quotient is "average hourly earnings."[9]

Hourly Wage Rates.—Our further discussion of the respective characteristics of the various measures of money wages may conveniently be divided into two principal categories, namely: hourly wages, and wages earned over longer periods. Statistics of hourly wages, in turn, are of two general sorts,

----

[7] These data come out first in abbreviated and preliminary press releases; later as a department of the *Monthly Labor Review,* and in somewhat fuller form in the monthly pamphlet series entitled *Employment and Payrolls.*

[8] See Ch. 11-A on relations among the current statistical measures of employment, unemployment, overtime, and short time.

[9] Nearly all the more frequently recurring and up-to-date wage-hour reports, such as the USBLS *Employment and Payrolls* and the National Industrial Conference Board series, are based upon *samples* of the industries and areas referred to, since complete coverage is very expensive and time-consuming; and it is doubtful whether the added precision (exemplified by our railway wage statistics) of an approach to 100% monthly coverage is worth the social cost, as compared with good statistical sampling.

Sample series, however, need to be corrected from time to time by comparison with census data. The USBLS, e.g., adjusts its *Employment and Payrolls* series for manufacturing industries to the biennial Census of Manufactures, and similarly for other census industries.

Another bench-mark for periodic adjustment of these current reports is provided by comprehensive and authoritative accumulations of payroll-tax reports made in connection with unemployment compensation and old age "insurance." The first compilation of these was issued under the title *Employment and Payrolls in State Unemployment Compensation Systems, 1938,* by the Social Security Board, Washington, April 1940 (mimeographed).

viz.: (1) wage *rates,* paid during normal or nominal working hours, and (2) hourly *earnings,* including overtime rates, bonuses, and other special earnings. Consideration of these two views of hourly wages will bring out some of the more general problems involved in seeking an average figure for an industry, group of industries, or whatever other unit of earning is in question. A highly important problem in the construction and interpretation of statistical averages, of course, is the factor of weighting.

One type of hourly wage statistics is derived from a wage "scale" which is taken to give the "prevailing" (or perhaps modal) rate for the place and time and occupational group concerned. Such are the trade union scales, which have been of particular historic importance in the statistical measurement of wages, e.g., in building trades. These hourly scales, of course, throw but little light on the weekly or annual incomes in employments which, like those in the building trades, are seasonal and otherwise unstable. Other statistics of wage rates (such as weekly rates in textiles, and monthly wages in agriculture, shipping, and elsewhere) show the rates of earnings of the persons covered, as long as they work the normal number of hours in the week or month.[10]

In localities where such scales are effective for a large fraction of, say, the employed building tradesmen, the occupational scales are close to the "average earned rates" for their respective occupations, unless an appreciable amount of overtime is worked (at punitive rates of pay). If data are desired with reference to non-union as well as union workers in these occupations, however, or on total earnings or averages covering two or more occupations (and weighted according to the numbers of hours worked in such occupations), these hourly scales must be supplemented by payroll reports from employers showing the number of dollars paid out within a specified period to

---

[10] See especially the bulletins and *Mo. Lab. Rev.* articles of the USBLS, classified as the *Wages and Hours Series.* This series includes, e.g., annual reports of union scales of wages and hours in building and printing as well as reports of union scales in some other trades in each of numerous American cities.

how many individuals (by occupations), and preferably for how many hours of work.[11]

Hourly Earnings; Breakdowns.—Besides the scales or tariffs of hourly wage rates mentioned in the preceding paragraph, many series of wage statistics, as told above, are based upon employers' reports of total wage payments and the numbers of hours paid for, so that average hourly earnings or earned rates can be computed. The most comprehensive data regularly published monthly on hourly earnings refer to "industries," such as the 90 manufacturing classifications of the USBLS *Employment and Payrolls* reports, and similar groups in Conference Board and State wage and employment statistics. An over-all average of hourly earnings in an industry, of course, is of rather limited significance. Most practical wage questions are concerned with sub-groups which lie buried in the grand averages; and even if we are interested in comparing a whole industry's wage averages at different times, or at one time with another industry or more than one, we still need to break the gross figures down, so far as possible, in order to discover what parts factors like overtime earnings, geographic location, skill, age, and sex composition of working forces are playing in the whole drama. A number of the "breakdowns" (sub-classifications) which have been made in wage and hour data are examined in section C of this chapter.

Average Weekly Earnings.—A staple and long-established figure in the field of wage statistics is "average *weekly* earn-

---

[11] Average building trade wages, collected more or less in the latter fashion, were published for some time by the F. W. Dodge Corporation, and utilized in the Conference Board's Wages and Hours series. In recent years, moreover, the USBLS has reported monthly certain averages of hourly earnings in construction industries, based on payroll data; further, a special field survey was made by the Bureau as of 1936 (using employers' payrolls), reported in *Mo. Lab. Rev.*, Aug. and Oct. 1937. As will be explained in Ch. 19 below, a number of governmental contracts require (as did, for a time, work-relief wage rates) public hearings or other official inquiries to establish local "prevailing rates of wages." These inquiries lead to publications or mimeographed records which constitute a prolific source of wage statistics.

For periods earlier than, say, 1914, union scales constitute the most comprehensive statistical records for a number of industries. (See Paul H. Douglas, *Real Wages in the United States, 1890-1926,* esp. Chs. 5-7.)

ings," as published, for instance, by the departments of labor of New York and other states, and by the U. S. Bureau of Labor Statistics in its *Employment and Payrolls* series. Every reporting employer can furnish at least two figures, viz., (1) total amount paid out as wages during the payroll period specified, and (2) the total number of workers whose names appear on this payroll. Dividing the total of wages paid (converted to a weekly basis if the actual pay period is not exactly one week) by the total number of names on the payrolls gives the figure often referred to as "average weekly earnings." In the New York reports, for instance, such averages are given separately for men and women, as well as for certain industrial and geographic divisions. This average of weekly earnings, however, is lower than the average earnings of all who work through the week, if (as is nearly always true) it is pulled down by individuals who have worked only part of the particular week in question.[12]

Another "weekly earnings" figure was prominent in the older U. S. Bureau of Labor Statistics occasional wage-hour reports—namely "full-time weekly earnings." Average hourly earnings were ascertained in certain industries (once in a year or longer interval)—by occupations and by sex and state— from sample payrolls; also the nominal or normal working hours. These two averages, multiplied, give the weekly earnings of "the average worker" if employed during exactly the normal working hours of the whole week. It gives no indication as to how earnings were actually affected by such factors as overtime, absences, and layoffs. These surveys of the USBLS, however, gave useful historical information on varia-

---

[12] The total number of names of *hourly* wage earners (excluding executive, professional, and clerical classifications) which appeared at any time on the August 1939 (for example) payrolls of Class I railways (some 95% of all American rail workers) was 666,095; whereas the number employed in the *middle* of the same month was 588,079. The latter figure best represents the average wage labor force actually employed during the month. Now, if we divide the former and larger total of workers into the average weekly wage bill of $17,807,587 (computed from the total payroll of that month), we get "average weekly earnings" of $26.73. If, on the other hand, we use the latter and smaller total as representing approximately the number of *jobs* which were continually filled, we obtain the substantially higher figure for "average weekly earnings" of $30.28.

tions and trends in nominal hours and weekly earnings, as did
and do the monthly reports of the Conference Board.

Monthly Salaries and Earnings.—No uniform significance
attaches to the distinction between weekly and monthly earnings or pay rates. The general difference pointed out above,
between wage *rates* and *earnings,* is fully applicable to the
weekly basis of pay, but in lesser degree to the monthly—since
monthly salaried people's earnings are very much less affected
by overtime and part-time work. The week is the most common period for which wage payrolls are made up (and hence
for raw material of wage statistics) : when the monthly basis of
pay is quoted, the inference is warranted that this occupation is
characterized by greater stability of employment than if payment is on an hourly, daily, or weekly basis. Such is obviously
the case with crews of ships, teachers, and executives and other
office workers. These simple verbal conventions, however, correspond very imperfectly with degrees of employment security
among industries and regions.[13]

In discussions of wage and salary statistics, payments actually made on a weekly or monthly basis are often expressed on
an hourly basis by dividing the total payment by the number
of hours worked; sometimes (as in the survey cited in the preceding footnote) on the annual basis. Such hourly or annual
rates of earnings imputed to weekly- or monthly- or annually-
engaged workers, however, are not fully comparable with
hourly earnings at the same kind of work and at the same place,

---

[13] All railway salaried people, for instance, including the highest executives, are classified in ICC reports as paid on the "daily basis," and the
U. S. Personnel Classification Board, in reporting a survey of remuneration
of some 30,000 stenographers, made the following observation (among
others) : "Although no factors associated with geography that might influence salary were discovered during the analysis of the data, one probable
reason for variations within a single area was revealed. Method of paying
wages was observed to have some intra-area effect. For example, in the
geographic area known as East North Central States, where weekly and
monthly salary payments are about equally popular, it is found that among
the concerns paying on a weekly basis a pay of $1,300 greatly predominates,
whereas among the concerns paying on a monthly basis a pay of $1,200 per
annum predominates. This would seem to lend confirmation to the theory
that in determining pay, executives are guided largely by accidental rather
than essential considerations."—*Report of Wage and Personnel Survey*
(1929), p. 94.

on shorter engagements, or with monthly or annual earnings
of employees hired by the year. Wage incomes in casual or
short-term engagements are usually much more insecure and
fluctuating than in weekly or monthly hirings, and (for each
hour *worked*) tend to be higher than through the longer terms
of employment. It is a commonplace, for instance, that farmers
are usually able to hire men by the month at lower average
hourly earnings than they can hire similar work for only a
fraction of a month during a busy season; and in some degree
the same applies to all occupations and industries. Everyone
knows that earnings in trades much affected by seasonal and
cyclical variations, such as building and mining, sound much
higher when expressed in hourly than in yearly terms. The importance of this factor of period of engagement or employment
security is becoming increasingly recognized, and will be discussed at some length in Chapter 11.

Annual Earnings.—Statistical information on annual earnings, by industries and occupations and locations, is obviously
of great importance. And, like the somewhat analogous geographic measure of annual rainfall, the distribution of earnings among people and months of the year is also very important. In general, a steady flow of earnings, week by week and
month by month, is of greater advantage to the worker than
feast-or-famine fluctuations, especially if the extent and timing of these be very uncertain.

Many statistical series purporting to show average annual
wages or earnings of various working groups are subject to
rather wide margins of error and/or misinterpretation, by the
necessity of resorting to a number of somewhat slippery assumptions. Estimates for earlier decades are sometimes computed from (1) records of hourly rates or earnings, by applying (2) estimates of percentages of unemployment during the
year in the group of workers in question. Over-all averages of
actual annual earnings, on the other hand, are readily available
for railroad employees and workers in many industries and for
years covered by relevant Census reports—e.g., the biennial
censuses of manufacturing industries.

The usefulness of these over-all averages, however, is limited in many ways. In computing such a statistical mean, the actual payroll for the year is divided by the number of employees, giving the "average annual earnings." Simple enough, until question is raised as to the *divisor*—"number of employees" at what period(s) of the year? In a national railroad wage dispute, the employing carriers presented a certain figure which purported to show annual earnings. This figure, derived from reports of the Interstate Commerce Commission, was obtained by dividing total compensation by the number of employees as shown by the average of the 12 mid-month counts.[14] The labor spokesmen, however, substituted for the mid-month count the total number on the payroll at any time during the month—obtaining thereby an "average annual earnings" figure lower by $150 or more. The latter side also adduced figures issued by the (Federal) Railroad Retirement Board, which divided total compensation by the total number of persons employed by any of these railroads at any time during the year. This latter "average annual earnings" figure was some $600 lower than that presented by the employing carriers. The Emergency Board, trying to reconcile these figures, marshaled still other averages, such as the average annual earnings of all who were employed six months or more, or all who had worked four or more months and had earned not less than $150,[15] but finally concluded: "It is the opinion of the Board that any one figure said to show the average yearly earnings of railway workers has rather less significance than such averages usually have. For, as regards rates of pay, there are very different classes among railway employees, and their work opportunities vary because of the nature of the industry."[16] That is, even if

---

[14] This method gives an annual earnings average nearly comparable with those easily derived from Censuses of Manufactures—in which "average number of wage earners" is usually computed from numbers on payrolls in one week near the middle of each of the 12 months.

[15] Yet other divisors could be the number of employees on the payroll at the end of the year; the peak number of employees; the number on the roll both at the beginning and at the end of the same year—all these are actually used by reputable wage statisticians.

[16] Report of the Emergency Board to the President (of the U. S.), appointed Sept. 27, 1938, under Sec. 10 of the Railway Labor Act in re Atchison, Topeka and Santa Fe, etc., p. 44 (See Ch. 12-B, also p. 49.)

you could agree that some one of these calculations best represents the over-all average of annual earnings of *all* railway workers, its significance would still be dwarfed by contrasts among occupational *groups* of such workers. Thus we are reminded of the great import of wage differentials, which are investigated in the following section.

In recent years, income and Social Security tax regulations have required employers of the bulk of American industrial wage earners to report to government agencies actual totals of wage payments to named individual employees. The reports for income tax purposes may not be used to arrive at the total of wages earned by any person who works for more than one employer in the year; but the announcements by large employers of annual earnings of their workers, based on these reports, constitute a significant recent addition to annual wage data. And, as will be noted below, Social Security Board data are beginning to close this last gap, since the Security Administration posts to each worker's record all his earnings from "covered" employers.

C. An Outline of the American Wage-Hour Structure

Rather by way of further illustrating the preceding discussion of types of wage-hour statistics available than for the purpose of giving a complete portrayal of the existing (exceedingly complex) structure of American wage incomes, there follow a few examples from, and generalizations based upon, the voluminous literature to which we have referred. The program in this section is (1) to exhibit some of the existing American *average* "hours worked," "hourly earnings," and "annual earnings" figures; and (2) to indicate some of the more important dispersions around these averages—i.e., wage and hour *differentials*.

Charts of USBLS Data.—Charts 1 and 2 show the course, respectively, of average hours actually worked per week and of average hourly earnings, for some principal industrial groups over a number of recent years (nearly the whole period for which necessary data have been published by the U. S. Bureau

AVERAGE HOURS WORKED PER WEEK
1933 – 1939

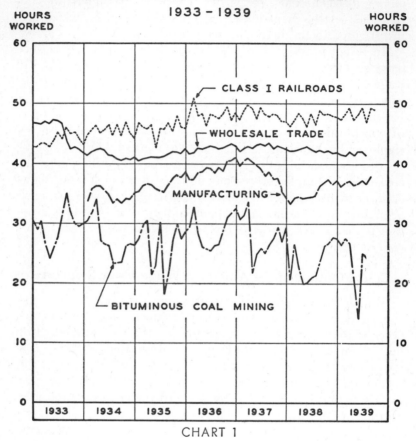

CHART 1

Sources: U. S. Bureau of Labor Statistics, Employment and Payrolls series; Interstate Commerce Commission, Wage Statistics series (Class I railroads).

of Labor Statistics.)[17] The numerical data used in these charts
may be obtained from compilations by the BLS[18] and (for
railroads) by the ICC.

Several "stories" are told by each of these charts, which also
may be pieced together to give a somewhat fuller account of
averages and variations among industrial groups during this
period. Fluctuations in "employment," to be sure, are not either
shown or implied in these exhibits,[19] but average *weekly* earnings of employed workers may be computed by multiplying
average hours worked by average earnings per hour. Our two
charts show, for example, that although the wage earners on
railroads obtained average *hourly* earnings only slightly (if at
all) superior to those in wholesale trade, the railway men employed averaged distinctly longer hours of work after 1933,
and thus obtained materially higher average *weekly* earnings.
At the other extreme is the case of the bituminous coal miners
—their *hourly* earnings leaped upward in 1933 and have continued to soar, as the union recovered lost ground; but their low
average of hours worked per week implies much more modest
average earnings in *weekly* terms, as compared with those
reckoned merely in cents per hour.[20]

---

[17] Both these series involve substantial sample reports, in each industry,
of man-hours actually worked during a week near the middle of each month.
Total man-hours divided by total number of persons who worked any part
of this sample week equal average hours worked per week. This latter average, therefore, is affected by labor turnover and absenteeism, as well as by
fluctuations in overtime and short time. Total dollar payrolls divided by
total man-hours worked equal average hourly earnings.

[18] *Hours and Earnings in Manufacturing and Nonmanufacturing Industries, 1932 to 1939*—mimeographed by the U. S. Bureau of Labor Statistics,
February 1940.

[19] "Employment and payroll" monthly indexes, respectively, for durable
and non-durable manufacturing industries, 1919-39, are shown in Chart 9,
below; and revised data, compiled in mimeographed form, are supplied on
application by USBLS.

[20] Chart 6, below, shows that hourly earnings in bituminous coal mining
declined more than in most other industries, 1920-33; this fact helps to
explain the great rise in hourly earned rates after 1933. (Average hourly
earnings and hours worked per week are affected, of course, by changes in
nominal hours and overtime rates. Bituminous miners initiated their 7-hour
day in April 1934.)

Another question suggested here, which I have not worked up, is comparative extents of work sharing—i.e., total vs. partial unemployment—
among such industries as railroads and coal mining.

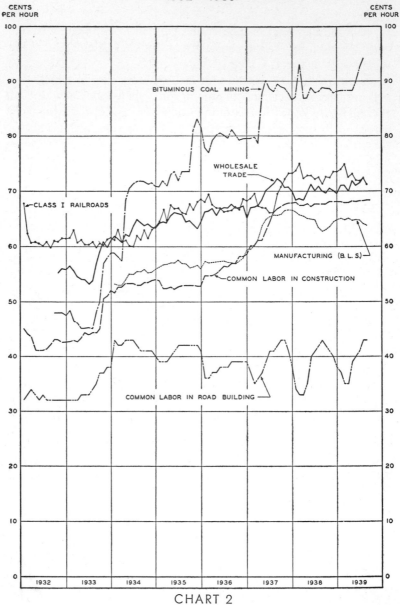

AVERAGE HOURLY EARNINGS
1932 - 1939

CENTS
PER HOUR

CENTS
PER HOUR

BITUMINOUS COAL MINING

WHOLESALE
TRADE

CLASS I RAILROADS

MANUFACTURING (B. L. S.)

COMMON LABOR IN CONSTRUCTION

COMMON LABOR IN ROAD BUILDING

CHART 2

Sources: U. S. Bureau of Labor Statistics, Employment and Payrolls series; Inter-state Commerce Commission, Wage Statistics (Class I railroads); Survey of Current Business (common labor in road building).

46

Annual Earnings Illustrations from Automotive Industry.
—The general nature of the data on average *annual* earnings
which have become available in recent years may be illustrated
by reference to wage earners in the motor vehicle manufacturing industry; and it is convenient here also to illustrate one of
the many types of investigation of *individual differences in
wages*—a topic receiving further brief notice in later pages of
this book.

ANNUAL EARNINGS OF MALE HOURLY-PAID FACTORY EMPLOYEES IN
AUTOMOBILE (MOTOR VEHICLE) PLANTS, MODEL YEARS 1934-1939

Model Year (ending Autumn of)	Average Annual Earnings of		Number of Steady Workers, as % of All
	All Men[a]	Steady Workers[b]	
(1)	(2)	(3)	(4)
1934	$ 749	$1,317	51%
1935	1,014	1,454	56
1936	1,294	1,618	79
1937	1,399	1,848	61
1938	906	b	b
1939	1,328	b	b

[a] All men on plant rolls at any time in year. If a man worked in more than one plant he is
counted more than once.
[b] Men who had 46 weeks or more in the 12-month model year. This statistical concept has
now been abandoned by the Association; hence the latest figures are not available.

Source: Payments to individual male workers by single plants of members of the Automobile Manufacturers' Association, which Association supplied data for the above table.
(Ford is not a member, but inclusion of Ford data would change these averages only slightly.)
Includes bonuses and special gift payments, except for first two years. Women constitute
about 5% of the nearly 500,000 motor vehicle wage earners. Average annual earnings of *all*
wage earners, both male and female, would run from $5 to $24 lower than the figures in col. 2
above.

For other data (and modes of calculation and inter-industry comparisons) see the AMA's
Automobile Facts and Figures yearbook. For the year 1937, for example, in which the over-all
average for men employed in any part of the year was $1,399, the average annual earnings of
other significant categories of automobile-and-body-mfg. workers were: of all employed at end
of model year, $1,600; of all earning $3,000 or less and employed during fourth quarter of calendar
year (Social Security data—see below), $1,531.—*Ibid.*, 1940 ed., p. 42.

The contrasts between entries in columns 2 and 3—and
comparisons added in note (b)—show how greatly the inclusion of the most temporary workers may pull down the grand
average of annual earnings, in a rather seasonal industry. Col-

umn 4 gives one indication of how greatly the ratio of "steady" workers to all workers has fluctuated in this trade during the years 1934-39.[21]

Wage-Earner Incomes from All Sources.—The motorcar industry may also be used to illustrate the problem of ascertaining total incomes which wage earners derive from all sources. With reference to 1934, a household canvass by Federal investigators, covering 3,538 motor vehicle workers, secured reports indicating that, on the average, these workers added very little, by other employment, to the wages they earned at the single plant of principal employment. Even the 25% of workers in this latter sample who received lowest incomes (all less than $527 in that year from their respective single plants) made an average of only $35 per year by finding additional employment *within* the industry, and an average of $29 more by securing employment *outside* the industry.[22] This picture differs somewhat from those yielded by other investigations of this problem in earlier times; but on the whole it appears that wage earners have had to rely largely on earnings within one

---

[21] This last index was affected, in the period covered, by such factors as: (1) variations in trade union policy, and power to enforce it, with reference to work sharing and seniority in layoffs and rehirings; (2) date of introduction of new models (much of the increase in percentage of steady workers in 1935-36 was due to the early model change in 1935, which was "planned that way"); and (3) fluctuations in production (in an unusually busy year more temporary workers are drawn in).

It is shown, a few paragraphs below, as well as in section B of this Chapter, that the "average annual earnings" of rail workers, too, is greatly pulled down when temporary workers are included. The rail industry is probably less distinctly seasonal than the automotive; both are strongly affected by fluctuations in general prosperity and depression; and the secular trend of rail employment has been downward since about 1920—of automotive employment, upward until 1930.

[22] N. A. Tolles and M. W. LaFever, "Wages, Hours, Employment, and Annual Earnings in the Motor Vehicle Industry, 1934," *Mo. Lab. Rev.,* March 1936, pp. 24-26.

In this article, too, the annual earnings in plant of principal employment (1934) are tabulated by sex and by $100-intervals of earnings. The lowest quartile for the 102,000 men, whose earnings in single automobile plants were ascertained for that year, fell between $500 and $600 (i.e., somewhat more than 25% earned below $600); and the median fell a little below $1,000 (i.e., a little over half these men earned less than $1,000). Comparison with the table above shows that this median was considerably above the arithmetic mean ($749) for the model year 1934.

industry, during any one year, and to a great extent on one employer.[23]

More complete evidence on the actual total earnings of workers from all sources is and will continue to be offered by the Social Security Board's figures for individual workers' incomes from all *covered* employments.[24] For the whole automobile and parts industry, the average annual earnings (including salaries up to $3,000) for 1937 and 1938 were, respectively and in round numbers, $1,400 and $1,180, which may be compared with $1,531 and $1,184 for similar employees of the automobile and body industry (excluding other parts). Even the Social Security Board data, however, do not reveal (1) earnings from part-time employment in non-covered industries, or from self-employment, and (2) the extent to which laid-off and otherwise unemployed men utilize idle time by work around their homes and gardens. Such work, especially on suitable "subsistence homesteads," may yield appreciable real income.

Annual Earnings of Railroad Workers.—The voluminous railway wage statistics already published permit more comprehensive exhibits of annual earnings, within each of the 128 occupational classifications standardized by the ICC. The accompanying ingenious Chart 3 shows the spread of annual earnings during 1929, in each of 12 such occupations—chosen as typical of the principal steps from lowest to highest.[25]

It will be observed that the lowest two occupations on this chart are (1) section and extra gang (including maintenance of way) men and (2) messengers and office boys, whose median annual incomes in 1929 were distinctly below $1,000,

---

[23] Some other data on this point are cited in my *Compensating Industrial Effort*, pp. 224, 225.

[24] The workers are classified by industry groups according to their fourth-quarter employment. See Social Security Yearbook—annual supplement to the Board's *Social Security Bulletin.*

[25] Reproduced from Maurice Leven, *The Income Structure of the United States.* Cf. U. S. Railroad Retirement Bd., *Railroad Wages and Months of Service, 1937,* 3 vols., Oct. 1938.

Leven's chart, showing the "array" from lowest to highest earnings in cumulative percentage terms, is based upon frequency-table "breakdowns" of annual earnings of all individuals in the particular occupations that are specified.

OCCUPATIONAL INCOMES OF RAILROAD EMPLOYEES IN 1929
CUMULATIVE PERCENTAGE DISTRIBUTIONS FOR SELECTED OCCUPATIONS

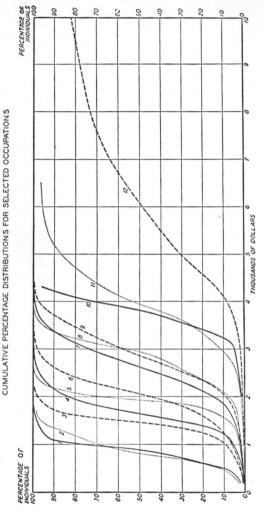

CHART 3

1. Section men and extra gang men
2. Messengers and office boys
3. Bridge and building carpenters
4. Clerks and clerical specialists
5. Signalmen and signal maintainers
6. Road brakemen and flagmen

7. Road conductors
8. Gang foremen and gang leaders
9. Road engineers and motormen
10. Chief train dispatchers
11. Division officers, assistants, and staff assistants
12. Executives, general officers, and assistants

Source: Figures from Federal Coordinator of Transportation, Annual Earnings of Railroad Employees, 1924-1933, pp. 137-170. Chart reproduced by courtesy of Brookings Institution from Maurice Leven, The Income Structure of the United States (Washington, 1938), p. 22.

and whose highest annual earnings were in the neighborhood of $1,700 to $1,800.[26]

Another sidelight on statistics of earnings classified by occupations is provided by this chart—especially by the contrast between the curves numbered 10 (chief train dispatchers) and 11 (division officers, assistants, and staff assistants). The more gradual rise of the latter curve is undoubtedly due mainly to the heterogeneity of the jobs thus grouped together; whereas the chief train dispatchers constitute a much more nearly homogeneous, sharply defined, occupational group—and hence the full-time workers have more nearly equal annual incomes. In statistical parlance there is much less "dispersion" about the chief dispatchers' average than about that of the more heterogeneous class of "division officers, etc."

Wage Differentials Summarized.—The foregoing presentations of automotive and railway annual earnings have led us over the threshold of the important statistical field of wage differentials. The sub-classifications or internal "breakdowns" of wage data which are now to some degree statistically feasible may be listed under three heads, viz., wages classified in relation to: (1) objective physical differences of the workers (*sex, age, geographical location, color,* and other physical or mental traits which produce *individual differences in earnings* within many occupations); (2) differences in skill and competence (as roughly reflected by statistical classification according to *occupation,* and *length of service*); and (3) the more largely institutional factors (e.g., wages classified according to *industry, hours worked, size of plant,* degree of *worker organization,* and *method of wage payment*).

To the extent that we can more finely sub-classify wage data, we not only progress with measurement of wage differences—we also make headway in accounting for such differentials. The general method used is cross-classification, or

---

[26] The median annual income, reached by just half the members of any group, if obtainable (from frequency tables), is likely to be a better measure, over the years, of the "average" full-time worker's earnings than is any arithmetic mean, since the former is not much affected by fluctuations in the working opportunities of temporary employees.

successive tabulations or breakdowns. For example, over-all figures giving average earnings of men and average earnings of women do not show the true sex-payment differential; for the women, as a group, are not working on the same jobs, are not equally skilled, of equal age, organized in equal degree, nor dispersed geographically in the same fashion. By successive breakdowns the chief causal factors behind any crude wage difference can be gradually revealed. This process cannot, of course, be completely carried out on the basis of present wage data. But it is this type of information that we are seeking when we attempt to discuss, statistically, existing wage differences.

In the remainder of this section will be given a broad summary of American wage differentials, as of the latter part of the 1930 decade—with incidental attention to differentials of nominal weekly hours and annual employment, since these are important factors in wage incomes.[27]

---

[27] Detailed citations of evidence will not be given, as the material is very voluminous; but the principal types of source (most of which have already been mentioned) may be here indicated. Among non-governmental investigators of these matters, a prominent place is occupied by the National Industrial Conference Board, which has brought together part of its own evidence in the volume *Differentials in Industrial Wages and Hours in the United States,* by M. Ada Beney (New York, 1938).

Another group of wage studies, utilizing original data, may be found in publications of the Department of Industrial Research of the Wharton School, University of Pennsylvania—e.g., titles by Bezanson, Hussey, Frain, and Alderfer. Some other university bureaus have also published original data on wage and salary earnings—e.g., the study by Elliott and Manson of the University of Michigan, Bureau of Business Research.

Most of the agencies collecting and publishing wage and hour statistics, however, are governmental departments and bureaus. Over-all averages of annual earnings, classified by such criteria as state, industry group, age, and sex, are now published by the Social Security Board. Another important source is the long line of censuses of various industry groups, notably of manufactures. Many wage data from the latter censuses were distilled by Paul F. Brissenden, into his *Earnings of Factory Workers,* 1899-1927 (Census Monograph X, 1929). The principal Federal agency, of course, is the Bureau of Labor Statistics of the U. S. Dept. of Labor. Most of its own investigations, and many publications by other authors and organizations, are summarized in its *Monthly Labor Review*—including its two important series of primary wage data, put out respectively by its Employment and Payrolls and Wage and Hour Statistics divisions. Especially for earlier years, the primary data published by various state agencies are important, e.g., those of the Massachusetts Census of Manufactures and of the New York Department of Labor.

Two competent summaries and commentaries on certain types of wage

One of the simplest and most obvious differences is that between *men's and women's* wages. The crude over-all figures (e.g., Social Security Board averages for all workers with social security accounts) tend to show men's earnings to be about twice women's (respectively $1,027 and $525 in 1937). Likewise the Census reports have shown comparable differences in magnitude. When, however, an attempt is made to eliminate other possible causes of wage differences (occupation, industry, degree of unemployment, etc.) we find that the difference shrinks to more reasonable proportions—in rare cases, it is even reversed.

In regard to wage differences by *age,* we have the recent Social Security Board figures showing peak earnings (in 1937) at about age 45. Other evidence is roughly confirmatory.

The subject of *geographical* wage differences has received particularly detailed analysis by statisticians, in part because of its importance for public policy in regard to minimum-wage legislation. Wages in the South are known to be generally lower (for similar work) than in the West and North. Also wages tend to be higher, within limits, in larger than in smaller cities, towns, and villages. Normal hours of work have some tendency to vary in the opposite directions, with respect to both of these factors; so that the differences in weekly and annual earnings are likely to be less affected by geographic variations than are hourly earnings. Part of the difference between northern and southern wages is due to the factor of *color,* since it is well known that, "other things equal," wages of colored persons are lower than of white. Part of the difference may also be due to differing compositions of northern and southern laboring forces in regard to sex, age, and skill.

The effect of the factor *skill* on wage earnings is hard to

differences have recently appeared. One, *Wage Differentials, the case of the unskilled,* by Carrie Glasser (New York: Columbia Univ., 1940), examines statistically and theoretically differences in "unskilled" labor's earnings among industries, geographic locations, etc. The other, *Hourly Earnings of Employees in Large and Small Enterprises,* by Jacob Perlman (Monograph No. 14 of Temp. Nat'l Econ. Comm., Washington, Gov't Ptg. Office, 1940) contains new tabulations of USBLS data on 16 industries, mostly manufacturing; with incidental treatment of such factors as sex, unions, size of town, plant, company.

measure. Presumably, skill is the result of aptitude, training, and experience. Hence, measurement of wage differences according to degree of skill can best be approximated by comparing workers according to their occupation and according to their experience under conditions suitable for acquiring skill. Whether outputs of workers on a given job increase as much after the first year or two of service as their pay frequently does is open to question; but the employer's interest in maintaining morale and reducing turnover, together with frequent worker insistence on seniority, often combines to cause a steady progression of earnings with longer service.[28]

Comparative wage rates of various *occupations* (which presumably call for various degrees of *skill*) have already been illustrated by Leven's chart (Chart 3, above) showing earnings of various classes of railroad workers. Attempts to compare wages in the frequently used broad classifications of "skilled," "semi-skilled," and "unskilled" work have hitherto met with indifferent success at best—at least this is true of inter-industrial comparisons with reference to degrees of skill. Some important difficulties are the frequent shifts in the contents of various jobs, and the lack of comparability of the work done in different plants and departments under the same labels. Nevertheless, these three degrees of skill are so frequently referred to that some attention needs to be paid to them. The Conference Board has published average hourly earnings series in 24 to 27 manufacturing industries, by sex and skill. Such data, which show unskilled wages in all manufacturing industries combined at about 73% of skilled wages, must be interpreted with a good deal of caution (especially for earlier years), in view of the size and composition of the industrial samples sometimes used, and of various difficulties which have produced anomalies in these averages. In part, the higher wage rates of skilled workers are due to the fact that such workers are generally men—and mature men at that—are mainly white, and tend to have better native abilities or aptitudes than the general run of wage earners. The differentials in favor of skilled persons have possibly narrowed slightly over the past generation or two, by reason of factors like vocational training at public expense, increase of egalitarian sentiments, diminished supplies, and rising organizational power of the "unskilled"; but fluctuations of such differentials within relatively short periods—notably the rise of "unskilled" by comparison with "skilled" wages in the 1914-18 war and immediate post-war years—are much more clearly evident than any long-term trend.[29] Doubtless the markets for particular skills become rather more unstable, with the increasing tempo of economic change.

In regard to wage differences by *industries,* the first two charts above have pictured hourly earnings and hours worked in various major divisions. Similar and additional data concerning a great many individual industries (especially manufacturing industries) are available—since about 1932, in reports of the U. S. Bureau of Labor Statistics, and for longer periods covering years prior to 1932 in (e.g.) the literature of the Conference Board.

A statistical wage factor which has been rather recently noticed is *size of plant.* In general earned wage rates are higher in larger than in smaller plants, even when other factors like size of city are allowed for. This rule appears to hold, not only in manufacturing and allied trades, such as bakeries, but also in other industries, such as building construction and motor carrier operations.

Any summary statement about wage differences on the basis of *hours worked* would be a generalization from insufficient evidence; but such data as do exist suggest that, within limits, wage earners in any occupation and locality who spend longer weekly hours on the job are likely to receive higher weekly, though lower hourly, earnings—as compared with similar workers having shorter work weeks. There is interaction here with the plant-size factor—the larger plants have some tendency toward shorter normal hours.

---

[29] See discussion of criticisms of Australian wage regulation, latter part of Ch. 18-B below.

Another important breakdown in some wage statistics compares average earnings of *union and non-union* workers. The evidence shows clearly enough that union hourly wages tend to be higher than non-union, in the same trade and area. The crude, over-all breakdown into union and non-union, however, exaggerates the real difference—because of the interaction of geographical, occupational, race and sex differences in the composition of the union and non-union groups. Although opponents of unionism contend that the higher hourly rates create more unemployment and hence cause lower weekly or annual earnings, scarcely more than fragmentary data are available at present to prove whether this contention has a solid basis in fact.

There remain, among others, two types of wage differentials not yet summarized—(1) according to *method of payment,* and (2) wage *differences among individuals* of the same age, sex, color, and experience, working in the same industry, plant and occupation, under the same (union or employer) rules as to hours, method of payment, etc. The foregoing discussion has been almost entirely concerned with *average* earnings of various classes and sub-classes of workers. Shifting attention to individual differences focuses attention on the deviations of individuals' earnings, within such classes, from the class averages. The matter of individual differences in earnings is, moreover, bound up very closely with the question of payment methods.

If method of payment is a straight time rate for all workers of a given occupational group, perhaps somewhat graduated according to length of service, there tend to be but small individual differences, if any. Such narrow dispersion may result from employer or from union insistence. If, on the contrary, suitable methods are used to measure individual differences in productivity (where such differences can exist and can be measured), and to fit payment to productivity, then important differences in hourly earnings will probably appear. Such differing individual earned rates are most commonly observed in connection with piecework and bonus payment methods—but they may occur also as differing time rates for different workers on the same job, graded according to estimates of their relative competence or worth.[30]

As to the general relationsnip between earnings of otherwise similar workers on a straight time payment basis and on a payment-by-results basis, American workers under the latter systems appear to earn 10% or more higher wages. Methods of hiring, placement, and supervision, however, are now more important factors in labor efficiency and earnings than are wage methods in the narrower sense.

D. Statistical Agencies; Trends toward Improvement of Wage Quotations

Some indication was given above of the considerable number and variety of government bureaus, trade associations, and trade journals to which we may now look for historical and current quotations of wages. No attempt is made in the present volume to survey in detail the agencies and methods involved; but a few remarks at this point may assist the reader to bear in mind the principal sources of wage statistics, and the lines of progress now visible. This picture has changed rapidly in recent years.

Censuses; Social Security Agencies.—Some references were made above to Censuses, such as those of manufactures. The latter Census provides (since 1919) biennial reports of employment and payrolls, classified by months of the year, sex,

---

[30] Cf. Ch. 15-C below. If individual wage differences do exist, and if they fully reflect individual differences in ability (no restriction by nature of work or otherwise), then the variation will tend (as number of workers on like work increases) to follow a normal probability curve. This is because, under the conditions specified, the outputs are strongly affected by innate physical and mental abilities, which occur in individuals roughly in accordance with the dictates of probability. Certain divergences from the bell-shaped probability curve, however, should be expected. The frequency curve of earnings will probably be cut off at the lower end, by the employer's weeding out of the least apt or fit applicants—perhaps at a point economically dictated by a legal or customary minimum wage. And actual individual earnings curves are likely also to be cut off at the top, perhaps by voluntary restriction of output from the worker side, or more probably by reason of factors like some physical feature of the job which imposes an upper limit on any worker's efficiency, or by inadequate wage incentive methods.

states, and various industries and subdivisions and groups. Such Census data on wages, however, have not been broken down by occupations within the smallest industry categories—except by wage and salary earners. Another group of sources likely to provide master-prints of the wage structure for *every* year after 1936 or 1937 are those connected with our social security system. The present practice of accumulating complete wage and salary data (in covered employments) on each of the fifty-odd millions of persons covered by old age and survivors' annuities is expensive, and may not persist indefinitely; but so long as it lasts it provides a unique, authoritative, and remarkably comprehensive record of earnings of individuals, year by year.

The most complete and lengthy series of wage statistics in a single industry, it will be recalled, is that which has been published monthly for many years by the Interstate Commerce Commission, covering payments for personal services to nearly all employees of the American steam railways, and classified by well-defined occupations.

Non-recurrent and Irregularly Recurring Wage, Hour, and Salary Surveys.—In the foregoing sections of this chapter we have been preoccupied with continuous and regularly recurrent wage and hour data—many of which are published monthly, some yearly, some at longer Census periods. Numerous other examples might be cited, such as the agricultural wage reports made by the U. S. Department of Agriculture. It is necessary now to recognize the existence of discontinuous surveys, made by all manner of commissions, bureaus, and individuals. An example, cited elsewhere herein, is the U. S. Personnel Classification Board's *Wage and Personnel Survey* (published 1929); another is the Conference Board's *Clerical Salaries in the United States* (1926). In general, the longer series, where carefully done so as to make clear the varying degrees of comparability from year to year, are most useful and significant. Outstanding importance, however, attaches to the somewhat irregularly recurring wage and hour surveys which the U. S. Bureau of Labor Statistics and its predecessors have carried out from time to time for four or five decades. These surveys take considerable time for collecting, editing, tabulating, and interpreting the data; hence each publication is likely to refer to events which occurred a year or more before the report reaches the reader. But this series is the master-key to other wage data; for in it wages are classified not merely by grand averages in industries, but are broken down according to place, sex, occupation, frequency distributions, and latterly into numerous other classifications. These occupational wage data, as we shall see, leave something still to be desired in the direction of unambiguous definitions of jobs. Improvements made in recent years, however, provide better information as to how earnings vary in relation to payment method, size of plant, union organization, and so on.

Before 1914, as stated, among the principal quotations and statistics of wages available by occupations were trade union rate scales. The U. S. Bureau of Labor Statistics continues publication of some such scales; but the principal advances in quantity and quality of wage quotations have come through reports secured by statistical agencies from cooperating employers.[31]

Trends in Improvement of Wage Statistics.—Some indications were given above of the shortcomings of available wage statistics. The same matter may now profitably be approached from the opposite direction, by inquiring what are the principal lines of improvement visible at the time of this writing. Outstanding among these current improvement trends are (1) the speeding up of collection and publication of wage records and analyses thereof, partly by the development of sounder and more economical sampling; (2) more use and understanding of "breakdowns" of mass observations—especially by frequency tables supplementing the various averages; (3) job analysis for

---

[31] The most frequently recurring and up-to-date wage surveys—of "employment and payrolls"—by government and trade association offices are conducted largely by the employer filling out, each month, a rather simple schedule and mailing it to the statistical office. The more intensive USBLS "wage and hour series," on the other hand, use as raw material data copied from plant payrolls (for the week or other sample period to which the survey refers) by field investigators of the Bureau.

development of more accurate identification of the type of work for which the wages are paid; and (4) more continuous and up-to-date interpretations of the technical data.

1. *"Sampling"* referred to under the first of the foregoing headings, means the collection of small but representative "random samples" of each type of industry and worker in question, with continual checking of the sampling procedure by comparisons with the much more costly and less frequent Census or other more complete coverages. It will doubtless be agreed that more up-to-date wage quotations, by industries, occupations, and areas, are desirable; though wage rates are perhaps sufficiently more stable than commodity and security prices so that daily wage quotations may never become important. In any case the most likely means of speeding up such labor quotations is through application of the statistical art of sampling. Public employment bureaus are necessary, in part for administration of unemployment benefits; and they have many advantages as agencies for continuously collecting and publishing labor market information. Some staple "business barometers" already include certain common-labor hiring rates, and this group will doubtless be enlarged.

2. Among the more extensive data now becoming available are *breakdowns and frequency tables* to supplement the old over-all averages of somewhat heterogeneous items. In the U. S. Bureau of Labor Statistics the trend toward speeding up is represented by the Employment and Payrolls Series, which endeavors to publish relatively quickly over-all quantities, indexes, and averages of earnings and hours with reference to as many industries and principal sub-divisions as possible; whereas the trend toward more significant supplementary information is typified by the same Bureau's Wages and Hours Statistics Series, which includes results of the Bureau's intensive investigations of payroll data.

In trade association labor research we see similar tendencies. The Conference Board, a creation of several such associations, has figured prominently in the field of wage-hour statistics since 1920—collecting and compiling primary data, reprinting others, and presenting business reactions to government and other private wage-hour reports. The NRA greatly stimulated wage-statistical work by individual trade associations, as in motor vehicle, automotive parts, chemical, electrical, metal, and paper industries. Many, if not most, of these compilations are circulated privately among association members; but they are apt to be accessible also to official wage fixers and to serious students.[32]

3. A third line of improvement is the development of *more widely-standardized occupational names and specifications,* by job analysis procedures. To a certain extent, occupational wage data have been made more meaningful by breakdowns according to objective distinctions, such as men and women, density of population, geographic locations—as noted above. Occupational names, however, are often employed in importantly different senses by different respondents to wage questionnaires and other inquiries. A crude but commonplace example: we all know there are innumerable grades and values of "stenographers," "typists," and "secretaries," as well as of positions offering work to these people. Similar observations will apply to many occupational categories as soon as we get beyond the confines of single shops and the relatively few occupations, such as linotype operators, in which the workmen to an unusual extent are literally interchangeable. Some series of wage statistics relating to occupations, for instance those of the U. S. Bureau of Labor Statistics, have long contained glossaries giving brief definitions of the jobs covered. Such descriptions and specifications, however, should be developed a good deal further for wage surveys, in part by utilizing occupational analyses intended primarily for hiring, training, or other personnel and social administration purposes. This extension will make occupational wage statistics more comprehensive and meaningful—the occupational names and grades will designate with increasing accuracy the respective skills, versatilities, and

---

[32] Among private wage-survey data available to the public are those for sample weeks in 1929 and some later years, as collected in the hosiery industry by George W. Taylor (impartial chairman), in cooperation with the trade association. See Univ. of Penna., Wharton School Industrial Research Dept., Hosiery Series (No. 1, Aug. 1936).

efficiencies of the various workers whose wage rates and earnings are tabulated.[33]

4. The trends just noted, which tend to make primary labor statistics ever more voluminous and complex, are paralleled in some degree by the development of more and better *nontechnical interpretive summaries*. Summaries and popularizations of technical matters are old stories, of course, and the multiplication of "press agent" activities has some dire possibilities; nevertheless, opportunities do change rapidly for quickly digesting and reporting to the public the net import of bewildering streams of events.

Illustrations of this trend are furnished by the monthly *Reports on Labor Market Developments*, issued by the Research and Statistics Division of the Bureau of Employment Security (Social Security Board), and by some (at least) of the affiliated state organizations. Under headings such as "Adequacy of Labor Supply" and "Trends in Hiring Practices," these agencies tell where and how and why supplies and demands relative to specified sorts of workers were changing during the previous few weeks. Little or no mention is made in these reports, however, of wage and salary rates and trends —which are obviously required to give a labor market report in a fuller sense. Materials of the latter sort are not difficult

---

[33] Full standardization of occupational nomenclature, as shown in Ch. 10 below, includes the two phases of: definition of job-type names (e.g., carpenter—general work), and grading or classifying degrees of skill within these occupations (e.g., carpenter A, or first-class carpenter).

A very comprehensive program of job analysis has been carried on for some years by the U. S. Employment Service—see its *Job Descriptions* series (automobile mfg., etc., industries—1935 and following years), and especially its *Dictionary of Occupational Titles* (3 vols., 1939). This dictionary contains miniature job descriptions of some 18,000 distinct occupations—29,000 job titles in all. In these titles, now used extensively in Federal employment work, appear some Roman numerals, e.g., "Pattern-maker, I"; but these numerals signify industries or materials, not degrees of skill.

All of this literature reiterates the warning, "The U. S. Employment Service has no place in the determination of jurisdictional matters or in the setting of wages and hours. Plans for the Occupational Research Program have never encompassed consideration of such things and no facts were collected on them." But, as these specifications are increasingly used for hiring and transfer (and extended to show some grades of competence beside "laborer," "apprentice," "foreman," and the like), it will be a short step to the use of them for wage-data tabulations.

to find; and it would seem feasible for such an interpretive "newsletter" to summarize briefly the current reports from other sources which most directly illuminate the issuing bureau's own primary data. The Federal Reserve Bank letters and the *Employment and Payrolls* pamphlets of the U. S. Bureau of Labor Statistics will serve as examples of this latter tendency.

E. Summary

Fruitful discussion of wage problems must grapple with quantitative data; and so this chapter is a very brief compendium and commentary relative to American wage statistics. The chief staple types of recurrently collected and published wage-hour data were analyzed—concerning wage rates and earnings per hour, week, and year. Our charts and tables illustrate these types and some leading "case histories" among them. We have also indicated summarily the import of wage differentials—by age, sex, region, occupation, etc.

These wage-hour statistics should also be regarded as quotations and should be correlated with other labor-market information. Labor quotations are being rapidly multiplied in quantity and improved in quality—especially by speedier publication of results of better sampling procedures, refinement of occupational nomenclature, and non-technical interpretive summaries.

PART II

FACTORS COMMONLY INVOKED IN COLLECTIVE WAGE ADJUSTMENT

CHAPTER 4

TRENDS IN ECONOMIC THEORY OF WAGES

The preceding chapters have sketched our main problems of wage policy, indicated the chief sources of quantitative information about wages, and set out a few facts of the American wage structure. In Parts II and III, into which we now enter, the organization is more largely theoretical, in the sense that it is based upon classes of causes and effects of wages. In the present chapter we outline briefly the outstanding factors or determinants of wage incomes, attempting to "see the wood," or rather to get an airplane view of relations among the various woods. We must neglect many very important clumps of "trees," such as the State as a wage factor, and relations between wages, mechanization, and industrial progress in general. A number of these wage factors, to be sure, are discussed in others of our chapters.

First, in section A we shall inquire further into relations between the income and the cost functions of wages; then in section B we shall proceed with the theory of wages under full competition among both employers and workers, as contrasted with section C, wage determination under imperfect competition.

A. Labor Units, Income and Costs

The concrete and practical facts of wages are so complex that we cannot hope to handle any considerable part of them all at once, but must attempt to progress through a series of abstractions or simplifications. In Chapter 2 it was pointed out that numerous items of real income of wage earners, such as services of public schools and recreational facilities, as well as the subsidized parts of health services, relief, and pensions, are not strictly wages. We have also noticed various crudities of "the labor market." It is therefore unnecessary to elaborate here the point that actual wage payments are in many cases different from what they would be in the perfect markets commonly assumed by economic theory. Such divergences are due not only to the exploitation of some workers, through their ignorance of what they could obtain from other employers, but also to similar ignorance on the part of some employers. Numerous rates of pay for personal services are also stereotyped by long use and wont; moreover, employers not infrequently base their payments in part on their human interest in the personal needs and circumstances of the people whom they hire. Nevertheless, in many important ways the labor market is analogous to commodity markets—wages resembling the "sticky" retail rather than the more volatile wholesale prices. Even exploitive and customary "wage" payments are influenced by other wage rates which are set under more nearly perfect market conditions.

Another way of bringing out the relation between the market-price and the human-being aspects of hired labor is to point to similar interplays of considerations with reference to other social groups, notably in agriculture. In order to understand and deal intelligently with problems of the agricultural population, one vital requisite is to study the objective and impersonal forces of supply and demand, with reference to farm commodities. But this sort of study is not sufficient; we must supplement it with studies of the human problems of the farmers, notably relations between their family incomes and family needs.

Units of Labor and Wage Differences.—In addition to these deviations from fully competitive market wages due to such forces as custom, ignorance, and sharp practice, the world of wages is made complex by diversities of skill and efficiency among workers and employers, and among equipment, production methods, and products. We are confused, moreover, by differing names for what prove to be very similar skills or jobs, and even more by the *same* names given to human and material factors which, on closer inspection, prove to be signifi-

cantly different. Before proceeding with further generalizations about wage forces, it will be well to recall some outstanding points which are thus suggested.

Wage Differences and General Wages.—Economists have
frequently treated wage theory under these two heads. Obviously it is much easier to be concrete and realistic when the
emphasis is upon *variations* among occupations and individuals;
indeed, some writers have protested that there is no such thing
as a *general* rate of wages—that wage theorizing which speaks
of *"the* rate of wages" and *"the* interest rate" is mystical, for
there are many types of wage and interest rates. The narrow
usefulness of economic generalizations based *merely* upon
highly simplified assumptions—such as Marx's implications
that all labor is homogeneous and that all real costs are labor
costs, and the classical doctrine of international trade, which
commonly gets too little beyond a similar abstraction—should
warn us against prescribing for a living patient on the basis
merely of anatomy of skeletons. The great diversities in the
world of wages and its history must indeed be emphasized; as,
for example, in Chapter 3 above and at greater length in the
chapters which follow. But it is also necessary, if we are to
understand the causes and conditions of wage changes as fully
as possible, occasionally to consider the interactions between *all*
wages considered as a group, and factors such as capital supply
and labor supply. Whenever reference is made to "wages" as
a type of distributive share, the context will show what sort
of composite of wage payments the author has in mind.

Labor Units and Labor Costs.—An associated problem of
labor economics is that of defining "labor" and "wages" for
purposes of quantitative discussion. There are literally innumerable varieties of labor units, when we take account not only
of hours, days, months, and occupations, but of variable efforts,
skills, equipment, processes, and management personnels and
methods associated with all these. Many such diversities, however, may reasonably be neglected while attention is focused
on the mere over-all fluctuations in man-hours worked in specified establishments, departments, and industries—particularly

if there are good grounds for assuming that no great changes are simultaneously occurring in proportions of skill, experience, and so on, among all these man-hours.

In general, the appropriate definitions and units of labor and wages are somewhat different, when we are most interested in wages as income to the workers, than when our focus is on wages as costs of production. For the former purpose, hourly, weekly, and annual *earnings* of individual persons, adjusted by reference to the best available index of living cost, give useful first approximations; and these can be supplemented in various ways, notably by information on averages and frequency distributions as to annual earnings, as well as on the nominal daily and weekly hours of work, their timing from the standpoint of the worker's convenience in relation to his various opportunities for use of "leisure," and actual overtime and "short time" worked in any given period. Other supplementary data, sharpening further the labor-income picture, include age, sex, marital status, and dependents of the wage earners.

When our preoccupation is with wages as the employer's cost of production, on the other hand, average hourly earnings, qualified by reference to production and price indexes, afford the best first approximation available. Such earned rates may be superior, for this purpose, to tariffs of wage rates—for the averages of hourly earnings reflect overtime penalties and other divergences of actual payments from nominal wage scales. The competent entrepreneur, as such, finds other aspects of wages secondary to their great rôle of *labor cost per unit of output.*[1]

A historical record of hourly earnings needs to be interpreted in the light of the schedules of working hours, if we are interested primarily in the employer's labor cost in all its significant relations with his total cost. A change to shorter hours, for example, may be associated with resort to two or more shifts, which tends to reduce certain overhead costs (such as

---

[1] Any actual person, to be sure, on the managerial or other wage-paying side, knows only within rather narrow limits what combination of wage and other arrangements, in his prevailing circumstances, actually will tend to minimize total cost per unit. The same observation applies to variations in marginal costs. Practical possibilities of experimentation are quite limited—especially in the direction of varying wage rates and other prices.

those incident to finance and taxes) of the plant. Furthermore, shortening of a working week from (say) 54 hours down to 44 or 40 rather commonly leads to an increase in labor efficiency per hour; for within such a range as this the worker can generally stand a higher rate of wear and tear on his muscles and nerves for the shorter than for the longer spell.[2]

Indexes of Labor "Productivity" and "Efficiency."—Such changes in physical output per worker and (better) per man-hour worked have been shown statistically for many industries, especially with reference to the last couple of decades.[3] These indexes, however, are somewhat heroic abstractions, easily misinterpreted, especially as to degrees, kinds, and causes of total change over long periods. The obvious measure of physical output of automobile manufacturing, for instance, provided by the mere count of number of cars and trucks produced, is very fallible as an indicator of long-term trend, in that qualities of cars and trucks, even within each price range, continually change—as do also the relative quantities in the various price-groups. Many other physical products change less than this, but some change even more—particularly in periods of early development and occasional rejuvenation from stagnation in the industry.

Supposing that this problem of defining units of output is comprehended and allowed for, there is another difficulty of great importance for labor economics. The mere averages of output per worker on payroll and per man-hour worked are often designated indexes of "labor productivity"; but it seems much less apt to mislead the unwary if we refer to these in-

---

[2] The relation between labor efficiency and hours of work is, of course, very complex; hence, simple generalizations in terms of over-all nominal weekly hours are apt to be misleading. In most work, efficiency increases during the first hour or so of each spell, as the individual "warms up"; and decreases during the last half-hour of the spell, as his attention is distracted by prospects of release. On the other hand, it appears that these latter factors and others have been handled by not a few managements and workers (in cereal and paper manufacturing, for example) so that as much, or almost as much, may be produced per worker in a 36-hour week composed of six six-hour days as in a 40-hour week, composed of five eight-hour days.

[3] See Ch. 8 and Chart 10, below.

dexes, or the thing they try to measure, as "physical output per worker employed" and "output per man-hour" respectively. Obviously, the gains of 50% or more in the latter variable, which have characterized most major American industry groups since 1919, are attributable to more skilful and faster working labor only in an uncertain or unknown degree—part of the growth certainly was due to more and better capital and management. The latter variables must be adequately controlled or allowed for, to arrive at a valid measure of labor *efficiency*.

If indexes of output or "productivity" and of hourly earnings are available for a given industry—as they are for many— then division of the former by the latter for each year or month in the series gives an index of "unit wage cost," of considerable social-economic significance. Piece rates of wages, or other wages based directly on current output, usually make for comparative stabilization of the employer's direct labor cost; and they tend to be adjusted in response to significant shifts in character of materials, products, equipment, or methods, as well as to time-wage rates in the same labor market. Only to a negligible extent, however, are long-term series of piece rates available for a whole industry, or intelligible to most economic researchers.

Employees' Services and Payroll Taxes as Labor Costs. —The employer's mere *wage* payments, over a long period, may imperfectly reflect the trends of his labor costs, in relation to the real incomes of his workers, for still other reasons. Prominent among these are private and public "welfare work."

With reference to the first, the perquisites which employers have often given employees in the past (notably "free" or "low-cost" housing) in addition to money wages have often been important items in the real income of such labor—though of course we are verging here on "truck" payment, which has been much restricted by labor legislation because some employers used such practices as scrip payments, coupled with high prices in company stores, to underpay their workers.[4]

---

[4] Adam Smith referred approvingly to anti-truck legislation (*Wealth of Nations,* Bk. I, Ch. 10). See Ch. 17-A, below.

The present emphasis on increasing minimum money wages puts pressure on employers to dispense with some types of "welfare work," such as free or subsidized housing; and to this extent the recent increases in money wages are somewhat greater than the gains in real wages. On the other hand, the continued spread of non-wage "free" benefits, such as vacations with pay and employer-supplied group insurance, tends to advance real wages faster than money wages.[5]

The great rise in payroll taxes, for support of old-age pensions, unemployment compensation, and other social services, which has occurred in many countries since 1913 also distorts many comparisons of pre-war and post-war labor costs. The employer may not unreasonably view "his" part of new payroll taxes as added labor cost, since these taxes ordinarily vary directly with wage payments (and, in part, also with salary payments). At present, all but very small American employers, in the majority of our urban types of private indus-

---

[5] Already the cost of payroll taxes plus voluntary labor benefits, such as vacations and sick leaves with pay, group insurance, and voluntary supplementary provisions for retirement income, to many progressive employers amounts to 10% or more of the payroll. A sample calculation of this sort may be found in the *1938 Annual Report* of Kimberly-Clark Corporation, Neenah, Wisconsin, and more comprehensive data in reports of the Conference Board; another, for the du Pont corporation, in U. S. Senate Hearings on S. Res. 215, Dec. 1, 1938, pp. 235-241.

Other varieties of compulsory social insurance, such as protection against loss of income from ill health, have been operative for many years in some other countries; and employers recently have been legally required to provide substantial vacations with pay in Sweden and in several other nations. In Germany, the birthplace of social insurance, under the Weimar Republic the employer's costs for compulsory and voluntary labor benefits, apart from wages, were competently estimated anywhere from 15% to 25% of the payroll. This high ratio may have been a factor of some consequence in the continuing mass of unemployment, which in turn was a prime factor in the overthrow of the Republic by the Nazis.

So long as paid vacations and other benefits are unusual and dependent on some sort of exceptional skill or efficiency of the worker, the employer's labor cost is apt to be affected favorably, if at all, by such increase of the employee's annual real income. If these benefits are widely generalized and made compulsory, however, it is doubtful whether there will be compensating changes in labor efficiency, and we may expect most of the cost in this case ultimately to be shifted to wage earners as a class by way of money wages lower than they would be but for such universal non-wage benefits—unemployment insurance, e.g., benefiting seasonal and casual workers in part at the expense of workers whose employment normally is highly stable.

tries, have to pay some 4% as payroll taxes (3% initially for unemployment compensation, and 1% for contributory old-age pensions); and when the program is fully in effect this total will be raised to some 5% or 6% (besides the employee's share of the tax to provide old-age annuities).

Do these payroll taxes constitute real incomes to the workers? They certainly do, for wage (and salary) earners as a class. So far as the annuity system is concerned, the covered workers and/or their dependents, moreover, all receive benefits made possible by their own and their employers' payroll taxes, with interest on the accumulations. As to the unemployment compensation system, on the other hand, the worker who is fortunate enough to have stable employment derives no direct and obvious benefit from his employer's payroll tax for this form of social security. Every covered worker does, nevertheless, derive real income from unemployment insurance, of the same general sort as the benefit to the insured house owner whose house has not actually burned down during the term covered by his fire insurance policy.[6]

B. Wage Adjustments under Full Competition

So much for general natures of labor and wages and their close relatives. We proceed now to develop some essentials of wage causation, beginning with the supposition that each industry consists of a large number of employing units and a still larger number of workers "attached" to that industry. In the present section let us also assume that all these units of employers and employed act independently, each for his own immediate economic interest and with full information about prevailing rates. Such would be the chief conditions of a "perfectly" competitive labor market—contrary to fact in many ways, as will be recognized even as we develop the simplified

---

[6] See, e.g., J. K. Hall, "Incidence of Federal Social Security Pay Roll Taxes," *Quar. Jour. of Econ.*, Nov. 1938, pp. 38-63, which concludes: "Labor, in the main, will bear the costs of social security as financed from pay roll tax revenue. To those who had hoped for a different result we may commend Professor Taussig's conclusion that 'obviously it is no objection to an insurance system that the premiums ultimately come from the beneficiaries themselves.'"

outlines of wage theory. In the next and last main section of the present chapter we shall make the picture more realistic by taking further account of imperfect competition on the sides of both management and labor.

B-1. Demand for Labor

Personal Services to Consumers.—It is sometimes convenient and legitimate to speak in terms of the supply and demand of labor in general, but such language leads almost irresistibly to ambiguous and even meaningless abstractions. Fundamentally, of course, demands for labor come from consumers' wants; and the great bulk of such consumers are themselves workers of one sort or another, during the greater parts of their lives. Thus, at bottom, the labor market is a great exchanging or bartering circle of personal services.

In this chapter we have not much occasion to deal with peculiarities among the industries which make or distribute commodities, but it seems expedient at this point to point to some differences *between* all the "commodity" industries, as a group, and the employments or "industries" which deal mainly in personal services which are rendered to the consumers directly, instead of through the medium of sale of commodities. Sometimes the consumer buys labor service by the piece, as from an independent bootblack; sometimes from an organization, for instance, in a barber shop; sometimes by a time period, as in the cases of chauffeurs and housemaids. In many instances, therefore, the consumer makes a direct judgment as to whether the laborer's services are worth the wage asked for them. The demand for each such type of labor in its own market is entirely analogous to the demand for each type of commodity. In both cases, statisticians may be expected gradually to determine elasticities of demand—i.e., to construct statistical schedules and curves showing (within limits) what quantities would be bought at each of a variety of prices—assuming other factors than price to remain constant.

Most employed persons, however, sell their services less directly to consumers. In some situations (for example, beauty shops, private medical clinics, and law firms), although one person may render service directly to the consumer, he does so in cooperation with other workers and perhaps with an employer, whose work and/or overhead expense for capital and land may also be important. And finally, the bulk of hired workers serve consumers only indirectly, through commodities and services—as in agriculture, manufacturing, trade, and in the operation of "utilities," such as transport and communication. In all these cases, including even very small enterprises, the utility and value of the work of the individual cannot be literally or unequivocally earmarked and measured in isolation from the contributions of services of other laborers and/or of property.

Marginal Productivity of Labor.—In these latter and more typical instances, in which one sort of labor cooperates with other sorts, and probably also with non-labor "productive factors," can each laborer's wage be, in any reasonable sense, based on *his own* production? Is there any realism in the "marginal productivity theory of wages"? Logically this problem involves two sub-problems, viz., (a) isolation of that part of the physical or technical product which is reasonably imputable to each of the factors producing it, and (b) valuation of these factor-products—finding what are often called the "value-products" of the labor and other cooperating factors.

The marginal productivity theory—or, rather, point of view as to valuation of distributive shares—may be briefly stated as follows: Suppose an experiment station arranges a series of productive processes in which all the conditions, so far as possible, are held constant except the number of homogeneous units of labor.[7] The results might be tabulated as in the table on the opposite page.

It will be observed that, in the series shown, increasing applications or inputs of labor in combination with constant inputs of other factors give diminishing proportionate physical

---

[7] For the simplest experimenting, the labor should be of uniform skill and quality; but variation in quantity could alternatively be made in terms of sets or squads of labor, each consisting of several varieties of skill, supervisory ability, and the like. The latter, more realistic, assumption should be considered for interpreting Marxian and other "labor theories of value."

HYPOTHETICAL DATA OF PRODUCTIVE EXPERIMENTS—
LABOR THE ONLY VARIABLE

Number of Workers	Total Product	Marginal Product of Labor[a]
4	80.0	. . .
5	86.6	6.6
6	91.0	4.4
. .	. . . .	. . .
8	96.0	2.5

[a]Number of units added by the "last" worker.

returns, i.e., increases in total output less than proportional to the increasing inputs of labor. Notice also how the last column illustrates the fundamental economic concept of marginal product. This marginal product is best defined as a comparison between two totals of physical output, with reference to a single variable factor. In this illustration, the marginal product of the *fourth* worker is not shown, because the output for a lesser number is not given; moreover, the marginal product of the *eighth* is here approximated by averaging the increase of five units of product which results from increasing the input of labor from *six* to eight—the average increase in product at this point, *per unit increase of labor,* is 2.5. Working backward, we may suppose the marginal product of labor when just *four* men are employed would be more than 6.6; but this inference might be false. Economists take three phases of output to be normal, if the combinations or proportions are sufficiently varied, viz., increasing, then decreasing, marginal and average products in relation to the variable factor; and finally diminishing absolute or total output. Under fully competitive equilibrium, full employment of all productive factors may be inferred —this is an implication of "fully competitive equilibrium." We here concentrate attention on the *marginal* aspect of the diminishing-return phase—the rate of change in totals between two adjacent points on the curve of total outputs, per unit of the factor whose input is variable.

The illustrative figures given in the above table have a certain historic interest, as they were used in one of the earliest expositions of the idea of diminishing returns per unit, when the factor *labor* alone is variable.[8] (The similar theory of diminishing returns of labor-plus-capital "doses," in relation to the rent of land was, of course, developed earlier.)[9]

Under the simplified conditions: (1) perfect competition among both employers and workers, (2) a given state of "technology," (3) constant demand curve for product, (4) insignificant changes (if any) in total output of *the whole industry*, and (5) labor the only variable factor of production, the following implications emerge from the analysis above summarized:

(a) Selling price of product, per unit, will not be affected by variations in output under the control of any one producer. Hence the value of labor's marginal product in each firm will vary directly and proportionately with the physical or technical quantity of such product.[10]

(b) The employer will strive to increase his gross revenue by successive applications or inputs of labor, up to the point where the addition thus made to his total gross revenue is counterbalanced by the increase in his total cost (i.e., until marginal revenue equals marginal cost).

(c) Thus, the value of the marginal product of labor in each firm tends toward equality with the wage of the marginal laborer.

---

[8] J. H. von Thuenen, *Der Isolierte Staat*, Zweiter Teil, 3 Aufl. (1st ed., 1826), 1930 ed., p. 570. (Cited by P. H. Douglas, *Theory of Wages*, p. 35.)

[9] It is very important to observe that this principle of average, marginal, and total outputs, in relation to variable inputs of factors, abstracts from discoveries, inventions, and improvements of methods, over even a few years' time. Actually, of course, "technology" (in a broad sense, including science, business methods, and the current state of knowledge of geographic locations of natural resources) is another very important variable. Here is an illustration of the numerous contrasts between "static" and "dynamic" aspects of economic affairs.

[10] In other words, each marginal physical product may be multiplied by the unit selling price (e.g., $1.00), to find the addition to the employer's gross revenue which results from the employment of the marginal worker.

(d) Since the workers are supposed to be homogeneous, or equally desirable employees, the marginal product of labor tends to equal the wage of each of the workers.[11]

Another way of stating the gist of (c) and (d) above: if we start with an equilibrium of five workers and a marginal "value-product" equal to a wage rate of $6.60, and then suppose that the supply of labor seeking employment increases to eight, *while other matters remain constant, and outputs vary as indicated in our hypothetical table above,* it follows that this enlarged labor supply can find full employment only at a wage rate approximating $2.50.

Some Retouches on Marginal Productivity Theory.—The doctrine outlined above is sometimes represented as a comprehensive theory of wage determination, but actually it is rather one approach or logical instrument among many required in the infinitely complex task of explaining exchange values of commodities and personal services. No lengthy statement of particulars in which the foregoing stark sketch falls short of being a lifelike portrait of the whole causation of wages is needed here; but a few additional lines will indicate more fully its relevance and importance with reference to the real world.

Among the qualifications demanded by realism are these: other conditions and factors commonly change simultaneously with inputs of labor; consequently, the "other things equal" basis is nearly always lacking in business firms for experimental determination of the amount of change in product attributable to each variation in quantity of each type of labor used. In many productive processes, in fact, a little more or less labor cannot practicably be used in relation to other factors, without reorganization of equipment, methods, and so on, which may entail expense and time.

---

[11] In other contexts we may speak, without confusion, of "super-marginal" and "sub-marginal" labor or land, in the qualitative sense—meaning individual workers or pieces of land which are better or worse in quality than the poorest which the current economic conditions make employable. In the "marginal productivity" context, however, emphasis is on *variable proportions among quantities,* each unit of each factor assumed to be interchangeable with any other unit.

So long, however, as managers *try* to get their money's worth in each purchase of a productive factor, and to neglect no opportunity to profit by buying labor and other resources and converting them into salable products, we have a general and powerful force tending toward equilibrium between each firm's marginal cost and marginal revenue. Naturally, managers make many mistakes in both directions; in particular, as will be emphasized in Chapter 13, below, during a depression they are especially in the dark as to the financial results to be expected from increasing or decreasing their expenditures for many sorts of labor. And in the last section of the present chapter we shall deal further with the significance of the many other ways in which both employers and employed lack the knowledge required for "perfect competition."

Partial and General Equilibria.—As was shown above, the marginal productivity approach, and its arithmetical illustration, has been a commonplace of economic science for several generations. It has, indeed, been the subject of much controversy, which has served to clarify essential points and qualifications such as were expounded in the foregoing paragraphs. More recently, mathematical and statistical economists have attempted to formulate the marginal productivity analysis, as well as many others, more precisely; and also, by statistical methods, to find actual quantitative relations among factors and products. It will be useful for us to notice very briefly some additions thus recently made to economic literature on wages.

The equilibrium between marginal labor cost and marginal revenue which was outlined above and illustrated by von Thuenen's hypothetical table, is often referred to as *partial* equilibrium, by contrast with more *general* economic equilibrium among a wider range of quantities and prices of factors and products.[12] This conception is reflected in numerous uses

---

[12] The mathematical exposition of general economic equilibrium apparently was first attempted by Leon Walras, at the University of Lausanne (Switzerland), who began publications on this matter about 1874. See, e.g., H. L. Moore, *Synthetic Economics*, p. 100 (Macmillan, 1929). An elementary treatment of essentials may be found in E. H. Phelps Brown, *The Framework of the Pricing System* (London: Chapman & Hall, 1934); see also "Wages" by J. Marschak, *Encyclopedia of the Social Sciences*.

of the abstract device of simultaneous equations, stating symbolically the quantitative relations among factors and products and their prices, in the writings of numerous economists.

Production Function.—Another mathematical-statistical development in this field is the idea of generalizing algebraically the effect on output of any given variation in input of *any* factor. Thus, Paul H. Douglas and associates have conducted very extensive researches on statistics of manufacturing outputs, in relation to inputs of labor and capital, over rather lengthy periods of time; and they have concluded that changes in these three series conform rather closely to a functional relation of the following type:

$$P = C^{\frac{1}{4}}L^{\frac{3}{4}},$$

in which P stands for quantity of total physical product, and C and L for total (physical) quantities, respectively, of fixed capital and of labor employed.

This illustrative function may be roughly translated thus: each *small* increase (increment) in the input of labor tends to increase the physical product three times as much as a similar proportional increment to the capital supply. (And *vice versa* for small decreases or decrements.) An increase in either factor alone, however, according to this equation, yields less than proportionate increases in total product. Another free translation: an increase of 1% in labor, if capital remains constant, tends to increase output on the average by three-fourths of 1%; and at any time the total product is related to the total quantities of labor and capital used, as shown by the exponents in the above equation—the fourth root (square root of square root) of total capital input, and the cube of the fourth root of total labor input. Douglas believes these propositions characterize the quantitative relations of labor, capital, and output (all expressed in physical terms) in American manufacturing during the epoch 1899-1922; and that thereafter a different functional relationship prevailed in this group of industries.[13]

---

[13] See P. H. Douglas *et al.*, *The Theory of Wages* (New York: 1934); also articles in *Quar. Jour. of Econ.*, Nov. 1937 and later, as well as in other

From such a function as the rather simple one given above, the mathematical process known as partial differentiation (familiar to all students of calculus, such as most engineers and statisticians) yields two other formulae for what economists call the marginal products of each of the factors (and what mathematicians call differential coefficients with reference to each factor). The function $P = C^{1/4}L^{3/4}$, for instance, implies that the respective marginal products of C and of L (let us designate these as M_C and M_L) may be computed as follows:

$$M_C = \tfrac{1}{4} \cdot \frac{L^{3/4}}{C^{3/4}}$$

$$M_L = \tfrac{3}{4} \cdot \frac{C^{1/4}}{L^{1/4}}$$

All these functions, moreover, standing alone imply a very small (theoretically infinitesimal) change in whichever is made the independent variable or "cause." Thus, if L in these equations stands for labor, the appropriate formula for marginal product of *labor,* applied to any specific inputs of capital

---

journals. For simplicity I have omitted the small modifying factor b from the Cobb-Douglas formula, which is held to apply to *American* manufacturing as a whole, 1899-1922.

There are several considerations which make it very difficult to judge the significance of this sort of attempt to check marginal productivity theory statistically. One is the changes in the great complex of "technology" which occur simultaneously with changes in inputs of labor and capital. Another is the problems presented by variable degrees of unemployment of the productive factors, from year to year. One way of expressing the meaning of the production function given above is to say that physical output in American manufacturing increased somewhat less than did fixed plant, and much more than did total labor inputs—one interpretation being that an increase of 1% in labor employed tended (within the limits explored) to raise output three times as much as did a rise of 1% in input of fixed capital.

But the two decades beginning in 1919 told a different story—much more complicated by post-war and other depression phenomena; perhaps also more affected by changes in "technology." From 1919 on, physical output showed a steeper upward trend than *either* fixed capital or labor employed (S. Bell, *Productivity, Wages, and National Income,* p. 47). Finally, consider the great reservation thus indicated by Professor Schumpeter (*Business Cycles,* vol. 2, p. 836): ". . . the fundamental theorem about marginal value productivity of labor is an equilibrium proposition that would at best apply (approximately) in neighborhoods of equilibrium, but cannot in the intervals between them. Profits in our [Schumpeter's] sense precisely arise and vanish in these intervals, hence, do not bear any definite relation to 'productivity wages.' "

and labor, may be solved for the marginal product of labor—in the sense that either addition or subtraction of an infinitesimal amount of labor, *at this point* on the curve of variable proportions of capital and labor inputs, would add or deduct the amount of output, per unit of labor, which is shown by solution for M_L.[14]

People having little or no acquaintance with mathematics and its engineering and statistical applications, especially those also not well schooled in economic principles, are apt to reject entirely the whole marginal productivity analysis because of its limited realism. They may point out, for instance, that variations in labor, capital, and so on are not actually infinitesimal in quantity; or, perhaps, that since capital without any assistance from labor could produce nothing, therefore the whole product must be imputable to labor. Doubts are also expressed that distribution as analyzed by marginal productivity would be exhaustive, i.e., that such fractions of the total product would be attributed to the cooperating factors as precisely to account for the total product.

It would take us too far afield if we attempted to clear up such difficulties thoroughly, but the following considerations may be helpful: (1) Functions and curves like these, based on higher mathematics, have the same general usefulness in economic theory and policy that they have in the various branches of engineering which relate to the practical arts. In the latter fields, too, variations by infinitesimal degrees are rare if not non-existent in practice, yet the infinitesimal calculus has proved an indispensable tool in dealing practically with finite and tangi-

---

14 Example: Suppose the input of labor is 100 units, of capital 100 units, and the quantity of output is also 100 units. (Each, of course, must be reckoned in its own appropriate physical or technical terms.) Then, substituting 100 for C and 100 for L in the illustrative formula given in the text above, we get $M_L = \frac{3}{4} \cdot \frac{100\frac{1}{4}}{100\frac{1}{4}} = \frac{3}{4}$ or .75 of one unit of product—i.e., addition (subtraction) of one unit of labor from this particular combination, if we have the correct production function, would increase (or decrease) product (P) by .75 of one unit.

Another way of expressing marginal product of (e.g.) labor is $\frac{dP}{dL}$, i.e., ratio of marginal increment (or decrement) of product or output to marginal increment (decrement) of labor input.

ble quantities in such pursuits as manufacturing, transportation, and communication. (2) The marginal concept in economics gives most consistent and reliable results when applied to variations which are small in relation to the total quantities involved—i.e., to data extensive enough to allow "the law of averages" scope. (3) As to accounting precisely for the total product, it is interesting that the production functions most commonly discussed indicate variations of output in relation to variable inputs, such that a uniform fraction of the total product is imputed to each type of factor, so long as the state of the art remains constant. Take, for example, the Cobb-Douglas function cited above (referring to American manufactures as a group, 1899-1922). Three-fourths of the total product is here always imputed to the labor factor, one-fourth to capital. Over-all totals of wages in all industries, too, remain rather close to a constant fraction in annual estimates of national income (see p. 180, below). These are too few indications, however, to show reliably whether variation in the relative labor and capital inputs—other conditions constant—would leave unchanged the fractions of total output tending to go to each class.

Elasticity of Demand for Labor.—What does all this signify, with reference to demand for labor? As was indicated above, if the supply of labor increases, relatively to the supplies of cooperating factors, the economic productivity of each unit of the former tends to fall, except as offsetting changes, such as introduction of capital-saving methods, may occur at the same time. If a particular productive process makes for a very slowly diminishing marginal product of labor, as the relative intake of labor increases, then that circumstance contributes toward (but does not assure) high elasticity of demand for labor. Such is the case with the Cobb-Douglas function reviewed above, in which an increased input of 1% of labor (capital remaining constant) results in a diminution of only one-fourth of 1% in the marginal product of labor.

Since the relation between quantity of labor sold and the price per unit is of great practical importance, we must here give further attention to the idea elasticity of demand, with special reference to a given type of labor.[15] One of the staples of economic science is the coefficient of elasticity, most commonly applied to the demand for a particular commodity. This coefficient is the ratio of a small percentage (i.e., *relative*) change in quantity sold, to the associated percentage or relative change in the price per unit. Thus, if lowering the price by 1% results in a precisely compensating increase in quantity sold (approximately 1%), then the coefficient of elasticity is —1.00, and it is said that the elasticity is unity.[16] It makes no difference which is regarded as the independent variable or "cause" —whether the change in price is regarded as the result of the change in quantity marketed, or *vice versa*.

Approximate actual coefficients of elasticity of demand for various commodities (within practical ranges) have been established by statistical researches, usually on the basis of records of prices and quantities sold over a number of years, with various allowances and adjustments designed to hold, as far as possible, "other things equal."[17]

It was stated above that the production function symbolizes one important influence on elasticities of demand for labor and other factors of production. But marginal product in the physical sense is one thing; its value in exchange is another, dependent in part on elasticity of demand for the product. These two aspects of "marginal product of labor" should be carefully distinguished. The production function used for

---

[15] See also Ch. 13, below, wherein this matter is discussed further, with special reference to wage policies in booms and depressions.

[16] Such elasticity of demand is usually negative, because an increase of quantity is associated with a *decrease* of price. The formula for E (elasticity of either demand or supply) is

$$E = \frac{\dfrac{dq}{q}}{\dfrac{dp}{p}}$$

where p stands for price and q for quantity sold.

[17] See e.g., publications of the late Professors H. L. Moore and Henry Schultz, of Holbrook and Elmer Working, Mordecai Ezekiel, and Mrs. E. W. Gilboy. Most of these relate to agricultural staples. A recent set of researches, by Dr. C. F. Roos and others, is presented in *The Dynamics of Automobile Demand,* General Motors Corp., 1939.

illustration above, and the output curve which it specifies, indicate how the *physical* product (or, rather, its total exchange value) will tend to be shared among the factors (under fully competitive conditions), but not how these "remunerations in kind" will stand as to purchasing power in terms of other services and commodities. The technology of coal mining, for instance, might be such, in the vicinity of a total labor input index of 100, that increase of the labor index to 101 would raise output proportionately—to 101. Such an observation, so far as it goes, indicates no fall in physical marginal product of labor. But this increase in total output might bring a decline in market value of coal per ton, and so in the value of the marginal product of mine labor.

Elasticity of Substitution.—The production functions, which naturally vary greatly among plants and processes, and also from time to time and from place to place, have the further important aspect of indicating the "elasticity of substitution" of one factor for another. In this sense, to increase the input of capital relatively to that of labor is to substitute capital for labor, per unit of output. If labor and equipment must be used in invariable proportions for each unit of product (as is often the case within the lifetime of a piece of equipment—e.g., one driver to each shift of hours within which a motor truck is used), then there can be no *immediate* reaction at this point in the way of substituting capital for labor, if labor becomes relatively higher priced. Over a longer period, however, any factor which becomes relatively cheaper tends very generally to be used more freely in relation to another factor which becomes relatively more expensive. The implications of this idea will be explored further, with respect to the "competition between machinery and labor" and between different types and locations of labor, in Chapters 12 and 13, below. There, as well as in Chapter 5 and still elsewhere in this book, it is shown that the apparently obvious proposition that increases and decreases of wage rates tend respectively to check or to raise employment is subject to important qualifications. It exemplifies the "partial equilibrium" or "other things equal" emphasis of traditional economic theory. But economists attempt progressively to take account of wider and later repercussions of particular events, such as spirals of upward and downward prices and wages. Such studies take us in the direction of "general equilibrium." On the other hand, the idea of a general or average elasticity of demand for all labor at once is so abstract, not to say vague, that its manipulation is attempted by few competent labor economists.

Labor's Interest in Capital Supplies.—How are wages influenced by the quantity of capital available? The preceding section, in connection with a few of the economic commonplaces assumed above, gives some help toward answering this question. When economists speak of a changing *productivity* of labor, especially of *marginal* productivity, they are very unlikely to be referring to changes in the skill or effort of the workman. The latter sort of development is rather known as increased or decreased labor *efficiency*. The marginal productivity economic apparatus, as explained above, also assumes constancy in the physical or technical unit of each factor.

A corollary of these propositions is the familiar economic principle that it is to the advantage of labor as a group that the supply of capital should increase faster than the supply of labor—not necessarily by multiplication of mere numbers of capital goods, for "capital" may also be increased along such avenues as new designs, increased precision, safety, comfort. Such relative increase of capital has, in the past, been a most important lever for raising real wages or standard of living, and all indications are that it will continue to be in the future. (Inventions, discoveries, and gains in skill and intelligence of labor and management are other great levers, more or less independent of capital supply.)

Is there, then, no reality underlying the popular idea of conflict between capital and labor? Such a conclusion by no means follows; the long-run general identity of interest between these two groups does not at all signify that no individual may gain at the expense of others. As is argued further in the latter part of this chapter, as well as in most other parts of this book, the suppliers of the productive factors do not obtain the values of their marginal products automatically, independently of any marketing and bargaining skill and effort. This marginal productivity scheme merely describes one important part of the framework within which wage bargaining must proceed. In the past, suppliers of capital and of wage labor have been largely in distinct, and hence often conflicting, social classes; but such need not always be the case. Thus, if a group of hired persons get the better of the wage or salary bargain, through their own saving this outcome may increase the total capital supply more than if the advantage had been reaped by their employers. It is sometimes argued that excessive profits tend to do less social harm than do excessive wages—since capitalists are usually more able and willing to invest surplus incomes in industrial plant and equipment ("other things equal"!) than are wage earners. The degree of truth in this type of argument depends, not only on the relative abundance of real capital equipment as compared with labor, but also on the amount and kind of new saving needed.

Conditions in Which Wage Equals Marginal Product.— The suggestion is often made that, in order that wages may be brought anywhere near labor's marginal productivity, workers as well as employers must know the production functions— must know what variations in product are attributable to what changes in inputs of production factors. This view is incorrect. The elements which are necessary in order that wages be adjusted to the true marginal product of labor are: (1) that the judgment of *employers* on the production functions or processes should be correct, so that they may bid for factors on the basis of the quantities of products which can be made out of such factors (in the existing technology); (2) that full and free competition should prevail among both workers and employers, implying (3) that workers as well as employers should know what wages are being paid for what types of work. If we add (4) that labor as well as capital have adequate mobility, the implication of (3) and (4) is that wage earners may take advantage of competition among employers for their services.

B-2. Factors in Labor Supply

Much of the foregoing account has been concerned with various aspects of demand for labor, one being the elasticity of such demand. Equally important in determining the wage rate (value of labor per unit) are forces influencing labor supply. To the latter factors we must now devote some analysis, and again it will be useful to raise the question of elasticity, i.e., to what extent labor supplies vary in response to wage rates and earnings. In this present section we shall continue to emphasize spontaneous or individualist actions, reserving comments on trade union and other collectivist influences for section C, below.

Two principal *general* factors which tend to influence supplies of all or many types of labor simultaneously may be first explored. These are: (1) the relative attractions of labor for the pay offered and of leisure "on one's own time"; and (2) population changes, by births, deaths, disabilities, and migrations.

Influences of Wages on Hours.—With reference to the first of these factors, two principles are indicated by the economic laws of utility and disutility: increases of an individual's real income (subject to some qualifications) tend to yield him decreasing marginal utility or net attraction; and (again within limits) increasing the hours of the week devoted to work for pay, and/or increasing the intensity of work, tend to raise the marginal disutility or repugnance of such work. Equilibrium among such forces as these has much significance for modern labor groups, though to many an individual worker or small employer there appears to be only Hobson's choice—he must (he thinks) accept the terms offered, or starve. Rates of pay for overtime and for work on unpopular shifts and holidays are resultants, not merely of any individual's balance between utility and disutility, but of all the factors contributing to the group behavior in question. If jobs are scarce and not well protected by union power, for example, most men can be required to work long hours and on nights and Sundays without premium wage rates; whereas if jobs are abundant, union or no union, liberalizing wages may lead the workers to give themselves more holidays, regardless of the boss's convenience. There is no simple or universal relation between rate of pay and supply of labor efficiency.

Outstanding variables in this feature of labor supply are the length of the normal work week and the intensity of work within each number of hours tried. The general shortening of weekly working hours which has occurred over the past century may be due in part to rising real incomes of the workers, and in part to the rise in marginal disutility of the more intensive work which has developed along with the shorter hours; but probably the most significant cause has been the widespread belief that shortening hours is a useful method of mitigating unemployment.

Still another angle of the hours-of-work question is indicated by the statistical finding that relatively long weekly hours, at relatively low hourly rates, have often been acceptable to the workers, provided that the weekly earnings were higher than they could obtain elsewhere—where they might work for higher *hourly* rates, but at hours so short as to yield lower *weekly* earnings.[18]

Gross Population Changes in Relation to Wages.—Somewhat arbitrarily I shall deal especially summarily with this venerable and important chapter of wage theory. The modern history concerned is complicated by policies oriented toward

---

[18] More inclusive data, for several sample years between 1890 and 1926, were analyzed by Paul H. Douglas, who found a well-defined association between higher hourly earnings and shorter working weeks (*The Theory of Wages,* Ch. 12). So far as hours of work are concerned, therefore, within limits the supply of labor appears negatively elastic with reference to earnings per hour. The true supply of labor efficiency is not given by mere man-hours worked, however, since more work is often done per hour in the shorter week. There is considerable ground for the view that shortening hours are, in the first instance, a form of real income made possible by rising output per man-hour; and that further reduction of hours, by restricting the effective labor supply, tends to enhance the latter's unit price. But see the argument, and statistical evidence supporting it, that in American urban industries as a whole, over the period 1919-1938 (characterized by phenomenal reductions of hours and gains in hourly earnings): *"The gains to labor proved to be chiefly in the form of greater leisure."* (S. Bell, *Productivity, Wages, and National Income,* p. 176—italics in original.)

such objectives as increasing the supply of cannon-fodder, maternal and child welfare, and attempting to combat local unemployment and raise wages by restricting international and intercommunity migrations. It is clear that the old and crude economic interpretation of "Malthusian" doctrines—to the effect that all gains in real wages per capita tend soon to be nullified (as to average or per capita individual welfare) by the growth in population which they permit—is subject to many important qualifications; while its optimistic antithesis is perhaps still more misleading. The outstanding facts appear to be the differential rates of net fertility (birth rates minus death rates) among and within social-economic groups. To a rather important extent, *within* such groups—especially within professional and other "white-collar" groups—the higher-income families tend to be the more prolific. *Among* broader occupational groups, on the other hand, differential fertility tends in the opposite direction, despite the advance of birth controls. Farmer and coal mining groups, for instance, with low average real per capita incomes, tend to have high birth rates.

Thus the reaction of gross labor supply to changes in wages is complex and uncertain. So is the reaction of real wages per capita to changes in total labor supply. Increasing population encroaches on "means of subsistence," in the sense of *ultimate sources* of raw materials; but advancing technology long ago reduced this particular "Malthusian devil" to a minor rôle.

Relative Labor Supplies: Age and Sex Groups.—So much for general influences on the amount of available labor. Let us now illustrate the innumerable particular influences by reference to the somewhat variable offerings of work by men, women, and children.

Populations of nations, cities, and other areas differ a good deal in their age compositions, and to a much lesser extent in the proportions of males and females. Hence, a mere count of heads is a rather poor indicator of labor supply; a better one is a count of males and females within the more active working ages. Yet the "active working ages" also vary somewhat with place and time. People's ideas and circumstances change with reference to such matters as how early their children or youth should begin employment, how early voluntary or enforced retirement should occur; and these ideas are often quite different with reference to the two sexes. We might have rationally expected that a rising level of real incomes would tend to lower the average retiring age; but the opposite tendency seems stronger at the present time—mass unemployment tends to make average incomes much lower than they would be with full employment, and such unemployment now leads to extreme demands that the retiring ages be lowered drastically, to make more room for younger people out of work.

The labor supply is also negatively elastic (lower quantities offered, as wages per unit rise), with reference to ratios of women and children employed. The percentages of women and children working for wages, in other words, tend to be higher (other things equal) in those nations and cities where men's real earnings are low than where they are high.[19] Throughout the world, for example, a great deal of hard agricultural work is done by unpaid family labor, which is accounted for but imperfectly, if at all, in statistics of employment, unemployment, and wages; such woman and child labor is due largely to the low real incomes of most farm families. Among many families above the lowest incomes, however, the last few generations have seen a great relative increase in employment of women, both married and unmarried, mainly for other reasons than absolute poverty. Thus the statistics of proportions of women gainfully employed show resultants of the opposing tendencies toward "emancipation of women": one (decline of prejudice against their employment) offering them more jobs for pay; the other (rising real incomes per capita) tending to release them from the necessity of working for pay.

The supply of youthful workers is also in a state of ferment. Our national Wage-Hour law of 1938 renews and presses

---

[19] In 1919-20, for example, the coefficient of correlation between average earnings in manufacturing in 41 American cities and the percentage of the respective populations aged 14 and 15 years gainfully employed was, for males, of the order of —.56 and for females —.47. (Douglas, *Theory of Wages*, p. 275.)

further the NRA prohibition of "child labor" under the high standard of 16 years;[20] this law is merely outstanding among numerous recent governmental acts tending to raise minimum ages for employment. In no small degree such legislation, like legal restrictions on the labor of convicts, women, old people, and aliens, is motivated by the group selfishness of adult workers who want to get rid of competitors for their own jobs. But, as pressure-group restrictive practices go, the raising of "child labor" standards is socially beneficent, especially so far as it is accompanied by positive measures for education and training of youth. Part of such training should consist of supervised and paid productive work.

C. Imperfect Competition; Implications for Wages

From wage theory based largely on the assumption of full and free competition among large numbers of workers and employing establishments, we turn to the less thoroughly explored field of value theory with respect to labor, using the more realistic assumptions which are commonly bracketed under the general heading "Imperfect Competition." One of our main objectives here is to find the principal ways in which trade unions can influence wages; another and almost parallel quest is understanding of the analogous powers of employers.

Meaning of Imperfect Competition.—What is the general nature and significance of imperfect competition? Everyone interested in economic studies, to be sure, has recognized various imperfections of the competition actually prevailing at various times and places. Such "lapses" include incomplete information as to the prices, quantities, qualities, and other terms of goods actually sold; also various restraints on competition imposed by concerted actions of groups of people who have tried to pursue what seemed to them a "live and let live" policy. One rather common incident of competition, which paradoxically operates in some cases to restrain and in

---

[20] Also 16 to 18, in employments deemed hazardous by the U. S. Children's Bureau.

other cases to intensify competition among sellers, is secret deals, by which virtually the same good sells in an imperfect market for more than one price at the same time. We are also familiar with the age-long efforts of governmental agencies to enforce competitive conditions by legal penalties and prohibitions against monopolistic combinations and "conspiracies in restraint of trade"; and with the less frequent recurrent efforts to deal with farmer and labor unions as monopolies or conspiracies.[21] In the older economics textbooks, the theory of value under conditions of outright monopoly, and even of duopoly (only two vendors), was contrasted with value or price under perfect competition.

In 1933 and 1934 were published Edward Chamberlin's *Theory of Monopolistic Competition* and Joan Robinson's *Economics of Imperfect Competition,* signalizing a "New Era" in economic theory, clarifying and unifying the analysis of value and price, especially under modern actual conditions.[22] I use here "imperfect" rather than "monopolistic" competition, not merely because the former is the more general term, but because it seems to carry less in the way of misleading connotations. Associations of business men, farmers, and laborers quite properly resent most of the charges made against them on the score of "monopolistic combination," since they are usually sincerely unaware of any intent to engage in anti-social monopolistic conspiracy.

Imperfect Competition among Employers, and Wages.— Among the innumerable types of influence of imperfect competition upon wages, a few are selected for brief discussion here, namely, (1) variations in size of employing unit, in rela-

---

[21] See, e.g., Thurman W. Arnold, *The Bottlenecks of Business* (1940).

[22] Mrs. Robinson and Mr. Keynes, however, appear not to realize how much of the difference between their own views of wages in relation to unemployment and the classical doctrines on these same matters are accounted for by differences in assumptions as to competition among workers and business men. Surely the Keynesians do not mean seriously to deny the classical idea that, if all wages and other terms of exchange were completely flexible and if there were full competition all around, unemployment would always be of a "dynamic" sort, and always tending to disappear. Some further comment on the Keynesian discussions relative to wages will be found in Ch. 13, below.

tion to local labor market; (2) joint activities among employers; and (3) significance of imperfect competition for the marginal productivity analysis of wages.

(1) The first point is often neglected, especially by conservative economists, who emphasize competition among employers as tending to *raise* wages. The Webbs (who, contrariwise, overstressed competition among individual laborers as tending to depress wages) quite reasonably criticized harder-boiled economists for pointing to the rising trend of real wages among domestic servants (such as cooks and housemaids) as proving that trade unions are not necessary to secure higher wages for workers. This domestic-labor illustration refers to a very large number of employing units, composed mainly of separate households, in each of which not more than a few servants are employed. It would thus be difficult for all these domestic employers voluntarily to combine to keep down wages, though their addiction to custom, and the numerous other imperfections of this labor market, do prevent domestic wages from responding promptly to slight changes in total supply and demand. Similar observations may be made with reference to other employments, as in agriculture and in part of the mercantile field, characterized by many small-scale employers.

But in most industries the employing enterprises which account for the bulk of employment have long been increasing in size. Any big employer automatically presents a united front to a large number of individual employees; the extreme case, perhaps, being the "company town," in which the employer may have other weapons, such as eviction from housing, in addition to his power of discharge from the payroll.

(2) As employment becomes concentrated into larger units, moreover, these managements find it feasible and natural to carry on many types of "cooperative" action. Some of these collaborative methods have been clearly anti-social if not illegal, such as blacklisting employees suspected of trade union activity. Many others, like the maintenance of statistical, research, and training organizations, may be managed so as to be advantageous to the general public as well as to the proprietors who conduct them.

Most types of collective action within any industry or trade, however, need to be safeguarded against activities which violate the letter or the spirit of anti-trust laws, though the dividing line is often very hard to establish. Cooperative interchanges of wage and price information have sometimes assumed forms which were open to attack as tending to bring pressure on the employer who "stepped out of line" by paying more or charging less than his competitors in the industry. In both the commodity and the labor markets, competition is made more effective by prompt broadcasting of information on prices, etc., concerning *bona fide* transactions; yet the history of trade associations, both formal and informal, shows instances in which interchange of information about prices of commodities and of labor has been carried on by means which tend toward anti-social controls of such prices and wages by the businessmen in the associations.

(3) Finally, we may notice how imperfections of competition among employers affect the relation of the wage to the value of the marginal product of labor. This is taken up in detail in the following paragraphs.

Wage Rate May Not Equal Value of Labor's Marginal Product.—The crucial point here is that, under the simplest sort of perfect competition, any employer arranges his volume of employment and output on the assumption that his own volume will have no effect on the unit price of his product; whereas, under monopoly and also in many forms of imperfect competition, the employer calculates that (within limits) an increase of his own output will depress the average price of his product, because his production accounts for, or influences, a relatively large fraction of the whole production of his industry. This point comes out most sharply, of course, by reference to a perfect and unregulated monopoly—let us say, of a community's water supply (for whose product the substitutes to which consumers may resort are very unsatisfactory).[23]

---

[23] In some degree each enterprise which cultivates a clientele of its own, by such means as trade-marks, advertising, and distinctive service, is a monopolist, because many of its customers consider there is no thoroughly satisfactory substitute for this firm's product and/or service. This case is

Chart 4 shows graphically some relations between wage rates and value of marginal product of labor, under highly simplified assumptions, including disregard of non-labor costs. Each of the diagrams refers to the demand for labor by a single firm; one (A) under perfect competition, the other (B) like A in all respects except that B hires labor under non-competitive conditions. Diagram A is based on the supposition that labor is bought at a going and uniform rate of $30 per unit; hence, the firm's average cost per "laborer" (AC) is equal to its marginal cost of labor (MC = cost of one-unit-more). Such a uniform price per (standard) unit of labor would characterize a perfect labor market. Diagram A also assumes perfect competition in the sale of the product, so that the unit selling price (not shown here) is fixed by the whole market, independently of the output or employment of this particular firm. Firm A, therefore, hires 30 laborers, getting diminishing product as shown by the "VMP" (value of marginal product of labor) curve; at the going wage rate of $30, represented here as being also the value of the marginal product of labor when 30 men are employed. Thus, this firm reaches employment equilibrium at the point where the value of labor's marginal product equals labor's wage rate.

Chart B shows the smaller employment and lower wage rate which would result if the selling price per unit of product is fixed by perfect competition in the commodity market, at the same rate as in case A, but if there is also the following type of imperfect competition in firm B's hiring of labor: The lesser the number employed by this firm, the lower is its wage rate. Accordingly the *marginal* labor cost (dashed curve marked "MC_1" = increase in total wage bill, as each addi-

known to economists as a variety of "monopolistic competition," and it is obvious that the monopoly which pertains only to trade-marks and/or other good will of a firm is subject to competition from substitutes (supplies of competing firms in the same industry) which are much more satisfactory than is the case with the "monopolies" (a single firm or tight combination "monopolizing" a whole industry) of popular speech.

Apart from the economic power to "administer" price control which goes with "product differentiation," or with any device for limiting the number of firms within a market, other "customary" factors affect price and wage flexibility. Thus, wholesale prices tend to be much more flexible than retail.

DEMAND FOR LABOR

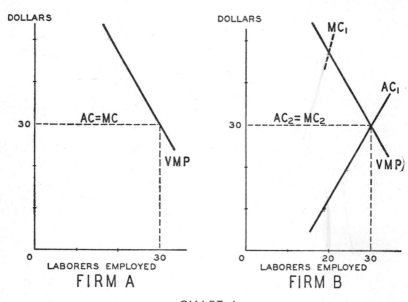

CHART 4

Hypothetical demand for labor in Firm A, under perfect competition in sale of product, also in hire of labor, and in Firm B, under perfect competition in sale of product, imperfect competition in hire of labor. **AC** = average cost (wage rate); **MC** = marginal cost (of hiring one more man); **VMP** = value of labor's marginal product. Adapted, by permission, from J. E. Meade and C. J. Hitch, An Introduction to Economic Analysis and Policy, graphs III and V, p. 156. Cf. data in ibid., appendix tables (New York: Oxford Univ. Press, 1938).

98

tional man is hired) rises faster than the average labor cost or wage rate, and the firm is shown as obtaining its maximum profit at the low wage rate of $10, which is here supposed to be contingent on hiring no more than 20 workers. With 20 workers, the value of the marginal product attributable to labor is materially higher ($48) than if 30 were employed ($30); and so the wage rate of $10 falls far short of the value of labor's marginal product. (But if firm B expanded production by hiring more labor, the added product would be worth less—under these assumptions—than the addition made to total wage bill by the joint effects of more labor to pay and the higher wage rate.)

Another type of imperfect competition in the hire of labor (not shown here) is discriminatory wage payments to different (equally productive) members of the labor force; for example, by hiring in new people at higher wages than are being paid to those already on the force. Personnel managers as well as unions have had to contend against such discriminatory wages, which may grow up spontaneously, not necessarily as the result of any deliberate policy.[24]

Under the conditions assumed for our diagram, a minimum-wage rate of $30 enforced on firm B would doubtless reduce this firm's net profit, but it would shift the point of maximum total net profit from employment of 20 to employment of 30 workers. For under this new condition, the *unit* labor cost cannot be driven below $30 ($AC_2 = MC_2 = 30); B, therefore, continues to hire until, with 30 men, he reaches the equilibrium where the added outlay for wages is barely covered by value of marginal product of labor.

This bit of economic geometry does not, indeed, signify much in a practical sense for the total range of minimum-wage problems; these are discussed realistically in Chapters

---

[24] Firm B's position as a purchaser of labor is very roughly analogous to the short-run power of the employer in a one-company town.

For other applications of imperfect competition theory to labor and wages, see J. Robinson, *op. cit.*, Chs. 25, 26; E. Chamberlin, *op. cit.* (rev. ed., 1939), Ch. 8; J. E. Meade and C. J. Hitch, *Economic Analysis and Policy* Pt. II, Chs. 5, 7 (New York, 1938); P. H. Douglas, *International Labor Review*, March 1939.

17-20, below. But the above diagram and accompanying discussion do show (1) that, apart from many other imperfections of a labor market, the average wage of labor *need* not be equal to the value of the marginal product of labor; and (2) that minimum-wage control does not *necessarily* lead to diminished employment.

Non-competing Groups Among Workers.—Imperfect competition also exists among workers, and takes a number of forms. Economists have given much attention to the idea, suggested by J. S. Mill and elaborated by J. E. Cairnes, that the various grades of "unskilled," semi-skilled, skilled, and professional occupations constitute "non-competing groups" or almost social castes—in that most workers remain within the social stratum into which they are born. Cairnes emphasized the analogy between exchanges of services between these skilled and unskilled labor groups and exchanges of products and services between nations. Many inhabitants of the poorer nations, like those of the less skilled occupations, according to this view, would like to migrate into higher-income territory, but are restrained by obstacles which to most of them are insuperable.

Some critics have pointed out that a sharp statistical definition of such "non-competing" labor groups is impossible; and others have urged that there is, in fact, a very considerable flow of relatively low-born individuals into higher-paid occupations.[25]

The great growth in public and philanthropic assistance to education and training of promising young people, which has occurred in Europe as well as in America during the past century, tends to reduce the importance of such social hindrances to full competition within the total supply of labor; but we are far from the goal of real economic democracy.

---

[25] Cf. F. W. Taussig and C. S. Joslyn, *American Business Leaders* (New York, 1932), for a statistical research into the social origins of executives in American companies. Professor Taussig has emphasized non-competing groups in his valuable writings on wage theory, but in the book cited here he reports that a significant number of powerful business men have risen from laborer families.

Even if handicaps due to low incomes were completely over-come, however, it is probable that non-competing groups would remain, based on inborn physical and mental differences among people.

Collective Bargaining.—The last phase of imperfect competition in labor supply to be considered in this chapter is the influence of organization on the labor side, i.e., of trade unions. Again many points must be neglected for the sake of brevity, the objective being to show the position of the principal elements in the larger pattern. In this discussion we must raise briefly the old question: What are the limits of power over wages to be secured by collective bargaining—that is, by organization among employers and employed respectively? And a larger question looms in not a few minds: Are we permitting non-competing castes or labor aristocracies to develop under labor organization and social legislation? Sometimes it appears that the gulf is widening between job-holders and jobless, and that restrictions upon hiring make the jobless person's plight hopeless. This last issue is largely a question of facts and quantitative relations; it will be touched upon at various points in ensuing chapters.

By abstract and simplified argument it may be shown that if *either* the supply or the demand curve is completely inelastic (meaning that over a range of prices, no more and no less will be offered—or taken), the price will nevertheless tend to be "determinate" if the other curve is elastic. Under these conditions only one price will just bring out the marginal increment of the elastic supply or the elastic demand. Thus, if a union controlled the whole labor supply of its industry and the demand for such labor were elastic, it could not enforce *both* its wage rate and a full volume of employment. If, on the other hand, there are overlapping ranges of inelasticity of both supply and demand—as may be the case, for a season anyhow, when both sides are well organized—then there may be a "range of practicable wage bargains," between the lowest the workers will accept and the highest the employers will pay, without a bitter fight; and any change within this range would have no soon-visible effect on employment.[26] This proposition gives some slight support to the "bargain theory," which holds that wages are determined, not so much by economic laws, as by bargaining skill.

But it must immediately be emphasized that the "range of practicable bargains" is primarily a short-term view, based considerably on existing commitments of both employers and workers. As time elapses, it may be found that the wage was too high, in the sense that it stimulated competition of other sections and industries, and checked or reduced investment in the industry directly concerned; or too low, in the sense that it provides inadequate incentive to maintain the needed labor supply in this industry or trade and area.

Other variables and factors involved in the query as to limits of trade union power over wages are very numerous; some of them are discussed elsewhere in this volume. Union officials, for example, tend to be specialized bargaining agents, whose functions are somewhat analogous to those of commodity brokers and also of attorneys; they utilize, moreover, labor market information collected through trade union channels. The union can give its members, or help them to secure, strike and unemployment benefits and public "welfare" allowances, moreover; can thus assist such members to hold out for better wages; and, hence, can bring labor bargaining closer to the commercial concept of "willing buyer and willing seller."

The outstanding practical question: How much advantage (if any) in real *annual* earnings is secured on the average by the union man for his dues and other contributions to his union? can hardly be answered in any simple and straightforward fashion. Those statistical wage comparisons between union and non-union workers, which are most plausible in that other factors appear to be not too dissimilar, quite commonly refer to the older crafts or skilled men's unions. These older unions, of course, had considerable opportunity to regulate the

---

[26] See, e.g., A. C. Pigou, *Economics of Welfare,* 1st ed., Pt. 3, Ch. 6 (1920); A. Marshall, *Principles of Economics,* Bk. 5, Ch. 14, Sec. 9; and W. H. Hutt, *Theory of Collective Bargaining* (1930). Hutt and Hicks argue that Edgeworth, Marshall, and Pigou exaggerated the power of trade union bargaining to control even wage rates, to say nothing of total labor income.

supplies of their skills, by such policies as apprenticeship, short hours and "work sharing," and by working rules which in some instances amounted to voluntary limitations on their members' efficiency. The higher *hourly* earnings thus secured are generally accompanied by shorter work weeks, so that weekly earnings are not as much higher; and there are many difficulties in the attempt to show statistically the effect of unions on *annual* earnings of members. It is plausibly argued that their high hourly rates are achieved, in part, at the expense of non-union workers, who are kept (for instance, by seniority rules) from developing their optimum skills and working opportunities, and whose living costs are raised by the high wages of the organized workers.

In recent years, organization has proceeded rapidly among the less skilled, largely through industrial unionism both in and outside the old unions. Such organization apparently enables the members of the lower-ranking occupations to aspire toward higher percentages of skilled wage rates, at least within their own organizations. The past decade has been so abnormal in other particulars, especially in the vast unemployment of many types of skilled artisans, that it is not yet apparent whether this rise of industrial unionism tends to reduce too much the wage differential for skill, so that the incentive to acquire skill is becoming inadequate. The skilled occupations are often strategically strong within industrial unions,[27] but it would seem that in the long run their smaller numbers would force them to share their advantages with the more recently organized masses of workers with much less skill. The pecuniary advantages of union membership may well be less marked under widespread industrial unionism than when trade unionism is largely confined to the skilled crafts.

As organization spreads and deepens, at any rate, the problem of extent of gains, by whom, and from what sources, becomes increasingly complex. The old craft unionism has often presented grave social problems in its controls of skill supply— as by working rules, apprenticeship regulations, high fees and

---

[27] E.g., tool and die makers in the automobile workers' union.

dues. These two latter problems scarcely exist in the newer industrial unionism; but work rules acquire increasing importance as union membership spreads, while the seniority regulations which buttress high union wage rates raise new questions as to how many wage earners can get their annual real incomes increased by the labor movement.

Wage Dynamics.—In the foregoing sections of this chapter, some references have been made to interdependence among wage "causes" and "results," and we have not altogether neglected connections between wages and industrial progress and stagnation. On the whole, however, the above analysis was confined within "static" limits; the emphasis has been on the various equilibria toward which the forces cited were tending to bring wage rates to rest. We have also passed from one factor or factor group to another, much as if these were independent in origin and in strength—independent of each other and of the wage rates which they help to determine. We must indicate further the "dynamic" and interdependent aspects of wage problems.

Actually the labor market is continually in evolution, and the "results" emerging at one time become "causes" with reference to the next step. One type of interaction is that pointed out by Adam Smith, Alfred Marshall, and many others: the vicious circle of very low wages and very low efficiency of the labor supply which is ill-nourished and ill-educated by reason of these low earnings.[28] The factor of custom may be cited once more; people tend to regard as "fair" the wages and wage-relationships to which they have become accustomed.

Two more examples will serve to give a more realistic impression of what is meant by dynamic aspects of wages. One is the variable behavior of the wage-determining forces in dif-

---

[28] "The liberal reward of labour, as it encourages the propagation, so it increases the industry of the common people. . . . Where wages are high, accordingly, we shall always find the workmen more active, diligent, and expeditious, than when they are low. . . ."—*Wealth of Nations,* Bk. I, Ch. 8 (Cannan's ed., p. 83; Mod. Lib. reprint, p. 81). Cf. discussion of "the economy of high wages," Ch. 20, below.

ferent phases of the business cycle. Employers' estimates of the marginal products of various types of labor, and especially as to the values which such products will have by the time they become marketable, become especially distorted during periods of extreme boom and depression.[29]

Another illustration of wage dynamics is the reaction of management methods to wage changes. It is very commonly held by labor advocates and reformers that an important result of raising wage rates by trade union and legal minima is to force employers to improve the efficiency of their equipment and management; and that the customers of those who cannot improve their operations tend to be taken over by the more efficient entrepreneurs. Thus, these people argue, each such increase of wage rates creates means of its own payment.[30]

Within limits this idea seems sound; but the limits are probably narrow. Any significant increase of labor costs is indeed likely to provoke employers into some sort of action; but where their choice will fall among various alternative courses will depend on circumstances. One possibility is that they will resort to labor-saving devices and methods; this aspect of wages is treated at some length in Chapter 12, below. Here is a rather obvious form of increased managerial efficiency; and while it may make for higher social productivity in the long run, it tends to produce technological unemployment in the present.

Other possible reactions have been well stated by another British economist:

[Employers faced with advancing wage rates] may concentrate their energies on securing a protective tariff, or, if they already have one, on increasing it; or they may agitate for a subsidy, a compulsory

---

[29] Cf. Ch. 13, below.

[30] "Trade unions ought consciously to try and keep wages not in exact adjustment with, but a trifle above, the current marginal productivity equivalent; to accept the fact that this is bound to produce a variable, but permanent, margin of unemployment, which is of their own deliberate making and no inherent fault in the capitalist system; to take all possible steps to increase the mobility and fluidity of labour, in order to facilitate the reorganization and improvement of technique which must ensue before a fresh advance in wages is possible. . . ."; J. W. F. Rowe, *Wages in Practice and in Theory,* p. 229 (London, 1928).

restrictive scheme or other forms of State assistance to help them out of their difficulties. If they live in an age, like the present, when governments have ceased to believe in the virtues of unrestricted competition and the survival of the fittest in industry, and are willing to give a helping hand to any industry of "national" importance that finds itself in difficulties, they may find government assistance a less arduous and therefore more attractive way of escaping from wage pressure than overhauling their technique and organisation. Alternatively, if they feel that very little is likely to be provided in the way of government assistance, they may resort voluntarily to semi-monopolistic schemes for raising prices by restricting output or allocating markets.[31]

There is also force in the suggestion that the customers and the employees of the firms forced out by higher wage costs will be absorbed by more efficient firms, but such possibilities, too, may have modest bounds. Some low-cost enterprises, for example, are based on limited natural resources, and so their costs tend to rise if their operations increase; to some extent, superior management ability is a natural resource of this sort. This high-wage argument is most realistic with reference to mass production industries. Many firms have been eliminated from the automobile industry, for example, in part by rising labor cost; and increasing shares of the industry, while the total was still growing, flowed to the more profitable firms. Thus, some of the industrial changes produced by wage increases may be favorable to an industry's wage-paying ability; but it is easy to press too far this type of theory.

D. Summary

This chapter has made sparing use of the various academic theories of wages; attention has rather been concentrated on the factors and processes which are thought important by present-day economists in our contemporary American situation. We have examined briefly a considerable range of factors and interactions, including some—such as changes in population, "non-competing" groups within the population, capital

---

[31] A. G. Pool, *Wage Policy in Relation to Industrial Fluctuations*, pp. 22-23 (London: 1938).

supply as a demand for labor—which have been emphasized by the chief historic wage theories. We have neglected many important problems, some of which, like business cycles and interest rates, are treated in relation to wage rates elsewhere in this book; and we have indicated how misunderstandings may result from inadequate attention to variations from short- to long-run, from static to dynamic, points of view, and between lesser and greater degrees of competition among employers or employees or both.

Because the market value of labor is of outstanding importance, the familiar economic apparatus of supply and demand provides a convenient framework for examination of the processes involved. Since the notions supply and demand scarcely make sense when applied literally to all labor at once, however, we can most hopefully seek understanding of wage determinations by comparisons among groups of workers. In many labor groups today, the supply of man-hours forthcoming will be somewhat smaller at higher than at lower rates—there are numerous ranges of *negative* elasticity of supply. Such man-hours, however, are somewhat inadequate measures of labor supply and use; some account must be taken of their skill and efficiency. On the demand side, the marginal productivity analysis is of great usefulness when properly understood, and its practical application has been made easier by the newer theory of imperfect competition, which emphasizes the balance between the employer's marginal revenue and his marginal cost. (This latter analysis, in turn, must be qualified with reference to shorter and longer periods, taking account of cyclical business conditions.)

CHAPTER 5

TRENDS IN PRACTICAL WAGE FACTORS

The foregoing chapter dealt in rather abstract fashion with wage-making factors and forces. In the remainder of this book we shall try to utilize these comprehensive abstractions to map the difficult terrain of practices and ideas of people on the various wage firing lines—including members of legislatures and of other types of governmental agencies. Naturally, factors or principles are more explicitly recognized and debated by the people concerned in *collective* wage determinations than in the pricing of labor under "individual bargaining," and more explicitly in arbitration and legislation than in ordinary trade union collective bargaining. Some favorite characters in *avowedly* theoretical discussions of wages, such as marginal productivity, do not cut much of a figure on the practical stage. This difference may be accounted for, in part by the obviously abstract and simplified nature of academic wage theory; and in greater part by the inability of practical people to realize that they, too, are inevitably theorists—that their arguments like "labor is pricing itself out of its market" and "increase purchasing power" involve many assumptions which may be contrary to fact.

The remainder of this brief chapter will develop in section A some main purposes of wage policy and a few more notes on interactions among wage forces, and then (B) will classify some leading factors commonly recognized in comprehensive wage settlements. These latter factors, each of which has a considerable history, will be treated at some length in succeeding chapters.

A. Some Main Purposes of Wage Policy

Goals and Criteria of Wage Determination.—What fundamentals do people seek through collective wage arrangements?

To an important extent, of course, their purposes conflict; but we may also discern a large area of identity of interests as well as some lines along which clashes may be compromised. The following list of objectives, which may be modified according to the reader's taste and outlook, includes a number of the main tendencies which a good wage structure will contain:

1. The wages should be high enough to secure and hold the needed labor supplies;
2. And to yield to each grade of labor earnings as high as that grade is tending to command through all industries in its own labor market;
3. "A *living* wage must be the first charge upon industry";
4. "Labor must have its rightful share of the national income";
5. Yet any industry's wage rates should not be so high as to burden it with excessive costs;
6. Nor so high as to contribute to excessive unemployment;
7. Nor should the whole industrial-relations structure of the industry tend to handicap improvements in equipment, processes, methods;
8. Nor offer chronic irritations to either managements or men such as to foster an abnormal degree of strikes or other forms of withheld cooperation; and
9. Finally, within limits wage rates should be flexible rather than rigid.

What are the more promising routes toward these goals?

Taking up, first, the points relating to adequacy and flexibility of labor incentives, we may observe that each of these slippery generalities is a complex of baffling problems. The outlook, moreover, appears to be for increasingly collective action and attempts at "stabilization" with reference to wages, production, prices, markets, and nearly everything else—and we can all find much to commend, as well as many dangers, in this world-wide drift.[1]

---

[1] Many employers and unions, for instance, attempt to standardize and stabilize labor costs, in the sense of preventing other employers from paying less than their own wage rates; and it is widely believed that employers who

Nevertheless, it is by no means idle to discuss current collective wage policies, *in part* with reference to an idealized fluid laissez-faire world. It is generally conceded that the long-range objectives of collectivist social organization are largely identical with those presupposed by the classical "individualistic" economists. Both hold, for instance, that productive resources should flow from this field to that, in response to changes in such factors as consumers' wants, locations of markets, technology, and availability of natural resources. And only a thoroughly utopian collectivism will dispense altogether with rising and falling prices, for labor and for other resources, as partial means of effecting such readjustments. (The practical result of eliminating entirely voluntary purchase and sale of labor would be intolerable regimentation under governmental authorities.) There are many signs that workers and employers both tend to favor wage flexibility operating only in one direction (the former striving to avoid all wage cuts, the latter hostile to advances)—yet we shall notice also a rather impressive history of "sliding wage scales," by which money-wage rates have been kept flexible both ways, with reference to certain price changes.

Employers' Acceptance of Unionism; Types of Labor Frictions.—Let us pass now to the criterion of industrial peace. Naturally, we should not suppose that any wage arrangements, of themselves, can or should entirely prevent the labor disputes which have handicapped the American economy more than those of many other democratic states. But the wage policies and practices of organized workers and employers reflect several main phases of their experience with collective actions; which circumstance affords some grounds for optimism.[2] While trade

---

pay less than trade union rates thereby secure unfair competitive advantage. Most employers, moreover, desire wage stability in the additional sense of knowing what labor costs they can count on during the season, or longer period, just ahead; and workers also value a season's (or longer) security against money-wage rate reduction. Such are some of the practical objections to extreme wage flexibility.

[2] I am indebted to George W. Taylor on this point, e.g., through his paper "Do Current Tendencies in American Labor Organization Tend to Promote Price Rigidity?" read at the American Economic Association meeting, Dec. 30, 1938.

union organization is gaining ground rapidly against militant resistance by employers, disputes are exceptionally numerous and violent; and wage negotiations tend to be conducted on a more frenzied basis than when the organizational relations are more seasoned—when employers are better resigned to the continued existence of *the unions then in being* (not merely resigned to model or ideal labor unions). It appears that the rapid rise of American wage rates in 1936-37 was due, considerably, to two such militant phases. First, many employers gave wage advances as a sort of "insurance against unionism," which had some inflationary effect; and later more than a few firms felt obliged to grant further wage increases, partly in order to maintain the current union officials in power, lest still more radical ones should oust them. The more secure unions in Britain and Scandinavia did not, as a rule, attempt to exploit 1937 prosperity in a manner as extreme as did our own labor organizations—many of which fought with whatever weapons were handy, for objectives not well thought through.

If a further illustration is desired of the difficulties involved in reconciling the main objectives of wage policy, consider this one: May the utmost security and comfort of the present generation of workers be provided without impairing capital supplies and other sources of industrial progress? Though such conflicts often become alarming, we must avoid becoming alarmists. Fortunately, workable compromises are also very common. It is widely realized among wage and salary earners that, however production be organized among "profit-making" and "non-profit" agencies, not *all* the current product can be consumed without danger to the future; and this realization holds the more radically left-wing interpretations of "equitable sharing of product" in check. On the other hand, the continued growth of mass political and labor movements, even in their fascist forms, tends to prevent the distribution of *material* income from becoming ever more unequal—if not actually to lessen the degree of inequality. Sincere and intelligent efforts toward more equitable sharing of resources, including special solicitude for the poorer and weaker folk, should tend to mitigate labor disputes; and such mitigation not only makes more continuously productive the labor and capital immediately affected, but also lessens the unemployment inflicted by strikes and lockouts upon non-combatants whose supplies and markets are thus interrupted.[3]

Repercussions and Stability of Wage Adjustments.— Another proposition which applies to our whole discussion of wage factors is that (in Bastiat's words of a century ago) the "seen" or immediate results of many economic events should be evaluated in the light of many "unseen" or more distant repercussions. Numerous disputes over wage matters can be resolved in part into these terms: each party contends, in effect, that the other is not taking account of enough consequences of the program it proposes. The advocates, for example, of the "purchasing power" or income aspect of wages have done useful service in reminding us all of some important reactions, particularly of general wage cuts in a time of business depression. These advocates, in turn, often become short-sighted

---

[3] USBLS records indicate crudely the extent and numerous classifications of overt labor disputes; see, e.g., the article "Strikes in 1939" in *Mo. Lab. Rev.,* May 1940, which article contains a chart of annual fluctuations, 1881-1905 and 1914-1939. Such data are analyzed, e.g., by D. Despain in Report on S. Res. 215 of 75th Cong., Chs. 3, 4 (76th Cong., 1st Sess., Senate Rept. No. 610), in an attempt to show the economic "cost of strikes."

The figures for the sit-down era of 1937 (4,740 strikes, involving 1,860,621 workers) are charged with causing some 26 million idle man-days—but very slightly more than in 1927, and equivalent to an average of about two days per annum for each of the 12 million industrial wage earners employed in 1937. But such calculations can only scratch the surface of the great family of problems of labor "unrest" or frictions or withheld cooperation. To some extent such stoppages as those in coal mining substitute "man-days lost through strikes" for man-days which would otherwise be lost by layoffs; but against this discount must be offset vast amounts of loss of potential production through minor slow-downs, restrictive practices, and many forms of "labor unrest" apart from "strikes," also the losses due to strikes in non-striking shops and groups. E.g., "In July a large group of Chrysler employees received payments covering monthly partial unemployment . . . as a result of the labor dispute at the Briggs Body Plant which lasted from May 22 to June 7. In July a labor dispute involving General Motors tool and die makers affected practically all General Motors production workers . . . the Commission determined that the production workers were not involved in the dispute and authorized the payment of [unemployment] benefits to these workers." (*Michigan Unemployment Compensation Bulletin,* July-Sept. 1939, p. 1.) Within a few months thousands of body plant workers were thrown out of work, in their turn, by the month-long Chrysler dispute. The disputes in these three large companies were all with various locals of the United Automobile Workers (CIO).

when they are asking for wage *increases,* which they are loath
to believe can threaten an *upward* spiral of wages and prices
or inflation.

Besides the cyclical fluctuations of business thus suggested,
there are various other types of industrial instabilities which
complicate our practical wage problems—notably the life cycle
of growth, maturity, and, in many cases, decline and death of
a whole industry. We may adopt a relatively new verbal
fashion among economists and say that wage settlements are
always forward-looking—are based in part on *anticipations* as
to what conditions the industry will see during the year or
other period for which the wage rates run. Numerous attempts
are made, as we shall see, to specify what contingencies may
call for a revision of the wage structure; but increasingly collective methods of wage determination almost necessarily tend
to make any general wage change a time-consuming matter;
also to "play up" the advantages (suggested in footnote 1,
above) of considerable stability in money-wage rates.

B. Classifications of Wage Factors

The considerations cited in the preceding paragraphs of this
chapter are perhaps wage factors themselves, but a more convenient framework for further treatment is supplied by the
vocabularies of several families of arguments commonly invoked in wage deliberations. We proceed to utilize these, according to the following scheme:

Chapter

    6. Cost of living in relation to wages
    7. Wages as per cent of total production cost
    8. Production, national income, and wages
    9. Wage-paying capacity, sliding scales, profit sharing
   10. Comparisons with other wages; job evaluation
11-13. Wages and industrial fluctuations (unemployment as a
       wage factor)

Some Alternative Formulations.—Numerous variations and
alternatives to the above outline may be found in the literature,

since such factors as are thus indicated may be supplemented, subdivided, combined, or differently expressed, according to the emphasis of the speaker or writer (which in turn is influenced by the conditions under which he talks or writes).[4] Especially influential in trade union and governmental wage determinations in the English-speaking world have been the "living wage," "fair wage," and "ability of the industry to pay" principles, as well as unemployment.[5] These principles and criteria are easily recognized in the titles of Chapters 6 through 13 of this book; and it is also evident that there is some logical overlapping among these factors—for instance, arguments concerning labor efficiency are certainly relevant to the wage-paying capacity of the industry.

An explicit list of wage factors was specified for consideration in railway disputes by our Federal Transportation Act of 1920. This set of statutory instructions, which in turn was based on a rather lengthy history of railway wage adjustments, included reference to "the degree of responsibility," "the hazards of employment," and "irregularities of increase of wages or of treatment, the result of previous wage orders or adjustments." The last of these is not logically coordinate with the others, but is rather an inquiry whether previous settlements have been erroneous or inequitable in some important respect. The first two (responsibility and hazards) are

---

[4] See, for example, a keen analysis, with special reference to British trade union policies and practices toward wages, in J. T. Dunlop, "The Movement of Real and Money Wage Rates," *Economic Journal,* Sept. 1938, p. 421 ff. This author remarks, for instance, that unions are apt to claim that "technical changes have imposed increased responsibilities and an increased nervous strain upon the employees. The widespread use of this argument is not usually appreciated."

[5] See especially A. C. Pigou, *Economics of Welfare,* refs. to "fair wages"; and E. M. Burns, *Wages and the State; a comparative study of the problems of state wage regulation* (London: King, 1926).

More recently-published discussions include commentaries on the forty years of public regulation of wages in New Zealand by E. J. Riches, of the International Labor Office, who says: "The policy adopted may be broadly summarised as an attempt to fix minimum rates of wages that would be uniform within each single grade of work, appropriately differentiated for work of different grades, adequate to provide a living wage, within the capacity of industry to pay, fair as compared with the shares of total product received by other factors of production, and stable over fairly long periods."— *Economica,* Aug. 1938, p. 316.

important wage factors, unusually difficult to define and evaluate, which are considered along with various other influences on market rates of wages in Chapter 10, below.[6]

A couple of other aspects of American railway wage settlements may be noticed, in part because this industry has the longest history of governmental participation in wage adjustments in our own nation. First, it is obvious that the injunction to consider "hazards of employment" in the Transportation Act of 1920 was responsive to emphasis on this point by railway labor, which emphasis in turn was based on the abnormally great danger to life and limb characterizing (or formerly characterizing) many railway occupations. It may also be recalled that, when Herbert Feis was writing on practical wage principles early in the 1920's, he featured "standardization" as a principle or policy or criterion of wage settlements.[7] No doubt Feis was influenced by the old trade union doctrine of "standard rate," discussed in Chapter 14, below; also there were bitter contentions in 1919 and years immediately following over what geographical area or areas should serve for wage rate standardization on American railways.

The Firm, the Industry, the Area.—Here are three points of view, from each of which wage problems are often considered. In the context of comprehensive wage determinations the small firm counts for little; each one must adjust itself as best it can to what happens to its section of its own industry. Large firms, on the other hand, such as the leaders in the steel and automobile industries, occupy a different position. To an important extent they are able to act independently in collective dealings with representatives of labor and of the general public —perhaps deliberately handicapping their weak competitors by making new concessions to labor.

---

[6] In its Decision No. 2 (1920), the Railroad Labor Board relied in part on some other considerations, notably the effect its decision might "have on other wages and industries, on production generally, the relation of railroad wages to the aggregate of transportation costs and requirements for betterments, together with the burden on the entire people of railroad transportation charges."

[7] *The Settlement of Wage Disputes* (New York, 1921); *Principles of Wage Settlement* (New York, 1924).

Business and Social Standpoints.—In discussions of wage factors and principles, moreover, there are two other outstanding points of view, which are often somewhat confused: the standpoint of business or supply-and-demand causation, and the standpoint of social welfare or social objectives. It would be entirely logical to classify wage factors, from this point of view, into (a) those which are business-like, and (b) those which require ethical or political sanctions to make them effective. Such differentiation, however, does not lend itself well to more detailed treatment, since most of the commonly recognized factors have both aspects. The "living-wage principle," for example, is largely ethical and political in character; yet living costs and real wages appear also in a number of business and economic contexts of wages. On the other hand, practical and business-like dealings with wages in relation to profits and losses and to other wages are influenced not a little by ethical and political currents. Yet the emphasis clearly varies between these poles, as we pass from one factor-group to others. In discussions of living costs, productivity of labor, unemployment, and, above all, of "labor's share of the total product" (in comparison with the shares going to management and property), the ethical and social points of view are predominant; whereas in talk about the industry's wage-paying capacity, also about reasonable relations among wages, the business point of view is predominant. The variable mixtures of these elements are well illustrated by the numerous versions of "purchasing power" as a wage factor. This phrasing frequently appears to be intended as an appeal to the self-interest of the individual employer; yet very little analysis shows that, if purchasing power is to be a practical and important factor in wage determinations, widespread collective action must be assumed.

CHAPTER 6

COST OF LIVING IN RELATION TO WAGES

Comprehensive wage determinations usually involve some references to living costs. Several centuries ago, the attempt was begun to make statistical, historical, and geographical comparisons of real wages; and in recent times it has become commonplace to divide periodic indexes of money wages by indexes of prices which purport to measure changes in cost of living. This is scarcely an exact science as yet, however: there remains much room for arguments over choice of data and methods of interpreting them.

One set of problems is that of "population differentials"— Are the lower money wages found in smaller towns adequately compensated by lower living costs? And, in times when living costs are rising, as a matter of course labor spokesmen cite this fact as an argument in favor of increased wage rates. When retail prices are declining and other business conditions are adverse, employers are apt to argue that the drop in living costs is one good reason for a reduction of money-wage rates—such wage adjustment would perhaps leave real-wage rates higher than they were in some previous, allegedly normal, year or years. But labor usually makes every effort to avoid any cut in money-wage rates, whatever may happen to the cost of living. Its view is that money-wage rates should always *at least* keep pace with living costs, and indeed should outstrip the latter as fast and as far as possible, to provide an indefinitely rising trend of real-wage rates. The past long trend of rising real wages makes it reasonable to hope for a continued rise hereafter.

Nevertheless, the world has seen not a little use of arrangements for automatically adjusting wages (also salaries) periodically, both upward and downward with reference to some standard index of living costs; and many of these schemes have been entered into voluntarily by organized labor, or at least accepted without great protest. Among important contributors to the whole movement toward determining wages by sliding scales keyed to indexes of living costs is the legal minimum-wage movement, which also has featured the demand for "a living wage." In its less ambitious form, this latter undertaking starts with a given legal minimum-wage rate in money terms in a base period; and then attempts to maintain this wage's purchasing power by tying it to some official index of cost of living. This endeavor encounters serious difficulties, as we shall see; but on the whole the task is easy, compared with the more ambitious enterprise of *determining statistically what is an adequate living wage,* for the workers concerned, in the base month or year.

Problems pertaining to legal minimum wages are explored in Part V, below. In the present chapter we are to study, in section A, the use and abuse of living cost indexes for mere comparisons of real wages; then, in section B, problems and methods involved in maintaining and increasing real-wage rates.

A. Comparing Real Wages

Some Recent International Comparisons.—The accompanying table of annual indexes of industrial wages, both "money" and "real," for the principal nations, 1927-38 inclusive, is of some basic importance, despite the lack of full comparability within most or all of its rows and columns.[1] This table does not give absolute money wages, nor data on variations in number of hours worked per week; hence, it does not enlighten us on comparative rates or earnings between countries in any one year.[2] But it does indicate the varying directions

---

[1] Real-wage index $= \dfrac{\text{money-wage index}}{\text{living-cost index}} \times 100$ when the base period of the two indexes is the same. Hence, the living-cost indexes implied by our table are easily found; e.g., for Australia, 1930:

$103 = \dfrac{98}{\text{living-cost index}}$; i.e., living-cost index $= \dfrac{98}{103} \times 100 = 95$ (base : 1929).

[2] On this extremely difficult problem, the technical reports published under the title *International Wage Comparisons* by Manchester Univ. Press (c. 1931), and the "Ford Wage Study" of the I.L.O. (*An International Enquiry into Costs of Living*—Series N, Study No. 17, Geneva, 1931), are exceptionally valuable.

INDEX NUMBERS OF INDUSTRIAL WAGES (MONEY AND REAL)[a]

Base: 1929=100, except for Japan real wages (1932=100)

Country	Nature of Data	1927	1928	1929	1930	1931	1932	1933	1934	1935	1936	1937	1938
							MONEY WAGES						
Australia	Hourly rates	99	100	100	98	89	84	81	82	83	85	89	96
Canada	Hourly earnings	97	98	100	101	96	91	86	87	89	91	98	102
France (Paris)	Hourly rates	84	86	100	109	108	104	104	104	102	116	165	172
Germany	Hourly rates	87	95	100	102	97	82	79	79	79	79	79	80
Great Britain	Weekly rates	102	100	100	100	98	96	95	96	97	100	104	107
Italy	Hourly earnings	..	98	100	99	93	91	89	86	85	90	101	108
Japan	Daily earnings[d]	95	99	100	87	91	92	91	92	91	92	95	100
New Zealand	Weekly minimum rates	97	100	100	100	93	85	82	82	84	93	102	106
Sweden	Hourly earnings	(96)[c]	(98)[c]	100	103	103	101	98	98	99	100	103	109
U.S.A.	Hourly earnings[e]	98	98	100	100	96	84	83	98	102	104	117	121
							REAL WAGES[b]						
Australia	Hourly rates	101	102	100	103	105	104	104	103	102	103	105	110
Canada	Hourly earnings	(99)	(99)	100	101	108	111	111	111	113	113	118	121
France (Paris)	Hourly rates	91	92	100	104	106	110	111	112	117	127	148	137
Germany	Hourly rates	91	96	100	106	109	104	104	101	99	98	98	97
Great Britain	Weekly rates	100	99	100	104	109	110	112	111	111	111	110	113
Italy	Hourly earnings	..	100	100	102	106	110	112	114		109	111	110
Japan	Daily earnings[d]	..	..	100	..	..	100	96	93	89	88	87	85
New Zealand	Weekly minimum rates	97	100	100	102	103	102	103	102	101	109	111	112
Sweden	Hourly earnings	(95)[c]	(97)[c]	100	106	109	110	108	107	107	107	108	112
U.S.A.	Hourly earnings[e]	96	98	100	103	110	108	111	124	123	123	133	140

[a] Figures relate to all workers (or to men only), employed mainly in mines and industry, but also in certain branches of commerce, transport or public service; for Great Britain and New Zealand, agriculture is included.

[b] Figures computed by applying the national cost-of-living index numbers to the index numbers of money wages.

[c] The figures in brackets are not taken from the latest revision of the series and are therefore not strictly comparable with the following figures.

[d] Statistical office of the Imperial Cabinet Series.

[e] National Industrial Conference Board series.

Sources: International Labor Office, Year-Book 1937-1938, p. 357 (Geneva: 1938); Year-Book of Labor Statistics 1938, pp. 127 ff. and sepn. (Geneva: 1938); International Labour Review, Vol. XL No. 4, Oct. 1939, p. 552.

and degrees of change of money and real wages in the respective countries in this 12-year period covering the "Great Depression" and that new "last pre-war year," 1938. Some important results, for instance, of the drastic 40-hour-week reforms under our own NRA in 1933, and in France and New Zealand in 1936-37, are here apparent. In Paris, for instance, the index of average hourly (money) industrial earnings rose from 116 in 1936 to 165 in 1937 and 172 in 1938—gains, respectively, of 42% and 48%, from the base of *1936*. Meanwhile living costs rose faster (not entirely on account of the great reduction in weekly hours with no reduction in weekly pay, of course), so that the rise in average real hourly earnings was distinctly more modest (127 in 1936 to 148 in 1937 and 137 in 1938 = increases of 17, falling to 8 *per cent,* using 1936 as the base).[3]

Before 1929.—Any index purporting to show degree of change in living costs oftener than once a year (e.g., monthly) must, of course, be constructed from *retail* price data, and should include housing as well as other major items. The technique of such construction has been tackled on a great scale in most nations only since 1914; and in spite of variations in detail, the rival indexes in the principal countries all tended to show modest gains, if any, in real-wage rates over that war period and the two inflationary years of 1919 and 1920.

In 1921 money wages dropped, but prices dropped more. After 1921, of course, in the United States (and in many, if not most, other areas) the steep upward trend in average hourly earnings, with declining trend in living costs, has not been fully offset by weekly-hours reductions—so that industrial weekly and annual average real earnings (taking no account of increased leisure as real income) were distinctly above

---

[3] The French weekly real wages might have lagged further behind, but for collective agreements and governmental pressures, calling for adjustments of wage rates, whenever living costs advanced by some minimal amount (usually 5% to 10%). In the economic and political circumstances then prevailing, these "safeguards" contributed somewhat to the upward spiral of inflation.

the 1913 level by 1938—for most wage earners whose employment was as steady as in 1913 and preceding years.[4]

Over some decades before 1914, gains in real wages appear to have been more substantial, at least in the more progressive nations. Competent estimates for Great Britain, Sweden, and the United States, for example, all indicate that real weekly and annual earnings at least doubled, 1860 to 1913; and of course hourly real earnings rose more, since working hours fell, by (say) 10% or more.[5] In all these long periods, to be sure, there were some setbacks lasting a year or more.

American Real-Wage Rates Since 1890.—Some further details, supplementing the foregoing remarks on the course of real wages in the United States, may be gleaned from two charts in later chapters of this book. One, Chart 10 in Chapter 13, gives (1) annual indexes of average money hourly earnings in manufacturing, 1909-39, and on the same chart are shown annual indexes of (2) wholesale prices and of (3) living costs for the same period.[6]

If we turn now to Chart 6, in Chapter 10, we find annual data on hourly wage rates or earnings for each of the principal industrial groups for which available records go back to 1916 or an earlier year; also the USBLS cost-of-living index

---

[4] The unsatisfactory data available indicate that percentages of unemployment have averaged higher in nearly all lands since 1920 than before 1914. Several international wage comparisons, 1914-38, are made in Ch. 18-B, below.

[5] A. L. Bowley, *Wages and Income in the United Kingdom since 1860* (Cambridge Univ. Press, 1937); G. Bagge *et al., Wages in Sweden, 1860-1930* (London: P. S. King, 1933); W. I. King, *Wealth and Income of the People of the United States*, Ch. 7 (New York: 1915); P. H. Douglas, *Real Wages in the United States, 1890-1926* (Boston: 1930). (King, and other students of these events before 1890, lean heavily on the "Aldrich" Senate Report, No. 1394, of 1893, for which Dr. R. P. Falkner was Statistician.)

[6] U. S. wholesale prices reached a peak of about 166 in 1920, as compared with 113 for the BLS living-cost index (1926 = 100). By September 1940, the same wholesale index was down to 75, the cost-of-living index to 80.6.

Even the long-run trends of retail and wholesale price indexes should not necessarily run parallel. For the retail prices which we pay, for instance, we may get increasing amounts of valuable services and of quality improvement. And since 1920 another powerful factor has tended to prevent retail prices from declining as far as wholesale—the rising labor costs of retail distribution services.

relating to wage earners and lower-salaried workers in 32 large cities. By comparing the slope or trend of this latter curve with any of the money-wage curves on the same scale, for any period, the reader can judge whether such money wages were outstripping or falling behind living costs. This chart is the ratio or logarithmic type, in which any two curves, so long as they run parallel, show growths or declines (if any) *at equal rates*. This device reduces in importance the query whether the base period chosen for any or all series was "normal."

Limitations of Living-Cost Indexes; Problem of Weights. —In the foregoing sections we have utilized indexes of living costs to obtain some bearings on the course of real wages, and have indicated a few of the principles and problems involved. These latter topics, including the main objections which may be raised against this and that particular living-cost index, are sufficiently important to warrant our further inquiry. This discussion will relate principally to the quarterly reports of the U. S. Bureau of Labor Statistics on "Changes in Cost of Living," referring to 33 large cities, and to the monthly indexes of the National Industrial Conference Board, covering 52 cities, which utilize USBLS monthly data on retail food prices.[7] Other American indexes are of much more restricted significance for the cost of devising, revising, and keeping up a creditable index of living costs is so great that there is not a great deal of competition for the job.

---

[7] Both agencies give index numbers, not only for "all items combined" for individual cities and for "all cities combined," but also individual city indexes for the chief budget categories. As of June 15, 1939, e.g., the BLS indexes for all its 33 cities combined ran as follows (1923-25 = 100) : all items, 81.7; food, 76.3; clothing, 80.9; rent, 69.5; fuel and light, 85.4; house furnishings, 83.2, and miscellaneous, 98.5. Beginning March 15, 1940, the BLS shifted its base to 1935-39 = 100; hence, the indexes for all its groups are now near 100.

The BLS issues reports—monthly on retail prices of food and certain other items, and quarterly on total "cost of goods purchased by wage earners and lower-salaried workers"—in press releases, separate pamphlets, and in a section of the *Monthly Labor Review*. In the autumn of 1940, the BLS began giving out *monthly* releases on "changes in cost of living" for 20 large cities. The Conference Board's monthly living-cost data come out in abbreviated form in its *Management Record*, and in full in its *Economic Record*. Each agency, moreover, has published various research monographs on longer-term behavior of living costs.

To the very considerable problem of securing sufficient retail price quotations from suitable areas and types of sellers
for adequately defined qualities and quantities of commodities,
also of services such as housing, must be added the disturbing
question of *weighting*. Obviously, the wage earner's total cost
of living is not decreased if bread increases 1% in price while
pepper decreases 3%; yet the simple average of these two
prices (each weighted as one) shows a decline of 1%. Since
the cost of living is made up of costs of a large number of
goods, consumed in varying proportions by different persons
and families, it is readily seen there is much opportunity for
argument as to which items should be priced, and how much
each price should be allowed to influence the final index number.
Differences of judgment and practice on both these matters
account, at least in part, for such divergences as may at times
occur between such indexes as those of the U. S. Bureau of
Labor Statistics and of the National Industrial Conference
Board, which attempt virtually the same task.

Two important aspects of this matter of weights may be
illustrated by the category food.

(1) One of Engel's laws, running to the effect that the
poorer the family (other things equal), the larger the *percentage* of its income which must be spent for food, is not in-
fallibly accurate but profoundly significant; and Professor
Douglas properly interpreted data showing a declining percentage of income spent for food as corroborating his conclusion, reached in other ways, that American real earnings
had advanced.[8] Some of the principal European living cost
indexes referring to wage earners have given food prices, as
a group, weights of 60% or more; while corresponding American indexes have assigned this group about 30 to 40 points
out of 100, depending on the city.

(2) The selection and weighting of particular prices within
such a broad group as "food" should also be modified to take
account of changes in consumption habits, based in part on
trends in relative prices and in incomes. Among these trends

---

[8] *Real Wages in the United States, 1890-1926,* Ch. 28.

were the widespread substitution of margarine for butter during the war period 1914-18. This *ersatz* was good enough to make the rise in butter price somewhat overstate the real rise in this particular branch of living cost. On the other hand, great declines in relative unit prices for such goods as electric current, fruits, vegetables, dairy products, radios, and automobile transportation have made these much more prominent parts of the living costs of American wage earners in the last couple of decades. Any single living-cost index for a given locality, moreover, must refer to a relatively fixed standard of living, and to a weighting which is not entirely appropriate to any single family. In the bigger families, for instance, expenditures for food and clothing tend to exceed those in smaller families of similar incomes.[9]

Attention to some of the expedients used by the U. S. Bureau of Labor Statistics in dealing with these problems enables us to judge better the significance of its indexes.[10] By 1917 this Bureau had developed a tolerably satisfactory retail-food price index for 1890 and later years. Then wartime demands for more inclusive measurements of living-cost changes led the Bureau to collect family-budget data from some 12,000 white families in numerous cities, in order to determine which objects of consumption should be regularly priced, and especially what weight should be given to each.[11] The families thus covered were selected to be representative of wage and lower-salaried earners; the minimum number of persons being three (husband, wife, and at least one dependent child); the average number, 4.9. From this "quantity-sur-

9 "Differences in climate as reflected in fuel requirements and the weight of clothing used, as well as differences in food consumption habits, make it impossible to use an identical budget from city to city. Although the list of items priced varies little from city to city, there are differences in the grades of goods priced and the weights assigned to each item." (*Mo. Lab. Rev.*, July 1938, p. 205.) Cost of housing construction is another item affected by climate.

10 A convenient official summary is provided by "The Bureau of Labor Statistics' New Index of Cost of Living," *Mo. Lab. Rev.*, Aug. 1940—reprinted as Serial R. 1156 and supplied by the Bureau on request.

11 This investigation of 1917-19 is reported in detail in USBLS Bull. 357, *Cost of Living in the U. S.* (May 1924). Ninety-two cities and towns in 42 states were covered—of which indexes for only 33 large cities have been continued.

vey" the list of 22 foods, 61 items of clothing, etc., was established in 1919—some 145 commodities and services in all, besides housing rents. Since the 12,000 families, on the average, spent about 38% of their incomes for food, this became the approximate weight for food in the national living-cost index—but the index for each city reflected proportional expenditures in its own sample.

The Bureau made rather minor revisions in its index, from time to time, as pricing procedure developed and budgetary studies accumulated; and finally, in 1934-36, very comprehensive surveys of family incomes and expenditures were made by the Bureau, in cooperation with other Federal agencies. These surveys led to major overhaulings in 1935 and 1940 of the Bureau's living-cost index, now specified as relating to "wage earners and lower-salaried workers in large cities." Apart from rents, prices of 98 commodities and services are now used; and the national average of weights had become, by March 1940: food, 33.9; clothing, 10.5; rent, 18.1; fuel, electricity, and ice, 6.4; house furnishings, 4.2; miscellaneous, 26.9; total, 100.[12]

Apparently no very drastic changes have resulted in the total indexes of living costs from these revisions, which however are important safeguards against accumulating errors. In the new series for years 1913 onward, but little change was needed up to 1925 (since the 1917-19 survey is still the best evidence for that period); and the indexes for years 1930-40 had already been substantially adjusted to the survey of 1934-36.

Interregional Comparisons.—These price quotations and indexes arouse some curiosity as to reasons for the variations among cities at any one date. For March 15, 1939, for instance, while the "all cities combined" or "United States" total living-cost index of the BLS was 82 (% of 1923-25), the roll of cities started off as follows: Baltimore, 85.7; Boston, 81.6;

---

[12] Within the "miscellaneous" group, prices relating to automobiles and their operation now account for 20%—hence for some 5% of the total living-cost index.

Buffalo, 84.1; Chicago, 78.5; Cleveland, 85.9; Detroit, 79.3. Birmingham, Alabama was lowest—76.5. Indexes of the main subdivisions of living costs, by cities and dates, show similar diversities. Warning is given that such data may not be interpreted as showing the relative expensiveness of a fixed living standard among the cities at one time. For each city, rather, the index shows how an approximately fixed type of living, appropriate to an "average" wage-earning or lower-salaried family in that locality (considering not merely climate, but also incomes, social customs, and available supplies) differs from its cost in the base period. Thus, money living costs in this sense by March 1939 had fallen in Baltimore to 85.7% of the 1923-25 level; in Birmingham to 76.5%. Such costs, of course, were not equally "normal" in all cities at any one base period—prices may (e.g.) have been in somewhat of a local boomlet in Birmingham in 1923-25, relatively depressed in Baltimore.

But of course the question is often raised—not least in connection with geographical wage comparisons—how does the cost of living differ, for families of about the same size and level of net comfort, between North and South, between town and village? Most men in the street have no doubt as to the general answers to these questions, and they suppose that statisticians should be able to make precise measurements. But our government officials claim that such measurement, if not impossible, is *not yet* possible, as shown in the following quotation:

The comparison of the cost of the same level of living from one part of the country to another presents serious technical difficulties for which wholly satisfactory techniques have not yet been developed. This is particularly true in attempting to measure differences in living costs from large to very small cities or from urban to rural communities, where consideration must be given not only to differences in such factors as climate and consumption habits, but also to differences in housing, the fuels available, and the means of transportation. In large cities with similar climate, comparisons are possible with the use of an identical budget and descriptive specifications to facilitate pricing identical commodities and services from city to city. Such studies, because of their great expense, are beyond the present resources of this Bureau.[13]

We have seen how important is the problem of revising the weighting of the index, for making living-cost comparisons over lengthy periods of time; but the problem of appropriate weighting is probably even more important in interregional comparisons. For the consumption habits of a single group seem to vary less, as time goes on, than consumption in one region varies from that in another region at the same time. These considerations are important for interregional comparisons, within any nation and also between nations. In comparing the cost of living in Detriot and New Orleans, for example, we should not use the same amount of coal in the "market basket" which is priced in each of the communities; and the clothing and food budgets should also be differently constituted. It should be borne in mind, too, that the markedly lower average expenditures of families in villages and on farms, as compared with cities, are due in large part to differences in income, and rather less to differences in cost of equally comfortable living.[14] Housing, defined merely as a given number and size of rooms, usually costs less in villages than in cities, in part because building and other wages tend to be lower, as well as taxes. The village cottager, too, can afford garden space and can easily walk to work. But one reason why his house is cheaper is that it lacks some conveniences of city housing. Moreover, the occupant lacks certain civic facilities—for in-

---

[13] *Mo. Lab. Rev.*, June 1939, p. 1360. Similar language appears in later living-cost reports of the BLS. The matter is somewhat complicated by political-economic pressures on statisticians, such as are suggested in Chs. 19, 20, below.

[14] "The differences in the per cent assigned to food can be largely explained on the basis of differences in income. New Orleans families, for example, with a low average income, allocate almost 40% of their total expenditure to food, whereas Washington families, with a comparatively high level of income, spend less than 30%. In New York, however, where the average money income is relatively high, food prices are high enough to bring the proportion of the total going to food to a percentage distinctly above the average."—"The Bureau of Labor Statistics' New Index of Cost of Living," *Mo. Lab. Rev.*, Aug. 1940. The weights of food, etc., in the index for each city are adjusted to local average budgets of wage earners and lower-salaried people, as indicated in this quotation.

stance education, health, and recreation—which the city dweller helps to pay for through his landlord's taxes. Such are but a few of the pitfalls in geographic comparisons of living costs.

Pricing Same Living in Different Cities.—In the face of these difficulties, statisticians have nevertheless ventured to compile and publish several series which indicate approximate differences, at the dates covered, in cost of a specified mode of existence for a standard family in each of numerous cities and towns. The results indicate somewhat lesser degrees and self-consistency among differences in living costs, according to region and population density, than many of us would expect.

In Australia, for many years, the key wages have been adjusted by public authorities, in part by reference to changes and local variations in living costs. One outgrowth of this system is the regular (quarterly) publication of comprehensive cost-of-living data for each of some 33 towns and cities. As of June 1939, these local indexes ran mostly in the low 70's, the extremes being 65.4 for an obscure town in South Australia, and 86.4 in Kalgoorlie, Boulder, in the State of Western Australia.[15] Thus living costs are officially reckoned, in the lowest-rated Australian town, as only 76% as high as in the highest-rated.

In the United States, the year 1935 marked the beginning of elaborate studies by the Works Progress Administration on intercity differences in cost of a fixed living level for a standard wage-earning family.[16] A four-person manual-worker family was assumed, and two budgets were defined. The higher of these, called the "basic maintenance level," was supposedly near the minimum necessary indefinitely to sustain normal health in this family. It, and the lower "emergency" budget, were priced for March 1935 in 59 cities, with adjustments in the fuel, ice,

---

[15] Commonwealth Bureau of Census and Statistics, *Labour Report, 1938,* p. 151 (Canberra: 1940). Base: weighted average of 6 capitals, 1923-27 = 81. See Ch. 18, below, for further discussion of Australian wage regulation.

[16] *Intercity Differences in Cost of Living, March 1935, 59 Cities,* by Margaret L. Stecker. Research Monograph XII, Division of Social Research (Washington, 1937). See also M. A. Beney, *Differentials in Industrial Wages and Hours in the U. S.,* pp. 36, 202 (New York, Conference Board, 1938).

and transportation items to fit local conditions. The WPA researchers were more impressed by intercity variations in cost of the standard budgets *within* major geographic regions than *among* such regions. The cost, for example, of the "maintenance" budget in the most expensive city (Washington, D. C., $1,415) exceeded that in the least expensive (Mobile, Ala., $1,130) by 25%; and "in more than half of the cities [such] living costs were within a range of $100 a year."[17] Costs were, however, distinctly lower in southern than in northern cities of comparable size—though below populations of 500,000 this WPA study found only a slight progression of living costs with increasing size of city.

The U. S. Bureau of Labor Statistics has repriced this WPA "maintenance" budget at various intervals in 31 cities;[18] and at the request of the Federal Wage-Hour Division, it made a comparison of five northern and five southern cities, all 10,-000 to 19,000 population, as of December 1938.[19] This last study showed only about 2% of difference, on the average.

Specialized Living-Cost Indexes.—As mentioned previously, families with higher incomes tend to spend a lower percentage of their incomes for food than do poorer families. Pursuing this lead further we may say that no one index number, however well constructed, will serve equally well for "deflating" the dollar-figures of all types and ranges of incomes, since all classes of people do not consume the same commodities in the same proportions and in the same markets. Our cost-of-living indexes relative to wage and lower-salary earners are much better instruments for such "deflation" than are still cruder price indexes; yet it is desirable to develop special indexes to fit various types among income, regional, population-density, and still other social groups. Use of these special-purpose living-cost indexes will make computations of real wages and other real incomes more significant. The National Bureau of Economic Research, for instance, in its studies

---

[17] *Intercity Differences in Cost of Living, March 1935, 59 Cities, loc. cit.,* p. xviii.

[18] E.g., in Dec. 1938, Feb. 1939, Sept. 1940.

[19] *Mo. Lab. Rev.,* July 1939, p. 22.

of national income in the United States, directed by W. I. King, adjusted the money-income figures by means of separate indexes for several types of consumers—viz., families spending $25,000 annually, families spending $5,000 annually, urban employees, farmers, and farm laborers.[20] Witt Bowden has recently published tables and charts comparing money annual incomes of factory workers, farm operators, and hired farm workers, 1914-38, in relation to indexes of living costs of farm and factory workers respectively.[21]

These pathfinding ventures indicate very considerable differences in degrees of change among such series, in periods of great instability. King figured, for instance, that, from 1913 to 1920, living costs of urban wage earners increased about 20% more than those of $25,000-a-year people. The indexes used by Bowden tell that "commodities bought for farm family living" declined in price, from 1924-29 = 100 to 67 in 1932, 68 in 1933. In the same period the urban wage earner's living-cost index (1924-29 = 100) declined to 79.4 in 1932, 75.4 in 1933.

The poorest and largest families, of course, have to spend the largest fractions of income for food; thus, if retail food prices drop more than those of other items (as they did, from 1925 to 1933), these poorest people are benefited more than is suggested by the grand average index, which is influenced also by comparative luxuries. And if housing rentals decline more than other items in the official budget (as they have, for "all American cities" as a group, almost steadily since 1924), that confers more advantage on some types of wage earners than others.

Suggestions on Making Real-Wage Comparisons.—Since the doctors disagree on the amounts of change of all types of living costs, it is unwise to rely too implicitly on any one calculation of real wages or other income, for any social group. "The truth" which we want, to be sure, is not necessarily

---

[20] W. I. King, *The National Income and Its Purchasing Power* (1930), pp. 68-69. Cf. King's *Index Numbers Elucidated* (1930), pp. 209-214.

[21] Articles in *Mo. Lab. Rev.*, June, July, Aug. 1939, published separately by USBLS under title *Three Decades of Farm Labor*.

obtained by splitting the difference between measures which give different results. When we are confronted by apparently contradictory measures of the living costs in which we are for the moment interested, we must attempt to analyze the respective materials and methods used, and form a reasoned opinion as to the probable degree of change and limits of error. Supposing, moreover, that we accept certain series of money-wage and living-cost data as the best available, and attempt to interpret their significance for real wages, we shall find that not one but several types of comparison are needed. Over the last two decades of sharp reductions in working hours, for instance, charts of real weekly and annual earnings show much less impressive advances than does the picture of real *hourly* earnings. The possibility that the percentage of unemployment, or its distribution, has changed over the period suggests another important footnote for any story of real wages. And, finally, different charts constructed from the same fundamental data may convey very different impressions. A natural-scale chart showing real hourly earnings, with all series based on 1913, for instance, appears to show an enormously greater gain than if the base is a later period. In general, if this type of chart is to be used, a base-period near the middle of a long series, or near the beginning of a short one, probably tends to minimize the distortion. Comparisons of series of index numbers with base periods in the same or closely adjacent years (illustrated by our table at the beginning of this chapter) are convenient for relatively simple arithmetical calculations; but for graphic exhibition of long-period comparative changes, semi-logarithmic charts (such as that on p. 233) have many advantages.

B. Maintaining and Advancing Real Wages

However we measure or estimate the respective courses of money-wage rates and living costs, none will doubt that a grave and perennial problem is presented by these questions: What provisions, if any, are needed to assure real-wage rates against decline? If labor is to merit such protection, may it reasonably be expected to give the employer "sauce for the gander"—protection against any, or undue, *rise* in real-wage rates? Especially against the rise which develops when living costs decline markedly while the wage structure is held rigidly up? The wartime inflation of 1916-20 saw a great development, throughout the world, of sliding-scale wage and salary schemes. Many of these later came to grief, but this sort of endeavor, to find a rational basis for utilizing "the cost-of-living factor" in wage adjustments, tends to receive favorable consideration again in each period of rapid and sustained advance in the price level.

In the following discussion we shall deal most explicitly with plans for recurrent and automatic adjustments, which attempt to "freeze" the real-wage rate for the next year or more. But some hints will also be given as to how the arguments relevant to these sliding scales or formulae can be adapted to the more familiar case, in which living-cost change is urged by one party or the other—not as *the sole basis* for wage setting, but as one factor along with others.

Living-Cost Sliding Scales; Difficulties of Real-Wage Stabilization.—Short shrift must here be given to the factual history of how the living-cost factor has been used in wage determinations, with and without statistical trimmings. One chapter in this story, for instance, would deal with cost-of-living war bonuses, kept distinct from wages and supposedly withdrawable after the war (for even in 1916-18 it was widely recognized that most wage rates were more rigid than most prices). Cost-of-living bonuses in wartimes, too, rightly tend to favor the lowest-paid as compared with higher-paid wage and salary earners.[22]

At this point, too, it will suffice merely to mention a very difficult problem of real-wage protection which is peculiar to

------

[22] For an account of American experiences during the first World War and early post-war periods, see Elma B. Carr, *The Use of Cost-of-Living Figures in Wage Adjustments*—USBLS Bulletin 369 (Washington, 1925). On the more widespread use of this wage policy in that war and post-war period, good sources are the volumes on labor affairs in the various nations, by A. L. Bowley and others, in the *Economic and Social History of the World War* series (J. T. Shotwell, Ed.), under auspices of the Carnegie Endowment for International Peace.

periods of war or similar sustained national emergency, since this matter will be treated in a later chapter.[23] In brief, to attempt to maintain real-wage rates unimpaired during a great national-defense effort means to try to exempt the mass of the population from the economic burden of the war; and so far as such attempt takes the form of adjusting wage rates automatically upward in the full measure of advancing living costs (many of the war taxes, of course, are paid by consumers), this policy contributes strongly to an inflationary spiral of wages and prices.

The exhibits of trends of money- and real-wage rates and earnings given in the table at the beginning of this chapter, and in the charts on pp. 233 and 358 below, indicate that industrial real-wage rates have usually been anything but stable, both in and out of wartimes. The rising trend of real wages caused living cost to become a less prominent factor in American wage policy during the 1920's, in which period the trade unions naturally placed increasing emphasis upon the productivity factor. The great depression of 1929 and following years, moreover, brought still another rival wage factor into prominence: "purchasing power." This type of high-wage philosophy had then become so powerful that industrial wage rates were sustained to a remarkable degree—for a year and more after prices had sharply fallen and unemployment had become catastrophic. By 1933, however, many private wages had been cut drastically (and prices of staple commodities and all agricultural incomes still more). Then the incoming Roosevelt administration dealt with the problem of government deficits, partly by cutting the salaries of Federal employees. In this connection it was understood that such salaries were to be automatically adjusted upward if and as living costs advanced. But the latter scheme soon fell into abeyance, as the emphasis shifted more strongly to price raising, "increasing purchasing power" by increasing wage rates, and as government deficits came to be regarded more indulgently. When recovery developed into somewhat of a boom in 1937, our employers and

---

[23] See Ch. 21, below.

workers became interested again in wage formulae keyed to living costs; and not a few agreements of this sort are still in force.[24]

Living Cost a Poor Index of Labor's Value.—Apart from such fluctuations in prevailing ideas and social conditions as the world has experienced since 1914, and apart from the common will that the long-term trend of hourly real wages, as well as annual earnings, shall be upward, there is an economic reason why particular wages will not long stay hitched closely to living costs. When we realize that any type of labor in a given time and place may be in much different bargaining power than are other types at the same time; that these market conditions may change within a week, while a cost-of-living index is bound to be a month or six months behind the times; and that labor has all too much reason for dreading the consequences of even the slightest cut in its money-wage rates—then we can begin to realize the difficulties facing employers, unions, or public officials who would stabilize real-wage rates for an extended future period.[25] An index of living costs, in other words, is a highly fallible barometer of the current market value of any one sort of labor; the latter is affected by many other factors besides contemporary living costs. In addition to the long-term trend of general real wages upward, there are innumerable cross-currents among supply-and-demand conditions for particular labor groups. At any one time some industries are growing vigorously, while others are declining, perhaps decaying. Transfer of labor from the latter employments to the

----

[24] See, for instance, "Adjustment of Wages According to Changes in the Cost of Living," *Supplement to Conference Board Service Letter,* Feb. 11, 1937. An early milestone in the Conference Board's work in this field was M. W. Alexander's address of April 27, 1921, in connection with the 9th annual meeting of the Chamber of Commerce of the U. S. In 1936 the U. S. Steel Corporation, in connection with a wage advance of 10%, provided that, thereafter, "If, as, and when the cost of living rises or falls a full 5% . . . a corresponding wage adjustment of 5% shall be made, either upward or downward, from the then existing wage level. . . ." (Mimeographed memorandum dated Nov. 7, 1936, Homestead Works, Munhall, Pa.)

[25] In the present section, "stabilizing real wages" or "real-wage rates" refers to hourly or weekly earnings, not to stabilization of annual labor incomes by steadying employment. This latter very important and practical line of endeavor is treated in Ch. 11-D, below.

former is generally facilitated by change in wage differentials, though many supplementary measures for modifying the relative labor supplies are likely also to be needed.[26]

The comparative stabilization of real-wage rates in Australia and New Zealand over the last three or four decades, however, should warn us against sweeping and dogmatic generalizations on this theme.[27] Real wages, as well as other labor benefits, have indeed risen in those Dominions over the long term, in part because the legal awards and determinations are for *minimum* wages, which fall somewhat below market rates in times of brisk trade. Wage differentials among occupations, industries, and regions, too, have shifted from time to time, more or less in accord with changing supply-and-demand conditions. Nevertheless, the tenacity with which these people have clung to the living-cost index as the main guide in wage fixing, even when it led to substantial wage cuts in 1920-22 and 1930-32, is very striking—especially considering the economic and political powers of the labor movements in both countries through these several decades. One reason why such a record was possible, of course, is that a living-cost index is in some sense a business barometer; when it is rising, employers usually can afford to raise wages, and vice versa. It seems probable, too, that rising real incomes have generally been more widely diffused through the whole New Zealand and Australian populations; while in America and some other nations, *industrial* real wages have risen faster than (perhaps at the expense of) other incomes. We may conclude that the living-cost wage factor, like several others, is more practicable when used on the national scale, in all industries simultaneously, as in Australia, than when a small segment of industry attempts long-term stabilization of its own real-wage rates.

---

[26] A locality in which a new industry is booming is apt to be characterized by high money wages and also high living costs—the latter due, in part, to the former. Perhaps the contrary tendency appears, to some extent, in declining communities. In a one-industry town, therefore, the cost of living tends rather directly to reinforce the influence of supply and demand of the industry's product. In more diversified towns, on the other hand, some industries will be unusually prosperous at almost any time, while others are in distress.

[27] See Ch. 18-B, below.

Should Labor Bargains Be in Real-Wage Terms?—Such are some principal reasons why stabilization of real-wage rates over more than a year or so at a time is an impossible and undesirable objective at present, in the United States. Much more cogent and realistic is the proposition that employers and employees would benefit by making their (annual or other-period) wage bargains in terms of stable-purchasing-power units. This argument was well expressed in 1887, for instance, by the great English economist Alfred Marshall:

. . . money is a bad measure in which to express any arrangement that is intended to last long: because the purchasing power of money is always changing. When trade is good and prices are high, the employer's fixed charges are light, and he borrows with a light heart: when trade is bad, the consequent fall of prices increases the burden of his fixed charges, and if called on to repay his debt he must make very great sacrifices of his goods. A perfect standard of purchasing power is unthinkable: even a nearly perfect standard is unattainable. But government could easily publish from time to time the money value of a unit of purchasing power which would be far more nearly constant than the value of money is. . . .

I think it ought to do that. And then nearly all wage arrangements, but especially all sliding scales, should be based on that unit. This would by one stroke make both wages and profits more stable, and at the same time increase the steadiness of employment. It would perhaps be a further improvement if a special unit could be made for wages: that should be based on the general unit, but differ from it by giving greater weight to the prices of the commodities chiefly used by the working classes.[28]

The official indexes of purchasing power thus recommended are now well advanced, and it is easily seen that a bargain for a year or two, providing for automatic adjustment of the money-wage rate by reference to some index of living cost, offers each side some desirable elements of protection. Take, for example, the clause cited on p. 384 below, from the 1938

---

[28] In his preface to L. L. Price, *Industrial Peace,* pp. xx, xxi (London: Macmillan, 1887) Marshall approved, of course, a rising trend of real wages, which he thought best secured by declining living costs. See J. M. Keynes' article in *Econ. Jour.,* March 1939.

hosiery agreement. It provides that wage negotiations may be re-opened and, if necessary, arbitration shall be resorted to, in certain contingencies; and in this connection cost of living is specifically mentioned—though only as a possible ground for union demand for *increase* of pay.

We Are Accustomed to Money Contracts.—There are several great obstacles in the way of even short-term automatic adjustments of money wages to any cost-of-living index, even if both parties agree that a given index does satisfactorily measure changes in the living costs with which *they* are concerned. We are all thoroughly accustomed to contracts in terms of *money,* and we need to know as definitely as possible the amounts of money we are liable to pay, and may expect to receive, at specified future periods. The immediate reaction of a vice-president of the Swedish federation of trade unions, when I spoke to him about automatic adjustment of wages to living costs, was in this sense: "Our members have obligations to make payments of money, for instance on purchase of homes. They want to be able to count on definite money wages for the coming year." Those who already have stable employment, moreover, would consider the argument that constant-purchasing-power wages would make for steadier work irrelevant to them—as well as of doubtful validity for any or all labor groups. The employer, too, has to make many forward commitments in money terms; and *he* wants to be assured in advance of his important money-wage costs.

If more and more business contracts were made in index-number terms, to be sure, it would become easier to apply the same principle to wages; but here we meet another major obstacle. At present, many economists, politicians, and others believe we are making real progress toward stabilizing the purchasing power of money, notably by governmental monetary and credit policies and by public works during depressions. To the extent that this objective can be realized, such progress will have many beneficent results. Protection will be afforded against undermining of real wages and other incomes by inflationary movements of prices; and lessening the severity of business depressions will tend to stabilize employment and annual earnings. Meanwhile, the hope of such reform weakens the will to experiment with purchasing-power wage contracts such as were suggested by Alfred Marshall, except for a very limited current usage, illustrated by the hosiery and steel agreements just cited.

A Floor under Real Wages?—Should each employer take the position which may be inferred from the hosiery agreement and set minimum real wages—guaranteeing that, during the ensuing year, wages shall *at least* keep pace with a specified index of living costs? Would that reduce his labor friction enough to make it worth while? In many cases it might work out so; but not always. If the market rate for a given type of labor, say common labor, for six months dropped faster than living costs, the employer who had made such a contract would at least maintain the quality of his labor force by keeping his wages abreast of living costs ("few would die, and none resign!"); and he would certainly build up some good will in his workers. But when an upward swing of wages took place, without a corresponding rise in living costs, many of his workers would not stay with him long, if other employers offered them higher money rates. In short, the employer is obliged to pay at least the current market rate of money wages, or submit to deterioration of the competence and morale of his labor force. If he proclaims that he will at least maintain his employees' real wages, he is committing himself to what might become a serious handicap.

Labor's Aversion to *Any* Wage Cut.—And we must reckon with an outstanding problem which runs like a refrain through this book: the firm conviction held by nearly all representatives of organized labor that they should firmly resist virtually any and every effort to reduce any wage rate, under whatever circumstances. This attitude is not merely "rationalized"—it is reasonably accounted for—by such arguments as these: (a) All experience shows that labor must struggle bitterly for any advance in its wage rates. (b) If it yields to wage cuts when prices and employment decline, total real-wage income *might* be somewhat increased—but probably only temporarily. (c) When prices and cost of living rise again, real wages are liable to be cut—the more so if money-wage rates have been cut during the recession phase.

This line of claims, convincing as it is under the conditions assumed by its advocates, and important as it is in accounting for labor's prejudices, is not a valid objection against a collective agreement providing for adjustment of the wage scale in accord with living cost. For, in this latter context, the foregoing argument disregards the employer's definite promise to restore money-wage rates, if and as living costs rise again. The kind of real-wage bargain, moreover, which we are just now considering, runs only for a short term—say a year, or until either side gives notice that it demands revision. Each party thus is free, after this short period expires, to press for a revised wage agreement, with or without a cost-of-living clause, but presumably altering the real-wage rate from its position at the end of the contract period.

We shall see (in Chapter 9, below) that other types of sliding-scale wage schemes have kept the wages which they regulate more flexible than most others; that the unions making such "sliding" agreements have proved willing and able to take drastic wage cuts, in large part because experience taught them they could rely on the employer's promise to raise money-wage rates without a struggle, if and when the agreed-upon price indicators called for such upward wage revision.

Real Wages and Business Fluctuations.—Even if all or nearly all wages were simultaneously adjusted to a living-cost index, however, it is doubtful how far this method alone could ease the social strains connected with business cycles. It is true, of course, that during a sharply-rising-price epoch (e.g., 1916-18) many employers make handsome profits and can well afford to make and fulfill promises to keep wage rates at least abreast of living costs. But adjustment of labor costs to living costs may not greatly mitigate the inflationary movement, for the total behavior of *these* employers' revenues and costs may still favor rapid expansion. One reason assigned for the

Australian Arbitration Court's advance of wage rates *further* than living costs alone would have warranted, in 1937, was desire to check the boom. And do not forget the many enterprises, private and public—such as railroads, cities, hospitals— whose prices are fixed by regulating agencies, custom, or other lagging factors. If these employers are to be bound to raise and lower wages in step with living costs, their revenues also should be made more flexible. Finally, in a war or similar stringency, gauging wage rates by cost of living can become distinctly inflationary.

In the downward phase of the cycle, on the other hand, wholesale prices tend to fall sooner and faster than retail; hence money-wage reductions keyed merely to a living-cost index (especially if the latter becomes available only a couple of months or so *after* the collection of the retail prices and rents which it reports) would be unlikely to respond quickly and proportionately to shrinkage in the employer's receipts. Such limited wage relief would, of course, be much more acceptable to the employer than none at all; but another type of sliding-wage scale (see Chapter 9) might be better, in the long run, for both employers and employed.

In brief, so far as it goes, the influence of real-wage stabilization tends to neutralize booms and depressions; but even if universalized it could not do better than moderate them.[29]

C. Summary

It is clear that wages and salaries cannot long be adjusted *merely* by reference to cost-of-living indexes, even in peace-times—and wartimes offer special difficulties to be examined

---

[29] The contrast between money- and real-wage rates is important for social problems and policies relative to business cycles in many ways, some of which are indicated in Ch. 13, below. Mr. Keynes has been the storm center, for instance, of controversies on the actual and the desirable wage policies, during rising- and falling-price periods. In this connection the question is often debated, whether some form of cut in real-wage rates is normally a necessary step toward recovery from depression. The Keynesians formerly, at least, held that it is; but that this step may much better be taken (under democratic capitalism, anyway) by measures for lifting prices, rather than by cutting money-wage rates.

below. Problems of construction and maintenance of a cost-of-living index are perplexing. Satisfactory retail price quotations, fully comparable over long periods, are difficult to obtain— particularly on housing rents; and the changes of weights assigned to various goods, which are required to adapt the index to changes in people's incomes and consumption habits, soon run beyond the layman's comprehension. When great dependence is placed on a cost-of-living index for wage setting, therefore, discontent with that index is pretty sure to develop. Questions as to relative cost of living between village and city, and between regions, have baffled statistical experts, but rapid progress on these problems is to be expected. Thus, our present indexes show approximately the degrees of change in living costs, *from time to time,* in each large city covered (from which some inferences can be drawn as to simultaneous changes in adjacent territories).

Among other serious difficulties inherent in the use of any cost-of-living index as the sole factor in wage determination are these: (a) changes in cost of living do not closely parallel changes in the supply-and-demand situation of any specific labor group; (b) organized labor's traditions are strongly against any money-wage cuts; and (c) so long as other business contracts run in terms of money, an important objective of both worker and employer is definite anticipation of *money-*wage rates. The first of these obstacles is not serious when the wage is tied to living cost for only a year or so at a time, which is the only type of automatic adjustment of wages to living cost now likely to receive serious consideration in America. Any steps in the direction of stabilizing retail purchasing power of money will simplify problems of wage bargaining, as they will tend to make the money wage a better measure of the real wage. Until price stability is more definitely assured, however, many collective wage bargains might advantageously be made in real-wage terms—money rates automatically adjustable to any change in the chosen living-cost index of (say) 5% or more, during the year or so of the contract's life.

CHAPTER 7

WAGES AS PER CENT OF PRODUCTION COST

The ratio of the employer's payroll to the whole of his costs is an important matter in every wage proceeding. The higher this fraction, the greater the immediate effect of a given percentage wage change on total cost, and ultimately on selling price and employment. After listening (as a visitor) to the arguments in a certain arbitration, I remarked to an official of the union that I had missed the expected claim that the price to the consumer would be but little affected, since wages are only part of the total cost. He replied that this omission was deliberate because, in his industry, wages constitute an unusually large fraction of total manufacturing cost. And the research director of one of the largest British trade unions mentioned this aspect of wages as one which his principals often emphasize, in their capacity as members of "trade" (legal minimum-wage fixing) boards.

In arguments intended for their membership and for other popular consumption, union leaders often argue, either that their demand for wage increase should not lead to any appreciable increase of price to the consumer, since it affects the employer's cost relatively little and should be absorbed by profits, or that a proposed wage decrease would not benefit the consumer appreciably (if at all), but would merely increase the employer's profits unnecessarily.[1] Employer spokesmen, too,

---

[1] Many years ago, Alfred Marshall gave some discussion to this matter, e.g., in connection with relations between demands for finished goods and for materials and factors of which they are made. He remarked: "Since the plasterer's wages are but a small part of the total expenses of building a house, a rise of even 50% in them would add but a very small percentage to the expenses of production of a house and would check demand but little." —*Principles of Economics,* Bk. V, Ch. 6, Sec. 2 (6th Ed., p. 385). And here is a similar proposition, derived from statistical studies: "In the manufacture of pig iron, direct labor costs, exclusive of labor costs in mining and transportation of materials, accounted in 1929 for approximately 5.4% of the

often take a similar line, intimating that their profits and
salaries constitute such a small fraction of total selling price
that a disastrous reduction in these property and management
shares would be of insignificant benefit to labor and other
consumers.[2]

The great weakness of this "wage factor" is that it assumes
the wages of a small part of all workmen may be changed,
without effect on other wages. Only to a limited extent is
this assumption realistic, for wage movements are often apt
to become general throughout many industries. As wage *increases* multiply, their inflationary influence is transmitted in
the guise of increasing costs of commodity materials. Any
wage *cut,* contrariwise, has some tendency to generate others
and to contribute to a deflationary, downward spiral of wages
and prices.

Whatever the direction and degree of total cost change
effected by a wage adjustment, however, the effects on the
employer's net income or profit, and on employment, are predictable only very roughly. Such reactions depend on many
circumstances: notably the extent to which the immediate competitors (if any) of the employing individual or group experience similar cost changes, and, in a longer run, on how consumers react to the price changes (if any) for which our wage
adjustment is responsible.

---

total value of the product. Hence, a relatively large percentage increase in
wage rates could be absorbed by a relatively small increase in prices or by
a decrease in other costs."—(C. R. Daugherty *et al., Economics of the Iron
and Steel Industry,* vol. 2, p. 1087.)

In recent years, numerous writings on these relations of wages and prices
have appeared. J. A. McInerney, for example, argued in the *American
Federationist* (April 1938) that wages in the building trades constitute only
a minor part of the total cost of housing construction. Several articles, pro
and con, appeared in *The Annalist* during 1937—one by John L. Lewis, entitled "The Effect of Moderate and Gradual Wage Increases on Prices and
Living Costs" (Nov. 12, 1937). Mr. Lewis pointed out that wage changes
have little indeed to do with agricultural prices; that building construction
involves many other charges, such as land and financing and selling, and he
claimed that "practically every important wage increase in the history of
the country has been secured by the pressure of labor, and lower production
costs have *followed,* not *preceded* the increase in wages." He did not call
attention to the coal mining industry, in which payrolls constitute some 65%
of all costs.

[2] See p. 197, below.

The remainder of the present chapter supplies further background for interpretation of this wage factor, by seeking answers to the following questions: in section A, What rôle do wages play in total costs, among various industries—in relation to the "value added" by the industry to the materials it buys? in section B, In relation to total values of products sold by these industries? and in section C, In what chief ways are wage-cost ratios significant for profits, taking account of production rates?

A. Wages as Per Cent of "Value Added" to Materials

Data from Census of Manufactures.—Many financial surveys of industries have shown the percentage which wages, and often salaries separately, form of the cost or expense of doing business in these groups. Examples are offered by most of the bureaus of business research in university schools of business administration, as well as by numerous trade associations and by governmental agencies such as the Federal Trade Commission. Such surveys, to be sure, often do not show directly or clearly relations of wage and profit net incomes; for sometimes cost of materials is omitted entirely, sometimes not all business taxes are included, and the profit margin between total costs and total revenues may be omitted. A further complication, important for many firms and industries, is the distinction between gross income or revenue from the normal operations of the enterprise and "other income," e.g., from investments owned.[3] In Chapter 9, below, further references will be made to such surveys, as well as to compilations of the published statements of individual corporations.

The more comprehensive data used in the present chapter

---

[3] An interesting though uncommon case is suggested by the report that, in 1939-40, some one-third of the net income of Cluett, Peabody (old-time "Arrow" collar and shirt makers) was derived from royalties on use of the Sanforizing process.

It may be plausibly argued that non-operating income and profits are (in many cases, at least) in effect derived from separate investments owned by the firm's stockholders; thus of no more direct concern to the firm's wage earners than the workers' private investments or other properties are to their employers.

are derived from Census reports, and show only relations
between: total wages and salaries and (1) total value of the
products, as made available by the industry for sale; and (2)
the "added value" attributable to the operations of the industry
itself—payments for materials and for services from other
industries being first deducted from the value of its products.
The phrase last quoted is derived from the procedure, developed
many years ago by the Federal Census of Manufactures, of
computing for each manufacturing industry the "value added
by manufacture," by the subtraction just mentioned. Thus, the
grand totals in question for all manufacturing industries combined in 1937 were: value of products, $60.7 billion; deducting
cost of materials ($35.5 billion) leaves $25.2 billion as the
total value added by manufacturing enterprises to the materials
and "outside" services which they purchased. This "added
value" obviously contains a minimum of the double counting
which makes the "aggregate value of products" difficult to
interpret, because products of many manufacturing industries
(e.g., iron and steel) are materials for many other manufacturing industries.

Each Census of Manufactures (now taken for every odd
year) shows various other particulars for each industry and
major group of manufacturing industries. One is average
number of workers and officials employed (by months); another is total payments of wages and of salaries. The "value
added" by each industry is distributed each year in wages,
salaries, interest, dividends, profits of unincorporated concerns,
rents and royalties, also in taxes—i.e., among the various people supplying services of work and of property for use in the
industry in question. A few such data, on wages as percentage
of "value added," will now be examined; and later we shall
see how the ideas outlined above, with reference only to manufacturing, have been extended to other industries and employments, to make up statistical estimates of all national production or income.

The accompanying table gives a few samples of the Census
materials available on the matters we are now considering. The
first five columns are rounded-off figures taken directly from

manufacturing Censuses of the years specified; columns 6 and 7 are computed from the others to show how different is "labor as percentage of production cost," depending on how you figure it. The following comments also cite some other Census data not shown in this table.

For all manufacturing industries as a group, total *wages* amounted to 42% and 43% of total "value added" in 1914 and 1923 respectively. This ratio gradually declined to 36% in 1931 and 1933, then rose again to about 40% in 1935 and 1937.[4] Among major divisions of manufacturing industries, the lowest rank is occupied by chemical and tobacco groups, whose wages have varied, during the past 25 years, usually between 19% and 23% of "value added."[5]

Similar comparisons among subdivisions of chemical types of industries also show considerable variations.[6] The wages of petroleum refining, for instance, have accounted in most Censuses for around 29% of the added value, but for only 22% in 1929 and 34% in 1931. The highest ratio of wages to added value, within the chemical sphere, is usually coke manufacture, for which the percentage represented by wage labor dropped to 25 in 1929, but usually is 35 to 40. Lowest are patent medicines and compounds, perfumery and cosmetics, and cleaning and polishing preparations—in these three groups, wages take only about 10% of the added value, i.e., difference between the manufacturers' selling prices of these goods and the cost of materials.

Our table also gives a notion of the importance of salaries, by comparison with wages; and the ratio of salaries (plus wages) to the added value in each manufacturing group and sub-group of the table is shown in column 7. This ratio undoubtedly also fluctuates a good deal from one Census to

---

[4] Col. 2 as per cent of col. 5.

[5] Comparisons of these percentages, through the series of manufacturing Censuses (biennial, 1919 and following years), show various fluctuations and some trends; but considerable research would be required to ascertain how closely comparable the data really are, among and within the different industries and groups, especially over the longer periods. Coverage, definitions, and classifications differ somewhat among successive Censuses.

[6] Cf. L. W. Bass, "How the Chemical Product Differs Economically," *Chemical and Metallurgical Engineering,* July 1930.

WAGES AND OTHER DATA, SELECTED MANUFACTURING INDUSTRIES AND GROUPS, 1935 AND 1937

(000,000's omitted)

	Total Value of Products (1)	Total Wages Paid (2)	Total Salaries Paid (3)	Cost of Materials (4)	Value Added (5)	Wages as Per Cent of Value of Products (6)	Wages and Salaries as Per Cent of Added Value (7)
All Manufacturing Industries: 1935	$44,994	$ 7,311	$ 2,253	$26,441	$18,553	16%	52%
1937	60,713	10,113	2,717	35,539	25,174	17	51
Selected Divisions							
Foods and Kindred Products: 1935	9,511	800	261	6,724	2,786	8	38
1937	11,266	978	282	7,911	3,354	9	38
Textiles: 1935	6,061	1,371	256	3,532	2,529	23	64
1937	7,062	1,550	268	4,089	2,972	22	61
Motor Vehicles: 1935	2,391	217	32	1,815	576	9	43
1937	3,096	316	49	2,394	702	10	52
Motor Vehicle Bodies, Parts: 1935	1,551	328	44	1,005	546	21	68
1937	2,080	440	66	1,275	805	21	63
All Chemicals: 1935	2,837	286	153	1,449	1,388	10	32
1937	3,722	381	169	1,928	1,794	10	31
Petroleum Refining: 1935	1,839	110	34	1,482	357	6	40
1937	2,547	140	36	2,064	482	5	37
Printing, Publishing and Allied Products: 1935	2,165	446	349	613	1,552	21	51
1937	2,586	533	422	793	1,793	21	53

Source: U.S. Censuses of Manufactures.

another; I have made only a few year-to-year comparisons. In the single Census year 1925, for example, the total salaries reported in manufacturing industries formed 27% of all wages; and wages plus salaries were 51% of the total added value (as also in 1935 and 1937). In 1925, to continue, the ratio of salaries to wages varied from a high figure of 56% in paper, printing, and allied industries, to low points of 18% in transportation equipment and 14% in railroad repair shops. In the last-named industry (rail shops), wages and salaries together accounted for 99% of the added value in 1925; whereas in the depressed year 1931, the Census showed wages alone to be 99% of the added value.

Reference to the table of estimated national income on p. 178, below, will enable the reader who wishes to do so to compute ratios of aggregate salaries to total wages, by major industrial groups, for 1937—according to one set of national-income estimates.[7]

B. Wages as Per Cent of Value of Product

We have indicated that, for many purposes, it is more significant to reckon wages as a percentage of the *net* social product of the industry (e.g., the "value added by manufac-

---

[7] Estimates of national income usually include some adjustment of Census data, but the discrepancy between the national-income table's figure of $3.4 billion, and the Census total of $2.7 billion, for salaries in manufacturing in 1937, is an unusually large percentage variation—due in part, no doubt, to publication of these national-income estimates before final Census data were available for 1937. The Census totals, in this case, make manufacturing salaries (1937) some 27% of wages, whereas they were nearly 35% according to the national-income table.

Comparisons of wage and salary aggregates, even in and among the few industries in which separate statistics are available, are of but limited significance. There is no uniform criterion for determining which workers are paid wages, which salaries; and within many firms the practice changes from time to time. The recent trend toward paying certain manual workers salaries instead of wages (tending to stabilize their incomes) should be considered, in interpreting statistics of earnings of salaried and wage employees.

The ratio of total salaries to total wages is highest in the government "industry"—in part because white-collar and professional services are prominent in such work, and in part because the salary basis of payment is traditionally regarded as appropriate for a great many manual workers in the public service. See Ch. 19-C, below.

ture") than as per cent of the gross value of products, since the former procedure avoids the double counting of goods which are products of one industry and materials for others. From estimates of national income ("produced," and "paid out") in our major economic divisions, we find that the total compensation of employed persons (in the industries other than Government) accounts for some 60%-65% of the aggregate values of net products, after excluding duplications by way of material costs so far as possible. Thus, if all wages and salaries could be increased by 10%, while other incomes (including those of working proprietors, such as tenant, as well as owning farmers) were kept constant, the prices of products would tend to be raised by something like 10% of 60%, or 6%. The respective amounts of wages and salaries have not as yet been reliably estimated for all industries, but obviously the total of wages is considerably more than of aggregate salaries. Perhaps their proportions are as two or three to one (about three to one, in manufacturing). Of course, if wages alone could be so changed, with salaries as well as entrepreneurial incomes remaining constant, the effect on costs would be less; but it is difficult to imagine a significant change in wages which is not followed or accompanied by change in the same direction in at least the lower salaries, such as those of office clerks and foremen.

The foregoing type of comparison, however, makes less appeal to representatives of wage earners than do comparisons of total wages with total value of products, within each industry or enterprise. This latter comparison is what people usually have in mind when they speak of wages as per cent of "production cost." In the languages of law and accounting, however, the total *cost* refers mainly to all elements, such as wages and materials, which are *paid or due to non-proprietors* (the latter term here including both common and preferred stock holders). Hence such costs, as well as depletion and depreciation of owned capital, must be deducted from gross revenue (or total value of products) in order to ascertain the net income or profit of these proprietors (before taxes levied on such net income or profit). Comparison of the wage bill alone with the whole gross receipts or value of products gives the lowest ratio, among all the comparisons thus far suggested; but, as remarked above, it is fallacious to argue that costs and prices are affected by wage changes only to the extent shown by this lowest ratio, unless there is assurance that wages elsewhere, and other costs too, will not be affected by the particular wage change contemplated.

Variations Among Manufacturing and Other Industries.—A few illustrations will be instructive, particularly to show the very great differences among industries in the way this wage argument can be applied. The table on p. 147 above gives, as of the years 1935 and 1937 for certain categories of manufacturing, data on total value of products (which approximates the gross incomes of all enterprises in each classification), totals of wages and salaries reported, and the wage bills as percentages of total values of products. It will be observed that the wage item alone accounts for only 5% to 23% of the total value of products in the manufacturing industries represented in the table—though much higher in railroad repair shops (not included in the table).

Among non-manufacturing industries, one of the high points of the wage ratio is found in mining. Among subdivisions of mining, the lower ratios are found in metal and oil and gas, in which wage bills usually amount to less than 60% of total payments other than for materials, and salaries to about 10% to 25%. Both percentages vary greatly through the business cycle, since the prices of products are extremely variable, as are also total revenues in relation to fixed charges, such as interest and taxes. The highest labor costs, in relation to values of products, in this industry are usually found in coal mines —where wages account (in the U. S.) for some 65% and salaries, for 8% to 12%, of all payments other than for materials.[8]

---

[8] Above data taken from U. S. Dept. of Commerce, *National Income in the United States,* 1929-35, p. 86—except the 65% for bituminous mining, which follows W. E. Fisher, *Am. Econ. Rev.,* June 1940, p. 296. In other nations, also, the great bulk of costs in coal mining is the payments for labor; moreover, salaries are lower in mining than in many other major industrial groups, in relation to wages.

For another major industry—steam railroads—very comprehensive and accurate data are available. In 1929 wages constituted 55.6%, and salaries 20.3%, of total payments other than for materials; then the wage bill sank in relation to other payments during the succeeding depression years, the low point being 47.6 in 1932.[9]

Another industry for which unusually comprehensive information is available on these points is the private electric light and power industry. Here the total wage bill usually runs a little below or above 20% of total operating income;[10] and combined salaries are not far below the same figure.[11]

One more illustration may be offered here: house-building. Recently the Federal Home Loan Bank Board has been collecting and publishing data on costs of building houses, endeavoring to secure comparable data on standard types of construction. Taking a six-room house, for example, this Board has found that the labor costs run from 25% to 50% of the total— the ratio varying greatly among the 90 cities. "Labor" for these computations presumably refers to labor at the site of the construction—which, of course, has shown a declining long-term trend in relation to *all* labor involved in house-building, as more and more preparation of materials is done in factories and shops. The data given below relative to automobile manufacture may suggest how low the percentage of housing cost accounted for by labor on the site of construction may sink, if and as house erection becomes much more largely a matter of assembling prefabricated standard parts.

Labor Costs of Automobiles.—The table on p. 147 also gives us some food for thought with reference to the two chief branches of the motor industry—motor vehicle (automobile

---

[9] *Ibid.*, p. 140. Spurgeon Bell's *Productivity, Wages, and National Income* includes convenient annual data on wages and other variables, for a number of industrial groups. His chart for railroads (p. 36), for instance, shows wages fluctuating between a high of 64.4% (1920) and a low of 46.4% (1933) with reference to railway *income payments and net business savings* —the latter base being analogous to "value added by manufacture." See Ch. 8, below.

[10] Exclusive of income from investments, etc.

[11] Bell, *op. cit.*, p. 41.

manufacturing), and bodies and parts for such vehicles. Referring first to car manufacturing, it will be noticed that in recent years salaries have amounted to about 15% of wages,[12] and that wages alone have constituted only about 10% of the gross value of the products. This latter ratio is higher for the bodies and parts industry, however—running around 20% in the last Censuses. To a very large extent, of course, the products of the bodies and parts industry are materials for the car manufacturing industry; and when we consolidate our data by deducting costs of materials from both these branches of manufacture, we find that total *wages* now constitute about 50% of the "value added" in the whole motor industry.[13]

Under present conditions, the union representatives, in bargaining with the car manufacturers, are not likely to argue that only 10% of any wage rise would affect the consumer, since this union also organizes workmen in the bodies and parts industry, and the wage scales are highly interdependent, though by no means identical.[14] And, in case of a wage rise of 10% or more throughout both of these affiliated industries (as has occurred several times during the last few years), it would also be fallacious simply to add the value of the parts to the value of the cars and compute the per cent which total wages form of this aggregate; for obviously any rise in the price of parts must be pyramided in the price of cars.

---

[12] Col. 3/col. 2 × 100—not computed in the table.

[13] In 1937, e.g., the "value added" by the car industry was $702 million and by the body and parts industry $805 million (col. 5 of my table); total, around $1,507 million. The corresponding wage bills were $316 million and $440 million; total, $756 million.

When this motor-industry consolidation is made for all the Censuses of Manufactures, 1904-37 inclusive, it shows remarkably little variation in the ratio. In 1904 and 1909 this ratio was about 42%; it was also in the lower 40's in 1919-27. In four Census years, however, it was in the range of 36.6% to 38.9%, namely 1914 and 1929, 1931, and 1933.

[14] See W. H. McPherson, *Labor Relations in the Automobile Industry,* Ch. 8 (Washington: Brookings, 1940). There are only a handful of car manufacturers, whose operations are largely concentrated in Detroit; and union power plus Ford high-wage philosophy and prosperity have produced especially high wage rates. The body and parts industry, by contrast, is more scattered and includes many small enterprises—some in villages—and is less thoroughly organized by the union. McPherson remarks (p. 91) that "wage rates in Chicago parts plants [not well organized by the union] are typically about 20% lower than those in Detroit."

C. Wage Ratios and Production Rates, in Relation to Profits

Wage Ratio Not Indicator of Profit.—It should be observed that comparisons of the percentages which wages constitute of values of products, or of "added value" or "national income produced," among industries have very little significance as to relative profitability of these industries. The lowest ratio of all, for instance, is found in agriculture—not because agriculture is exceptionally profitable, but because most of the value of agricultural products is attributable to other factors than hired labor, notably to the land and capital used plus the labor of independent and tenant farmers. Year to year fluctuations of the wage ratio within an enterprise or industry, moreover, are certainly not reliable indicators of relative profitability, as anyone may infer from the data in the table above, relative to motor vehicles and bodies and parts. In the parts industry, wages form the highest percentage of total value of products in the boom year 1929, and in both branches of the industry they were as low in the depressed year 1933 as in any other. In industries such as coal mining, whose wage bill is a large fraction of its total cost, fluctuations in the ratio of wages to value of product may have more significance with reference to profit or ability of the industry to pay wages.

Wage Ratio Affected by Rate of Production.—Many employers would emphasize one respect in which the foregoing discussion is unrealistic—the lack of reference to variations of costs and profits, according to the extent to which optimum or best capacity operation of each plant is approached. The following table will illustrate concretely the sort of calculation often made on this point (see p. 154).

It will be noticed that the labor costs shown in this table include all manner of work—direct and indirect wages and also salaries. Actually, in this industry piece work is very general, and of course piece work gives the employer highly stable *direct* labor cost per unit of output. Even with piece work, however (and bonus systems which similarly stabilize direct labor cost), variable rates of plant operation produce differing *unit costs for indirect labor,* such as plant maintenance, as well as for salaries.

The considerations sketched above are crystallized in the phrase "break-even point," referring to a percentage of operating capacity. This expression is most commonly used with reference to the iron and steel industry, whose current percentage operating rate is an important business barometer. When this industry has enough orders to operate at say 60% or more of capacity, it is able to earn current returns on much

FACTORY COSTS PER UNIT, AT VARIOUS RATES OF OPERATION

Rate of Production	85%	60%	50%	40%
Fixed Charges:				
Depreciation................	$0.286	$0.402	$0.486	$0.608
Rent, Insurance, Taxes........	.19	.267	.323	.406
Variable and Semi-Variable Costs:				
Heat, Light, Power...........	.115	.151	.157	.159
Salaries and Wages...........	.109	.153	.153	.180
Repairs and Maintenance......	.074	.091	.093	.095
Supplies....................	.026	.031	.031	.031
TOTAL COST PER UNIT.......	$0.80	$1.095	$1.243	$1.479

Source: Brief of employers' association in a wage arbitration, 1938. Refers to an actual plant, said to represent the average for the association.

of its invested capital; whereas operating rates of (say) 50% or less spell mere "break-even" or worse for the owners. In other industries, such as old-fashioned coal mining, in which capital and other overhead costs are much less prominent (i.e., the ratio of labor costs to all costs is high), the break-even point would be lower, for as sales and operation decline, total costs fall nearly as much—at the expense, chiefly, of the disemployed labor.

Thus it becomes clear that this factor "wages as per cent of production cost" is an abstraction, best handled as a long-term average. About this average will be innumerable fluctuations, due to changes in (e.g.) accounting and statistical definitions and other practices, and in rates of wages and other costs, and

not least to differing volumes of production or operation and
sales.

Labor Cost and Price Policies.—It is time now to come
down still closer to earth, and make some applications of our
findings. Let us consider the implications of the following paragraph from a bulletin on a single firm's industrial-relations
policy:

COMPETITION SETS THE PAYROLL

. . .

For example: Years of experience have shown that 50 cents of every
sales dollar can and should go to payroll. We see to it that it does.
The policy is not to buy labor as cheap as possible and sell it as high as
competition allows. Rates of pay are not determined arbitrarily, nor
yet by horse-trading. They are set by the company's position in the
highly competitive industry in which we operate. That is management's
contribution.[15]

This statement indicates that an employer may consider his
own long-term average ratio of labor cost to total revenue a
significant and even controlling figure. Since in this case he
views selling prices as determined by outside competition, the
50%-of-gross-income figure is regarded in effect as a normal
budget for total payroll, supposedly fair to both employees and
owners of the business. If and as rate of operation fluctuates
materially from year to year, however, so must the labor-cost-
ratio. The latter is a practically useful wage factor only in
relation to a normal volume of sales and employment.

Obviously, the standard ratio of labor to other costs may
be changed, too, if an unusual degree of mechanization or other
input of new capital occurs. Here the possibility of displacement of labor by capital rears its head, and suggests urgent
social problems. A mere comparison of the average wage
ratio of electric light and power concerns with those of other
industries (see above, in this section) shows that varying pro-

---

[15] From a circular entitled *Behind the Guns,* issued by the Waverly
Press, Baltimore, in 1940. This concern has about 240 employees, and has
long used an efficiency-bonus wage plan.

portions of capital and labor employed must affect the wage ratio.

A few further precautions as to interpretation of this factor may be briefly suggested. It goes without saying that the ratio of labor costs is the same to total cost and to total revenue, only if there is no profit realized over cost, or if "normal return" to capital and management are regarded as costs. The latter view is sound economics in the long run, with reference to fully competitive industry—though not in accord, as explained above, with legal and accounting vocabulary. And of course profit in the latter sense—the difference between gross revenue and the costs incurred toward non-proprietors of the business—vary a good deal in most concerns, through phases of the business cycle. In general, wholesale prices fluctuate widely with prosperity and depression, retail prices less widely, and wage rates still less. Hence labor costs tend to have a more stable relation to total costs than to total revenues. These phenomena give some basis of fact for the argument that prices vary, not mainly *because* of wage variations, but vice versa—that wage movements merely tend to follow price movements, and usually with a distinct lag in time.[16]

The immediately foregoing remarks, moreover, refer primarily to unregulated industries. In railroads and other industries whose prices and/or wages are controlled by public authorities, changes in wage costs naturally receive some consideration by these authorities in connection with moves from either side for changes in rates of charge to customers of the industry—though perhaps often not sufficient consideration. It appears, therefore, that wage movements are more directly the causes of price movements in the regulated than in the unregulated industries. Where the ratio of labor cost to total cost is moderately high, as in the railroads, a given percentage of wage change will naturally tend directly to produce more change in price of product to the consumer than in an industry,

---

[16] It will be argued, however, in Ch. 13, below, that this is in the nature of a half-truth, and that to an important extent inflationary and deflationary spirals of prices and wages can be avoided or slowed down by wage policy alone.

such as electric power production, in which the wage cost is a smaller element in total cost.

Wage Changes Tend to Spread.—The last sentence in the preceding paragraph must immediately be qualified, as indicated at the outset of this chapter. A great many, if not most, arguments as to how much effect a proposed change in a particular group of wages, salaries, or prices will have are fallacious—because they give too little (if any) consideration to the question: "What *total* changes in wages and prices would the move under consideration bring in its train?" Of course, such forecasting is unreliable; of course, we can usually argue that nearly everyone else's position has already been improved—now it's *our* turn. Nevertheless, here is an outstanding limitation of validity of wage-ratio arguments, which limitation becomes increasingly important with the growth and coordination of labor organization.[17]

D. Summary

This chapter has sketched the variations among industries, in fractions which wages and salaries constitute of (1) total values of products (or gross revenues) of such industries, and (2) of the "value added" to materials bought. The latter wage ratio is important raw material for consolidations of all industries into the national-income data to be considered in our next chapter.

Wage-determination arguments which run in terms of wages (or salaries, or both) as per cent of the employer's total cost or revenue have considerable long-run importance. The average wage ratio in the firm's or industry's history, qualified by reference to a standard operating rate and by inquiry whether the capital investment has changed enough to call for alteration of the old wage ratio, gives one norm or criterion for standard payroll.

The most serious qualification of the significance of these ratios for wage adjustments lies in the possibility that any

[17] See also Chs. 13-B and 20-A-5, below.

wage change may be compounded or pyramided, thus appearing in succeeding industries as changes in costs of raw materials. There is seldom any assurance whether a general wage revision in any industry or section will be the occasion for (what sorts of) changes in labor costs in other industries and sections; but each change tends to make other groups contemplate the possibility of following suit. This possibility should be seriously considered in connection with each wage adjustment; and it should not be lightly assumed that the ratio of any group's wages to total cost of product is an adequate measure of the degree in which any change in this group's wage rates will be transmitted to price of product—and thus, perhaps, to degree of employment of this group.

CHAPTER 8

PRODUCTION, NATIONAL INCOME, AND WAGES

From time to time, considerable discussion has been given to production or productivity, as a principle or factor in wage determinations. Like other factors, this one is susceptible to various interpretations and applications. Let us begin in section A with a few words on its most obvious significance—in piece work and wage plans of similar effect; then pass to a fuller discussion of the more novel arguments as to how wages are or should be related to indexes of physical output (section B); and to other elements in national income (section C). These two latter approaches utilize much the same fundamental materials as were discussed in the preceding chapter, and they lead us to the outstanding problem of "labor's share," in relation to shares of capital and other claimants.

A. Individual and Small-Group Wages Based on Productivity

Essentials in a Wage System.—This topic I treat very briefly here, partly because most of its phases are likely to be familiar to the reader, partly because I have dealt with it at some length elsewhere.[1] Starting with the simplest scheme of individual piece work, we might investigate a rather complex-appearing family tree of "payment by results" or "incentive" wage systems. But of course these numerous plans, after translating their differing terms into a common language, amount to differing patterns of rather few elements. These elements are: (1) the measurement of the worker's efficiency or accomplishment, (2) standard (hourly) accomplishment for his occupation and shop, and (3) the basic (hourly) wage rate assumed

---

[1] In *Compensating Industrial Effort* (1937). See also Ch. 15, below, for discussion of the outstanding problem: standards of labor efficiency.

for such standard efficiency. No. 2 divided by (3) gives a piece rate—if (2) is explicitly stated in units of standard output; otherwise (3) is apt to be the day rate paid to workers whose total service to the employer (No. 1), in the foreman's judgment, is up to standard (No. 2).

Is the worker's efficiency measurable or not? If it is not perfectly measurable, must he then be paid *entirely* by reference to the time he works? The latter alternative would be a slacker's paradise; it implies that neither boss nor workers have any idea, either of what the individuals do or what they may reasonably be expected to do, to earn their wage. In truth, jobs and shops differ by many small degrees, between the best-measurable work (repetitive—but not necessarily *short-cycle* tasks, *under standard conditions*) and work in which tasks or conditions or both are highly variable, so that there is much room for reasonable difference of opinion as to labor efficiency.

Day work, therefore, is really a form of payment by results; and since day work became nearly universal in the automotive industry, numerous bitter disputes over alleged "speed-ups" and "slow-downs" testify to the importance of more or less explicit production standards under this oldest and simplest wage plan. At the other extreme, many individual piece-work systems assume their labor-efficiency measurements to be by no means infallible—they provide guaranteed day rates, in part to protect the worker if conditions beyond his control throw his piece earnings too low.

Partial Indicators of Individual Productivity.—Other wage plans falling between straight piece work and plain day work also tend to base payments on some index which is thought to *reflect*—though not accurately to measure—the individual's output or efficiency during the pay period, better than any available alternative. Group piece work or bonus, for instance, under some conditions may supply a fairer indication of the current performance of each member of the group, and a more effective incentive to the worker, than would day work. Such a result is probable only if members of the group can adequately supervise one another—which is usually possible only in a small group—otherwise the comparison as to fairness and incentive may be more favorable today than to group payment.

Many other partial indicators of relative efficiencies among individuals are employed to supplement the foreman's off-hand judgment, particularly in reference to layoff, rehiring, promotion and demotion. Among such criteria are seniority and "merit-rating" procedures.[2] These latter factors are seldom used directly for individual wage rate or weekly-earnings determinations, but obviously they have important bearings on the relative annual earnings and other satisfactions of individuals.

The foregoing propositions may be summarized in the following slightly different terms: (1) the individual's productivity must, in some fashion, be measured or estimated to determine his wage; (2) apart from the current opinions of foremen (and others, in case of dispute), systematic recourse is often had to one or more among partial indicators which can be counted, weighed, or otherwise measured; but (3) piece rates, standard time allowances ("tasks"), and other labor efficiency indicators must be reset whenever any significant change occurs in the conditions of work—for example, when a new model goes into production.

Piece Work in Totalitarian Nations.—The most extensive national use of incentive wage methods is made in Soviet Russia and Nazi Germany,[3] which fact doubtless accentuates American trade union prejudices against such wage forms. Trade unionism of the British and American sort was scarcely known in Russia before 1917; and in Italy and Germany the fascist destruction of independent labor unions was somewhat facilitated by previous leftist political activities of many of these unions. Workers in the totalitarian countries, organized into party-dominated "labor fronts," were the less likely to object to piece work, too, because these regimes have greatly reduced, if not abolished, outright unemployment. These totalitarian

---

[2] See Chs. 14-C and 15, below.
[3] Other aspects of the wage policies and practices in these regimes are treated in Ch. 18-C, below.

"labor fronts," of course, have many of the undesirable characteristics of "company-dominated" unions, including the lack of effective avenues for expression of labor grievances against particular piece rates or production standards. But if trade unions in democratic nations attempt not merely to safeguard their grievance procedures (i.e., "democratic control" of wages and other conditions of work and pay), but to resist the whole principle of payment by results, they may thereby handicap their own industries in the international struggle against dictatorships.

Piece Work and Labor's Share.—Not a few people, on the other hand, have naïvely supposed that mere adoption of piece payment is a complete solution of the problem of sharing proceeds among all the parties. In particular the Nazis seem to view their more or less frozen piece rates in this light: "the workers can always get more by producing more." This notion is a gross oversimplification, of course—even as to relative wage rates, and much more as to the general wage level. Individual piece rates and other production standards need continuously to be resurveyed, to see if particular industrial changes have put them "out of line" with other wages; and the whole wage structure of each industry must also be frequently checked, to see that real wages per unit of time, skill, and effort are kept advancing as fast and as far as the national productivity makes possible.

B. Broader Production Indexes, in Relation to Wages

Workers paid by the piece (or otherwise according to measured efficiency) tend to earn 10% or more above the average of day workers under otherwise comparable conditions. But "whether you work by the piece or by the day," you naturally want your full share in the total product of your industry. Among discussions of the latter problem, which appeal to quantitative evidence, are arguments based on physical outputs in broader senses than those considered above. Various American trade unions had invoked statistical production data, in reference to wages, as early as 1913;[4] British labor soon became interested in this possible use of the then-novel indexes of national industrial production; and the AFL in 1927 proclaimed emphasis on "productivity" as its "Modern Wage Policy."[5]

Despite the many absurdities to which proposais of this sort easily lead, labor advocates very frequently cite statistics of output per wage earner as evidence of these men's "productivity" and wage deserts. Among impartial labor economists, moreover, all but doctrinaires agree that total real wages in a nation, though they obviously cannot exceed total national output, sometimes do not keep proper pace with national real production. Thus, it seems expedient to indicate here: (1) what sorts of production data are and will be available; and (2) their relevance and meaning, with reference to wage problems.

Physical Outputs and Other Wage Factors in U. S. Manufactures, 1899-1917.—Many of the standard statistical series in this field begin with 1919; but a number of fairly reliable production indexes are available also for earlier years. Many of these were utilized by Professor Paul Douglas, in his two books to which reference has already been made.[6]

From 1899 until the wartime distortions became serious, about 1917, composite indexes show a growth of total physical volume of American manufacturing of well above 100%. Taking 1899 as 100, the Day-Thomas index used by Douglas rose to 227 by 1917. Meanwhile, the index of number of wage earners employed in manufacturing rose more slowly—to 196 by 1917.[7] Here is indicated a gain of some 16% in annual output per wage earner employed. During this period, real earnings in "all manufacturing industries," as calculated by the

---

[4] See H. Feis, *Principles of Wage Settlement,* Ch. 7, and p. 402 f. (New York: 1924).

[5] A. G. Pool, *Wage Policy in Relation to Industrial Fluctuations,* Ch. 9 (London: 1938); AFL Research Series pamphlet No. 1, *Organized Labor's Modern Wage Policy* (1927).

[6] *Real Wages in the United States, 1890-1926,* and *Theory of Wages.* See Ch. 4, p. 82 f., above, for comments on Douglas' view of the significance of "productivity" in relation to wages.

[7] *Theory of Wages,* Ch. 5.

same author on both hourly and annual bases, showed little if any upward trend.[8] These figures, and similar comparisons for other periods, are readily interpreted as showing that labor did not obtain a fair share of the social gains of increasing productivity.

Why Real Wages May Lag Behind Output per Man.— Several other circumstances, however, obviously call for consideration. One is the great flow of capital into manufacturing. According to Douglas, the supply of fixed capital (in "real" or physical terms) employed in American manufacturing trebled, 1899-1916, and quadrupled by 1920. However critics may deal with this particular set of indexes, there can be no doubt that up to 1929 the growth of American manufacturing capital was very great—much greater than the increase of labor employed.[9]

Man-Hours; White-Collar Workers; Technology.—Several other adjustments and comments are in order, moreover, with reference to such data on labor inputs and physical outputs, in relation to real wages. The American manufacturing labor market, for instance, though characterized by a rapid growth in demand, may have been especially affected by the great tide of immigration which was running in during the 15 years just preceding 1914. And the *average number of wage earners employed,* month by month and year by year, is of course a very crude measure of labor input—though the best we have, for earlier years. The average working week in manufactures

---

[8] *Real Wages,* pp. 108, 246.

[9] Since 1929, the value of capital invested in U.S. manufacturing has tended to decline, and perhaps more than is to be accounted for by lower prices and write-offs attributable to adverse business and political conditions. (See Bell's book, cited in the following section, p. 47; and, for detailed treatment of this statistical problem, with many international comparisons, Colin Clark, *Conditions of Economic Progress,* Ch. 11.) Among problems to be faced in construction of indexes of real or physical capital invested after 1929 are: obsolescence of older buildings and equipment, lower replacement costs on many improved designs, the "wringer" effect of all manner of debt deflations, and the rapidly declining interest rates presumably used for capitalizing expectations as to earning power.

The inputs of labor in American manufacturing, as will be shown in the following section, have also shown a stationary or downward trend since 1919 or a little earlier, and total physical output a strongly rising trend until 1929.

declined from some 59 hours in 1899 to about 55 by 1915; meanwhile, the number of white-collar, salaried workers employed in manufacturing grew faster than the number of wage earners. Douglas figured that these trends offset one another; his index of man-hours *worked by both wage earners and clerical workers* runs nearly parallel to his index of mere number of wage earners employed.[10]

Finally, to advancing technology and methods is due no minor share of the increase in output per man-hour employed. This last factor can scarcely be sharply distinguished from the labor and machines through which it takes effect, but it is clear enough that "industrial progress," in the sense of mere multiplication of labor and equipment, will increase output less if techniques and methods are too conservative, than will progress in the larger sense, including steady advance in ways of utilizing labor and capital. Government agencies, such as the Bureau of Standards, assist in technical development and in many other ways.

The record of physical output, therefore, needs to be studied in relation to inputs, not only of wage labor, but also of other work, including that of development and research; and furthermore in relation to inputs of the non-labor factors, land and capital goods.

Outputs, Wages, Etc., 1919-38.—For the two decades just preceding 1939, statistical materials are more abundant and reliable. Infrequent Census reports, for instance, are now supplemented and checked by information published by various agencies, for example the USBLS and the national income tax administration, also by various researches, such as those of the WPA. This period is comprehensively treated, from our present point of view, by Dr. Spurgeon Bell, in his *Productivity,*

---

[10] Hence, his index of labor inputs refers most significantly to man-hours of both manual and factory-office labor. "Output per man-hour" in the more usual sense (referring only to wage-earner hours) in U. S. manufacturing increased some 32%, 1899-1916—as compared with the 16% gain in output *per wage earner employed,* according to Douglas. (See also later estimates, such as those cited in note 12, on the next page.)

Wages, and National Income,[11] and his chief findings must be noticed here.[12]

The accompanying table shows the industries covered by Bell—railroads, electric light and power, all-manufacturing, and all-mineral, as "major groups," and five large industries selected from the ranks of manufactures.[13] The base and beginning of this table is the 1923-24 average, since 1919-22 were judged too abnormal; and the periods 1928-29 and 1936-37 were selected as later bench-marks, to avoid the worst abnormalities.[14] This table is subject, of course, to many corrections and revisions, but it is representative of the statistical information now available, relevant to industry-wide productivity in

---

[11] Washington: Brookings, 1940.

[12] After this chapter was completed, other important compilations and researches were published. One is the rather drastic revision of the Federal Reserve Board's Index of Industrial Production, reported in the *Federal Reserve Bulletin,* Aug. 1940, which, taking better account of the newer types of production, showed total industrial output (manufactures and minerals) in 1937 and 1939-40 running a little above 1929 levels. An outstanding part in demonstrating the need of this revision was played by the elaborate researches of the National Bureau of Economic Research, most fully reported in *The Output of Manufacturing Industries, 1899-1937,* by Solomon Fabricant. This series shows the over-all gain in total manufacturing physical production, 1899 through 1937, of some 276%—nearly a quadrupling. The U.S. population, meanwhile, increased only 73%; and the number of wage earners in manufacturing was not quite doubled. The National Bureau is now conducting parallel studies of output in non-manufacturing industries.

Using Fabricant's estimates for manufacturing, and the standard data for mining and railroads, Witt Bowden and associates in the U.S. Bureau of Labor Statistics have made some valuable researches; see, especially, "Wages, Hours, and Productivity of Industrial Labor, 1909 to 1939," *Mo. Lab. Rev.,* Sept. 1940, and article in *ibid.,* July 1940. Cf. Chart 10, Ch. 13, below.

[13] These four "major groups" account for a majority of the American "industrial wage earners," though for less than one-third of all "gainful workers." Less complete data are given by Bell for another large category of "industrial wage earners"—the one and one-half million in construction.

[14] From 1916 through 1922, Douglas' indexes (1899 = 100) for all-manufacturing show a continued rise in fixed capital (298 to 431), a declining trend of employment (182 to 161), and a slightly rising trend of total output (225 to 240). According to the same estimates, employment increased slightly, 1917 through 1919; but output per wage earner employed diminished somewhat, and output per man-hour more, during this three-year period.

These few data give an inkling why many exhibits of "increasing productivity," which use 1919 as a base, exaggerate the actual trend thereafter.

Bell's charts for the individual years 1919 through 1923, of course, show no significant gain in rail traffic. They do indicate a great increase in output of electric energy, and also a 25% advance in the production of "mineral industries" (mainly of oil wells).

PRODUCTIVITY, OUTPUT, AND EMPLOYMENT

Percentage Changes Between Designated Years

I. IN MAJOR GROUPS OF INDUSTRIES

A. FROM 1923–24 TO 1936–37

Item	Manufacturing	Mining	Railroads	Electric Lt. & Power	
Productivity................	+50	+89	+43	+111	
Physical volume of output.....	+25	+12	−17	+141	
Man-hours of employment.....	−16	−41	−42	+ 14	
Number of wage earners.......	+ 3.5	−14	−39	+ 36	
Average hourly earnings.......	+12.9	+ 1.5	+12.7	+ 30.1	
Wholesale price index........	−13.5	− 9.3	−14.6	− 24.2	
Capital invested.............	− 3.6		+ 3.1	+ 97.7	
Total annual earnings of capital	− 8.3		−29.8	+ 87.1	

B. FROM 1923–24 TO 1928–29

Item	Manufacturing	Mining	Railroads	Electric Lt. & Power	
Productivity................	+25	+32	+16	+31	
Physical volume of output.....	+27	+16	+ 5	+71	
Man-hours of employment.....	+ 1.8	−13	−10	+31	
Number of wage earners.......	+ 2.8	− 5.8	− 9	+41	
Average hourly earnings.......	+ 5.6	− 8.9	+ 6.3	+ 7.6	
Wholesale price index........	− 2.6	− .9	− 3.4	− 5.0	
Capital invested.............	+18.3		+ 9.1	+77.0	
Total annual earnings of capital	+33.7		+26.3	+95.0	

II. IN SELECTED MANUFACTURING INDUSTRIES

A. FROM 1923–24 TO 1936–37

Item	Automobiles and Parts	Iron and Steel	Paper and Pulp	Cotton Textiles	Tobacco
Productivity................	+47	+56	+52	+39	+140
Physical volume of output.....	+46	+16	+50	+ 7	+ 17
Man-hours of employment.....	− 0.7	−25	− 1.5	−24	− 51
Number of wage earners.......	+25	− 1	+12	− 7	− 35
Average hourly earnings.......	+19.3	+28.2	+ 8.4	+ 4.4	+ 15.7
Wholesale price index........	− 8.5	−18.0	−15.3	−18.6	
Capital invested.............	− 5.3	−14.9		− 7.5	
Total annual earnings of capital	+21	−18.0	+24.0	−31.7	+ 17.6

B. FROM 1923–24 TO 1928–29

Item	Automobiles and Parts	Iron and Steel	Paper and Pulp	Cotton Textiles	Tobacco
Productivity................	+31	+35	+22	+ 2.8	+32
Physical volume of output.....	+50	+30	+31	+ 5.3	+11
Man-hours of employment.....	+15	− 3.5	+ 7	+ 2.4	−16
Number of wage earners.......	+13	− 4.3	+ 5	− 3.8	−15
Average hourly earnings.......	+ 2.8	+ 5.5	+ 5.2	−13.5	− 2.3
Wholesale price index........	+ 5.7	−16.9	−11.4	−14.0	
Capital invested.............	+20.2	+ 3.7		− 6.6	
Total annual earnings of capital	+43.8	+50.8	+50.0	−33.7	+34.2

Source: Compiled from S. Bell, *Productivity, Wages, and National Income*, p. 167, and appendices, by courtesy of Brookings Institution.

"1923–24" = average of estimates for years 1923 and 1924, etc. For manufactures and mining, Bell's main source was the Federal Reserve indexes, before they were considerably revised, as told in footnote 12.

"Productivity" is here used in the sense of physical output per man-hour (worked by wage earners).

relation to wages. Bell's volume charts annual fluctuations, by industries, of all the data shown in this table, as well as various others—several of the others being derived from the fundamental series here summarized. His index of hourly earnings in each industry or group, for instance, divided by his corresponding index of "productivity" (equals physical output per wage-earner-hour) gives his index of "unit wage cost."[15]

May Each Industry's Wages be Pegged to its Own Physical Output-per-Man?—Despite this rapid growth in quantity and quality of physical-output statistics and indexes, it is very doubtful if "productivity" in the sense or senses thus suggested can become a factor of much practical importance in collective wage determinations, except perhaps those of widest scope. Among the many difficulties which we may here barely mention are rival ideas as to how changes in quantity, quality, and usefulness of each type of product and factor, and their weighting, should be handled in index making and interpretation. Differing measures and estimates of outputs of the innumerable commodities and services may be combined or weighted in a host of plausible ways, as may also the inputs of other important productive factors besides wage labor—notably services of capital and of work other than that of wage earners—for instance, managerial and inventive work. Physical output per man-hour, too, is influenced not a little by the intensity of utilization of natural resources; here is another obstacle to any simple keying of wages to output per wage earner.

And if we attempt to regulate each industry's wages by its

---

[15] This important index is not shown in the table above; but its trends may be derived by the operation indicated above. In "all manufacturing," for instance, Bell's index of "productivity" rose 50%, 1923-24 to 1936-37; while average hourly earnings were gaining 13.3%. Applying our formula, we get the following index of "unit wage cost" (1923-24 = 100) : $\frac{113.3}{150} \times 100$ = 75.5. The newer indexes, indicating as they do a greater rise in industrial production, 1923-37, imply a greater reduction in the "unit wage cost" index. See Chart 10, below.

Comparisons of real wages are made by Bell and others with output-per-worker data assembled as herein indicated, and with dollar-returns on dollar-capital. The problem of real earnings of capital has been much less adequately handled, in researches thus far published.

own output per wage-earner hour, we face the added and grave difficulty that we shall prescribe very different *rates* of wage change in the various industries—conceivably, at times, opposite *directions* of change. Reference to the Bell table, p. 167 above, will give only the faintest idea of past variations among industries and periods, in outputs per man-hour and in other factors.[16] We may not presume, of course, that wages should be equal among industries, at any one time, or that wages should change by equal degrees in all industries during each period of time; but the notion that each industry's wage rates should be pegged to its own physical-output-per-man index, from the standpoint alone of the degrees of wage inequalities that this scheme would entail, is quite fantastic.[17]

What Share of Production Gains Should Go to Labor?— Possibly we should set out more explicitly the chief interpretations or proposals, as to how "productivity" should govern practical wages, and the problems faced by each. But the reader will doubtless recognize that, at present, data are most nearly adequate for fruitful discussions of relations between *real wages* (hourly rates or earnings) and physical outputs

---

[16] The charts and tables in Ch. 29 of Douglas' *Real Wages* are particularly instructive on variations among industries and times, in rates of growth of average real earnings and of physical output per worker. In general these cover the years 1890-1924, and in most cases show "productivity" rising much more than average real wages. The outstanding case is "land vehicles," in which industry, 1899-1925, average real annual earnings increased by 44% (more than in most other industries), while output (cars and trucks) per worker grew by 1,207%! Over this same long period, Douglas shows that average real earnings in coal mining and in a few other major industries grew *more than* average output per wage earner.

Bell's data on "mining" (= "mineral industries"), in the table on p. 167, above, should be interpreted in the light of these further qualifications: (a) the physical-output data are influenced enormously more by inclusion of the vast production of petroleum than the average earnings figures are affected by wages of the comparatively small number of petroleum workers; and (b) the coal miners' wage rates, which dominate the "hourly earnings" average, were well above their wartime peak in 1923-24. (Cf. chart, p. 233, below.) After 1923-24, moreover, mechanization proceeded much more rapidly than before, in coal mines.

[17] In any one industry, moreover, indexes of output per man-hour are apt to show considerable fluctuations from time to time, in part due to variable relations among productive and operating and plant maintenance and extension work. Most labor leaders now realize that, however attractive this index may be for any of them at the moment, it may turn sharply against them in the future.

per man-hour. The preceding section indicates difficulties enough in the way of establishing a firm tie between these two; cruder doctrines which ignore such factors as changing living costs and work weeks are so much the harder to appraise scientifically. What further fundamental problems are faced by the proposal that real wage rates should keep pace with output per man-hour? One obvious line of objection, already suggested, is that this demand seems to credit wage labor alone with rise in output per man; to ignore the reasonable claims of capital, management, and still other contributors, such as clerical and professional workers. This commonplace conservative argument is, of course, valid within reasonable limits; and indeed labor spokesmen usually concede this point in advance —asking only that labor should have a *fair share* of increasing productivity.

And how may we determine what is labor's fair share? We may not hope to settle that question, but we may go on to consider a few relevant and important matters which are easily overlooked.

The simplest of these is that some plans for hitching total wages to total product are based on erroneous application of the philosophy of piece work. Restoration of output per man in British coal mining after 1918, for instance, was widely felt to be a great social need; and the "proceeds-sharing" scheme applied to that industry in 1921 was expected to give the miners a new material interest in increasing production. Profit sharing also often raises similar hopes.[18]

Now there remains much room for individually and socially beneficial extension of payment-by-results principles to all manner of labor and capital, but only where the connection between a man's reward and his effort is reasonably clear and direct. To neither profit sharing nor other large-group-reward schemes can significant effects on wage earners' efforts be confidently traced—and much less to the still grander ventures in adjusting wage rates to statistics of output which are here under consideration.

---

[18] Proceeds sharing is discussed further below (see p. 191); profit sharing, at p. 213.

How About Consumers?—As stated above, labor advocates usually demand only a *fair* share of the results of increased productivity in their industry; and naturally they do not want their employers to monopolize such gains. But what share, if any, may fairly be claimed by "outsiders"—especially the consumers at large?

One principle of classical economic theory is that competition tends to diffuse the benefits of economic improvements throughout an exchanging society.[19] This proposition, in any of its numerous guises, may be demonstrated convincingly if we assume full competition among all suppliers and all buyers; but its relevance to the actual world of imperfect competition is often disputed. Few will gainsay, however, that there is *some* actual tendency toward such diffusion: nearly all of us, for example, have benefited by improvements in the radio industry, though only a minority invest substantially their labor and/or capital in carrying on that industry. And Bell's table, shown above, indicates (his charts, much better) that, to an impressive extent, the lowering of unit wage costs has been paralleled by declining unit wholesale prices, in all the industries and groups studied.[20] Surely the social ideal lies in the direction of more prompt and complete spread of the gains attributable to discoveries, inventions, and more general improvements like applications of mass-production principles, rather than in the opposite direction of reserving as much as possible of each productivity gain for the particular capital and/(or) labor already in the industry when and where it is achieved.

Productivity, Hours, and Wages, in Relation to Leisure and Unemployment.—We have observed that, during the past 40 years and more, our problem of actual and proper connections between output and wages per man is complicated by a decline in the normal work week, from 60 hours or over to

---

[19] This point is well expounded, for instance, by F. M. Taylor, in his *Principles of Economics* (8th and 9th eds.), Ch. 2 (iii).

[20] One complication is that in many cases (for instance, tobacco and electric power), increased taxes on consumption prevent the consumer from benefiting proportionately to the reduction in unit wage cost. And retail prices cannot be expected to fluctuate completely parallel with wholesale, unless the numerous other retailers' costs do, too.

40 or less. The reason why we have discussed the main issue chiefly in terms of *man-hours* is that the pay per man-hour (i.e., "average hourly earnings") is obviously limited by the output per man-hour.

But the hours complication is not so easily disposed of. In the first place, decreasing the work week *may* tend (sooner or later) to raise real hourly *labor efficiency*—by such avenues as greater skill, effort, and attention. (Whether it *does,* however, depends on many circumstances, such as the weekly hours before and after the cut, the relative strain of the work, as well as methods of payment and of management generally.) A second difficulty will arise if we tell a labor advocate that, since 1923, "the gains to labor proved to be chiefly in the form of greater leisure."[21] Discounting extravagant claims from leftist circles, it would remain true that the decline in normal work hours, and still more in "average hours worked per week" means, in part, work sharing or distribution of unemployment, as well as gains in real leisure.[22] And trade unions having many unemployed members (which ones have not?) still tend to demand ever higher hourly wage rates and shorter weekly hours, thinking thus to make more jobs for their unemployed. They admit that this is merely a choice among evils, and that the policy in question must have some limits short of a universal week of zero hours; yet the unemployment problem staggers us all—it is a desperate case, for which desperate remedies are bound to be prescribed.

Although some restrictive measures, as well as direct financial public assistance, are no doubt needful temporary expedients for cushioning economic shocks to such classes as farmers and unemployed, "stabilizing" and "planning" policies should attempt to modernize, not to scrap, liberal economic policy. If we try to pass on more fully and promptly all productive

---

21 Bell, *op. cit.,* p. 176 (and elsewhere).

22 Those who realize most fully the burdens on wage earners of unemployment, however, often tend to exaggerate the security of "employment" of capital. Receivers of the most stable and assured property incomes, of course (wage earners' savings should be and often are so invested), buy such security at the cost of allowing common stockholders and other "venture capitalists" to take the major portions of both feasts and famines as they occur.

gains by lowering prices to consumers as far and as fast as such gains make it possible, and to allow wage rates among all industries to find their level by fair competition among the whole body of workers, then the industries in which productivity is advancing will expand still more rapidly and will absorb labor faster than they are absorbing it now. If we try, on the other hand, to temper this principle by giving the labor, or both the labor and the capital, in each industry an *extra* share of the benefits of progress as it occurs in this industry, then prices will be reduced less rapidly, consumption will expand less freely, and less than optimum employment of capital and labor will be maintained.[23] Here is a final and fatal fallacy in "industry by industry" comparisons of real wages in relation to physical production.

Production Index as Guide to National Wage Policy.— Although physical output would be an irrational guide for individual craft or industry wage determinations, indexes of production may become significant for comprehensive treatment of the whole national wage complex. In Australia, for example, where wages are to a large extent explicitly regulated by public authorities, records of physical output have quite properly received serious consideration, among all evidences as to whether the nation can afford a general rise of real wages. And even where wages are not controlled in more or less socialist fashion, national leaders of labor, industry and government find such output indexes significant straws, showing whither the wind of national wage capacity is blowing.

Yet mere output indexes can at best be only a partial indicator for such comprehensive wage policy. They are necessarily best standardized for industries which are comparatively mature and important, and cannot cover as well the newer and smaller sources of livelihood. Furthermore, however accurately physical outputs and operations of each type are measured, there remains always the problem of weighting each type, for boiling them down into one index of production, or a few. And the "industries," such as government and other social services,

---

[23] This theme is treated further in Ch. 12, below.

which produce no tangible commodities, employ a large and increasing share of the nation's labor.

C. Values; Wages in the National Income

The shortcomings of output indexes, for purposes of checking the adequacy of the share taken by wages, may to an important extent be offset or neutralized by resort to estimates of wages in relation to national income. The latter are based not on physical products but on the *exchange value* of such products, as well as on the values or prices of labor and other factors.

Production Data and Real National Income.—This value point of view is obviously of the greatest importance in any critique of wages, and something of the sort would remain vital even in a socialist or totalitarian regime with very different institutions as to property, money, and exchange. If farmers, for example, increase their output per man until their staple products (subject to inelastic consumer demand) have very low values in exchange, that means agriculture's total contribution to national (money) income also becomes low. If (under these assumptions) we looked at physical output per man alone, we might be tempted to reward farmers by raising their wages indefinitely, encouraging them to ever greater heights of over-production. This latter policy would not only be impossible for the employing farmer; it would retard the redistribution of labor among all industries of the nation which would be socially advantageous.

Yet physical output and consumption data are most useful as supplementary materials, toward answering questions as to how wages and other elements in the national income are behaving, in "real" as distinguished from money, terms. They point, for instance, to lagging and vanguard industries and occupations; and they tend to show which types of consumer demand are most and least elastic.

Nature and Limitations of Estimates of National Income.—In making up these estimates, each industry is treated by the same logic as was explained in Chapter 7 with reference to the Census of Manufactures. The first objective is to determine the value which it adds to the materials and services it buys from other industries. (Usually all governmental agencies together are regarded as the "industry" of "government.") Other objectives include addition of these "contributions" of the respective industries to arrive at the total national income; and estimation of the shares taken by wages, rent, interest, dividends, and so on.

We encounter various difficulties as we try to work with this material. One danger is that we may confuse "income produced" and "income paid out," in each industry, with the accounting concept of aggregate net incomes of all its enterprises. The gross value of each industry's products is, indeed, approximately equivalent to the aggregate of gross revenues of all its enterprises—for this purpose reckoning self-employed individuals, such as physicians, as "enterprises." But the aggregate of what accountants and income tax collectors call "net incomes" of these business firms represents the *share of the added value which is available for distribution among proprietors and shareholders of the industry.* The expenses of these enterprises, which are deducted from their gross receipts to show the net incomes of such proprietors, consist not only of payments to other industries for materials, but of payments for personal services and use of property employed within this industry—in other words, for wages, salaries, interest, rents, and royalties, all of which are reckoned by national-income statisticians as part of the "income paid out" within this industry. In short, the "contribution" or "value added" by each industry is composed of wages and property incomes of people "attached" to that industry; and the sum of all these is the national income.

Wages, as Per Cent of Income "Produced" and "Paid."— The other chief difficulty referred to above is the distinction indicated by the terms "income produced" (replaced, in the latest Department of Commerce estimates, by the phrase "national income") and "income paid out" (or "income payments" or "income realized by individuals"). The difference between incomes "produced" and "paid" is simply the total of "business savings," or undistributed profits, which in depression years become negative items, because dividends and other out-payments from enterprises to proprietors tend to exceed current earnings or profits. Thus, according to estimates of the Department of Commerce, in 1929 the total of "national income" produced by all American industries (including Governmental agencies) was approximately $82.9 billion, of which $80.6 billion were paid out in wages, interest, rents, and dividends: hence, net business savings of $2.3 billion were retained as undistributed profits.[24] The other extreme is represented by 1932, when the income produced was estimated at $40.1 billion, the income paid out at $49.3 billion; and so the payments to wage earners and others exceeded by $9.2 billion the total value of the current production of 1932.[25] In such a year, therefore, total wages and salaries constitute very different percentages of these two widely separated bases. For 1932 the "total compensation of employees" was estimated at $31.5 billion, which is 64% of the *income paid out,* but a much higher percentage (78) of the total value of *current production* (i.e., "national income"). For all other years on record, the discrepancy between these two bases of calculation is smaller; indeed in most years undistributed profits, or the contrary excess of out-payments over current earnings, are rather small in relation to the value of current production.

The majority of the official tables, showing "total compensation of employees" as a percentage of national income, give the percentage which such labor incomes constitute of "income paid out." The latter total gives less room for technical statistical and accounting arguments than do the estimates of net value

---

[24] And as current profits "plowed in," by unincorporated proprietors.

[25] Such "negative business savings" as this $9 billion in 1932 (dividends paid from surplus and other "entrepreneurial withdrawals") amount to return of capital to its owners or (in many cases) loss of capital, rather than to *income* payments in the strict economic sense. For most of the years since 1929 (all industries combined), the estimates have shown negative business savings, which apparently were not fully offset by new investments. In part, a negative total of business savings is due to write-downs to lower price levels; in part to depreciation and obsolescence.

of current production for each year, since this latter figure involves somewhat disputed methods of reckoning depreciation and other declines in values of assets—and sometimes of opposite "write-ups" or appreciation of inventories and other property values. Moreover, there are difficult problems as to how far governmental payments measure the current productivity of this "industry." In the following sections I shall speak mainly of wage and salary payments for labor in relation to *income produced,* which corresponds in principle with what the Census of Manufactures calls "value added by manufacture."

Variations in Labor's Percentage Among Major Industries.—The accompanying table gives a bird's-eye view of the relations among payments of wages and salaries in relation to value of current production, by each of our major categories of industries, for 1937, which was our most prosperous year between 1929 and 1940, and was characterized by strongly rising wage rates. For only a few industries are wages and salaries available separately;[26] but the table gives estimates of total wages and salaries together in every one. With reference to the Government "industry's" place in the national income, there are many puzzling questions, but in general the category "government, excluding work-relief wages" is the aggregate of governmental payments of wages, salaries, and rent and interest —for "value received" in services of labor and property. The cash income which any person derives by supplying such services to his own industry he normally spends, mostly to acquire products of other industries (including services, e.g., "purchasing" governmental services by fees and taxes).

How may we account for the variations shown in column 3, among industry groups, as to payments for labor in relation to value of current production? Wages and salaries form the lowest percentage in agriculture, for two obvious reasons: (a) much of the value added by this industry is attributable to the

---

[26] In the four groups for which aggregate salaries were separately estimated, for 1937, they formed the following percentages of wages: mining, 10%; manufacturing, 34%; contract construction, 30%; transportation, 40%.—*Income in the United States, 1929-37,* Table 18 (U.S. Dept. of Commerce, Nov. 1938).

ESTIMATED U. S. NATIONAL INCOME, 1937

By Major Industrial Groups and Certain Components

($ billion)

Industry, etc.	National Income (1)	Total Wages and Salaries (2)	Wages and Salaries as % of Income Produced (3)
Agriculture....................	6.4	.8	13
Mining.......................	1.5	1.3	87
Electric Light, Power and Gas......	1.4	.7	50
Manufacturing.................	17.0	14.0	82
Contract Construction...........	2.0	1.5	75
Transportation.................	5.1	3.8	74
Communication.................	.8	.6	75
Trade........................	9.1	6.5	71
Finance	6.2	2.0	32
Service.......................	8.5	5.5	65
Miscellaneous.................	3.1	1.9	61
Government—Excluding Work Relief	7.4	5.6	76
All Industries.................	68.5	44.2	64
Social Security Contributions of Employers.....................	.9	.9	....
Other Labor Income [a]............	....	.6	....
Total National Income, Exclusive of Work-Relief Wages..............	69.4	45.7	65.8
Work-Relief Wages..............	1.8	1.8	....
Totals.	71.2	47.5 [b]	66.7

[a] "Other labor income" appears to consist mainly of private pensions and workmen's compensation for injuries.

[b] This $47.5 billion is the Department of Commerce's figure for "total compensation of employees," which (in 1937) formed 67.7% of the "total income paid out" (see below).

Source: Cols. 1 and 2 condensed from U. S. Department of Commerce, *Survey of Current Business*, June 1940; col. 3 computed from cols. 1 and 2. In this article (by R. R. Nathan) will be found also corresponding data by years, 1929–39 incl. "Total income paid out" is given, for 1937 (*ibid.*), as $70.3 billion, as compared with "total national income" shown above of $71.2 billion—indicating net business savings of about $.9 billion in 1937.

services of property, notably land, and (b) much of the labor is contributed by the farm operators ("entrepreneurs") and unpaid members of their families. Normally the other extreme is represented by the two major groups—manufacturing and mineral production—in which compensation of employees amounts usually to 80% or more of the value added to materials and services bought from other industries. A parallel table for 1935 (not given here) would show in column 3 a very high figure (about 97) as the percentage which total employees' compensation formed of the value of 1935 production in "mining" (including petroleum and metal extraction). Evidently the aggregate of current net production in this group of industries in 1935 was very little in excess of wages, salaries, and other payments for the benefit of employed persons. The corresponding figure for the same industry and year (1935), however, with reference to "income paid out," was only 79%. Apparently a large part of the remaining 21% must have been in the nature of return of (not to) capital, by depletion, depreciation, and the distribution of any accumulated corporate surplus.

Two major groups of industries in which employee compensation is relatively low, in relation to both current production and "income paid out," are electric and gas public utilities, and finance. In these industries, of course, the services of capital are unusually important in relation to labor. Much of the labor, moreover, is paid by salaries and commissions (notably in sales of insurance) rather than by wages. It might be expected that the commercial, merchandising, or "trade" industries also would show low ratios of employee compensation to total national income produced, since there are many small mercantile enterprises (like "corner groceries") in which the labor in done by the entrepreneurs and unpaid members of their families. The absolute number of such small trading concerns is very large; but their aggregate production must be small in relation to that of larger firms which do employ considerable help, for no less than 71% of the income produced (value added) by trading industries in 1937 was compensation of employees.

Wages and Salaries in National Income.—Should total payrolls show a rising trend, not only in relation to number of workers and living costs, but also as a fraction of national income? Enough has been said above to indicate why the share going to *hired* labor varies: (a) among types of industry, and (b) among years—and that (c) in boom and slump years you get one sort of per cent figure by comparing wages and salaries with *income payments,* and another and very different figure if you take as 100% *national income produced.*[27] We must now go a bit further into the trend of wages and salaries, as percentages of total national income. The following data and comments amount to a slight elaboration of (a), (b), and (c) above in this paragraph, though I shall not keep these points entirely separate. A few comparisons, moreover, will be made between American and foreign estimates of hired labor's share.

A number of investigations have shown the remarkable stability of the relative shares, among *all national-income payments,* taken by (a) wages and salaries and (b) management and property, through all phases of the business cycle. The over-all percentage of 67.7, cited in note *b* of the above table (which "total compensation of employees" formed of total income *paid out* in 1937), comes within a point or two of the corresponding percentages for each year since 1932, when the low mark of 63.9% was hit, as compared with 65.5 in 1929.[28]

More or less similar percentage series have been published by other investigators, and for other years and nations. These estimates differ sufficiently in methods and definitions so that comparisons are difficult; but each investigation tends to show

---

[27] In the long run, of course, "income paid out" must equal "income produced"—if each is adequately measured.

[28] Nathan, *op. cit.,* Table 3. The apparent rise of "labor's share" shown by this latest official series is, however, largely attributable to the great growth, since 1932, of work-relief wages. If we exclude this latter non-economic factor, and compare remaining total labor income, year by year, with total national income produced, the fluctuations are greater among individual years since 1929 (low: 64%, 1929; high: 79%, 1932; usual range: 65% to 70%) ; and no upward or downward trend appears within these 11 years.

considerable stability of percentage shares for the period and group to which it refers.[29]

Wages in the National Income.—The question has often been raised, have total *wages* increased in proportion to other incomes? This, of course, is one interpretation of "labor's share." The eminent statistician Bowley, for instance, studied this problem, with reference to Britain.[30] He estimated that, between 1880 and 1913, "The proportion of the national income received as wages diminished from about 41½% to 35½% . . . ;" but he also found that, whereas wage earners formed 83% of the British gainful population in 1880, they made up only 73% of it in 1913. Taking account of the rise of a "middle class" of salaried and other incomes, Bowley reckoned the shares obtained by work and by property to be respectively 62½% and 37½% in each of these years, 1880 and 1913.

The table on p. 182, which I have derived from King's estimates, indicates that a somewhat different yet significant change went forward in the United States after 1909.

It appears, moreover, that salaried people have increased more in numbers than in share of income—from 13% to 18% of the gainfully employed is a larger relative change than their concurrently rising share, from 15% to 19% of the national income. Enterpreneurs have become a relatively less numerous class in the population, due both to the rise in importance of large business enterprises, and to the decreasing relative rôle of farmers (much the largest single class of entrepreneurs) in our national economy. Since it was, in general, the smaller fry among business proprietors who became employed by others (or were not replaced as entrepreneurs when they died or retired), it is not remarkable that the share of "entrepreneurs

---

[29] See, e.g., the publications on national income of the National Bureau of Economic Research (New York), notably works by W. I. King and Simon Kuznets; M. Leven *et al.*, *America's Capacity to Consume*, pp. 147 ff. (Brookings, 1934); and Colin Clark, *Conditions of Economic Progress*, pp. 407 ff. (London: 1940).

[30] A. L. Bowley, *The Change in the Distribution of the National Income, 1880-1913* (Oxford, 1920).

ESTIMATED SHARES OF WAGE EARNERS AND OTHERS IN AMERICAN
NATIONAL INCOME, 1909-13 AND 1924-27

Period		Entre-preneurs	Salaried Persons	Wage Earners	Total
1909-13 avg...	Per cent of gainfully occupied population	28	13	59	100
1924-27 avg...	Per cent of gainfully occupied population	22	18	60	100
1909-13 avg...	Percentage share of national income	48 [a]	15	37 [b]	100
1924-27 avg...	Percentage share of national income	42 [a]	19	39 [b]	100

[a] Includes share of "other property owners," some of whom are salaried and wage-earning persons.

[b] Includes pensions and workmen's compensation. As explained in Ch. 2 and elsewhere herein, the definitions of "wage" and "wage earners" by employers are somewhat variable and shifting.

Source: Computed from W. I. King, *National Income and Its Purchasing Power*, pp. 56-62, 80 (New York: 1930).

The percentage of national income taken by wages should be lower in U. S. A. than in Britain, since agriculture accounts for a much larger fraction of our population. As industrial and other urban types of industry grow, relative to agricultural and other small-scale economies, a rising fraction of national income is distributed in the form of payrolls. King's earlier book (*Wealth and Income of People of U. S.*) indicated this trend. Wages and salaries, he estimated, rose from 35.8% of the national income in 1850 to 53.5% in 1890, 47% in 1900 and 1910.

and other property owners" in the national income did not decrease as much as did the relative numbers of business proprietors.[31]

---

[31] Statistical differentiation of work income from property income is very difficult. Clark (*op. cit.*), following Kuznets, includes all professional incomes with wages and salaries, thus obtains a higher percentage than given above as the "share of employees." But this procedure is illogical: no doubt professionals do earn their incomes largely by work, but proprietors of all manner of unincorporated enterprises—notably farmers—also earn their incomes in large part by work.

The Department of Commerce computes "percentages which dividends and interest represent of income paid out," by industries. For 1937, all industries, this total was 13.8%—leaving some 20% which is largely rents, royalties, and "profits" of unincorporated enterprises. (Interest accounted for 18% of "income paid out" by government—excluding work relief—in 1937.)

Bowden gives some valuable data and comments on distributive shares and capital formation in American manufacturing, mining, and railroad industries, 1919-39 (*Mo. Lab. Rev.*, Sept. 1940). In these three industries taken together, it seems that wages formed 65% or more of total income paid out, in 1919 and 1920; thereafter mostly between 57% and 62% until

Real Incomes of Work and Property.—The relative stabilities thus indicated, of incomes of wage earners, in proportion *both* to their numbers in the whole population and to the total national income, may seem to indicate stagnation, or be inconsistent with other indications that real wages per capita have risen. Such an interpretation is unwarranted. Since the national income has shown a rising trend *per capita,* after allowing for variations in the purchasing power of money, the stability above referred to merely means that all labor's share has, so far as the scanty evidence available goes, about kept pace with other income shares. Naturally, many people desire to see labor's share increase faster than others, and this sort of trend may develop in the future. Two factors, however, work in an opposing direction: (a) increasing public expenditures for social benefits like education, relief of destitution, increased aid to children, the aged, and the blind (sometimes called part of the "social wage"), and (b) the tendency in most modern periods for capital invested to increase faster than the labor supply. Many other indications, such as records of physical outputs of consumers' and producers' goods, support (in general) Professor Paul Douglas' finding that in American manufacturing, 1899-1922, the fixed capital invested (adjusted for changing price level) increased about 330% (from the index 100 to 431); while the man-hours worked by wage earners and clerical workers in manufacturing increased only about 60% (from index 100 to 161). If the *unit* rates of return to capital and labor had been constant throughout this period, the share of labor in the total "value-product" of manufacturing would have declined greatly. The annual estimates beginning with 1909 indicate an approximately level long-term trend in the share taken by wages in the urban industries,

the years 1930-32, when this percentage slumped to 52%-53%. For years 1934-39 it was in the 57%-59% range.

It should be noticed that in this series by Bowden, (a) the per cent taken by *wages,* not wages plus salaries, is calculated; and (b) 100% is "income paid out," which in depression years includes large payments out of surpluses earned in preceding years. Contrariwise, in boom years like 1919 and 1920, part of current property earnings are retained as business savings, not paid out. And these relative distributive shares are affected by variable conditions like taxes on "excess" and/or undistributed profits.

though there are great oscillations from one year to another. Moreover, non-wage labor benefits, such as group insurance, paid vacations, pensions, and other Social Security services, have greatly increased. Interest rates, to be sure, appear to have declined greatly since 1929. Their fluctuations constitute a factor of no small importance in determining the proportionate shares of labor and property in industry's current product. It is doubtful, however, whether the percentage-share estimates hitherto available have adequately dealt with the capital which is lost after investment.[32]

D. Summary

In this chapter we dealt first with estimates and indexes of physical outputs, in relation to inputs of labor and wage rates. We found the strongly rising trends of output per man-hour which have been characteristic of most industries during at least the past 40 years to be of great social significance, and potentially important for *very comprehensive* wage determinations. For annual wage bargains in particular employments, however, such "productivity" data are far from reliable indicators, either of this particular labor's deserts or of the industry's capacity to pay.

Increasing productivity per man and per machine should be accompanied in full measure by savings to consumers. The property and labor in the progressive industry may naturally feel entitled to higher earnings than such consumer gains would permit, but such special earnings mean that consumption and employment will expand less rapidly than is reasonably possible in these progressive vocations.

National-income estimates bring us closer to practical wage factors, since they take account of values and costs. A few of their many problems in relation to wages were discussed. We

---

[32] "It should also be noted that the available data come from 'going concerns.' Losses which such concerns suffer presumably are deducted from profits. But the losses of enterprises which go into bankruptcy or 'fail to succeed' in any year are not likely to be reported in our sources, and such losses fall mainly, though not exclusively, upon 'management and property.' "—W. C. Mitchell *et al., Income in the U. S.,* vol. I, p. 96 (New York: 1921).

found that norms as to "labor's share in the product" are very hard to come by. The pattern differs greatly among industry types, for instance between agriculture and mining; hence, as a nation becomes industrialized, the percentage of its national income distributed in the form of wages and salaries tends to rise. The share of wages alone, estimated by King at 37% to 39% of the whole U. S. national income in 1909-13 and 1924-27, is affected by changing occupations and methods of payment, as well as by changing wage rates. Over each whole business cycle, the fraction of all *income payments* taken by labor is remarkably constant; but within the cycle, total payrolls tend to become a declining fraction of *national income produced,* as business activity increases.

CHAPTER 9

WAGE-PAYING CAPACITY, SLIDING SCALES, PROFIT SHARING

The factor "productivity," we have seen, is susceptible of interpretation and application to wage problems in various ways. When it is taken in the sense of value-product, it becomes roughly equivalent to the subject matter of the present chapter—the economic or financial position of the industry and its ability to pay wages. Talk about productivity, however, is apt to run in terms of rather broad statistical series, based considerably upon physical and Census data; whereas discussions of an industry's wage-paying ability are conducted more largely in accounting vocabulary—costs, profits, and losses.

Let us consider the general relevance of the employer's prosperity (profits and losses) to wages, and notice relations among several of the different senses in which wage-paying capacity has been interpreted. The following headings will serve to bring out some of these ambiguities and confusions and means of dealing with them: section A: How is the criterion of wage capacity to be adjusted to the criterion of a "living wage"? Section B: If wages are to vary with the particular industry's ability to pay, are "sliding-scale" indicators adequate? Section C: Can wages be adjusted to profits at all, in view of the variability of profits among different firms? If so, how may accounting data on actual net profits and losses be used in wage determination? Section D: May labor incomes and industrial peace be promoted by profit sharing? Should wages tend to favor contraction, expansion, or stability of employment in the industry concerned? Discussion of these questions will be undertaken in this chapter, which closes by summarizing and showing a few further connections with matters discussed in other chapters.

A. Living Wage and Wage Capacity

It has often been argued that "the payment of a living wage to the lowest grade of employees and the maintenance of the standard of living of all employees . . . must be regardless of the financial condition of any industry or any unit of it";[1] and that "if an industry cannot pay the workers engaged in it a reasonable wage it is in the interest of the community that it should cease operations."[2] But, as is indicated in Chapter 17, below, faith has been declining in the ability of officials and experts to determine the amount of a practicable "living" or "reasonable" wage, *independently* of industry's capacity to pay. And when profits are understood to be rising, even out of the cellar of losses, there is a widespread tendency among labor advocates to use this trend as an argument for increasing wages.

Nevertheless, there is an important sense in which the New Zealand court's dictum cited above may be defended. It is sometimes practicable for a state or nation to enforce minimum wages which will condemn all or most of *one industry* (*or more*) to extinction—practicable, that is, so long as these wage minima are within the current ability of that nation's *industry at large* to pay.

One of the ambiguities we face, then, is this: "wage capacity" may refer to the prosperity or wage-paying ability of a single firm, of a group of firms constituting an industry or section of an industry, or of all industries in the nation or section. In general, our concern in this chapter is with arguments and endeavors toward adjusting the wage scales in an industry to profits and losses within that particular industry (group of firms).

In Australia.—The following passage in an early and celebrated Australian wage arbitration case presents an interesting mixture of considerations:

---

[1] J. N. Stockett, *The Arbitral Determination of Railway Wages,* p. 188 (Boston: 1918).

[2] New Zealand Industrial Court, *Awards,* vol. 19, p. 1061 (gold miners).

The remuneration of an employee is not made to depend on the profits of the employer. If the profits are nil, the fair and reasonable remuneration must be paid; and if the profits are 100%, it must be paid. As at present advised, I shall certainly refuse to pry, or to allow others to pry, into the financial earnings of the manufacturers, or to expose their financial affairs to their competitors in business. If it has to be cards on the table, it ought to be all cards on the table; but, having regard to tariff protection given, the excise exemption offered, and the admission which I have mentioned, I shall ignore any consideration that the business will not stand what I should otherwise regard as fair and reasonable remuneration.[3]

The "basic wage" for common or unskilled labor, varying only with the index of living costs, and added differentials for skilled trades, are still outstanding elements in Australian wage policy. The whole national wage structure, however, the state and Commonwealth arbitration courts attempt to adapt to the prosperity and prospects of all industries as a group. Hence, the basic or minimum real wage is not really as firmly maintained as might appear. Material wage cuts were, in fact, made in nearly all Australian industries in the depression following 1929; and national defense burdens bring even more urgent necessity for temporary lowering of living standards to all countries from time to time.

As a result of this comprehensive and deliberate governmental control, the wages in any segment of Australian or New Zealand industry have been somewhat less closely related to the current prosperity *of that particular segment* of the economy than is the case in most other countries. In another chapter it will be pointed out that this result may be a favorable influence on national employment.[4]

B. Sliding Scales for Industry-Wide Wage Adjustments

The ability of employers to pay wages, therefore, is an outstanding, if not the chief, practical determinant of wage levels.

---

[3] *Ex parte,* H. V. McKay, 2 Commonwealth Arbitration Reports, p. 5, cited in George Soule, *Wage Arbitration,* p. 174. (This is the famous "Harvester Case."—See Ch. 18-B, below.)

[4] See Ch. 20-A-5, below.

As has been intimated, all manner of wage-paying abilities
may be discovered among the various employers, according to
the point of view. Two principal points of view are discussed
in the present and the following sections. The first is variations *among* industries, and of each industry from year to
year, in prosperity or wage capacity. The second is variations
among firms or enterprises *within* each industry. Both of these
matters may be investigated by reference to whatever accounting data on prices, costs, profits and losses may be available;
or by other and less direct indications, such as volumes of employment, production, sales, and so on. The former type of data
we may briefly designate as "accounting"; the latter as "statistical."

Wages Keyed to Selling Prices.—Organized employers
and workers have not infrequently adjusted wage rates by
reference to one or more among certain indexes of the prosperity of the employing industry. Such schemes are often
referred to as "automatic" or "sliding-scale" plans for wage
adjustment. We shall here examine briefly the chief classes of
such schemes, and compare their results with each other and
(at chapter's end) with sliding scales which make wages vary
with indexes of living costs.

Wage sliding scales based on selling prices of the products
of the wage-paying industry have seen most use in iron and
steel trades, and mainly in Britain.[5] As early as 1840, an
English ironmaster (Thorneycroft) was paying his puddlers
one shilling as wages for each pound (sterling) of selling price
of marked bars, which relationship persisted in some branches
of the trade down to 1919.

A more representative scheme was that of the Cleveland
and Durham (England) blast furnace workers, whose agreement (of 1919) provided that certain basic or minimum wages
—mostly tonnage, piece, or bonus rates—were to be paid when
pig iron was 54s. a ton or less. For every 3d. by which the

---

[5] In the U.S. in recent years, "plans for the automatic adjustment of
wages to the price of the commodity are rare except in non-ferrous metal
mining and smelting."—*Mo. Lab. Rev.*, Jan. 1940. This article gives excerpts from the current Anaconda Copper Mining Co. agreement.

price exceeded 54s., ¼ of 1% was added to these basic wage rates. The details have been revised from time to time; for instance, the basic price had become 67s. 6d. by January 1924, and then was lowered several times, reaching 50s. by April 1934. The average selling price in this plan is ascertained quarterly by two firms of accountants, named respectively by the employers and the trade union; these accountants secure the data from the accounts of seven specified firms which are parties to the agreement, and presumably the wage rates of each quarter are thus based on the average selling prices of the previous quarter, except that there is a minimum rate below which wages may not fall, except by revision of the fundamental agreement.[6] Widespread use of sliding scales, similar in principle to this one, was also made in British coal mining, particularly between 1870 and 1900—with very different results, as will be explained below.

Wages Keyed to Profit Margins.—A variant of this principle of adjusting wages periodically to product selling prices is found in "profit-margin" sliding scales. The latter have been used, for instance, by British tin-plate and galvanizing trades. Such a margin plan depends on a formula by which, from the average selling price of the standard products, is deducted the current cost of a batch of standard raw materials supposed to be normally used in making a unit of the finished product. A scheme of this latter sort was seriously considered in British cotton manufacture, 1899-1900, but was not consummated.

---

[6] I take the above details, and many other materials for the present chapter, from A. G. Pool, *Wage Policy in Relation to Industrial Fluctuations* (London: 1938). Mr. Pool's is doubtless the most up-to-date and searching account of sliding wage scales of all sorts.

Similar sliding wage scales have been long employed in certain branches of American iron and tin-plate trades, notably hand puddling. The latter type of scale "involves the setting of base rates of tonnage wages for various occupations and grades of product at annual conferences between employers and union representatives, after which the wage rates are adjusted up or down every two months in accordance with changes in realized sales prices (of individual companies), determined by a union-management committee which examines the company's books. The scales of selling price-wage adjustments, i.e., the percentages of corresponding changes up or down, are also agreed on at the annual conferences."—C. R. Daugherty *et al.*, *Economics of the Iron and Steel Industry*, Vol. 1, p. 143 (New York: 1937).

In 1905 such a plan was adopted by organized employers and workers in cotton mills of Fall River, Massachusetts; and it remained in operation until 1910.[7]

Economy Sharing.—What other plans have been tried, for making the workers' labor income vary in more or less automatic relation to the employer's ability to pay?

Instances are supplied, in American experience, by Henry R. Towne's practice of "gain sharing," begun (by Yale & Towne) in the 1880's; and by the "collective economy dividend" feature of John Leitch's "industrial democracy" employee representation plans, about 1915-25.[8] These latter devices, however, are essentially group bonuses for economy in the use of materials, lubricants, and the like; Mr. Towne explicitly excluded price changes, on the ground that the worker should not be required to speculate on price movements. The sliding scales with which the present chapter is concerned, on the contrary, are based on the idea that the worker inevitably must speculate, as to job security and annual real wages, on price movements in his industry. These latter schemes attempt to give him unusual gains when economic conditions are most favorable, and to minimize unemployment by reducing his money wages when these conditions are unfavorable. Some firms and employees, to be sure, enjoy the benefits of relatively stable employment with little or no conscious effort and cost toward that end, and others *achieve* stability; both classes naturally do not find this objective of sliding wage scales of importance for themselves.

"Proceeds Sharing."—Much more like price and profit-margin sliding wage scales is "proceeds sharing," used on a broad scale in British coal mining since 1921. The background includes long and almost universal collective bargaining; sev-

---

[7] S. E. Howard, *The Movement of Wages in the Cotton Manufacturing Industry of New England Since 1860.* (Boston: National Council of American Cotton Manufacturers, 1920.)

[8] Mr. Towne's procedure was described in a paper which he read to the American Society of Mechanical Engineers in 1889, reprinted in *Economic Studies,* American Economic Association, Vol. 1, No. 2 (1896). Cf. my discussion in *Compensating Industrial Effort,* pp. 285-290.

eral decades of experimentation with selling-price scales; legal minimum-wage fixing under a Parliamentary Act of 1912; government control of the industry and national standardization of wages during the first World War; then return of the mines to private ownership in 1921, followed by periods of exporting which afforded a few feasts but mostly famines.

Details of this proceeds-sharing institution, in the eighteen districts of bargaining, have been changed several times. As of 1936 they provided, first, for minimum-wage rates—in most cases those prevailing in 1914 plus 30% to 40%. (Presumably these minima refer to hourly-earned rates, and are payable only if the hourly rate of earning at the current tonnage piece rate is less.) After payment of these "standard wages," and "costs other than wages," the remainder of the proceeds which neutral accountants ascertained to be received by all the mines in each district were to be divided between the workers and the operators in the ratio (usually) of 85:15. Such "ascertainment" of proceeds was made usually at periods of one to three months, sometimes annually.

For these purposes, no serious attempt was made to compute the total investment in property, nor to determine a fair rate of return on such investment. The standard adopted for "profits" (equals all property income) was the percentage (13% to 17%) which pre-1914 profits were supposed to have formed of the pre-war total wage bill, in British coal mines as a group. The proceeds-sharing plan, therefore, made standard "profits" a claim on gross proceeds junior to standard wages and other costs (exclusive of accrued depreciation and depletion, with reference to property of the operators); and, after standard wages and other costs had been paid (including deficiencies in standard "profits" brought forward from previous years), the remaining proceeds were shared according to the ratio of standard wages to standard "profits." British economists have regarded this scheme as a very promising experiment in industrial relations; the parties directly concerned think well enough of it to revise their local versions from time to time; and yet in only a few years since 1921 have there been any net proceeds (above standard wages and standard

"profits") to share. The following comment is that of a dis-
cerning analyst:

It is unfortunate that this first experiment in proceeds sharing
should have been tried in an industry confronted with the necessity of
adapting itself to what is generally admitted to be a permanent shrinkage in demand. The distinction between a minimum wage based on
the lowest standard of living acceptable to the men, and an economic
wage normally fluctuating above the minimum, has been lost from
sight, so that the arrangements for sharing surpluses have, for the most
part, been a dead letter. But there is no reason why such a distinction
should not be maintained if this method of wage adjustment were tried
in an industry liable to the usual short-period fluctuations, but not burdened with a productive capacity which is excessive in relation to any
foreseeable demand.[9]

Some Lessons from British Sliding Scales.—Several criteria may be applied to all wage policies and methods, including: (1) the tendency of each to promote industrial warfare
or peace; (2) effect on volume of employment and aggregate
earnings; and (3) tendency to equalize earnings of the workers
in question with earnings of similar skills and efforts in the
bulk of other industries.[10] When these three standards are
applied to the "automatic" wage variation plans we have been
discussing, some important contradictions are discovered. These
contrasts are attributable, in large part, to differences in economic characteristics of the industries concerned. Outstanding
is the contrast between the successful application of sliding
wage scales in British iron and steel trades, and the much less
satisfactory experience of both selling-price and proceeds-
sharing scales in British coal mining. In the former, labor
warfare has been well below the average of organized industries; wages have been variable with selling prices, but on the
average have been higher than those in other shrinking industries; and although employment in these ferrous trades has
increased less than the average since 1920, the flexibility of

---

[9] Pool, *op. cit.*, p. 217. The minimum wages which have been, in nearly
all years, all the industry could pay, were almost incredibly low, and unemployment was very high in Welsh and other sections.
[10] Cf. Ch. 5, above.

their wages may well have sustained such employment at a higher level than more rigidly fixed wage rates would have permitted. In coal mining, on the other hand, considerable use of selling-price and proceeds-sharing scales has not prevented stoppages, low wages, and low employment.

Clues in Inter-industry Economic Comparisons.—This contrast is attributed by Pool [11] to three technical-economic differences between the two industries: (1) Output per man increased strongly in the iron and steel industry, both before and after 1914-18; whereas the coal raised per man employed in British mines had declined from over 300 tons in 1879-83, to about 260 by 1913. By 1929-33, despite considerable spread of mechanization, the average had recovered from the post-war low of 195 to only 262. (2) In both industries, piece work is prominent; and the readjustment of piece rates is often a rather sluggish process. With increasing output per man, this sluggishness is to the workman's advantage; with decreasing output the contrary. In both cases, the wholesale price of the product tended to decline and thus to set limits on wage-paying capacity; but, by reason of the differing trends in rates of output per man, the downward pressure of price declines upon wages was much greater in coal than in iron and steel. (3) The wage bill is a much higher part of total cost of mining coal than of producing iron and steel products. This circumstance aggravated the downward pressure on coal wages, as compared with iron and steel. The efforts of the miners, therefore, were of necessity concentrated on protecting minimum rates of hourly earnings as best they could; and in most years since 1921, they have secured earnings which were seldom as much as 50% higher than they had in 1913. American coal-mining wage rates have been relatively less depressed, in part because our mines did not have a large export trade to lose, as did the British. In both instances, the rise of competing sources of heat and power in the home market was a leading difficulty.

Both American and British miners have used political tactics

---

[11] *Op. cit.*, p. 174 ff.

to bolster up their employers' wage capacity. These tactics include our NRA, Guffey Act and its successors; also comparable British measures of concerted action in marketing coal and an outright government subsidy to the industry early in the 1920's. Within recent years a rise in coal prices, intended partly to benefit the miners, was voluntarily conceded by most of the larger British consumers. These latter expedients illustrate an important general proposition: organized wage earners are not content to accept employers' wage capacity as it exists at any and every time, but tend to thrust employers into measures for increasing their gross incomes—for instance, by raising the price of the product—or for decreasing non-wage costs.

Sliding Scales Increase Wage Flexibility.—Among numerous other features of these sliding wage plans, briefer notice may be taken here of a few which will serve to introduce our next main section. One aspect of such scales is their simplicity, which in some cases was clearly excessive. A rise in iron and steel prices, for example, which is materially less than the concurrent rise in other costs than labor signifies, not an increase in wage-paying capacity of iron and steel firms, but the reverse. While the "profit-margin" and "proceeds-sharing" plans mitigate this difficulty, it is obvious that none of these schemes attempts to change wages in any very exact accord with changes in the economic condition of either individual firms or the aggregate of all firms in the industry. They are avowedly rough and ready wage indicators. Hence, revisions have been made frequently in the formulae or scales, so that their "automatic" character is easily exaggerated. They define the scope of recurrent collective bargaining; they do not at all dispense with rather frequent wage bargaining.

Especially striking is the record of wage-rate fluctuations accomplished by the sliding scale in British iron and steel trades, since 1918 as well as before. Thus, the average earnings of all such workers were 108s. 5d. (a week) in December 1920; but they declined to 66s. 9d. by December 1921 and to 55s. 9d. by December 1922. Most years since (up to and

including October 1935), they have averaged in the neighborhood of 62s., but the depression carried them down to 55s. by
October 1932.[12] These wage changes, of course, are based on
corresponding fluctuations in the basic iron and steel prices.[13]

Similar schemes in industries characterized by stabler prices
would make for less wage variation; but an industry in which
prices and wages are relatively stable would be less disposed
to consider a sliding wage scale plan at all. The industries,
moreover, whose chief products are sufficiently standard in
quality from year to year so that wages can be pegged to their
prices are perhaps in the minority.

With all such qualifications, it remains a striking fact that
well-organized workers in British iron and steel, through the
1920's and '30's, should stand by their sliding wage scales,
since the latter not infrequently produced smashing wage-rate
reductions. Most other labor organizations, in this period, resisted strongly any sort of wage cuts, and assigned as a leading
reason for such resistance, the difficulty of securing wage
advances when business conditions warrant them. Workmen
long habituated to the iron trade sliding scales, on the other
hand, felt much greater assurance that their wages would be
advanced as soon as the general body of employers could afford
such increases, and they were willing to accept reductions when
product prices indicated that the industry's wage capacity had
declined.

But Who Wants Wage Flexibility?—Such fluctuations in
money-wage rates, however, are not welcome to most people.
In general, wage earners greatly need more stable *incomes*. But
the adherents of these wage plans believe that prompt reduction
in wage *rates* on the signal of weakening prices tends to sustain
employment in larger volume than would inflexible wage rates.
Many other persons, who refuse to accept this argument, like

---

[12] Pool, *op. cit.,* p. 176.

[13] American steel producers, for a number of years, followed the lead
of U. S. Steel Corporation in maintaining inflexible prices on a number of
products—though of course their profits and losses and employment of labor
fluctuated greatly with business cycles. Employers, doubtless, would be
less apt to try to keep their own prices constant if all or most of their
wage rates were pegged to them.

Mr. John L. Lewis, are apt to advocate price stabilization schemes, on the ground that such stabilization is favorable to labor incomes.

It should not be taken as axiomatic or sufficiently demonstrated, to be sure, that the volume of employment (including short time and overtime) in any industry is a simple function of its wage rates, or even of the particular wage as a fraction of some aggregate of wages or prices. As Pool points out (p. 185), it may be plausibly contended that the demand for labor in the making of capital goods (of which staple iron and steel products are leading elements) is unusually inelastic. The optimism and pessimism of booms and depressions seems to override moderate changes in prices of such goods; and wages constitute such a minor fraction of their total costs in many instances that a 10% reduction in wages might lead (say) to only a 2% cut in prices of such products—particularly products like new factory buildings.[14]

This objection is perhaps convincing, if we suppose that only the iron and steel men (for instance) allow their wages to be cut during the slump. If such a cut is but part of a general downward wage (and price) movement, however—that is another and more complex problem; and this consideration shows that the effect of these sliding-scale wage plans on volume of employment depends a great deal on how widespread is their effective scope.

Such wage schemes, too, may be powerless to affect volume of employment, if the prices to which the wages are pegged are controlled by monopolistic means; for the monopolist's volume of output is much less directly affected by his costs than is that of the competitive producer.[15]

---

[14] On behalf of the U. S. Steel Corporation it was urged that, since "the cost of steel is about 10% of the delivered price of a low-priced automobile, a 10% reduction in the price of steel, therefore, would only mean a 1% cut in the price of an automobile . . . hardly enough to increase automobile sales."—*Business Week,* Feb. 3, 1940, p. 15. Observe that this representation runs quite parallel to the very common trade union argument for wage maintenance or advance, whose limitations are shown in Ch. 7, above.

[15] Some further remarks on sliding scales and proceeds sharing appear below, p. 222.

C. Variable Wage Capacity, Within an Industry

The differing financial conditions of the various firms concerned is an outstanding problem in most collective wage determinations. In a few instances, indeed, the problem is simplified because a single employer does not appear to be directly in competition for much of his labor with other nearby employers conducting similar operations. Instances are governmental enterprises and public utilities—at least with reference to occupations peculiar to themselves; also "company towns." Or the firms immediately affected may present very similar financial pictures. Much more commonly, however, the wage structure of the single employer must interlock with those of other employers hiring at least some types of similar labor in the same market. In the present section, therefore, we are shifting emphasis from the average wage capacity of a whole industry, or local section thereof, to the variability of wage capacities of individual enterprises within a group of employers who are directly competing both for labor and for sales. Not infrequently the profitability of the *plant* will be a crucial matter; for a profitable company will be disposed to close down a plant that is making less money, if any; which may be a vital matter to the workers concerned.

Published Profit-Loss Data Transform Wage Negotiations.—Another consideration also distinguishes this section of our chapter from the preceding one: From the former's emphasis on relatively crude statistical indicators of the industry's wage capacity, we now transfer attention to the growing mass of accounting or financial particulars which are cited by representatives of labor, employers, and the public with reference to variations in wage capacity.

One important reason, in fact, why sliding-scale wage plans like those discussed above are not likely to be widely used hereafter is the great transition from relatively small employing units, which could and did keep their current rates of profit and loss secret, to large employing companies whose financial conditions are published quarterly (or even oftener) in a variety of ways. In the heyday of the old sliding scales, organized

labor had to be content with indirect indicators of its employers' current earnings or losses; now, to a much greater extent,
these unions may cite recently published accounting-statistical
data which show explicitly the current financial positions of
particular employers.

In some ways this trend toward greater publicity of entrepreneur finances has aggravated industrial relations problems.
Trade unions tend to demand wage increases when they learn
that profits are increasing, even though such increases of profits
may be from positions of loss or of abnormally low earnings.
Many trade union leaders, however, are quite capable of learn-
ing to interpret financial data in reasonable and far-sighted
ways, though they may be obliged to present these matters in
superficial guise to the rank and file of their constituents.

These topics are to be further discussed in the present section under three principal heads, viz: (1) differing rates of
profits and losses, among firms within an industry; (2) union
policies and practices on relation of wage rates to such variability; and (3) some applications of history and theory of
profit-sharing plans.

Variable Rates of Profits and Losses, Among Firms.—One
type of difference of earnings, which is important in many
ways, relates to time: virtually all concerns have their better
and their worse quarters and years. This problem, already
touched upon in the previous section, will be further developed
in the following paragraphs. But the outstanding difficulty
which we are now facing is that of persisting differences in
profitability of competing companies. Such persistence, of
course, is not sharply defined. To some extent competitor A is
more profitable than B this year, whereas B does better than A
next year; these temporary and short-run variations do not produce serious strains on wage structures. It is much more difficult to deal with competitors X, Y, and Z, who are safely above
the margin of impending bankruptcy only when the whole industry is booming.

An unusually prosperous firm, moreover, is able to put an
extra handicap upon its less profitable competitors by a "gen-

erous" increase of its own wage scales, which forces these rivals to grant similar wage advances. If the prosperous employer is also resisting union organization of his labor (as are, for instance, some of our steel concerns), then he has a double motive for such a "generous" wage boost.

Should Marginal Concerns Be Forced Out?—One approach to this problem of variability of finances within an industry is to assume that increased labor costs will be bearable by the industry as a whole, either through improved management by the marginal and sub-marginal concerns, or by their elimination and the transfer of their operations to the more profitable employers. We have already given some attention to this argument in Chapter 4 above, wherein it was pointed out that increasing labor costs may bring other reactions (such as more use of labor-saving methods and appeals for government aid) rather than, or in addition to, improvement of managerial efficiency. In almost any industry at any time, nevertheless, there are sub-marginal concerns; and, however low wages may sink, there will always be (or come to be) some enterprises in some section of the industry unable to maintain themselves. Thus it is easily possible to exaggerate the significance of unprofitable members of any industry, as to the ability of that industry to bear a given wage structure. As the weaker units are eliminated, to some extent their sales and their employees *are* taken over by competitors who are better able to pay increasing wages and to make profits. The recurring problem is to determine (in shifting circumstances) how far such wage pressure may go, in any group of producers, before reactions such as higher prices of products and unemployment for workers, as well as undesirable political activities of overburdened employers, will outweigh the gains to the receivers of higher wage rates.

Supposing that the highest-cost producers are eliminated by increase in labor cost, various circumstances may prevent the lower-cost producers from expanding operations to a compensating degree, *while still maintaining their lower costs.* This is most obviously the case in an industry of long-run diminishing returns, such as mining; and, recognizing this difficulty, many coal miners have favored public ownership and operation, hoping that profits from the better mines would (in effect) be used by the State to subsidize employment in the marginal and sub-marginal mines. Differences in profitability among railway companies and operations are well known; but railway labor hesitates to favor government ownership, lest unemployment be aggravated by consolidation of operations. And in almost any type of business there are factors tending to increase each firm's marginal costs as its production expands beyond its own optimum point. Unless there is some assurance that new low-cost operators will enter the field to take the place of the high-cost people forced out, progressive increase of unit costs will tend to leave fewer and fewer firms within the field. This result, in some cases, would make for operating economies and lower prices; but (perhaps more commonly) it would increase both the power and the need of these firms to raise the prices of their products.[16]

Statistics of Profit and Loss Variations.—Before proceeding to further consideration of their significance for wage problems, it will be well to sketch the general nature and extent of sources of quantitative information on profit and loss variations among business firms.

For industries whose finances are most closely regulated by governmental authorities, profit and loss data may be published by the regulative bodies—by the Interstate Commerce Commission for the railways, for banks and insurance concerns by state and Federal supervisors, and so on.

For other sorts of business, the most detailed continuous

---

[16] It must be borne in mind, however, that the relations between wage rates, efficiency of management, and prosperity, among firms and regional sections of industries, are very complex. The low-wage payers are not necessarily the most prosperous, nor yet the least efficient. A management which is efficient is sometimes handicapped by an unfavorable financial structure, which in turn is a menace to both its wage capacity and the employment of its workers. As shown elsewhere herein, wage comparisons are often vitiated by lack of standard definitions of occupations and by varying efficiency of labor, equipment, and methods. Hence, firms in which earned rates are low not infrequently pay highly for the labor efficiency which they get.

and up-to-date information of this sort available, of course, pertains to the larger corporations, whose relations with security exchanges and their own investors require recurrent publication of voluminous financial data. These particulars may be studied in various compilations, such as the Moody manuals and Standard Statistics reports; and every daily newspaper contains various current items, which trade union offices and others interested are apt to clip out and file.

One important comparison is between profits (or deficits) and the current net worth of stockholders; this comparison shows profit or loss as per cent of net worth or book value of outstanding stock. Another significant comparison, suggested in Ch. 8 above, is between all current earnings of property (interest and rent, as well as dividends), and total "invested capital," in the more general sense of current value of *all* property utilized in the industry. The returns (especially rents and interest) to *hired* property fluctuate considerably less, from year to year, than does the return on net worth or proprietors'-equity capital; and the latter bears the first impact of losses. Hence, in a moderately good business year like 1922 the rate of return earned by equity capital is higher than that earned by all capital;[17] in depression years the former is lower, or negative. Capital structures change, from time to time, not only as to total investments but as to proportionate relations between debt or loan capital, and the equity or share capital or net worth. If the equity capital is but a small "shoestring" in the total property used by the enterprise, such equity has high "leverage," and its profits and losses fluctuate more wildly (as percentage of net worth) than when the proprietors use largely their own, rather than borrowed or leased, capital.

One other elementary principle of business finance is that *dividends* paid to stockholders during a given period should

---

[17] See Federal Trade Commission, Report on National Wealth and Income, p. 211 ff. [Washington: 69th Cong., 1st Sess., Sen. Doc. 126 (1926).]

The stockholders of a corporation collectively correspond to the proprietor or partners of an unincorporated business unit, in owning the equity or net worth, by which current value of all assets is reckoned to exceed liabilities to creditors. But the net profit of an unincorporated enterprise commonly rewards its proprietor, not only for his invested capital but also for his work.

not be regarded as evidence of the exact amount of profits or earnings of such enterprises during the same period. Corporations not infrequently pay cash dividends in excess of *current* earnings, provided that there is sufficient accumulated earned surplus and that such dividends do not encroach unduly on working capital. As shown in Chapter 8, above, in the worst depression years the aggregates of dividends and other entrepreneurial withdrawals in cash and kind exceeded by several billions of dollars the current earnings of capital during those same years.[18]

Indexes of Profits.—Corporate profit data, classified by industries, are compiled by many organizations; and some of these are widely regarded as indexes of stockholders' earnings. The AFL's *Monthly Survey of Business,* for example, sometimes charts such an index for 120 manufacturing corporations, issued by Standard Statistics, as well as the Federal Reserve industrial production index.[19] A somewhat similar comparison is shown by Chart 5, which exhibits the quarterly index of industrial corporation profits of the National City Bank of New York. This index is based on 200 industrial corporations (not including rails or utilities), and shows (for these 200 companies as a group) quarterly earnings before dividends *in relation to current net worth.*[20] Exhibits merely of successive

---

[18] So-called stock dividends merely hold down or reduce the equity represented by each share of stock—they do not give the recipients cash or affect the total equity of all stockholders.

[19] These two curves were also shown, 1924-39, on the same chart in Cleveland Trust Co.'s *Business Bulletin,* Feb. 15, 1940.

[20] This Bank's April letter (each year) also tabulates combined profits and losses, for the two preceding years, of a much larger sample—in April 1940, for 2,480 concerns, with aggregate net worth of nearly $56 billion. For each of the 66 industrial classifications, net profit or loss is shown as per cent of net worth. Up-to-date samples of corporate gains and losses, however, are almost necessarily drawn from the comparatively small number of large companies which, for various reasons, publish annual (sometimes more frequent) financial statements. If we want fairly complete coverage of corporations, we can have it—as of two to three years ago—in the *Statistics of Income,* published annually by the U. S. income tax division of the Treasury. These consistently show that corporations whose reports are published, hence available more promptly, as a class earn decidedly higher rates of profits on net worth than do the average of *all active* corporations. In 1936, for instance (an unusually prosperous year, by post-1929 standards), the 1,720 manufacturing and trading corporations of the

INDEXES OF BUSINESS ACTIVITY AND PROFITS

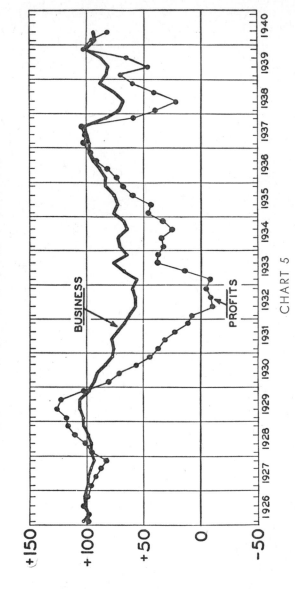

CHART 5

Source: Monthly economic letters of National City Bank of New York—reproduced by courtesy of the Bank. The "Business" curve is The Annalist index; the quarterly "Profits" indexes are prepared by the Bank from reports of 200 leading industrial (mainly manufacturing) corporations.

absolute figures of profits (or losses) are almost meaningless. We must have some appropriate "yardstick" for comparison, one of the most significant of which is *current net worth* or investment of the stockholders—not merely the amount of capital they may have "dedicated" to the business, perhaps years ago, or even their own net worth two or three years ago.

Since the N. C. B. profits index reproduced in Chart 5 takes account of net worth changes, is based on concerns more prosperous than the general run, and is a composite of industries whose feasts and famines are timed somewhat differently—this index's gyrations are less extreme than some others. Nevertheless, it illustrates graphically and quantitatively our commonplace knowledge of fluctuations in earnings of capital, especially of the "venture capital" which on the whole is most satisfactorily measured by net worth.[21]

Statistics of Profit and Loss Variations Within Industries.—Remarkably few comprehensive statistical studies have been published on short- and long-term differences of prosperity among directly competitive concerns. Employers and workers usually know which are the outstandingly profitable and losing members of their trades; but systematic comparative analysis of profit and loss variations among such companies, year by year, is a baffling undertaking. Some of the difficulties were thus stated, in a private letter, by a leading business statistician:

Taking companies which are all engaged in the same industry, the difference in rates of return [on net worth] might be found to reflect merely differences in capitalization ("share" capital vs. borrowed capital); or differences in accounting procedure as to depreciation, de-

National City Bank's list earned a consolidated return on net worth of 10.2%; and the whole 2,280 concerns in the same compilation (including $14 billion worth of 1.2%-earning railroads) earned an average rate of 7.3%. Crum's investigations cited on p. 208, below, indicate that American corporate industry as a whole earned less than 5% on net worth in 1936.

21 One reason why this index has been below its 1926 level since 1929 (except during four quarters) may be the low interest rates which have prevailed. But perhaps these low interest rates are due, more fundamentally, to the low earnings obtainable, on the average, by business ventures. The N. C. Bank uses net worth on Jan. 1 as base for computing percentage return for each year. Others use Dec. 31 or some average between the two.

pletion and other reserves and year-end adjustments; or differences in investment income (interest, dividends, profits and losses); or differences in corporate set-up (branches, or subsidiaries here and abroad); or differences in valuation of plants (excessively high, or ultra-conservatively low)—to enumerate a few of such factors that come readily to mind.

Continuing the discussion, this analyst called attention to intercompany differences, within industries, in treatment of "good will" as an asset; also to varying methods of distributing product (e.g., by sale of tangible product, or of mere lease of same), and to the complications produced by ancillary undertakings, such as refrigerators made by an automobile company.

Trade Union Interpretation of Financial Data.—References to accounting and statistical materials purporting to show the financial position of employers, and the outlook as to profits, are rather commonly employed in wage negotiations and arbitrations. This is one use to which statistical compilations of accounts, kept according to methods standardized by (for instance) a trade association, can be put. Such use has been illustrated by several bargains and arbitrations in the closed shop (Printers' League) branch of New York book and job printing, notably in 1919 and immediately following years. Agreements made by this employers' association with several of the unions in 1919 provided that after one year wages might be readjusted, "such readjustments to be based upon the increased cost of living and the economic condition of the industry at the date of readjustment."[22] In this connection, at least one arbitration (press assistants and feeders) made extensive use of financial data, gathered by accounting surveys under joint union-management arrangements, and compared with Census reports and with a much broader survey in the same trade and city by the printing trade association. These comparisons showed rather material differences in prosperity among firms, the larger (as usual) being in general the more profitable. The

[22] D. R. Craig, *The Economic Condition of the Printing Industry in New York City*, p. 1 (New York: New York Employing Printers' Ass'n, 1925). Cf. George Soule, *Wage Arbitration*, esp. pp. 85-94 (Macmillan, 1928).

slight wage reduction which resulted from this arbitration was based, in part, on the arbitrator's inference as to the financial outlook of the smaller employers.

Government Data on Profits and Losses.—In this field as in others, labor representatives are apt to be suspicious of exhibits prepared by persons who seem to them under the control of the employers. Hence, they tend to discount the showings of published financial statements and of trade association surveys; and to have rather more faith in statements and data emanating from government agencies. We touch here, it would seem, one reason for the wide acceptance of official living-cost indexes in wage adjustments. The statement quoted from Mr. John L. Lewis below in this chapter reflects labor distrust of private financial statements. Apparently, if accounting materials are to be constructively used in reference to collective wage settlements, some extension of joint or impartial machinery for their construction and interpretation is needed. The New York printing case and the sliding wage scale schemes, cited above, are significant in part because they exemplify such collaboration.

A few further comments may be useful here, on the annual statistics of corporate earnings which are byproducts of our national income tax—all corporations, profitable or losing, being required to file annual returns conforming to government accounting standards.

Through all categories of industry runs the great division, each year, therefore, between corporations reporting profit or net income for that year, and the others reporting deficits instead of profits. For the unusually prosperous year of 1937, for example, 192,029 active corporations reported a total of some $9.6 billion of net income (this was before Federal income tax), while the much larger number of 285,810 active and unprofitable corporations in the same year reported an aggregate deficit of $2.3 billion.[23] This mass of losing companies is made up, to a great extent, of relatively small concerns, many of which are but recently organized; some, perhaps, as Mr.

---

[23] *Statistics of Income for 1937, Preliminary Report of Corporation Income* (etc.), pp. 4, 5 (U.S. Treasury, 1939).

Lewis says (see below), were organized for the sole purpose of showing losses.

In the detailed annual official *Statistics of Income,* corporation tax returns are also summarized within industrial groups, according to amounts of assets. Professor W. L. Crum, who has given long and effective study to the matter, finds a very general tendency for the rate of return on stockholders' equity to be higher in the larger than in the smaller corporations— even though this "rate of return" in many cases (especially in such years as 1931-34) is a rate of deficit instead of profit. He argues, too, that this difference is not due in large measure to the better opportunities of the larger concerns for "monopolistic" practices.[24] This is the most extensive evidence available on the nature of variations of rates of profit and loss within industries; and the obvious corollary is that large enterprises tend to have higher wage capacity than their smaller competitors. It should be recalled that wage rates and earnings usually run higher in larger than in smaller concerns,[25] a tendency apparently found in both union and non-union establishments.

Union Wage Policies, in Relation to Profit Trends in the Firm and Industry.—A statement issued by the American Federation of Labor contained the following passage:

Rising production means decreasing unit labor costs, enabling industry to pay higher wages. It is essential that labor receive its full share of the increasing national income if recovery is to be maintained. Wage increases must, however, be based on decreased labor costs per unit of production, for labor wants permanent gains. No general rule can be laid down for the amount of wage increase which will give labor its just share. This must be determined by examining the operating records of each company.[26]

The first proposition in this excerpt gives one among many applications of the idea that each *industry's* wages should be as

---

[24] See his *Corporate Earning Power* (Stanford University, 1929) and later publications, especially his *Corporate Size and Earning Power* (Harvard University, 1939).

[25] See Ch. 3, p. 55, above.

[26] *Monthly Survey of Business,* Sept.-Oct. 1939, p. 4.

high as its own capacity will bear. In many trades, and within limits, increasing the rate of production does tend to reduce the unit cost of production and to react favorably on profits.[27] Permanent gains for labor, however, obviously depend on more sustained upward trends in real-wage capacity than can be established near the beginning of an upturn in sales, operations, and profits. The first upswing from even a minor recession is likely to react favorably on unit costs, since indirect labor and various other expenses are usually not cut as much as the rate of operations, and there is much idle plant to be used. But, since the rate of net profit is abnormally low or negative during very low rates of operation, it is not reasonable to expect an advance in wage rates with any and every advance in profits or profit rates. Sound interpretation of profit advances, as of wage advances, involves the troublesome questions: What, in the circumstances, is a *normal* rate? Are profits (or wages) just climbing up *toward* normal—or above?

The AFL's statement quoted above suggests further that "the amount of wage increase which will give labor its just share" "must be determined by examining the operating records of each company." And in innumerable trade union journals and other communications of labor leaders appear references to the prosperity of individual employers. Do trade unions, then, attempt to "charge what the traffic will bear," in the sense of adjusting each company's wage to its own wage capacity? Or, in less opprobrious terms, do they "temper the wind to the shorn lamb" (that is, allow lower labor costs to the less prosperous concerns)? Such policy would run counter to the statements made and cited in Chapter 14, below, to the effect that trade unions demand "standard wage rates" for each occupation, industry, and section; and also counter to numerous arguments like those cited at the beginning of this chapter, to the effect that the individual employer's current

---

[27] Chart 5, reproduced above in this chapter, reflects the usual association between rates of output and of profit. Among other statistical exhibits, see C. R. Daugherty *et al., Economics of the Iron and Steel Industry,* Vol. I, Chs. 8, 9 (1937). The chart on p. 402 of this latter volume shows the inverse variations of man-hours per ton and rates of blast furnace operations, 1929, 1931, 1933.

ability to pay should not be considered in determining the wage rate. We should discount heavily the claims of inexperienced unions, who do not stop to think how the profit argument may later turn against them; yet we still have here a profound problem.

Some Modifications of Union Standard Wage Policy.— The standard or union wage rate philosophy is no doubt still dominant throughout the trade union world; and it is obvious that differences in wage rates among employers of the same industry and section must be very much smaller (if any) than the differences in the employers' rates of profits. Nevertheless, appreciable differentials of labor earnings, and still more of labor costs, between employers, in accordance with their respective abilities to pay, have existed in various sectors of the trade union world for some generations; and the trend toward greater publicity of finances of individual employers appears to promote increasing differentiations of labor costs.

It is difficult, however, to secure comprehensive and detailed information on these points. The numerous obvious differences in wage rates, earnings, and labor costs may be due to any one or a combination among factors such as were mentioned in Chapter 3, above; and many others may be due merely to inadvertence and ignorance. It appears, though, that labor costs are to some extent adjusted to the employer's prosperity under collective bargaining, by such means as: interregional differences in wage rates; wage differences within a region, partly based on employers' finances; and differences in labor costs which are not indicated by basic wage rates. The motion-picture operators, for instance, have used a wage tariff graduated according to the seating capacity of the theatre, the opportunities to work in the bigger, higher-wage places being allocated largely by seniority. This scheme makes earnings vary more directly in relation to the employer's ability to pay than in relation to the skill and exertion of the worker—though in this case, as in the somewhat analogous train-service custom of allocating "runs" by seniority, the men receiving higher pay tend to bear heavier responsibility.

In Coal Mining and Elsewhere.—Well-established for many years in the American bituminous coal industry has been the "Principle of Competitive Equality," which works out so that the poorer coal fields tend to have lower tonnage wage rates than the better fields. This result is approximately the opposite of what would be expected under conditions of perfect and individualistic competition among workers and employers, even when the somewhat different economic effects of width and depth of seams and of accessibility to markets are allowed for. The purpose of this policy of the miners' union apparently is to enable the poorer mines to continue operating, and thus to afford continued employment for the miners in their own localities. It may also have some tendency to enable the workers in the better mines to secure gains which would otherwise go to profits or royalties or to both.[28]

Other unions, perhaps all at times, have made various concessions to marginal employers, often through practices which concealed the resulting labor costs and net earned rates. In the latter cases, the nominal day or piece rates may be the same for all employers in the area and trade, but those in the greatest financial difficulty get any or several among a variety of aids from the union so that, in effect, they receive more efficient work for their wage dollar than do their more prosperous competitors.[29]

---

[28] Among published accounts of this "Principle of Competitive Equality" are: I. Lubin, *Miners' Wages and the Cost of Coal*, Ch. 4 (1924); International Labor Office, *Wage Determination in the Coal Mine Industry* (1931).

This union, of course, may have neglected some other phases of wage capacity. The "Jacksonville" union scale, providing a minimum of $7.50 a day, was a severe handicap for the organized sections of the industry; and the percentage of coal produced by unionized mines declined rapidly while it prevailed. Partly by political methods, e.g., through the NRA and Wagner and Guffey Acts, the union recovered its position and secured almost complete organization of American coal mining. It is very plausibly argued, however, that its success in maintaining and advancing wage rates has accelerated the trend toward substitution of other sources of heat and power. See Ch. 12, below.

[29] Labor-cost concessions have even been made by a union with the warning to the employer that *he must not pass on the saving to his customers,* but must use it to strengthen his own finances.

Within a local area, a union must usually keep inequalities of wage rates within rather modest bounds. The Hosiery Workers, for example, made headlines by declaring "unfair" a group of members who had taken over a

Wherever separate wage bargains are made, especially at separate times, in the same industry, some differences are apt to appear among wage rates, over and above those to be expected by reason of varying skills and efficiency in the work. Such has been the case in the printing trades, where one association of employers has frequently bargained separately with various printing unions; and also in the automotive industry, in which one union has bargained separately with various employers. Naturally the side which is most nearly unified attempts to use its best previous bargain to secure at least equally favorable treatment from the other parties. Such variations in labor costs, of course, have no necessary relation to differing financial capacity among different enterprises in the same industry.

Nevertheless, some of the differences in wage rates, which may be found by comparing scales for similar work in different firms, may be traced to disposition by the union to secure higher rates from the enterprises which are at the time the most profitable.

Union-Management Cooperation for Improving Wage Capacity.—The modern movement designated by this headline will receive more extended treatment in later chapters (14 and 15). Here we may merely note that one of its sources is the circumstance that, in concerns or plants having unusual difficulty in paying current union wages, both management and workers are most likely to be hospitable to cooperative measures for improving the employer's wage-paying capacity. Here seems to be *one* root of the "B & O Plan"; also of other progressive management-engineering and financial-aid activities

mill to operate as a cooperative shop, and had cut their own wages materially in order to get business. (*The Hosiery Worker*, Mar. 8, 1940.) This action seemed unreasonable, at first blush; yet if employers are to help the union uphold wage rates, the union must assist in maintaining prices of products; moreover, this union's research director held that "because most of the hosiery co-ops are creatures of desperation in which unemployed workers buy stock as a last straw, most of them are at the mercy of the buyers because of insufficient working capital."

Among the coal mining industry's numerous problems, in recent years, has been the tonnage mined and sold by unemployed men out of abandoned or marginal pits.

of such unions as those in the men's clothing, hosiery, and steel industries.[30]

D. Profit Sharing

Labor incomes may also be varied with the prosperity of the particular employer by means of a profit-sharing scheme. Profit sharing has hitherto been used by only a small minority among both employers and wage earners, though practices more or less akin in principle have been widespread. Some of the latter, such as bonuses and private pension plans, are now somewhat menaced by the rapid rise of trade union organization and social legislation. On the other hand, it appears that the principle of profit sharing is favorably regarded by good-sized percentages of all social classes,[31] so that from the standpoint of public relations (if no other), both employers and unions have reason to reconsider their positions with reference to the matter. Many unions, no doubt, would be more favorable to some sort of pooling of the whole "dividend to labor," for the benefit of all their members, than to each firm's sharing its profits with its own employees; but such pooling would be unwelcome to nearly all employers and also to many wage earners; hence, only single-firm profit sharing will be considered here.

Many features of profit sharing are of interest in other connections, such as the affiliations among numerous related practices, their respective influences on industrial disputes and on customer good will, and causes and treatments of business cycles. Particularly important are the comparisons to be made between profit sharing with executives (and other higher-salaried personnel) and with wage earners. In the following paragraphs we shall adopt the wage-earner standpoint, and this largely with reference to the following matters: (1) predetermined percentage methods, in comparison with other means of sharing profits; (2) cash payments, in comparison with applications of profit sharing to employee-income stabilization, with

---

[30] See, e.g., H. J. Ruttenberg, "The Strategy of Industrial Peace," *Harvard Bus. Rev.,* winter 1939; "The Fruits of Industrial Peace," *ibid.,* spring 1940.
[31] See *Fortune* magazine's Survey of Public Opinion, March 1940.

or without management-sharing plans; (3) trade union attitudes; and (4) the general economic significance of profit sharing.

(1) Profit Percentage, Wage Dividend, and Other Profit Sharing.

—The following excerpts from a statement by Senators Vandenberg and Herring gives some of the staple principles, which have been widely recognized during the past century: "Profit sharing with employees is not profit sharing unless a fair and just wage is paid before there is a division of net profit and, technically speaking, the shares should be a percentage or sum fixed in advance. . . . Profit sharing will not succeed if undertaken by the employer as a sudden strategic alternative to unionism or to legitimate collective bargaining as established by law. . . . It must contemplate the full, free disclosure of facts respecting the profit operations of an enterprise."[32] One other characteristic often insisted on as an earmark of "true" profit sharing is that at least a substantial fraction (say, one-third or more) of the employees must be profit sharers.[33] Without splitting hairs we may here focus attention on profit sharing which is actually available to all but temporary and short-service workers—for it is practically necessary

---

[32] *Survey of Experiences in Profit Sharing and Possibilities of Incentive Taxation,* and *Report of Sub-Committee of the Committee on Finance,* U. S. Senate, pursuant to Sen. Res. 215, 76th Congress First Session, Report No. 610, p. 4 (June 1939). The research reported in this document was directed by Mr. D. Despain.

[33] The definition proposed by the International Cooperative Congress in Paris, 1889, specified that not less than 75% of employees must be profit sharers. When Boris Emmet prepared *Bull. 208, Profit Sharing in the United States,* for the U. S. Bureau of Labor Statistics in 1916-17, he confined attention to American plans which provided predetermined profit shares for at least one-third of all employees. Emmet found only 60 such plans in operation, and of the 38 for which he obtained details, 71% employed less than 300 people each.

I have discussed profit and management sharing, with respect to both wage earners and executives, in Chs. 16 and 17 of *Compensating Industrial Effort.* In addition to the references given there should be mentioned various reports issued by the National Industrial Conference Board, including Mr. H. F. Browne's *Profit Sharing* (1935), also C. C. Balderston, *Profit Sharing for Wage Earners* (New York: Industrial Relations Counselors, 1937). The last-named volume gives a relatively recent survey of profit sharing in England as well as in the United States. The British Ministry of Labor has issued reports on profit sharing and copartnership from time to time, e.g., Cmd. 544 (1920).

to require an employee to complete a year or so of service in order to qualify for any real profit-sharing plan.

Another problem of definition of industrial profit sharing is suggested by Senator Vandenberg's remark, "Technically speaking, the shares should be a percentage or sum fixed in advance." Various forms of extra-wage expenditures by employers for benefits to their workers, such as vacations with pay, group insurance, pensions, and bonuses, in various degrees amount to profit sharing in principle, so long as these expenditures are truly voluntary and additional to the wage rates the employers would have to pay if they did not provide these labor benefits. In the same diluted sense, any firm which pays higher wages than are required to attract and maintain its actual labor force is sharing profits. Naturally, it is often difficult or impossible to determine whether such expenditures for labor benefits are in any fundamental sense additional to the current market wage rate, especially when many employers offer the same types of benefits beside wages. At other times, as in the case of the Ford "profit sharing" when initiated in 1914, there is no doubt that the benefits to the employees are added to market rates of wages.[34] The profit-sharing employer, of course, does not intend that the profit share shall be entirely (if at all) additional to market labor earnings *for the labor efficiency he gets from his employees*—since the employer usually expects profit sharing to stimulate his workers to extra zeal. Whether it is likely to, in fact, is often very doubtful.

Likewise, a common personnel practice has been the employer's subsidy added to employees' contributions to some thrift or savings plan, whereby it is expected that in the long run the employee will receive a higher rate of return, and a larger capi-

[34] Mr. Ford's minimum total payment of $5 a day, initiated in 1914, is often referred to by Ford representatives and others, as the company's minimum *wage*. The arrangement is also commonly referred to as profit sharing; but it was not a predetermined-percentage-of-profit plan. For the lowest grade of labor, about half of the $5 total was regarded as wages, the remainder as "profit share," for which the employee had to qualify by conduct satisfactory to the company's Sociological Department. For various higher-rated employees the total payment was also $5 a day, larger fractions being wages and smaller fractions ·being the profit shares.—See S. M. Levin, "The End of Ford Profit Sharing," *Personnel Journal,* Aug. and Oct. 1927.

tal sum available in the future, than his own saving out of his wages alone could produce. When the employer subsidizes purchase of his company's stock by his workers, it becomes a sort of sharing of profits and of management; a plan of this type has had a long and successful experience in the Procter and Gamble Corporation, which plan is also the basis of a guarantee of annual earnings to the profit-sharing employees.

The schemes referred to in the preceding paragraph—aimed at more than ordinary provision to employees of security of income (present and future), participation in profits, and perhaps also in management—provide no predetermined percentage relationship between these non-wage labor benefits, in any one year, and profit or loss of the employing firm in that same year—except so far as the workers have already become stockholders. Other plans, with the same general objectives, are built upon a *contractual obligation* of the profit-sharing firm to make payments, additional to wages, for the direct benefit of the profit-sharing employees, in a specific proportion to either (a) the net profits before dividends, or (b) dividends paid to stockholders—usually on common stock. Schemes of the (a) type may be called profit-percentage sharing; of the (b) type, wage-dividend plans. The former is much the more common, an illustration being the Sears, Roebuck arrangement; the latter is illustrated by Eastman Kodak's practice.[35] Usually profit shares for employees are contingent on some minimum return to capital. The Endicott-Johnson Corporation plan, for example, provides that all employees with two years' service or more shall obtain a 50% share of net profits (if any) above $5 per share on the common stock.

(2) **Cash Payments, or Employee-Income Stabilization?** —Another dimension in which these "industrial partnership" plans have varied greatly is the time and method of paying the additions to wages. At one extreme is the practice of putting the "profit share" into each pay envelope, as was done by Ford for some years, beginning in 1914. Westinghouse Electric &

---

[35] For further particulars, see Despain *et al.*, *Survey of Experiences, etc.* (76th Cong., 1st Sess., Sen. Rep't 610), esp. Ch. 19.

Manufacturing Company established a predetermined profit-and-loss-sharing plan in 1936, which also puts the employees' profit share into their pay envelopes on a quarterly basis—regular wages are (or were) increased by 1% for each $60,000 by which the average monthly earnings of the corporation for the previous three months exceed $600,000; and, contrariwise, wages are reduced toward their own minimum rate, as earnings fall short of the same standard. Annual distribution of cash profit shares is more usual; and a rather high fraction of profit-sharing plans are intended to kill two big birds with one stone—to assist the employee to build up an estate for protection in case of death or in old age, and to develop his interest in the employer's problems—by distributing the profit shares in the form of stock in the employing corporation, which stock is expected to yield cash dividends of either the preferred or the common type.

People interested in profit sharing are often somewhat credulous on the number of birds which can be brought down by a profit-sharing stone—i.e., on the extent to which numerous objectives, such as industrial peace, increased zeal and management sharing by the workers, and savings for old age, can be accomplished at one stroke. Since the disastrous experience of many workers and employers with employee ownership of stock, in 1929 and following years, it has become apparent to all that the very laudable objective of applying profits in the profitable years to building up financial cushions for the employee's premature death or disability, or for his age of retirement, is not as a rule best promoted by assisting him to purchase even preferred stock in the concern for which he works. Such profit shares are best drawn off into some sort of investment trust, whose assets are safeguarded by laws applying to trust funds.[36] Commonly these various forms of profit-assisted thrift plans provide that an employee who quits may take out at least some part of the employer's contribution; and there are good grounds for arguing that he should be allowed to take out

---

[36] The reports resulting from Senator Vandenberg's resolution recommend issuance of special governmental savings certificates to be used for this purpose. See Rep't No. 610 (cited above), Ch. 16.

the whole of such employer contributions and accumulated interest on the same—which contributions will commonly be made only after the first year or so of his employment. These credits are made by the employer each year for value received; moreover, "strings" attached to the employee's mobility and freedom to join a strike are very questionable means of improving industrial relations.

The objective of sharing management with wage earners appears to be achieved as adequately as is usually feasible (especially in large concerns), through trade union or other bona fide employee-representation organization. And the objective of "partnership spirit," for increasing the employee's efficiency, is a rather remote one at best, since so many other factors beside the individual workman's efforts contribute to the firm's net profits and losses.

(3) **Trade Union Attitudes.**—Trade union leaders have generally opposed profit sharing—if not in theory, at least as they considered it to be usually practiced. This hostility is easy to account for in the United States—where enthusiasm for profit sharing has not infrequently been associated with opposition to trade unionism (at least, as the employers considered *the latter* to be usually practiced), and where profit sharing has often been recommended on the basis of its alleged tendency to reduce industrial disputes. It is not so easy to account for a corresponding coolness of organized labor's attitude in Great Britain, where trade unionism has been longer established and where the more militant, not to say savage, forms of employer opposition to unions disappeared long ago. There are some indications, however, that the opposition of trade unions to profit-sharing principles is tending to diminish; at any rate a few of the factors involved merit some attention here.

Does profit sharing tend to promote industrial peace? Does it necessarily tend to impede the growth and operations of trade unions? It is true that a number of the American concerns noted for profit sharing have had little experience with trade union organization; and in some of these cases the profit sharing is part of a larger program and practice of industrial relations which has been—perhaps still is—intended to keep labor contented and to retard or avoid the development of trade union organization. In most of the latter instances, however, unionism has not been handicapped also by espionage and violence on the part of the employers. On the other hand, not a few instances of profit sharing are found in fully organized concerns, such as the big American electrical manufacturers and many or most of the British profit-sharing concerns.

Profit sharing, moreover, is necessarily part of the more ambitious industrial partnership or productive-cooperation plans, such as those of Leclaire (in France) and the Columbia Conserve Company (Indianapolis), in which many or most of the working employees exercise a high degree of ownership, control, and management over the business. Such "self-governing workshops," to be sure, have never become (quantitatively) more than interesting experiments in the industrial world; and the many disappointments in this movement, despite much missionary zeal spent in promoting it over the past century and more, suggest severe limitations of profit sharing in the sense of workmen's acquiring total or majority ownership of the enterprises in which they work. As mentioned above, experiments with subsidy of employees' stock ownership, which superficially look in this same direction, have demonstrated the great danger of putting the workman's two eggs of job and savings in the same basket.[37]

The survey of profit-sharing experiments, made pursuant to Senator Vandenberg's resolution, included a statistical investigation of industrial disputes and other indexes of industrial relations, in establishments with practices in the nature of profit sharing.[38] This study revealed that, among all degrees of "profit sharing," disputes have been distinctly fewer in concerns with profit-percentage and wage-dividend plans, which are the most thoroughgoing among practicable species of profit

[37] See the history of the "Cooperative Plan" of Mitten Management of Philadelphia Rapid Transit Co., 1921 and following years, for illustration of possibilities and dangers of workers' collective ownership of stock, in a large concern. I have given a few particulars in *Compensating Industrial Effort*, p. 360 n.
[38] *Op. cit.*, Ch. 18.

sharing. Companies sharing profits only with executives and higher-salaried employees were found to have their full share of disputes with wage earners, as might reasonably be expected. The number of cases, however, of each type of profit sharing is too small, and the economic conditions in the years, locations, and industries of their trial too variable, to permit convincing statistical demonstration of their respective results. Freedom from industrial disputes, of course, is far from an infallible sign of the best industrial relations; moreover, it would be shallow to argue that unions cannot exist without strikes, hence that trade unionists will oppose profit sharing in proportion to its record in averting such disputes.

Statements of Messrs. Green and Lewis.—In 1938 the presidents of our two national labor organizations gave statements and testimony relative to the Vandenberg resolution, which must be summarized here.[39] William Green, President of the AFL, was favorable to profit sharing, provided that all its details be worked out by collective bargaining and that "all records must be equally available to both sides," including those dealing with "production costs, sales, salaries, and financial policies." Naturally he insisted that "the standard wages of producing workers . . . should be fixed by collective bargaining at the highest level industry could reasonably be expected to pay, and should provide for customary standards of living proportionate to productivity as human labor power is increased by mechanical power and machine tools, and reflecting lower unit-production costs. The standard wage is the cost item which is the first charge on industry and which is necessary to the sustained consuming power upon which all business depends." Less expected were such remarks as:

Profit sharing or a partnership wage is the share which labor would have in the net income of the enterprise. In reality, labor is a partner in production, not from the investment of capital but from the investment of experience and work ability. . . .

Recognition of real partnership and frank acceptance of the privi-

---

[39] 75th Cong., 3rd Sess.: Hearings on S. Res. 215, Nov. 21-Dec. 14, 1938, pp. 104 ff., 189 ff.

leges and rights derived therefrom would be the greatest incentive to
sustained efficiency and work that industry could devise.

Mr. Green further testified that, in his opinion, most profit-
sharing plans of the present and past have been anti-union in
inspiration; and that he did not know of any existing plan
which is adequately based on joint control with organized
workers. If developed in full partnership with trade unionism,
he said, "I am sure it could be made a success." He raised no
question as to how labor attitudes and policies might be affected by higher total annual earnings of workers in profitable
enterprises, as compared with similar workers in unprofitable.

John L. Lewis, President of the CIO, had little or nothing
good to say about profit sharing in practice or in principle;
and a number of his criticisms were shrewd. Naturally he ob-
jected to profit sharing as "insurance" against unionization,
and suspected that the tendency of these plans is to lower wage
rates. In profit sharing, he said, "There is too much of a theory
of the distribution of largesse," of paternalism. He had no
objection to arranging, by collective bargaining, for "an immediate participation of any amount in the profits" of an exceptionally profitable year, but he was inhospitable to any
continuing plan of variable labor income.[40]

The following passages in Mr. Lewis' testimony point to a
leading difficulty of all the systematic variable-labor-income
schemes discussed in the present chapter:

In some ways this profit-distribution proposition is related to the
so-called flexible wage scale, or what we used to call the sliding scale.
The sliding scale in the anthracite-mining industry was introduced as
far back as 1869 or 1870, and the wages of the men were tied to the
price of coal at certain points, and from time to time through the
years the wages would fall or rise, but always the workers had no
power of influencing the factor of change; that power always rested
with the industry, with the operators. If they came to an agreement
that for reasons of their own they would reduce the price of anthracite
at destination point or the basing point 25 or 50 cents a ton, or for any

---

[40] The CIO Automobile Workers union, e.g., has lately demanded "CIO
dividends" from employers currently making large profits.

reason that seemed to them valid, down went the wages. The workers were not consulted; they had nothing to do with it. If they were making good margins of profit and wanted to satisfy a local situation they would raise the price and raise the wages 25 cents a day.

The workers were constantly at the mercy of a few statisticians employed by the operators who computed the tonnage and set down the factors that controlled the wage scale.

That same proposition runs into any kind of a sliding scale, any kind of a flexible wage, any kind of a profit-sharing patronage. . . .

We have thousands and thousands of corporations in this country which are organized as operating concerns and designed to show no profit. In the coal industry, for instance, one of our large industries, we have thousands of corporations that have been organized by the same people who own the land and who own the coal rights, and they function as operating companies, and they are designed always to show either a loss or no profit, while the holding companies levy charges and royalties against the operating company, which eats up its substance as it makes it, so the coal company can always show that it is in a terrible financial condition. . . .

. . . the average individual who works in one of these plants cannot follow the complexities and intricacies of the corporate set-up, the corporate structure, the relationships of holding companies, operating companies, service charges, bonuses and salaried executives, and all these sorts of things. It is a realm he is not permitted to enter. He cannot feel secure about what its executives will do at the next board meeting or what the stockholders will do at the annual meeting, providing some one group gets control of the proxies and are able to dominate the situation. He is merely a pawn.[41]

One difficulty in the proceeds-sharing plans in British coal mining, outlined above, has been the varying financial relations of the coal mining enterprises. The miners' union has often argued that proceeds to be shared should include revenues from selling and coke-producing affiliates (and perhaps others). Even if this position were accepted by the employers, there would be further difficulty in relations between earnings of workers in selling organizations and coke-making enterprises, with and without corporate connections in coal mining. One

---

[41] However accurate may be Mr. Lewis' strictures on anthracite sliding wage scales, most or all the sliding scales cited above in this chapter have been operated by true and full collective bargaining.

inference which may be drawn from all this is that profit
sharing may tend to be most successful in small enterprises,
and in larger ones with comparatively simple financial structures.

(4) General Economic Significance of Profit Sharing.—
Attitudes of labor leaders and others will be influenced by the
gathering and analysis of information on some further points.
One point: Is profit sharing equitable, or in the long run
feasible, since apparently employees are unable, even if willing,
to share losses? Another: Profits and losses vary greatly from
firm to firm; is it reasonable that labor earnings should vary
correspondingly—as profit sharing would require?

We find some evidences that thoroughgoing profit sharing
tends to be associated, to some extent and for the long pull,
with loss sharing. One method of accomplishing this result
is the wage dividend plan, by which profit shares are paid or
allocated to labor, only to the same extent that profits are *paid
out in dividends to stockholders.* The more fluctuating yearly
earnings and losses, therefore, have their first impact on surplus and other undistributed profits.[42] The principal means
of loss sharing, however, is wage reduction when business conditions are adverse. It may be that profit-sharing employees,
like those working under sliding-scale wage schemes, tend to
be more willing to submit to wage reductions than others, who
perhaps have more reason to apprehend that wage cuts will be
terribly difficult to get restored.

Another observation which bears on both queries is that,
whatever the firm's rate of profit would be in the absence of
profit sharing, its profits can be increased (or losses reduced)
by concerted attempts of the profit sharers to increase the efficiency of operation. Some observers have reported a general
tendency for the installation of profit-sharing plans to increase
profits or turn losses into profit. But the more common view
among well-informed students is that, except in small establishments, the profit-sharing workman, like others, will be so much

---

[42] Any political pressure toward more prompt distribution of business
earnings, as by taxation, of course makes this arrangement less feasible.

inclined to "let George do it" that profit sharing (at least in its initial stages) may not be expected sensibly to increase total efficiency of labor. If, with the passage of time, the workman's savings fund grows by accumulation of profit shares, he may develop more of an attitude of proprietorship in the enterprise (and possibly also become less enthusiastic about left-wing "solidarity" with all workers in his industry or "class").

It is difficult or impossible to imagine the whole net effects of profit sharing on rates of wages, total labor incomes, profits to the various types of capital, and prices to consumers, if profit-sharing plans should become general throughout an industry or all industries. If the view is adopted that profit sharing does not materially affect the efficiency of the ordinary wage earner, particularly in the larger (and generally more profitable) establishments, and if we assume that real wage rates may be held as high as they would be without profit sharing, then apparently the only source from which profit shares can be paid to workers are real incomes that otherwise would go to capital, or to consumers (not themselves profit-sharing workers), who would perhaps have to pay higher prices for products of profit-sharing firms.

The objection that labor incomes in each occupation should not vary as greatly as do profits and losses, among establishments within an industry, is not a weighty one *at the inception of profit sharing,* since each plan may set standards based on past performance and offer both workers and capitalists in both high- and low-profit companies little to lose and something to gain. Unless these standards (e.g., as to how much payment to capital, if any, must be made before any profit shares are added to wages) are revised from time to time, however, trends of rising and falling profitability among firms will gradually bring about very considerable differences in labor incomes within occupations, between the more and less prosperous concerns. Such variations, moreover, in incomes of the workers (and perhaps also of owners of capital) will be based considerably on luck rather than on skill and effort.

This result, to be sure, would be only an exaggeration of some of the existing inequalities among labor incomes. As we have seen, labor earnings differ from industry to industry, from plant to plant, and from department to department, due to many other factors besides skill and effort; and to some extent these differences are recognized and tolerated by trade unions. Many such differences are inevitable. The workers in the more prosperous plants are bound to have steadier work and less exposure to complete unemployment, by liquidation of their enterprises, as compared with employees of the less prosperous firms.

Profit sharing's best rôle seems normally to be in the building up, by the profit-sharing firm, of trust funds, during seasons of better business, to supplement governmental social-security provisions against such hazards as disability and unemployment, and for protection of old age. This result is (of course) available only in a small degree to the chronically marginal firms; moreover, it would appear that only within rather narrow limits, if such practices become general, can the more prosperous companies expect profit sharing and other employee-benefit programs to pay for themselves through improved selection, morale, and security of their workers.

Another social aspect of wage determination, related to the individual industry's ability to pay, is the effect of labor costs on prices—and, through prices, on employment in the industry. There is danger that wage arrangements (with or without profit sharing) will be held satisfactory in any industry, merely because industrial disputes, unemployment, and employers' financial difficulties are no worse—if not better—than in industry at large. But it is possible that wages, or prices or profits (or any combination) may be kept unduly high by obstacles to entry of labor and/or capital, especially in the case of a young and progressive industry. This point, already touched upon above, will be most explicitly developed in a later chapter.[43]

Comparisons and Summary

This chapter began with a contrast between the "living-wage" and "wage-capacity" principles. We then surveyed sev-

---

[43] See Ch. 12, below.

eral types of sliding wage scale schemes of the older sorts, which raised and lowered wage rates with reference to those prices of staple products (sometimes qualified by prices of cost goods) which have served as rough indexes of fluctuations of profits and losses within the respective industries.

These crude measures have been largely superseded by increasing publicity of accounting and financial data on profits and losses of individual firms—which movement has been slightly assisted by the slow growth of profit sharing. The profit-sharing principle, like the older selling-price sliding scales, adjusts labor incomes upward and downward with the industry's prosperity; but such adjustment of the individual firm's wages to its own financial position sets up conflicts with the objective favored by trade unions and many others—that equal work should draw equal pay, irrespective of the particular employer's current profit or loss. It appears likely that labor unions will try to hold variations of labor income (especially actual wage scales) within rather narrow limits, in each occupation of each industry and section thereof; also that the most promising field for profit sharing is in providing trust funds for the benefit of the firm's personnel, particularly in unemployment and old age.

With occasional revivals of the schemes noticed above in this chapter, go also some continued experimenting with scales which make labor-money incomes change by reference to cost-of-living indexes. The General Electric Company, for example, maintains both a profit-sharing plan and a cost-of-living sliding wage scale. There is a rough correlation between the movements of the cost of living and of business profits; hence automatic adjustment of wages to cost of living tends in some degree to adjust wages to the industry's wage capacity. Continuance of rather widespread use of short-term cost-of-living scales shows that many workers are willing to accept *some* wage cuts, particularly within a framework of collective bargaining, when they are convinced that they can thus secure protection against *rising* living cost. Thus, such scales stand somewhat in the way of further increasing rigidity of labor costs—particularly rigidity against any sort of downward movement. But in the long run all these principles are now acceptable to labor only so far as they seem to yield each group *a rising trend of real labor incomes.* The latter objective is also generally accepted by management, which of course is often over-cautious—though sometimes reckless—as to how much advance (if any) it can manage *now.* A primer of corporation finance was offered in this chapter, indicating why wage rates do not—probably cannot—fluctuate as far and fast as profit rates; and indicating where we may look for indexes of sustained and real wage-paying capacity.

In Chapter 12, below, it will be shown that the current tendency to gauge wage rates chiefly by reference to the factor of the particular industry's wage-paying capacity may be an important root of the unemployment problem.

CHAPTER 10

COMPARISONS WITH OTHER WAGES;
JOB EVALUATION

The factors investigated in preceding chapters have come in for a good deal of discussion in connection with large-scale wage settlements, especially in recent years; but practical people are always more clearly conscious of the factor to be treated in the present chapter—prevailing or "going" wage rates. This latter criterion is the heart of the "fair wages principle" of British tradition, and one of its applications is indicated by the slogan "equal pay for equal work." Differentials in pay, among different occupations, present problems which must be tackled by reference to the rates prevailing in the market for these occupations—or for related and more common jobs.[1]

It may be plausibly argued, indeed, that all other wage arguments are only window-dressings. Should not (some will say) the prevailing market wage always be paid, and is it not the only basis for wage setting which is business-like and practical? In the course of this chapter we shall review various actual and possible uses of the prevailing-wage criterion, and shall incidentally bring out many of its limitations. Though the idea of the going, or market, wage is simple enough, every one has been puzzled at times by the real or apparent existence of more than one wage rate for the same sort of labor in the same locality at the same time. Which of these contradictory quotations, if any, should be taken as the real prevailing wage? Procedures for collecting and interpreting such quotations will be considered in these pages.

---

[1] In this chapter we are concerned primarily with *business* methods directed toward finding the "prevailing wage." Progress in this sphere will no doubt also be reflected in legal procedures for governmental determinations of "prevailing" or "fair" wage rates, considered in Ch. 19, below.

In this chapter we shall usually be most concerned with the
local labor market or region in which the wage adjustment is
made, for obviously the idea of prevailing wage makes sense
most clearly with reference to such an area. It should never be
forgotten, however, that wages paid in distant markets and in
other industries are of great importance in the long run.
Neither employers nor employees carry out all their threats to
migrate unless their wage conditions are improved; nevertheless, very considerable migrations do take place, in response to
wage differences, provided that such regional and industrial
shifts are not prevented by ignorance or other effective barriers.
The American population is largely composed of immigrants
attracted by higher wages, plus descendants of others; and in
recent decades we have witnessed great migrations within the
nation—notably southern labor moving toward the higher
northern wages, and northern industry "migrating" toward the
lower southern wages.[2]

For simplicity, moreover, we shall usually speak merely of
comparative *money* wages; but it should be remembered that
the latter are subject to various qualifications in the direction of
estimated comparative *real* wages. A high money wage—in a
northern metropolitan city, for example—may represent less
purchasing power than a lower cash wage in a location where
the cost of living is not so high. Jobs may also differ in one
or more of a great many other factors which contribute to the
real wage. Examples are vacation and sick leave privileges,
pension expectations, perquisites in commodities, transportation, etc.; some jobs are relatively blind alleys, while others are
stepping stones to higher things; and above all, some are comparatively permanent sources of income while others are temporary or insecure. This last-mentioned factor—unemployment, in relation to wage policy—will be discussed at some
length later.

The present chapter, which contains a few further comments on real-wage factors of the types just mentioned, is
organized, first, with reference to wage quotations, through two

---

[2] See Ch. 12, below, for discussion of specific instances of larger industrial changes, in relation to comparative earnings of labor.

steps : in section A, some uses of the wage statistics and surveys
hitherto available; and in section B, job analysis and evaluation
methods for improving such quotations. In section C, we then
proceed to consider various applications of such wage quotations and job evaluations, notably with reference to differentials
among skills and occupations, and general increases and decreases of wages, as compared with relative or particular
adjustments. In the latter connection we shall touch upon the
degree of autonomy suitable for local managements and unions
in dealing with wage problems.

A. Interpretation of Wage Statistics and Surveys

In Chapter 3, above, the wage statistics and quotations
hitherto available were discussed at some length, but it will be
useful to summarize here the relevant points. We must fix
firmly in mind the relations among the various wage measures
which are used, for various types of averages and high and low
figures often have to be pieced together because of incomplete
data. A few pages below will also be found a chart of wage
trends in certain industries, over rather long periods.

Workers, Wage Types, and Periods Compared.—Several
obvious steps may be taken toward making significant comparisons between the wages of the people whose pay scales are at
the moment under adjustment, and other wages. First, published wage data are usually classified on the basis of the earner's
sex, and quite commonly are also classified between juniors or
learners and the more mature and experienced people. Equally
obvious are the factors occupation and skill. Over-all averages,
such as are obtained by dividing total payrolls by mere numbers of employees or man-hours worked, are of some significance when the effects on such averages of variable proportions
of sexes, ages, and occupations of workers can be allowed for ;
but actual wage classifications of wages paid in these categories,
and averages for each, are usually much more significant than
over-all average earnings by industries or even by plants. In
addition to *averages* of either of these types, attention should
also be given to minimum rates or earnings—data on which

are rather commonly available for women, for juniors, for the least skilled men, and for various other classes of work and workers.

The wage types referred to in the preceding paragraph are simply the various forms in which wage rates and earnings may be expressed. In "day work," and within the normal hours, the hourly wage rate and the hourly rate of earnings are of course the same; whereas in piece work the wage rate is expressed by the piece, and the hourly rate of earnings (or "earned rate") is computed by dividing hours worked into dollars earned. Quotations of hourly earnings are often affected to an unknown degree by higher rates for overtime, but a good many wage data now are classified so as to give the overtime earnings separately from earnings during normal hours. Normal hours, in turn, sometimes may be classified according to the shift, since the less desirable shifts may be paid premium rates. These hourly rates and earnings, moreover, it is desirable to supplement by information as to the weekly and annual earnings for each class of worker. In some instances, only rough "average weekly earnings" data by industries are available, computed by division of total weekly payrolls of the reporting establishments by the total numbers of names on such payrolls. The more this average can be supplemented by indications as to how it is affected by proportions of men and women, skilled and unskilled workers, and of overtime and short time, perhaps also by relative efficiency of piece or bonus workers, the more clear will be its interpretation.

Areas Compared.—Wage comparisons are made within and among various areas and regions. The basic unit, of course, for collective wage determination is usually the individual plant or establishment: there are also many occasions to compare the various minima and averages among companies or other employers. Trade union bargaining is most directly concerned with wages within its own industry, but no small interest attaches to comparative wage movements among industries. As stated at the beginning of this chapter, comparisons within the locality or region of the workers immediately concerned are usually most relevant, yet not a few wage adjustments have to be made over larger areas—in some cases, involving changes throughout many parts of a country.

Examples of Comparative Wage Trends.—Among the many important questions which wage data of these sorts serve to clarify are these : Is there any base year in which wages were at their normal or proper level, for the industry and occupation(s) in question? To what extent do wages in the principal industries tend to keep step with one another? Do wage quotations in one industry have any significance for problems of wage adjustment in any other industry? These queries may be briefly examined, with reference to the accompanying chart of annual averages of hourly wage rates or earnings in some leading American industrial groups (Chart 6). It will be observed that this is a ratio or semi-logarithmic chart, a great merit of which is that inclined lines which run parallel to one another represent equal *proportional* changes—rises or declines at the same percentage rate.

Most of the series here shown are average hourly earnings (of workers in the industry), expressed in cents. Apart from many other questions of statistical accuracy, however, these series are not entirely comparable, since building wages are here expressed as an index, and others as cents per hour. Too, for the New York Typographical Union and for common labor in road building, the averages are in terms of *minimum* wage rates rather than average earnings per hour actually worked in a whole industry. It is obvious that a number of important occupational and industrial groups are not represented in this chart, which (nevertheless) includes many of the standard series which are available for many years past.[3]

---

[3] The national index of building trade rates was recently prepared by the U. S. Bureau of Labor Statistics, from its collections of trade union scales by cities. This index is supposed to be weighted according to the numbers of workers in the various localities and occupations. These local union scales are not infrequently higher than other quotations for the same trades and localities—the latter statistics (especially those prepared by F. W. Dodge Corp. and published by the Conference Board until 1935) presumably including non-union building labor; moreover, it is generally conceded that building unions on not a few occasions have accepted employ-

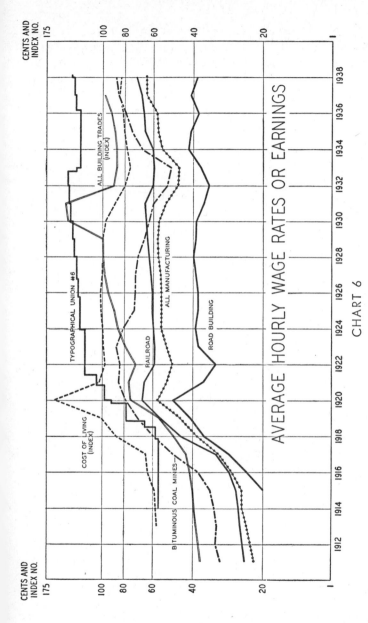

CENTS AND
INDEX NO.

CHART 6

AVERAGE HOURLY WAGE RATES OR EARNINGS

Source: Typographical, N. Y. Employing Printers' Ass'n.; building, USBLS Bull. 657; bituminous mining, Statist. Abstract of U. S.; manufacturing and railroads, S. Bell, Productivity, Wages, and National Income, p. 234, and P. H. Douglas, Real Wages, pp. 108, 167, 168; common labor in road building, Survey of Current Business; cost of living, USBLS (reports issued before 1940 revision). Railroad series is average earnings per hour paid for, of all hourly-paid workers except professional, clerical, and general.

This chart confirms common knowledge that, over periods like 1914-20, 1922-29, 1932-39, wage rates and earnings either move or remain in relatively constant relations throughout all major industrial groups; but it also gives an approximate historical record of several instances of unusual wage trends, e.g., the considerable decline of hourly earned rates of bituminous coal miners from 1922 down to 1933.[4]

This exhibit thus serves to bring out the highly important point that, besides the latest snapshot of prevailing wages which is available for any wage adjustment, should be considered the *trend* of prevailing wages. This trend, moreover, should be taken over not too short a period, if we are to arrive as nearly as is practicable at normal relations among wages. The bituminous coal miners, for example, might reasonably defend the unusually sharp upward trend of their earnings since 1933 by reference to the great deflation which they had taken between 1922 and 1933.

B. Job Analysis and Evaluation

The foregoing comments have taken occupational and industrial titles and the wage data pertaining to them, at their par or face value. Attention was centered on periodic collection of wages paid for the same-named occupations in specified localities or regions, and averages based on such units. We

ment, even on new construction jobs, at less than their current nominal scales. (On steadier work, such as factory maintenance, the earnings of craftsmen, such as electricians and carpenters, have averaged distinctly lower; see Ch. 11 below.) The comprehensive field survey of building trade earnings, made by the USBLS in 1936 (see p. 38, above), gave averages by localities very similar to those of the building trade union scales of that year. The top curve in my chart, for New York Typographical Union No. 6, derived by dividing the weekly wage scale by the corresponding scale of normal hours, of course is only roughly indicative of the trend of *all* printing wages in New York City. A weighted national index of printing wages, 1907-37 (base 1929) runs a course very similar to the index of building wages in my chart. (See USBLS Bull. 655.)

[4] During most of the period 1922-33, the organized sector of bituminous mining was losing ground to the unorganized, in part by reason of the high union scale symbolized by the "Jacksonville Agreement" of 1926, which provided a minimum rate of $7.50 a day. In 1933, assisted by the NRA (and later by the similar "Guffey" Acts), this union began a remarkable drive, by which it secured over 90% organization of the national bituminous industry within a few years.

shift the emphasis now to the limitations and inadequacies of these older types of wage statistics and surveys, and notice some modern efforts to improve the wage-setting processes, in part by improving the job of wage surveying.

Job evaluation is a particular application or type of job analysis (or compilation of "occupational descriptions" or surveys); job evaluation is also otherwise referred to as "wage and salary standardization" (or grading or classification). Other applications of job analysis include development of hiring specifications, such as are now used in public as well as private employment offices, and of training and promotion programs. To some extent job information for more than one of these purposes can be obtained in a single survey. In this chapter, however, we shall refer only to data which are important for improving wage and salary administration, and more particularly to those parts of the philosophy and practice of job evaluation which seem most useful toward improving *collective* wage determinations.[5]

---

[5] More detail on job evaluation processes, however, is given in this chapter than would be needful if the subject were better understood, particularly in trade union and unionized employer circles. This movement appears to have gained headway first in civil service or public personnel administration, notably through the work done by E. O. Griffenhagen from 1909 onward. Principles and methods of salary surveying and classification are expounded ably, and at length, by the Federal Government's Personnel Classification Board; see especially its *Report on Wage and Personnel Survey* (Washington: 70th Cong., 2nd Sess., House Doc. 602, 1929). A great many articles in periodicals and association reports devoted to private and public personnel administration have described the work of various specialists; and brief analyses with reference to the individual management and worker may be found in Ch. 9 of my *Compensating Industrial Effort,* as well as in various textbooks on labor management or personnel administration. Among the more extended and recent treatments may be recommended: J. W. Riegel, *Wage Determination, Salary Determination* (Ann Arbor: Univ. of Mich. Bureau of Industrial Relations, 1937 and 1940); and C. C. Balderston, *Wage Setting Based on Job Analysis and Evaluation* (New York: Industrial Relations Counselors, Inc., 1940).

Among the phases and problems of job evaluation which would be elaborated in a fuller treatment are the personnel, routines, and organization best suited to the task, and relations with other labor policies and techniques. A job evaluation program, for example, needs to be carefully correlated with the local provisions for measuring the individual employee's accomplishment from time to time. In case such measurement is attempted through merit ratings or progress reports by supervisors, a good deal of the job analysis employed for setting normal pay ranges should be used in the procedure for such merit ratings. (See Ch. 15, below.)

Provocations and Objectives.—Two principal phases of occupational surveys are emphasized herein, which might be symbolized respectively by the two names, job analysis and job evaluation. The first refers to the numerous difficulties which flow from misleading job titles or occupational names, i.e., from misconceptions which are fostered by lack of any approach towards standardization of contents of jobs called by the same name. Three girls, for example, may be doing essentially similar work, one being called a typist, another a stenographer, another a secretary. The one who is called typist is apt to get the lowest pay, unless her immediate boss is a good bargainer with his superiors. Such inequities are commonplace within every large organization, and they have constituted the chief provocation to the job evaluation movement. Of scarcely less importance is a related source of irritation: one of our girls hears that another company is paying more for "stenographers," not realizing that these outside workers are subject to more stringent requirements as to speed, accuracy, and versatility. Thus, the first phase of job analysis with reference to the wage structure is overhauling job titles, to see that within the organization each grade of each type of work has the same payroll title; and also to make these titles match as closely as possible with the outside labor market, so that both inside and outside comparisons of wage rates and earnings are made more significant.

The second phase—job evaluation proper, we might call it —concerns job analysis with reference to the qualifications required for the various jobs, and study of these requirements in an attempt further to rationalize the wage and salary structure. Such rationalization applies, not merely to the "common jobs" which are found among various departments and employers, but to all jobs, including those which are peculiar to the department or company.

It is readily perceived that careful job evaluation is especially needed with reference to new occupations, such as are created by new industries and processes. Scarcely less vital, however, is its function in periodically checking the contents of older occupations which often insensibly change in their relative worth. On this basis, probably, may be explained part of the variations, within any large labor market, in wage earnings of "standard" occupations such as toolmaker, millwright, wood pattern maker, and engine lathe operator.[6] Trade unionism has been a conservative influence in maintaining old crafts or occupations, with names pertaining to them; and in general real apprenticeship develops comparatively versatile craftsmen according to the trade's traditions. Nevertheless, in large establishments unionized craftsmen, such as members of the printing unions, have become much more specialized than the old-time craftsman of the small shop.

General Procedures in Job Evaluation.—The important steps which are common to most systems may be outlined as follows:

1. Have a competent staff prepare descriptions or analyses, as indicated herein, with reference to all jobs which *appear* to be distinct;
2. Establish finally revised list of titles for genuinely distinct jobs—considering possibility of sub-classes, such as "Toolmaker A";
3. Record descriptions or analyses of all jobs on this final list, showing dates of surveys and approvals of results—for future reference, especially if controversy arises as to whether and when any job content is changed;
4. Show, by each job description, the minimum "objective" qualifications normally *required* by each job (as distinguished from the "subjective" qualifications—e.g., educational—*possessed* by workers who at the moment are

---

[6] An early research on this point, in which surprising differences in *average plant rates* of the same occupation in the same city were demonstrated, was that of H. L. Frain, *Earnings in Standard Machine-Tool Occupations* (Univ. of Penna. Press, 1929) ; one of his charts is reproduced in my *Compensating Industrial Effort,* p. 226. A recent confidential survey of metal trade wages showed such anomalies as these: automatic screw machine operators were paid (on the average) markedly less (70¢) than "all-around" machinists (95¢) in a large Alabama industrial city, while in an important Connecticut manufacturing center these occupations received the same wage (84¢). Such tabulations, to be sure, most commonly do not distinguish earnings of time and piece workers; the latter, of course, are usually much more variable.

filling such job), and also the *degree* in which each job requires each such compensable factor; and

5. Grade or zone jobs according to ranges of pay found appropriate, in the light of qualifications and duties—disregarding existing wage and salary rates until the preliminary grading is done.[7]

A few comments will clarify the foregoing list, and further indicate its implications. We begin with steps 1 and 2, on *job titles*. Throughout this chapter, as in most of this book, I use the term "job" in the sense of a distinctive occupation, rather than in the other common senses of (a) employment opportunity for one person, or (b) a given piece of output. At best, however, the problems of defining and naming jobs are difficult, and the best solution varies somewhat with the conditions and purposes. Earlier experiences with job analysis and evaluation, as was suggested above, invariably turned up many instances of more than one payroll title for substantially similar work. In the Federal Government survey of 1928, for example, some 54 titles were found in use, to designate what these analysts considered to be essentially a single class of positions (a "position" here meaning an *individual* employment opportunity or single person's job), which class was finally designated "junior stock clerk." This problem becomes less serious as job analyses and evaluations are made recurrently; nevertheless, one objective of every job evaluation should be to make titles or job names keep pace with job contents.

All persons covered by a single payroll title need not necessarily be immediately interchangeable, in the sense of being

---

[7] The actual procedures, and especially the names given to their parts, differ greatly among the various job evaluators. In one very large corporation, for example, with many diversified plants, little or no emphasis is placed on step 2 above (standardization among plants, of job nomenclature); attention is rather focused on standard processes tending to place each job in the proper wage grade, no matter what it is called.

It must be borne in mind, too, that each "common" or key job (which can be priced "outside" the company or group making the evaluation) must be evaluated in part by reference to such outside-survey data; whereas the "uncommon" occupations, more or less peculiar to the one employer or group, must be evaluated by more largely "synthetic" methods, whose principal types are indicated below.

engaged in identical operations, but the work of all such persons should be very similar. Most essential are the following characteristics, emphasized by the governmental analysts just referred to, who defined a "class" in the same sense as "job" is used by most analysts as:

> a group of [single-worker] positions which are sufficiently similar in respect to their duties and responsibilities that—
> (a) The same requirements as to education, experience, knowledge, and ability, are demanded of incumbents.
> (b) The same tests of fitness are used to choose qualified appointees.
> (c) The same schedule of compensation can be made to apply with equity.[8]

Such a class, therefore, was defined with reference to convenience in civil service examination of applicants and in fixing brackets of pay. For many other administrative purposes, however, such as training and distribution of work assignments, separate titles need to be used to identify detailed work elements, for example sub-classes of craftsmen and operators of specific machines. Whatever be the roster of job names or payroll titles in the final outcome, naturally every job must be provided with normal rate or rates of pay, which is the goal of job evaluation. Job evaluation, therefore, begins with existing job titles, and collects such data as are needful for the whole program, with reference to all distinct types of work found under each title. Such analysis is likely to show that some people doing essentially similar work have been designated by two or more titles, and that (on the other hand) two or more types of work, of differing values, have been erroneously designated by the same job title.

A brief explanation will perhaps suffice for point 4 (*job requirements*) in the above outline. Obviously a high-grade person may be working on a job of low value; and so long as he is thus occupied, this person's economic possibilities cannot be realized. Hence, the educational and other qualifications of the workers found in each job are scrutinized carefully, to

---

[8] *Wage and Personnel Survey* (full citation in note 5, above), p. 20.

determine what degree of each qualification is *really necessary* for minimum and maximum efficiency within such job. Generally some individuals will be found, whose long service with the employer or other qualifications have seemed exceptionally valuable and have caused them to become overpaid for the work they are actually doing. It is a separate problem (not an integral part of *job* evaluation) to determine whether and how such people can be helped into work at which they can earn the pay they have been getting, if not more; or whether the employer really wishes temporarily to overpay them for the sake of having them available when their capacities can be fully utilized.

Though employment officials must have considerable latitude in hiring, normal requirements can be determined for each job, with reference to the factors which have most influence on compensation. It is usually necessary to state these job requirements partly in terms of "work" factors (identified by reference to equipment, materials, products, and processes) and partly in terms of "worker" qualification factors (such as age, training, and experience). The problem of choice and definition of these compensable factors will be discussed in our next section.

Finally, point 5 of the above outline must be clarified. It indicates the final aim as "grading or zoning" the various jobs, in the sense of determining normal minimum and maximum rates for each (account being taken of rates suitable for beginners and for others, who have passed the appropriate probationary period). The whole process of job evaluation is therefore often spoken of as wage or salary "classification" or "grading," or "standardization." This objective naturally involves equal payment for (equal efficiency in) work which is found to be identical; also equal payment for all the different jobs which are finally agreed to be of equal value. All such jobs, then, belong in the same grade or zone or level; and actual money prices must be set for each zone, probably also somewhat variable money limits for each single job within each grade or zone. Problems and principles relevant to this matter of normal spread of rates within each job are discussed below; here let us note merely that occupations which are paid by piece rates or other output bases, must be *graded* on a time-earnings basis. If there is to be a guaranteed minimum day rate, that furnishes one point for defining the grade—which, however, should also be set with reference to normal variations in hourly earned rates. Naturally, it should be assumed that the efficiency of piece workers averages distinctly higher, other things equal, than workers paid only day rates in the same occupations.

The last clause of point 5 must also be emphasized. This clause specifies that the process of grading jobs according to appropriate ranges of pay should be carried out, "disregarding existing wage and salary rates until the preliminary grading is done." Of course the data concerning present rates and earnings form an important part of any job analysis or description; but the very purpose of job evaluation is to determine whether these existing rates are correct. In order that opinions and judgments may be pooled as to what ranking of occupations is rationally defensible, it is best to keep the existing rates of pay apart from the descriptions of qualifications and duties until tentative agreement has been arrived at, as to how the various jobs should be ranked or graded. Then the jobs can be plotted according to the two scales of (1) existing pay rates and (2) the ranges of pay suggested for them by analysis of job contents. Further consideration and consultation will show that in some cases it is the rates of pay which need resetting; while in other instances of disagreement, it is the tentative grading of the job which is incorrect.

Security and Perquisites.—Such are the chief phases of job evaluation. What further consideration must we now give to its crucial phase—selection and treatment of the factors or characteristics applying to all jobs which are most suitable for rationalizing rates of pay?

Before dealing with five outstanding factor-groups, with which job evaluators are commonly preoccupied, it will be well to refer briefly to a point stressed frequently in this book—that *real* wage comparisons are most significant when they take account of comparative security of employment, especially in relation to annual earnings and various "perquisites"—attractive or unattractive—such as vacations on pay, health service, insurance, pensions, opportunities for advancement. These important elements of real wages may not need explicit evaluation *in comparisons of jobs within one company*—all such one-company jobs may be similar in security and perquisites; but they should certainly be specifically considered in *intercompany* and *inter-industry* comparisons.[9]

A Job Evaluation Form; Use in Wage Survey.—The accompanying example, supplied by courtesy of the Elgin National Watch Company, will serve to illustrate concretely the sorts of data which are collected and considered in present-day job evaluation, and in the more careful wage surveys.

The significance of such information for a plant or company program of job evaluation will be discussed in a moment, but first let us consider the somewhat simpler application of job analyses in *outside* wage and salary surveys. The Elgin company used the third class toolmaker job description, and a number of others, in the course of a wage survey in other companies as of December 1939. Copies of each such job analysis, referring to "common" occupations, were submitted to employers cooperating in the wage survey. The latter were

---

[9] Numerous aspects of unemployment and overtime and short time, in relation to wages, are discussed elsewhere herein, notably in Chs. 11-13; and here it may be said that the blank forms and other routines of job evaluation ought to provide for estimates of comparative stability of earnings through the year, especially for wage surveys in which quotations of wage rates may be sought from other employers and on the same job in other industries. To a considerable extent, perquisites such as housing, food, clothing, and transportation can be given cash values and added to the cash wages to arrive at approximate annual real earnings; and comparisons with other employers and industries should allow for any variations in important elements like vacations and other time off with pay, pensions, insurance, and savings subsidies provided by the employer. The Federal Government survey of 1928, cited above, in its comparisons between government and private wages and salaries collected data on many of these matters—like working hours, provisions as to overtime pay, and "welfare" contributions of employers; and its tables of earnings of institutional employees (e.g., in hospitals) naturally included estimated values of food, housing, and uniforms. Its non-institutional comparisons of public and private wages and salaries, however, appear to run entirely in annual-basis cash rates. Apparently these surveyors did not devise means of allowing systematically for the values of "perquisites" outside of institutions. It is perhaps symptomatic of the spirit of 1928 that this Federal survey made little if any reference to the great factor of job security, which would now seem obvious to all as a prime point of comparison between public and private wages.

JOB DESCRIPTION

Operation name: Fine Tool Maker—3rd Class

Method of payment: Day Work

Duties: Make simple plug gauges, bushings, pins, cutters, and detail parts for fixtures. Replace pins and bushings in chucks and jigs. Repair fixtures.
Example: Bushing a small jig
   Drive out old bushing, inspect hole in jig to see that it has not been damaged. Cut off piece of drill rod in chuck. Chuck piece in bench lathe, face, spot, drill, and ream hole. Turn down outside if necessary, leaving stock for grinding and lapping. Have hardened. Lap hole to proper diameter, put on arbor and grind outside diameter to proper size. Tap in jig.

Tolerances: ± .0002. Each part inspected 100%.

Machines and equipment used:

Bench lathe	Lapping machine
Engine lathe	Special cutter making machine
Grinder	Machinists tools

Operator sets up own machines and sharpens all tools except drills, counterbores, reamers, and taps, which are sharpened in tool crib.

Training period: 3 years [as apprentice].   Supervision exercised: None

	Mach. & Equipt.	*Materials*
Normal damage that may occur at one occurrence which worker is responsible to avoid..........	Less than $5	$10
Damage not likely to occur. Little attention required.		
Damage easy to avoid. Ordinary attention required........X		X
Damage fairly easy to avoid. Close attention required.		
Damage difficult to avoid. Extreme care required.		

Hazards: Minute metal chips in eyes. Not much hazard of cuts to hands.

Working conditions: Clean   Standing
                    Bench   Sitting
                    Machine   Occasional dust from grinder.
                              (Emery grinders are all exhausted.)

Education and experience required: High school graduate or equivalent.
                                   Must serve 3 years as apprentice.

Physical strain: None.   Eye strain: None.

asked to report how many men they were employing in each such job, and the hourly wage rates—assuming day work and year-round employment. The tabulated reports from nine companies in a certain area included six such rates for third class fine toolmakers, the lowest being 62½ cents, the highest $1.02, and the weighted average 96 cents. In general, of course, the companies whose rates were low for one job tended to pay low rates for other jobs also, and vice versa for those on the high side. A somewhat lesser number of quotations was secured in this survey for first and second class fine toolmakers, the respective weighted averages being $1.04 and $1.01. The spread within each of these classes is rather surprisingly broad, undoubtedly due in part to lack of complete comparability of jobs within classes; but these spreads are naturally less than that between the minimum of 62½ cents for third class toolmakers as compared with the maximum of $1.33 for first class. Similar results were secured and tabulated for three classes of die makers and machine builders; and for various other occupations, not sub-classified. More comprehensive surveys based on the Kress job rating plan (mentioned below) secured similarly overlapping quotations for two or three sub-classes in other common occupations, such as maintenance carpenters and electricians. (Such jobs, for which the most reliable "outside" market quotations can be secured, are referred to herein as "common" or "key" jobs—e.g., adult male common labor, and inter-industrial maintenance and tooling crafts.)

Wage surveys are of rather limited value towards rational wage setting, unless the surveyors are rather intimately familiar with the jobs in question, and collect data by interviews and observation of the work, not merely by questionnaires.[10] Undoubtedly routinized methods of collection, even when based on excellent job analyses and specifications, will not be interpreted in like fashion by all the people who send in data; and here is a serious weakness of most occupational wage surveys. Careful and competent interviewing and inspection is necessary for the most adequate interpretation of wage quotations.

---

[10] First-hand inspections and interviews were an important part of the Elgin Watch Co.'s job evaluation program, for example.

Analyzing Job Factors.—What problems remain, after the wage survey based upon job analysis? A great many difficult decisions must still be made, including interpretation of the spread of quotations for even sharply defined jobs. There remain for evaluation, too, the numerous "uncommon" jobs on which reliable market quotations cannot be secured, because these jobs are new or are otherwise peculiar to the organization or trade in which the job evaluation is being made. Wages in the latter jobs may be checked in relation to the rates of "common" or "key" jobs by comparative evaluations of job contents.

The great variety of vocabularies employed in different job evaluation plans may suggest that a chief requisite for devising and applying such a plan is "the gift of gab." The selection and handling of job factors for such evaluation, however, is not primarily a logical or a verbal problem; it is rather a problem in business economics. The objective is to concentrate attention on those characteristics of jobs which (1) are few enough to be manageable in the innumerable conferences which should be held among the various parties concerned, and (2) are also of outstanding importance in spontaneously determining wage variations and changes in the labor market. In other words, the task of naming and listing the factors to be studied must be carried out simultaneously with the task of deciding approximately the weights, or comparative importance, of all job factors which are examined.

A study of the sample Elgin job analysis form reproduced above, in connection with many examples from other sources, shows a marked concentration of job factors (or factor-groups) which may be designated under the following headings:

1. Working conditions, hazards, and efforts;
2. Errors—probability, character, and seriousness (an important aspect of "responsibility") ;
3. Problems and decisions (of the typical worker in *this* job) —frequency and difficulty;
4. Training and experience required;
5. Supervision received and/or exercised; other personal contacts.

Measuring the Factors.—The widespread agreement that these five characteristics of jobs—however they are named—are of outstanding importance in job evaluation means that, collectively, they are weighted heavily by all or nearly all evaluators. But how heavily is *each one* weighted? And is it possible to determine how much each job possesses of each factor?

Taking up the latter point, we may observe that industrial psychology has supplied the suggestion that such qualities as these should be assessed as nearly *objectively* as possible, in terms of literally measurable quantities; or (when that is impossible) by comparing each job, one factor at a time, with a few standard jobs which represent the principal degrees of the factor in question. Usually no attempt is made at many fine gradations, but from three to half a dozen steps ought to be recognized. In the toolmaker description cited above, completely objective measurements are represented by the tolerance or accuracy required (in this case two ten-thousandths of an inch) and by the statement that each part must be passed by a specialized inspector; and the normal damage on any one performance which is practically within the worker's control is estimated to be less than five dollars in equipment and not more than ten dollars in materials. It is stated also that this third class toolmaker should be a high school graduate or equivalent, and should have served three years as apprentice.

In the many instances in which job factors cannot be objectively measured, a scale can be devised for each factor, using several common occupations to illustrate the principal degrees. Our third class toolmaker job would thus illustrate a low degree of whatever premium may be awarded for adverse working conditions, hazards, and efforts; but it involves a higher degree in the error or responsibility factor (since this job is characterized by much self-direction, and skill is required to avoid spoilage). Our toolmaker also ranks high in the factors problems and decisions, training and experience; and he stands in a middle ground with reference to the supervision factor, since he is not so closely supervised as are routine and "production" workers—yet only heads of tool and die groups are responsible for supervision of other workers.

Assuming that we have determined tentatively some such methods of rating each job within each factor or factor-group, how shall we determine whether a low or middle rating in one factor is more important than a high rating in some other factor? How compare (for instance) the values of unusual bodily strength and unusually good eyesight? This problem of weighting among factors meets us at every turn of the road of job evaluation—as distinct from the easier task of job identification.

It is very generally realized that the great differences in wages and salaries among occupations are due much more to differences in the characters of the problems, decisions, or judgments involved in these jobs than to variations in working conditions and physical or mental efforts. To a large extent the three other factors in my list (errors, training and experience, and supervision) are merely practical subsidiary indicators of the importance of the problems and decisions required of the job holder.[11]

Weighting the Factors.—Job evaluators have long been divided between two schools: (1) those who contrive "point" schemes to represent the various degrees in which jobs are judged to possess the various factors (and thereby definitely and formally to establish weights among these factors), and (2) those who favor the less formal weighting which is implied by conferences which interpret, without such quantitative rules, the results of the various factor comparisons. One member of the former school is A. L. Kress, whose evaluation system's maximum score is 500 points. Of these, 250 may be assigned

---

[11] In some industries and occupations, to be sure, wage rates are quite strongly affected by very unusual hazards to health, life and limb. Work, for example, on the high levels of skyscraper construction, and under air pressure in caissons, tends to be highly paid; as do sailors venturing into war zones. Wages of airplane crews also vary partially in relation to relative danger, e.g., with respect to day and night flying. In railway train service wage proceedings, the hazard factor is argued strongly by the workmen's representatives.

I have not undertaken or seen any comprehensive statistical study of earning rates in relation to hazards, for which workmen's compensation insurance data would supply one set of valuable materials. It would be very difficult, however, to disentangle the effects of this factor from the other wage determinants.

on the basis of his four skill factors (education, experience, initiative, and ingenuity), and 150 on the basis of his four factors relating to effort and job conditions (physical and mental or visual demands, working conditions, and unavoidable hazards). The remaining 100 points are distributed among the four responsibility factors (equipment or process, material or product, safety and work of others).[12]

In the Kimberly-Clark Corporation, on the other hand, where a great deal of intelligent effort and collaboration with employee representatives has been spent on job evaluation (beginning about 1930), the industrial relations staff abandoned point schemes. In place of points or other formal quantitative factor ratings, the Kimberly-Clark analysts conducted long series of conferences with employee representatives on the basis of job descriptions, each somewhat like the toolmaker description given above. They concluded that working conditions, efforts, and even hazards (all lesser problems in such paper mills than in numerous other plants and industries) are practically of so little influence on market wages that they should determine job ranking only when other factors are found approximately equal. Of the six remaining factors (supervision, errors, experience, initiative and resourcefulness, cooperation with associates, and education) emphasized by Kimberly-Clark, moreover, they considered the first three to be the outstanding keys to proper job evaluation.

An important point seldom mentioned in the literature is that the weighting of factors is determined in part by the mere formal listing of them. Thus, if we regard "physical effort" and "visual effort" as separate compensable factors, we are apt to attach more importance to the two taken together than if our analysis called for only one rating on "effort— physical and visual." The attempt to split complex factors into simpler components is most defensible, as was suggested above,

---

[12] Details of Mr. Kress's procedures and results are given by literature of the National Electrical Manufacturers Association and National Metal Trades Association; and brief accounts may be found (for example) in *American Machinist,* Sept. 6, 1939, and in *Factory Management and Maintenance,* Oct. 1939. The Elgin analysis cited above is similar to that of the Kress system.

with reference to strategic complexes (such as "skill," or problems-and-decisions) than for factors, however complex, which have but small effect on the job's value.

Job Ranking vs. Job Grading in Money Terms.—By comparing jobs, each with several others, it is possible to build up a rank order, almost independently of the existing rates of pay. This rank order shows merely in what directions the jobs should be paid relatively to one another—it ranks them from lowest to highest, probably with numerous "ties," or jobs rated as about equal in value. But of course it is necessary to get on to actual job evaluation in dollar terms, i.e., to determine how much each one should be paid.

This problem may be tackled through application or development of a point rating scheme (which gives a rather specious appearance of precision and scientific authority), or by some other method (which is likely to have more of a bargaining flavor). In any case, job evaluation entails a great deal of trial and error, working back and forth between the job descriptions (with particular attention to factors which are believed entitled to most weight) and the "keys" or "bench-marks" in the labor market—i.e., the wage quotations for occupations that are "common" to a sufficient number of employers so that significant "prevailing rates" are available. If the grading into dollar terms is to be finally applied by reference to points of difficulty or importance of jobs, this point system must be wrought out first in trial-and-error fashion so as correctly to evaluate the key jobs—to give them proper ranking and money differentials in relation to the outside market. When a point system finally passes this test, then the weights which it assigns to the various degrees of the various factors are entitled to some confidence with reference to interpolations of wage rates for the non-key jobs, for which outside prevailing rates cannot be had.[13] If point systems are distrusted by the parties

---

[13] I.e., a point system is derived from the money-wage differentials found in the outside market. The weighting of each factor must, indeed, be a matter of pooled judgment; but the points finally assigned to the "common" or "key" jobs available must be proportional to the wage differentials found in the market.

making the evaluation, it is still necessary for them to find by experimenting a procedure which will evaluate satisfactorily the key jobs.[14] In Kimberly-Clark Corporation, as stated above, the outcome was to weight most heavily the factors of supervision, errors, and experience. Thus, where a job was found to differ notably in one or more of these factors from the nearest key job, it was considered deserving of substantially different pay also. Where the decisions were closer, involving resort to the less heavily-weighted factors, whatever wage differences resulted would tend to be small.

Another point of procedure is emphasized by the Kimberly-Clark representatives. They think it expedient to restrict their job-evaluation conferences to pay relations *within* major departments—such as production, inspection, and maintenance. They use this technique for inter-plant comparisons *within* these major departments, but do not attempt by such conferences to make job-factor comparisons *between* departments, even in the same mill. The reason given is that both employee and management conferees should deal with jobs of which they have fairly intimate knowledge. Naturally interdepartmental wage relations have to be surveyed, and some jobs are found in more than one department. On the whole, however, these evaluators rely on outside quotations of the key jobs of each department as primary data for each departmental wage structure.

Grades and Ranges of Occupational Rates.—Whether or not a point system of evaluation is used, the endeavor of any program of systematic job evaluation must be, not to bargain about the rates of individual workers or occupations helter-skelter, or merely to compare two at a time; the work must lead to a classification of all jobs into groups or families and zones, whose relative remuneration can be rationally advocated by comprehensive and recorded information. The trial and error processes might begin by tentatively throwing individual jobs

---

14 In view of the great difficulties, discussed further below, of interpreting prevailing-wage data, we may say that factor analysis tends to influence the selection of quotations to be adopted even for key jobs. But if evaluation of all jobs were undertaken with complete disregard for outside wage structures, neither management nor workers would accept the results.

(Kimberly-Clark recognizes 700 hourly-paid occupations) into a rather small number of main boxes or grades, deferring the problems of exact amounts of wage differentials within and between grades, as well as of final rate relations among individual jobs. Such a beginning would characterize the simplest sort of grading *or* ranking scheme. After a standard evaluation procedure has been developed for a given plant or group, then the data supplied by any one of its individual job descriptions can be immediately interpreted in money-wage terms—i.e., "classified" as to wage or salary bracket.

Throughout these endeavors graphic representation is very commonly used and is helpful to many people, though doubtless not a few are allergic to it. Chart 7, by Balderston, is relevant to a number of the problems and practices with which we are concerned in this section. Based primarily on a survey of 91 Philadalphia metal plants in June 1938, it was prepared to illustrate several propositions. First, the sample occupations named at the bottom of the chart are here graded according to their average relations found (among all plants covered in this research); and the solid heavy diagonal line, labeled "market slope," indicates the average relations of pay among these occupations in the market at large. (Emphasis was placed on the intracompany relationships, each firm's lowest wage— usually paid to janitors and common laborers—being taken as the base. If the reader finds this "code of cents per hour" too baffling, let him substitute, for the Detroit area, about 75 cents for janitor and $1.25 for toolmaker A.) It will be observed that three occupations (toolmaker A, electrician A, and stockkeeper) are considered borderline cases and elsewhere their grades are given as 1 ½, 3 ½, and 7 ½. Balderston used this particular chart mainly to exhibit graphically: (1) by the lower dashed line and the *crosses* showing the occupational averages from which this dashed line is derived, an instance of poor wage relationships within the first firm; and (2) by the top dash-dot line and *circles* showing occupational wage averages from which this line is derived, a "good alignment of rates," in the sense that this second firm's structure is similar to that of its own labor market, with the exception that its rates are

EXAMPLE OF CHART USED TO STUDY
ALIGNMENT OF RATES IN EACH FIRM

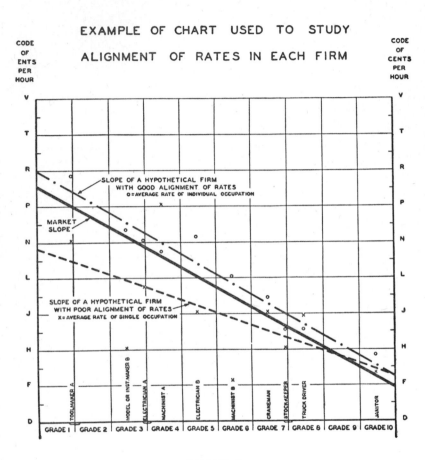

CHART 7

Source: C. Canby Balderston, Wage Differentials, a study of wage rates in Philadelphia metal plants, p. 23 (Industrial Research Dept., Wharton School, Univ. of Penna., Sept. 1939). Reproduced by courtesy of author and publisher.

a little higher than those of the other firms surveyed, in most of these occupations.[15]

In the foregoing paragraphs the discussion of wage rates has run mainly in terms of plant *averages,* by occupations. The further problem must be faced, however, of proper *variations from such averages,* and of overlapping ranges between high and low rates; as well as the important matter of relations between day rates and piece rates or other remuneration on the basis of output. Only some main clues can be indicated here. A chart like one given above is easily adapted to show wage ranges by occupations. One simple device is to draw a vertical line through each circle or cross, the top of the vertical line showing the highest wage paid in this occupation, and the bottom the lowest. Still better is a scheme of dots which will make clearer how many people are being paid which wages. In most organizations and industries it is preferred by all concerned that there should be, not complete uniformity of wage payment for all members of each occupation, but rather differentials in favor of the most competent workers in the job.[16]

A usual result of the early stages of job evaluation in a firm is to reveal unreasonable spreads of earnings—perhaps within occupations, almost certainly within the grades in which occupations are grouped by any proper evaluation. One purpose of job evaluation, therefore, is to establish ranges within occupations and grades (overlapping, probably, between grades) which are rationally defensible, and which will hold in check such forces as carelessness, timidity, and favoritism in wage setting.[17]

The percentage by which the highest earnings among ex-

---

[15] Balderston's monograph from which this chart is taken, contains brief definitions or specifications for each of the 44 service occupations and 92 productive occupations covered by his survey.

[16] A single chart showing all these data for even fifty occupations would, of course, be too complex to be helpful to many people. Separate charts can be made, like the one given above, for departments or other subsidiary groups; and master charts can show relations among all these components.

[17] The percentage by which the highest wage in an occupation or grade exceeds the lowest often becomes greater than is rationally defensible, by excessive premiums or automatic advances for mere length of service. See, e.g., the Thorndike article, cited on p. 265, below.

perienced workers in an occupation may reasonably exceed the lowest, however, depends on opportunities within the plant for one member of the occupation to be worth more than another. In some repetitive productive operations, which may be paced by conveyors or other plant routines, after a very brief breaking-in period the worker of longer service or better aptitude may have little or no opportunity to produce more for the employer than the shorter-service man. The main rational grounds for wage differences among such workers are their adaptability, versatility, and reasonable promise of development into higher skill. At the other extreme are most of the occupations suitable for individual piece work, in which experienced workers of high aptitude and zeal can easily earn twice as much as the least productive group. The final result of job evaluation should take all such matters into account; hence, some occupations may reasonably show very narrow spreads of normal rates, others a comparatively low base or guaranteed hourly rate, with opportunity for high piece or bonus earnings.[18]

Labor Organizations and Job Evaluation.—Such is the broad picture of the aims and accomplishments of industrial relations specialists in the field of job evaluation. It is clear that job analyses or descriptions, together with revisions of job titles based on such studies, tend to make wage quotations and statistics more meaningful and reliable. And, so far as "collective wage determination" includes direct governmental wage

---

[18] Balderston found that the average spread between productive day rates and piece work earnings was, in the lowest grade (No. 10), about 20%; and that this differential, in percentage terms, narrowed steadily to about 12½% in the highest grade of occupations. Very likely this phenomenon is due partly to the widespread tendency to make wage adjustments in terms of cents per hour, with rather little attention to proportions or percentage relations. Balderston quite rightly warned that the best piece and bonus workers in the highest-paid occupations should be able to make more than 12½% more than their day rates. He also observes, with reference to guaranteed base rates for incentive jobs, that usually such guaranteed rates are lower than the hourly day work rate in the corresponding grade of work and market; and he argues reasonably that "when day workers must be taken off incentive because of a delay in production or a change in process or equipment, it is only fair that they be paid rates at least equivalent to the day rates being paid in other occupations requiring a similar amount of skill, experience, responsibility, etc."—(*Wage Setting Based on Job Analysis*, p. 56.)

setting, it is obvious that some part (at least) of the ideas and methods of job evaluation are apropos. Has the job evaluation movement any other significance for collective bargaining? What trends may be discovered here among labor unions and employers who deal with them?

In general, organized labor has had but little contact as yet with the job evaluation movement, for several reasons. Many job evaluations have been confined to salaried work; many have been carried out in plants and industries where collective bargaining was rare or non-existent or fought; and the older mechanical trade unions still see in most branches of personnel administration the horns of the devil of Taylor's scientific management. Even the widespread practice of job evaluation in municipal, Federal, and other governmental services has had very little impact on labor unions, although such wage and salary surveying in government service has not infrequently extended to occupations in which there were and are strong unions.

The labor attitude, moreover, is likely to be different as between craft and industrial unions. A homogeneous, traditional, tightly organized craft like that of the locomotive engineer offers relatively little scope for job evaluation. As craft unions, however, adapt themselves to changing conditions by organizing people who do more than one type or grade of work, and as industrial unions multiply, the case is changed —for these industrial and quasi-industrial unions face difficult problems of internal relations of wages among occupations. These problems cannot always be solved by the simple expedient of general wage advances for every one. Various unions, too, have now obtained full recognition and collective bargaining with employers, such as General Electric Company, in which job analysis and other features of scientific management had previously been domesticated; and this great gain in union status has tended to mellow such unions toward the employment practices to which workers in such plants had become accustomed.

An important avenue by which job analysis and evaluation is brought into the sphere of collective labor dealing is illustrated by the experience of Kimberly-Clark Corporation (paper makers). From the very beginning, this company's persevering work in wage and salary rationalization has been carried on by means of conferences and agreements with employee representatives. In the earlier years such collaboration was with a "company union" whose expenses were borne by the employer, and recently it has been taken up again, principally with an independent, self-supporting union of employees in this concern.[19]

In both AFL and CIO unions, moreover, and apart from the union-management-cooperative practices cited in Chapters 14 and 15, below,[20] several acceptances of job analysis and evaluation procedures may be found. The contract negotiated between the United Automobile Workers (CIO) and General Motors Corporation, during mid-June 1940, contained the following endorsement of the comprehensive job survey which had been initiated by the Corporation some months before:

> . . . a sincere attempt will be made to properly evaluate the jobs in the plant on the basis of work done, skill required, and rates paid in the past and now being paid in the plant. It is recognized that rates may be found to be out of line on the high as well as the low side, as a result of the constantly-changing nature of the products manufactured, the processes and equipment used, and changes made from piece work and group bonus methods of pay to straight hourly rates.

> However, no employee's current rate will be reduced as a result of re-rating as long as he is working on the same job, unless he has been offered another job at the same or higher rate and prefers to

---

[19] The Corporation also recognizes orthodox unions in some occupations and locations, but these have not materially affected the job evaluation program. The wage agreement of Nov. 7, 1936 between management and employee representations of the Homestead Works of the Steel Corporation approved results of the local job evaluation plan. Later the CIO union was recognized by the Steel Corporation as the employees' bargaining agency.

[20] Job analysis for purposes discussed in this chapter overlaps the time-and-motion type of job study needed for setting piece rates and work assignments. All these purposes involve, for instance, researches for constant improvement of equipment, layout, methods, standardization and written specifications of what is regarded (between such overhaulings) as "the one best way" for each job. Job evaluation studies are likely incidentally to reveal where some changes in job contents and articulations are needed; and as such revisions are made, of course wage standards should be made to accord with them.

remain at his present job at the new rate . . . the final result of this program of wage adjustments and the establishment of wage scales in the plants under this agreement will be the equivalent of an average increase of 1½ cents per hour for all of the employees covered by this agreement as of May 1, 1940.

Here seems to be an important milestone on the road toward collective wage dealings based upon more comprehensive and relevant facts.

Some beginnings of job analysis have also appeared in craft unions. As will be noted, the modern tendency to classify skilled occupations into grades (ABC) was anticipated long ago by some craft unions which graded their own members according to degrees of competence.[21] Under older industrial conditions, such grading and job defining could almost be done once for all. And no doubt it is still true that skilled and versatile occupations like that of toolmaker change more slowly as to job contents than do the less skilled "specialties"; hence, analyses of the former, for purposes of improving both wage statistics and wage administration, require less revision from year to year after the grading is once well done. Nevertheless, specialization continues to go forward even within the traditional crafts, and instances may be found of craft union co-operation along lines somewhat similar to those considered in this chapter.[22]

C. General and Relative Wage Adjustments

The principles developed in the preceding sections may now be applied to several problems which are important in collective wage determinations, e.g.: How should differentials between occupations be handled? In case general changes in rates are to be made in all or most occupations, to what extent is it advisable to raise or lower each occupation the same number of cents per hour? What sorts of wage adjustments are appropriate for local officials of managements and unions, as compared with the head regional or national offices? Among the

---

21 See Ch. 15-C-2 below.
22 See, e.g., the account of certain TVA procedures, in Ch. 15-C, below.

numerous rates to be found in the outside market for "key" jobs, which should be taken as key wages in any wage settlement? These questions will be briefly examined.

Occupational Differentials.—Although many careful job evaluators, while making their preliminary grading, almost disregard the existing rates of pay, another large factor in collective wage problems is the strong presumption which exists in most people's minds in favor of wage relationships which have long existed. Higher-paid people are jealous of their prerogatives, and they attempt to maintain the advantages to which they are accustomed.[23] Hence, an employer tends to refuse a wage advance for a single occupation, which otherwise he would be disposed to grant, because he knows that other occupations would immediately begin to agitate for restoration of the previous wage relationships. Contrariwise, if one labor group accepts a wage reduction, it incurs ill will from other groups, who know that such an act may threaten reduction of their wages too—for the employer also is prejudiced in favor of customary occupational wage relations. Employers and skilled workers join in the cry "What incentive is there nowadays for anyone to learn a skilled trade?"—the employer meaning that wages for the less skilled are too high, the skilled men meaning that their own wages are too low.

In the Chicago dispute over wages of closed-shop printing-press feeders in 1921, for example, which occurred after the employers had agreed on a new wage scale with the pressmen, the employers were able to show that, during the preceding eight or ten years, the feeder's wage in percentage terms had crept up very considerably on the pressman's—from some 70% to over 80%. Since the pressman's wage for the next season had already been fixed by mutual agreement, the employers argued that the feeder's wage should be reduced, so that some part of the old relative differential should be restored.[24]

---

23 Whiting Williams has well emphasized the material and social-psychological bases for this attitude. See, e.g., his *Mainsprings of Men* (1925).

24 See F. Meine (ed.), *The Chicago Press-Feeders' Wage-Arbitration Case* (Univ. of Chicago Press, 1922); and abstract of arbitration decision in *Mo. Lab. Rev.*, May 1922, at p. 125.

On the other hand, capable advocates for almost any occupation can argue plausibly along such lines as : the work is more arduous, hazardous, responsible, and skilled than is commonly realized, it has never been adequately paid by comparison with others, and the wages with which it is now being compared are themselves too low. Collective wage controversies quite commonly involve *ex parte* job analyses and evaluations of this sort.

Too little evidence was actually offered on this point; but it is easily conceivable that the job of the Chicago press feeder had become more valuable relative to that of the pressman in the decade in question; a rather expensive and time-consuming job analysis would have been required to supply the most convincing evidence; but, once done, it could be kept up to date with comparatively little difficulty.[25]

What guides in such circumstances may be suggested? An indispensable criterion for the wage rate for each job is an exhibit of prevailing rates paid for this job in other establishments (if any) than those involved in the controversy. If such information is not collected by careful job analysis and other statistical methods, then misleading comparisons of rates, which are really paid for dissimilar services—or for similar work in essentially different market and/or living conditions—are sure to be made. But even this latter process of crude examination of market rates is a useful adjunct to more abstract evaluation—e.g., that which tries to show merely how much more skilled, let us say, the locomotive engineer's job is than the fireman's, and tries to deduce what the relative wage rates in money terms should be. The prevailing-wage criterion, however, is applicable only to "common" or "key" jobs. Some occupations are so specialized, or the wage settlement may be so comprehensive, that outside quotations have little meaning. In the latter cases it is necessary to apply some sort of job evaluation principles. The relative wages which existed before the adjustment was made are bound to be important data for this problem; yet this *status quo* is also sure to contain in-

---

[25] See also Ch. 18-B, below—on world-wide rise of wages of "unskilled" relative to those of skilled workers.

equities, many of which may be eased by suitable wage evaluation procedure.

General Wage Changes, in Cents and Per Cents.—All

collective wage determinations are at once general and relative. As was indicated in the preceding section, even if only one— perhaps sharply defined—craft is at the moment involved, any revision of its pay rates will throw a strain on the remainder of the wage structure. And if the main contention is for a general wage or salary change, perhaps occasioned by a strong movement in prices and profits, the objection is likely to be raised that not all individuals and occupations are equally in need of change. The latter point may be expressed otherwise: a general upward or downward movement of wages or salaries offers opportunities to correct the numerous inequitable situations which are always developing within a wage structure. Whenever a general wage change is planned, a very common method of making the revision is an *absolute* or flat advance or deduction applied simultaneously to all wage rates. In Great Britain, e.g., soon after 1914 began a long series of "cost of living bonuses," of equal amounts for all occupations affected, some of which bonuses still appeared in many wage scales at least as late as 1937. General salary revisions, on the other hand, are much more apt to be made in terms of *percentage* increases or decreases, except that in the depression following 1929, sharper percentage cuts were often made in the higher salary brackets, and in many instances no reductions at all for salaries of perhaps less than fifteen hundred dollars. What are the merits of these approaches to wage and salary changes?

In the first place, the strict application of a uniform *percentage* change will give rise to many awkward odd figures, in terms of cents per hour. Thus, it is most convenient for both managements and workers to adopt wage changes in simpler terms. The simplest is a uniform addition or subtraction of so many cents per hour with reference to every wage. And, although the greater range of salaries makes percentage revisions seem preferable, yet rounding-off of odd figures is soon felt to be necessary when salaries are thus revised.

A glance at such bits of history as these shows that, while each general wage or salary change may be tolerable by itself, succeeding changes in the same direction are not unlikely; and if a series of further flat additions—for example—are made to all wages, we presently arrive at a profound modification of percentage differences. Such modification, in favor of the less skilled, was the cause of much strain in Britain and in most other nations by 1920; and similar distortions were created in the American wage structure by the succession of absolute rises in wages which began in 1933. It is emphasized elsewhere herein that by no means all existing differentials in favor of the more skilled occupations are justified; on the contrary, all differences should be recurrently scrutinized by adequate job evaluation processes. But such careful overhauling or revision of wage differentials is a very different thing from the ill-considered change in the relative advantage of the skilled man which is produced by a series of flat-rate wage advances or decreases. The best solution of the problem appears to lie in taking the trouble to work out a scale of conveniently rounded wage changes for the various occupations concerned, which will make for as little difficulty in computation of the new wage or salary as is compatible with approximately uniform per-centage revisions to the extent which is agreed to be necessary. The individual rates which have worked out of line with others should be taken care of by a continued program of job evalua-tion, rather than by being left until a general wage change.

Responsibilities of Central and Local Officials in Wage Adjustments.—The foregoing discussion of general, as com-pared with relative, wage revisions needs supplementing by con-sideration of another practical problem of collective bargain-ing on wages. This problem is the varying authorities and dis-cretions which are appropriate for managers of local plants of large enterprises, also for the local union officials with whom they have constantly to deal. As one central union official expressed it, "We want to talk with someone who can say yes or no quick"; meaning a chief official of the whole corporation. It is vexatious to a member of either side to be subjected to "run-around" and "buck-passing" in search of some person or group of persons who will not only make a decision but prove capable of carrying it out.

In the past, wage complaints and negotiations have been somewhat embittered by confused thought on the bones of contention which are analyzed in the present volume. Wage earners are always conscious of apparent inequities of pay within their own group, and also of many seeming instances of higher pay for similar work by other employers, perhaps in other localities or industries. To the extent that these wage earners possess strong organization over a wide field, they are likely to attempt a succession of fairly general wage advances, perhaps first achieving advances in one company and then using that advance as a lever in other companies. The top management of the large concern, on the other hand, tends to think of the company's wage problems in terms chiefly of local inequities, which the chief managers may think should be ironed out by the local plant officials and unions. The employer, moreover, realizes better than do many trade unionists that local and regional variations in wage levels are of long standing and are not easily reduced or abolished. The union officials take this talk about local adjustment of wage complaints to be evasion of the real issue, which in their eyes calls for all-around and general wage advances. They know that the local plant managements are usually without power to make any substantial increase in their whole wage bill.

These controversies will become less acute as experience shows which types of wage adjustment problems are really suitable to the responsibilities of the various levels of organization on both sides. It is clear enough that substantial changes in the *average* of wage rates in any one plant cannot be left to the discretion merely of the local people, to say nothing of general changes in rates of *all* plants. Some national unions and some large managements have policies of rather rigid central control of occupational rates in all locations. These central officials usually do and should content themselves with a rather low degree of detailed control of the local wage structure, and leave to local collective bargaining the determination of particular rates and handling of exceptional cases—all within strict limits as to the local minima and averages of wage rates and labor costs. It is disingenuous for top officials of any large concern to say that *all* wage problems can be settled by local agreements.

Which "Prevailing Wage" the Standard?—We have stressed the difficulty of ascertaining *the* prevailing wage for an occupation within a labor market, except where the trade union scale for a well-defined craft is also the rate at which the majority of workers in the occupation are actually employed. In the other common situation, where a number of rates are paid for each occupation, which of these rates should be taken as appropriate for any key job? We have also seen that job analysis is tending to make wage quotations more meaningful, in that the work for which the wage is sought is more carefully specified; and that one means of securing more dependable wage and earned rates is establishment of A B C classifications within occupations. But at best there will often be found a considerable spread among the wage rates and earnings, even within rather sharply defined jobs.

One reason for this situation is that some firms consider it good policy to pay on the high side of the market, at least for some occupations. A certain amount of customer good will may be attributable to a reputation for a liberal wage policy; furthermore, such a policy means an adequate labor supply, from which careful selection may be made, low voluntary turnover, and relatively high efficiency—provided that the concern recognizes and insists upon such efficiency. At the other extreme, some concerns maintain themselves on the lower side of many or most wages, perhaps by unduly optimistic representations as to the prospects for advancement, and in any case putting up with a relatively high labor turnover. Still another factor is that of the prosperity or wage-paying capacity of the firm. When this is low, even if the workers are strongly organized, they may be obliged to accept somewhat lower wages than their fellows in more prosperous concerns, or to give higher efficiency for standard wages.

Still another angle is internal wage relations within the various firms surveyed. As Balderston has shown, when a study is made of occupational rates, taking each firm's common-labor rate as a base and concentrating attention on the differentials between this and other occupations, some of the more skilled occupations show consistency of ranking and differentials above payments for least skill, throughout the market. This basis of comparison, however, is rather too complex and sophisticated to impress wage earners' representatives, who are much more impressed by absolute rates paid by competitors. Hence, emphasis must be placed, in collective bargaining, on information as to how many workers, doing specified work, at what probable degree of efficiency, are receiving specified wage rates in this market. The union which includes members of more than one occupation is practically obliged to aim for a good showing to its present and prospective members, particularly in terms of its minimum and average wage rates and earnings. And, if it is an industrial type of organization, a rather high fraction of its members are of low skill and thus are concerned with rates not much above the minimum. Employers must make special efforts to collect and study wage data for common labor and other occupations of low skill. Their importance is due not only to the considerable number of workers affected, but to the maladjustments to be expected if the rates for low skill are pushed up too high relatively to occupations of higher skill.

Although most people's ideas as to what constitute "fair wages" are dominated by the two factors, (1) wages paid by other employers and (2) customary relationships within the local wage structure, there is no doubt that wage structures nearly always need much improvement. One reason is because supplies and demands often change at different rates among occupations; for instance, the sharp restriction of immigration after 1914 markedly affected the common-labor supply in many of our industries and locations. Another reason is that wage relationships are greatly influenced by forces other than business-like competition—such as custom and habit, ignorance and poor management, differing opportunities for monopolistic action on both the supply and demand sides, and variations in intelligence and aggressiveness of leadership.[26] If men of substantial skill earn less than 50% more than men of low skill, other things being similar, there is a presumption that the supply of such skill is not likely to be kept up; and of course if the particular skill is becoming obsolete, this result is socially desirable. On the other hand, if the skilled trades make over twice as much as the least skilled, there is a presumption that public and philanthropic effort should be directed toward the "bottle-necks," such as restrictive practices of employer and employee associations concerned, and too-expensive or time-consuming vocational training for young people. Naturally, individuals and small groups among wage bargainers and administrators have but small power toward rationalizing or reforming the whole wage system; but everyone can exercise some influence in the directions indicated in this paragraph.

Summary

In this chapter we have resumed the story of prevailing wages, which is discussed from economic and statistical angles in preceding chapters, and in its political setting in Chapter 19, below. The older types of wage data were further examined, and it was shown that long-term trends should be studied, as well as inter-trade and inter-industrial wage comparisons for the latest months available. We have dwelt at more length

---

[26] See, for instance, E. L. Thorndike, "The Variation of Wage Ratios," in *Quar. Jour. of Econ.*, May 1940, pp. 369-383. This distinguished psychologist reports a study of ratios of occupational wages, within and among firms and nations, for each of numerous years. A recent survey of union building trade scales, for instance, shows the painter's wage to be 55% of the plumber's in one city, and at the other extreme 100%. Such variations are no doubt in part rational, due to such factors as loose definitions of occupations, varying efficiency of workers within them, varying costs of living, fluctuations in local and regional occupational supply and demand, and the like. But we may agree with Thorndike that the differences seem greater than can be thus accounted for, and that there is good reason to believe that "irrational" factors also play important parts. Both private and political actions, for example, often lead to undue advances of payment with increasing length of service; moreover, as Thorndike remarks, "the psychological law of gravitation of a person's thoughts and acts toward what makes him comfortable has many economic consequences. One is that any solution of a corporation's wage problems which is easy for the management to operate will seem to those who operate it more reasonable than it really is."

upon modern practices of job analysis and evaluation. These
are of great significance for improved collection and interpretation of wage quotations and statistics, particularly in view of
the increasingly rapid evolution of job contents. Such job
analyses have to be revised frequently; and surveys of prevailing wages by occupations become more meaningful when
anchored to competent job analyses. We have also seen how
job evaluation overhauls wage rates, not only for the "key"
jobs on which significant prevailing rates can be secured, but on
newer and more specialized occupations for which no guides
of outside prevailing rates are available. For the latter purpose,
attention is concentrated on certain job factors, degrees of
which may be estimated to check the adequacy of remuneration. "Point systems" are commonly used, but there are also
strong arguments in favor of somewhat looser methods of
job grading.

Job evaluation of the better sort has had but little application as yet in trade union collective bargaining. It is repug-
nant to several craft union traditions, but even these unions
must face the increasing rate of change of their skills and the
need of recurrent analyses of significant job factors as a check
on other guides in wage adjustments.

None of these methods of research, however much it may
utilize specialized skills and scientific foundations, can alone
eliminate strikes and lockouts over wages. Trade unions, however, are finding it needful to develop further understanding
and use of such methods, if only for the sake of putting their
case in as favorable a light as possible before the public. The
fundamental objective of labor and of management in general,
of course, is the same as that of the general public—establishing more reasonable relations among the pay rates of the various classes of workers and among all industries and occupations.

PART III

WAGES AND INDUSTRIAL FLUCTUATIONS

CHAPTER 11

SEASONAL AND CASUAL UNEMPLOYMENT AS WAGE FACTORS

In the foregoing chapters we have analyzed most of the major factors which have influenced collective wage bargaining. There remains for our consideration the great factor unemployment.

In the older days of collective bargaining the per cent of trade union members unemployed was accepted by most practical people as a principal barometer of bargaining strength. As this per cent rose, non-seasonally, the chance of obtaining an advance of wage rates declined—and even passed into a rising chance that wage cuts would have to be taken. It is generally recognized also that seasonal unemployment tends to have an opposite effect on wage rates—the longer the spell of seasonal unemployment on which the worker has to count, the higher should be his rate of earnings during the busy season.[1]

From time to time over several generations, however, the economic heresy has gained great influence in labor circles, that any sort of unemployment should be combated by shortening the work day and simultaneously raising hourly wages so that weekly earnings should not be impaired. The high hourly rates in the building trade scales are in some measure convincingly defended, by reference to *seasonal* unemployment; though in this case, too, conservative to reactionary opinion holds that building trade unemployment to a great extent is *caused* by too-high wage rates. These issues are so vital in wage policy that I am devoting to them three chapters, which will show that both wage raising and wage lowering are comparatively

---

[1] In Chs. 11-13 "wage rates" will frequently be used in the comprehensive sense of "hourly earned rates," i.e., average hourly earnings, whatever the method of payment.

ineffective measures for reducing total unemployment—but that
each is useful for that purpose under appropriate circumstances.

In the present chapter, after section A, some further discussion of the chief types of employment fluctuations, we proceed to consider, in section B, casual and decasualized labor,
in section C, wages in seasonal employments, and in section
D, interactions of work- and income-stabilization plans with
hourly-earned wage rates.

A. Types of Employment Fluctuations

Man-Hours a Superior Measurement.—As every wage
earner knows, the flow of his income is affected not merely by
outright *un*employment, but also by *under*employment (i.e.,
part-time work or "short time"). There are, in fact, several
administrative stages of lowering employment in the sense of
total man-hours worked, notably: (1) "spreading the work,"
by working the plant less than the normal number of shifts per
week; (2) short layoffs (the worker's name is retained on
the payroll, as he is expected to be recalled when volume of
work increases); and (3) unemployment in the full sense
(when the able and willing worker is not on any payroll).
All these stages, of course, must be distinguished in principle
from loss of work due to the initiative of the employee—e.g.,
by reason of illness or voluntary layoff; and of course vast
numbers of people are "employable" only when labor is exceptionally scarce. Reference to "unemployment" without qualification in these chapters should be understood to include all
the above three stages of involuntary lack of working opportunity, below the normal weekly hours.

Fluctuations in employment, for purposes of our discussion,
are best measured by changes in total man-hours worked per
week—allowing for normal growth of the population and industry concerned. Statistical indexes of total man-hours worked
by industries are becoming increasingly available, sometimes
sub-classified into man-hours for which "straight-time" or
normal wage rates are paid, and hours of overtime, now usually

paid for at penalty rates. Indexes of "employment" usually refer simply to the number of names on the weekly or other payrolls in question. But some of these payroll names belong to people who worked less than the full week, for lack of work in the plant, or for other reasons—such as being hired or quitting or absent sometime during the week. The U. S. Bureau of Labor Statistics also publishes monthly, as we have seen, data on "average hours worked per week" and "average hourly earnings."[2] These latter two indexes are based in part upon reports of total man-hours actually worked; for instance, "average hours worked per week" is the quotient derived by dividing the total man-hours worked, in establishments reporting such data, by the total names on the sample weekly payrolls of these same plants. Hence, it is possible, for any month and industry and place for which we have indexes of "employment" and also of average hours worked per week, to derive an approximately comparable index for total man-hours worked, simply by multiplying these two indexes (and dividing by 100).

This computation was made, for instance, by Witt Bowden for each of a number of industries and groups, January 1933 to January 1935, inclusive.[3] A few monthly comparisons within that period for automobile manufacturing will illustrate how far the index of "employment" is likely to understate the degree of fluctuation of total man-hours worked, in a seasonal industry recovering from severe depression: Taking the average of the year 1932 as 100 for both series, Bowden's index of *number of employees* in automobile manufacturing showed a low point of 81.4 in March 1933, for which month his index of *total man-hours worked* was still lower—76.4. At the other extreme during this (NRA) period is the month of April 1935, for which Bowden's index of number of employees (1932 = 100) was 189.0, and his index of total man-hours worked the much higher figure of 233.6.

---

[2] See charts on pp. 44 and 46, above, for samples of these averages for several large groups of industries; and p. 39 for a sample contrast between all-names-on-payrolls and number working on one day.

[3] *Mo. Lab. Rev.*, March 1935. Other historical indexes of man-hours worked, such as those referred to in Ch. 8, above, are usually derived in this fashion.

Estimates of Unemployment Are Improving.—Statistical data of the sort discussed above now give fairly adequate and up-to-date reports of fluctuations in *employment* and *"underemployment,"* by means of these counts of names on payrolls and of total man-hours worked—especially in the older and better-defined industries. Our statistical information on *unemployment*, on the other hand, is still much less accurate, especially in the United States; because only rather fragmentary data are available on the number of *employable* people seeking work in the respective industries, locations, and occupations. Now that we have comprehensive systems of unemployment compensation in all states, with the Federal Security Administration at Washington correlating their activities (including the public employment offices), we shall rapidly develop comparatively exact, continuous, and recent measures of unemployment. These reports will include not only numbers of job seekers registered in the employment offices, but also counts of the people (by industries and locations) who are currently receiving or qualifying for unemployment compensation, and who are thus shown to have been employable only a few months earlier.[4]

At best it is scarcely possible to classify the actually unemployed people neatly into theoretical categories, such as casual, seasonal, technological, and cyclical. Statistical approximations of these types, however, can be made. Determination of normal seasonal fluctuations in employment, by industry and location, is a rather commonplace statistical accomplishment; such analysis must be made in order to adjust any series (such as the Federal Reserve index of production) for normal seasonal variation.[5] The measurement of long-term trends is also a staple statistical procedure. A long or secular rising trend of per cent unemployed suggests growing technical and/or special market maladjustments; the seasonal factor may be separately allowed for; and most of the remainder of the actual unemploy-

---

[4] A few estimates of recent American unemployment data are analyzed in Ch. 21, below.

[5] For an example of calculation of normal seasonal variation of employment in a particular industry, see W. Bowden, "Farm Employment, 1909-38," *Mo. Lab. Rev.*, June 1939.

ment at any time may be taken as cyclical—moreover, the cyclical factor may be checked by other indexes of waves of general prosperity and depression.

This elementary statistical discussion may seem to take us afield from collective wage determination, but a moment's reflection will show that the current state of unemployment is meaningful, with reference to current wage problems, only by reference to some sort of standard or "yardstick," as to how much unemployment is normal for the current period. If no records are available, extending some years into the past, then the most accurate survey of unemployment in the industry just before the wage determination would be inconclusive, for no one would know whether the percentage of employables found unemployed was unduly high for that industry, area, and season. Furthermore, the *trend* of employment up to the most recent survey is a valuable indication whether more or less employment may be expected in the near future; and prospective, as well as actual, unemployment should be considered in large-scale wage adjustments.[6]

B. Decasualizing Employment

Let us proceed to a brief examination of implications for wages of some of the more promising schemes for giving greater income security to casual labor. This term "casual" commonly refers to irregularly available jobs, many of which last only a few days or a few hours, and it points especially to hiring which is done on the spot from whatever applicants present themselves. Casual work is thus characterized, not only by the short period for which the individual employer usually hires the employee, but also and especially by contrast with jobs in which the worker maintains a place for months or

---

[6] As we proceed to the discussion of variations or fluctuations and stabilization of wage earners' incomes, it should be borne in mind too that the worker is generally more benefited by an income which is steady, from week to week, than by a somewhat higher average of annual earnings which comes in "feast and famine" spurts. Even if these two annual averages are equally secure or assured, most wage-earning families are ill able to husband the receipts in peak weeks and make reasonable provision for weeks when income will be low or lacking.

years on the employer's payroll, even though he may be laid off frequently for lack of work. Casual work is found in many locations and industries; for example, innumerable agricultural crops are cared for, harvested, and processed to a considerable extent by migrant labor casually hired—such work is obviously seasonal also. Not many years ago it was rather common for American factories to hire the commoner types of labor in casual fashion, i.e., from the crowd at the gate, depending on the number of men wanted at the moment. The following remarks will be based, however, on the outstanding example of casual labor and associated decasualization schemes—the labor of longshoremen and other occupations on the waterfront, mostly engaged in the work of loading and discharging cargoes of ships.

Decasualizing Waterfront Work.—It is readily apparent why this work should be a leading example of casual labor. Vessels arrive and leave, require loading and unloading, in very irregular fashion, during all hours of the days and nights of the week;[7] use of the dock and other shipping plant and facilities is so expensive that there is great economic pressure for moving the cargoes within the fewest possible hours; this means strenuous work for many men during these hours, even at highly mechanized docks; and the ports are usually cosmopolitan centers of population in which are congregated many men who may be expected to join the crowds at the gates seeking work whenever a ship is at the dock. Worse, much longshore labor is comparatively unskilled.

Waterfront wages have long been regarded as dismally low, but not usually in terms of hourly rates of pay—on the contrary, hourly rates are apt to be high. Casual methods of hiring such labor, however, make for vast inequality of weekly and annual earnings, depending on the individual's luck or cunning in being chosen from the queue or "shape." (The men making highest annual earnings, to be sure, owe their relative success in some degree to their steadiness in presenting themselves

---

[7] There are seasonal variations in each port's traffic, but the fluctuations in man-hours demanded is non-rhythmic within any week.

whenever there is likely to be work, and to their being preferred by employers who have learned that they are unusually satisfactory men.) The problem of annual earnings, too, is not merely one of faulty distribution among all the waterfront workers. There are apt to be too many men attempting to secure such work (in part because the hourly earnings look attractive) to permit of a satisfactory average of annual earnings throughout the whole group.

The essentials of improvements hitherto devised for these conditions have been thus summarized:

The practical application of a scheme of decasualization, methods of organization, composition of central agencies, systems of distributing and dispatching the workers to the various piers, etc., may vary in accordance with the conditions and the needs of the individual ports. London has one scheme; Liverpool another; and Hamburg still another. In this country the system used in Seattle is different from that used in Portland, which in turn is different from the one used in Los Angeles.

In all cases, however, decasualization does or should accomplish the following:

(1) It guarantees to all the employers an equal chance to obtain workers as needed.

(2) It guarantees to all the longshoremen an equal chance of getting a job when work is available.

(3) It tends to eliminate the power of the hiring foreman and the abuses and favoritism that go with it.

(4) It gradually reduces the total number of longshoremen in port to that approximating the actual needs of the port and thus raises the average earnings of the men left on the register.[8]

In a port not fully decasualized, a trade union organization may have sufficient control of eligibility to employment so that

---

[8] B. Stern, *Cargo Handling and Longshore Labor Conditions, 1932,* p. 74 (Washington: USBLS Bull. 550, 1932). See also Marvel Keller, *Decasualization of Longshore Work in San Francisco* (Philadelphia: WPA National Research Project, 1939).

Cf. J. Hilton *et al., Are Trade Unions Obstructive?* (London: Gollancz, 1935), pp. 87-128, for a sketch of labor relations in the British "dock industry" in the early 1930's.

it can hold up the hourly wage rate, and probably also distribute the available work more or less equitably among its members. Other outstanding steps in decasualization have come from employers' organizations, which have established centralized employing and dispatching of labor from association offices in place of the traditional hiring of labor at each vessel from the "shape" or crowd of men seeking work there. A conspicuous example of such decasualization from the employers' side was provided by the port of Seattle, beginning in 1921. Nearly all longshore labor was hired through this association, which restricted all work except peak overflows to men on their eligibility list, among whom the work was alternated with a view to equitable distribution of earnings. These two policies—restricting employment, normally, to men on an eligible list, and rationing it within such list—thus serve both to increase average annual earnings of the regular workers and to make them approach equality among these men.[9]

In more recent years, considerable strife has marked the further rise of labor organizations in American ports, part of this strife being due to rivalry between the AFL and CIO unions of longshoremen and other occupations (such as teamsters) concerned in moving cargoes within and between vessels and warehouses. These unions tend to demand, and in some degree to obtain, powers like these: restriction of eligibility to employment to their members in good standing; control by the union of the hiring or dispatching halls—i.e., the union officials assign individual workers to each shift of work; and similar control over assignment of waterfront clerks and other auxiliary workers. Particulars of the labor warfare sometimes involved are not essential to our present purposes, nor greatly different in principle from labor struggles in other industries.[10]

---

[9] The larger employers, however, can generally rely on being supplied with services of the same men for all their work, these men being known to the supervisors and accustomed to work with the employer's particular ships and facilities.

[10] Clashes between labor unions, usually over jurisdiction or demarcation as to work, are especially prominent in American trade union history; and dispatching of individual workers by the union to individual employers, recalling them and substituting other union men on short notice, is a method tried by some unions (see section C below). This procedure, if the union

Decasualization Tends to Stabilize Wages, Perhaps Too High.—Although such work as that of longshoremen may not be thoroughly regularized, by reason of wind, tide, weather, seasons, and business trends, organizations of employers and employees have made great strides in decasualization by application of modern features of personnel and trade union administration, such as more adequate notification of each worker where and when there will be how much work for him. The result of decasualization which is most important for our present purpose is the raising and comparative equalization of weekly and annual earnings, accomplished by rational distribution of opportunities to work.

This improvement of average amount and steadiness of earnings, however, is by no means a sufficient justification, from the social standpoint, for any particular decasualizing scheme. Ideally, the stabilization should be brought about at the point where average hourly, as well as weekly and annual earnings, are just high enough (over several-year periods) to attract a sufficient qualified labor supply under conditions of really free competition. This result, of course, is not likely to be realized if there are arbitrary barriers shutting out able men who would like to enter the occupation. If there are such barriers (e.g., unduly high union fees and dues, or an anti-union restrictive policy of employers), and if the elasticity of demand for the casual labor in question is very low (little less of it demanded at a higher than at a lower wage rate), then stabilization may be reached on a basis of none-too-high average annual income, but an abnormally short average work week (even when adjust-

---

can enforce it, does tend (honestly administered) to equalize (among members) hours worked over the year; and it is also a potent instrument of power in the hands of the union officials. Probably it usually tends to make labor efficiency lower than when each employer can keep a more stable force of his own—and such lower efficiency can be regarded only very shortsightedly as "making work" for the union members.

Such equalization of employment, by not permitting a man to work when an employer in the union's good graces would be willing to have him, should not be confused with other closed—or preferential—or union-shop requirements for hiring and eligibility to work. It should be noticed further that the Seattle waterfront employing association, which in 1921 and some following years appears to have been anti-union (at least it was not bound by union regulations), nevertheless adhered to the principle of equalizing opportunity to earn, among the eligible men.

ment is made for work outside normal hours) with an abnormally high wage per hour. It would seem that decasualization, by tending to assure greater continuity of employment to the individual worker, should tend to make for higher average weekly and annual earnings *and also for lower hourly earnings*. At any rate, the dock industry shows that merely to increase the hourly earnings in any occupation is not necessarily to increase the welfare of the workers—it may rather have a lottery effect of increasing the number of seekers for the "prize" of such a job, despite the highly irregular employment which accompanies the alluring rates.[11]

I gather that decasualizing measures have not usually decreased hourly earnings, though, as stated above, they have decidedly tended to increase, equalize, and stabilize weekly and annual earnings. The employers have probably benefited, mainly by more and better service for their wages. Whether the consumer has been benefited and stimulated to buy more longshore services is doubtful—thus, it is also doubtful whether in practice these programs have contributed as constructively as they might to the problem of total unemployment.

The United States longshore industry's national wage structure appears, incidentally, to contain a number of anomalies, as well as to possess many features in common with foreign ports. Among the latter characteristics are numerous "wage extras," such as penalty overtime rates for work done outside of normal daylight hours, and also for innumerable supposedly disagreeable or dangerous types of cargo handling. The most puzzling feature of American rates reported as of 1927 and 1928 was the small regional variations. On the West coast the basic rate was 90 cents an hour; on the Atlantic, at Baltimore and more northerly points it was 85 cents, and below Baltimore, 80 cents. Some of these, however, were trade union but not fully prevailing rates. The most conspicuous instance of politi-

---

[11] The starvation wages for some casual agricultural work, featured in Steinbeck's *Grapes of Wrath,* indicate with what qualifications the above argument must be understood. A local, and perhaps temporary, oversupply of desperate seekers for work may be due to such factors as misrepresentations as to the work and wages available, *and extremely poor alternative opportunities for earnings.*

cal wage rates was thus illustrated (and notice that the time was in a Coolidge, not a Roosevelt, administration) :

The longshore labor in New Orleans is very much confused by the existence in the port of large bodies of union and non-union labor with different rates of wages. The union longshoremen do all the work for the United States Shipping Board, while all other companies use non-union labor. It frequently happens, therefore, that a stevedore company operating on a pier uses one kind of labor for one ship and a different kind of labor for another ship.[12]

In this case, the going non-union rate was perhaps half the union rate. Both union and non-union longshoremen in the deep South, I believe, were and are mainly Negroes.

C. Wages in Seasonal Employments

Seasonal Unemployment as a Cause of High Hourly Rates. —Do we encounter any new questions of principle as we proceed from casual unemployment to seasonal unemployment? These cases certainly present essentially similar, if not identical, problems of wage policy; there is much overlapping in the phenomena which these terms designate. As was stated above, casual labor is employed in many types of agricultural and horticultural production, and of course a primary reason is the largely uncontrollable seasons of planting, caring for growing crops, harvesting, canning, and other processing. Labor is said to be decasualized, we were told, when modern methods of labor administration are used to minimize street-tramping and irregularity of income for the workers, with reference to employment which, despite such measures, still shows marked short-term fluctuations, from seasonal and other causes. As we have seen, statistical records and analyses permit of increasingly accurate predictions, on the basis of average or normal seasonal variability and the current longer trend, as to the state of demand for labor in each industry in the *near* future. All, or nearly all, lines of business show some normal seasonal variation, making for corresponding fluctuations in employment and production; but of course some industries are outstandingly

---

[12] B. Stern, USBLS Bull. 550, p. 87.

seasonal. In the following discussion we shall use three well-known examples—the building trades, bituminous coal mining, and automobile manufacturing. Elsewhere in this book will be found statistical data and charts relating to earnings in these industries. For the sake of brevity no further detailed examination of such data will be included here.[13] Suffice it to say that these industries all show *hourly* earnings which are rather high, in relation to the grades of skill and effort involved; and, on account of seasonal unemployment, *annual* earnings which are low or not so high.[14]

Since opportunities for work during the off-season, in the localities where such seasonal operations occur, are poor or non-existent (at least, work in which the seasonal skills are in demand), hourly rates and earnings during the busy season have to be high in order to attract a competent labor supply.[15]

Unemployment Which Does Not Call for Higher Wage Rates.—The principle that, in seasonal employments, hourly earnings in the long run tend to be high enough to tide the

---

[13] The charts on pp. 44 and 46, above, are most significant in this connection, since they give *monthly* data over a number of recent years—of average hourly earnings and of average hours worked per week. It will be observed that the average hours worked per week by coal miners tend to decline in the summer months and to rise in the others. This index—average hours actually worked per week—however, understates the degree of seasonal fluctuation in employment, since during the off seasons a number of names are dropped from the payrolls.

Another factor influencing the average-hours-worked-per-week record is changes in normal hours. In bituminous coal mining, e.g., the seven-hour day with penalty overtime rates has been in effect since April 1934.

[14] These three industries are also strongly affected by cycles of general prosperity and depression; hence, the unadjusted statistical records show considerable fluctuations in average annual earnings, and still more variability in earnings among all individuals attached to these industries, due to the joint effect of seasonal, cyclical, and secular unemployment, and variable policies as to work sharing. Some other seasonal employments, such as those in college towns, are very much less subject to the additional impact of cyclical fluctuations.

[15] The more calculable demands for seasonal employment, especially those affecting workers who are well paid during the busy seasons, have very different significance from less predictable unemployment. Thus, no one wastes much sympathy on school and college teachers by reason of their summer "unemployment." Yet not a few teachers and other seasonal workers are actually unable to save during their season of payment in such fashion as to adjust their consumption through the year to reasonable expectations as to annual income.

worker over the off season, is perfectly sound within suitable limits. It is easily stretched, however, beyond these limits into fallacious arguments. This principle, for example, obviously "justifies" some sorts of high hourly rates for building tradesmen during their active season. But does it "justify" a progressive shortening of their normal working hours during their busy season? Or the maintenance of high wage rates through the inactive season? Seasonal workers are apt to press demands in all these directions at once, especially those most influenced by the traditions of old-style craft unionism. In the middle 1930's, for instance, the New York electrical workers organized a great demonstration at the City Hall (addressed by a sympathetic mayor), to urge widespread acceptance of the seven-hour day and five-day week which they had won (in their case, with an hourly wage scale of $1.70).[16]

Another example of fallacious "high wage prescription" for relief of unemployment was given (in 1917-18) by the advocate of some organized bakers in Boston—presumably not a pronouncedly seasonal trade—in the course of a wage arbitration. He argued that one ground for the high wage scale sought was the high unemployment existing among these bakers. Each member of the union was required (he said) to give up his job one day a week in order that some other member might have it —a policy of work rationing also used by printing, structural-iron, and other unions, which we have seen (within limits) to be suitable for decasualizing longshore work, but inimical to industrial efficiency so far as it clashes with the employer's reasonable aim of developing a stable working force accustomed to his own facilities and methods.

The main point to notice in this connection is that, to no small extent, high hourly rates may operate like a habit-forming drug. They may attract workers into the industry and locality, even over the bars of high trade union fees and/or other obstacles (where such exist). With numerous members of their trade unemployed or on short time, labor advocates often attempt the solution of shorter hours at still higher hourly rates,

---

[16] As of May 15, 1936.

influenced in part by the commonplace theory of high *seasonal* wage rates as dictated by seasonal unemployment. But seasonal fluctuations in demand are due chiefly to causes other than the price of the commodity or service, and such fluctuations make it necessary for consumers in the busy season to pay high wage rates in order to fortify the workers against the off season. This off season, moreover, of low earnings or none, serves as a barrier to hold down over-supply of workers during the busy season.[17] But when an industry is characterized by *chronic high unemployment,* in season and out of season, in good times as well as bad, there is a presumption that both its wage rates and its prices to consumers are unduly high and are tending to aggravate the unemployment.

One great danger easily overlooked in this connection is from competition of other industries and trades, offering commodities and services which are (in effect) substitutes for products of our first industry, from the consumer's point of view. However well each industry thinks it is doing, and has done, by the consumer, the latter fickle personage may be on the point of thinking that other services suit him better—at the existing prices.

Thus, not any and every sort of unemployment should be taken as evidence that the occupation and locality concerned needs higher hourly wage rates and shorter hours.

D. Stabilization of Employees' Incomes—Pressures and Plans

Many of the evils of industrial fluctuations have long been recognized, and a good many steps have been taken in the direction of steadying wage-earner incomes. What more may be done to increase real annual wage incomes, in industries which have hitherto been especially casual and seasonal? What importance have hourly or piece rates in this problem?

In considering these matters, we shall notice both "pressures," in the sense of penalties and inducements which are

---

17 In conjunction with other "natural" barriers, such as cost of migration of workers to do seasonal work.

thought to make for stabilization of work and wages; and some "plans" which appear to have accomplished significant degrees of stabilization.

Short Hours, Overtime Penalty, Annual Wage.—Employers in industries marked by exceptionally feast-or-famine conditions have always had some inducements to try to operate with greater regularity—notably the persistence of overhead costs of unutilized and underutilized plants or other assets owned or hired for long periods. More recently there have developed, in addition, various artificial or outside pressures, such as legal and trade union requirements tending to shorten normal hours and to increase penalty rates for overtime work, and experience-rating clauses of unemployment compensation laws. It is often argued that such provisions will force employers to find means of providing steadier work.

The Federal Wage-Hour Act of 1938 reapplied short-hour pressures after the lapse of national government control with invalidation of the NRA. In general, this 1938 statute now requires payment of time-and-a-half for hours worked over 40 in a week; but it specifies some important exceptions. Among these are provisions for straight time up to 12 hours in a day and 56 hours in a week,

(1) in pursuance of an agreement, made as a result of collective bargaining by representatives of employees certified as bona fide by the National Labor Relations Board, which provides that no employee shall be employed more than one thousand hours during any period of twenty-six consecutive weeks,

(2) on an annual basis in pursuance of an agreement with his employer, made as a result of collective bargaining by representatives of employees certified as bona fide by the National Labor Relations Board, which provides that the employee shall not be employed more than two thousand hours during any period of fifty-two consecutive weeks, or

(3) for a period or periods of not more than fourteen work-weeks in the aggregate in any calendar year in an industry found by the Administrator to be of a seasonal nature. . . .[18]

---

[18] From sec. 7 (b). Notice the work-sharing philosophy in clause (1), which stresses only the *maximum* of 1,000 hours for any employee, during

Clause (2) of this sub-section probably enabled the annual wage plan of Geo. A. Hormel & Co. (Austin, Minn.) to survive after 1938, since its meat-packing operations are necessarily somewhat irregular by reason of fluctuations in livestock marketing, as well as in demand of consumers. If this company had to pay for all work beyond 40 hours in any week, at 50% penalty wage rates, it would be more likely to call in temporary workers during the rush periods, and thus would be able to guarantee work up to 2,000 hours a year to a smaller number of regular workers.[19]

In many industries, however, the seasonal fluctuations are not yet legally considered sufficient to entitle them to the 14-week exception; yet these fluctuations are so great as seemingly to make annual wage plans prohibitively costly. In industries of this sort, it is probable that the legal shortening of normal hours and requirement of overtime penalty wages tend to spread work at the cost of reduced annual incomes for many of the better workers. Voluntary annual wage guarantees, and to some extent compulsory payroll taxes, have rather the opposing tendency—giving employers incentive to concentrate employment on as small a number of workers as possible. In their initial stages, therefore, the latter pressures tend to reduce the spreading of work and to aggravate the unemployment of workers who do not have steady jobs.

Experience Rating for Unemployment Tax.—Another type of pressure, acting as a lure or goad, according to your point of view, is provided by experience or merit rating in the unemployment compensation laws of a majority of the states.

"any period of 26 weeks," also in clause (2), which provides an incentive for an annual-wage guarantee—provided that the employee with such security is not allowed to work more than 2,000 hours in any 52 consecutive weeks. (Some railway unions have argued that certain clauses in their recent agreements, providing for abandonment of "work-sharing practices," entitle workers with seniority to employment for 48 hours a week!)

[19] More than 90% of this plant's 3,000 workers are employed on a straight-time basis, which means that, regardless of the number of hours worked in any one week, each such employee receives 52 weekly pay checks based on his hourly rate.

Many particulars of a plan of this character are given in publications of the Minnesota American Legion Foundation's Employment Stabilization Service, Historical Building, St. Paul, Minnesota.

Such a plan provides that the individual employer's payroll tax for unemployment compensation may be reduced, if the record of claims for such compensation filed by his workers during some immediately preceding period—say the past three years—is sufficiently favorable. This scheme is often defended by analogy with legal workmen's compensation for industrial accidents and diseases. Many insurance companies and funds have graduated premiums for such death and disability-compensation insurance according to the statistical experience of the individual employer or group of employers; and there is little doubt that this pecuniary motivation has been a factor of some importance in the promotion and development of safety engineering and allied practices.

There are, however, many controversial features of experience rating in unemployment compensation taxes. Many of these doubts may be traced to the fundamental question of the extent to which unemployment or irregularity of work is within the control of the employer. An associated aspect of the problem is expressed by this question: Is it not inevitable that the plants and industries of steadiest employment should contribute substantially to unemployment compensation in the unsteady industries? Do not the people whose houses never burn pay most of the expense of fire insurance? In life and accident insurance, rates of premium may vary over a wide range, if the insurers quote such rates on the basis of classification of risks, e.g., by medical examination for eligibility to life insurance. The administrative cost might be excessive if the attempt were made to adjust each employer's tax *closely to his own employment-stability experience;* comparatively broad and simple classes are probably necessary on this account.

Such experience rating is recommended, however, by no means *merely* because of its pressure on the employer toward stabilization of his own working force. Another of its advantages appears to be a tendency to assess costs of unemployment compensation equitably between the more and less seasonal industries. In the long run, the cost of social insurance is and must be mainly borne by wage earners as a class; and it is perhaps equitable that the workers who earn high hourly and weekly wages in the peak months of seasonal employment should pay higher premiums per dollar of such wages, for the unemployment benefits for which they are almost sure to become eligible during their dull season, than the workers who receive more modest hourly wages by reason of their more secure employment the year around, and thus are much less likely to become recipients of unemployment compensation. This particular equity problem, to be sure, would be the more serious but for the rather modest rates of unemployment compensation, the limited term for which it runs, and the waiting period before it begins.

Employers' Plans—Demonstrations of Income Stabilization.—The results attributed to such pressures as were referred to above are not based entirely on abstract theory; they are also supported by some instances of firms which have notably smoothed the curves of their workers' incomes through the year and through the years. The most desirable methods of income stabilization, of course, are those founded upon increasing regularity of the "work supply"—which methods may add to security of employment after decasualization has done its utmost. Among measures which have been found feasible in this direction are "dovetailing" (operation by an employer of enterprises or departments which have peak demands and/or materials supplies at different seasons), manufacturing larger quantities of goods for stock, and varying sales efforts so as to sell relatively more in the slack season, relatively less in the normally busy season. The automobile manufacturing industry, for example, has achieved a significant degree of seasonal stabilization of employment, beginning about 1935, by a combination of the last two of these methods. The sales campaign has been modified, chiefly by changing the date of introduction of new models; and during the dull season employment has been increased by greater manufacture of parts which are stored for use when the demand for cars increases.

A transitional method of improving the seasonal worker's position is also illustrated in automobile manufacture (General Motors plan): a loan of money is made by the employer on exceptionally favorable terms to the needy and laid-off worker, to supplement his legal unemployment compensation—perhaps without any interest, and repayable by work when and if the employer recalls the worker—and then by instalments, so that when he is recalled, the bulk of his then-current wages will be available for his current living. A loan plan of this sort amounts to self-applied pressure by the employer toward further regularization of his own work.[20]

The employee-income stabilization movement is also apparent in the growing practice of paying "manual" as well as clerical employees weekly salaries, instead of hourly rates, and giving both white- and dark-collar workers similar privileges as to vacations, sick leaves, and certain other absences without loss of pay. This latter trend has been under way for several years, for instance among the large petroleum refiners;[21] and it is a trend which may well be encouraged by suitable flexibility in wage-hour laws and regulations, with respect to hours worked in any day or week, in relation to overtime pay.

Building Seasons and Builders' Wages.—It is frequently asked, Why do the building trades cling so stubbornly to their high hourly wage rates in and out of season? Why do they not stimulate building, and increase their own annual earnings, by lowering these wages? As one employer put it, "Building wages are too high by the hour; too low by the year." The problem,

---

[20] The unions concerned have a reasonable claim to be consulted in the formative stages of any such income stabilization plan, and are able, if they are really cooperative, to offer much sound advice. And they have a motive to be cooperative, since if they can properly claim some credit for the completed plan, it adds to their prestige. Contrariwise, if the employer devises and announces his plan without consulting the union(s), he offends them by seeming to undermine their position.

[21] The annual wage and guaranteed-employment plans of the Procter and Gamble, Nunn-Bush, and Hormel companies are summarized in *Mo. Lab. Rev.*, July 1938; and the loan plan of General Motors in *ibid.*, Jan. 1939. See also *ibid.*, Aug. 1940, "Annual Wage and Guaranteed-Employment Plans in Union Agreements."

Cyclical stabilization of employment is of course most difficult, and in any full sense doubtless impossible. Within limits, coming events influencing employment cast shadows a year or more ahead; and if prospects are adverse, the employer can gradually reduce the income-stabilized part of his force by normal quits, deaths, and retirements. (Naturally, it is rarely prudent for a large employer to guarantee full yearly employment to each person at the time of first hiring.)

however, is very complex. One factor, for example, is the great impact of cyclical as well as of seasonal unemployment on this industry; another is the continuing prevalence of small employers and of much building to suit the tastes of individual customers; yet another, the maze of organizations among workers, contractors, and building materials people, some of which are being investigated under anti-trust laws. It appears probable that at least the more grossly anti-social restrictive practices which a few of such groups—singly and in collusion—have hitherto practiced will be reduced by governmental intervention, and that the rather archaic structures of wages and working rules of the crafts, which are symptomatic of the arrested development of the industry, will be undermined by the growth of factory-like methods of construction, carried out by larger and more progressive employers. These employers may well make greater use of specialized plant and equipment, as well as of semi-skilled occupations; and they may be more ingenious than the conventional builders have been in stabilizing the work and income of employees. The cooperation of organized labor is naturally essential to the most satisfactory kind of progress.

Meanwhile, a few particulars may be offered, showing that the AFL construction unions are somewhat more flexible in wage policies than is commonly realized; also some necessary limits of such flexibility. It is reported, for instance, that such unions in some cities have offered substantial wage reductions on government-aided, low-cost housing construction. Such reductions would assist in testing the elasticity of consumer demand for housing construction. Another recent concession is double-shift operation at straight-time wage rates—on national defense housing.

Lower Hourly Rates for Maintenance Work.—For many years, moreover, crafts which are prominent in the building trades have been employed for maintenance and service work by factories, mines, railroads, and various other industries not primarily concerned with miscellaneous *new* construction. These maintenance carpenters, painters, electricians, bricklayers, and the like very commonly had year-round work, or at least much steadier employment over the years than the same men could obtain by following new construction jobs. I have not found any comprehensive comparisons, but it is noticeable that quotations of wages of maintenance and service craftsmen of large employers usually run below the corresponding building trade scales and earnings in the same localities.[22] The latter "union scales" seem usually to exceed the hourly-earned rates of service craftsmen with more regular employment by at least 10% ; and I have been told by several employers' representatives from different industries and localities (including public institutions) that the trade unions concerned made no objection to moderate differentials of this character.

In some cases the union agreements provide that the local union building scale is to apply on all *new* construction, and a lower rate to the regular repair and maintenance craftsmen. By this scheme the employer *can* use his maintenance workers on new construction, but has little pecuniary inducement to do so.

The compromises sketched in the preceding paragraphs may seem incomplete, if not otherwise unsatisfactory. Why, it may be asked, do not the construction unions charge several different hourly rates, depending on how many days' work are offered during the year? The absurdity of expecting hourly rates in any occupation *fully* to reflect continuity of employment is obvious. In the construction trades, one obstacle is that but few contractors are able or willing to guarantee more than a few weeks' work to building tradesmen. Another is that, as a union's "standard wage-rate" structure becomes more complex, the union's enforcement problem is aggravated, and soon becomes impossible. Thus, we cannot reasonably expect any

---

[22] One brief discussion of this matter is in Daugherty, DeChazeau, and Stratton, *Economics of the Iron and Steel Industry,* Vol. 1, at p. 145.

Voluminous materials are available on hourly, weekly, and annual earnings of craftsmen in railway service, which materials appear not to have been carefully analyzed from this point of view. For the first six months of 1938, for instance, one calculation showed the following averages: bridge and building carpenters, per hour, 68.3¢—per week, $29.23; electrical workers (A), per hour, 88.3¢—per week, $39.52; machinists, per hour, 88.8¢—per week, $36.39. (*Report of Emergency Board*—discussed in Ch. 12, below—p. 52.)

union to sanction more than a few rates for any one occupation, time, and locality. Hitherto, building unions have tended to evade these issues, when the local labor market became strongly adverse, by making secret concessions. Experimentation with openly defensible wage-rate gradations would seem better.

Craft Union Hourly Rates for Year-Round Public Employment?—Because public opinion has not been well informed on this matter, governmental bodies are frequently maneuvered into paying the full new-construction union *hourly* scale for year-round work in skilled crafts. This is by no means true of all public employers; moreover, skilled craft workers are perhaps paid no more liberally (often less), by these public employers, as compared with many white-collar employees. Nevertheless, we have here another indication that the factor of stability of earnings through the year receives distinctly less attention than it deserves in the setting of rates of pay in public as well as in private employment.

This problem has been consciously studied by the unusually efficient personnel management of the Tennessee Valley Authority. Employees of the TVA in construction and temporary operating and maintenance work are paid hourly rates, in accordance with officially determined prevailing-wage scales; they have the 40-hour week and are paid time-and-a-half for overtime. Other members of the same occupations, doing regular and continuous work, are paid annual salaries and are allowed a month's vacation and two weeks' sick leave with pay (like other Federal Government salaried workers), but no penalty rates for overtime.[23] In its attempts to find a suitable relationship between annual and hourly wage rates, the TVA has been unable to discover any approach to uniform practice in private employment. Its own wage scales, based on prevailing construction and maintenance wages in its own area, show very small differences in hourly earnings (in the lower wage crafts), between men paid respectively by the hour and by the year. Skilled craftsmen on annual salaries of $2,000 a

---

[23] This last exemption is allowed to private employers by the Federal Wage-Hour law, only for non-routine salaried employees.

year, for example, earned $1.11 an hour (working 1,800 hours); while hourly-paid men in the same crafts received $1.12½.[24] This differential appears inadequate for a long-run policy.[25]

E. Summary

In this chapter we have opened up some connections between wages and unemployment, beginning with the short-term fluctuations in working opportunity that are characteristic of casual and seasonal labor. In a "free market" in which there was full and well-informed competition, hourly wage rates and earnings would have to be relatively high in such irregular employments, to compensate for the unsteadiness of earnings and to equalize annual earnings among occupations—skill and other net attractions assumed equal. In the actual world we find some evidence of this tendency; for instance, *hourly* earnings of longshoremen and building tradesmen compare much more favorably with those in similarly skilled but steadier work than do *annual* earnings. In recent decades a number of methods have been developed for giving greater stability to wage earners' incomes, for instance, by decasualizing work at the docks, by reducing seasonal variations in total hours worked for particular employers, and by still other means of providing greater constancy in the workers' cash receipts.

Such employment stabilization might proceed more rapidly if hourly wage rates were more free to be lowered in return for assurances of steadier work. Usually, however, continuity of workers' incomes is increased by somewhat irregular and gradual stages, for this and that class of earners; moreover, the same processes tend to assist the employer with his overhead costs and by lowering turnover and improving morale of labor. Yet unions have often, if not usually, acquiesced in the wide-

---

[24] These rates refer to 1938. In 1940, as told in Ch. 19-C, below, TVA hourly rates for skilled crafts ranged from $1.12½ to $1.50.

[25] It should be added that part of the TVA's enlightened personnel program consists in transferring temporary employees from one project to another, which practice has given them unusually full employment, and enabled some to earn more in a year than the salaried craftsmen.

spread and long-standing practice of paying (especially in private employment) lower hourly rates to maintenance and service craftsmen, who have relatively steadier work the year around, than to similar workers engaged in seasonal building construction. This history suggests that building labor costs (for example) might be significantly lowered, and volume of work — especially during off-seasons — stimulated by lower prices of products, through measures assuring seasonal and casual workers distinctly greater continuity of income.

CHAPTER 12

RISING AND DECLINING INDUSTRIES; TECHNOLOGICAL UNEMPLOYMENT AND REGIONAL COMPETITION

Business men strive to minimize labor as well as other costs. The markets in which they purchase labor fluctuate dynamically, and among these fluctuations are cyclical waves —partly due to, partly causing, new technologies and methods of management which compel some older industries to die away and permit newer ones to enjoy luxuriant growth. Upon these labor markets, too, strong pressure from outside is frequently exerted by the exigencies of nationalistic competition or actual warfare. We have surveyed those deviations from "normal" or "static" wage determination which are most directly connected with seasonal variations and the casual nature of particular employments. Chapter 13, below, will deal further with *all-industry* cyclical movements.

In the present chapter we take primarily a *single*-industry approach, and moreover focus attention on technological and regional factors which are responsible for the rise or decline of specific industries or sections thereof. Our first glance, in section A, will be at the general relationship of these long-run or secular industrial changes to the business cycles which we shall be discussing more fully in subsequent chapters. Next, in section B we shall try to discover how wage policy may best be adjusted (1) to secure maximum employment opportunities in industries enjoying secular *expansion,* and (2) to ease the pains of unemployment in the *declining* industries. Section C will seek wage policies appropriate for those industries whose expansion or contraction is influenced by economic competition between nations;[1] while section D will develop these principles

---

[1] Wartime and national defense adjustments will be further treated in Ch. 21, below.

in more detail with reference to interregional competition within industries and within a single nation.

In real life, of course, the pressures of inter-industrial, interregional, and technological competition cannot be sharply differentiated; to many intents and purposes, for instance, the wage principles of inter*national* and other inter*regional* competition run parallel; moreover, regional "migration" within such an industry as cotton textiles has implications for wages which are in many respects similar to those of technological changes.[2] But separate discussion of the factors outlined under sections B, C, and D, above, will nevertheless be useful for diagnosis and prescription on any actual local industry which is suffering from one, or some combination, of these maladjustments.

A. Secular Industrial Change in Relation to Business Cycles

Economic development under "capitalism" always has been more or less cyclical in character. Particular firms, single industries, and often whole national economies have experienced wavelike flows of prosperity and depression. As the range and accuracy of our studies have increased, it has become evident that "the business cycle," which roughly describes the fluctuation of an economy as a whole, is actually a complex of many types of waves. The fortunes of individual firms and industries are all part of the larger complex, often participating both as cause and as effect.

A leading authority on business cycles, Professor Joseph Schumpeter, emphasizes that the capitalistic process evolves through a continuing series of technical and business innovations; and the "immediate and ulterior effects of innovations, and the response to them by the system, . . . cause a multiplicity

---

2 Indeed, geographical "migration" is apt to involve hastening of technological changes in the whole industry, if only because the growing region as a matter of course tends to adopt the *newer* apparatus and methods, since it naturally is always much less burdened with antiquated facilities and traditions.

of simultaneous waves. . . ."³ These novelties come irregularly, although some are appearing at any one time; and, of course, the effects of those innovations which are introduced simultaneously will extend over periods of varying duration. Amid this tangle of cycles, Professor Schumpeter sees three rather regular sequences predominating—waves with periods respectively some 50, 9, and 3⅓ years.

Whether great weight should be given to his particular system of cycles, certainly there are long and medium and short waves, continually operating somewhat like the cross currents set up by tidal and wind forces. And like these natural forces acting upon large bodies of water, the various types of economic waves combine their effects, sometimes to offset, at other times to augment, each other. But we cannot carry this analogy too far; those who predict the forces of wind and tide have much more reason to feel confidence in their calculations and predictions!

Beneath or within these various undulations of the entire economy, changes are always going on in particular industries. Such variations are analogous to those for the economy as a whole, but they cannot be adequately analyzed by the macrocosmic or over-all study of general business cycles. Proceeding from a number of causes, among which technological developments, improved management techniques, and other innovations figure prominently, industries themselves undergo long-run changes similar to those which Schumpeter calls "Kondratieff waves" in a study of the whole economy. Rising industries are necessary by-products of the increased activity which follows the beginning of any particular innovation of large influence, such as the steam engine; and declining industries result from the decreased activity which follows the wearing away of the influence of another.⁴ It is useful for us to examine some of the microcosms or individual industries which make up the

---

³ J. A. Schumpeter, *Business Cycles* (New York: 1939). This statement is pieced together from phrases on pp. 171 and 172 (vol. I).

⁴ The Roman philosophic poet Lucretius reiterated the maxim: "Nothing arises in nature except through the death of some other being." So in an important sense, do new industries sound knells of old ones.

whole economy; and to study their long-run changes in relation to their wages.

B. Compensation of Labor in Rising and Declining Industries

We shall begin this study of wages in relation to life cycles of single industries by treating first the characteristics of those industries which are in the expanding phase. After a few notes on causes of such expansion, we proceed to a statement of the problem of wage policy in rising industries, then to a theoretical solution of the problem, and finally illustrate the problem and solution by discussion of some bits of "case material" from particular instances—the aircraft and automobile industries. Following the review of expanding industries, there will be a similar survey of the wage problems of more or less stationary or declining industries, using bituminous coal and railroads as illustrations.

What Causes an Industry to Expand?—There are three principal types of change, any one or combination of which may cause an industry to expand (apart from still broader factors like the rise of all industrial activity in recovery from a general depression, mere population growth, and the relative successes and failures of particular firms within each industry): changes in demand and in two aspects of supply—technology and materials.[5]

An increase in demand may tend to expand any industry. Such stronger demand may be due to shifts in tastes, perhaps associated with rising consumer incomes; such changes paved

---

[5] Of course there is much interaction among these. Silk hosiery, for instance, could be sold in increasing quantities at decreasing prices, as growing volume enabled producers to improve quality and style, and to advance technology. Migration of industry, too, is usually affected much less by mere discoveries of natural sources of raw materials than by advancing technology for extracting and processing these materials. Industrial location is also greatly affected by shifting costs of transporting products and materials (including labor). There is enormous variation in the percentage which all transport charges form, of the final price paid by the consumer. Facilities for transmitting information on all these matters, to actual or potential capital, labor, consumers, form another very important variable.

the way for larger-scale production of the silk stocking. The industry, moreover, may be supplying a newly discovered or greatly improved product—many of us have seen the automobile, radio, and airplane industries actually begin their phenomenal growths. The total markets for many sections of many industries, too, are affected by exchange depreciation, reciprocal trade agreements, and other forms of international competition, to be discussed in the next section.

New techniques, so far as they result in a lower price of product, tend to stimulate volume of production—how much, depending on the elasticity of demand for the particular good and market. So new machines, methods, and processes give rise to expansion of production; and in doing so they create technological *employment,* as well as "technological *un*employment." The plywood industry, for example, has grown out of new techniques in wood and lumber processing; the western citrus fruit industry's expansion is attributable in part to cost-reduction factors like the development of irrigation techniques in the Imperial Valley and improved transportation and marketing methods.

The phenomenon of "technological unemployment" usually develops in the older industries, if and as output per man-hour increases faster than growth of consumption of such output.[6] To an extent more difficult to show statistically, employment is at the same time growing in new and/or small undertakings. Employment by railways and coal mines and by the manufacturing that is surveyed by official statistics (for instance) has either declined or grown less than our total population, since about 1916. To an important extent, apparently, these slackenings were part of a secular growth in the total rate of unemployment; yet the concurrent *rises* of employment in such industries as electric power and automotive services are but outstanding representatives of the expansion rates that are characteristic of new and revived industries.

---

[6] Output will tend not to expand sufficiently to maintain employment (as output per man-hour grows) if (1) the price of the product is not proportionately reduced, or if (2) price is proportionately reduced, but elasticity of demand for it is less than 1.00.

A third type of rising industry follows the discovery of new raw materials, or improved sources of old ones. The western copper and the Mesabi iron mines, for example, were rapidly developed because these deposits became less expensive to mine than many older sources, when transportation and other technology reached a certain stage.

Why Is Wage Policy a Problem in Rising Industries?— It may seem that there should be no difficulty about wages in rising industries. Jobs are abundant, by comparative standards; wage increases are common; and we who are examining the industry may be content to leave our examination with that glimpse, or more likely with praise for the industry blessed with both high wages and expanding output and employment. A moment's reflection, though, will disclose profound social issues that are closely concerned with this industry's wage structure.

The national interest will be best served, and usually also the long-run interests of the capital and labor directly involved, if no industry's wage rates are allowed to rise (or fall) very far or long above (or below) wages in the area concerned for *all* labor of similar skill and efficiency. Admittedly, this goal is never fully attainable in practice, partly because almost none of the terms can be sharply defined for labor pricing. But we can become clearer as to objectives and methods by considering a number of plausible cases in favor of allowing particular wages to hold, either above or below those prevailing in the general labor market, and showing limits within which such arguments are valid.

Consider first, what is likely to happen if an "infant industry" is helped to grow by some low wage form of protection? One difficulty is that the workers, when they organize, will find the industry over-expanded. Their hard choice will then be: continuing these low wages, or raising wage rates and probably having fewer jobs. If the latter course prevails, capital also will become unemployed, and much of it lost. In this case unduly low wages during the period of growth have allowed the expansion of investment and employment to go too far, and added to the normal problems of slackening growth or actual decline which sooner or later face every industry.[7]

In rising industries, on the other hand, wages higher than those in the general labor market are common—a result of our habit, especially where union power is strong, of adjusting wages more largely with reference to the particular industry's current wage capacity than to any other factor. The entrepreneur knows that the period of innovation is the only time in which he makes profits in excess of the mere compensation for his labor of management and the returns he might have secured by lending out his capital.[8] During this joyful period, he can pay wages above the current value of his labor's grade of skill rather than suffer any delay in his realization of the profit which will disappear when his industry reaches the economic limits of its expansion. One argument, indeed, sometimes advanced in favor of above-market wage rates in a growing industry, is that high wages tend to prevent *over*-expansion.

But as investment and output go on, and prices of products decline, these high wages come to be regarded as a dangerous handicap to most firms in the industry, and the industry's growth is stopped too abruptly. The business man may introduce labor-saving machinery, which will absorb more capital but tend to reduce the number of workers needed. Or, if labor-saving machinery is not resorted to, the high wage rates will dictate a higher price of the product, and so more sharply limit expansion of the industry than would wages more nearly in line with those in the general labor market. Whichever of these alternatives is taken, the result is a lesser expansion of employment in the industry, and higher prices of its products, than the nation's resources and wants make desirable.

It is readily conceivable, moreover, that wage rates may be maintained within an industry at an unduly high level, without

---

[7] We touch here upon "parasitic industries" arguments, usually advanced in favor of trade-union and legal minimum-wage standards. These matters are examined further in Ch. 20, below.

[8] The entrepreneur does sometimes enjoy unforeseen windfalls, as well as losses; but the time he can most confidently expect handsome profits (averaging troughs and peaks of business cycles) is during innovation, while his industry is growing. (Gains attributable to more or less monopolistic factors are another matter.)

the symptom of excessive unemployment appearing *in that industry*. The abnormally high unemployment rate which is one of the obvious and important evils to be expected from too-high particular wage rates may be lacking (for instance) in an industry with a long and strongly rising demand—if insufficient time has elapsed for an overgrown labor force to become attached to it, or if there are "artificial" barriers preventing many workers from entering competition for jobs in this trade. Under conditions of free competition for labor and capital, on the other hand, above-market earnings of workers and/or of investors will tend toward a continued flow of new resources toward these high earnings, which in turn will increase production and bring down prices of the products—until these movements have swung to an opposite extreme and the industry becomes less attractive than others. Thus a condition of very high wages, high prices, and high profits, can be *maintained* in an industry only by placing obstructions in the way of flows of new labor and capital into it—in short, by policies and practices which are, in effect, restrictive of nation-wide competition, though doubtless not so intended.[9]

Temporarily High Labor Incomes Required for an Industry's Growth.—It is also argued that relatively high wages are socially required—if labor is not to be conscripted—in order to attract adequate labor supplies into each sizable new industry, particularly as at best there must be some uncertainty as to how long the new types and locations of jobs will last. Such deterrents as these, as well as the actual costs of new training, self-equipment, and actual movement of workers, should indeed be allowed for in any attempt to compare real-wage rates for work of a given grade in different industries and locations.

Yet it is easy to exaggerate the extent, and still more the duration, of the wage premiums socially needed to secure needed growth of a new industry. One offset, for example, is suggested by the availability of unemployed men; probably not *all* the workers drawn into each new industry have to be hired

---

[9] "High," that is, when all relevant factors such as skill, effort, seasonality, and risk are taken into account.

away from other jobs—some, if not many, of them may be had
from the ranks of the jobless. Growing industries, too, in the
aggregate are the best prospects for new hiring of young persons and immigrants as they first come into the labor market.

Wages and Employment, under Imperfect Competition.
—How may wage policy operate to facilitate rather than to retard this continual distribution and redistribution of the total
labor supply? The following analysis and succeeding "case
studies" will show further why conditions which allow individual-industry wage rates to oscillate about the general market
rate are likely to maximize both total employment and consumer satisfactions. As recognized above, industrial expansion
is affected by any one or combination among numerous demand
and cost factors. In attempting to trace connections between industrial expansion and wage rates, for instance, we are faced
with greatly varying elasticities of demands for products and
with numerous degrees of competition among employers.

The reader may have suspected that, even if the arguments
we have maintained above were valid in the old economic abstraction of "perfect competition," they are inapplicable to the
real world of imperfect and monopolistic competition. It is
quite true that competitive conditions greatly affect the *degree*
of reaction of product-price to labor-cost change.[10] But the
direction of change in employment which may be expected to
follow any perceptible shift in demand or in cost is the same,
whatever the type of monopoly or competition among employers. An upward shift in demand (for example) produces the
increased quantity of output and employment which characterizes an expanding industry, whether the industry itself is
eventually monopolistic or competitive. This increase in output,
to be sure, which will be less in a monopolistic than in a fully
competitive situation, appears only when the cost curve does

---

[10] Even under perfect competition, (1) labor cost is practically always
less than total cost, hence an isolated wage change will not tend to affect
the particular product price *proportionately;* but (2) as wage rises spread,
their effects are transmitted through material and plant costs, and then
product prices rise more nearly proportionately to the wage rise.
  Labor cost per unit of product, of course, does not change directly and proportionately with wage rates, if (e.g.) labor efficiency also changes.

not move to offset the rise in the demand curve. In both cases, if there were a sufficient rise in the wages and/or other costs per unit of output, the volume of production and employment would *decrease*—after rising product prices had reduced sales. If, on the other hand, all the productive factors were paid more than formerly, but just enough to compensate fully for the higher product price at which the old volume of production could be sold (with increased demand), there would be no change in output at all. So this industry would miss its opportunity to expand, if the vested interests were simply to exact proportionally larger payments for themselves. If wages, for example, were continually adjusted to give more and more to those who were in the industry at the beginning of an upward trend in demand, "wages would steadily rise in any industry enjoying an expanding demand for its product, no unfilled vacancies would ever appear, and it would be impossible to absorb any of the workers thrown out of employment, or receiving lower wages, in industries suffering from declining demands."[11] There would be no long-run increase in each new industry's employment, under these conditions, and the percentage of unemployment (in all industries) would mount ever higher, as each new industry discovered the advantages of such policy to itself.

Such extreme results seem unlikely to be realized, unless very exceptionally. The foregoing argument shows, however, that in the interests of increased output, at lower unit prices,[12] and correlatively in the interests of increased total national employment and of optimum rate of rise in real standard of living for the whole community, it is important that no substantial and long-continued departures should be made from general market rates of payment to productive factors. Par-

---

[11] A. G. Pool, *Wage Policy in Relation to Industrial Fluctuations*, p. 14. Cf. similar argument in W. B. Reddaway, *Economics of a Declining Population*, pp. 65, 66.

[12] In some cases, the upward shift of demand, while always causing increased output and employment, might do so only by increasing the prices charged—for example, it might become necessary to bring poorer land into use. And in an industry of one or a few firms, the employer might be able to exploit increased demand by increasing output but little, and continuing to sell at a price higher than would prevail under full competition.

ticularly while our economy is burdened with abnormally high unemployment, the correct policy surely is to make our resource markets more nearly perfectly competitive, than to give indiscriminate approval to high wage industries and sections of industries, without inquiring too closely as to whether these high wages are symptoms of some sort of restricted entry, rather than (or as well as) highly progressive labor and management.

The theoretical case is in essence the same, with reference to an industry in which a marked decrease in cost occurs, without change in its demand curve. Such decrease in costs, under either perfect or imperfect competition, tends to bring both lower prices and increased production, so that the industry's output and employment will expand. Once more the *degree* of drop in price and of increase in production will probably be much greater in the perfectly competitive situation, but the *direction* of change is the same in both cases.[13] If, however, after the costs have been reduced, they are immediately raised by increased unit payments for labor or capital or both, then prices must rise toward, or be held at, the former levels; and the industry's expansion is prevented, curtailed, or wiped out. Thus, no matter what the originating cause of expansion, the industry cannot obtain its fullest, socially desirable growth until prices equivalent to those which would be set by *full competition over all industries* are paid for the land, labor, and capital required.

Windfall Bonuses Preferable to Too-High Wage Rates.— High wage rates in a thriving industry are sometimes referred to as *de facto* profit sharing, analogous to the bonuses very often paid to executives in these firms. We can all sympathize with labor's desire for a share in prosperity which it has helped to create. The analysis here developed looks more approvingly on bonus distributions to employees, *after* high profits are real-

---

[13] A complete monopoly on the employing side might even decrease production as a result of lowered costs—but under very exceptional demand and cost conditions. The factor elasticity of demand is (of course) independent of the degree of competition in the supplying industry. Imperfect competition or complete "monopsony" among buyers, on the other hand, very much affects (at least short-term) elasticity of demand.

ized, than on mark-ups of wage rates which carry such rates well above the general labor market.[14] Such bonuses, even though they come to be expected year after year, are less in the nature of rigid costs than are high wage rates, and so the former have less tendency to put up or keep up product prices, and to limit production and employment below the points which generally prevailing wage rates would permit.

Some Instances of Wages in Expanding Industries: British Experience.—Pool has extended a valid, if commonplace, warning to all those who attempt to subject such a thesis as the foregoing to statistical tests: "Any inductive investigation of the effects of wage pressure on the efficiency of entrepreneurs and on unemployment would appear to be virtually impossible, owing to the difficulty of isolating this particular factor from all the others which may possibly affect technological progress and unemployment."[15] His own statistical summary of wage rates and employment in the English engineering and textile trades, and in other expanding and contracting groups of industries (after 1921), shows that in general average weekly earnings were (in 1936) about 10% higher in the expanding than in the contracting industries.

This difference, Pool argues, should be reduced:

> Such an adjustment of wage rates would have a threefold effect on the depressed industries: (1) by increasing the number of vacancies in the expanding trades, it would speed up the transfer of surplus workers from the overcrowded industries; (2) by stimulating a still more rapid expansion of the industries which are already fairly prosperous, it would help to increase the demand for the products of the depressed industries; and (3) in so far as the depressed industries incur costs by buying the products of the flourishing trades, it would help to reduce the costs of the former.[16]

It is interesting further to observe, although he passes over the implications of this fact in his own review, that in British

---

[14] This would be true even if the high profits were due to monopolistic practices; for high wage rates would be more apt to perpetuate this monopolistic control.

[15] Op. cit., pp. 29, 30.

[16] Ibid., p. 61.

building and similar construction, there was a "huge expansion" during a period in which the wage rates of these occupations steadily declined toward the average rate for the shrinking trades. On the whole his British data tend, as far as they go, to verify his argument that expansion of output and of employment opportunities will be greatest for the nation when wage rates but little higher than those prevailing for comparable grades of work elsewhere are paid in the flourishing industries —i.e., when wages are allowed to find this level by free entry of labor and capital into the expanding trades, after the earliest years when high returns to both labor and capital are actually required by reason of the uncertainties and adaptations required of labor in a really new industry.

American Data.—In the United States, too, there is some statistical support for this proposition, though as yet the evidence is inconclusive.[17] In the period from 1933 to 1935, for example, when nearly all manufacturing industries were recovering from extreme depression, the greatest expansion of output tended to be enjoyed by those whose wage rates increased most slowly. Not only did output increase the most, but total employ-

---

[17] Mordecai Ezekiel, for instance, analyzed materials in Bell's *Productivity, Wages, and National Income* (see Ch. 8, above) on nine industries, 1923-37, and concluded that changes in volume of employment showed no consistent relation to wage-rate changes. ("Productivity, Wage Rates, and Employment," *Am. Econ. Rev.*, Sept. 1940, pp. 507-523.) As Ezekiel intimates, several slips are possible between the cup of wage cut and the lip of employment expansion (especially if other wages and prices are held constant), e.g.: (1) wages may be a minor fraction of total cost for the particular industry, (2) product prices may be reduced (if at all) less than total cost is reduced by the wage cut, and (3) demand for this product may be inelastic.

But while this research by Ezekiel demonstrates anew (as one result) that we may not expect any and every sort of wage cut to increase employment of the workers affected, it does not invalidate the general thesis discussed immediately above—for Bell's nine industries include at least two (minerals and railroads) in which demand, especially in 1929-37, was abnormally inelastic.

And even if the return of rates of wages and profits in a thriving industry toward those in the wider market should not affect employment, there are other and still stronger reasons why such an equalizing tendency is good social policy. So long as an industry is in the real pioneering stage, prospective high rewards to its capital and labor are socially useful; but as the industry "matures," the equitable claim to higher-than-average gains is correspondingly weakened.

ment and total payrolls also rose farthest and fastest, in the industries of most moderate wage-rate increases.[18]

Aircraft and Automobile Cases.—These two industries, manufacturing new types of transportation equipment, provide us an unusually simplified "case study" on relations of wages and employment, though still too complex for confident interpretation. Costs, prices, and demands have operated to evoke rapidly increasing output and employment—most notably in automobiles—from the turn of the century to 1929. The following remarks refer to the years 1929-38, before influence of the European War became overwhelming. In 1929, when reasonably comparable data begin for both industries, the automobile industry had become very large, and thereafter there was no secular trend upward or downward in output and employment. In 1929 automobile employment and payrolls were only about 10%-12% higher than in 1923-25, and output (in number of cars and trucks) was about 50% higher.

Since 1925 the rise of production in the newer aircraft industry has been remarkably rapid and sustained. By 1929 employment and payrolls were both 400% above the 1923-25 mark; and by mid-1940 employment stood at some 2,300% above the same early '20's base.

The accompanying table gives further particulars as to wages and employment, 1929-38, for the two industries, bringing out the sharply contrasting advantages—of the automobile workers, as to hourly earned rates, and of aircraft workers, as to employment. (See opposite page.)

The striking differences between these records testify, first, to trade union power: the automobile workers were (in the period covered, especially by 1936) much the more strongly organized.[19] To most trade unionists it seems self-evident that

---

[18] The above calculation was made from Witt Bowden's series, "Employment, Hours, Earnings, and Production, Jan. 1933, to Jan. 1935," *Mo. Lab. Rev.,* March 1935. Waldo Fisher, after studying the BLS data for 71 manufacturing industries in 1933 and 1939, reached substantially similar conclusions—see his "Union Wage and Hour Policies and Employment," *Am. Econ. Rev.,* June 1940, pp. 290-99.

[19] The United Automobile Workers (CIO), to be sure, claims the mission of organizing the scattered aircraft and auto parts workers; but in

AIRCRAFT AND AUTOMOBILE WAGES AND EMPLOYMENT, 1929-38

(In index numbers, 1929 = 100)

YEAR	AIRCRAFT				AUTOMOBILES			
	Employ-ment	Total Man-hours	Pay-rolls	Average Hourly Earnings (cents)	Employ-ment	Total Man-hours	Pay-rolls	Average Hourly Earnings (cents)
	(1)	(2)	(3)	(4)	(5)	(6)	(7)	(8)
1929..	100	100	100	67.4	100	100	100	69.5
......	.....	.....	.....	.....	.....	.....	.....	.....
......	.....	.....	.....	.....	.....	.....	.....	.....
1932..	46.5	.....	46.7	.....	54.4	36.7	34.8	68.0
1933..	53.2	.....	47.1	.....	54.4	40.9	34.3	39.3
1934..	68.3	55.9	56.6	63.6	84.9	60.5	41.1	70.0
1935..	77.5	65.9	68.1	65.0	99.2	98.5	60.2	73.9
1936..	124.8	109.2	100.1	63.2	102.3	84.2	92.1	77.4
1937 .	173.1	152.2	163.1	66.6	115.3	88.7	111.2	89.1
1938..	164.5	137.2	198.8	72.8	67.4	47.4	34.7	92.5

Source: Computed from USBLS mimeographed "Revised index numbers of factory employ-ment and payrolls, 1923 to 1938" (Sept. 1938) and "Hours and Earnings in Manufacturing and Non-manufacturing Industries, 1932 to 1939" (Feb. 1940); and Bull. No. 523.

Cf. Ch. 3-C above, for data on *annual* earnings of automobile workers and some others.

aircraft wages should have risen as much as automobile—except to the extent that aircraft labor (especially during this industry's expansion after 1935) was "diluted" with green labor. But, on the other side, it may be urged: (1) although average hourly earnings in aircraft production advanced more slowly than in the automotive industry, still they increased more rapidly than did industrial wages in general; and (2) the more moderate rise in aircraft wage rates had the virtue (as far as it goes) of aiding, not handicapping, the other forces which were causing expansion of output and employment in this industry.

Another factor in these wage and employment records, of course, is the profits of employers, which appear in this period to have averaged distinctly lower (as percentage on net worth)

---

both these cases the union has been much less successful than in the Detroit area, whose labor market is led by the large motor-vehicle plants.

In 1940 the great war demand for airplanes assisted the union to organize aircraft workers and operated otherwise to raise their wages; but by early 1941 automobile wages were still sufficiently higher to produce many anomalies as to aircraft parts made in motor-vehicle plants.

for aircraft than for automobile production—yet high enough in both cases to provide substantial funds for expansion, as well as to attract new investment funds into airplane production. Superficially, at least, it appears that in this period the sharing of advantages, in the aircraft production industry, between capital, labor, and consumers was reasonable.

Wage Policy in a Declining Industry.—The foregoing hints must suffice with reference to wage rates in expanding industries, whatever the causes of such expansion. Let us now attend to the problems of languishing industries, and work through several types of cases. In later sections, some peculiarities of international and intersectional competition within industries will be considered; but in the present section we shall assume that there has been a relatively long period of declining employment in a nation-wide industry, relative to most others. This latter condition corresponds roughly to industry-wide "technological unemployment." In this situation it will appear that departures of wage rates from the general prevailing level should be made—on the downward side—but again that such deviations should be but moderate and temporary. This proposition will presently be applied to some important industries, but first it must be explained and supported in somewhat general terms. Let us notice some confusions of interpretation to be avoided, then how labor policies may interact with price and capital policies to assist the readjustments required by declining industries.

The phrase "declining industries" as used here does *not* refer: (1) to the weak firms which exist in any section of any industry, nor (2) to a year or more of adversity for most firms in the trade, which can be attributed to general depression or temporary causes. These latter two sorts of "adverse economic conditions" are not, as a rule, reasonable grounds for even moderate and temporary wage cuts;[20] but at present we are focusing attention on decline in employment which has gone

---

[20] Cf. Ch. 9, above, on weak firms, and Ch. 13, below, on wage reductions (a) in all industries, and (b) in the specially affected durable-goods industries, during a general business depression.

on for some years in a single industry, and threatens to continue.[21]

And again be it noted that the *wage rate* is only one of the elements of production costs which are more or less within control of labor. Some unions have cooperated with employers, not only to effect cost reductions by rationalizing antiquated union work rules—e.g., on wage methods—but even by inventing improved production and business methods (union-management cooperation). Hence, when we speak of change in wage rates or labor costs in this chapter, let us assume that costs appear to have been reduced as far as is (for the time being) practicable along these other lines.

Wages and Capital, in Declining Industries.—Many factors affecting use and cost of capital are wholly outside the field of labor bargaining, and even of labor politics; but numerous others will be considered in farsighted labor dealing. Two of these are the employer's incentive and his ability to compare returns to himself from expenditures for capital and for labor respectively.

If labor costs rise, relative to capital costs, and without simultaneous changes in technology and/or business methods of a capital-saving sort (such as adoption of multiple-shift plant operations), then the employer is given new incentive by this wage rise to "substitute capital for labor"—as economists say. One commonplace way of making such substitution is "mechanization"—modernization or new purchases of plant and equipment, to economize the labor factor, which has become dearer. By such means the employer whose labor costs are raised *may* feel able to avoid raising product prices, which would also court decreased volumes of sales and employment.

Various obstacles, however, may prevent the business man

---

[21] A case in most respects similar is "technological unemployment" of an *occupation,* such as Morse telegraph operators, rather than of a whole industry. Workers possessing semi-obsolete skill are much better off if their old employers are still prospering, than if the whole industry (or section of it) is drifting toward bankruptcy. Yet such craftsmen are more likely to be retained *in jobs which utilize their old skills,* if they effect reduction in cost of their production to their employers than if they cling to old wages and working practices.

from accomplishing such capital-for-labor substitution. Legal barriers, old or new, may thwart him; wages of capital-goods producers may advance, too, and mark up the price of further "mechanization." Still another difficulty is that a rise in labor cost, if it is not recouped from buyers of the product, may contribute toward impairment of the employer's working capital—particularly in a declining industry—so that, however badly he wants to "mechanize," he has neither the cash nor the credit therefor. Some labor and public leaders "laugh off" the "return to capital" issue in wage determinations by criticism of the existing capital structure—pointing out innumerable errors and excesses of the industry's capital suppliers and owners in the past, and recommending that the properties be put further "through the wringer"—that the fair-return-to-capital be written down by the simple process of marching further toward or through bankruptcy. For the older men whose jobs are most secure, this may be at least momentarily advantageous. But if any industry is even to *maintain* its present employment, it cannot rest on the oars of former capital investments—it must attract renewal, if not expansion of capital investment.

A few of the more progressive labor unions have shown remarkable vision and restraint, in this connection. Whereas the usual concern of labor, when any reduction in labor cost is conceded, is that all capital shall make at least equal sacrifices, I am told on good authority that unions have made the opposite stipulation: binding the hard-pressed employer *not* to pass on his cost reduction to his customers, but to use it to improve his financial position.[22]

The Case of Coal Mining.—Some concrete illustration and qualifications of the foregoing "theory" are afforded by even a superficial study of the wage problems of coal mining, especially since 1918. Expansion, under the direction of thousands of competitive mine owners after 1914 and until the '20's, caused an extremely unstable condition. The problem became aggravated by two major factors: (1) the development of

---

22 This policy, of course, could easily be pushed too far—in vain attempts at labor's expense to revive a hopelessly weak firm or industry.

alternative fuels was decreasing the proportionate amount of heat and energy supplied by coal;[23] and (2) the development of new techniques made possible more economical use of coal. The industry, over-expanded for even its maximum market, had to contend with a secular decline in demand. With that drop came a great reduction in the total value of production, a great drop in employment, and a drastic shrinkage in payrolls. The "Jacksonville" union scale of 1926, providing a minimum wage of $7.50 a day, represented the post-war attempt of the union to maintain, in the face of these factors of industrial decline, higher-than-wartime wage rates. Unfortunately for the miners, labor cost looms large among the total costs in their industry. This wage policy, therefore, helped to maintain a severe and chronic depression for the industry throughout this otherwise prosperous decade, as well as to increase the resort of coal operators and buyers to unorganized fields, non-union labor, machines, and substitute fuels. During the Great Depression of the early '30's, the industry perhaps suffered greater decline than industry in general; but the end of its deflation was not clearly in sight even by 1940. The union has continued strongly to resist lowering of wage rates and prices, partly by political actions, notably in the NRA and in the price fixing of the Bituminous Coal Commission. The NRA period saw phenomenal success in the unionization of the industry, but the problem of supporting a high wage and price structure is still most baffling.[24] Almost an economic miracle would be necessary to avoid the necessity of operating (except during a war boom) on a plane much below the former output and the present capacity of the industry.[25]

[23] This factor has applied also to anthracite mining, in which output is much more easily controlled, due to the smaller number and restricted area of the mines. Additional factors of great importance in European coal-mining troubles were the World War's upsets of export-import markets.

[24] As noted above, since 1934 unemployment has been spread by means of the seven-hour day, five-day week.

[25] Literature of coal mining and its wages is exceeding voluminous. A recent, well-informed, and rather conservative commentary is W. E. Fisher, *The Seven-Hour Day and Wage Changes in Coal* (Philadelphia: Univ. of Penna. Press, 1939).

Although the wage bill is an unusually high per cent of total cost in this industry, and so wage policy is particularly vital to employment, even a

These workers, like many others, demand high wage rates, in part on the score of the high rate of unemployment in their trade; and they have no little reason to distrust the efficacy of lowered wage rates actually to revive their employment. But a lowering of wage rates in such a case not only tends (however little) to check the decline by cheapening the product: it also tends to diminish (or to check the increase) of labor supply attached to such an industry. Falling wage rates convey a more effective warning away from a distressed industry, I suggest, than does the more rapid rise in rate of unemployment which is likely to occur if wage rates are not cut.

The Railway Industry.—During the last two decades, in Europe as well as America, this industry too has had many difficulties, as competing transport agencies have developed. Since the high peak of employment in 1920 total man-hours worked per annum on American railroads has been almost cut in half, yet over a million men are still attached to the industry. The financial distress of most of the companies is well known. This downward economic trend was masked or neutralized by the general business prosperity of the 1920's, but thereafter a succession of very lean years landed nearly one-third of the mileage in the hands of trustees or receivers.

It will be useful for us to examine some points of the wage history and policy thus involved. We must keep in mind, however, that the railway industry has many peculiarities which make its wage problems not fully comparable with those in other employments. One of these is its powerful labor organiza-

---

very cursory survey of domestic and foreign coal mining since 1918 shows that extreme wage cuts may not suffice to neutralize the other sources of the industry's distress. See, e.g., remarks on British mining wages, p. 191f., above.

The anthracite section of this union, according to Fisher, has not taken a wage cut since 1903. The geographical and economic concentration of this branch of coal mining, and the comparative inelasticity of demand for anthracite, have favored wage and price maintenance; yet one symptom of the industry's difficulty was rather widespread "bootlegging" of coal dug from old pits by unemployed miners. Because of imperfect competition among anthracite operators, it may be questionable if wage savings (if allowed by the union) would have been passed on to consumers; but apparently the miners' union did not wholeheartedly attempt a policy of thus catering to consumers.

tions. Another, is that we regard railroads at once as exceptionally vital necessities and as quasi-monopolies. Therefore, we regulate their rates and services, supervise their labor relations, and intervene in their finances—all by public authorities. But in this brief discussion let us center attention on wage problems which appear not only on railroads but also in industries less "affected with a public interest." Some of the relevant economic data were discussed earlier in this book.[26] A more comprehensive summary may be found in the Report, made to the President of the United States, of the Emergency Board which settled the nation-wide dispute of 1938, in which the employing carriers (who had voluntarily granted wage advances averaging 7% to 8% in the autumn of 1937) demanded a reduction in all wage rates of 15%.[27] It will be recalled that the boomlet of 1936-37, marked by the rise of aggressive unionism and of wage rates in many industries, turned swiftly into a deep recession in 1937-38, which recession was beginning to pass into the recovery of 1939 as the Board deliberated. The Board settled the dispute without any general change in wages.

Among arguments or factors of wider significance which were aired in this tribunal's inquiry were (1) (physical) "productivity of labor," (2) ability of the employers to pay, (3) alternative means of cost reduction, and (4) comparison of rail with other wages.

1. The employees advanced the "productivity" argument in somewhat more elaborate form than when they began appealing to it nearly thirty years earlier; but the Board of 1938 was not impressed.[28] Apparently no attempt was made to examine trends in output per man-hour on the railroads, by comparison with such trends in other industries. This would have been another way of showing the weakness of this index, as a criterion for wage adjustment.

---

[26] See Ch. 8-B, above, esp. reference to Bell's book.

[27] This tribunal (W. P. Stacy, chairman) was appointed Sept. 27, 1938 under Sec. 10 of the Railway Labor Act (see Ch. 18-A, below) in re A.T. & S.F. Ry. *et al.* Page references in following text are to the report of this Board, dated Oct. 29, 1938. (Washington, Gov't P't'g Off., 1938.)

[28] Emergency Board Report, *loc. cit.*, p. 42.

2. A vital factor, of course, is actual and prospective wage capacity, or finances of the employers. As was noted above, one factor which saved the day in 1938 for the railway wage earners was the recency of relative prosperity in 1936-37 and the faint economic recovery already stirring by September 1938. But the Board did not minimize the seriousness of the industry's financial position—indeed, it intimated that a wage cut might become necessary yet. On two (perhaps minor) points in this connection, however, the tribunal's reasoning may be questioned. First, as it inquired "whether railway employees as a group should be indirectly taxed to keep the roads running upon a specified level of equipment and service and upon a basis that will afford a moderate return on investment," [29] it might well have added that, while the employees would find it to their immediate interest to make capital already sunk go further "through the wringer," their future bread and butter depends in no small part on attracting *new capital* into the industry. Reliance on public funds (as the Board itself remarked) cannot go on forever. A second query is concerned with the respective capacities of strong and weak companies. On one hand, the Board approved past arbitral decisions which held that an exceptionally weak road may not be granted wage rates below standard, because of its relative financial incapacity; yet, on the other hand, it argued that a major weakness of the employers' 1938 case was that a wage cut would give to the more prosperous roads some financial improvement which they could do without. This last point seems in harmony with the abortive "Recapture Clause" of the Transportation Act of 1920; but so long as our railroad corporations are legally regarded as private properties, it is hard to see how their wage funds can be pooled, or that standard wage rates should be held not too high so long as they can be paid by the most prosperous carriers.

3. Under the head of union-management cooperation for improving railway finances, the celebrated "B. & O. Plan" was not mentioned, perhaps partly because so few railways have

---

[29] *Ibid.,* p. 46.

imitated it in detail. One very important outgrowth—and partial solution—of our railway wage problem of 1938, however, was the work of the national union-management Committee of Six, whose activities helped greatly to promote passage of a new Transportation Act (1940). This law promises to relieve the financial pressure on railways, in part by a new coordination of public regulations concerning the rails and competing means of transport. In the 1938 wage case, the unions of course declined to support employers' efforts to mitigate costs attributable to certain legal regulations, such as full-crew and train-limit laws. The Emergency Board, however, gave expression in a few words to common knowledge that such laws are, to some extent, political make-work devices of train-service unions.

Quite properly the Board commended the many evidences of cooperative spirit displayed by both sides. And it dropped the following hint:

> Consideration of savings in labor costs could also focus upon certain problems that should engage the attention of management and men more openly than has hitherto been the case. These flow from regulations prevalent in the operating service that call for pay not commensurate with the amount of additional benefit rendered. Some of these regulations have been relaxed or dropped, but a frank, candid inquiry as to their equitable nature could well be made the obligation of both management and men.[30]

Apparently reference is made to the great and long-growing body of working rules and practices, symbolized but by no means comprehended by the ICC statistical categories "time paid for but not worked," "miles paid for but not run," and "constructive allowances." Working rules and practices, which strike outsiders as excessively protecting the insider's job security and income, are but symptoms of the conservatism and traditionalism which characterize many other industries as well as railroads. They seem especially noticeable in older industries in which trade unions have long been powerful; but doubtless they are the resultant of interactions of long series of

---

[30] Emergency Board Report, *loc. cit.*, p. 56.

abuses, by no means all on one side. If the hands of the more progressive managers and labor leaders can be strengthened, rationalization of these old practices may be a promising source of cost reduction. At least, efforts to modernize them will tend to win sympathy from the consumers, taxpayers, and unemployed who have a stake in every industry.

4. Finally we come to the problem of most direct relevance to the present chapter—railway wages in relation to those in the most fairly comparable outside employments, and in relation to the current trend of employment in the railway industry. Our 1938 Board made a serious and able investigation of these matters (and had to do it within one month), reaching the conclusion that railroaders were not overpaid by comparison with men in other industries. I have not attempted the arduous task of independently assembling and weighing evidence on this point, but a few important considerations may be briefly noticed. My chart on p. 233, above, is crude, but it affords a certain limited support for the Board's presumption that rail wages were in proper relations to others in 1920.[31] It should be added that despite their exceptional economic and political power, our railway workers have acquiesced in several general wage reductions (or "deductions") since 1920—the latest (10%) in 1932-34. On the whole, however, they have followed the old union tradition of obtaining maximum wage *rates,* without worrying too much about where these rates are to come from—a policy most obviously advantageous to the

---

31 See also Bowden's article in *Mo. Lab. Rev.,* Sept. 1940. But the further back we try to push such comparisons, the less clearly are the data comparable within, as well as between, the industrial groups. Among the many other warnings which might be given as to statistical pitfalls for such inter-industry comparisons is this one: the all-manufacturing average hourly earnings figure in my chart was (by 1936) two or three cents lower than the Conference Board average for *males* in manufacturing (the railway average refers almost solely to men).

One is puzzled, moreover, in interpreting for this purpose the contrast between policies of rail and many other unions with reference to "work sharing." Some, at least, of the rail unions still tend to regard anything less than a six-day, 48-hour week as work sharing, to which they are strongly opposed. This policy has sustained the weekly and annual earnings of fully employed railway men at a level distinctly high in comparison with men obtaining similar hourly earnings in most other industrial employments. Cf. Ch. 3-C, above, for some added particulars on rail wages.

rather numerous men on whom seniority rules and operating requirements bestow unusual job security.

(a) Are railway wages in part responsible for the plight of the industry? (b) Should they be reduced? The foregoing discussion in this chapter shows that the answer to (b) is not prescribed in any simple fashion by the answer to (a). Let us suppose that the wage rates of the railway men were (in 1938) just about in line with those in the wider labor market, so far as factors like skill, hazards, and annual earnings are concerned. Then the case for wage reduction would be certainly weaker than if they had been paid above such an average; and, if the finances and long-term outlook for employment in their industry were up to par, there would be no good reason to consider a wage cut. But since these latter factors were much below par, it was reasonable to consider a temporary wage cut as a means of transition to the lower level of operation to which the industry seemed destined. Naturally, the men with the most secure jobs would be hurt, for the duration of the cut; but their own economic future (and still more, that of the junior and more irregular workers) would be better secured, if such a cut operated to restrain capital from being squeezed out of the industry and to make rail services and prices more attractive to consumers. It is true that the practical elasticity of demand for products is apt to be low in a declining industry (notably in a general depression); yet each industry must certainly beware of standing still while others are constantly giving customers more for their money.

Dismissal Compensation and Associated Practices.— These may partially solve problems of relative wages in growing and declining employments. Such compensation, as now voluntarily made in several hundred American companies, is defined as "payment of a specific sum, in addition to any back wages or salary, made by an employer to an employee for permanently terminating the employment relationship primarily for reasons beyond the control of the employee."[32] It is usually graduated

---

[32] E. D. Hawkins, *Dismissal Compensation, voluntary and compulsory plans used in the U. S. and abroad* (Princeton Univ. Press, 1940; 390 pp.).

according to length of work for the employer (say one week's pay for each year of service, up to ten years). Such a plan may cover separations on account of premature disability, and of course it must be coordinated with superannuation or normal pension provisions. But at the moment we are here concerned with dismissal pay as a cushion or insurance against technological and economic-change *unemployment.*[33]

When this device is widely used, it may (in effect) impound some of the high earnings during the rising phase of an industry, in trust funds which can be later drawn upon, when the industry is "permanently" contracting, for dismissal payments which will much facilitate transfer of the younger and middle-aged workers.[34]

Various difficulties and dangers, however, would remain. An industry with wages and prices above full competitive levels, for example, would be *assisted* to contract employment and output, and to raise wages and prices still higher, if it could squeeze workers out of the industry (and out of the union) by dismissal compensation. But of course any sort of unemployment insurance must be safeguarded against many possible abuses; and experience shows that adequate safeguards can be found when the dangers are realized.

C. Wages under International Competition

Our analysis of the general cases of rising and declining industries cannot take up each of the many factors affecting the health of individual industries. But there are two more great influences which operate so broadly and so powerfully that a few pages must be given to each of them. One is the

---

[33] The same objective is also sought, in some voluntary and compulsory schemes, by requiring a certain length of notice from the employer for these types of employee separations.

Doubtless such labor benefits will some time be made compulsory as part of our unemployment compensation systems. Meanwhile, employers feel handicapped because the unemployment compensation administrators tend to look upon dismissal allowances as prepaid wages or salaries, which make the recipient (for the time being) ineligible even to begin his waiting period for unemployment compensation.

[34] See Ch. 21-B, below, for a suggested application to national defense industries.

force of inter*national* competition, which has been in many
ways heightened during the last decade; the other is the inter-
regional shifting of industries within the nation, which renders
some areas flush and flourishing while forcing others to lean
more strongly upon the WPA. Generally, these geographic
"migrations" of industry involve some speeding-up of technological changes, and generally they mean a rising tide of
prosperity for some section(s) of one or more of our nation's
industries, while they spell decadence if not death to others.
We shall devote the remaining two sections of the chapter to
certain wage aspects of these two sorts of "industrial
migrations."

Are Our Wages Affected by Those of Foreigners?—
Since 1918, despite some backwashes, the nations more and
more have felt obliged to forego the bird in the bush—long-
run rewards of free trade—in favor of the immediate present
gains or stop-losses of nationalistic competition. Various
American industries have found themselves challenged in several ways. Home markets have been invaded by foreign producers, many of them producing at lower labor costs. Some of
our foreign markets dried up, as these nations reduced their
imports when the United States ceased its large-scale foreign
lending. Markets abroad were also diverted to other sources of
supply under the pressure of ever-widening exchange controls, and of clearing and compensation agreements between the
hard-hit South American, Balkan, and Central European countries. Each nation, like the old "mercantilist" regimes, strug-
gled to increase its exports, to avoid an "unfavorable" balance
of imports.

One important means available in some countries, for fur-
thering the sale of their wares, has been wage control. We
Americans have long been told by our orthodox economists
that cheap foreign wages mean no danger to us, because they
are but the result of low man-hour productivity abroad; but
we have always dreaded the competition of foreign "pauper
labor," and lately have found grave new reasons for this fear.
The impact of this competition is spread over a larger por-

tion of the American economy than first meets the eye. We have, to be sure, no large "unsheltered" industry, producing almost solely for export; yet a large proportion of our industries do some exporting, directly or indirectly. A loss of export markets, then, does not mean that several industries are wholly forced out of existence; it does mean that many producers are forced down to lower levels of output and wage capacity. Consider, for example, what our losses of export markets for wheat and cotton have meant to us; and how many readjustments become necessary when imports of—say—cheap shoes rise to the extent that our domestic production is seriously curtailed. Efforts to deal with such problems by political measures—such as import barriers or export bounties— may not suffice; then those who are menaced by new or increased foreign competition must face the question whether they shall accept wages and profits below our general level, in order to allow the price reductions which must be made if the customary domestic and foreign markets are to be preserved for American products. The McNary-Haugen principle of discriminatory prices for farm products, according as they are consumed at home or abroad, finds a sort of parallel in the contrast which has occupied many Europeans since 1920: wages higher in the "sheltered" industries (catering to domestic demands for commodities and services not economically importable in significant quantities) than in the "unsheltered" industries which are fully exposed to foreign competition.[35] This contrast threatens to grow in significance, especially if our quasi-"sheltered industries" develop more barriers to the free entrance of capital and labor which would expand them.

Contemporaneously with this intensification of foreign competition, and to minimize its disturbing effects on our own economy, the United States has lately pursued two programs designed to defend our exports and maintain or enlarge the total volume of our foreign trade. These are our exchange depreciation of 1933-34, and our reciprocal trade program, begun in 1934.

---

[35] Bowley, however, finds reason to doubt the validity of this generalization. See his *Wages and Income since 1860*, p. 16 (1937).

Exchange Depreciation as an Alternative to Wage Reductions.—Exchange depreciation has a temporary effect similar to that of wage reductions in all the exporting industries, so far as international competition is concerned. By cutting the gold content of our dollar we made dollars (for the time being) easier for foreigners to secure with their own currencies. With these cheaper dollars they could buy more from us just as readily as if the listed prices of all our goods had been reduced, with exchange rates held constant.[36]

Exchange depreciation by one nation, however, usually leads very soon to offsetting or retaliatory depreciation by other nations, as in the series of depreciations of 1931 and following years in which Great Britain, the United States, and France, successively played the leading rôle. It may be combated, too, by combinations of exchange control, exchange depreciation, and barter deals, such as those in which Germany has engaged. At best, exchange depreciation can only forestall the eventual competitive wage cutting and tariff raising which must appear everywhere that there is a battle for markets outside the walls of trade agreements.

Thus, wage cuts may take up the task which exchange depreciation can fulfill only transiently, of increasing exports in relation to imports. The great importance of securing or increasing a favorable balance arises in part from the stimulation this process gives to home employment, which usually seems offset only by a very minor shrinkage (or failure to gain) in the demand for home labor by importers. And this initial increase of employment may produce still further increases in total employment and in the national income through the action of "The Multiplier."[37]

---

[36] Germany after 1918, forbidden to engage in exchange depreciation, found it impossible to increase exports (to pay her war debts) unless wages were decreased at home. The necessary contraction of at least 40% in "gold-efficiency" wages was never accomplished, in part because of trade union power and an expensive program of social legislation.

[37] The multiplier principle, treated further in the next chapter, is a recent reformulation of the old common-sense notion that initial increases in employment tend to produce a series of further demands and outputs. Those individuals first given new work spend their earnings; those who receive the money from these purchases also spend; and so on until the

Another reason for the stimulation of exports is to secure the foreign funds which may be used to purchase essential raw materials abroad. The great push in German trade during the past eight years, for example, has been largely motivated by the desire or necessity to purchase war supplies. For such a purpose, wage reductions may be less expensive than exchange depreciation; the latter tends to raise the effective price of *all* foreign goods and to enable foreigners to carry off any and every sort of portable commodity, as from Germany during her great inflation.

What sort or sorts of protection do American workers need, under present conditions, against low-paid foreigners? As always, "it depends"—mainly on prospects as to future international relations. Other arguments for handicapping imports have declined in rational importance, but the rise of war dangers makes it more imperative than ever that we should (a) foster home production capacity of vital goods in which imports may be cut off by war, and (b) protect all our industries against ruin by imports of foreign-made goods, sold below long-term costs, under *temporary distress* conditions. Does this mean that all imports should be cut down to the vanishing point? It is hard to believe that the dangers of interruption of all foreign trade are so great as to make an affirmative answer correct. The greater our national self-sufficiency, the less we profit by the numerous specializations of trading nations, on production of goods in which each has comparative advantage (or least disadvantage). In any case our exporting industries, hard hit as they have been, will (as a group) be deflated still further, with corresponding downward pressure on wage rates, if we deliberately restrict imports further. Hence, the efforts of such exporters as the automotive manufacturers to combat extreme protectionism, within reasonable limits, are good for our collective living standards, as well as good business for such exporting trades and for the workers employed by them.

Another way of putting the same point: A lowering of

total increase in consumption and income is much greater than the amount paid out for the initial increase in employment.

either a nation's production cost or of the international value of its currency gives a stimulus to its exports, which might go far enough and last long enough to wreak havoc in the competing industries of customer countries. Hence, the latter nations are well advised to consider protective measures, such as retaliatory currency depreciation or wage reductions (to try to keep on exporting) and/or import restrictions (which, alone, tend to handicap *all affected nations'* exports). In this sense, low foreign wages threaten our own labor. If, on the other hand, the long-term outlook were for stable currency and trade relations, our currency and exports and imports would find levels which would tend to maximize our standard of living—no matter what money or real wages were paid by foreigners in producing the goods we imported. Whatever the foreign wages may be, our trade can adapt itself to them, to mutual advantage. It is the readjustment to any substantial *movement downward* of foreign real wages that our workers actually have to fear.

Wage Policy under Reciprocal Agreements.—This program involves two very difficult problems. The first one arises when the officials in the Department of State have to decide what actual changes should be made in duties and in import quotas. The second, which involves wage policy directly, arises when industries have to decide what to do after the agreements affecting them have been completed.

As for the first, no simple formula is defensible. Naturally care must be taken, as each pragmatic decision is made, that we do not precipitate a general depression at home by letting too many bars down at once. Such a result is possible, as we eagerly try to gain access to foreign markets for some of our products by agreeing, with inadequate safeguards, to invite other foreign goods into our markets to compete with our own. The minimum disturbances arise, so far as we export goods which foreigners do not produce, and import commodities that we do not produce. But there are many complications. Most of the imports of any nation are goods which are producible—at a price—at home, but can be obtained more cheaply by exporting other wares and services to pay for them—much as a modern farmer will often sell wheat to buy butter. The objective has been reformulated for practical reciprocal trade bargaining in terms of the "leading supplier" principle. This means that we secure new markets for those of our industries which furnish a large proportion of the total supply of their product on the world market. We arrange, by a mutual reduction of tariff duties, to permit a moderate, and practically a controlled, expansion of certain industries (which properly should be selected as having long-term comparative advantages for exporting) ; and, in turn, we agree that our home firms, in industries in which another nation excels, will gradually be subjected to new competition from foreign producers in our home market.

As for the second problem, whatever the mixture of factors which have developed the import-export trade of any industry, the livelihood of the people who are in that industry is bound to be an important political consideration; and the only real choice is between measures which try to keep an adversely affected industry indefinitely up to its old level, as compared with measures which are designed to be temporary and to ease the decline of the industry.

Barring government subsidies—which have their good uses but, more than the reciprocal trade program, tend to make matters increasingly worse by increasing world productive capacity—the only way to keep an adversely affected industry up to its former level is by "rationalization."[38] In this way the employers attempt to make themselves better able to compete in the international market—perhaps because political protection of their domestic market is insufficient to relieve their distress. Rationalization will make it possible to maintain wages and employment only if the improvements in technology at home are enough greater than foreign technological development to

---

[38] This is the term popularized in post-1918 European experience. It means modernization, especially in technology; and in practice it is often associated with cartellization and domestic competition-restraining organization. The British Cotton Spindles Board, for instance, whose main objective was to scrap redundant productive capacity of the most antiquated sort, illustrated all of these elements.

counterbalance any wage cuts which may be imposed on foreign labor in the industry.[39] The wholesale reductions in the wages of employees in our West coast pulp and shingle industries, following our trade agreement with Canada, foreshadow what may follow when increased efficiency does not solve the problem for an industry whose tariff protection is removed or reduced. Under such conditions union-management cooperation for other cost reduction may suffice to maintain employment without wage cutting; if not, labor faces the hard choice.

Trade agreements, however—or rather the international competition with which such treaties grapple—do not only force domestic industries to decline. They also give encouragement to some other home industries, and in two principal ways. This trade program, by securing wider markets for our "leading supplier" industries, encourages their expansion. And even the closing of foreign markets outside our trade agreements fosters some industrial growth at home—we turn, for example, to rayon and nylon, or to synthetic rubber, as a means of meeting the needs of the domestic market independently of the uncertainties of these unstable foreign supplies. Both these types of expanding home industries present the wage problems examined in the first part of the preceding section.

D. Interregional Movement of Industries

The fallacy of assuming that a single price or wage prevails for comparable labor throughout any large nation has often been demonstrated. Differences in the remuneration to a given level of skill and energy in different shops and places do indeed set up labor migrations tending to reduce such inequalities; but labor's information and ability to move are very imperfect. Moreover, shifts of labor demand are occurring with increasing frequency and degrees.

When some areas, otherwise about equally suitable, offer

---

[39] In England after 1918, e.g., rationalization was not very successful because many competing foreign manufacturers had too nearly equal, if not greater, technical efficiency and paid much lower wages. Hence, in spite of increasing efficiency, England was greatly handicapped by her resumption of the 1914 gold standard and her 1920 wage structure. Depreciation of the pound in 1931 afforded relief until other nations followed suit.

different scales of prevailing wages, that difference also becomes a factor in the location and relocation of industries. Labor does move, but only haltingly; and capital often moves more freely toward cheaper labor. In international competition, wherein both labor and capital are least mobile, wide sale of the product brings the market, in effect, to the immobile labor and capital.[40] Besides regional wage differences, of course, there are many other determinants of industrial location, such as the presence of unions, or certain kinds of unions, in one area and their absence from another, as well as suitable climate, transportation facilities, and nearness of markets.

There are some possibilities of preventing competing regions of one nation from undercutting each other in wages in order to secure increased employment. Thus, in the interests of securing minimum standards of subsistence, our Federal government has attempted to provide "a floor for wages"—which measure will be discussed in Chapters 17 and 20 below. We also hear much today of our interstate trade barriers. These are not defensible in the same terms as regulation of international trade; notably because domestic commerce is not endangered by wars to nearly the same degree that foreign commerce is so threatened.

Wage Policies to Mitigate Internal-Industry Migrations.
—Suggestions on this matter have already been given implicitly, in section B, above—on wages in rising and declining industries. There it was indicated that unduly rapid flow of capital from one area into another can be checked only if the developing area will quickly bring wages up to the nationally prevailing level for comparable work, while the declining area reduces wage rates to ease the pains of transition. In those cases of regional migration which are brought about by the existence of wage differentials, there is little reason to expect that the first part of the expansion in the newer section will be unduly cur-

---

40 "Movements of goods and of factors [of production] may be regarded as substitutes for one another; trade in goods reducing the stimulus to interregional transfer of the factors, and movements of the latter lowering the incentive to trade."—P. T. Ellsworth, *International Economics,* p. 124 (1938).

tailed by high wage rates. But as time goes on and labor organization develops in the "new" sector, this social problem may raise its head, in a form similar to that discussed above in connection with rising industries. At any rate, interregional migration of labor and of capital and management will tend to reduce the wage differentials which provoked such migrations.

For the area in which the industry's growth is slackening, or has turned into an actual decrease in employment, our argument for declining industries applies. It may be that wage rates in this older section have been run up above the general labor market, considering all relevant factors such as skill, speed of work, continuity of employment, and living costs. If so, the sooner these rates are brought down into line, the better. But the more common ailment, as suggested above, is more perplexing as to treatment when correctly diagnosed: the wages are not above—they may even be well below—wages elsewhere, but the demand for labor in this industry and location is becoming abnormally low. If so, old-time managers may try to cut wages as the first expedient. An opposing labor claim is perfectly reasonable: let us explore every other possibility before we resort to any general wage reduction. And actually we see organized employers and workers making common cause in fighting off competition from other industries and sections, by such means as political subsidies or loans for the group, handicaps for its competitors, advertising and labor-organizing campaigns, and perhaps by improved production and commercial methods. In such a stressful period the managements will do well to demand searching reconsideration of union working and employment rules, for some of these are apt to inflate production costs beyond the legitimate claims of labor (in the circumstances), and may prove boomerangs on the volume of employment.

If all this bag of other tricks proves insufficient—within the few months or years which can be afforded for trial—a general wage reduction may be accepted by or forced upon the workers. This cost reduction, if passed on to consumers as more of what they really want for their money, will probably assist in slowing down the local industry's decline. The labor objective then becomes the double one: (a) working for the earliest possible restoration of these wages to the all-industry market level; for which purpose (b) humane and far-sighted measures of public and private assistance (including dismissal compensation) for reducing the labor force attached to the industry in the losing area are greatly needed.

Such squeezing-out of "surplus" labor and plant may be attempted without cuts of prices, rates of property returns, or wages; but of course that procedure is apt to be more difficult. "Outsiders," moreover, should inquire from time to time whether the capital and labor in our declining industry have already become too successful in controlling numbers of employers and workers, and have thus raised rewards to themselves above wider market rates.

Hosiery and Clothing "Cases."—Among the many American trades which have been rent by North-South and urban-rural-area competition are the needle, clothing, and textile industries, whose northern sections have long had powerful labor organizations. These unions, in various ways, have sometimes beat strategic retreats in wage rates, intended of course to be temporary, pending their efforts to organize labor and raise wages in the newer sections. The hosiery workers, for instance, decided in the latter 1930's to ". . . accept a temporary reduction in wage rates and the hazard of technological unemployment for some of its members in order to enable northern hosiery manufacturers to install up-to-date machinery to compete with the more completely mechanized southern plants."[41] One of the

---

[41] Morris L. Cooke and Philip Murray, *Organized Labor and Production,* p. 170 (New York: 1940). Cf. *The Hosiery Worker,* June 24, 1938; H. Ober, *Trade-Union Policy and Technological Change,* p. 35 (WPA National Research Project, 1940). Notice that this wage retreat is part of a "rationalization" program of union-employers and union. The hosiery union has been unusually bold and prompt in using wage cuts as well as other means to restore unionized employers' costs within hailing distance of non-union (the latter are apt to be in another area—often hitherto in more southern and less densely populated regions). Not a few other unions have underestimated this danger until it was too late—for instance, the Philadelphia tapestry carpet weavers in the 1920's. Lately, both the men's and women's clothing unions have worked actively on "stabilization" plans, which in part are directed at lowering costs in the large northern cities, so that these industries should be under less pressure to migrate.

newer tendencies in trade unionism is to heed the protests of workers who have become unemployed at high wage rates.

"What the traffic will bear" without causing unemployment becomes very important in collective bargaining. There are not many situations where continuous gains to labor represent merely a diversion of excess profits and have no compelling effect upon the needed flow of capital into an industry or upon prices and the volume of goods purchased by consumers. Moreover, the very spread of membership in the labor movement has led to a growing recognition that the position of a relatively small number of skilled workers is less crucial to the national economy than the improvement of the real wages of labor generally.[42]

In other words, progressive unions are not content with putting the burden of proof on any one who says that too-high wage rates will limit employment opportunities for their members, nor do they administer their affairs primarily in the *immediate* interests of those members whose jobs are most secure.

The Cotton-Textile Migration.—The decline of cotton-textile manufacturing in New England and its concurrent rise in various southern states is an outstanding illustration of interregional migration of industry. Cheaper southern labor was one factor; others included the development of electric and steam power, and the nearness of the new locations to raw materials. A vivid picture of the problem with which the northern, more strongly unionized, workers in cotton manufacturing have had to contend is presented in Chart 8.[43]

This chart shows three indexes of the decline of the northern section—total spindles, active spindles, and total man-hours worked. The average hourly earnings curve reflects the downward pressure on northern wage rates until NRA wages began to handicap the South in 1933; and the following table shows

---

[42] Cooke and Murray, *op. cit.*, p. 191.

[43] This chart is an adaptation of that on p. 21 of A. F. Hinrichs, *Wages in Cotton-Goods Manufacturing* (USBLS Bull. 663, 1938), which shows only the spindle data. I have added the two curves of indexes of average hourly earnings and total man-hours worked, in *northern* cotton mills, as reported by the Conference Board (to 1936, in *Wages, Hours, and Employment in the U. S., 1914-36*, pp. 72-75).

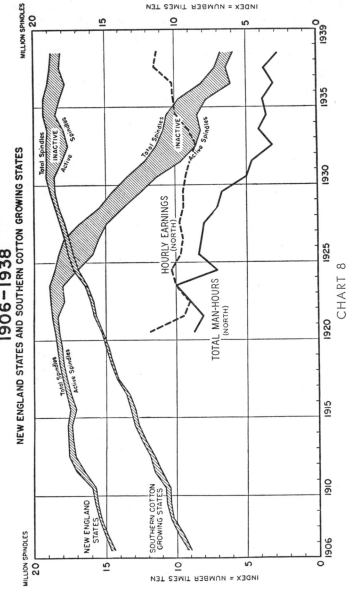

TOTAL, ACTIVE AND INACTIVE COTTON SPINDLES
1906–1938
NEW ENGLAND STATES AND SOUTHERN COTTON GROWING STATES

CHART 8

Source: Adapted from U. S. Bureau of Labor Statistics, Bull. 663, p. 21, by addition of indexes of annual averages of hourly earnings and man-hours worked (1923 = 100) from "Cotton Manufacturing, North" reports of National Industrial Conference Board.

relative trends of northern and southern average hourly earnings:

COMPARISON OF AVERAGE HOURLY EARNINGS IN NORTHERN AND
SOUTHERN COTTON-TEXTILE MILLS, 1928 TO JULY 1937

Period	Unweighted Averages			Weighted Averages
	North (cents)	South (cents)	Per Cent: South of North	Per Cent: South of North
1928.	39.4	27.3	69.3	69.6
1930.	39.7	28.1	70.8	71.9
1932.	32.3	23.9	74.0	79.5
July 1933.	27.6	20.5	74.3	72.2
August 1933.	41.1	33.7	82.0	86.3
August 1934.	42.2	35.6	84.4	85.5
1935.	42.2	34.8	82.5	Not available
July 1936.	41.8	34.6	82.8	" "
July 1937.	50.0	39.7	79.4	" "

Source: N. A. Tolles, "Regional Differences in Cotton-Textile Wages, 1928 to 1937,"
Mo. Lab. Rev., Jan. 1938, pp. 36-47. See Chart 13, below, for other North-South wage comparisons in cotton manufacture.

This table and chart show that the rise of southern, relatively to northern, wages, arrested the migratory movement somewhat after 1932—indeed, many of the northern supporters of the NRA "planned it that way," as they tended later to prescribe other wage-hour legislation and unionization for their southern competitors. Our table also supplies a fragment of the statistical basis for the generalization made earlier in this chapter: that "migration of industry," so far as it is promoted by regional wage differences, itself tends to neutralize those differences. Southern wages, as per cent of northern, rose from 69.3 in 1928 (when this comparison begins—the differential may have been greater before 1928) to 74.3 in July 1933, just before the NRA raised this percentage to 82.0. And by July 1937, after the NRA's effects had worn thin and before the 1938 wage-hour legislation was seriously expected, this percentage was 79.4—markedly higher than in 1928. This rise in the ratio of southern to northern wages was due in part, no doubt, to growing labor organization in the south; on the other hand, the increasing competition of southern employers for labor was and is a most powerful aid to labor organizers. As the regional wage differential narrows, of course, the pressure lessens for regional migration of any industry.[44]

E. Summary

This chapter has continued the consideration of unemployment as a wage factor and of wages as a factor in causation of unemployment. We have observed that the three categories into which unemployment is often theoretically classified—seasonal, technological, and cyclical—are helpful only within limits; for several other variables of large import are interwoven with them. "Cyclical unemployment," for example, is attributable to a large extent to technical changes; and technological changes (in turn) affect employment in conjunction with other economic developments, notably in locations of materials and markets and in the technologies incident to transportation. We have lately been jolted, too, into realization of the profound consequences of political forces. The latter include international relations; also group politics within nations, whereby various labor, farmer, business, and other interests influence the economic relations among our domestic trades and regions. Here we broach the great phenomenon of migrations of labor and of industries, for instance between northern and southern states. Both international and domestic stresses, as we have seen, profoundly affect and are affected by comparative wages, and all —of course—are complicated by discoveries in natural resources and in technology and marketing.

A great problem which reappears in countless places, times, and forms, is the struggle of older groups of producers to resist encroachments on "their" markets and jobs by rival in-

---

44 I have not investigated, however, the rôle played by the cotton manufacturing unions in these events. At least one cotton union (in the Naumkeag Company's Pequot Mills, Salem, Mass.) attempted, in 1929 and some following years, to safeguard their own long-term employment opportunities by a rationalization program which included drastic increases in work loads. The immediate effect of this program was to *decrease* employment.— See R. C. Nyman, *Union-Management Cooperation in the "Stretch Out"* (Yale University Press, 1934), and Ch. 16-C, below.

dustries. In the foregoing discussion we have used "industry" in the usual sense of a common product or material, such as "cotton textiles" (yarn and cloth) or "hosiery" (full-fashioned and seamless branches). But "industrialization" also has another significance—referring to the urban types of employment, by contrast with agricultural. An outstanding series of inter-regional conflicts has occurred and persisted, between nations and within nations, as agricultural and other materials-producing regions—generally characterized by higher birth rates and often also by lower average real incomes—have aspired to industrialize themselves (or as "foreign capital" has aspired to industrialize them).

It is to be expected that workers will find many ways of collaborating with their employers to improve or protect the markets for their products, as well as to meet competition from the other end—by lowering production costs. Neither political protection nor wage cutting below the wider labor-market level are to be commended, from the standpoint of public policy, except as temporary expedients—not as permanent shelters for an industry or section which is socially uneconomical as to labor, management, or location with reference to materials or markets.[45] Thus, when other expedients are inadequate for the moment to put the industry onto an economic basis, political subsidies or other protection and wage cutting of limited duration should be considered as means of easing the descent of a stranded industry and population.

On the more cheerful side of the picture—the growing industries—we need also to distinguish temporary from longer-term policies. Liberal wage rates and profits are generally equitable and necessary in the earlier days, and some applications of profit-sharing or wage-dividend philosophy may indefinitely be in the public interest. But it is clearly advantageous to the whole body of consumers (who are also obliged to sustain the burden of total unemployment) that competitive costs,

---

[45] Some industries, no doubt, may well be subsidized indefinitely as quasi-public services of education, health, defense, or what-not. In such cases, of course, prevailing wages should be paid and other tests of efficiency should be devised and applied.

prices, and profits should prevail within expanding industries as soon as they have become firmly rooted. This objective spells wage rates not necessarily as high as the particular industry's current capacity to pay at existing prices of its products; and it also means that representatives of the consuming public interest should continually work for free entry of capital as well as labor, and for price reductions, within all such fields. Among other arguments in favor of such policies is their remedial effect with reference to total unemployment.

CHAPTER 13

PURCHASING POWER, PRICES, AND CYCLICAL EMPLOYMENT

As was indicated at the beginning of the previous chapter, discussions of causation among wages, prices, purchasing power, and employment are apt to invoke various theories of business cycles other than those whose main emphasis is on differential rates of expansion and contraction of particular industries. As was also suggested above, we need to consider these interrelations with reference to long industrial trends, as well as to the more or less cyclical surges of business waves, above and below such trends.

In this chapter we shall sketch briefly the implications of some relatively staple and simple points of business-cycle theory, with special reference to people's behavior as private individuals and through their voluntary associations, which appear important for understanding the cause-and-effect connections of wages and cyclical employment. The two outstanding functions of wages—(1) incomes and (2) costs—are reviewed successively, in sections A and B, in relation to business fluctuations. Subsidiary topics include some further reflections on elasticity of demand for labor, as well as renewal of the query, What kinds and degrees, if any, of wage plasticity or flexibility are socially desirable? Some bits of statistical evidence will be considered.[1]

A. Wages as Incomes, and Cyclical Employment

Wages as Cart; as Horse.—Whenever unemployment becomes an increasingly serious world-wide problem—as in the depressions of 1920 and 1929—public interest tends to flare up

---

[1] In Part V, below, some hints will be developed as to governmental policies designed to mitigate booms and depressions.

with reference to connections between wage rates and unemployment. The theories most widely considered are naturally expressed in simple terms, for mass-consumption; but behind these over-simplifications lie abstruse and technical arguments, supporting more or less opposing practical conclusions. Among the more popular notions with which we are here concerned are these:

1. Competitive real wage rates are determined by the marginal productivity of labor.

2. If wage rates are raised without compensating increases in labor efficiency, the volume of employment will fall; if the wage rate per efficiency unit is lowered, employment will rise.

3. A long step may be taken toward re-employment of labor and general recovery from depression by a general rise in wage rates—which increases labor's purchasing power.

We have already noticed that proposition 2 is not necessarily true with reference to *general* wage changes, though it is subject to but few exceptions when *other wages and prices remain constant*.[2] Proposition 3—which owes not a little of its popularity to its ambiguity (raising wage *rates*, if it results in a sufficient decrease in employment, will obviously *lower* the total purchasing power of wage earners)—is not adequately refuted, of course, by fallacious applications of No. 2. Anyhow it will be instructive to review very briefly a few of the pre-1929 popular doctrines which were similar in effect to this No. 3. Into this class fall numerous representations—for example, those of Robert Owen, early in the nineteenth century, and of the German economist Lujo Brentano, from about 1875 onward—to the effect that shorter hours and higher wages tend to be advantageous to employers and consumers, as well as to workers—because the latter are more productive in short-hour and high wage regimes. This "steam-engine" wage argument[3] has suffered diminishing returns as a basis for ever higher

---

[2] See esp. Ch. 5, above.
[3] Cf. Ch. 20, below.

standards of wages and hours; but other varieties of high wage theories have emerged in its train.

One of the latter, often expounded by Henry Ford, also asserts that the orthodox wage doctrines put the cart before the horse. According to these dissenters, too, wages should be regarded, not only as the *result* of labor's productivity, but as a *condition* of such productivity. Obviously, the employer cannot operate his plant satisfactorily unless there exists a market for his goods; and such markets depend greatly upon the incomes of workmen. The more prosperous these workmen become, through receipt of higher wages, the greater is the volume of sales by employers and the better will their businesses thrive.[4] Mr. Ford, of course, expects high efficiency of his men; but he has emphasized the purchasing-power aspect of wages in many utterances like the following:

> I believe . . . our own sales depend in a measure upon the wages we pay. If we can distribute high wages, then that money is going to be spent and will serve to make storekeepers and distributors and manufacturers and workers in other lines more prosperous and their prosperity will be reflected in our sales. Country-wide high wages spell country-wide prosperity.[5]

Some Merits and Limitations of Purchasing-Power Wage Theories.—The idea that employment and general prosperity can be increased by raising wage rates, becomes less paradoxical and preposterous as we explore its more sensible interpretations. Assuming conditions of complete competition and full employment, for example, if the workers are ill-nourished and/or chronically over-fatigued, their efficiency may be increased by higher real wages—in the course of time—and in such a case wage raising by even a single employer would become profitable for him. But purchasing-power wage theories

---

[4] Another ambiguity should be noticed. The "higher wages" and "greater volume of sales" here referred to might be largely inflationary—higher *money* wages associated with, and perhaps causing, higher living costs.

[5] Ford and Crowther, *My Life and Work,* pp. 124-125 (1922). Cf. P. H. Douglas, "The Modern Technique of Mass Production and Its Relation To Wages," *Proceedings of Academy of Political Science,* vol. 12 (New York, 1927), p. 34. This article gives the quotation from Ford cited above, and others of the same tenor.

now usually assume a great mass of unemployed labor, and generally do not claim that it is practical for a few small employers alone to help themselves or the general employment situation by wage-rate increases. The argument is rather that, if a *general* rise in wage rates can be brought about, this change will increase employment and prosperity by raising consumer purchasing power. Obviously, if Ford workers alone have their total wages raised, they will spend this increase for many objects, whose vendors in turn will use their new purchasing power to save and to buy many types of goods; so that only a fraction of his additional wages would (under these conditions) return to Mr. Ford via new purchases of Ford cars.

These views had obtained so much currency in America by 1929 that a concerted and sustained attempt was made by business leaders and President Hoover to maintain wage rates, despite the catastrophic drop in employment.[6] References to the charts in this book will show that average hourly rates and earnings, in manufacturing and several other principal industries, were largely sustained for a couple of years after 1929, in sharp contrast with the prompt and radical cuts of 1921.[7]

---

[6] As of December 1, 1929, the Ford Motor Company *raised* its minimum wage from $6 to $7 a day. It remained at that figure until October 1931, when it was reduced to $6. On the first of October 1932, this minimum was more drastically cut, to $4; in March, 1934, it was raised to $5, and in May 1935 to $6—where it remained, early in 1940. (Data obtained by correspondence with the company.)

[7] The USBLS primary monthly data on hourly earnings and average hours worked by industries do not yet go back to years before 1929, but the Conference Board's data on average hourly earnings of all wage earners in 25 manufacturing industries, for this period, include the following: 1920 (June-Dec.), 60.6¢; 1921, 52.4¢; 1922 (July-Dec.), 49.4¢. The Board's monthly series, which began with June 1920, shows the peak of 61.1¢ in September and October 1920, and a decline each month thereafter until 48.6¢ was reached in December 1921. Here appears a gap of six months in the series, during which earnings in the sample plants probably reached their low point; for when reports were resumed as of July 1922, the overall average for all wage earners was 47.8¢. Thereafter, earnings rose, to reach 56¢ by September, 1923, at which approximate level they remained for about three years before rising further.

Rough calculations show that total payrolls fell by about the same percentages, in 1921 and 1930; hence, that the immediate effect of the wage cuts of 1921 was no more favorable to aggregate labor incomes than the wage maintenance of 1930.

In 1921, and still more in 1930 and 1938, wage rates tended to continue rising in the organized trades (such as railways, printing, building), mainly

Neither this sustaining of wage rates, of course, nor the sharp wage cuts which followed in 1932 and 1933, brought visible results in industrial recovery; and many other maladjustments could plausibly be blamed for the deepening and persisting world depression.

With the rapidly rising political power of labor and socialist factions, particularly in the United States, France and New Zealand, after 1931, it was inevitable that further efforts should be made to promote industrial recovery by increasing the purchasing power of wage earners. Far-reaching reductions were made of weekly working hours, usually without reduction of weekly wages, and in many other ways upward political pressure was applied to hourly wage rates. The NRA-PRA, in 1933, accelerated sharply the upward movement in wage rates, production, and employment (which had already begun, abroad), as Americans quickly became confident that labor costs, purchasing power, and prices soon would make widespread and rapid advances.

Spirals of Wages and Prices.—This revival of 1933-37, and the recession of 1937-38, illustrate some further significant interactions between money wages, prices, and profits. From superficial analyses of these relations, flatly contradictory recommendations have emerged. At one extreme is the argument that any increase in wages sets up a spiral of inflation, so that wage earners are said never to benefit from increase of money wages. This latter conclusion has been drawn, not only by a few employers' advocates, but even by Karl Marx's comrade Weston in the "First International."[8]

The opposite emphasis, on the baleful effects of a *downward* spiral, was attributed (for example) to John L. Lewis, in the following utterance:

All we need now in this country to encompass and insure a complete and most devastating economic, social and political *debacle* is to reduce

because the unions had initiated demands during the preceding phase of prosperity. The increasing sphere of governmental agencies in wage determination, discussed in following chapters, also makes for greater inertia in wage rates and proceedings.

[8] According to Marx's *Value, Price, and Profit,* Chs. 1 and 2.

the prices of commodities and reduce the wage structure of this country.

I hope that those in this country who are charged with the responsibility of leadership, both in the industrial field and in the financial world and in the area of statecraft, will not permit themselves to be lured to follow this economic will-of-the-wisp price slashing and wage reduction."[9]

An intermediate type of argument, extremely common in labor circles, was examined in Chapter 7, above. Here the claim is that a given advance (or fall) in wages to a particular group —say 10%—will, even under full competition, result in only a much less than proportional change in the price of the product to the consumer, because the labor cost is only a part (perhaps a small part) of the total cost of production. As we have seen, this intermediate argument is most fully valid only if the wage change in question can be localized and kept from spreading to other working groups. Undoubtedly, many wage changes do stimulate demands for similar wage revisions elsewhere.

Although these spirals of wages and prices must receive grave consideration in all collective wage determination—and the more attention, the larger the group of workers whose wages are likely to be affected—it is easily shown that such spirals do not continue either upward or downward indefinitely. Historically, money wages (in all senses—hourly rates and earnings, average annual earnings, and total payrolls) have increased much further than costs of living and other prices; hence, it is clearly fallacious to argue that advances in wage rates never do the workers any good. On the other hand, few realistic persons will maintain seriously that no wage rate should ever be reduced.

Monetary Flows of Purchasing Power.—The attempt to evaluate wage arguments emphasizing labor incomes is assisted, I believe, by attention to a sort of schizophrenia or split personality which has afflicted economic science for several generations. I refer now to the opposing tendencies to carry through economic analysis with very little or very much emphasis upon

---

[9] *The New York Times,* Jan. 26, 1938.

pecuniary phenomena. In general, the English classical school of Ricardo, Mill, Marshall, and Pigou, as well as prominent Austrian economists, conducted their discussions of general economic principles largely in "natural" terms, of the two general varieties: (1) physical or technical quantities (such as number of workers or of man-hours, pounds or yards of commodities and acres of land) and (2) mental states (utilities and disutilities of various sorts). They were bent on expounding the great economic truths in these terms, including the master truth that we are all fundamentally bartering services with one another, and striving to use all resources to maximize our satisfactions.

From time to time, however, not a few economists have challenged this emphasis, and have argued vigorously for economic principles stated more largely in terms of monetary stocks and flows. They have thus devoted themselves more heartily than has been the orthodox bent to social bookkeeping, tracing relations among the innumerable prices and payments, incomes, expenditures, and capitalizations. Such was the bent of the physiocrats. Among modern representatives of this monetary preoccupation are Foster, Catchings, and various disciples of J. M. Keynes.

Such writers have often adopted (rather illogically, in this connection) the classical "static" or "equilibrium" assumption that the aggregate of selling prices of the commodities and services produced in any period is equal to the aggregate of entrepreneurs' costs—thus assuming also the consummated tendency of complete competition throughout the economic system, and counting under costs the necessary rates of profit on all capital (including land), as well as normal remuneration of the personal services of all active proprietors. These somewhat heterodox theories further argue that recurrently the money incomes distributed to wage earners become inadequate for such people to buy all the goods suitable for wage earners' consumption currently produced, at prices which cover costs, as defined above; and that the growing mass of profits during a boom results in "over-investment," in relation to the rational outlook for consumers' goods, wants, and incomes.

Say's Law Applied to Unemployment Causation.—Thus a proposition often stressed in "under-consumption" types of business-cycle theories is that a primary force tending to end prosperity and to bring on depression is deficiency in wage purchasing power—that too much of the total national income during a boom goes to profits, too little to wages—hence, there develops a general glut of consumers' goods. Orthodox replies to these theories often follow lines laid down by the "Law of Markets" of the French economist, J. B. Say, near the beginning of the nineteenth century. Say's Law, or the substance of it, is also frequently invoked to demonstrate the fallacy of the idea that technical progress necessarily leads to an accumulating and permanent mass of technological unemployment.[10]

Applied to the argument that depressions tend to be initiated by disparities between wage and other incomes, the reasoning behind Say's Law shows that, if all incomes are being spent with only normal time lags, and if there is full employment at the outset, the total dollar-volume of sales will not necessarily be altered by any change in wage rates, or by redistribution of total national income as between wage earners and other groups. For if, after such a change, the wage earners have less to spend, other people have correspondingly more to spend. To the extent that wage decreases are passed on by employers to consumers by way of lower prices, real wages are cut less than money wages, if at all. But even if prices are unaffected by a rise or fall in money wages, the other income receivers may readjust their purchases to compensate for the changes thus imposed on the spending of wage earners. Labor and plant can be diverted from producing wage earner consumer goods, and devoted to producing consumer and/or producer goods for "capitalists."

This application of Say's Law points to important funda-

---

[10] See, e.g., P. H. Douglas and A. Director, *The Problem of Unemployment*, Ch. 10 (1931) (and Douglas' article in the AFL's *Federationist*, August 1930); also criticisms by A. H. Hansen in *Quar. Jour. of Econ.*, Aug. 1931, pp. 684-697, reprinted in his *Economic Stabilization in an Unbalanced World*. These points are briefly restated by Douglas in his *Controlling Depressions*, pp. 37-41 (1935).

mentals of the case, but of course it is a highly simplified and unrealistic model. One sort of complication is practical impairments of competition among laborers and among employers, in part by way of ignorance and imperfect mobility—these are obstacles in the way of prompt readjustments to any departure from existing economic relations. Hence, the Say's Law analysis is more useful as a statement of long-run "static" tendency, dependent on a high degree of competition and fluidity in the economic system, than as part of the "dynamic" science of business cycles. In the short term (of a year to a decade), an appreciable change in any person's real income is likely to affect his use of money income—as to how much he saves and (perhaps) invests, and how he readjusts his current consumption expenditures. To this latter theme we must now give some attention.

The Acceleration Principle.—It is convenient first, however, to take account of certain more or less technical relations between the consumers' and producers' goods industries. As is now widely realized, cyclical unemployment is heavily concentrated in the construction and other producers' or capital-goods trades; and competent students agree that the causes of this concentration are clarified by "the acceleration principle." This principle may be briefly stated thus: comparatively small changes in output of consumers' goods tend to bring about much greater *relative* changes in output of producers' goods.

The following highly simplified arithmetical example will illustrate the point. Let us suppose that, in a normal year, the value of the total output of a given non-durable consumers' good (such as school supplies) is $10 million, and that this output is just the capacity of productive equipment valued at $10 million. Suppose also that this "plant" has an average lifetime of ten years and that we may disregard repairs to it. Then, so long as the annual output remains at $10 million, and prices and technology remain constant, there will be an annual demand for equipment worth $1 million, to replace that which is worn out. If, on the other hand, the demand for the consumable good rises sufficiently so that its output must be increased by 10%

(to $11 million), then (if the higher rate of consumption is believed to be "permanent") the output of equipment for this industry must be stepped up much more than proportionately. There must now be produced at once, besides the normal $1 million worth (for replacement of worn-out plant) *another* $1 million worth of equipment—i.e., enough to produce the extra $1 million worth of the consumable good. Thus, under these conditions, an increase of 10% in output of the consumers' good tends to call out a temporary increase of 100% in the output of the corresponding producers' goods. Now suppose that in the third year the expected annual sales of the product have increased to $11.5 million—sales are still growing, but at a diminishing rate. Then the total value of new equipment required to be installed this third year amounts to not over $1.6 million ($1.1 million replacement, and $0.5 million to provide the expansion of $0.5 million in output of the consumers' good. But this means a marked decline from the preceding year in the equipment industry—from $2 million to $1.6 million, or 20% decrease.

When this sketch is retouched into a more lifelike picture, the essential fact remains that annual outputs of durable capital goods vary much more from year to year than do the outputs of non-durable consumer goods; and so this acceleration principle evidently accounts in part for the concentration of cyclical unemployment in the former industries.[11]

It must also be observed that demands for *durable consumers' goods* also fluctuate greatly, for reasons somewhat

---

[11] It should be noticed that such acceleration (and deceleration) of employment and unemployment is not characteristic of *capital* goods production, in response to changing outputs of consumers' goods, in all circumstances. If, for example, the productive equipment is durable, and if the rate of change of demand for the consumers' goods were constant, either upward or downward—then the rate of supply and of upkeep of the producers' goods would adapt itself to such constant and one-directional variation, and would become so stable and calculable that no unusual unemployment would characterize that particular producer-good industry. If, on the other hand, the equipment of buildings, machinery, etc., were non-durable—if they wore out and had to be replaced at the same rate as the consumable product—in that case changes in the demand for the consumers' good would be reflected in *proportional, not magnified,* changes of demand for the productive apparatus. Hence, the greater the durability of the latter, the greater is the magnification of changes in its demand.

similar to those just discussed in connection with durable producers' goods. Dwellings, automobiles and mechanical refrigerators are examples of such goods; their production and merchandising show fits and starts through cycles of years
somewhat like the construction and equipping of factories and
transportation enterprises, and other types of "plant."[12] All
durable goods, too, have the common characteristic that they
may be used for long periods, even when more or less obsolete,
if the users want to conserve liquid resources to an unusual
extent. And not only is the rate of purchase of new durable
consumers' goods unsteady over the years; the peaks and
troughs of demand for these tend to accentuate the booms and
slumps in producer-goods industries, for the simple reason that
when employment and payrolls rise in the latter, great numbers
of consumer incomes are favorably affected, and many people
then feel able to gratify their pent-up wants for new cars and
new houses, as well as for new clothing.[13]

Employment Multipliers.—Another business-cycle principle which overlaps that of acceleration is the "employment
multiplier," greatly emphasized by the adherents of John May-
nard Keynes. This multiplier doctrine—which also puts emphasis on wages as income or purchasing power of laborers—is most
commonly applied to new "investment," in the sense of construction of private capital goods or of public works or both.
In these discussions it is usual, moreover, to assume depression
conditions, involving reserves of unemployed labor, and hence
less than the optimum rate of production and use of consumers'
goods.

The multiplying process here referred to is the widening
ripples of new employment which tend to result from any
initial increase in employment. The increased incomes which

---

[12] Public works, such as roads and parks, and religious and philanthropic
construction and equipment, are other durable collective consumers' goods,
so far as they are not directly revenue-producing.

[13] Professor Slichter has well remarked that the variable rates at which
so many consumers' goods can be purchased—services like haircuts, cleaning and laundering, and house painting, in addition to more or less durable
commodities—is a great factor in elasticity of demand for labor.—*Am.
Econ. Rev.*, March 1939 Supplement, p. 126.

PRODUCTION EMPLOYMENT PAYROLLS AND EARNINGS

IN AMERICAN MANUFACTURING

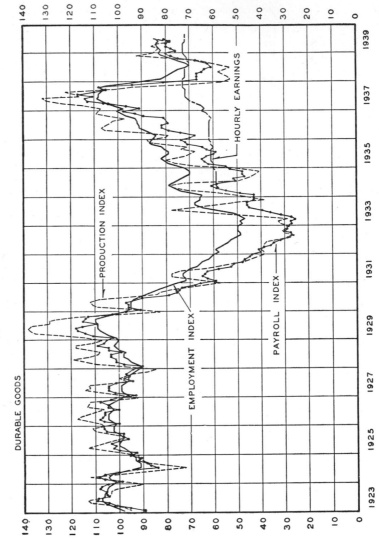

DURABLE GOODS

PRODUCTION INDEX

EMPLOYMENT INDEX

PAYROLL INDEX

HOURLY EARNINGS

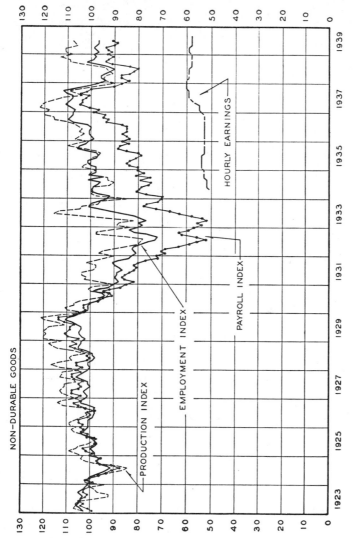

CHART 9

Sources: Various issues of Survey of Current Business, 1938 and 1939 (including 1938 supplement). Production indexes are those of Federal Reserve Board before the 1940 revision, and are not adjusted for seasonal variation. The other indexes, and averages of wage earnings (in cents per hour), are those of U. S. Bureau of Labor Statistics. Base of indexes: 1923-25.

the hitherto-unemployed workers receive—e.g., when they are hired to make new capital equipment or other durable goods—tend to be spent by those workers immediately on consumption goods, thus increasing the rate of such consumption. This increase of consumption, in turn, tends to create additional employment for producing the consumers' goods—and in widening circles, as each industry's new orders enable and induce it to give fresh orders to its own suppliers. Carried a step further, this reasoning leads to the theory of "pump priming." The literal suggestion conveyed by this latter metaphor is that after such impetus to employment is provided by a public works program, the pump of private industry will require no further priming but will continue to operate. The employment multiplier idea is involved, too, in upward and downward spirals; but the latter concepts suggest rising and falling wage rates and prices as well.

Employment on Durable vs. Non-Durable Goods.—We have seen that, if many of the potential buyers of durable goods become unusually frugal and make their old goods do for a longer time than normal, the producers of such goods will fall upon evil days and unemployment will develop. Chart 9 brings out statistically and historically the great contrast between durable and non-durable manufacturers, as to volume of employment and rates of physical output.[14] (See pages 346 and 347.)

Any study, moreover, of long-term charts relating to building construction, mining, railway carloadings, and other physical "business barometers" shows that such types of business, which produce (or are ancillary to the production of) durable goods show spasms or cycles of activity and depression more or less similar in amplitude and in timing to the *manufactures* of durable goods represented in this chart. Reference to Chart

---

14 The curve labeled "Employment," of course, refers to numbers of persons on payrolls about the middle of the month in question. The more fluctuating curves of "payrolls" (equals total wage payments of employers), read in relation to the curves of "average hourly earnings," imply the full impact of unemployment and underemployment on the durable-goods industries in terms of total man-hours. (See Ch. 11-A, above.)

1 in Chapter 3, above, will give a partial demonstration of this point. There it is shown, for example, that average hours worked per week fluctuate much more widely in bituminous coal mining (in part by reason of its large dependence on durable-goods industries) than do hours in wholesale or retail trade.

Some Interrelations of Acceleration and Multiplier Principles.—These two generalizations are important instruments for attacking problems of cyclical unemployment and wages; yet a few cautions should immediately be suggested. The acceleration principle, in its simplest terms, suggests continuous full utilization of productive capacity—though a moment's reflection will recall that, as the rate of consumption actually declines, under-utilization of the more durable plant used for producing consumers' goods will soon appear.[15] It may also be pointed out that, whereas the rate of total production and sales of staple and non-durable consumer goods is relatively steady, year in and year out, there are a number of industries contributing to the production of these finished and consumable products.

Thus, at the trough of a depression, those industries which are relatively remote from consumer goods (e.g., blast furnaces) tend to show the lowest degree of utilization of existing capacity. As a *Fortune* journalist has put it, the industry of producing freight cars is one of the crackers on the end of a long whip composed of producer industries, and shows "feast or famine" fluctuations of activity of the wildest sort. The machine tool industry is another prince or pauper. As a result, in the process of recovery from deep depression a considerable rise may occur in the production of non-durable goods before the capacity of such industries as iron and steel is sufficiently utilized to encourage enlargement of the latter facilities. The acceleration principle is thus most easily recognized in connection with *de*celeration at the downswing from the boom phase of the cycle, when the mere slackening of rate

---

[15] Contrariwise, increase of consumption may only lead to fuller utilization of existing plants; not immediately to more plant construction.

of increase in output of consumer goods is likely to cause a marked decline in orders for new plant and equipment.

The applications of the "multiplier" idea soon become more complex, but this language is more novel than is the general idea that any expenditure tends to set up a chain of purchases and employment. Some users of the "multiplier" tongue do not sufficiently warn their readers that the real problem is to create new upward spirals of employment by means which do not provoke offsetting (or more than offsetting) downward spirals elsewhere.[16]

Spending, Saving, and Investment, in re Employment.— Some reference has already been made to investment as a factor in employment and wage fluctuations. Since this term "investment" is heavily charged with meanings in contemporary business-cycle discussions, it deserves some attention here. As usual, we must fight our way through some ambiguities and mere verbal disputes. In ordinary language, "investment" serves as a noun which refers alike to the processes and the results of investing. The emphasis, in this common usage, is on income-yielding *property,* generally acquired by a process of saving part of current income.[17]

Income-yielding properties, of course, are of many sorts. Fundamentally, they are equities or legal claims to expected future incomes—e.g., from lands, buildings, franchises, copyrights, and obligations of persons, firms, and governments. This property-right point of view should be carefully distinguished from the social-wealth point of view—the latter is the physical assets side of the social balance sheet; while property

---

[16] Here we touch on questions of social psychology, which are vitally important for predicting effects of "economic" causes. Up to the present time, deficit financing of governmental expenditures for relieving depression victims, etc., has tended to hold in check "business confidence." Longer and wider experience with, and study of, such deficits in public finances may cause conservative people to view them with less alarm—in which case pump priming would become more nearly a net and long-run addition to the employment which would exist in its absence.

[17] An individual or a firm may also *reinvest* the liquid proceeds derived from the sale (or partial sale, as in amortization and depreciation reserves) of any property or investment; and an individual may acquire property by inheritance or other "capital" transfers—not necessarily by saving out of his own current income.

rights would mostly be accounted for on the other side, in an accurate enumeration of the equities in such social assets.

When business-cycle theorists, on the other hand, speak of investing and investment, many of them nowadays refer primarily to new "real investment," in the sense of *new commitments, by individuals, business firms, or governmental agencies, for the construction and/or alteration or reconstruction of durable goods.* Such investment in the business sense comprehends (a) construction of private capital goods, such as factories; but many of the essential elements of real investment appear also in (b) provision of revenue-producing works (e.g., toll bridges) by public authorities, (c) non-revenue-producing public and non-profit works, and (d) construction of durable goods for account of consumers thereof—notably residential housing.[18]

Marginal Propensities to Consume, to Save, in Relation to Income.—Many other important propositions might be added, as to how wages and incomes affect each other and cycles of prosperity and depression. It must suffice here, however, to inquire briefly wherein wage earners spend their incomes differently, as compared with higher-income people, in the various phases of "the business cycle"; and whether such comparisons suggest how wage policy may affect cyclical fluctuations in employment.

Let us begin by defining the Keynesian phrases in our headline. These "propensities," in present-day economic discussions, are generally conceived statistically. The simpler *average* propensities or rates of consumption and of saving, respectively, can be stated as the two percentages which together account for the total income of all the people. Thus, according to a recent official estimate, of the $59.3 billion received, in the year 1935-36, by 39.5 million American families and in-

---

[18] The term "real" or "new" or "social" investment may be used to designate *production* of durable goods, of any or all of the above categories. The individual's investment of liquid funds does not necessarily signify new or social investment—the person from whom he acquires income-yielding property may then use the purchase money for consumption or "hoarding." In either of these two cases no addition is made to the social stock of capital or durable goods.

dividuals, some 90% was consumed the same year, and about 10% was saved.[19]

But for our present purpose these over-all averages are much less significant than the *marginal* percentages consumed and saved—meaning how many dollars of an *additional* hundred of income would be used in these two ways. Only somewhat fragmentary data on amounts of savings, by income groups, are available; but they add precision to the common-sense view that the higher your income, the higher *percentage* of it you tend to save. Thus, the research just cited also indicates that the "savings" of the poorest two-thirds of our families and individuals (1935-36) were negative in the aggregate—that the 20 million units receiving under $1,450 a year consumed nearly $1.5 billion more than their aggregate incomes. At the other extreme, of the $7.5 billion gross savings of the upper one-third of people, some $2.8 billion (37%) was accounted for by 178,000 families and individuals—a minute fraction of the total earning population.[20]

How are these differences in amounts and in timing of "capital" and "labor" incomes concerned in depression causation? Two well-established points of diagnosis are apparent. The first diagnostic point is that wage earners tend to spend their small and fluctuating incomes promptly for consumption, year in and year out; whereas better-to-do people are able, and are inclined, when business prospects are for declining trade and prices, to try to play safe in two ways: they tend (1) to cut down current consumption, and (2) to get their assets into more liquid forms. Thus, in depression, we hear much of inactive bank balances, and a relatively strong market for high-grade bonds.

The other clear diagnostic point is the commonplace proposition that, during recovery and boom periods, people with

---

[19] National Resources Committee [now National Resources Planning Board], *Consumer Expenditures in the U. S.*, p. 77 (Washington, Gov't Printing Office, 1939). Gifts and personal taxes are included here in current consumption.

[20] These data are not directly comparable with national income estimates for the same year. The former, e.g., take no account of undistributed profits of business enterprises. As shown in Ch. 8, above, "business savings," both positive and negative, become very large in booms and depressions.

higher incomes tend freely to invest their current profits, other incomes, and borrowed funds too, in rapid extensions of productive facilities. Such extension is finally carried too far, and leads to depression. Why? According to some commentators, mostly because too little of the social income goes to wage earners, who are therefore unable to buy all the products of these new plants and other capital goods.

Would Shifts in Incomes Avoid Depressions?—The idea contained in the foregoing sentence has led the more left-wingish theorists to argue that equalization of incomes would greatly alleviate, if not abolish, economic depressions. This heroic treatment, especially when buttressed by some scheme of "planned economy," may be plausibly presented. But a strong presumption that inequality of wealth and income *as such* does not necessarily give rise to business cycles is afforded by medieval feudal society, which was characterized by marked inequality, stable technology and consumers' wants, comparative self-sufficiency of each manor or village—and only rudimentary booms and depressions. Apparently two factors—tempo of technical and consumer-want changes, and interdependence among producers—are the principal villains in the causation of the economic cycles which have developed in modern times. Hence, it may be more forcibly argued that certain types of diversion of income from profits to wages would *check a boom already under way* than that the problems of business cycles may be permanently or increasingly solved merely by progressive equalization of income.[21]

---

[21] The relations between inequality of income and economic cycles are much affected, too, by the absolute average productivity of society. It is generally recognized that one factor in the unusually spasmodic business activity of the United States is the high average of American incomes, which permits many people two great types of luxury: (1) consumer purchases are much influenced by style and appearance, and (2) large stocks of durable goods are built up in consumers' hands, and the less durable, such as clothing, are often replaced before they are worn out. By contrast, one reason why the economy of Soviet Russia has been less subject to business cycles is that the level of consumers' incomes there is so low that these two sorts of luxury could not be afforded. A society which was both rich and egalitarian, and in which there was a high degree of division of labor, characterized moreover by rapid changes in technology and in consumers' wants, might be subject to even greater extremes of prosperity and

B. Wages as Costs—Should They Be More Flexible?

The foregoing reference to the idea that excessive profits, or savings, or both, constitute a leading cause of depressions— and that the remedy is further diversion of income to wage earners—brings us to the rôle of wages, in business cycles, as costs of production. When we take this point of view, several further lines of inquiry are opened up, all bearing upon the great practical question: How much, or what sort of, wage plasticity (if any) is desirable—for the unemployed, if not for the labor with greatest job security?

Let us proceed through these stages: (1) general arguments about elasticity of demand for labor, including relations to capital supply; (2) historical-statistical relations of wages, prices, and employment; (3) business employment policies in boom and depression conditions; and (4) the questions, Should and could particular wages (especially in depression-vulnerable industries) be engineered to give greater industrial stability?

1. General Theories of Employment; Fallacies.—It was suggested above[22] that, among the many too-simple theories of connections between wages and unemployment must be classed the one that is entertained by most business men and by conservatives in general—the idea that unemployment is in large part due to labor's unwillingness to work for its real value. According to this view—which has been more plausible since than before 1929, because of the remarkable extent to which high wage rates have been maintained in the face of widespread unemployment—many kinds of labor have been "priced out of the market," and so higher average annual labor incomes could be secured by the fuller employment which is alleged to be available at lower wage rates. This view, with special reference to the persistent high level of British unemployment after 1920, was thus expressed by the late Professor Edwin Cannan:

---

depression than have yet been known—at least if production were organized to a large extent through private property and free enterprise. All this is highly speculative, in part because there is little historical ground as yet for supposing that a large society can be at once rich and equal and free.

[22] E.g., in Ch. 5, and earlier in this chapter.

General unemployment [he said] is in reality to be explained almost in the same way as particular unemployment. In a particular unemployment, provided demand for its product is elastic, more persons can be employed if they will work for less remuneration. In all employments *taken together,* demand is indefinitely elastic, and consequently indefinite numbers can be employed if they do not ask for too high a remuneration. General unemployment appears when asking too much is a general phenomenon.[23]

Most economists who have thought much about the subject, however, now realize that the matter is not nearly so simple as this. There is little doubt that the quantity demanded by buyers of any particular commodity or service tends to be greater at a lower than at a higher price, *so long as other things are expected to remain approximately equal;* but it is quite illegitimate to generalize this "law of inverse elasticity of demand" so broadly as to apply it directly to general wage or price changes. Even in the realm of commodity prices, an "economic paradox" which has often been noted is that demand may dry up in a falling market, since buyers may hold off for still lower prices; and vice versa for a strongly rising market.

No doubt at any moment there are levels of money-wage rates so high or so low that, if they could quickly be made to prevail in the labor market, they would result in substantial changes in employment. On the other hand, the well-known spirals of wages and prices during strongly inflationary and deflationary epochs show that it is easily possible to mark up or down all prices for commodities and services—and that in these spirals the volume of employment tends to move (if at all) directly rather than inversely with the wage-rate trend. Hence, our problem is often refined, in economic debates, into this form: Does employment tend to be increased by any fall in *real*-wage rates, and to be lowered by a rise in real wages? On this revised version, no clear consensus of economic opinion

---

[23] *Economic Journal* (London), Sept. 1932, pp. 357-370. Reprinted, under the title "Not Enough Work for All," in his *Economic Scares* (London: 1933). In its context this remark is more defensible than is indicated in the text above. Cannan was combating other popular fallacies—e.g., that increased population tends progressively to increase the *rate* of unemployment.

has emerged, because there are too many possibilities as to attendant circumstances that may affect employment independently.[24]

Interest Rates and Capital Efficiency, as Factors in Employment.—These factors are still more emphasized in current economic debates on the "general theory of employment." To probe far into such matters would take us too far afield; but the above headline is a reminder (a) that capital costs are mingled with labor costs, in nearly all production, and hence affect the volume of employment; also (b) the rate of production of capital instruments is dependent on the demand for such goods, which in turn depends upon their estimated "efficiency" or prospective profitability for their owners. Such "marginal efficiency of capital" varies, not only in response to labor and other costs, but also in relation to factors like new developments in technology and/or in consumer demands. In the preceding chapter, we explored some of the problems of "competition between machinery and labor," and in the next section below attention will be called to the temporary stimulus to employment in the "machine"-producing industries which may be given by a general rise in wage rates. Here it must suffice to mention that another moot and subtle question among economists is whether a general change in real-wage rates is likely to affect employment *indirectly,* through the possible effects of such wage changes upon interest rates.[25]

---

[24] This topic runs through the recent controversies growing out of doctrines and remarks in Mr. Keynes' *General Theory.* In the *Economic Journal,* March 1939, he recognizes that recent statistical researches show that the volumes of output and employment do not so *universally* respond (inversely) to rises and falls of real-wage rates as is commonly assumed. The bases of this latter generalization are the well-known facts that, very often if not usually, (a) rising employment is associated with falling real-wage rates (money wages lagging behind living costs); while (b) in business recessions the contrary lag appears. But even were there fewer statistical exceptions to these "rules," it would still be arguable as to what sorts of changes in real-wage rates (if any) *cause* increase or decrease in employment.

[25] Among technical economic discussions of this last point are those in *Econ. Jour.,* several of which were launched by Pigou's article "Real and Money Wage Rates in Relation to Unemployment," in the Sept. 1937 issue.

The non-labor costs of capital are quite complex. In a depression, for example, most people rush toward more liquid and "safe" forms of prop-

2. Historical Courses of Wage and Unemployment Rates.

—Several efforts have been made to prove statistically that too-high wage rates have been a main cause of the mass of unemployment—particularly in Europe and in the United States—since 1920. One of the earlier among these attempts was that of the French economist Jacques Rueff.[26] He charted British quarterly data, 1919-30, on (a) wage rates, (b) whole-sale prices, (c) the ratio of these wage/price indexes, and (d) per cent of insured workers unemployed. The wage/price ratio Rueff apparently regarded as an index at once of real-wage rates and of real labor costs;[27] and he showed that, in the 1920's, the percentage of insured workers unemployed in Britain rose and fell in almost perfect sympathy with the wage/price index. Rueff and various other European econo-mists, moreover, reasoned that the increasing scope of British social legislation after 1918 had strengthened the bargaining power of labor, thus put up and kept up labor costs, thus caused abnormally high unemployment.[28]

This proposition, though soon shown by the critics[29] not

---

erty, like passengers toward one side of a boat. This increased demand depresses "the interest rate," in the sense of yield on fixed-income securities generally supposed to be of highest grade of safety (e.g., U. S. bonds). But the other side of the boat—gross price of "venture capital"—simul-taneously rises, especially in the sense that there is little market, if any, for new issues of stock shares.

Many economists look on the first of these markets—supply and demand for money and quasi-money—as *the* capital market, whose state they sup-pose to influence the current rate of investment (construction of capital goods), and so of employment. The money supply, of course (including bank credit), is increasingly "managed" by governments. Business-like de-mand for money seems less manageable politically; however, as wage rates rise or fall, such changes tend to increase or decrease demand for payroll funds, and thus to exert some pressure on interest rates.

[26] *Revue Politique et Parlementaire*, Dec. 10, 1925; and *Revue d'Écono-mie Politique*, Vol. 45, No. 2, March-April, 1931, p. 211.

[27] Isles, *op. cit.* below, calls this ratio the index of "product wages."

[28] The title of Rueff's 1931 article, cited in the preceding note, is (trans-lated) "Unemployment Insurance—the Cause of Permanent Unemploy-ment." Other articles on the same theme appeared in the same issue (of *Revue d'Économie Politique*), and in *Soziale Praxis*, 1925 and 1926.

[29] Especially Pigou (see his *Theory of Unemployment*, pp. 298-301—London, 1933), who argues that the correlation shown by Rueff is spurious—that changes in unemployment, wages, and prices are all produced by out-side business-cycle factors, and do not much influence one another directly. One type of evidence on which Pigou relies is that German unemployment, 1920-30, was not consistently associated with wage/price ratio changes.

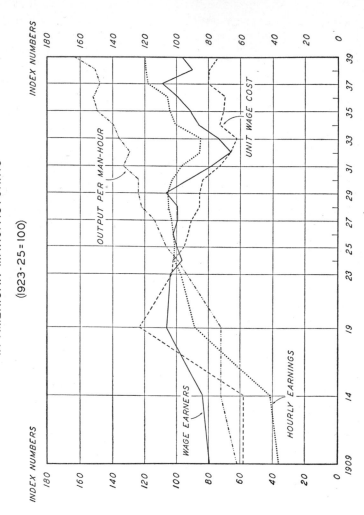

EMPLOYMENT, WAGES, AND RELATED FACTORS
IN AMERICAN MANUFACTURING

(1923-25=100)

INDEX NUMBERS

OUTPUT PER MAN-HOUR

UNIT WAGE COST

WAGE EARNERS

HOURLY EARNINGS

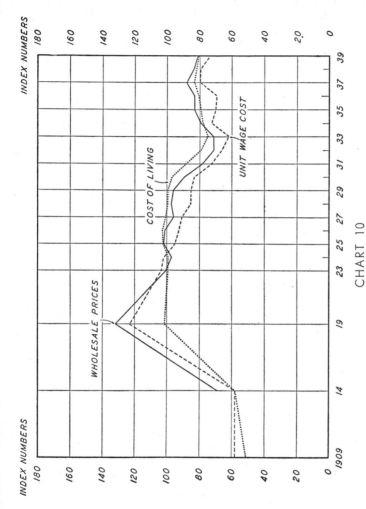

CHART 10

Sources: Data on employment ("wage earners"), output per man-hour, hourly earnings, and cost of living from Witt Bowden, "Wages, Hours, and Productivity of Industrial Labor, 1909 to 1939," Mo. Lab. Rev., Sept. 1940; on wholesale prices (finished goods) from Survey of Current Business. Index of "unit wage cost" computed by hourly earnings index/hourly output index.

to be so readily proved, served a useful purpose in redirecting attention to international comparisons among indexes of wages, prices, unemployment, and production. Professor K. S. Isles, for instance, published such charts with reference to Great Britain, 1851-1910 and 1922-31; also for Australia, 1913-30.[30]

Chart 10 shows estimated movements of hourly wage earnings, employment, and some associated variables in American manufacturing, 1909-39. As shown in this chart's top section, physical output per man-hour (worked by wage earners) rose only very moderately over the decade 1909 to 1919 (mainly because of the first World War); and since 1919 it has more than doubled. Indexes of total output and of total man-hours worked are not shown here; but the trend of "wage earners" (i.e., of "employment," or number of people on "hourly" payrolls) is exhibited as almost stationary, despite a marked decrease in average hours worked per week,[31] and despite a considerable increase in the nation's industrialization. These latter two factors raise a presumption that the number of wage earners employed in American manufacturing should have increased in these three decades *more* than proportionally to our total population growth—instead of materially *less,* as was actually the case.[32] No reliable measures of *un*employment in American manufacturing industries as a group exist for the larger part of this period;[33] but it is clear that employment

---

[30] *Wages Policy and the Price Level,* Part IV (London, 1934).

[31] Average hours per week declined from 52.7 in 1909 to 37.6 in 1939, according to the Bowden article on which our chart is based.

[32] Total population grew from about 90 million in 1909 to some 130 million in 1939—a gain of nearly 45%. The average number of wage earners employed in manufacturing rose from about 6.3 million in 1909 to 8.4 million in 1919 (about 20%); and the latter figure was not reached again until 1937. Discussions of "employment" in any industry over such a long period, however, should take cognizance of the trend of white-collar as well as of wage-earner employment. In 1937 1.2 million of salaried people were employed in manufacturing. Comparable data are not available over previous decades, but probably not over half to three-quarters of a million were so employed in 1909; hence white-collar employment in factories has increased some 100% in the past 30 years.

[33] See, however, Paul Douglas' "Estimated percentages of unemployment in manufacturing and transportation, 1889-1927," in his *Real Wages,* p. 445—which table indicates that in this group of industries the American unemployment rate during the years 1923-27 inclusive averages about the same (around 5%) as over the pre-war era, 1889-1913.

in these industries as a group failed to expand at a normal rate after the comparatively normal base years 1923-25.

Why this "arrested development"? Many rival explanations or hypotheses have been suggested, of course; and our Chart 10 presents evidence relevant to a few of them. The remaining two curves in the top of this chart, for example, show average money earnings per hour ("hourly earnings"); and an index of "unit wage cost" derived by dividing this earnings index by the output-per-man-hour index. In the lower section of the chart, moreover, the movements of this "unit wage cost" index are compared with two others: urban wage earner "cost of living" and "wholesale prices" (of finished goods). The living-cost index is shown for two reasons: it keeps pace approximately with retail prices, and, together with the "hourly earnings" curve, it affords a basis for computing indexes of "real wages" per hour. (Observe that hourly money earnings rose somewhat more than living costs from 1909 to the base period 1923-25; and that by 1937 the average real wage per hour in manufacturing was nearly 120/80—i.e., 50% above 1923-25.) Finally, our curve marked "wholesale prices" (of finished goods—raw materials prices excluded), since its beginning in 1914, shows a downward trend very similar to those of living costs and unit wage costs. These (not-fully-comparable) data suggest that wholesale prices of manufactured goods have declined less than the unit wage costs incurred by such manufacturers. Perhaps manufacturers unduly impeded growth in output and employment by reducing prices (1919 to 1933) less than their declining unit wage costs warranted— though their other costs (such as taxes and white-collar salaries) may have increased even more than their labor costs decreased.[34]

---

[34] Compare the numerous charts for manufacturing and other industries in Spurgeon Bell's *Productivity, Wages, and National Income,* Chs. 4 to 10. (See Bell's table, reproduced on p. 167 above.) My own chart, modeled upon some of Bell's, utilizes later estimates (e.g., those on output secured by Bowden from Fabricant of the National Bureau of Economic Research), and covers a greater span of years. Bell's data for certain industries (e.g., tobacco manufacturing) segregate the indirect tax from remaining components of gross wholesale price per unit.

Paul Douglas' paper, "The Effects of Wage Increases upon Employ-

Historical Correlations Inconclusive.—Thus the attempts of Rueff and others to demonstrate high wage rates as a leading cause of general unemployment have been unsuccessful. Correlations of unemployment with the ratio of the wage index to the wholesale price index, in particular, must be interpreted in the light of behavior of unit wage cost during the period— which unit wage cost is a function of output per man-hour as well as of the wage rate. Data like those in Chart 10, above, however, are liable to be accepted too readily as proof that high wage rates bear *no* responsibility for our present mass of unemployment. (See pages 358 and 359.) For it may still be plausibly argued:

1. That output per man-hour increased more in manufacturing than in all our nation's sources of livelihood taken together—also that such increase was mainly due to technical and other reasons largely beyond the control of the wage earners; and

2. That a more rapid decline of wholesale prices of manufactures—one requisite for which, since 1936, was a less rapid increase in manufacturing wage rates— would have kept average annual real earnings of factory earners in a more reasonable relation to national average earnings in all occupations, and also would have increased total employment and total real national income. (Similar arguments, of course, would apply to various other industries when their real hourly earnings rise exceptionally far and long—e.g., coal mining and certain public utilities.)[35]

---

ment" (*American Economic Review,* March 1939 Supplement, pp. 154-157), is another example of statistical research on this problem which utilizes recent estimates of "productivity" (per man-hour).

[35] Compare Ch. 8, above, where, by another route, the same conclusion was reached, viz.: that a single industry's record as to output per man-hour is much less significant for its own wage claims (from the social standpoint) than the general (all-industries) average output is significant for the all-industries average real-wage rate. See also Ch. 12, above, for elaboration of the point, implied in the foregoing text, that a low rate of unemployment in a particular industry does not necessarily prove that its wage rates are not—socially speaking—too high and tending to hinder its optimum expansion.

Study of such charts, and of other international wage and employment data,[36] shows:

1. Rather marked contrasts as to relations among these variables before 1914 and after 1918. Before that earlier World War, wage rates were more plastic and they fluctuated more nearly in sympathy with commodity prices than since 1918.

2. There is no simple causation running from general wage rates to general unemployment. Some significance, however, may attach to the following contrast in the period 1932-38, when our indexes are most reliable in quality: Unemployment in Britain and Australia declined rapidly (from some 23% and 29%, respectively, to the range of 10% to 13%), despite maintenance of or slight increase in the real-wage rates of the latter 1920's; whereas the great upsurge in American real hourly wage rates after 1932, which carried these well above all previous peaks, was associated with a more stubborn persistence of unemployment.[37]

All, or nearly all, western nations showed upward secular trends of real-wage rates (to the onset of the present war), whose social benefits were only in part offset by higher percentages of unemployment after 1918. No country, however, provides us reliable and comparable data over a sufficiently long term to demonstrate any conclusive correlation or the lack of it between general wage rates and general unemployment.

3. How Do Employers React to Wage-Rate Changes?— Since arguments from history and statistics are inconclusive, let us try to carry a few steps further a qualitative investigation, invoking common-sense impressions as to how wage in-

---

[36] Cf. Ch. 6-A, above.

[37] British and Australian recoveries after 1932 were favored, however, by the fact that these countries had not experienced a 1928-29 boom of American proportions. The effects on employment of the drastic increases in hourly wage rates produced by the French and New Zealand 40-hour week laws (1936) were almost immediately masked by the march of these nations into the war whose bombing began in 1939.

creases and declines affect hiring and layoff rates in recession and recovery conditions. Such arguments suggest (a) that abnormally high uncertainty as to future events tends to make any general change in wage rates more likely to decrease than to increase employment; also (b) that one cause of the spasmodic operation of capital-goods industries is the temporary boom that is given to production of labor-saving equipment by any general and material advance in wage rates.

EFFECT OF UNCERTAINTY ON WAGE RATES. Economic analysis such as that contained in Chapter 4, above, while it emphasizes the value of the marginal product of labor in the long-run philosophy of real-wage-rate determination, should not be interpreted as holding that employment is *quickly* responsive to wage changes, least of all during boom and depression conditions.[38] When business activities are contracting in ways that suggest or prove a general recession, the employer becomes less confident than in stabler times as to how much he can increase his total profit (or cut his total loss) by increasing or decreasing his output. He can still calculate fairly accurately how increasing or decreasing inputs of man-hours (and other factors) will affect his *physical* rate of output; but his abnormally high uncertainty about future prices and costs makes him disposed to avoid commitments, and to limit his immediate objective to keeping his regular customers supplied with goods, his most regular workers supplied with work. Thus, during rapid downswings of general business, employers become less likely to increase their volumes of employment in response to declines in wage rates—particularly in response to *small* wage changes.[39]

---

[38] For simplicity, I here assume (a) a high degree of competition among both employers and workers, and (b) no consistent change in labor efficiency associated with increases and decreases in wage rates and employment. Innumerable qualifications would be necessary, to take account of all of the variations found in the real world under both of these heads.

[39] At the outset of a recession, a decrease of labor costs may stimulate output; but, as the depression deepens, greater proportionate reduction in wage costs may be required to have any effect on employment—and, presently, general wage cuts will probably *reduce* production by operation of the downward spiral of wages and prices. The usual effect of recession, therefore, appears to be to decrease elasticity of demand for labor in most enterprises—at least with reference to wage-rate declines. (See footnote 41.)

In this connection "psychological" theories of business cycles are plausible; both bearish and bullish sentiments appear to spread through somewhat irrational contagion—somewhat like the exaltation of a religious camp meeting—and when prices and other prospects become more unstable than usual, the employer has no choice but to act more speculatively, more on "hunches," than when his prospects are clearer.

An expansion of employment is not likely to precede an increase in sales unless the employer is convinced that better times are ahead or assumes that he can sell the increased output at a satisfactory price. In a period of [general business] contraction these conditions are not likely, and a wage reduction will not lead to an increase in employment immediately, even though the new wage rate is (unknown to the employer) lower than the marginal productivity of labor.[40]

In the earlier stages of *upswing,* on the other hand, so long as unused capacity exists, increases in production and employment will proceed unchecked by any considerable upward spiral of wages and prices. The unused plant capacity means that total overhead costs are but little increased with the rising output, and unemployed labor will attempt to restrain demands for wage advances which might nip the recovery in the bud. If wage rates do, nevertheless, increase markedly during such incipient recovery, the result may well be to decrease employment; for business prospects are still highly uncertain, and the dangers of forward commitments and of high-cost inventories are still fresh in business men's minds.[41] In short, the duration of a wage-price spiral is unpredictable.

------

[40] E. Ronald Walker, "Wages Policy and Business Cycles," *Internat. Lab. Rev.,* Dec. 1938.

[41] In this phase, therefore, the factor uncertainty seems to *increase* elasticity of demand for labor—in the sense of making quantity demanded shrink abnormally in response to *rise* in unit price. It seems likely that the recession of 1937-38 was initiated or aggravated by the rapid, general, and material advance of wage rates in 1936-37. Other recessions as well as this one, moreover, have indicated that the laggard tendency of wage adjustments is apt to make average wage rates rise for several months after business activity has turned down. This inertia of costs has contributed to instability of profits and of employment; and the trend toward public and other larger-scale collective wage determinations tends to give still greater inertia to wage rates.

HIGH WAGE RATES MAY PROMOTE MECHANIZATION. As recovery reaches the point when existing capacity is inadequate (after a long depression, much of it is semi-obsolete and undermaintained), the accompanying wage-rate increases are apt increasingly to stimulate installation of labor-saving equipment and methods. As Walker remarks, "For the moment the production of the new equipment may involve increased employment; it is a form of investment and therefore exerts an expansive influence upon business activity. But . . . this influence may later be reversed when the installation of the new equipment is complete."[42]

The discussion in this section has dealt with only a few of the many practical reactions to wage changes, but it indicates why neither a widespread rise nor fall of wage rates is consistently followed by decrease or increase in employment. Any reduction in total unit production cost which the employer considers material in relation to his prospective selling price tends of itself to stimulate his output; and a wage cut that is expected to be localized and definitive, in an industry in which labor cost is (say) at least 25% of total cost, is likely to stimulate not only output but employment. The qualifications in this last sentence suggest many other cases in which wage changes may have no appreciable effect on employment. Various "paradoxes" are also possible, such as: (a) when wage rises or cuts are sufficiently general, they are likely to be parts of upward or downward spirals (of booms and depressions); and (b) the upward spiral may be partly attributable to the boom in production of labor-saving devices which is stimulated by rising wage rates—while the downward spiral is accentuated by unemployment in those industries which supply facilities for "mechanization."[43]

---

[42] *Ibid.* Another comment in similar vein: "A wage rate high enough to induce substitution of labor by other factors—or labor of the 'manual' kind by other labor—will at first tend to increase employment, because it engenders additional demand for labor-saving devices, most of which have themselves to be produced. . . . This possible source of treacherous 'verifications' of high-wage theories should always be kept in mind whenever the effects of wage rates on employment are being discussed."—J. A. Schumpeter, *Business Cycles*, pp. 841, 842.

[43] Another "paradox": If wages should follow more closely on the heels

4. Should Wages in Depression-Vulnerable Industries Be More Flexible?—Not a few economists, perceiving both the danger of a deflationary spiral and the concentration of economic depressions in durable-goods industries, have argued against greater general wage flexibility, but in favor of *more plasticity of labor costs (and product prices) pertaining to capital instruments.*[44] Let us consider this possibility briefly, utilizing our results in Chapter 11, above. I shall argue that certain sorts of wage plasticity or differentiation do offer practical possibilities of reducing cyclical fluctuations—at first, mainly by combating seasonal unemployment.[45]

We have noticed the concentration of cyclical unemployment in durable-goods industries; and that some types of durable-goods production (notably erection of buildings) have also been strongly characterized by seasonal activity. Hence, the suggestion has been made, even in high New Deal quarters, that reductions of wage rates in off-peak seasons in such trades would help promote industrial recovery, as well as increase the annual earnings of the workers concerned.

Two important questions are hereby raised: (a) Does deseasonalizing employment in any industry tend toward long-term general economic stability, or to be only a "single shot," reducing total unemployment only at the time the seasonal or casual peaks and valleys are first leveled? (b) Is there reason to think that wage policies can be applied in this direction, under present American conditions?

---

of prices during the upswing, as recommended by labor advocates, this increase in total purchasing power of wage earners might drive up prices and production of consumer goods to greater heights than have characterized past booms; and, through the acceleration principle, create more extreme speculative markets for productive equipment.

[44] An example of abstract theoretical argument along these lines is supplied by the paper "Wage-Rates, Investment, and Employment," by E. M. Bernstein, in *Jour. of Pol. Econ.*, April 1939, pp. 218-231.

[45] In this discussion attention is concentrated on factors more or less characteristic of all business cycles, and furthermore on *recurrently available* economic expedients for dealing with them. In practice, of course, the widespread despair generated by a major depression inevitably leads to political opportunism, and to use of methods which do not of themselves tend toward long-term stabilization of useful and economical employment. A vast increase of military preparations is such a means of reducing unemployment.

It must be admitted that each deseasoning measure must be directed at an objective much less broad than preventing general depressions. We may hope, for example, to minimize *seasonal* fluctuations in building-trade employment, even though, so long as there are long building cycles—due, in part, to general business cycles—the best that can be hoped is that unemployment during general-depression winters will be less than heretofore, because *every* winter there will be more jobs than in the past for building tradesmen in the corresponding phase of the long building cycle. Yet, as more and more occupations have their employment "regularized" over all seasons, it seems to me that such accumulating job-stabilizations must constitute a powerful resistance to whatever (possibly growing) forces still make for alternations of general booms and depressions. Since the compounding of many subsidiary cycles of employment into "the business cycle" may lead (merely by chance) to occasional synchronization of many *unemployment phases* and thus produce a main ingredient of a great depression, it can hardly be doubted that each smoothing of a seasonal curve is a contribution toward lessening the cyclical swings of general prosperity and depression.

When we proceed to ways and means of using appropriate wage plasticity or differentials, "industry by industry," for promoting more stable employment, we encounter two major difficulties: (a) Many seasonal industries are not producers of durable goods, and, on the other hand, doubtless not a few capital-making trades show no marked seasonal rhythm. (b) In these trades (and others), trade unions tend to resist any sort of wage cut; and we have reviewed many "good reasons" for such resistance—leading to the further reflection that, even if we could readjust wage rates of workers in both the seasonal and the durable-goods classifications, such workers are so numerous that we might thereby initiate a downward spiral into worsening depression.

The last sentence suggests what are perhaps insuperable obstacles to any wholesale and sudden attempt to dampen business cycles by wage flexing, but it does not bar the way to evolutionary advances. If the principle of stabilizing employment (by "annual wage" and "salary" plans, for instance) were generalized widely throughout many industries, the salutary effect on business cycles would gradually become very profound. In most discussions of business cycles, we assume realistically that industrial wage earners are hired subject to layoff and discharge on short notice (if any) when the employer decides he has no work for them. Comparatively recently the contrast in this respect between agricultural and other industries has been emphasized: farm labor is largely family labor, and therefore is (in effect) part of the farmer's overhead cost, not much affected by variations in his output. This circumstance helps to explain why agricultural production tends to remain high in the face of great declines in prices of farm products. A trend is now discernible toward longer-term engagements of labor among most urban industries, which (if it continues) will doubtless tend to stabilize industrial production and employment—at the expense of industrial price stability. It was remarked in Chapter 11 that employment-stabilizing plans hitherto have not led to many actual wage-rate cuts; and perhaps rigid wages stand somewhat in the way of more rapid spread of employment stabilization. Yet the wages of steadily employed maintenance craftsmen demonstrate that hourly earnings already are, to a significant extent, lower, in jobs offering relatively high security or continuity of employment. If employers study carefully the reasons for organized labor's wage policies, they can devise many types of bargain in which the workman gets a higher and more assured annual real wage, the employer greater volume, the customer more for his money.

How far wage and price flexibility is now practical in non-seasonal capital-goods industries is a matter I have not investigated. It is obviously impossible—to take an extreme case—for a locomotive builder to promise long-term employment to more than a small percentage of his peak-year force; and who can assure these workers increased employment, as the result of wage cuts, in a depression year? On the other hand, stabilizing employment through the seasons promises, not only to reduce the severity of the longer cyclical depressions, but to point out further methods (wage engineering and other) of increasingly stabilizing the production even of capital goods.

Summary and Transition

In these three chapters we have been wrestling with several outstanding and interlocking questions, notably: How does unemployment affect wages? How do wage rates affect employment? What sorts and degrees of wage plasticity or flexibility are desirable?

As to effects which unemployment has had on wage rates, we find that it depends on the type and amount of unemployment. Seasonal employments, and other sorts of hirings which offer especially low probability of continuous employment through the year, tend to command higher hourly pay than the same skill and efficiency commands in more continuous jobs. But widespread and unpredictable technological and cyclical unemployment have a depressing tendency on wage rates. Before 1914, when wage rates were more plastic than since, a sustained increase in the rate of unemployment was commonly the signal for wage cuts in the trade affected. Since 1921 hourly wages have been more rigid on the downward side, so that hard times have served rather to check their rise than to reduce them.

Our other main question—How do wage rates influence employment?—is more difficult to handle. Most competent critics or judges of wage policies from the social standpoint certainly include, among their criteria or standards, the probable effects of particular wages on employment—and upon *general* employment, not merely upon the jobs of some smaller group(s) of workers.

Here we may begin with the terrific unemployment that is characteristic of a general depression, and note the conclusion that, under conditions hitherto prevailing in American and many other "capitalist" societies, a crumbling wage structure is part of a downward spiral of wages, prices, and employment, which will go no one knows how far. It is very doubtful, therefore, whether in this situation more wage plasticity is needed, in the sense of less resistance to wage cutting.[46] And, since wage rates have become so resistant to reduction, it is also very doubtful whether a large increase of such rates should be the chief method of checking a boom. Especially if profits are shared with employees by bonuses and with consumers by more for their money, there is much to be said for a *gradual* upward trend in real wages. Inertia of wage rates—lag behind movements in prices and profits—is still one cause of business cycles, and this fact supplies one argument in favor of greater wage plasticity in the sense of more speed in making whatever wage changes have to be made.

Some popular high wage theories, which assume that raising wage rates is equivalent to raising the total purchasing power of the wage earners affected, of course beg all these questions of possible effects of wage-rate changes upon employment. Variation in total labor income, however, *is* a most important factor in the business cycle—in part because the prompt spending of such income has a strong "multiplier" effect. In a good many cases—notably in "declining industries" —the cutting of labor cost and product prices constitutes a sound means of spreading work and of minimizing unemployment. And even in some thriving industries, decline of wage rates into line with the whole labor market would ease the social problem of unemployment.

Since cyclical unemployment is largely accounted for by fluctuations in the capital-goods industries, the question arises whether greater wage flexibility in these industries in particular is desirable. It is doubtful; wage cuts in the heavy industries, once a depression is under way, would probably tend toward a further downward spiral. Some very promising attacks on this problem, however, are being made by annual wage stabilization plans. Job security may be often increased by means which, unlike the old make-work rules, tend to *decrease* production costs and thereby to stimulate consumption of products. Anything which tends to iron out cyclical fluctuations of total incomes of people connected with the heavy

---

[46] See Ch. 20-A-5, below.

industries, such as suitable unemployment compensation, tends also to mitigate booms and depressions. The simple wage-raising and hour-shortening programs hitherto stressed by many trade unions are likely to make these fluctuations greater rather than less.

PART IV

WAGE POLICIES AND PRACTICES IN PRIVATE COLLECTIVE BARGAINING

CHAPTER 14

COLLECTIVE AGREEMENTS; ELIGIBILITY TO WORK; STANDARD WAGES

In the preceding two Parts (Chapters 4-13), the main basis of organization was those principal factors which consciously or unconsciously enter into the determination of wage rates and total labor incomes—with incidental references to the respective rôles of private and public agencies. In Part IV we now explore further the causes and effects of wages which are most directly connected with the first of these groups of agencies—i.e., with characteristics of *private and voluntary* organizations of labor and employers. In Part V, below, we shall push the inquiry further into the field of *public or political* organization.

In the present chapter, after section A, a brief characterization of trade unions and employers' associations and their interactions, we proceed to section B, some outstanding features of collective agreements between them; and then take up, in section C, two great families of policies and practices which affect wage incomes and labor costs, namely (1) those bearing on the eligibility of workers to work (taking cognizance of problems of closed shop, seniority, etc.), and (2) wage methods, in both the narrower sense of time and output bases of payment and the broader sense of wage structure over occupations, shops, and areas. In the next chapter we shall follow this last trail into the field of measurement and standardization of labor efficiency, which must be considered in the light of working rules and practices.[1]

---

[1] Most of the matters treated in these two chapters (14 and 15) are dealt with much more fully in S. H. Slichter, *Union Policies and Industrial Management* (Brookings, 1941), which appeared after the script of this book was completed.

A. Some Characteristics of Unions and Employers' Associations

Trade unions, and those trade associations of employers which are important for collective wage bargaining, both may be studied historically and comparatively as to nations and other regions—as these strands interweave, not only with each other, but with numerous somewhat different types of human organizations. Among useful clues to the origins and natures of these wage-dealing associations are the three "methods" or types of labor union activity which the Webbs emphasized, half a century ago: mutual insurance, political pressure, and collective bargaining. The first of these three has greatly diminished in importance, as compulsory social insurance has grown; but the second and third remain the right and left arms of both trade unions and labor-dealing employers' associations.

Political and economic activities are also the right and left arms of numerous other special-interest groups, such as the remaining trade, professional, and farm organizations, many of which are (economically speaking) hybrids between trade associations and labor unions. The familiar contradictory views of unions and employers' associations can be explained by the maxim that almost any virtue can be enlarged into a vice, and almost any vice within adequate limits becomes a virtue. As we have recognized, especially in Chapter 4 above, there are many ways in which wage earners can cooperate within trade unions for mutual protection and self-development, and also in the general public interest; the same is true of all other human groups. Such organization, however, can be carried through many slight gradations of methods and results, until it arrives (usually without members realizing the fact) at monopolistic restrictions and other perversions which are anti-social if not illegal. Among the worst plagues of trade unions and trade associations are doubtless the racketeers—corrupt and vicious bosses. In some instances, the "unions" and "business associations" of such racketeers are mere parodies or impostors—composed, in one small part, of their hired gangsters, and in the other, of their victims from whom they extort money for "protection" against these gangsters. But, unfortunately, racketeers have also developed within legitimate associations of business men and wage earners, and some of their illegal exploits have been in the nature of collaboration between union and employer bosses.

Characteristics of More and Less Progressive Associations.—It is well known that the AFL-CIO schism in the American labor movement was produced not merely by the clash of craft and industrial organization principles; that various other factors, such as rivalry for union offices and power, contributed to the cleavage. Let us notice some of the other important differences among unions, which make easy generalizations of but limited validity at best.

Consider the following opposing characteristics:

CONTRASTS AMONG LABOR UNIONS

1a. Older	1b. Newer
2a. Dominated by skilled craftsmen; contriving artificial scarcity	2b. Industrial unions, effectively organizing both skilled and unskilled males and females, and not attempting monopolies of skills
3a. Centralized power—e.g., of business agent	3b. Democratically controlled
4a. Traditional methods—of production, bargaining, apprenticeship, working rules and methods of combat	4b. Offering less resistance to innovations in all these; tending to adopt new methods, both of cooperation and of resistance
5a. Striving for highest hourly rates —restrictive practices — "what traffic will bear"—skilled wages small per cent of total cost	5b. More conscious of consumers and of reaction of labor costs on the industry's prosperity and on annual real incomes of workers

This diagram contains a good-sized sample of the stuff of which industrial-relations problems are made, especially where trade unions are important. Collective bargaining offers opportunity for give and take, for concessions and counter-concessions, along these lines and many others, in addition to the familiar *quids* and *quos* such as wages, hours, and eligibility to work.

It would be a great mistake to suppose that the so-called craft unions—in and out of the AFL—are *all* accurately characterized by all the phrases in the left or (a) column above, or that the right-hand (b) column contains plans and specifications which apply with equal force to all industrial unions—in and out of the CIO. One instance shows how fallacious such a hasty conclusion would be: The United Mine Workers is an old industrial union which has not been universally commended at all times as to the democracy of its administration. Its situation as to distribution of skill among its membership, and as to the ratio of labor to total cost in its industry, is very different from that of the ordinary craft union; yet the UMW appears still to be rather strongly characterized by the high-wage-rate philosophy; also by other mixtures of traditional and advanced union ideas and methods. Another blend of the old and the new may be cited on the AFL side: it was the craft union of machinists which laid the foundations of the modern union-management cooperation movement.[2]

The newer industrial unions, like those in the steel, rubber, and automobile industries, are comparatively unhampered as well as unhelped by old traditions, and hence tend to be relatively open-minded on wage and other management methods. As their powers are consolidated and as they grow older, quite possibly they will grow more conservative, more resistant to change.

The variations among employers are perhaps as great as among unions, in such matters as these. Here is one ground for the saying that managements get the unions they deserve—also for the counter-proposition that unions tend to get the employers they deserve. Many employers and/or members of their supervisory forces were previously union members in the same industry; this is particularly true (of course) in the long-organized industries, such as railways, building, printing, and mining. While the self-made boss who has turned violently anti-union is a familiar figure, I think he is more than offset by the personnel on the employing side who uphold many of the

---

[2] See below, in this section and in Ch. 15-C.

traditions which they absorbed while they were union members. Whatever may be the number of the latter people, their influence is to confirm these unions in their old policies and philosophies.

Among other factors helping to account for diversities in the labor world are the great variations among industries in such matters as sizes of plants, rapidity of goods turnover, per cent of women and juniors among the employed, and especially the degree of competition for the customer's favor. Thus, the firms enjoying high profits because they are relatively sheltered from inroads by substitute goods of any sort are apt frequently to face demands from labor for a share of these advantages; whereas if competition is keen and average profits low, labor leaders tend to cater more to the consumer of their product, also to encourage or even to initiate new methods of cost reduction. In other words, although economists usually think of wages and other costs as determining product prices, practical wage-making often works backward—determining wages by reference to the estimated margin between prices of product and of non-labor factors of production.

Favorable and Unfavorable Possibilities of Union-Management Collaboration.—The foregoing remarks on union-employer relations may be usefully supplemented by a preliminary characterization—developed further in the next chapter —of some practices which are as yet nearly all to the good. Some of the newer methods by which employers—thus far, I believe, *individual* firms—have worked with trade unions on matters of mutual interest have been called "union-management cooperation." The best known family of such endeavors is that which was established in 1922 in the repair shops of the Baltimore and Ohio Railroad.[3] The cooperative plans of the B & O and certain other railways operated through joint committees quite distinct from the older collective bargaining machinery, which continued to function very much as before. Many other attempts have been reported in the direction of

---

[3] The most comprehensive report is that of Louis H. Wood, *Union-Management Cooperation on the Railroads* (Yale University Press, 1931).

new methods of concerted attack on the common problems of the industry.[4] Somewhat less systematic, but outstanding in their novelty, courage, and constructiveness have been aids given to able and well-disposed employers, temporarily in need, by clothing and hosiery unions. In the early 1920's, for example, the Amalgamated Clothing Workers are said to have underwritten one of their employing firms to the extent of $100,000.

Even this extremely laudable line of action has its better and worse forms, from the standpoint of general social effects. Compare, for example, preoccupation with clever advertising (or other price-maintenance devices), with increasing service and economy to the consumer; and notice the anti-social possibilities of excessive union-management collaboration for protective tariffs, or for imposing other artificial disabilities on outside competing firms and industries. It is the proper business of "outsiders," despite their handicap of meager information, to help keep union-management *collaboration* within proper bounds, as well as to support suitable legal limitations for capital-labor *conflicts*.

B. Salient Features of Collective Agreements

Collective bargaining leads to collective (or trade) agreements or contracts, (usually reduced to writing). In many cases, however, such agreements are verbal;[5] moreover, we may assume that the makers of written labor agreements do not

---

[4] One sort of cooperation is exemplified by the Chicago laundry industry, in which labor unions are contributing substantially to an advertising campaign—*Time* Magazine, Sept. 9, 1940. The cooperative program of the Steel Workers' Organizing Committee, described by H. J. Ruttenberg in *Harvard Bus. Rev.*, winter 1939 and spring 1940 issues, is more significant, since it emphasizes cost reduction. So did the railway-shop cooperative movement; though the broader campaign on these railroads attempted also to inspire all employees to become salesmen of these carriers' services.

[5] Usually with reference to terms which are written out somewhere, such documents supplying *prima facie* evidence as to the customs which are adopted by the verbal agreement. Thus, a powerful needle trade union is said to control an important market without any written agreement in that city; and in many unionized building jobs the working rules of the unions are accepted by the employer without any complete written agreement for his own case.

as a rule wear their hearts on the open sleeves of these semi-public documents—that in most cases there are private understandings which supplement the written terms. Agreements with larger unions are commonly printed or mimeographed and are not difficult to obtain. Many researches have been published, in various countries, based on comparative studies of them.[6]

These agreements may be usefully classified in numerous ways, for instance according to types of makers and scope of terms. There are all manner of permutations among such variables as geographic area, craft, unit of union and of employer, and subject matter within the total agreement. In the trades in which unionism has long been established there has been a tendency toward widening areas of bargaining—that is, a trend away from purely local agreements between one employer and one union toward national agreements between employer associations and industrial unions and federations of craft unions.[7]

---

[6] See, for example, International Labor Office, *Collective Agreements,* Studies and Reports, Series A, No. 39 (Geneva, 1936) ; Great Britain, Ministry of Labor, *Report on Collective Agreements* (1934). Many issues of the U. S. Dept. of Labor's *Monthly Labor Review* during the last few years have contained articles based on these agreements. This journal has also published numerous surveys concerning collective agreements in foreign countries, in some of which such agreements are legally required to be registered with the public authorities. Collective agreements on American railroads are required to be filed with the National Mediation Board in Washington. The National Labor Relations Board released early in 1940 a study of trends in American labor agreements.

[7] A survey of the current American position is afforded by Helen S. Hoeber's "Collective Bargaining with Employers' Associations," *Mo. Lab. Rev.,* Aug. 1939, pp. 302-310. She finds that the industries in which such associations play leading rôles in labor agreements are breweries, building, retail butchers, cigar making, coal mining, fishing, glassware, longshore work and shipping, motion picture production, and various clothing and needle industries. She also clarifies relations among the areas involved, remarking that "most of the instances of association dealing occur on a city-wide basis."

It must be emphasized that the employer associations here referred to are usually not the general trade associations in the same industries, but are additional or subsidiary associations formed especially for labor bargaining, by only those employers who do make agreements with unions. The names of some of the older employer labor-bargaining associations, as well as of some old trade unions, include designations like "defense" and "protective."

Individual Companies and Unions as Makers of Agreements.—Most of the newer collective bargaining, on the other hand, is between individual companies and unions—though the union to a great extent tends to secure agreements in identical terms (or nearly so) with the various employers in its industry. The independent local employer commonly has to deal with officials of a national union or unions; except that (1) there are some nascent local "outside" unions, including the numerous small unions directly affiliated with the AFL or CIO; and (2) some successors of "company unions" appear to be adapting themselves for survival under the Wagner Act.

Further illustrations of the permutations mentioned above are afforded by variations among the agreements applying to differing crafts and locations within some of the larger units of industry. A large corporation in a recently unionized industry may make a variety of agreements for its several plants, and some of these shops may remain so poorly organized as to achieve no collective agreement at all. The opposite extreme is exemplified by the General Electric Company's corporation-wide agreement with the CIO's United Electrical, Radio, and Machine Workers Union. And, although the industrial unions do tend to bargain simultaneously for all crafts and degrees of skill, such is not invariably the case. The United Automobile Workers, for instance, in 1939 made an agreement with General Motors Corporation applying specifically to tool and die makers in most, if not all, the Corporation's plants. And it is very common for a collective agreement which covers many localities to standardize other aspects of employment but to leave actual wage rates for local adjustment—supervised, of course, by the higher authorities on both sides.

Finally, what is nominally local or regional bargaining among single concerns and unions, or within local or regional groups, may in practice amount to wider-scale dealing. In bituminous coal mining, for instance, the labor negotiations have developed from relatively independent transactions with regional employers' associations to what are in effect national-scope agreements. In this case, of course, there is but one national union. A similar evolution has occurred in our railroad industry, wherein the agreements are formally between individual companies and some 21 unions; but in recent years the dealings have been carried on between the Association of American Railroads and the Railway Labor Executives Association.

Hosiery Agreement as Illustration.—The agreement between the Full Fashioned Hosiery Manufacturers of America, Inc. and the American Federation of Hosiery Workers, effective on and after September 1, 1938, may be used to illustrate some of the more important characteristics of the collective labor contract. This one is known in the hosiery industry as the master agreement; it is supplemented by local agreements on further details, such as wage scales. These local variations are presumably known and approved by all members of the Association as well as by all the interested members of the unions.[8]

This master hosiery agreement, for example, established a "preferential shop" for production employees. On this point the contract read as follows:

. . . no new employees will be hired unless they first become members of the Union, excepting as to inexperienced help, commonly known as learners or apprentices, who may be employed, but who shall have four months after employment within which to join the Union. . .

In the event that the Union cannot supply competent workers within 48 hours after formal request is made, the Association and/or Members thereof may secure such workers from other sources, it being understood however that such workers shall become members of the Union within 15 days after their employment; should however such workers fail or refuse to become members of the Union, then and in that event whenever the Union will replace them by competent help from the Union, such outside workers shall be discharged by the Members [of the employers' association] immediately upon such replacement.

---

[8] Such a union and employers' association, however, will often conceal the exact terms of their bargain from non-union competitors—the latter are thereby deprived, for example, of whatever competitive advantage they might derive from knowing precisely the labor costs in the union shops.

Another section conceded the employer

. . . the free exercise of the right to employ or discharge any worker in accordance with the necessity of his or its business, provided in the case of a discharge from employment such discharge is in good faith, . . .

—subject, however, in case of discharge or other disciplinary treatment, to appeal machinery, culminating in the impartial chairman for the unionized section of the industry.

The section headed "Rates and Hours" provided formally for an important change in policy—from pressure for uniform *piece rates* among all mills toward uniform *hourly earnings for equal skill and effort*. Several years of research had convinced this union (1) that differences among mills in equipment, materials, and management methods made uniform piece rates yield substantially different earnings to a given skill and exertion; (2) that the union was able to deal with the difficult administrative problems of adapting the piece rate to take account of these inter-mill variations; and (3) that this change would be one means among others of stimulating unionized manufacturers to strengthen their competitive position by continuous modernization of plants.

The "Rates and Hours" section of this master agreement also provided:

. . . if there shall occur a general decline or fall of earnings of full fashioned hosiery workers in the industry, or if the cost of production on the same type and condition of equipment shall decline, or if general conditions shall warrant a decrease, then any member mill whose competitive position is adversely affected thereby, may request, in writing and in detail, a specific revision of its rates of pay. In the event there shall occur a rise in the earnings of workers in the industry, or of the cost of living, or if conditions generally shall warrant an increase in earnings, then the Union may request, in writing and in detail, a specific revision of the rates of pay in any member mill. In either event, the Union and member mill involved shall negotiate the request, and if they cannot agree, within thirty days after receipt thereof, then that matter shall be submitted to arbitration by a Wage Tribunal, composed of three persons, . . .

Apart from a short paragraph providing a "check-off" system (whereby the employer, upon a written order from the employee, deducts union dues from the employee's wages each pay day), the remainder of this agreement was concerned with provisions for the agreement's interpretation and administration. It was stipulated that

. . . for the full period of this agreement, there shall be no strikes, stoppages, boycotts or lockouts, nor picketing of any kind or form whatsoever, however peaceable, nor demonstrations, displays or advertisements tending to excite sympathy or protests, and that neither of the contracting parties will authorize, permit, countenance or suffer the existence or continuance of any of the acts hereby prohibited . . .

provided that each party should abide by the decision of the Impartial Chairman in case of any dispute; and each was to post a bond whereby the Impartial Chairman might, if he deemed it necessary, levy fines on an offender.

The term of this contract was three years, and it automatically renewed itself unless either party gave 60 days' notice of intention to terminate it after the end of three years.

Significance of Hosiery Agreement.—This document is significant both for what it contains and for what it omits. It is brief and simple, by comparison with many collective agreements; and therefore does not crystallize in writing many controversial policies and practices which might become difficult either to retain or remove. Such simplicity is an important aid to industrial efficiency—if the principals are capable of composing any differences that may arise without resorting to formal written "laws" covering all manner of detailed points connected with the work. The three-year term is unusually long, and presumably would not be acceptable if the master agreement contained more rigid particulars of wages, hours, and working conditions. The latter, it will be observed, are subject to negotiations on comparatively short notice from either side.

A collective agreement should always contain some provision for its own interpretation, and some procedure to be followed in the event of dispute. The arbitration machinery of the hosiery industry is very similar to the system long employed in the clothing or needle trades, but these have not as yet been widely copied throughout the trade union world. In some nations and industries special public authorities undertake to settle disputes which arise as to interpretation of voluntary collective agreements; examples are the Labor Court of Sweden, the Arbitration Court of New Zealand, and our own National Railway Labor Adjustment Board.[9]

C. Policies and Practices Affecting Wages

C-1. Eligibility to Work, as Influence on Labor Incomes and Costs

Among the matters to which these labor treaties or contracts are devoted, a prominent rôle must be assigned to specifications as to eligibility for each type and place of work involved. These stipulations are not only concessions by the employer, important for the union's functioning if not existence, which may sometimes be balanced against wage claims; they also profoundly affect both labor incomes and labor costs. We may examine them under the heads apprenticeship, "closed shop" and probation, and layoffs and rehiring. The latter topic, in turn, involves consideration of seniority systems and schemes of work sharing and employment stabilization.

Entrances to a Trade.—Control over the number of men in the craft, of course, was a chief source of the old trade union's power over wages. Such control was exercised commonly by regulation of the number of apprentices in any shop, usually as a maximum percentage of the number of journeymen. Apprenticeship was of variable duration among crafts and unions, three or four years being common. By 1920, however, several comprehensive American vocational surveys revealed that these

---

9 Collective labor contracts are also enforceable, to some extent, by the courts like individual business contracts; but there are several peculiarities of these labor agreements, from the standpoints of law, public policy, and other practical considerations. Hence, private conciliation and arbitration arrangements, and special labor courts, seem best fitted to interpret and enforce them.

old apprenticeship ratios were becoming moribund, and that in rather few shops were there as many apprentices as the union regulations allowed. It appears, therefore, that control over real apprenticeship is no longer an instrument of outstanding importance for trade union wage policy.

The entrances to modern trades and vocations are now more largely controlled by other arrangements, notably by public and other schools for vocational training and by service as helpers to more skilled practitioners. Trade unions naturally exercise influence over these avenues, e.g., by nominating or electing committeemen and other public officials concerned with vocational training and licensing; also by political pressure toward enactment of governmental regulations governing various vocations.

"Closed Shop" and Probation.—The most obvious control of eligibility to work by trade unions at present is through "closed," "preferential," and "union" shop clauses in formal collective agreements—to which should also be added informal and unwritten practices tending to give preference in hiring or holding jobs to union men.[10]

Regulations as to union membership are often supplemented by understandings on a probationary period of employment. The unionized hosiery employer is obligated to accept from the union only *competent* workers. Within limits the employer may be the sole judge of competency; but if he wishes to discharge any worker for alleged incompetence without challenge from the union, such discharge must be made within the probationary period. After the probationary term expires, any discharged employee in a union shop is likely to have rights to due process of appeal, through which some higher official or tribunal determines whether the employer's agent acted fairly in discharging him. It is to the employer's interest, and

---

[10] The older type of "closed shop" agreement requires the employer to hire, as journeymen, only men already union members—who thus have seniority in their trade. The "preferential shop" clause is similar in effect—only union members may be hired—"as long as supply lasts." The "union shop" desired by the newer mass-production unions gives the union least control over hiring—it only requires, after a probationary period, that a worker must belong to the union to *hold* his job.

probably (in long run) to the union's, that the probationary period should be adequate—relative to the complexity and variety of the work—so that the employer may have reasonable opportunity to judge a new man's competence. In many cases six months would not be too long. It is also obviously possible to handicap an industry by making it too difficult to dismiss a workman who has *become* slack or inefficient—as often happens to workers who did good work throughout their probation.

Problems of Closed Shop and Check-Off.—A well-conducted union which has demonstrated its ability to organize the majority of the employees in any "bargaining unit" (craft or shop) can make out a strong argument in favor of an agreement requiring all steady workers to belong to the union, implemented by effective assistance from the employer in dues collection. Such an argument is apt to call the non-union man or delinquent member a "tax-dodger": " 'We are tired of having these "scabs" get all the benefits of the union and let us pay all the bill,' the union president, who is also the borough burgess, complained, 'You can be sure that they pay their taxes to the borough or they'd lose their property, if they have any.' "[11]

Such considerations may seem merely to relate to equity as among the employees; but the issue cuts deeper into the employer's immediate self-interest. So long as he supports the union in this crucial way, its officials can afford to devote more effort to constructive cooperation, less to contriving an endless series of minor victories designed to persuade workmen to join. Above all, the union is then free from temptation to use strong-arm tactics toward the "scabs."

There are other sides to the story, of course. Employers accustomed to union-hating naturally yield as little as they can, hoping for a turn in their luck. And even if an employer considers the existing leadership and constitution of the union

---

[11] H. J. Ruttenberg, "The Strategy of Industrial Peace," *Harvard Bus. Rev.*, Winter 1939, p. 172. In other contexts labor advocates stress the voluntary character of unions; hence the tax-dodger analogy should not be pressed too far.

satisfactory, he may with some reason dread the effect on this union of a monopoly position. If the union officials are no longer obliged to persuade men to belong to the organization, or even to collect dues (this manager may reflect), do not their jobs become sinecures? How can the employer be expected to underwrite a union, in whose affairs he has no voice?

Like associated problems, these difficulties are overcome in varying ways and degrees, as intelligence and patience are brought to bear upon them. In practice, of course, union officers and agents are not relieved by a check-off from the necessity of continuously "selling" their union to its members—the latter people always have strong incentives to demand their money's worth. Some flexibility on methods of dues collection —even on membership by a few real "conscientious objectors" —is often if not usually conceded by the union if the employer cooperates on the essential point: disciplining union members who will not pay their share of the union's expenses. A union which becomes corrupt or dictatorial or slothful under union shop protection is, to be sure, hard to reform or get rid of. But not impossible: the employer who turns and fights such a perverted body will be assisted by the many workers who have become dissatisfied, and who want to reorganize or supplant it.

Rather than fight bitterly any arrangement savoring of "closed shop" and "check-off," therefore, the far-sighted employer will play the trump card of assisting in dues collection in return for such valuable concessions as adequate probationary period, reasonable working rules, and not-too-onerous conditions within which an incompetent or uncooperative worker may be discharged. He should also warn the union leaders, from time to time, that his help in collecting their dues will be contingent on their maintaining decent standards in union administration—e.g., avoiding unreasonable penalties for individual members or would-be members.

Layoffs, Rehiring; Work Sharing and Seniority.—Many trade unionists regard a definite and written program for the contingency of short time and layoffs in slack seasons as a matter of the first importance. Such workers are apt to insist on some sort of seniority and/or work-sharing provisions in their contracts. The silence of the hosiery master agreement on this subject does not mean that no definite programs are agreed upon in this industry; this silence rather testifies to the difficulty of drafting a definite plan that will sufficiently satisfy the various union locals and union shop employers. The emphasis on rather rigid seniority rules in layoffs and rehirings, which spread rapidly among American unions during the depression years of the 1930's, has long been characteristic of our railway train service organizations. The railway industry, it would appear, took over this philosophy along with others from the still older traditions of military and maritime forces. In the latter organizations—especially regular Army and Navy officers—we find promotions based very much on seniority, which is not nearly so much invoked for this purpose in trade unions. For all these personnel problems, however (layoff, rehiring, promotion, demotion, and pay-rate change) there is a continual jostling of more or less incompatible principles, notably (1) work sharing, (2) seniority (variously interpreted, as within departments, plants, companies), (3) family responsibilities, and (4) individual competence. Each of the first three of these is an objective criterion, little susceptible to use for covert discrimination against union members, nepotism or favoritism. Hence, we find unions, with their general predilection for personnel methods whose operation they can practicably audit, favoring various combinations among these three, and tending to frown on the employer's favorite—"individual merit." The employer, of course, usually has great need to select a few "key men" of low seniority but with particular versatility or competence, for retention in any drastic layoff; on the other hand it is natural that, when unions which have been savagely fought finally gain the foothold of recognition, they should use rigid seniority as a device for protecting their members against discrimination. Other factors which influence union policy and practice in this field of eligibility are the percentage of women among the workers and their marital status, and degree of seasonality of the industry. In a distinctly seasonal employment, straight seniority tends to make the short-service workers bear most of the burden of unemployment; hence the latter are apt to press for work sharing. (The automobile union agreements usually provide for work sharing down to a certain specified point, then for layoffs by seniority.)

A recent research on these problems concludes:

Industrial workers want job security. In large measure the success of any union organization drive is dependent on the degree to which the union can claim credit for protection of the members' jobs. Union officers attempt to afford such protection in two ways: by insistence on straight seniority, or "legislative control" over employment policies or by continuous negotiation through joint union-management committees, which might be termed "administrative control."[12]

The latter (more flexible and adaptive "administrative control") method naturally is possible only when a high degree of mutual confidence between union and employer has been achieved—and even then, many undesirable heritages of past labor struggles in the whole industry will be hard to get rid of. In the following pages we shall observe some of the methods by which joint "administrative control" of eligibility to work has been sought—one outstanding problem being merit ratings of individual employees.[13]

Eligibility to Occupations, to Retirement, and to Other Indirect Wages.—In various further important ways labor incomes and costs are bound up with methods of determining who may work, and when, at a given job. One example is supplied by the occupational paths toward higher or lower wage rates which a labor agreement may require many workers to traverse, during expanding and contracting labor requirements, in accordance with their respective seniority rights. Such regressions ("bumping") and progressions are common in the mass-production unions. As stressed in previous chapters, labor

---

[12] F. H. Harbison, *The Seniority Principle in Union-Management Relations,* p. 38 (Princeton Univ., 1939). See also the same author's *Seniority Policies and Procedures as developed through Collective Bargaining* (Princeton, 1941, 63 pp.).

[13] Discussed in Ch. 15-C, below.

costs of growing importance are vacations with pay and employers' contributions toward unemployment compensation and toward annuities or "pensions"; still another (as yet unusual) is dismissal pay to personnel which must be prematurely let out of a declining industry or section of industry. This last provision has been made in a few unionized industries, such as men's clothing manufacture, and by joint financial contributions, as well as in non-contributory fashion by individual employers.

Some Social Problems of Eligibility.—As is generally realized, there are many profound issues involved in various conceptions and policies relative to "the right to work," in addition to those explicitly mentioned above. Extreme applications of the work-sharing principle, for instance, were made in many plants after 1929, and to a deplorable extent our NRA and Wage-Hour legislation have been promoted by misconceptions as to how far shortening of hours and raising of wage rates can be remedies rather than palliatives of unemployment.

Still more dubious, perhaps, is the long-term effect of simple and sweeping seniority rights to employment. They help to produce a growing body of unemployed young people whose youthful tendencies toward radical social programs are thereby fortified. Again, seniority work rights, especially when coupled with excessive protection against discharge, tend to develop a steady, stable, elderly working personnel, of somewhat mediocre competence and effort. It would be a large task to prove charges of this sort against any particular group, such as the railway industry, whose low-seniority and maintenance workers have certainly suffered keenly as the great depression added its weight to the already declining trend of rail employment.[14] No easy method is likely to be found for determining the best complex of provisions for the workers' security; but it will be

---

14 Among numerous complications of the problems of railway work, incomes, and labor costs were the old voluntary pension systems, which had grown up (in many cases) without adequate actuarial foundations. These schemes have been more or less salvaged by the (Federal) Railroad Retirement Board program, which, like the railway traditions on employment rights, is now beneficial chiefly to the longer-service workers.

helpful in evaluating each actual or proposed plan if we try to remember that the practical alternative to it is not necessarily the degree of insecurity which afflicts such employees when they have no protection from either labor unions or social legislation.

C-2. WAGE METHODS; STANDARD UNION RATES

Eligibility to work is, of course, eligibility to earn labor income, through the immediate pay envelope and through indirect pay, such as pensions. Now let us notice some additional policies and practices, which even more directly affect labor incomes and costs. One of these is suggested by the formula which has been current for many generations: "A fair day's work for a fair day's pay"; others by the phrases "standard (or union) minimum wage rate" and "working (or shop) rules and practices." The "union rate" specifies what the organization regards, for the time being, as fair (minimum) pay for a given type of work in a given vicinity; it also often means that the union members doing similar work must earn at least this minimum, whether they work for the same employer or for different employers. "Working rules" are intended to protect this wage standardization, in particular to safeguard the worker from being obliged to do more than a "fair day's work" for his day's pay. Problems of wage standards will occupy the remainder of this chapter; problems of work standards, Chapter 15, below.

Work and Pay Relations Analyzed.—Any work-and-pay situation may be further analyzed into the following four essentials :[15]

> (a) The method of measuring or estimating the individual worker's *actual* accomplishment, productivity or efficiency during any pay period.
> (b) The *standard* or *minimum* efficiency which is supposed to apply to this worker so long as he holds this job.

---

[15] For fuller discussion of this analysis see my *Compensating Industrial Effort,* Part II.

(Such standard or theoretical labor efficiency is fixed, for relatively long periods; while naturally the actual efficiency of each worker fluctuates from day to day.)

(c) The money-rate of remuneration, per hour or other time period. (In piece work, this time rate is implicit, being the amount which it is assumed that the average competent piece worker is able to make under normal working conditions.)

(d) The formula or method by which the foregoing three elements are related, to determine the worker's earnings in any pay period (e.g., piece work or day work).

These four threads, of course, are in practice very much intertwined; and for purposes of the following brief discussion it is unnecessary to distinguish them sharply. In particular we need not give a separate treatment in this chapter to (c) above (hourly earned rates), since that is the chief subject matter of this whole book. Our present task is rather to make clear what implications time and piece rates of earnings have with reference to methods of measuring labor's accomplishment or efficiency, and of utilizing whatever labor-efficiency measurements are available to determine the amount of earnings.[16]

British and American Union Policies re Payment Methods.—It is commonly but erroneously supposed that employers usually prefer piece work, unions day work. The Webbs properly emphasized, more than 40 years ago

. . . What the trade unionists are aiming at, in the one case as in the other, is uniformity in the *rate* of remuneration. In some industries this can be maintained only by insisting on time wages. In others, covering, as it happens, a far larger number of organized workmen, time wages would produce just the opposite result, and the trade unionists accordingly insist, with equal determination, on payment by the piece.[17]

---

[16] See also Chs. 2-A, 4, and 8, above, on usages of "labor productivity." "Labor efficiency" or "accomplishment" is used throughout this book to designate the physical or technical result attributable to *the worker's* proficiency and effort.

[17] S. and B. Webb, *Industrial Democracy*, (1920 ed.), p. 285.

These authors proceeded to tabulate three lists of (British) trade unions, with their respective memberships in 1894. The first group of 49 unions insisted on piece work; this list included 322,000 coal miners; also various textile, shoe, and garment workers; cigar makers, and certain workers in metals and ceramics. Their second list comprised 24 unions which "willingly recognized in various departments both piece work and time work." These craftsmen included metal tradesmen, printers, and cabinet makers. The third list, covering 38 unions which insisted on time work, covered building tradesmen, machinists ("engineers"), and some other metal tradesmen.[18] The Webbs also gave some reason to suppose that "among trade unionists a larger percentage worked by the piece than among the workers in unorganized trades." At the time they wrote, individual piece work was almost the only prevailing form of "payment by results," though Halsey, Rowan, and other managers and engineers were already experimenting with their now well-known bonus methods. Since that time a majority of the "engineering" or machinist workers in Britain have come to accept piece work and bonus methods.[19]

To a remarkable extent the Webbs' old classification of methods of payment by industries applies not only to Britain but to the United States today. Among the important points in which it is not applicable are: the more general present use of payment by results in British iron and steel ("engineering")

---

[18] These lists purported to include all trade unions in the United Kingdom (as of 1894) having more than 1,000 members, except unions of unskilled laborers and transport workers. The memberships, of course, are only very rough measures of the relative incidence of piece and time work. In the miners' unions, for instance, there are always many workers, such as surface laborers and maintenance crafts, whose work is not sufficiently standardized to be paid for by measurement of output. As of 1924, 59% of British miners were paid by time rates; and in 11 of 22 mining fields in 11 countries, 50% or more of coal miners were paid by time rates. (Internat. Lab. Off., *Principles and Methods of Wage Determination in the Coal-Mining Industry,* Geneva, 1931, p. 18.) The British position as to methods of payment by industries, unions, and reasons therefor, was re-examined by G. D. H. Cole in 1918; see his *Payment of Wages,* Ch. 2. More recent material may be found, e.g., in J. Hilton *et al., Are Trade Unions Obstructive?* (1935).

[19] L. M. Yates, *Wages and Labour Conditions in British Engineering,* Chs. 5, 6, (1937). Cf. my *Compensating Industrial Effort,* pp. 83 n, 132-134, 141 n.

trades, mentioned above; and the tendency of many American craft unions to promote day work in place of "incentive" wages.[20] The latter attitude is no doubt strongly attributable to the prominence in the AFL of building, printing, and machinist tradesmen, all of whom have had day-work predilections in Britain as well.[21]

Variations of Piece-Work Principle.—Trade unionists in all lands have tended more strongly to oppose the various "fancy" bonus plans of payment[22] than plain piece work. The former are somewhat more difficult to understand; moreover, they have been rather more used by anti-union employers. Another important objection to most of these bonus schemes is that, beyond a certain point, the workman's earnings increase less than proportionately to his output; still another, that some bonus plans are so complex that the workers cannot satisfactorily check the employer's computations of their earnings.[23]

Many wage earners favor piece work over day work, on the other hand—not only because the more competent men are thereby enabled to make higher earnings, but because of the relative freedom from supervisory discipline which piece workers often enjoy. When the work, moreover, for technical reasons is difficult for the employer closely to supervise, there is a special advantage in payment by results. Hence, we find the tonnage basis of payment nearly universal for those coal miners who work in small and scattered teams; moreover, we

---

20 See, e.g., Matthew Woll, *Wage Negotiations and Practices*—a pamphlet published by the AFL, 1925.

21 The British "engineering" unions also resisted (especially the newer types of) incentive systems; but, obliged to accept them, redirected their efforts to achieving joint control over methods of administering these wage methods.

22 The systems of Halsey, Rowan, Emerson, Bedaux, and so on. Cf. D. A. McCabe, *The Standard Rate in American Trade Unions*, Ch. 4 and App. B (Baltimore: Johns Hopkins Univ. Press, 1912); and Ch. 15-B, below.

23 F. W. Taylor was devoted to the straight piece-work principle (sometimes recommending a "differential piece rate"—i.e., a higher rate for performance at and above (the Taylor) standard of efficiency than below); and he strongly favored notifying each worker, early every day, how much he had earned the day before. Thus, obscurity and complexity with reference to computation of earnings are by no means inherent in incentive wage systems.

find coal miners prizing the comparative freedom which they enjoy.[24] The mechanization of mining doubtless decreases the scope of individual piece work; it may, however, lead to more applications of group piece work.

Merits and Applications of Day-Work Principle.—In the printing industries, particularly for the work of compositors (type setters), piece work was very common until mechanical composition developed rapidly, around 1900. The Typographical Union was brilliantly successful in maintaining employment of its members at operation of the new machines; and its policy has long been opposed to piece rates for machine work. In these circumstances not a few employers also recognized many advantages to themselves in the day- or week-work system.[25]

In many cases, moreover, where payment is made with direct reference to the worker's current output, there is a guaranteed time rate. This guaranty tends to minimize grievances when workers are handicapped by lack of materials, faulty equipment, or other maladjustments; furthermore, it is often necessary to employ, at day work, a person who is normally on an incentive basis—perhaps because there is no work available in his normal occupation, or because he must be put on a new model job for which output standards have not yet been fully established. In the latter case a conscientious and competent worker is needed, who may well be assured the average rate he has earned per hour when on piece work.

---

[24] See Carter Goodrich, *The Miner's Freedom* (1926).

[25] "[Newspaper] publishers in New York generally assert that, irrespective of the union, they prefer the time system to the piece system, because it permits greater elasticity in shifting a man from one kind of work to another. When paid by the piece the swift compositor wishes to be kept at one kind of work. Intricate records are required in order to compute wages. The abolition of the piece system has removed one of the main sources of friction in offices, as under that system a large part of the time of the foreman and chairman of the chapel is consumed in dealing with the adjustment of extras, "fat," etc. The piece scales are very elaborate and minute in details. All of these grounds of friction are abolished by the adoption of the time system. Moreover, the machine is really a pace maker, as stated by one employer. It has a motion of its own, which, as it were, draws the operator along."—U. S. Bureau of Labor (C. D. Wright, John R. Commons, *et al.*), Eleventh Special Report, *Regulation and Restriction of Output,* pp. 49, 50 (1904).

Pay Methods in Rail and Building Trades.—Among the older and quantitatively important occupations in which payment methods reflect these principles of payment by results, qualified by guaranteed time earnings, are the railway train services:

The wages of engineers, firemen, and conductors, except those in the switching service, are commonly paid at mileage rates with guarantees of payment for a certain number of miles per hour for the time worked. The rates are expressed in terms of cents per mile, not in hours, and for the most part, except in local and slow freight service, payment is in fact for miles actually covered. The railway unions have favored the system of payment by mileage and have done much to extend it, and they are largely responsible for the present form of the guarantees.[26]

In these occupations the combinations of mileage and time bases of compensation have become extremely complex. Besides the guaranty of minimum rates of earnings per hour, there are also guaranties of minimum total earnings, for each day or part of a day worked—though not guaranties of minimum earnings per month or per year. There are also rather elaborate regulations regarding overtime payments, and these higher overtime rates have sometimes accounted for an appreciable fraction of the total wages received, especially in the freight service.[27] It is not clear whether much of the logical ground for payment by results is left in this train-service wage structure, since the number of miles run in any day is largely, if not wholly, beyond the control of the worker. Apparently the chief argument in favor of it has always been that the running of each type of train for 100 miles is worth a given wage bill to the employer, even if it may be run in a lesser

---

[26] McCabe, *op. cit.*, pp. 72, 73. The mileage basis of payment, however, has been uncommon among British trainmen. (Cole, *op. cit.*, p. 9.)

[27] McCabe, *op. cit.*, p. 74. Taking at random the month of April 1939 as a sample, however, payments for overtime constituted only 5½% of the total remuneration of train and engine service personnel; and a lesser fraction for other major classes. The "time paid for but not worked" category in ICC wage statistics reflects guaranties of minimum earnings for any day in which the employee is called to work; "constructive allowances," the "hours" paid for, represented by miles actually run in less than the time paid for.

number of hours than some slower train. The system may also
give some incentive to crews to keep trains on time.

It is rather obvious why the building trade unions have always been opposed to piece work. Most of these tradesmen
have been employed in comparatively short engagements by
rather small employers, under extremely variable conditions as
to materials, weather, and so on. For the same reasons not many
building employers would care to assume the expense and other
difficulties involved in establishing satisfactory piece or bonus
rates. Hence, there has been no widespread demand on the employing side for thorough-going payment by results in the building trades. It is said that American building contractors get
relatively high efficiency from their labor, by reason of the comparative freedom allowed them by the trade unions to pick and
choose among (union-member) workers in hiring and in laying
off. (Seniority and work-sharing rules have been rare or non-
existent in these trades, though their short-hours movement is
no doubt motivated considerably by work-sharing philosophy.)

It is by no means unthinkable, nevertheless, that piece work
should in the future become widely used in unionized building
trades. Nearly every contractor, however small, is obliged for
estimating and bidding to ascertain his approximate standard
costs per square foot for putting on lath and plaster; and so on
for all the other more or less standard building operations.
Self-employed building workers, such as lathers, commonly
take contracts at piece rates; moreover, contractors sometimes
make temporary bargains with their building workers which
amount to payment by results. As the development of larger-
scale employing agencies proceeds in the construction industries, and as the position of trade unions becomes more firmly
established throughout American industry, it is quite possible
that methods of payment based more immediately upon output
will be developed in construction as well as elsewhere. Perhaps,
however, this tendency will work out rather in the form of adjustment of salaries of individuals to their apparent competence,
as has been the trend in retail merchandising.[28]

---

[28] Cf. *Compensating Industrial Effort*, pp. 305 f.

Do Workers Want the Simplest Wage Methods?—A few more words are in order here on simplicity and complexity of wage plans, from the wage earner's point of view. An objection often put forward against bonus systems is that it is too hard for the worker to understand them and compute earnings; doubtless it is true that simplicity of a wage scheme is (within limits) a great virtue. Ordinary day work is outstanding in simplicity; and "it is highly probable that the greater convenience in bargaining and enforcing and the greater solidarity of interest engendered by a single rate, also make the uniform minimum rate of pay attractive to the unions."[29] A good many seemingly arbitrary classifications are reasonably defensible on this ground of administrative practicability, in most human affairs.

Yet even the few particulars given above concerning union wage methods, especially in the old piece-working industries and in the railway train service, show that union control does not necessarily lead to extreme simplicity. On the contrary, over a long period it tends to build up piece-work structures— as in the textile, needle, and shoe-manufacturing trades—which to outsiders are exceedingly complex. One result of such complexity is to make it increasingly difficult to resort satisfactorily, for arbitrators or umpires, to individuals who have not had long experience within the industry.

Scale and Type of Production, in re Wage Method.—The similarity of the pictures of payment methods by industries in Britain and the United States over the last four or five decades also leads to several further reflections. To a considerable extent, as was indicated above, the industrial distributions of unions and their traditions in these two nations are similar. Certain technical conditions, like those applying to coal mining, also tend to produce their characteristic wage methods, wherever the industry is located.

Another outstanding factor, of course, is the volume in which a relatively standardized good is produced. In this sense repetition of operations is a factor making for payment by re-

---

[29] McCabe, *op. cit.*, p. 89.

sults. Payment according to output is not economically feasible for a very small volume of production, like samples, novelties, early outputs of new models, and goods produced under highly variable difficulties. Payment by some piece rate or bonus plan has been much more characteristic of larger than of smaller plants or operating units, particularly before the rise of the mass-production unions.[30] Among reasons for this difference are the following: The larger employers can best afford the cost of the engineering work necessary to establish and apply standards of output to the various jobs. Such employers, moreover, characteristically have groups of people working in similar occupations and under very similar conditions. Here is one clue to the importance of piece work in railway shops, textiles, boots and shoes, and others of the earlier-established factory trades.

Two qualifications, however, are important with reference to this factor of scale of production. First it should be noticed that a good many types of work done for *small* employers are paid in part, if not wholly, by results—such as hair cutting, typing, and agricultural plowing and harvesting. In these instances the volume of work for a given employer may be small, but the volume of similar work in the aggregate is large and the local rates reflect collective experience with the special local difficulties under which the work is done, as well as the local supply of and demand for such workers.

The second qualification, in reference to repetition as a factor in wage methods, is suggested by the continuous processes which have become so important in mass production. Here the employing establishment is apt to be large, but payment by results is less common than in the textile and other *older* repetitive factory employments. The Ford automotive plants supply leading examples; here only time rates are used in wage payment; there are no piece rates or bonus arrangements.[31] An outstanding reason why day work is often preferred in such

---

[30] See, e.g., National Industrial Conference Board, *Systems of Wage Payment,* p. 9 (1930); also the Board's *Studies,* Nos. 217 (p. 17) and 221 (p. 12).

[31] The Ford wage structure, too, appears to be unusually simple in the sense of relatively few "brackets" of hourly rates among all occupations.

mass production is the comparative inflexibility of the rate of output of each individual member of each group—there is little practical and immediate opportunity for the individual to do either more or less in a day than is prescribed by the schedule. The publisher's remark of 1904 or earlier,[32] "The machine is really a pace maker; it has a motion of its own, which, as it were, draws the work along," has been echoed by innumerable other observers. By use of day work in this situation, the management saves much of the cost of inspection of goods in process and of counting the outputs of individuals. Such costs are commonly involved in administering individual piece-work or bonus plans, especially under intermittent processing arrangements.

Although much of mass production is therefore unsuitable for *individual piece work,* it is well suited to *group piece-work and bonus methods,* which largely prevailed throughout the automotive industry (except at Ford's) a few years ago. The unions favored the change to straight day work in this industry, chiefly because it simplified their drive for increased *minimum* day rates, and to a lesser extent because of accumulated irritations with the group payment plans. One defect of some of these was managements' attempts to get the benefits of mutual supervision among group members in pay groups which were too large for that purpose.[33]

Day work as practiced in the mass-production industries, however, is a very different matter from the old day work of small employers at variable tasks and under variable difficulties. The former's working schedules are based on detailed engineering studies, of the same types that are used for the more advanced piece-work systems. Hence, these industries, with their conveyors and professionally set schedules, get high labor efficiency for their day rates—and will get still more, as they solve the problems of "speed-ups" and "slow-downs" discussed in the following chapter.

A somewhat more general factor influencing wage methods is the relation between the overhead cost for plant and equip-

---

[32] Cited on p. 397, above.
[33] Cf. Ch. 15-C, below, for further comments on group wage incentives.

ment and the wage bill for direct or variable labor.[34] When the overhead costs are high relative to cost for direct labor, the management has a special motive for trying to increase the latter's efficiency—that is, to secure use of the expensive machines, salaried overhead and so on, at as near full capacity as possible. This effort may take such forms, for example, as piece-work and bonus wage methods, and multiple-shift operation. The instance of the motor-car industry, however, shows that supervisory and other production control methods can secure high utilization of expensive overhead facilities without necessarily paying the workers in immediate relation to the rate of output.

Do Unions Tend to Secure a "Dead Level" of Work and Pay?—It is often charged that the net result of trade union policies and practices is to encourage each member to do just enough work to avoid discharge—in effect to hold down the performance of all workers to the level of the less capable and more lazy individuals. As usual, there are at least two sides to this story. One obstacle, for example, in the way of easy and accurate generalizations is the area-differences within unionized occupations, noticed below in this chapter—and the differences in efficiencies of workers among such areas. Another complication (among many) is that often it is the nature of the job (e.g., on a conveyor line), or poor equipment or management, which more or less limits the outputs and efficiencies of the more competent individual workers, rather than any trade union policy or practice. Still another is the fact that jobs in which individual efficiencies can be most easily measured are apt to be piece-work jobs—hence comparative efficiencies of day workers—union or non-union—have as yet received but little careful statistical treatment.

Contrasts between piece-working and time-working unions with reference to the "dead-level" question, therefore, are very unlikely to be fair and adequate. For both types, the working rules and practices discussed in the following chapter (found among non-union as well as union workers) give all too much

---

[34] These matters are treated in Ch. 2-A, above.

color to the sweeping indictment referred to above; but at least for piece-working unions there are available numerous published data showing that members of these unions do not, save in exceptional cases, hold down their best workers very close to the pace of the poorest.[35] Hence the complaint of "low dead level of output" applies least to the "union standard wage" when the latter is a *piece* rate.

Time Rates Graded by Competence.—But what if it is a day rate? Then, a close approach to uniform hourly-earned rates within the occupation and area (see below) *appears* to be the practical result of union pressures, despite the usual formal freedom of the employer to pay more than the union minimum day rate to extra-competent union men.[36]

Many union leaders have long been struggling with this problem, which usually appears to them in this guise: How can we get wage rates high enough to benefit a majority of our members, without dooming our weaker brothers to unemployment because no employer will have them at our standard rate? And some unions have tried to solve the problem by grading, or allowing employers to grade, their members by competence, and permitting suitable differentiation of day rates for such grades.

A few cases will show further how these matters have been handled. One instance which seemed to bear out the assertion that the union's *minimum* wage does not hold the able and ambitious man down was the high percentage of "premium men" in New York (closed-shop) book and job printing, before 1930. While the regular scale for compositors was $50 a week in 1922, and $54 to $55 in 1926, surveys by the Employers' Association in these two years showed that, among

---

[35] Individual differences in output, as well as in other human traits, are discussed in Ch. 3-C, above; also (in more detail) in *Compensating Industrial Effort,* Chs. 2 and 8, and in W. D. Evans, "Individual Productivity Differences," USBLS Serial No. R 1040 (published in part in *Mo. Lab. Rev.,* Feb. 1940). The most efficient union piece workers not infrequently produce twice as much as the least efficient—who are able to hold their jobs and who work under fully comparable conditions.

[36] See McCabe, *op. cit.,* p. 106 ff. on various aspects of theory (and practice, before 1910) relative to "the union rate and actual wages."

all the crafts, some 45% were "premium men," receiving from
$1 to $10 a week above the standard rate. Since 1930, however, such "premium men" have been rare.[37]

To some extent other differentiations of day rates are formally permitted by the unions within occupations and areas.
Individuals who are either newly fledged journeymen or are
handicapped by age or otherwise, and are recognized as below
standard competence, are not infrequently allowed to work
at sub-standard rates. Various crafts, moreover, such as the
lathers, woodcarvers, stonecutters, carpenters, and railway shop
crafts have sometimes tried grading their experienced, non-
handicapped members according to competence, and prescribing standard rates for such grades.[38]

The majority of day-working trade unionists who have considered such plans, however, have opposed such grading, usually
on the ground that it offers too much temptation to fully
competent or extra-competent men to accept employment at
low-grade rates. Hence, the orthodox union position is that,
within any trade or occupational group and locality, there is to
be but one standard minimum union rate applying to all but
(perhaps) a very small minority of probationary and handicapped workers; and the employers are allowed to make individual bargains at *higher than* the standard rate. In practice
such individual bargains appear seldom to be made, and trade
union earned day rates seem to have tended toward uniformity
—within occupations and normal working hours, and within
standard wage areas.

A principal obstacle to grading day workers as to compe-

---

[37] Information from New York Employing Printers' Association.

[38] "The Post Office is an example of a time-work industry with an
elaborate system of remuneration based upon graded incremental scales of
salaries and wages. . . . The trade union standard rate is continually attacked by employers and economists on the ground that it tends to ensure
the same remuneration to the less capable and to the slacker as to the more
capable or more energetic workers. This argument has not been without
its force among trade union leaders of the individualist school. For instance, it was strongly emphasized by Mr. W. J. Davis, General Secretary
of the National Society of Brassworkers, when he was arguing in favour
of the scheme—now in force in the Birmingham brass trade—of grading
workers according to capacity."—Cole, *op. cit.,* pp. 14, 15. Cf. McCabe, *op.
cit.,* p. 94 ff.

tence or efficiency is the difficulty of devising satisfactory measures of comparative "merits" of such individuals.[39] Some of the older grading schemes, referred to above, operated through collaboration between managers and union committees. This principle also underlies the clothing industries' use of "week work with production standards." In the latter type of plan, the individual worker's weekly wage rate is graded according to a count of his output over comparatively long periods —for instance, his weekly rate in one month may be determined by his production record in the preceding month. These needle trades, of course, have also had extensive and comparatively satisfactory experience with individual piece work, under rather long and complete acceptance of collective bargaining by their employers. Such conditions are favorable to union acceptance of incentive payment.

As unions study the pro's and con's of alternative wage methods, under increasing security of their own existence, and as various income-security measures are developed, they are likely to cooperate with fair-minded employers in the development of pay incentives—including use of merit ratings of day workers and other *partial* indicators of individual efficiency, for purposes of wage payment. Cole is undoubtedly right in saying that trade unions primarily desire effective participation in the wage-setting processes, rather than either the day or the piece type of payment as such.

It is often suggested that labor organizations tend to foster the collectivist, at the expense of the individualist tendencies of their members; and that, although there are many good features of group loyalty, it becomes a vice when it represses the inclination of the more able and vigorous people to earn as much as they can by exerting themselves to the full of their powers. The communistic or egalitarian ideal is not, in my judgment, an important factor in American trade union attitudes toward wage methods. Their "collectivist spirit" is rather a disposition to protect the employment and earnings of fellow-workers who are weak—in working capacity or otherwise in

---

[39] See next chapter, section C.

liability to discharge or layoff.[40] The payment of individuals (except, of course, employer-subsidized "pace-makers") according to their respective efficiencies appeals rather strongly to the majority of workers, union and non-union; and this is a force tending to promote both time rates graded according to the workers' competence, and piece-work and bonus plans.

Areas of Union Wage Rates.—Some further problems pertain to the geographical or industrial area of the union minimum wage rate. It must suffice to say here that virtually all unions which have members distributed over wide territories are obliged to vary the terms of remuneration in their local contracts, in some sort of relation to local conditions. Union scales of wage rates and hours are published from time to time by the U. S. Bureau of Labor Statistics—for example, with reference to building and printing unions. These scales are classified according to cities as well as occupations—and the practical uniformity of earned rates within each craft tends to define the "prevailing wage" sharply in each city. At the top of the following page is a small segment from such a table.

In the building trades, the usual unit of jurisdiction is the city local union, whose geographical area often reaches beyond the municipal limits. Frequently it includes suburbs as well, as in "Greater New York," sometimes "within a 25-(or 30 or 40) mile radius." Frequently the county is designated as the area, but occasionally several counties are included.[41]

In some industries, such as coal mining, the areas within which union wage rates apply are in many cases larger; for example, state and even interstate regions. Certain automobile manufacturers maintain very similar wage scales in their local plants, scattered throughout the land. Thus, the hourly earnings (or at least the *minimum* wage rates) in such plants in low wage areas may be far above those in the most nearly comparable local occupations. Such anomalies, however, have frequently

---

[40] As shown in the following chapter, these motives of more or less benevolent and enlightened self-interest sometimes pass, by easy stages, into group restrictive practices which the men can justify to themselves only by elaborate sophistries.

[41] *Mo. Lab. Rev.*, April 1936, p. 13.

UNION SCALES OF WAGES AND HOURS IN CERTAIN CITIES, MAY 15,
1937, AND MAY 15, 1936—BRICKLAYERS

	May 15, 1937		May 15, 1936	
	Rates of wages per hour	Hours per week	Rates of wages per hour	Hours per week
Atlanta, Ga...............	$1.250	40	$1.125	40
Baltimore, Md..............	1.250	40	1.100	40
Birmingham, Ala...........	1.500	40	1.250	40
Boston, Mass..............	1.500	40	1.300	40
Buffalo, N. Y..............	1.500	40	1.250	40
Butte, Mont...............	1.625	30	1.625	30
Charleston, S. C...........	1.000	44	1.000	44
Charleston, W. Va.........	1.500	40	1.333	40
Chicago, Ill...............	1.500	40	1.500	40
Sewer and tunnel.........	1.750	48	1.750	48
Cincinnati, Ohio...........	1.625	40	1.375	40
Cleveland, Ohio...........	1.625	40	1.375	40
Sewer and caisson........	2.000	40	1.750	40
Columbus, Ohio...........	1.563	40	1.300	40
Dallas, Tex...............	1.500	40	1.125	40

Source: *Union Scales of Wages and Hours in the Building Trades in 70 Cities,* USBLS Bull. 657, April 1938. This bulletin contains statistical analysis, including that relating to variations in scales by regions and by size of city. In general, the southern scales for journeymen were some 10% lower than for northern and Pacific cities of the same size; and the southern scales for helpers and laborers were some 30% below those of northern cities of comparable size. In both regions the scales tended to vary directly with size of city, though not quite consistently.

As is well known, craft unions (like other business organizations) sometimes make secret concessions to their customers, which occasionally will undermine the nominal "union scale" seriously. The extensive payroll survey by E. P. Sanford in 1936, however (see *Mo. Lab. Rev.,* Aug. 1937), showed average hourly earnings by crafts and localities which were similar to the most nearly comparable union scales, as given in Bull. 657.

developed independently of trade union power. They testify once more to the tendency of the larger and more prosperous employers to pay higher wages; and no doubt are due in part to the employer's need, occasionally, to shift workers back and forth among his plants.

The areas of standard rates of railway workers, particularly in train service, have become very wide. During government control of all American railroads in 1918-20, the unions were able to secure national agreements which tended to level wage rates upward throughout the nation; but after return of the roads to their private owners some reversion toward sectional differentiation occurred. In still more recent years, national scale bargaining on railway wages has turned the tide once more rather strongly in the direction of nation-wide standardization of occupational rates.

Most national trade unions have avowed policies of bringing upward the lower wage areas toward equality with the better-paid. In general, they do not formally concede that wages should be lower in smaller towns and in milder climates, by reason of lower living costs; yet this latter consideration dampens somewhat their militancy in leveling upward, as does also the argument that higher wages in big cities have attracted superior workmen into these high wage territories. In practice, furthermore, the variable degrees of success which most unions experience in different regions tends to increase wage differences between the more and less strongly organized regions.[42]

Comparing areas of time and piece rates about 1909, McCabe made the following observations:

> The usual area of the *time rate* is the locality. . . . The tendency toward wider than local areas of rate application is not nearly so strong among the time-working as among the piece-working unions. This is due to the fact that the areas of competition are not so wide for the time-working trades [e.g. building] as a group as for the piece-work trades. . . . Non-uniform piece rates, where conditions are similar, are standing evidence of differences in labor costs. . . . Where minimum time rates differ, proportional differences in labor costs do not necessarily follow.[43]

It is doubtless still correct to say that there is a stronger tendency toward uniformity in piece-work earnings over intercity regions, than of day rates. Exceptions, however, on both sides

---

[42] "The fact that the union has as yet been unable to develop any significant organization in the low wage regions has prevented it from reducing these differentials. In fact the union has increased them (except in the motor-vehicle branch) since its greatest wage gains have been won chiefly in the regions where the rates were already highest."—W. H. McPherson, *Labor Relations in the Automobile Industry*, p. 88 (Washington, 1940).

[43] *Op. cit.*, pp. 163, 181-182 (italics added). See also *ibid.*, pp. 134, 171 on arguments in the *Molders' Journal* over the policy of wide-area uniform piece rates, regardless of variations in living costs.

were noted above—for example, nearly uniform day rates in some widely scattered automobile plants, the recent modification of the hosiery union's policy away from uniform piece rates, and national bargaining in railway train service, over what are essentially day rates.

Social Problems of Standard-Wage-Rate Philosophy.— The foregoing sketch, together with our discussions in Chapters 9 and 12 (on wage paying capacity and the special wage problems of rising and declining industries), shows some of the guises in which problems of wage standardization appear; and we shall encounter still others when we deal with public wage controls. The interpretation of this standard-union-wage principle which will meet with most general approval identifies it with the local prevailing wage, as outlined in Chapter 10 above —*within each locality,* every wage should be kept closely in line with the current earnings in the corresponding grade of skill and efficiency. Within such a locality, moreover, workers should be wary of taking lower wages to enable their own employer to survive, except as a last and temporary resort.

Between regions, however, which differ markedly in such factors as climate, population density, and industrial history, the "principle of wage standardization" becomes increasingly difficult of satisfactory interpretation—and more attractive to people who insist on simple solutions than to those who try to take broader and longer views. One of the oldest over-simplifications in economic thought is the notion that commodities and services which are *physically* alike should have the same value, wherever, and whenever found. It is indeed a reasonable and feasible objective to assist workers in low wage territories by trade union, legal, and other ways to obtain the full *local* value of their labor. But if we insist further that they must be paid as much as any member of their grade in any part of the nation, then we are usually attempting what is not only impracticable but undesirable. We are, in effect, trying to freeze the existing geographic distribution of industries, and to bar the low wage, agricultural regions from the rate of industrialization which is necessary to give them increasing employment as well as increased earning power. Many measures are needed, as recognized particularly in Chapters 12 and 20 herein, to ease the pains of geographic readjustments—including various sorts of cost reduction in the sections which are losing too many industries. These lowered costs, and the rising wage rates which tend to be produced by increasing competition for labor in the newly industrialized regions, will make for a higher national average of real earnings (for the nation's *whole* working population) than could be achieved by the degree or rate of wage standardization upward which would obstruct such redistribution of industry.[44]

D. Summary

This chapter, and the one which follows, treat of wage factors in the framework of collective bargaining. Some re-

[44] As shown elsewhere (see Chs. 6, 19, 20) in this book, different living costs offer a less convincing ground for area-differences in wage rates than is commonly supposed, since part of the *apparent* differences in living costs are due to different living standards—people with lower real incomes have to put up with lower living standards. Nevertheless, if the actual differences in living costs are disregarded, equalizing of *money* wage rates certainly signifies creation of new inequalities in real wages. The areas of highest wage rates, too, may be those in which monopolistic practices of labor and/or employers flourish most freely. But the most important objection to too-hasty leveling upward is that it tends to promote geographical redistribution of industries in the opposite direction of that corresponding to demands and supplies of all consumers and workers, through the nation as a whole. Regional differences in wage rates are in part symptomatic of the social need for two flows—one, of workers toward higher wages, the other, of employers toward lower wages. If wage rates were suddenly equalized over all regions, these flows would be checked, if not reversed.

Whether upward leveling has actually gone to the danger point or above in any American industry is a more difficult question. A trade union critic of the foregoing paragraphs says, in part, "The trade unions have not been sufficiently strong in this country to seriously affect this [rural industrialization process]. . . . The minimums established by the NRA . . . [and by] the present Wage-Hour Law were and are to a large extent operative only against the sweatshop operator or the sub-marginal plant. Unless there are standards of payment, the tendency in depressed industry is for a flow away from any area which has created any type of standard into some section where no standard prevails at all. . . . The type of plant that moves to a lower and lower wage area is almost invariably one with a short life." On the other hand, unions and unionized employers may form powerful political pressure groups, invoking the national government's power to restrain their competitors, many of whom are in lower wage areas. See the latter parts of Ch. 12, above, and of Ch. 20, below, for data and arguments on northern and southern cotton manufacturing wages.

marks were added to those in previous chapters, warning against generalizing too broadly from the experiences of or with a few unions or employers. In this connection perhaps we should have placed still greater emphasis on the degree in which employers have sincerely accepted real trade unions as "here to stay." Fortunately, a virtuous circle often develops, as time passes after the militant struggles of a union's rise to power. The employer may become, not merely resigned to the inevitable, but increasingly cooperative, and thereby earn and teach constructive cooperation from the union's side.

The bulk of this chapter consists of a survey of practices, problems, and principles in two great divisions of organized industrial relations—eligibility to a job, and method and scale of pay. Under the former head, we have found much that is sound in such union policies and practices as seniority, work sharing, and "closed shop"; and we have argued against obstructive and anti-social applications of the wholesome general principles of increasingly equitable distribution of opportunity to work. Undoubtedly union-management cooperation will develop safeguards to the workers, within which incentive payment systems acceptable to labor unions can grow.

The areas of wage standards, as the labor movement is consolidated, now present more dubious prospects. Trade unionists, and the many others who assist them in writing concrete social legislation, seem to have a tendency to level upward wage-rates as fast as possible over wider and wider areas, and to underrate the *economic* differences of our diverse areas.

CHAPTER 15

MEASUREMENT AND STANDARDS OF LABOR EFFICIENCY

In this chapter we are to deal further with policies and practices of both managements and workers relative to the quantity and quality of work done for the wage. We begin, in section A, with a brief survey of problems which, from one point of view, are commonly designated "restriction or limitation of output," from another point of view "working rules and practices." This survey sketches trade union traditions of dealing with the working pace and allied matters. Next, in section B, we outline still more briefly the earlier impact of the scientific-management or industrial-engineering movement on these problems, in various types of shops; and, finally, we devote the latter half of this chapter to section C, consideration of present-day constructive efforts to safeguard both industrial progress and labor welfare, under full collective bargaining.

This dual problem of labor effort and labor cost often appears in the simple form of alleged "speed-up" or "stretch-out": the work conditions are fixed, the only question is, How many pieces per man-hour? (or, How many man-hours per piece?) But before this point in the road of work loads or assignments is reached, many ancillary issues may have to be decided, such as, Which workers may be employed on this job? During what hours? With what number and kind of helpers—if any? What equipment, materials, processes are permissible? (Union labels may be required on machines and stock, as well as on products.) These queries give a faint idea of what is meant by the "working rules and practices," and "management methods" referred to below.[1] All these matters naturally tend to affect

---

[1] Many of these practices and regulations are formally codified, by sundry employers and/or unions. The Typographical Union refers to its written rules as "laws"—which term may perhaps also embrace numerous

the employer's labor costs; they also influence real labor incomes in many ways. In the preceding chapter we have studied eligibility to work. Hence, that group of work rules will receive little or no attention in this chapter, which is concerned primarily with problems of *measuring* a particular worker's net contribution to production, and with *determining an appropriate standard of efficiency* for this worker's occupational group. For simplicity we shall often concentrate attention on mere quantity of output, assuming a more or less repetitive job; but the difficulties connected with the changing characters of jobs—which changes appear to become ever more drastic and rapid—run like a refrain through the whole exposition.[2]

A. Production Standards in the Older Unionism

How Piece Work May Protect Workers from Speed-Up. —Several of the recurrent problems in this field were clearly

---

of its unwritten practices, many of them traditions of long standing. A collective term is suggested by the title of Sidney Webb's essay, *Restoration of Trade Union Conditions* (1917), which shows in brief compass how profoundly the voluntary suspensions of many of their rules by the unions (for the duration of the war) affected post-war industrial-relations problems.

[2] One very useful treatment of this large chapter in trade union history may be found in Harry Ober, *Trade-Union Policy and Technological Change* (Philadelphia: WPA National Research Project, 1940). Ober reminds us, for example (p. 41), that the problem of "labor displacement" is apt to be brought more explicitly to the union's attention in connection with mechanization and other changes in methods than in connection with work loads under given productive conditions: ". . . The changes in work assignments considered in this section of the report have a direct and observable effect on the number of jobs available before and after the change (for example, the change from streetcar operation with two men to the one-man car, the assignment of two hosiery-knitting machines to one knitter, or the elimination of the fireman on Diesel engines). The other phase of the problem of limitation of work loads (the determination of how many units of a product a worker is expected to produce in a given time . . .) arises more frequently in connection with rate setting and wage determination. Here questions of speed of operation, intensity of labor, health, and safety are more prominent in negotiations. Although the rate of performance has a bearing on the number of jobs available, the relationship is more obscure." And in analyzing numerous illustrations of craft union declines due to poor adaptation to changing technology, Ober finds that as a rule the union leaders have shown awareness of the problem and of the need of action other than stubborn insistence on the old union policies. The frequent failures of such leaders to obtain adequate support from their followers toward making needful readjustments throws a sidelight on broader questions of "democracy" and "dictatorship" in trade union government.

apparent to the Webbs, nearly two generations ago, as is shown
by the following passage:

> On asking a leading official of the cotton-spinners' union why he
> objected to time wages, he replied that, in his opinion, it was only the
> system of piece-work remuneration that had saved his trade from the
> evils of sweating. The work of a cotton-spinner, he explained, varies
> in intensity (and his product in quantity) according to the number of
> spindles which he has to attend to, and the speed at which the ma-
> chinery runs, conditions over which the operative has no control.
> Owing to the introduction of mules bearing an increased number of
> spindles, and the constant "speeding up" of the machinery, the amount
> of work placed upon the operative is steadily, though often imper-
> ceptibly, increased. If he were paid by the hour or the day, he would
> need, in order to maintain the same rate of remuneration for the work
> done, to discover each day precisely to what degree the machinery
> was being "speeded up," and to be perpetually making demands for an
> increase in his time wages. Such an arrangement could not fail to
> result in the employer increasing the work faster than the pay.
> Under a system of payment by the amount of yarn spun, the opera-
> tive automatically gets the benefit of any increase in the number of
> spindles or rate of speed. An exact uniformity of the rate of re-
> muneration is maintained between man and man, and between mill and
> mill. If any improvement takes place in the process, by which the
> operative's labor is reduced, the onus of procuring a change in the rate
> of pay falls on the employer. The result is, that so effectually is the
> cotton-spinner secured by his piecework lists against being compelled
> to give more work without more pay, that it has been found desirable
> deliberately to concede to the employers, by lowering the rates as the
> number of spindles increases, some share of the resulting advantages,
> in order that the trade union may encourage enterprising mill-owners
> in the career of improvement.[3]

These authors may have painted a rosy picture of the textile unions of their day, perhaps in part because of their own
satisfaction that the days of old-fashioned craftsmen smashing
new-fangled machinery seemed (and still seem) to be gone by.

---

[3] S. and B. Webb, *op. cit.*, pp. 288 and 289. Cf. Ch. 9-B, above, on the
greater advantage of piece work to iron and steel workers than to coal
miners, because output per man-hour in iron and steel rose markedly, over
many years.

Their chapter "New Machinery and Processes" took a more optimistic view of trade union tendencies and influence in these matters than has been taken by many another observer down to the present time. The last sentence in the passage quoted does, however, still apply to the more far-sighted trade union members; and their influence is frequently great enough to mold the union's policy.

The Webbs were also correct in emphasizing the factor of industrial change in relation to labor effort and reward. Many, if not most, disputes over "a fair day's work" are precipitated by some innovation on the employer's part (as in model of product, character of supplies, equipment, methods), and by somewhat novel work assignments which the union regards as unreasonable. Thus, railway unions have used both economic and political power to prescribe minimum crews to be used on trains, in part because trains have grown ever bigger (lately, they have worked for and secured laws limiting size of trains); organized painters have fought the introduction of compressed-air sprays; and so on through an endless series of difficult adjustments. When he investigated (just before 1914) the relations between organized labor and the industrial-engineering movement led by Frederick W. Taylor, R. F. Hoxie emphasized that scientific management was devoted to rapid as well as progressive evolution of labor methods, whereas the old skilled crafts and their unions were best adapted to relatively static industrial conditions.[4] Fortunately, as we shall see, trade unions have already displayed much capacity to replace this static craft tradition with more progressive outlooks.

Regulation and Restriction of Output by Workers.— Apart from recurrent crises (of all degrees) connected with innovations of materials, products, equipment, methods, and

---

[4] *Scientific Management and Labor* (1915). Hoxie's investigation was made on behalf of the United States Commission on Industrial Relations, of which Professor Commons was a member. Commons was also a chief investigator in the old U. S. Bureau of Labor's elaborate research published in 1904 under the title *Regulation and Restriction of Output*. This report, covering European as well as American experience, is a rich storehouse of data and analyses bearing on the production-standards complex in industrial relations.

skills, there are also chronic difficulties about standards of labor efficiency, even in any well-managed shop and operation. We sometimes encounter the phenomenon of wilful limitation or restriction of output in its simpler and cruder form. In case a considerable number of operators or craftsmen are working under closely comparable conditions, and provided further that reliable measurement of individual output is available and also that his output is largely under control of the individual's dexterity and effort, it is relatively easy to detect voluntary restriction. Such limitation results in a "frequency-distribution" or "curve" of outputs among individuals, markedly different from that which may be expected by reason of the differing capacities of different workers, even when the poorer ones are eliminated by good selection methods or by failure on the job.[5] If, under these conditions, all members of a good-sized group produce within a few per cent of the same rate, there is good ground for suspecting voluntary restriction of output.

Trade union working rules in a very few cases have been shown plainly and explicitly to limit the output or earnings of any individual member. Somewhat similar restrictions, furthermore, are not infrequently enforced by employers, apparently usually on the theory that any worker who tries to exceed the shop limit is likely to scamp his work or waste material. And there is abundant evidence that *unorganized workers* are also susceptible to secret understandings among themselves which result in lower rates of output than are easily within the capacities of many of the workers.[6]

Motivation Prompting Union Efficiency Standards.—We have already examined some sources of these trade union methods for dealing with production or efficiency standards, but it will be useful to consider somewhat further the motivation involved. A minor factor is the worker's desire to make the work as easy and comfortable as may be. Other and more

---

[5] Cf. *Compensating Industrial Effort,* Ch. 2 and pp. 126 ff.
[6] See, e.g., S. B. Mathewson, *Restriction of Output by Unorganized Workers* (1931); F. J. Roethlisberger and W. J. Dickson, *Management and the Worker* (Harvard University Bureau of Business Research, 1934).

important causes appear to be (1) concern for the health and safety of the workers (especially of the weaker), (2) suspicion that the explicit or implied terms of the labor contract are being evaded, and (3) efforts of the wage earners to mitigate unemployment and part-time employment.

1. Employers and employed, of course, each tend to talk about these matters in terms of high-sounding moral principles, each of which is of some real importance but is usually quite inadequate as a practical guide. Thus, wage-earner groups really are more or less activated by sympathy with their older or weaker members; and here is one reason why such a group sometimes holds back the more vigorous and capable individuals—so that the latter shall not expose the others' deficiencies. The employer, naturally, is better able to see the point of view of the individualistic workers (and of employees who consciously or unconsciously curry his favor); thus the boss tends to be a champion of the "pacemaker's" "individual liberty." No doubt, also, a number of labor demands, with reference to matters such as size of crew and limits within which mechanical, electrical or chemical devices may be used— which demands are explicitly defended on health and safety grounds—are also aimed in part at "making work."[7]

2. Friction over the rate of work is also produced by the feeling that the other party is attempting in some degree to alter the terms of the wage bargain. This is most obviously the case when the day worker complains that he is being speeded up by such means as faster conveyors, inadequate tools, or less assistance from fellow workers; and one of the weapons in the arsenal of organized labor is the mild form of sabotage commonly known as "slow-down." Especially are wage earners bitter against secret bonuses alleged to be paid by some employers to exceptionally capable people to act as pacemakers. The same fear of over-speeding has prompted the building and clothing workers in their opposition to extreme sub-contracting

---

[7] "[The railway employees'] attitude with reference to these matters [full-crew and train-length laws] springs mainly from the employees' concern over the declining trend of railway employment."—Report of Emergency Board to the President, appointed September 27, 1938, p. 41. (See Ch. 12-B, above.)

of work. The opposition refers particularly to sub-contractors who otherwise would be foremen, and who are (in effect) mere labor middlemen, the amount of their profits depending chiefly upon their ability to get more work out of the rank and file. A union rule which prohibits the employer from working on the job is perhaps intended both to "make work" and to prevent the manager from serving as his own pacemaker.[8]

Disputes over working tasks are especially apt to grow out of changes in technology and management methods, and to some extent (as the cotton spinner argued to the Webbs) piece work tends to mitigate such arguments. Nevertheless, there are abundant opportunities in almost any shop for suspicions of "chiseling" or sharp practice and bad faith with reference to the rate of work, whatever be the method of payment. Piece workers often fall into some form of restricted output, in part because managers are rather prone to think that high piece earnings indicate that the task was wrongly set—and often, when high earnings are made, the employer is also revising the job in ways which arouse suspicion of rate cutting.

3. A motive of the greatest importance for restrictive practices by workers is the desire to secure steadier and fuller employment. The evils feared in this connection include unemployment by reason of age or lowered work capacity, displacement by unorganized or unskilled workers, by other skills, by machinery, or simply by the job running out. Fear of displacement by unorganized workers, for example, prompted rules against "shop" (i.e., prefabricated) work in certain building trades; whereas other sections of the same trades, which had organized these "shops" as well, did not make corresponding demands. Fear of loss of jobs to other trades and to the unskilled is obviously the explanation of demarcation and "antispecialization" rules. If there is not enough work for existing members of the trade, any narrowing of this trade's boundaries apparently will mean still more unemployment for some of them. Fear of displacement by machines is, of course, at the

---

[8] A hoary joke among New York women's clothing workers relates that a workers' shop chairman telephones the union headquarters, "Our boss is cutting, himself!" To which the reply is made: "Call the ambulance!"

bottom of numerous restrictions on their use, including the "full crew" type of rule.

An interesting modern example of union methods of fighting displacement of labor by machines is provided by the musicians' union. The widespread use of "canned music" in radio broadcasting, theaters, restaurants, and so on, has threatened the livelihood of many members of this union—whose Chicago Federation, according to press reports, at first prohibited its members from making any phonographic record. Later this regulation was modified to allow the making of records, but requiring that such records be not used by any radio station unless the station, while broadcasting, kept the same number of musicians standing by as the number used in making the record. Likewise, it is said, the rule insists that any theater charging more than 25 cents admission may not use sound films produced in Chicago unless the theater employs the same number of musicians as were used in making the original sound recording.[9]

Finally, fear of the work running out, so that short time and layoffs will be necessary, is also the ground for a great variety of restrictive regulations. Of course, excessive devotion to this "lump of labor fallacy" is disastrous, from the individual worker's as well as the social standpoint. Yet this potent and widespread fear of "over-production" within one's customary and immediate market will probably always plague both employers and the people who work for them, as well as self-employed

---

[9] The hosiery agreement, discussed in Ch. 14, above, contains this clause: "All knitting machines shall be operated as single jobs." This requirement is no doubt due in part to the growing complexity of these machines; but it is also a barometer of the union's current economic power, for like most other craftsmen the knitters are keenly conscious of an employment problem, particularly in the better-organized and higher wage territory. At various times past this union has permitted the knitter and a helper to operate two machines, which was advantageous to the employer when lower output per man did not counterbalance the helper's lower wage, but distasteful to knitters, both because the double-machine practice spells immediate limitation of employment for skilled knitters, and because it trains helpers into knitters. (See G. W. Taylor, *The Full-Fashioned Hosiery Worker* (1931); H. Ober, *op. cit.*, pp. 45 ff.)

Every old union has been through a succession of technical and economic upheavals which have left imprints on its working rules as well as on its wage structure.

people like professional workers and farmers—in fact, humanity. Only in rather extreme and unusual instances, however, does this fear result in trade union requirement of clearly useless work, as in the "dead-horse" type of rule (for instance resetting type already available in stereotype)—or in the outright destruction of agricultural and other produce or productive capacity, in order to support a price or wage structure.[10]

To some extent these motives to "make work" are reduced if the employment contract specifies not only the rate of pay but a large total amount of work to be done. Salaried persons, with the most secure tenures of jobs, are distinctly less exposed to temptation toward restrictive practices than are wage earners, with their age-long experiences of being out of work—*for part-days as well as for weeks and months*. Yet salaried workers also frequently see, or think they see, their positions being undermined by technological or organizational developments and the activities of other groups; hence, policies designed to protect the jobs of established bureaus and divisions are commonplace enough in all large organizations, governmental as well as private.

B. Labor Trouble in Premium-Bonus and Scientific-Management Wage Plans

Between the older piece-work systems represented by cotton spinning and coal mining, and present-day wage incentive practices, fall two transitional movements whose significance is often misconceived by people interested in labor problems. These are (1) "premium bonus" and (2) "scientific management" wage plans and practices. Let us notice how these products of engineering minds have dealt with production methods and standards.

Premium Bonus Schemes.—These older bonus methods were attempts to minimize the disputes and output restrictions

---

10 Some "useless work" union requirements—like sending a truckload of materials 40 miles back to its source, to be "properly" loaded and hauled again—are regarded by the unions concerned as penalties for alleged wilful violations of labor contract by the employer or his agent.

often encountered in old-fashioned piece work. One bonus plan was introduced by David Rowan into Great Britain; another by F. A. Halsey into the United States, both in the 1890's; and a little later Harrington Emerson popularized his bonus plans. More recently, C. E. Bedaux has promoted widespread use of wage schemes which incorporate certain elements found in the older bonus systems.[11] What are the fundamental problems, attacked and created by the premium-bonus school?

One point which usually characterizes premium plans is a guaranteed minimum day rate—often equal to that prevailing in the local market for similar work on the straight time basis, but often lower, sometimes higher. Are not piece workers also guaranteed minimum time rates of earnings? They are —more commonly now, than when these bonus systems were born. The latter, moreover, attempt to solve a problem often posed by the slow piece worker, with guaranteed day rate. For if this slow man is unable or unwilling to turn out enough work to earn his day rate at the piece price, he "might as well be hung for a sheep as for a lamb"—he is paid just as much, if he falls (say) 10% or 20% below, as if his piece earnings fully equal his day rate.[12] Some bonus wage plans deal with this prob-

---

[11] Wage systems are described in many publications, e.g., C. W. Lytle, *Wage Incentive Methods.* Cf. *Compensating Industrial Effort,* Ch. 13.

In this section of the text above, the discussion runs in terms of bonuses based upon mere *quantity* of output—and in fact the older bonus plans were largely restricted to this somewhat crude measure of the worker's accomplishment. The last two decades have seen considerable development of bonuses based upon other indexes, such as quality, economy of materials, punctuality in attendance, and so on. An ideal measure of the worker's accomplishment or total efficiency would have to take into account a considerable range of such factors.

[12] "At one of the shipyards previously referred to, I obtained striking evidence of general output limitation. The workers at this yard were paid at a piece rate, but they were likewise guaranteed a somewhat liberal minimum wage, whatever their output. Before the war, when there were plenty of men available, this system worked fairly well, for if a worker persistently failed to earn his guaranteed time rate, he could be discharged. During the war, however, the demand for shipyard workers, and especially for riveters, became greater than the available supply, and the men now controlled the situation. They found it easier to receive their guaranteed time rate than to try and earn their piece rate, and at one period scarcely a riveter earned the money he was paid."—H. M. Vernon, *Industrial Fatigue and Efficiency,* p. 132 (London, 1921).

lem by guaranteeing low minimum hourly earnings, and applying a graduated tariff of bonuses for accomplishments
(called by Emerson and others "percent efficiency") up to the
standard work load above which a *uniform* scale of bonus in
relation to output may be earned. If the worker, for example,
is paid a guaranteed or base rate for performances up to 67%
of standard efficiency, he may be advanced by an "empiric table"
to 120% of his base rate for just 100% efficiency.

The most controversial feature of bonus systems, however,
is their tendency to pay, for output above that required to earn
the guaranteed time rate, less than proportionally to the
worker's efficiency.[13] Halsey's premium-bonus plan, for example, assumes a guaranteed prevailing day rate and a rather
roughly set standard of output ("100% efficiency," to Emerson), above which bonus would be paid. This bonus is computed for each pay period, by means of a comparison between
the hours the man actually worked and the "time allowed" for
all the pieces of his output. If the "time allowed" exceeds the
"time taken," the worker is paid, at his day rate, for the time
taken; and he is paid in addition and at the same rate for some
standard fraction (usually half) of the excess.[14] Thus, under
the Halsey bonus systems, for production above standard efficiency the worker's earnings increase at a constant rate, but less
than proportionately to his increase in output. The ordinary
workman would make about the same hourly earnings under
Rowan's bonus scheme.

No doubt it was realized by all concerned that these old
bonus plans appeared somewhat unfair to the worker; but the
great argument in their favor was that they tended to enable
the operative to exert himself freely without fear that the employer would unreasonably cut the time allowance for the job.
Such plans were designed to minimize the harm done by the

---

[13] This feature is not essential to a bonus plan; in fact some of the systems actually installed by Emerson and Bedaux—and all of certain other
bonus schemes, such as those of Wennerlund and Estes—pay in full proportion for extra-standard output.

[14] Thus, if, in a 40-hour work week a man performed an amount of
work for which the time allowed was 48 hours, he would be paid his regular day rate for 40 hours, and in addition that rate for, say, 4 of the 8 hours
"saved."

old crude methods of setting time allowances, and to share between the employer and the worker the saving in processing time which often comes about very gradually through improved equipment, materials, general shop methods, also through short-cuts found by the individual workman.

Taylor's Approach to Production Standards.—As Harrington Emerson used to say, Frederick Winslow Taylor's methods began where his own (Emerson's) left off. Taylor's far-sighted and fundamental solution of these problems (and many others) was based on his revolutionary "time and motion study" technique.[15] His plans for "scientific management" (which are most clearly advantageous for mass or repetitive production) prescribed detailed research upon, then standardization of, equipment, layout, and human motions, training operators with good aptitude for each job into high competence, and determination of the *necessary* time, usually by means of stop-watch observations.[16]

The bitter struggles that ensued between the Taylorites and organized labor are attributable in large part to the former's lack of appreciation of the background of labor problems and trade unionism—and to Taylor's impatience with opposition generally. Later collaboration among students and practitioners of such fields as labor economics, labor organization, personnel administration and industrial psychology and engineering have smoothed many of these rough edges, and prepared the ground for the better solutions surveyed in the following section.

---

[15] Frank and Lillian Gilbreth were the leading pioneers in motion study, which they, too, "began where Taylor left off."

[16] An associated procedure favored by the scientific-management movement is relegation of the less skilled operations to less skilled people, a process exemplified by Gilbreth's brick-laying system. This policy (called, in Britain, "dilution" of skilled labor) goes against the grain of those trade unions which are based on traditional crafts, each of which desires at least to retain all the working opportunities which it has. The opposition of such unions is reasonable and not anti-social, so far as it extends only to ruthless disregard of the livelihood of the present generation of skilled men, and/or to changes which really endanger quality, health or safety. "Dilution," moreover, should be accompanied by public and private training programs for upgrading the less skilled workers so far as they have the requisite aptitudes.

C. Production Methods and Standards under Present-Day Collective Bargaining

This "story" of more recent trends will develop through the following phases: (1) Evolution of the stop-watch and bonus-curve problems; (2) partial measures of an individual worker's accomplishment (particularly in merit ratings and in group wage incentives); (3) union and management policies and practices on production standards in the newly unionized mass-production industries; and (4) the more elaborate methods developed, over a longer period, by progressive labor unionism and progressive labor management, notably in the industries which have accustomed themselves to permanent voluntary arbitration machinery.[17]

1. What Now of Stop-Watch and Bonus?—To many workers reared under American trade union traditions of a generation ago, an industrial engineer's stop-watch is still a cause for war. This uncompromising attitude is softening, however, as the workers and their officials grow in understanding and in control of not only the stop-watch but the several alternative methods of standard making—such as electric clocks, motion-picture cameras, and output-and-cost statistics.

Fundamentally similar observations apply to incentive wage plans. There is still a strong current of preference for day rates, and especially of hostility to most bonus systems, in American trade unionism; but on these matters, too, growing confidence in the ability of their own officials to see that the workers are not dealt with unfairly in such schemes makes these unions increasingly open-minded.

It is very doubtful whether any management should now compute earnings by a bonus curve which pays the worker less than proportionally for his output above the standard efficiency; for the guesswork in "time-allowance" setting which was the main justification for the old premium-bonus curves has been largely replaced by careful and accurate time-study standards,

---

[17] A conveniently accessible and useful reference is H. Ober, *op. cit.,* esp. Ch. 2, Sec. on "Limitation of Work Loads," and Ch. 3.

more or less checked by worker representatives. Some force, to be sure, remains in the managerial argument that the time normally required for any operation tends to be reduced by many sorts of improvements, none of which alone may seem to justify a revision of the formal time allowance. It remains true also that the normal, day-in-day-out time required by a thoroughly experienced worker can seldom if ever be determined with fine and objective precision—however well standardized are the conditions. These considerations, so far as they go, favor premium-bonus plans which "share savings."

On the other hand, the employer tends to benefit by lower overhead costs from a worker's high rate of production; and with competently set and maintained production standards, the employer can well afford to pay each worker or small group in full proportion to his or its output above the average man's standard. Such payment may be made by either a piece rate or by an equivalent "100% bonus" plan. (In the latter system, the worker receives his own day rate for all the "standard" hours represented by the work he turns out.)

2. Partial Indicators of the Individual Worker's Efficiency.—The foregoing discussion of wage methods has almost "begged the question" of measurement of the individual worker's efficiency or net accomplishment for his employer, within a given pay period. Obviously, in any piece-work or bonus job there are units of output which are accepted as sufficient means for such measurement; though it is also generally recognized that no count of such pieces is a *completely* satisfactory index of the individual's or group's total service during that period, even if he or it has done nothing but piece work under normal conditions. Many of the more superficial objections to payment-by-results schemes concentrate attention on the imperfections of the measures of labor efficiency hitherto used, without raising the question whether the imperfections of alternative wage methods may be on the whole still greater. It is true that the pure time basis of payment (day work or salary) to a large extent lets this "sleeping dog lie,"—does not often raise explicitly the question of how little any given worker may do, and still avoid discharge. Incentive payment, on the contrary, necessarily makes explicit every payday the method of efficiency measurement which is to be used for computing earnings. As was indicated above, piece-work earnings usually are adjusted, in cases where a straight application of the ordinary piece rate would be inequitable—for instance, by reason of short supplies of materials or other abnormal difficulty encountered temporarily by the worker. One common method of safeguarding the incentive wage earner is a guaranteed day rate. Another is temporary revision of the piece rate, to take account of the current difficulty of the work—the foreman, the worker, and perhaps the local union representative sometimes make such temporary revisions.

Apart from these older features and adaptations of individual piece work and bonuses on mere quantity of output, there are various other indexes of the worker's efficiency during any pay period, which, singly or in combination, may adjust pay to work to the mutual advantage of employer and workers.

Increments with Length of Service.—One indirect or partial indicator of the worker's worth is the time he has been in his employer's service. Such automatic increments in pay (or in perquisites, such as vacations or pensions) with lengthening service are not very common (beyond advance from the probationer's rate, a month or so after first hiring) in American collective bargaining; but especially in some foreign countries (notably the Austrian state railways, under the socialist governments in the early 1920's), this principle has been pushed to absurd lengths.[18] This practice is obviously a member of the

---

[18] See E. L. Thorndike, "The Variation in Wage Ratios," *Quar. Jour. of Econ.*, May 1940, p. 380. Noting that the Austrian locomotive engineer's wage, by the increments then used, would be doubled by 34 years of service, Thorndike remarks: "He would probably be at [age] 69 less fit for work as a locomotive engineer than at 59 or even at 49. . . . The reasonable ratio in relation to age will vary according as the work depends upon strength, skill, speed of reactions, knowledge, judgment, etc. It will also vary widely with individuals. But for most occupations and most persons a ratio that increases a man's time wage after 55 is unreasonable, it being more reasonable to begin reducing it gradually from then on until the time of retirement on a pension." Over-emphasis of seniority is still more pernicious in promotions to the higher ranks of administration work; and it has been

seniority-rights family, and, like its cousins, appeals to labor interests in part because length of service is an objective factor —it cannot easily be rigged or manipulated in a discriminatory fashion. Within modest limits there is a fair presumption that an employee becomes more efficient with increasing service; but at best it is a very indirect criterion of individual merit.

Standards for Quality, Economy, etc.—In many jobs the worker's total accomplishment is sufficiently well measured by units of output, as in ordinary piece work—such counts of output, of course, being restricted to pieces which pass inspection for precision and other quality factors. But many managers have felt the need of establishing supplementary standards for various other features of the worker's performance besides mere quantity of output—such as quality of product, "scrap" or economy in materials (including power, lubricants, etc.), punctuality of attendance, versatility, cooperativeness, and constructive suggestions. The reader will recognize these illustrative work factors as frequently forming bases for bonus payments or penalties, especially in non-unionized firms or occupations.[19]

Group Wage Incentives.—Another partial measure or index of the individual's efficiency is available if the efficiency of the group in which he works is measured. In mass production the products of departments and other groups are sufficiently standardized so that records of their outputs are easily come by, and scores for quality and economy are apt to be feasible also, for each group.

In these industries and numerous others, group piece-work and bonus plans have often been preferred to either individual piece work (if feasible at all) or to day work. Among potential

---

responsible for much dry rot in the older types of large organizations—such as business corporations and military and naval services.

[19] The Joseph and Feiss ("Clothcraft") clothing plant, for example, simultaneously paid separate bonuses for output, quality, attendance, and length of service. This and other partial-bonus schemes are discussed in *Compensating Industrial Effort*, Ch. 13. Group incentives (see below) are treated in *ibid.*, Ch. 14, and service ratings in Ch. 7. Some references to the respective literatures are given in each of those chapters.

economies of group remuneration are: less counting and accumulation of pieces, less capital locked up in such accumulations, simpler wage calculations, passing work promptly in line of production (savings in motions and transport), and more regular scheduling of interlocking operations. Such work appears on the surface to be done equally well by straight day work; but searching comparison will show that, under straight day work, the foremen and assistant foremen must be more vigilant taskmasters; under group incentives the group members supervise each other, and many like this relative freedom from foremen's prodding.

In the eyes of many labor advocates, these advantages of the automotive group wages were more than offset by various disadvantages. Several types of complaints, in turn, are traceable to the employer's error in using too large groups for these wage plans. In the latter case the more capable and energetic workers tend to be discouraged by lack of cooperation from other members of their group. Experience in a number of companies has indicated that the individual worker will generally be more effectively rewarded through a group measurement of his efficiency if the group is small (say 50 or less) and if each member is able to know how well the other members are working. Technical conditions, such as conveyors, have great pace-making possibilities; nevertheless it is usually possible for a malingerer to abuse whatever flexibility is necessary to allow for variations in materials and in health of the workers; hence some reward for standard and extra-standard production of a group is usually in the interest of both management and labor.

Merit or Service Ratings.—Such ratings or reports, and the "scales" generally employed therefor, have received much attention in private, and still more in public, personnel administration—especially since the war period of 1917-18. Many trade union leaders are suspicious of any sort of merit ratings of individuals by private employers, because merit rating reports cannot be fully objective and proof against either foolish or knavish applications. Such labor leaders may be reminded that merit ratings, like trade unions themselves, are fundamentally protective devices, especially needful in large employing organizations, in which some forms of "red tape" and "bureaucracy" (i.e., formal routines, reports, checks and audits, specialized personnel) are inevitable. The longest experience with formal service records, moreover, is not only in both military and civil governmental agencies (including postal service), but also in railway employment—the latter is certainly a leading example of powerful trade unionism. The old merit-demerit scales, to be sure, now appear too narrow, and too rigid in routines of evaluating the factors they did consider. The tendency is to emphasize routine in gathering data, and collective human judgment in determining how such data shall be evaluated for laying off, promoting, rewarding or penalizing, the individual worker.[20]

Applications of Ratings.—This discussion of merit ratings and other methods of estimating the parts and the sum of the individual's efficiency may seem beside the point of collective *wage* determination. The whole story of these families of techniques is, indeed, complex and confusing. Superficially trade unions are opposed to all manner of "fancy" bonuses and personnel routines, as formerly they were to medical examinations by "company doctors"—all seemed tarred by the stick of wily, discriminatory, union-baiting employers. And, if we point out that the powerful train service unions for many years have

---

[20] The theory and practice of merit or service ratings include the following chief points: (1) The whole procedure should be adapted to the main purposes—e.g., the personality traits, mental alertness, education of the individual may be much more relevant for purposes of vocational selection and training than for wage or salary setting. (2) The blank forms, and the study and discussions required for use of such forms, tend to call the attention of the foremen and other supervisors to the chief factors which affect each employee's promise and performance—from the standpoint of the employer. (3) Such ratings should be made and recorded, somewhat like a school teacher's record of marks, at fairly regular intervals. Thus the immediate supervisor's opinion of the individual employee's worth is recorded at other times than in crises pertaining to the employee's discharge, disciplinary penalty, layoff, promotion, demotion, or pay revision. (4) Such ratings or reports are commonly made by more than one supervisor, with reference to each worker; and a strong case may be made out for inviting each ratee to confer with the official or officials in charge of the records pertaining to him, in order that he may know his own points of strength and weakness, according to his supervisors' systematic judgments.

acquiesced in service-record routines—including merit-demerit scales—the easy reply is that this was a hangover of military penalties, and had no connection with wage setting.

The rating techniques hitherto applied to industrial wage earners, moreover, have been generally used for purposes other than wage setting—such as training, transfer, and promotion. For the latter purposes individual "progress reports" should deal especially with the worker's personality traits and other human assets and liabilities from the standpoint of his best placement and development potentialities. Trade unions are already manifesting a cooperative spirit in this line of endeavor.[21]

Attitudes Toward Efficiency Estimates.—Although the line of least resistance under collective bargaining is the traditional practices in the industry—old-fashioned day work or piece work, as the case may be—it is nevertheless probable that progressive managers and unions will study the problems sketched in this section, and will gradually apply scientific methods toward better measurements and standards of individual accomplishment, during each pay period. For many years efficiency or merit or service ratings (stressing compensable factors like quantity and quality of work done, initiative shown, cooperativeness, punctuality) have been used for adjusting salaries in both private and government enterprises.

Whether incentive or day-work payment is used, it seems probable that systematic individual service records will be increasingly desired by unions as well as by managements. Such records, suitably devised and maintained, tend to restrict the area of controversy when the foreman claims a man is incompetent or otherwise deserving of penalty, as well as when pro-

---

[21] One sort of union-management cooperation in the Tennessee Valley Authority has been concerned with a "Job Performance Record" for the individual worker. In the Dept. of Chemical Engineering, where experiments along this line have most advanced, the blank for carpenters, for instance (marked by the foreman, and checked by union representation), refers to relative experience and competence in sash fitting, setting frames, and eight other types of work; also to "attitude toward work," "cooperation on job," "attitude toward safety." These records have no reference to payment—only to placement. There is little or no variation in wage rates, among different members of the same occupation.

motion is made from the ranks. The negative function (protection against discrimination) is no doubt the chief appeal of such techniques to the old-time day-working trade unionist, who may favor a single time rate for all men in the trade since that system is easiest to police and seems not to drive his people into working themselves out of jobs. But the broader gauge union member or official, more conscious of the significance of costs and selling prices for employment and annual incomes, will welcome such merit-rating devices as will fairly enable the more efficient workers to get correspondingly more pay, within sensible health precautions. Day rates, thus graduated according to individual competence, are essentially like "week work with production standards." The former scheme, in fact, has this advantage: the "production standards" used for such needle-trade "week work" are based solely on counts of (acceptable) output; whereas, merit ratings should compel the attention of all parties to all important aspects of each worker's performance, such as quality, economy, punctuality, and versatility.

3. **The Newer Unions and Production Standards.**—Let us now resume the main road of experiences in progressive determination of *standards* of labor efficiency. Henceforth, we may concentrate attention on number of acceptable pieces of output per hour (or time per piece) as *the* measure of production (in this connection, of *labor efficiency*) ; and try to remember that measurement of such efficiency may be indefinitely improved. Yet whatever measure and reward are—for the moment—applied to any hour's "task" of a person or a group, the question must be recurrently faced: In the present circumstances, is this "task" reasonable?

Unionism has come only recently to the industries in which industrial engineering has had its most striking successes. In automotive production, in rubber, and in iron and steel, for example, efficiency standards and rapid and continuous technological innovations have been part and parcel of the mass-production processes with which such industries have astonished the world. And, prior to the advent of the new industrial unions in these great plants, their managements were able to proceed virtually unhindered in the development of novel methods of operation. Not surprisingly, the promise of control over labor "speed-up" was among the more telling arguments for organization addressed by union organizers to the employees in these industries—particularly as unemployment itself "went into mass production" after 1929.

In their earlier days there was some talk among these newer unions of sweeping away all the appurtenances of industrial engineering. Piece-work and bonus payment systems, in fact, were largely abolished in the automobile industry (about 1935), partly as "union insurance." The basic structure of efficiency standards however, and of interlocking production schedules in these heavily mechanized plants, has never been seriously attacked by labor. The unions have only insisted that the speed at which men are asked to work does properly fall within the sphere of collective bargaining; in some cases they have asked for (and in a few cases have achieved) the right to participate jointly with management in setting production standards.[22] Otherwise, the pre-union methods of initially determining a "fair day's work," as jobs were changed, by means of time studies and engineering data have not been modified by the advent of labor organization.[23]

Commonly (though the precise method varies from plant to plant) the unions in the mass-production industries play their part in determining output standards by criticism—through some type of grievance procedure. If the fairness of the rate of production as established by management is disputed by the workers involved, there ordinarily is an initial, informal attempt at settlement by the union officials and management representatives in the immediate department. Failure to reach an agreement at this stage may bring a retiming of the operation, perhaps with a union official acting as an observer. From

[22] The extent to which the union should participate in predetermination of production standards was one of the matters nominally in dispute during the strike of the United Automobile Workers at the Chrysler Corporation plants in the fall of 1939; but in this case the demand appears to have been partly a "nuisance bid"—at least no well-considered plan is known to have been proposed by the union.

[23] Automobile and body plants are doubtless afflicted by more of such job changes than are most other industries, on account of yearly models.

this point, if no settlement can be had, the dispute can be carried through successive steps to the top executives of the union and the company.

While not a standard feature of union contracts in the automobile industry, the clause governing speed of operations in the 1940 General Motors-United Automobile Workers agreement illustrates the general framework of the procedure in use in most of the well-organized plants:

(1) The policy regarding speed of operations is that time studies shall be made on the basis of fairness and equity consistent with quality of reasonable working capacities of normal operators. The local management of each plant has full authority to settle such matters. If an employee or group of employees claim the timing of their work is too fast and the foreman is unable to adjust the matter, the job will be restudied and if found to be unfair, an adjustment will be made.

(2) If after the job has been restudied, the employees still protest the timing, the committeeman for that district may, upon reporting to the foreman of the department involved, examine the job in order to negotiate the complaint, and the foreman or time study man will explain all of the facts of the case to the committeeman. Should a satisfactory adjustment not result, the matter in dispute may be appealed in accordance with the grievance procedure.

Under this system of dealing with production speeds, if the workers do not object to a standard introduced by management, there is an implied agreement that the standard is fair. Much less common are instances where an explicit agreement is reached *before* any production standard is promulgated by the management. Here the union and management representatives time the operations together, and agree on the production standard in advance. The feasibility of such an arrangement in a large plant where hundreds of standards must be set at the beginning of a production season is open to question. In various smaller plants, provided there is a spirit of give-and-take on the part of both principals, it has been found a workable method of avoiding disputes—any one of which may become bitter and disastrous—over the speed of operations.

The difficulties involved in collective negotiations over production speeds are rather obvious. First, it presupposes some knowledge on the part of the employee representatives of the techniques of industrial engineering. Unless the union steward or committeeman has some understanding of the principles of time and motion study, disputes may drag on interminably, in part because of his ignorance.[24] Again, the delays which are inherent in even a smoothly working system of grievance procedure make it peculiarly inappropriate to disputes which should be settled with some dispatch. If a production standard results in overstrain, the employees involved need an adjustment immediately rather than several weeks hence. Conversely, where employees refuse to meet a standard until it has finally been proven reasonable, management may meanwhile suffer a serious competitive disadvantage.

Nor is arbitration yet available in these mass industries, in any form well adapted to this type of dispute. The technical knowledge necessary to arrive at a fair decision is not of the kind possessed by the ordinary arbitrator, however impartial he may be.[25] As we shall see, other industries in which impartial-chairman machinery is of longer standing, have used it to settle questions of work loads as well as others.

This vital need for *prompt* settlement of the inevitable differences over the "fair day's work" suggests: (1) serious investigation of the possibilities of joint initial determination of tentative work assignments (which, in any case, should be subject to correction after they have been given fair and long-enough full-scale trial); and (2) "speed-up" of procedures for final settlement of this type of dispute.

4. Union-Management Cooperation in Efficiency Standards.—Although F. W. Taylor insisted that time study and work-standard setting were purely scientific or engineering functions, and that there was no more occasion for bargaining

---

[24] After the 1940 General Motors contract had been negotiated, the United Automobile Workers instituted its own course of instruction dealing with the principles of time and motion analysis. This "school" was attended by a group of committeemen concerned with adjusting disputes over production standards.

[25] Although the 1940 General Motors contract provides for a continuing umpire as the final stage in the grievance procedure, it also specifically provides that he shall not "rule on any dispute regarding timing operations."

with trade unions about these things than for bargaining over the time of sunrise, even before his death a number of management specialists began to work sympathetically with trade unions in the attempt to reconcile the respective claims of progressive unionism and progressive management. One of these pioneers was the late Robert G. Valentine, who served as an impartial expert in a unionized market in one of the clothing industries.[26] Some of the more general aspects of union-management cooperation were noted in the preceding chapter. Up to 1929 this movement had displayed its great potentialities for constructive collective dealing with other labor problems connected with technological and management innovations, but it had not really opened the old sore of determination of work loads.[27]

"The Naumkeag Experiment."—In 1929 an industrial engineer was jointly employed by the management and the union in the Pequot Mills of the Naumkeag Steam Cotton Company, Salem, Mass.[28] Within a few years this arrangement broke

[26] Valentine's precept and example gave a major inspiration to Tead and Metcalf, for the significant chapter "Joint Control of Job Analysis" in their *Personnel Administration.*

[27] In the long run the former is probably the more ambitious and important undertaking. Whereas most labor organizations (rightly) consider themselves virtuous and public-spirited when they "do not *oppose* progress in productive methods," the B & O and similar cooperative schemes undertook to stimulate and assist their managements to *find and use* new devices and methods. One reason for this contrast in attitudes was the original orientation of the B & O plan toward conserving working opportunities for the men—reducing the management's incentive to contract out work to non-union shops.

A symposium on these matters, entitled "Scientific Management and Organized Labor Today," was reported in *Bulletin of the Taylor Society,* June 1925. In this symposium, for instance, Geoffrey C. Brown reported favorably on work he had done for a plate-glass union and its employers. "No attempt was made to install any form of piece work or bonus system," he said. "All other elements of modern production control including an adequate time-keeping system, a perpetual store inventory, a cost system, advance scheduling of orders through manufacture, time study, etc., were, however, successfully introduced."

The articles by H. J. Ruttenberg, cited above, and the book *Organized Labor and Production* by Cooke and Murray are further testimonials to the deep roots this movement has taken.

[28] This episode is reported in detail in R. C. Nyman's *Union-Management Cooperation in the "Stretch-Out"* (Yale Univ. Press, 1934). It was a dramatic incident, not only of the Great Depression, but also of the southward migration of the cotton-textile industry discussed in Chs. 12-B, 20-B, and elsewhere in this book. A brief account of how other of the textile

down, after weavers had finally been required to operate some 20 or more looms (at somewhat higher weekly wages), instead of the 10 or 12 they had been tending before the collaboration began.

The adversity of business conditions confronting the Pequot Mills, growing worse steadily for four full years after the scheme was launched, might well have wrecked the best-conceived plan; but other unfavorable factors are also apparent. The chief of these, I gather, was the circumstance that no time study, and perhaps few other scientific management procedures, had been used in this mill before; so that upon the "Technician" sponsored by the union agent fell the double and impossible burden of quickly demonstrating to the executives and supervisors, as well as to the wage-earners, that his methods were sound. Taylor was fond of saying that the essence of scientific management is a "mental revolution" in employers and their staffs. Probably this revolution must be well begun on the managerial side before there is a reasonable chance of its inspiring organized labor.[29]

In the earlier phases of union-management cooperation it is the function of the management to propose work loads; of the labor organization, to criticize constructively the management's standards. If the employer induces the union officials to assume too early any positive responsibility for the working pace, such officials are all too apt to be repudiated by their constituents.

In Needle Trades.—Apparently the longest, and perhaps the most successful, experience in union-employer collaboration on work-load or labor-efficiency-standards problems is in the clothing trades (including hosiery), where impartial chairman and other voluntary arbitration systems have existed for some 30 years. The Amalgamated Clothing Workers' constructive attacks on management problems, especially in their industry's weaker firms, were mentioned in the previous chapter; and the

---

"stretch-out" problems were tackled during the NRA period is given in J. W. Nickerson, "Work Assignment," *The Annals*, March 1936. This author pays tribute to the cooperativeness of unions concerned—notably in New England silk textiles, with which he was connected.

[29] Such was my own comment, in *Compensating Industrial Effort*, p. 141. Further attempts have been resumed, in the Pequot Mills, at constructive handling of these problems. See S. H. Slichter, *Union Policies and Industrial Management*.

American Federation of Hosiery Workers assists some employers with what amount to industrial engineering services.

The most elaborate union-employer scheme for the establishment of production standards now operating is in the New York dress industry.[30] The International Ladies Garment Workers Union, which is a sort of federation of unions in a number of allied crafts and industries, has a long background of piece work and of problems of all manner of contracting and sub-contracting, of home work and "sweat shops." The agreement structure of 1936 (and immediately following years) provided for a uniform piece rate for each garment operation throughout the New York market, in whatever shop such garment might be made. The union has an industrial-engineering staff, which apparently keeps records of the many "job-units" (somewhat analogous to the "elemental times" of Taylor's time study); and the impartial chairman's office also has a similar apparatus, which serves to settle disputes over piece rates—perhaps to initiate rates in some shops sometimes.

That the new system of settling piece rates has been successful is demonstrated by the fact that since April 1936, when it went into effect, piece rates for over 400,000 different styles of garments have been determined. The overwhelming majority of rates were set without need for intervention by the arbitration machinery maintained jointly by the employer and the union in this industry to adjust their differences.

The tendency in collective bargaining is now away from the old trade union goal of an identical piece rate or work load, over the widest possible area, for each variety of product. The unions are increasingly recognizing that, due to variations of equipment and management, a given sort of product can be turned out more quickly—perhaps also more easily—in some shops than in others.[31] Hence, one of the basic principles enun-

---

[30] This system is briefly described by Anne Gould, "Fixing Wage Rates in the New York Dress Industry," U. S. Dept. of Labor, *Labor Information Bulletin,* April 1938, pp. 1-5. The quotation in my text is from this article.

[31] See Ch. 14-B, above. It seems doubtful whether the I. L. G. W. U. system in New York, mentioned above, gives the employer adequate incentive to improve equipment and methods.

ciated by Governor Winant's textile board in 1933 ran to this effect: work assignments should be based on equality, not of pieces but of effort. Such effort, in turn, should be that which a normal employee can daily handle without impairing his health.[32]

Summary

In this chapter we have tried to bring down to date the old story of employer-employee controversies over fair work loads. But instead of assuming that the individual worker's performance either is or is not rather accurately measurable—as do many treatments of this topic—we have stressed: the numerous aspects or dimensions of any worker's service to his employer (such as quantity, quality, and versatility of work, reliable attendance and cooperation); and the gradual development of methods of measuring these partial efficiency factors, also of estimating them, as in merit ratings.

Wherever piece rates or output bonuses are used, the work must be already somewhat standardized and repetitive; and so these jobs bring into focus the problems of production or efficiency *standards* (or work loads or tasks); and in such work also, various types and degrees of "speed-ups" by employers, "slow-downs" or output restrictions by employees, are most easily studied.

It was convenient to notice certain facts of history—both American and foreign—notably with reference to the respective attacks (years ago) of premium-bonus and scientific-management systems on these problems. But our main thread was the progress of collective bargaining with reference to workload difficulties. Possibly we have not sufficiently explored the various aspects of job security in this connection; but at least we have found plausible the argument so frequently advanced, that as employers safeguard their workers against unemployment, these output-restriction difficulties diminish. Certainly a local trade union's position on its work loads is much more apt to be constructive and cooperative when the management sin-

---

[32] Nickerson, *op. cit.*

cerely accepts it than when the union feels obliged to seize every weapon in a fight for life.

But the latter two factors are not enough. Many unions, American and foreign, are secure and have employment about as well stabilized as is now feasible, yet are "restrictive" in the sense that they are inhospitable to progressive technical and management methods. Here lies the great hope of "union-management cooperation" and of progressive management and trade unionism under any other title—to work together to protect the *future* as well as the present of the industry, by seeking constantly for efficiency methods which (at each step) best reconcile the interests of labor, employers, and consumers.

CHAPTER 16

VOLUNTARY WAGE ARBITRATION

The preceding chapters have outlined some essential features of collective bargaining, which rather directly affect wage rates and the contents of the jobs to which these rates apply. But two crucial parts of our background have not yet received sufficient attention: wage disputes as causes of "strikes", and State regulation of wages and other labor conditions.[1] Some types of governmental determinations of private wages are made primarily as a means toward maintaining or restoring industrial peace; this theme will be prominent through our succeeding chapters. In the present chapter, on the other hand, our attention is mainly occupied with voluntary or private settlements of wage disputes by conciliation and arbitration—processes which developed historically in very close association with various types of State intervention.

Whether the intervening "third party" can exert any governmental pressure whatever, the chief issues in the particular dispute must be made clear to him or them (conciliator, arbitrator, or board). Hence, the written decisions or awards, and ancillary documents, which are usually produced by such proceedings, constitute a very important body of information on

---

[1] Government statistics of industrial disputes classify them by major issues—warning that accurate classification is impossible. For the period 1927-39 inclusive, proposed wage and/or hour changes accounted for 25 to 50% of "strikes" and workers involved in U.S.A.; and "union organization" (usually recognition) for a larger share—in most years. ("Strikes in 1939," *Mo. Lab. Rev.,* May 1940.) Wage issues are, in the long run, much more prominent among causes of actual or potential labor warfare than these figures suggest. Strife over union organization is largely motivated by the union's power over wage rates; and where unions are more firmly established—as in Britain—the percentage of disputes directly attributed to wage issues generally runs well above 50.

On the innumerable and heavy social costs of labor frictions—very imperfectly reflected by strike statistics—see, e.g., P. S. Florence, *Economics of Fatigue and Unrest* (1924).

wage facts, factors, and arguments.[2] It would unduly enlarge
and delay this book, however, to include illustrative factual
data; and for the same reason no further comments are made
herein as to how various arbitrations have dealt with the wage
principles and factors surveyed in Chapters 4-13, above.

In the following paragraphs we shall examine arbitration
(including allied procedures) from three standpoints: in section A, features by which it is related to, and differentiated
from, other wage settlements; in section B, its chief forms;
and in section C, evaluation of its significance for our whole
subject.

A. How Arbitration Is Related to Other Methods of Collective Wage Determination

Essentials of Arbitration.—Voluntary arbitration implies
that some person or persons, in their private capacity, undertake as impartially as possible to consider the evidence and
arguments submitted by the parties to a dispute, on the understanding that the decision of such arbitrator(s) will be accepted
as final. In labor as in commercial arbitration, a very common
method of procedure is for each party to select one arbitrator,
experienced in its own affairs and obviously somewhat biased
in its favor; these two to agree on a third arbitrator, who presumably has no private economic interest in the particular controversy.[3]

At first thought it seems that a strict line could easily be
drawn between collective bargaining on the one hand and arbitration on the other. Likewise, it would seem simple to decide
when the State had intervened in a wage settlement, and when
the matter remained solely in the hands of private parties. But
neither line can be so sharply drawn. Some gradations, all
within the sphere of private and voluntary action, are suggested
by the following classification of methods for the settlement

---

[2] See Note on American Wage Arbitration Series, at the end of this
chapter.
[3] The neutral member, on whom chief responsibility for the decision
commonly falls, may be called "umpire," "referee," or "impartial chairman," instead of merely "the arbitrator."

of trade disputes which a British Royal Commission of 1891 found at work in British industry:

(1) negotiations between individual employers and deputations or representatives of their own workmen;

(2) negotiations between individual employers and trade union officials acting on behalf of their workmen;

(3) negotiations between officials of trade unions and officials of employer associations;

(4) occasional meetings between committees of trade unions and committees of employers' associations, with possibly at the same time a standing joint committee to settle minor questions of a judicial nature;

(5) more or less regular and periodical meetings between such committees;

(6) formation of joint committees or wage boards either for a whole trade or for the section of a trade in a particular district or for a single establishment, with regular constitution and rules of procedure;

(7) provision for reference of special cases to an arbitrator approved by both parties;

(8) embodiment in the constitution of joint committee or other negotiatory bodies of a provision for referring questions to arbitration in the event of disagreement.[4]

Conciliation and Arbitration.—Clearly, only methods (7) and (8) can well be called arbitration; and methods (1) through (4) are collective bargaining in the more ordinary senses of the term. But where permanent joint committees or boards exist, to which particular disputes can be referred, we find something midway between. Especially is this true when the board or committee is industry-wide, representing numerous employers, and perhaps several unions of employees. Any particular dispute coming before such a "board of conciliation and arbitration" may find neither party to it directly represented on the board. To a particular employer and a particular worker or group of workers, every member of the board may be an outsider—although the two halves of the board represent the

---

[4] Quoted in International Labor Office, *Conciliation and Arbitration in Industrial Disputes,* Studies and Reports, Series A, No. 34, p. 146 (1933).

two larger industrial groups to which the respective parties to the particular dispute belong. In many of the older organized trades, such bi-partisan boards of men, each member intimately familiar with problems and technicalities of his industry, have settled in the aggregate many more local disputes than have "impartial" or "neutral" arbitrators. Thus, certain forms of conciliation approach very near to the process of arbitration; and frequently, for disputes of a relatively minor or partial nature, such methods have achieved excellent success in adjusting controversies.[5]

Conciliation and arbitration, as practiced in the United States, may be regarded as phases of collective bargaining in the broader sense, since they rest formally on voluntary action. Very often such processes develop *ad hoc* or extemporaneously after an impasse occurs; but collective agreements in growing measure include provisions for settlement of any type of dispute—if possible by "grievance" machinery, within the family; if this does not suffice, then by resort to "outsiders." In the latter event the industry's bi-partisan or conciliation board or council may solve the problem; in which case it is (in effect) an arbitration board; otherwise or alternatively some method of resorting to a neutral arbitrator may be predetermined by the labor agreement.

Where Does Arbitration Become State Regulation?—The boundary between voluntary arbitration and State wage control is also rather difficult to set; again we must recognize certain hybrid cases. What, for instance, is the State selection and reimbursement of arbitrators, or the existence of a permanent court of arbitration, to which recourse is voluntary? Or State enforcement of arbitral awards? Or public authority granted to arbitrators, allowing them to compel attendance of persons and production of other evidence? All these mixtures, and many more, have actually contributed to the world history of labor arbitrations.

---

[5] "Conciliation" is also used in much the same sense as "mediation"—to denote the efforts of some outsider (often a government official) to help the parties to a dispute to find a settlement which each will accept as a bargain, not as an arbitration or court award.

By many stages and methods, as will be further indicated in the next several chapters, the public authorities can influence if not dictate private wage scales. These methods include systematic and recurrent "compulsory arbitration" of labor disputes; also more opportunistic legal, social, and economic pressures, as when a mayor, governor, or president intervenes in a stubborn and important stoppage of work.[6]

Although any sort of governmental participation in particular disputes thus gives some degree of political sanction, even to what is nominally an entirely private settlement, yet not a few modern State activities with reference to industrial relations tend rather to *facilitate voluntary methods.* Such, for instance, are the research and educational work of our public authorities with reference to collective bargaining and handling of grievances. And while the usefulness of the Whitley Councils and Industrial Court in Britain may be attributed in some part to the "big sticks" of potential government rewards and coercions in the background, it seems probable that these bodies have been really vital in proportion as they have leaned in the laissez-faire direction—providing resort to tribunals containing public as well as employer and worker representatives, only after all reasonable recourse to wholly voluntary methods has been exhausted. It will be argued further below, in this chapter, that voluntary arbitration now tends to grow in use and significance, in part as a means of avoiding resort to public labor tribunals.

B. Types of Voluntary Arbitration

Apart from the above-cited variations in general methods of wage settlement, we may classify arbitration itself on the bases of (1) subject matter and (2) the nature of the machinery.

---

[6] The conciliatory functions exercised, e.g., by U. S. Dep't of Labor and by the National Labor Relations Board are not buttressed, I believe, by any compulsory powers intended explicitly to restore industrial peace; but one may guess that officials of such agencies can bring to bear many indirect pressures which are beyond the reach of most private mediators.

1. Subject Matter.—Analysis of labor disputes—after union is recognized—reveals two outstanding types: *grievances* relating to past events (e.g., payment for work already done) and impasses over *new terms of employment* (e.g., wage rates for the ensuing year).

Of Grievances.—The Webbs (who were none too sympathetic with the high hopes often expressed for arbitration) thought that arbitration of grievances was seldom satisfactory. In the first place, they said, grievances could be easily settled by direct collective bargaining, or by the appeal to some higher joint conference which represents the older usage of "conciliation." Hence, arbitration in the narrower sense they considered unnecessary for settlement of grievances. In the second place, they held, a neutral arbitrator must be a man of wide reputation, whom both parties can trust because of his record of accomplishment and integrity in important public or semi-public employments; such men cannot be secured to arbitrate minor grievances.

The first of these propositions has proved to be only partly correct. In the printing industry, for instance, agreements have long existed to arbitrate both types of controversy; yet in this case arbitration of grievance cases was formerly somewhat rare.[7] But this and other industries have shown abundantly that the arbitration of grievance cases through continuously functioning arbitration machinery is not only possible, but contributes substantially to the achievement of successful and harmonious industrial relations. The Webbs seem to have underrated the potential importance of such "minor" controversies; and they did not have the experience of such unions as those in the needle and hosiery trades to prove that arbitrators can be secured for such cases who can command the confidence of both parties over many years.[8]

---

[7] J. F. Bogardus, *Industrial Arbitration in the Book and Job Printing Industry of New York City.* (Philadelphia: Univ. of Penna. Published under date 1934; but latest events and literature mentioned are of 1926. On later years, see footnote 9, below.)

[8] Confidence of the general public is important, too. The arbitration policy of a union or employer is no mean part of its public-relations program.

Of New Terms of Employment.—In the arbitration of disputes over terms of future employment, arbitration seems best suited to handle questions of wages. The other features of the labor contract appear to demand specialized knowledge that the ordinary impartial arbitrator does not possess—that is, unless and until he acquires such technical knowledge through his continuous employment in permanent arbitral machinery of the industry in question. In printing arbitrations, for instance,

. . . almost all parties concerned regard arbitration as much better fitted to deal with wages than with shop rules or working conditions. The Presidents of Typographical Union No. 6, Pressmen's Union No. 51, and Press Assistants' Union No. 23, and the officials of the Printers' League [employers' association] all state that in the formation of a contract they consider arbitration best suited to deal with wage disputes and would with great reluctance allow other disputes to be arbitrated. Shop practices and working conditions, they say, should be settled within the industry and in the past have always been settled satisfactorily by the parties concerned.[9]

The process of arbitrating industrial disputes has often been compared with the practice of submitting other disputes to a court; or with the practice of business men in submitting their inter-firm disputes to commercial arbitration. These analogies are enlightening, yet each is inexact. A grievance dispute, arising from the interpretation of an existing labor agreement, is much more similar to a commercial complaint which may either be submitted to the State's courts or to private arbitration, than is a controversy over future employment. Labor grievances arise, either because the wording of the agreement is not sufficiently clear so that both parties can agree on its meaning, or because something has occurred which seems not to have been specifically provided for at all in the agreement. Since the labor agreement is an important part of the employment contract, arbitration of disputes under it can be compared very accurately

9 *Ibid.*, p. 61. Between 1924 and early 1940 the New York union book and job printing industry had 9 arbitrations for new contracts or agreements, and 30 arbitrations on grievances—i.e., interpretations, discharges, etc. The New York newspaper industry also had (in 1940) contracts with 6 crafts providing for arbitration of succeeding agreements, and with 3 other crafts, without such clauses. (Information from employers' associations.)

to that of commercial arbitration, which in turn is based on the
desire to avoid part of the expense and time required for
authoritative litigation. But in the arbitration which relates to
new terms of employment, there is almost no law or contract
for the arbitrator or judge to interpret; this is more a legislative than a judicial problem.[10]

In not a few cases, however, there are some rather definite
principles which both parties agree should be used by the
arbitrator in determining the terms of the new contract. If it
were not so, would arbitration be used at all over new terms?
The Webbs, for instance, attribute the success of arbitration
in the iron trade of England to the fact that both employers and
workers were fully agreed that wages should be based upon the
price of the product; hence, the work of the arbitrator was to
interpret and apply this accepted sliding-scale principle—which
is analogous to the work of a judge.[11] But even where the
so-called principle seems thoroughly agreed upon, it may be
argued that the work of the arbitrator still partakes of that of
a legislative body—determination of policy on the basis of
independent judgment and choice. For instance, turning again
to the printing trades, agreement was general that wages should
be determined upon the basis of changes in living costs and
upon the economic condition of the industry. Although the
first of these is capable of moderately objective determination,
the second is much less so. The judgment of the arbitrator as
to the condition of the industry required first the decision—on
independent grounds—as to what constituted a "reasonable" or
"fair" rate of profit.[12] It was a question of attitude and
opinion, as well as of fact.

----

[10] In his *Industrial Arbitration in Great Britain,* p. 67 (London, Oxford
Univ. Press, 1929), Lord Amulree (William W. Mackenzie), who headed
the chief British labor tribunals during the 1914-18 War and also in later
years, points out that neglect of the above important distinction is at the
bottom of many blunders in public labor policy. Disputes over past events
are susceptible of settlement by arbitration or by the State, on lines suggested by the traditional courts of justice; whereas terms of employment
for the future, which are more immediate and vital issues in many "strikes,"
demand for treatment powers quasi-legislative as well as judicial.

[11] See Ch. 9-B, above.

[12] David R. Craig, *The Economic Condition of the Printing Industry in
New York City,* pp. 72, 73. (New York Employing Printers' Assn., 1925.)

Separation of Powers?—This contrast between arbitration of grievance cases (like decisions of a court of justice, because of the existence of a definite body of "law" or contract to be interpreted) and arbitration of new terms of employment (analogous to the creation of law through a legislative process), to be sure, can easily be over-stressed. In practice, a decision as to some new terms of employment does not necessarily involve the making of a wholly new employment contract. The lives of many other parts of a labor agreement are, in fact, normally longer than the life of any particular set of wage rates. The agreement will perhaps merely state that wage rates, during its lifetime, are to be determined by joint negotiation, with arbitration provided in case the negotiators at any time fail to agree. Or, as we have seen was the case in the hosiery industry master agreement,[13] the contract may state the reasons or conditions which justify either party, before expiration, in asking for a rate revision.

The distinction between "legislative" and "judicial" functions, nevertheless, is of enough practical importance to call for, and sometimes to produce, a certain amount of "separation of powers" in labor arbitrations. The famous Amalgamated Clothing Workers-Hart, Schaffner and Marx agreement of 1916, for example, provided what were in effect separate arbitration tribunals for each type of case—which system was soon extended over the whole unionized men's clothing industry in Chicago. The Trade Board, with its neutral chairman or arbitrator, functioned continuously and on the spot to deal with the multitude of grievance or interpretation cases which arose in the shop. The Board of Arbitration had jurisdiction only when disputes over future general policy occurred, or in case of appeal from the decision of the Trade Board. The text of the original agreement said,

. . . that questions of fact and testimony shall in the main be considered by the Trade Board while the Board of Arbitration will concern itself mainly with questions of principle and the application of the agreement to new issues as they arise. But this is not to be con-

---

[13] Ch. 14-B, above.

strued as limiting the power of the Board [of Arbitration], which is broad enough to make it the judge of facts as well as principle when necessary, and to deal with any question that may arise whose disposition is essential to the successful working of the agreement.

. . . In reaching its decisions the Board is expected to have regard to the general principles of the agreement; the spirit and intent, expressed or implied, of the parties thereto; and, especially, the necessity of making the instrument workable, and adaptable to varying needs and conditions, while conserving as fully as possible the essential interests of the parties involved.

If there should be a general change in wages or hours in the clothing industry, which shall be sufficiently permanent to warrant the belief that the change is not temporary, then the Board shall have the power to determine whether such change is of so extraordinary a nature as to justify a consideration of the question of making a change in the present agreement, and, if so, then the Board shall have the power to make such changes in wages or hours as in its judgment shall be proper.

This somewhat ponderous and legalistic machinery has been simplified. Most labor arbitrations do not try to draw lines of subject matter quite so sharply.[14] Yet the implicit recognitions of the special difficulties attaching to arbitration which in effect legislates on anything so vital as future wage scales are rather common. Our hosiery agreement, it may be recalled, referred *general* wage disputes to a special tribunal—not to the regular impartial chairman.[15]

We may now see an important limitation of the proposition that good grievance procedure tends to remove the ground for other disputes. Even if personal relations are of the best, and even if officials of employers and union are convinced that the wage scale must be cut or not advanced, the parties may

---

[14] At this point it is high time to remark that some labor and employing groups are allergic to any procedures savoring of lawyers or litigations; also that some labor tribunals (e.g., the British Industrial Court) staffed by learned judges, omit "opinions" from their decisions, to avoid developing too many arguments about precedents.

[15] See Ch. 14-B, above. A leading purpose in calling in a special wage tribunal is to enable the continuing impartial chairman to survive the shock, to union membership or individual employers as the case may be, of a general wage revision. (The neutral member of the special wage tribunal will, in all probability, not be acceptable again to one side or the other.)

resort to arbitration to enable the union officials to appear sufficiently aggressive in the eyes of their rank and file. Here seems to be an important reason for persistence of "legislative" wage arbitrations.

2. Types of Arbitration Machinery; Impartial Chairmen.

—Methods of arbitration may be usefully analyzed, not only upon the basis of the subject matter of the cases, but also according to the machinery used. We can conveniently distinguish three chief types. The first is *ad hoc* or improvised arbitration of specific cases which appear insoluble by ordinary bargaining methods. Mediators in industrial disputes who are unable to bring the parties to any sort of amicable agreement frequently urge that the core of unsettled points be submitted to arbitration; and not infrequently one side or the other proposes arbitration mainly in an attempt to put onto the other party the onus—in public opinion—of refusing arbitration. Should the parties agree, they then must determine who the arbitrator shall be, how he shall be reimbursed, what issues are to be arbitrated, what procedure shall be adopted in presenting arguments, and so on. In a second type of arbitration the procedure for selecting the arbitrator(s), and perhaps also the scope of his or their activity, are agreed upon before it is known whether any dispute will occur. In the third type, the complete arbitration machinery, including the arbitrating personnel, is provided in advance of any particular controversy, hence this last apparatus may be called "permanent."

Such permanent arbitration facilities, in turn, may be entirely the product of agreement between the parties themselves. The "impartial chairman" systems in the needle and hosiery trades are leading examples; others are mentioned in the note at the end of this chapter. Permanent provision for investigation, conciliation, and/or arbitration of industrial disputes is also a commonplace feature of present-day governments, particularly with reference to industries in which the consequences of disputes to the public are considered especially serious.

A leading example is the railway industry. The American and

British national governments, for example, over the past half-century or so have set up various types of arbitral machinery for the settlement of disputes between rail carriers and their employees. Once the disputing parties agreed to accept arbitration (e.g., under the Erdman or Newlands Acts), the procedure was automatically settled upon. In this case the machinery itself was not permanent—it was set up anew for each controversy; but the form which the machinery should take, and many other details were provided in advance by law.

Another type of governmental provision of arbitration machinery is exemplified by the British Industrial Court. This court is for the use of any industry, and for any type of labor dispute. Recourse to it is voluntary; lack of other sanctions than public opinion is one factor tending to make this court continue to emphasize voluntary agreements. Disputing parties can either refer the controversy to a permanent panel of judges, or they may be supplied with the procedure for selecting an *ad hoc* arbitral authority. On a local scale, a few American cities have established panels of citizens continuously available for mediation and arbitration of local labor disputes.[16]

C. Evaluation of Arbitral Methods

Permanent Arrangements Compared with *ad hoc* Machinery.—There is much to be said in favor of permanent industry mechanisms for the arbitration of labor disputes; yet it is not quite all to the good. In its favor is the fact that it makes unnecessary a further wrangle over the selection of the arbitrator or over other procedure, at a time when tempers are already ragged. And if the arbitrator has been chosen in advance of any controversy, it is more likely the parties will continue to have confidence in any decision that he might make, than if he is chosen in a hurry. Another objection to *ad hoc* machinery is that the arbitrator is too apt to be a stranger to the industry, and much time must be spent in acquainting him with technical details—if indeed it is at all possible to acquaint him in so brief a time, and under such conditions of stress, with

---

[16] At least Toledo, O., and Newark, N. J.

enough of the traditions, customs, and intangible factors which
are so important in industrial relations. A permanent arbitrator
becomes increasingly conversant with all these. When an
experienced neutral is recurrently used, much of the uncertainty
involved in any unpremeditated resort to the decision of an
amateur is avoided.

Objections to Arbitration.—But steps leading toward permanent arbitration machinery meet many resistances. Some of
these, for instance, arise from passions for old-fashioned indus-
trial-anarchistic freedom; others from disillusioned experience
with arbitration. It is also said that the existence of permanent
machinery unduly encourages its own use; that if the parties
know that in case of deadlock they must have recourse to
arbitration, they will be less ready to bargain in the necessary
spirit of give and take.[17] Some people find objectionable the
tendency, remarked upon earlier in this chapter, to make an
arbitrator the scapegoat for an unpopular action which leaders
on both sides privately concede to be necessary. And opposition is sometimes raised to the use of *any* voluntary arbitral
methods. One ground is that their use promotes a contentious
spirit between the two parties. In an effort to present its case as
convincingly as possible, each side is led to express its arguments to the arbitrator in vigorous terms, and to overlook no
opportunity to bring in any point, however minor, or to challenge any argument of the opposition, however well-founded it
may be. This strong statement and spirit of challenge are said
to engender a certain unnecessary rancor. While the irritations
thus aroused are certainly less than the ill-feeling engendered
by a strike or lockout, they may be more severe than the discords incident to conciliation—the completion of which is the
more likely, in the absence of an easy recourse to neutral-
arbitral procedure.[18]

---

[17] A. C. Pigou, *Economics of Welfare,* pp. 377-378 (1st ed.).

[18] Pigou, *op. cit.,* pp. 376-377; Bogardus, *op. cit.,* pp. 80-81; and L. L.
Price, *Industrial Peace,* pp. 44-48, all emphasize this allegation that arbitral
proceedings tend to cause a contentious spirit. Whether harmoniousness is
cause or effect of the successful working of the arbitration machinery may
be argued; but the experiences of the clothing and hosiery industries, for

Still another undesirable feature of labor arbitrations, according to some observers, is that arbitrators tend merely to split the difference between the demands of opposing parties. Knowing this, both sides tend to ask for more than they expect, and to make demands more frequently than if arbitration were not easily available, knowing that at least a part of what they ask for is sure to be granted. While a certain degree of merit must be allowed to this objection, it seems to lose force as the arbitrator becomes permanent and experienced. For he thus gets a longer view of the conditions of the industry, and the history of past wage movements; and he has many means of penalizing a party which manifests an attitude of "everything to gain, nothing to lose" by asking too much and too often.

Yet another criticism of the arbitral settlement of wage disputes is that the arbitrator merely sizes up the bargaining strength of the two parties, and makes an award which approximates that which a trial of force would have secured. He tends to "award the lion's share to the lion," as one experienced arbitrator frankly says. The chief objectors on this ground are persons who have some definite idea of how wages *should* be determined, some pet principle which they feel a real wage tribunal ought to employ in an attempt to reform the world. It is indeed true that any successful arbitrator cannot and should not ignore the economic powers of the opposing parties. For any settlement which does too glaringly ignore their relative strength will not be accepted or will soon collapse. Thus, what some see as a weakness of arbitration others see as strength. This point of view is well stated by George Soule:

Wage arbitration is therefore primarily an instrument of collective bargaining. It is resorted to by both sides of the bargaining process as a way of settling disputes which they find difficult to settle by direct negotiation. They could, if they liked, fight out the issue by a strike

example, seem to indicate the arbitration as at least a partial cause, the relative harmony as result.

Arguments similar to those examined in the present section are reviewed in Ch. 18-B, below, relative to compulsory arbitration in Australia and New Zealand; and a similar conclusion is reached.

or lockout, and settle it by a test of strength. But such a process would
be so costly and injurious to both that they prefer the peaceful uncertainty of an arbitral settlement. The arbitrator is thus not a superior
sort of dictator, dispensing justice from on high, but an agent of the
two sides to the collective bargain. His job is to reach a solution
that will be satisfactory enough to both sides to be workable. He has
to take into consideration their relative strength and their relative
necessities. He has to remember not to depart so far from a possible
compromise, consistent with the respective power and desires of the
parties, that one or the other of them will be likely next time to prefer
open hostility to peaceful settlement. He has also to remember that
a decision is useless if it cannot be enforced, and that the power and
ability of the respective parties to administer a decision successfully
is an integral part of the decision itself. A decision which cannot be
carried into effect or which will create lasting dissatisfaction is not
really a decision at all. On this account a wage arbitration is not an
exercise in pure reason, and a summary of merely logical arguments,
as stated in the opinion accompanying the decision, does not tell
the whole story. Arbitrators frequently do not, of course, understand
these limitations, but the more successful ones do so.[19]

Securing Fulfillment of Labor Agreements and Awards.
—An extremely important problem is suggested by this headline—a problem which runs through the whole gamut from the
simplest and most temporary voluntary labor bargains to the
most extreme State regulation of labor relations. At all these
stages this question is never far in the background. (Really
voluntary arbitration, of course, depends upon a doublesided
agreement to accept arbitration; hence this is but one form or
clause under a general collective labor agreement.) Are there
adequate rewards and penalties to secure that these undertakings and/or decisions will be carried through? The legal histories of each of the chief sanctions—e.g., fines, forfeits,
deprivation of seniority or other employment status, directed
at individual employers and workers, and/or their respective
leaders and group properties—are (of course) extremely com-

---

[19] *Wage Arbitration, Selected Cases, 1920-1924,* pp. 6-7 (1928). Somewhat similar opinions are expressed by Bogardus, *op. cit.,* pp. 75-76; and
E. W. Morehouse, "Development of Industrial Law in the Rochester Clothing Market," *Quar. Jour. of Econ.,* Feb. 1923, p. 261.

plex. The upshot of the matter, however, is that (in democratic societies) :

1. Each party has very often charged the other with breach of labor contract or award;
2. Unions, more than employers, have relied mainly on economic weapons (notably strike and boycott) to punish such alleged breaches, but sometimes such a legal remedy as the injunction has been successfully used;
3. Governments have succeeded, by various ways, in narrowing the field in which *this sort* of labor warfare operates, if not in abolishing it. A leading example of this last tendency is the Labor Court of Sweden, which, since 1928, appears very successfully to have used its broad powers to interpret and enforce voluntary labor agreements, once they are entered into.[20]

The outstanding sanction making for peaceful settlements of labor disagreements, of course, is enlightened self-interest —whatever may be the formal machinery of interpretation or adjudication. But this "glittering generality" needs much elaboration as to conditions which tend to make self-interest take peaceable forms of expression, and yield tolerably equitable results. For a few years while any major factor is new—such as effective union or employer organization, or a "permanent" arbitration scheme or important labor laws—we must expect exploratory reactions from both the employer and worker sides, as both leaders and rank and file convince themselves where is the line between mere prudence and too-sharp practices and irresponsibility. There must be built up a complex of provisions which tend to reward and penalize their individual

---

[20] Under this system, all industries and occupations, subject to rather minor limitations, are legally free to strike or lock out after each agreement expires; and under the system the parties are perhaps unlikely to agree to arbitrate a renewal of contract—which might signify renunciation for an indefinite period of the right to strike.

Sweden also has a tribunal called the Labor Council, which adjudicates difficulties relating to hours of work and overtime pay—see U. S. Commission of Industrial Relations in Sweden *Report*, pp. 8, 9 (1938). As is told in Ch. 18-A, below, our Nat'l Railroad Adjustment Board has a function, in its own industry, similar to that of the Swedish Labor Court.

members, in proportion as the acts of these members contribute to or threaten the welfare of the industry.

An example of expedients hitherto used for this purpose in voluntary arbitration is the posting of surety bonds by both parties, these funds being one means available to the arbitrators or umpires to enforce their decisions and to indemnify the persons who have suffered from breach of agreement by the other party. Such bonds have been maintained since 1895 in the British boot and shoe industry, and they are also found at least in the British pottery and American hosiery industries.[21]

Other outstanding conditions within which pressure of self-interest operates are the various sectors of public opinion. State industrial-peace agencies rely heavily on their special opportunities to influence public opinion (generally through publishing results of investigations, made perhaps during a compulsory "cooling-off period"). In a lesser degree, private and voluntary arbitration machinery can utilize similar pressures.

The social costs of unrestricted labor warfare are so great that a trend must be expected toward compulsory adjudication of disputes not peaceably settled within a reasonable term— at least of grievances arising during the lifetimes of labor agreements. This trend gives added incentive to political activities of both employers and workers; yet it also supplies a new and added inducement toward provisions for voluntary conciliation and arbitration. So long as the latter operate successfully, differences are settled privately and expeditiously within the family, rather than more publicly and cumbrously through governmental machinery.

D. Summary

This chapter concludes our treatment of the chief means by which voluntary collective bargaining directly affects wages, and it also begins our survey of the intervention of third parties into disputes over wages—the outstanding bone of

---

[21] U. S. Commission on Industrial Relations in Great Britain, *Report*, p. 36 (1938); Ch. 14-B, above.

industrial contention. Numerous stages were distinguished, including many hastily improvised arbitrations by amateurs; but our interest centers on the more permanent machinery, especially that which serves a whole industry, or at least more than one firm. The older variety in this latter line is bi-partisan "boards of conciliation and arbitration" (or "industrial councils"); such boards supply the chief key to British industrial peace, and in a few industries have had long and successful histories in America. In our land, however, preference now seems to run rather to a continuously retained arbitrator, umpire, or impartial chairman.

In any case voluntary arbitration of grievances (i.e., interpretation of an agreement still in force), presents notably less difficulties than does arbitration of a "strike" due to inability to agree on a new contract. Yet disputes over what are essentially new terms, such as general wage scales, are in fact sometimes successfully arbitrated—within limits suggested by precedents and the agreement to arbitrate.

This transitional chapter has also supplied occasion for discussion of sanctions to secure fulfillment of collective agreements (including agreements to abide by arbitration) and awards; for labor arbitration is a twilight zone between purely voluntary action and actual or easily possible State intervention. An experienced and continuing arbitrator is a bulwark against bureaucratic regulation of labor relations, for such a person helps to work out various private rewards and penalties which tend to make his decisions accepted. On the other hand, he is better qualified than any well-meaning amateur to make wise decisions and—what is extremely important—to state such decisions persuasively.

Yet these great merits (of private settlements at their best) by no means justify a general opposition to State labor courts. Such courts have many constructive possibilities, notably for guaranteeing the fulfillment of expert and neutral interpretations of existing agreements. But they function best, perhaps, as "stand-by capacity"—when they are little used because each industrial family composes its own differences promptly and in accord with its many peculiarities.

Note on American Wage Arbitration Series

Besides the titles and industries cited above in this chapter, the following may serve as an introduction to the literature most relevant to the present position in U.S.A.:

H. Feis, *Principles of Wage Settlement* (Wilson, 1924); and G. Soule, *Wage Arbitration, selected cases* (Macmillan, 1928), present excerpts from decisions and briefs in various industries. Nearly every number of the *Monthly Labor Review* of U.S. Dept. of Labor for many years has contained material of this sort, and occasional summaries, e.g., in the November 1939 and February 1940 issues. (See also BLS bulletins and other U.S. Dept. of Labor publications.)

The longer series of single-industry arbitration records are rather scattered and heterogeneous in form. Perhaps the longest-lived is that of the Anthracite [coal mining] Board of Conciliation, over which an umpire presides (Hazleton, Pa.). Of outstanding importance are the records of the various railway arbitration and adjustment boards, discussed briefly in Ch. 18-A, below. Much if not most of this railway tribunal material has been printed in government documents. Among commentaries for these two industries are: A. E. Suffern, *Conciliation and Arbitration in the Coal Industry of America,* and J. N. Stockett, *Arbitral Settlement of Railway Disputes* (both published by Houghton Mifflin, 1913 and 1918 respectively).

Other series, more or less continuous, pertain to certain sections and areas (usually) of at least the following industries: (1) various needle and knitting trades—coats, suits, headwear, hosiery, fur garments; (2) printing trades; (3) boot and shoe industry; (4) meat packing (Judge Alschuler, early 1920's); and (5) Pacific waterfront workers. The 1940 contract between General Motors Corporation and the automobile union, providing for a permanent umpire with reference to most classes of grievances (Cf. Ch. 15-C, above), appears to indicate a rising trend of use of such machinery.

The American Arbitration Association in recent years has promoted labor arbitration arrangements.

PART V

INFLUENCES OF PUBLIC POLICY ON WAGES

CHAPTER 17

LEGAL MINIMUM WAGES

In our discussion of arbitration we noticed that public intervention is a likely possibility if voluntary negotiations (including arbitration) do not suffice to settle labor disputes; also that various States have contributed money, prestige, and power to the support of certain forms of arbitration. We proceed now with further consideration of government agencies, as factors helping to build and maintain the national wage structure. Succeeding chapters in this group will treat modern political pressures, direct and indirect, upon wages at all levels of skill (within the industries affected), and some chief economic effects of public wage controls. In these later chapters the cost aspect of wages will be most prominent.

In the present chapter the income aspect looms larger—for the contemporary minimum-wage laws here treated are intended primarily to raise the real incomes of workers in the lowest ranks.[1] We proceed, in section A, to deal summarily with certain further background materials, disentangling minimum-wage legislation from superficially similar affairs; then, in

---

[1] "In current British [and much other foreign] usage a *minimum wage* does not necessarily mean a *subsistence wage* or even a *living wage* as it usually has in the United States. A minimum wage is exactly what the words say, simply the lowest wage legally payable in a trade. The level of living which it provides may vary somewhat from trade to trade. Actually, however, the minima fixed by the different wages boards represent the *prevailing* rate of wages in the industry for which they are fixed and they are determined with that objective in mind."—Dorothy Sells, *British Wage Boards, a study in industrial democracy*, p. 6. (Brookings, 1939.) The more complete and centralized systems of public control of wages (including those of skilled adult male workers) investigated in our next chapter are therefore treated in some foreign literature under the title "Minimum Wages." Where rock-bottom wages are legally established respectively for (unskilled) women and men, these rates are sometimes designated by the Australian term "basic wages." As was pointed out above (Ch. 14), trade union wage rates are often considered as minimum—not necessarily usual or maximum—for the occupation and area concerned.

section B, we sketch the development of the legal minimum-wage movement itself, through (section C) our national NRA and Fair Labor Standards systems; and, finally, in section D, we examine some problems of enforcement.

A. Background, Including Older Wage Legislation and Family Allowances

Direct legal wage control springs from a complex of conditions and theories, some of which were studied in previous chapters. As we shall see, for instance, the employer and employee representatives on State wage boards have often caused the function of such boards to be referred to as "collective bargaining"—despite the fact that they are instrumentalities of government rather than voluntary associations. Another and more vital factor is widespread grinding poverty —among many families of low-paid workers, and in other families who have no workers or whose workers have not jobs. No section of the present book is devoted to exhibits on this point, since my readers are likely to be familiar with such facts; but some data are offered incidentally on how many people have received how low earnings, for instance in Chapter 3, above, and Chapter 20, below.

Two further bits of background seem to be less familiar to Americans, and to call for more extended mention at this point: (1) pre-modern State wage controls, and (2) the family-allowance or endowment movement, which illuminates some of the joints between minimum-wage and social-security programs.

Wage Regulation before Nineteenth Century.—Through most of the nineteenth century, as well as the first two decades of the twentieth, direct legal control of wages was very unusual, and widely regarded as improper as well as futile. During that period, legal determination of minimum-wage rates, for various classes of weak workers, gradually got under way. In some earlier centuries, on the other hand, legal regulation of wage rates was rather widely practiced—usually in the sense of prohibitions of remuneration *above official maxima.*

The so-called Statute of Laborers[2] in Great Britain appears to be the earliest such instance on record; it arose out of the scarcity of labor produced by the Black Death pestilence, and —like most labor legislation down to about 1825—it was based in part upon the old philosophy that no seller of either a commodity or service should be allowed to advance its price or "profiteer" by reason of dearth. Some of the earlier of these laws specified actual wage rates for the chief classes of workers throughout the Kingdom. "The penalties attached to those who should give or take more and not to those who gave less, the latter class being apparently non-existent."[3] From Elizabeth's time to the early nineteenth century, this policy was made more workable in several directions: wage determinations were to be made locally by county groups of justices of the peace, mainly by reference to local living costs; and penalties were prescribed for paying less as well as for paying more.

By 1776 such laws had become honored most in the breach. Adam Smith quoted approvingly the remark of the then standard author (Burn) on local *Justice:*

. . . it seems time to lay aside all endeavors to bring under strict regulations, what in its own nature seems incapable of minute limitation; for if all persons in the same kind of work were to receive equal wages, there would be no emulation, and no room left for industry or ingenuity.

And in this context Smith made these further observations:

Whenever the legislature attempts to regulate the differences between masters and their workmen, its counsellors are always the masters. When the regulation, therefore, is in favor of the workmen, it is always just and equitable; but it is sometimes otherwise when in favor of the masters. Thus the law which obliges the masters in several different trades to pay their workmen in money and not in goods is quite just and equitable . . .[4]

---

[2] 23 Edw. III, c. 1, 1349.
[3] Amulree, Lord (Wm. W. Mackenzie), *Industrial Arbitration in Great Britain,* p. 2 (London, 1929).
[4] *Wealth of Nations,* Bk. I. Ch. 10. Cf. *ibid,* Ch. 9: "We have no Acts of Parliament against combining to lower the price of work; but many against combining to raise it."

The Family Allowance Movement.—In the preceding paragraphs we have sought perspective on modern minimum-wage legislation through its historical background—conditions out of which it arose later in the nineteenth century. Among those conditions were (1) widespread sympathy for low-paid workers, in especially weak bargaining position; and (2) the view, popular especially among trade unionists, that these low wage rates are a menace to all other wages. At this point, however, it is well to remind ourselves that the evil of excessively low family incomes can only in part be relieved by higher minimum-wage rates; and that more direct attacks on the low-family-income problem have modified somewhat the earlier minimum-wage movement.

Family allowances, in the sense of payments in specific relation to the wives and other actual dependents of employees, have been made by some employers over many decades. In the United States the chief precedents of this sort have usually been non-profit employers, such as church organizations and military or naval forces. But in Europe this custom appeared in certain private industries, even before 1914—as in the French railway and mining industries. After 1918 practices of this sort spread rapidly on the Continent, among both public and private employers, so that by 1925 it was estimated that some 6 million workers were affected. Gradually several national governments consolidated and made more uniform the diverse family-wage pools of voluntary origin, and supplemented what had amounted to unofficial "payroll taxes" by contributions from government funds.[5]

Proponents of such schemes generally realized that they were feasible only when the deductions from wages to form the pool for payment of dependents were made on a uniform plan by all employers in the industry or region; otherwise non-cooperating employers would be able to skim the cream of the available workers with few or no dependents.

---

[5] Especially in France, Belgium, and Italy—see Mary T. Waggaman, "Family Allowances in 1937 and 1938," *Mo. Lab. Rev.*, May 1939. In the 1920's voluntary family-allowance funds were a prominent part of the German industrial landscape.

It would take us too far afield to recount further the facts and theories involved.[6] It is apparent that we have here an interpretation of the need or "living-wage" factor which has been widely used in collective wage determinations. Undoubtedly, poverty was thus ameliorated in many large families, who drew their allowances without any stigma of charity or pauperism.

The movement received much attention among middle-class labor sympathizers in the English-speaking world (trade unionists were more suspicious of its implications for practical freedom to organize and strike) ; and the family-endowment systems which have been operated for some years now by Australian and New Zealand governments—also the scheme proposed for Britain by J. M. Keynes[7]—were partly inspired by these voluntary wage pools.

But family allowances from *wage* pools have several characteristics which have made the north Europeans, the British Dominions, the United States, and even Nazi Germany and Fascist Italy supplement their legal minimum-wage programs by methods which are, in several fundamentals, different from the voluntary family-allowance systems. The latter have two especially grave limitations, from the humanitarian point of view : (1) they do nothing for poor people in whose immediate families there are no employed wage earners; and (2) the family allowances are, in effect, raised entirely from wages— i.e., from funds which otherwise would be paid out as ordinary wages.[8] Obviously these objections are avoided by national social-security programs which prevent and relieve destitution throughout the population, by resources drawn not only from payroll taxes but from levies upon other incomes.

---

[6] See, e.g., USBLS Bull. 401 (1926) ; Paul H. Douglas, *Wages and the Family* (Univ. of Chicago Press, 1925) ; A. Gray, *Family Endowment, a Critical Analysis* (London: Benn, 1927) ; articles in the economic journals; and numerous reports in International Labor Office publications.

[7] See his *How to Pay for the War,* and Ch. 21, below.

[8] In some cases no doubt critics were correct in claiming that family allowances, pacifying workers with large families, impaired labor's bargaining power and enabled employers to get off with lower total labor payments than they would have had to make in the absence of such allowances.

B. The Legal Minimum-Wage Movement

So much for what minimum-wage laws do *not* accomplish or try to accomplish. Now for a sketch of their actual province. Where, when, and how have they operated?

Development in English-Speaking Nations.—Such laws provide for official determination of the lowest money-wage rate which may be paid to each class of workers covered. In the first modern proving-grounds of such control, New Zealand and Australia, much attention has been given to the "basic wages" for unskilled labor—a rate for each sex, and more or less qualified for age and experience—which was supposed to be a "living wage," determined in some cases by reference to statistical evidence on the living costs and needs of such workers. The implication, moreover, was accepted that the minimum *money* wage should be reviewed periodically by public authorities, to see that the official minimum *real* wage was maintained in the face of price changes.

In our next chapter we shall notice also the Australasian controls of wages of skilled workers—mainly incidental to prevention and settlement of labor disputes; but just now we are concerned only with public regulation of wages of low-paid labor.[9] This is the best-known form of legal minimum wage. In 1909 Great Britain inaugurated boards for determination of legal minimum wages in certain industries; in 1912 Massachusetts followed suit, and now minimum-wage laws are found in many nations.[10]

The Anglo-American legal philosophy which prevailed during the nineteenth century favored State control of employ-

---

[9] Some voluntary minimum real-wage standards have been put forward, notably by Quaker employers. See e.g., B. S. Rowntree, *The Human Needs of Labor* (London: Nelson, 1st ed., 1918; rev. ed., 1937); also M. E. Leeds and C. C. Balderston, *Wages, a Means of Testing Their Adequacy* (Univ. of Penna. Press, 1931).

[10] See International Labor Office, *Year-Book for 1937-38,* pp. 356-368, and *The Minimum Wage, an International Survey* (1939). Good historical and analytical accounts of the world-wide development of State wage controls may be found (e.g.) in E. M. Burns, *Wages and the State* (1926); Barbara Armstrong, *Insuring the Essentials* (1932); and H. A. Millis and R. E. Montgomery, *Labor's Progress and Some Basic Labor Problems* (1938).

ment conditions for *adult male* workers, only in extra-hazardous industries. Hence, legal regulations of hours of work were, for half a century and more, directed primarily at the protection of *female and child* workers; likewise the earlier minimum-wage legislation. The English Trade Board system was applied first to only four industries, in which female and juvenile labor and very low earnings were characteristic;[11] and the more than one million workers now employed in the 49 industries over which this System has spread are still predominantly (about 70%) women and minors. The minimum-wage laws of the 15 American states which had passed such laws up to 1933 were confined entirely to women and children; moreover, two of these had been repealed and some others were enforced but weakly, if at all.

In Britain, to be sure, this legal minimum-wage movement was not *restricted* to women and children. By 1912 minimum-wage legislation was already applied to skilled as well as unskilled coal miners; and during the War of 1914-18 nearly all wages became formally State-controlled, to a greater degree than in the United States. After 1919 such control either was repealed or became ineffective in most instances except those covered by the expanding Trade Board system; but soon various forms of public regulation of wages of various grades appeared again in several British industries, notably agriculture, road haulage, and cotton-weaving.[12]

The leading criterion for the selection of industries in which the Trade (minimum-wage) Boards were established in the British Commonwealth was originally the prevalence of very low earnings; but the qualification is now commonly added that lack of effective trade union organization among the workers makes it unlikely that their earnings will be raised without State regulation.[13]

---

[11] Tailoring, paper box making, lace finishing and chain making.
[12] See Ch. 18-B, below.
[13] "Parliament amended the Trade Board Act of 1909, which had limited the application of trade boards to 'sweated' industries, to permit the Minister of Labor to set up a trade board in any trade in which, in his opinion, 'no adequate machinery exists for the effective regulation of wages throughout the trade, and that accordingly, having regard to the rates of wages prevailing in the trade or any part of the trade, it is expedient that the acts

C. U. S. National Wage-Hour Control: NRA, FLSA

The disastrous depression which began in 1929 brought unparalleled unemployment and many miserably low rates of earnings (particularly, as always, among industrial home piece workers). And by this time there had also developed widespread approval of these two propositions: (1) The employer who pays decent wages (and observes other adequate labor standards) should be legally protected against the competition of other employers paying less—wage cutting should be outlawed as a form of business competition. (2) Only Federal regulation of labor standards can fully protect these fair employers, for it is impossible to make effective legal standards operative through the state governments alone. Employers, dazed by the depression and yearning for the governmental repression of "destructive price-cutting" which was promised through the NRA, were ready to accept the stringent labor clauses of the NRA's "codes of fair competition."

Thus the New Deal's National Industrial Recovery Act and Administration of 1933-35 marked an outstanding change of American policy with reference to authoritative regulation of

---

should apply to that trade.' Thus, although there are no laws to compel union recognition, or to compel collective bargaining, and the Government consistently maintains the principle of non-interference with voluntary collective bargaining, yet in industries having no effective organization and excessively low wages the Government may, and does, set up trade boards to determine minimum standards by legislative and administrative processes." —U. S. Commission on Industrial Relations in Great Britain, *Report*, p. 15 (1938).

American state wage boards have been set up in some of the same industries in which minimum wages are prescribed by law in Britain, e.g., laundering and dry-cleaning, hotels and restaurants, and brush manufacture. Important differences may also be discerned. In Great Britain in 1938 there were 49 trade boards, in addition to sundry agricultural district wage committees. These industries included, for example, "retail bespoke tailoring," and a number of other garment-making trades. (Sells, *op. cit.*, p. 353.) American garment workers, who have been much more solidly organized by trade unions and (in the larger factories, at least) have secured moderately high earnings, have been less subject to legal minimum wages— doubtless in part by reason of the difficulties arising out of interstate competition, of which more will be said below. Merchandising salespeople or shop assistants, on the other hand, who are little organized in either nation have received relatively more attention in American state minimum-wage legislation; though in 1938-39 it appeared probable that the British system would soon be applied to these workers, too.

labor conditions. For the first time our national government asserted power over minimum wages and maximum hours— as well as the right to ban child labor, in nearly all industries engaged in (or producing for) interstate commerce. The wage, hour, and child labor standards, too, which were required in all the NRA codes applied to male as well as to female and juvenile workers.[14] The NRA, of course, was intended to accomplish many purposes at once; establishment of labor standards on a national basis was only one objective.

Despite the failure of this grandiose scheme as a whole, the NRA did demonstrate that compliance with labor standards which seemed fairly high could be secured on a national scale, to a degree which realistic opinion had previously held impossible. A great many industries in which wages are low, of course, are spread over two or more states; so that minimum-wage regulation by any one state in a free-trade area is greatly handicapped by the absence of similar legislation in some other state or states in which competitors are hiring similar labor. These forces, added to the increasing will and ability of American organized labor to use political methods, are among the leading forces which produced the Federal Wage-Hour law of 1938, discussed below. This Act sets a "floor for wages" in each industry covered. This law is thus less ambitious than were the codes of the NRA, which prescribed increases also in many wages above the minima applying to skilled or low-skilled people. The 1938 National law, however, like the NRA system, in addition provides "a ceiling for hours and a break for children." These regulations are now much more uniformly applied to all interstate industries than were the somewhat variable codes of NRA. The present hours restrictions, furthermore, are less absolute than were many under NRA—the employer is now legally privileged to employ

---

[14] At least one precedent might be claimed, namely the Adamson Act of 1916 (39 Stat. 721), by which the Federal government established a "basic 8-hour day" for railway train service, and indirectly raised the wages of such men. This statute, however, was rather in the nature of improvised and emergency industrial-peace legislation than of State fixation of minimum wage rates; though it is also a landmark as a far-reaching curb on hours of work by application of penalty rates for overtime.

workers for hours longer than 40 in a week, provided that he pays a penalty wage of time-and-a-half for overtime work.

Recent Minimum-Wage Legislation of U. S. States.—In 1937 the United States Supreme Court held constitutional the minimum-wage law for women of the State of Washington, in effect reversing its previous adverse decisions on the District of Columbia and New York laws. Immediately more states began enacting minimum-wage legislation, so that by the end of 1939 a total of 26 states, in addition to the District of Columbia and Puerto Rico, were thus regulating the wages of low-skilled workers. During 1937 and 1938, moreover, 58 wage orders were issued in these states, a number which exceeded all the orders of the 26 years elapsed since the Massachusetts law was passed in 1912.[15] The present Federal law is explicitly intended to assist low-earning *men* as well as women and children, and it supplies a model with high prestige for state legislatures. The recent Oklahoma and Connecticut laws illustrate the present tendency to make state acts apply to men, as well as to women and minors. Most of the more industrialized states except Michigan, Indiana, and those in the Old South had (by 1940) passed minimum-wage acts; and in place of the small group of heterogeneous state minimum-wage laws and regulating bodies which had characterized this movement in our country before 1937, the United States appears to be moving rapidly toward a comprehensive and comparatively integrated system of minimum-wage regulation by public authorities.

The wages of agricultural and domestic-service workers, everywhere among the lowest, have not yet been subjected to public control in the United States.[16] Among the more important reasons for these omissions are the great administrative difficulties, and the large political powers of employing and self-

---

[15] See Ch. 20-C, below, for data and comment relative to two recent wage orders, in Ohio and New York.

[16] Abroad (as in England, Sweden, and New Zealand) public control of agricultural wages is now established (in part through the leverage of protective duties and subsidies to farmers). "Industrial home work" for manufacturers or contractors is quite generally regulated by law; but wages of domestic *service* (maids, cooks, and the like) are only exceptionally fixed by public authorities.

employed farmers and housewives. Our national government, however, has utilized the leverage of its aid to agriculture to regulate wages and child labor, e.g. in sugar beet growing.

A few particulars are offered below as to outstanding principles and practices of this American governmental regulation of minimum wages (the details of which are always changing). The remaining remarks in the present section deal with the make-up and general powers of wage-regulating authorities, and with their use of cost-of-living data. In the following section we shall consider problems of sanctions or enforcement.

Principles, Constitutions and Powers of U. S. Wage Boards.

—How is our minimum-wage machinery constructed? This movement has seen many interactions between (a) the principle of universal statutory dollar-minima, applying to wage earners in many (if not all) employments, and (b) the principle of "industry by industry" wage boards, each with power to set a minimum or minima for its own workers. Some statutes of the former type have been provided with little or no administrative machinery, and hence are entirely ineffective; yet there is a tendency to extend and coordinate wage boards in the direction of establishing a "floor" of uniform height for an ever-widening circle of wage earners. One important duty usually assigned to the administrative authorities concerned, in all lands, is to authorize exemptions of learners and of workers handicapped by old age or otherwise. Such exemptions may permit the employment of these low-value workers, when the legal minimum-wage rate is high enough to offer real protection to experienced and normal workers.

Our Federal Fair Labor Standards Act instructs the Administrator to appoint, for each industry covered, a committee composed of equal numbers of representatives of employers, employed and the public.[17] Such an industry committee is in some ways similar to the wage or trade boards of Victoria, Great Britain, and Massachusetts—in that its recommendation

---

[17] Cf. my article, "The Organization and Functioning of Industry Committees under the Fair Labor Standards Act," *Law and Contemporary Problems* (Duke University), Summer 1939, pp. 353-367.

initiates the setting of a minimum-wage rate (or rates) for its
industry. The new American national type is unlike these older
boards, however, in several important respects, notably: (1) it
has no administrative function, in fact is dissolved soon after
its recommendation is made; (2) its recommendation is confined to the wage rate; and (3) the range within which its
recommended rate may fall is rather narrowly prescribed by
the statute, namely between 30 and 40 cents.[18] By this latter
requirement, therefore, the statute coordinates the minimum-
wage rates among all industries covered.

The State minimum-wage laws have been hitherto much less
comprehensive—applying usually only to such industries as
laundries and dry-cleaning, retail trade, beauty shops, and hotels
and restaurants—low-wage industries, characteristically employing many women and minors.[19]

The "Living Wage," in Theory and in Practice.—To what
extent are legal minimum wages based upon living-cost data,
adapted to the needs of the workers? How far should they
be? Here are outstanding questions of policy and administration. The principle that such a law should assure a "living
wage" in earlier decades was usually interpreted as requiring
the public authorities to investigate the costs of living of the
types of workers covered. Thus, the officials interpreting and
administering these statutes would make up budgets held necessary for a self-respecting and self-supporting single woman in
the industry concerned, and would apply the current prices of
articles in this budget, to determine such a worker's need. In

---

[18] In the first year, October 24, 1938 to 1939, the blanket minimum for all
industries covered was 25 cents; thereafter, 30 cents. After seven years
(i.e., by Oct. 1945), the initiative is reversed, and an approved recommendation is necessary to *reduce* any minimum from 40 cents toward or to 30 cents.

[19] In 1938 the laundry wage board of New York State started a "guar-
anteed-minimum-wage" movement, which has spread into several other industries and states (see *Mo. Lab. Rev.*, Feb. 1938, p. 294). Under this form
of wage order the employer's legal obligation is to pay a specified minimum
weekly sum, e.g., "to any employee who has been employed up to and including 40 hours," or "for weeks ranging from 17 through 44 hours" (with
a few exceptions, such as substitutes for absentees and starts and quits during the week). Work beyond 8 in a day or 40 in a week, of course, is still
likely to call for a higher hourly rate.

recent years, for example, such budgets have been calculated, for American women workers, with the following results:

BUDGETS FOR WOMEN WORKERS CALCULATED BY U. S. STATE
MINIMUM-WAGE AUTHORITIES

State	Per Year	Per Week
Arizona....................................	$1,032.34	$19.85
Colorado...................................	975.08	18.77
District of Columbia.........................	1,118.49	21.51
New Jersey.................................	1,147.82	22.07
New York..................................	1,192.46	22.93
Pennsylvania...............................	1,094.83	21.05
Utah......................................	924.28	17.77

Source: "Recent State Minimum-Wage Legislation," *Labor Information Bulletin* (of U. S. Dept. of Labor), March 1939, p. 9. This article continues: "In making the survey on adequate minimum standards for working women, the Minimum-Wage Division of the New York Department of Labor, for example, had in mind a budget which would provide an adequate standard of living for self-supporting women and not for emergency use for persons or families in temporary economic distress. It also found it necessary to establish the required minimum budget on an annual basis, as workers must maintain themselves not only when actually employed, but also during partial employment and during periods of temporary unemployment." The implication of this last sentence seems to be that, if the New York industry usually operates only half the year, the legal minimum weekly wage should be well above the $22.93 shown in the table—perhaps nearly $46.

Procedures similar in principle have been followed for many years by the Australian minimum-wage authorities; though there was great variation in the statistical details. In nearly all countries, however, the wage-fixing authorities have felt obliged to compromise between this standard of a "living wage" and the apparent wage-paying ability of the industry.[20]

Our Federal Fair Labor Standards Act conforms to the trend away from the attempt to enforce a statistically determined "living wage," and does not emphasize cost-of-living data (see Chapter 20, below). It directs (Sec. 8) that

With a view to carrying out the policy of this Act by reaching, as rapidly as is economically feasible without substantially curtailing employment, the objective of a universal minimum wage of 40 cents an hour in each industry engaged in [interstate] commerce or in the production of goods for commerce, the Administrator shall from time to time convene the industry committee for each such industry, and

[20] "No board, however, has as yet recommended a minimum wage as high as the amount needed to meet this standard."—*Ibid.* Cf. E. M. Burns, *op. cit.*, Chs. 13, 14.

the industry committee shall from time to time recommend the minimum rate or rates of wages to be paid . . . The committee shall recommend to the Administrator the highest minimum wage rates for the industry which it determines, having due regard to economic and competitive conditions, will not substantially curtail employment in the industry.

Thus, the criteria are the somewhat arbitrary limits of 30 and 40 cents per hour (similar to those of the NRA),[21] and a reasonable prospect as to what rate (within such limits) can be set "without substantially curtailing employment." The latter, of course, is equivalent to the twin factors, otherwise known as "the ability of the industry to pay"[22] and "unemployment."[23] Under our present national law, therefore, legal minimum-wage rates vary among industries, in accordance with judgments of the committees and of the general administrator as to effects on employment;[24] and no formal attempt is made to see that the minimum wage should cover statistically ascertained needs of the workers.

Why this trend away from the statistical "living wage"? Several reasons were suggested under Section A of this chapter, in the discussion of the family-allowance movement. Here we may pick up another thread in the treatment of problems of poverty in modern democratic states. The older appeal to "the living-wage principle" commonly proceeded upon the assumption that an adult male employee should receive as minimum annual earnings enough to support a "standard family" of (perhaps) five—man, wife, three children. "Minimum subsistence" and "minimum health and decency" budgets, of some $1,500 to $2,500 are still put forward as endorsed by high governmental authorities; and in the last table exhibited above may be seen corresponding estimated "living wages" required by women supporting only themselves.

---

[21] Thirty cents an hour, however, is a higher *national minimum* than was prescribed by the NRA codes. NRA's minimum under its Cotton Textile Code No. 1, e.g., applying to southern outdoor common (frequently Negro) labor was well under 30¢. Some NRA minimum rates for unskilled, on the other hand, were above 40¢. Lyon *et al., The National Recovery Administration*, Ch. 12 (Brookings, 1935).

[22] Discussed in Chapter 9, above.

[23] Chapters 11-13, above.   [24] Subject to court review.

Wages based upon such budgets, however well they are prepared, are now known to be inadequate for social policy toward labor incomes, for several main reasons. (1) When applied to a concrete industry, there is usually widespread agreement that legal wage minima measuring up to these calculations would produce too much unemployment. (2) The average Census family in the United States is now less than four persons, not five. (3) If each woman worker were paid at the rate of at least $1,000 to $1,200 a year and each man at least $2,000, the total national income (estimated at about $70 billion a year in 1937 and 1939; about $75 billion in 1940) would hardly suffice to remunerate the 50-odd million people who now are actual employees, working employers, or self-employed. (4) And finally, even supposing that such "living wage" minima could be practically guaranteed to all workers, those with unusually heavy burdens of dependents would still be inadequately protected.[25] By another route, therefore, we arrive again at the conclusion that other social-security and employment measures are needed to meet the social problems connected with poverty (particularly the great problem of the high percentage of all children who belong to poverty-stricken families)—after we have done our utmost by political means to raise the *wages* of the poor.

First Two Years of Fair Labor Standards Act.—A few official data will give an idea of the task set by our national law—apart from its ban on labor of "children" under 16 years of age.[26] The number of workers in the interstate industries covered was estimated at about 11 million when the law took effect, at 12.7 million in April 1939. (The difference in these figures is doubtless due in large part to general business recovery from the recession of 1938.) As the third year of the law's operation began on October 24, 1940, bringing into effect time-and-a-half for work beyond 40 in a week and continuing the

---

[25] See reference to the Australian Royal Commission on the Basic Wage of 1920, p. 494, below.

[26] Employment of persons under 18 is forbidden in any occupation certified as too hazardous by the Chief of the Children's Bureau—see Sec. 3 of the Act.

national minimum-wage rate at 30 cents, official reports were thus summarized by a journalist:

Under the escalator provisions, 300,000 workers received wage increases in 1938, and 690,000 in 1939, while the work-week reduction [to 44 hours] benefited 1,400,000 the first year, and [the further cut to 42 hours] 2,382,500 the second. Now the formal inauguration of the 40-hour week means shorter hours—or time-and-a-half for overtime—for about 1,950,000 workers.[27]

To the calculations as to numbers of workers whose earnings in normal hours were brought up in the first and second years, respectively to the statutory 25-cent and 30-cent minima, should be added the wage orders which established minima higher than 30 cents for specific industries, after recommendations by the respective industry boards.

MINIMUM-WAGE ORDERS BY INDUSTRY, DATES, RATES, AND COVERAGE, AS OF JULY 31, 1940

Industry	Date Effective (1)	Minimum Hourly Wage Rate (2)	Coverage		
			Wage Earners in Industry (3)	Wage Earners Directly Affected (4)	Percent of Workers Affected (5)
Hosiery....................	....	......	150,000	47,400	31.6
Seamless..............	Sept. 18, 1939	32½	a	a	....
Full-fashioned........	do	40	a	a	....
Textiles..............	Oct. 24, 1939	32½	668,000	179,700	26.9
Millinery.............	Jan. 15, 1940	40	22,000	3,600	16.4
Shoes................	Apr. 29, 1940	35	234,000	60,100	25.7
Knitted underwear and commercial knitting..	May 6, 1940	33½	62,000	17,000	27.4
Woolen................	June 17, 1940	36	159,000	12,500	7.9
Hats.................	July 1, 1940	40	25,000	5,500	22
Knitted outerwear......	do	35	26,000	8,500	32.7
Apparel b, d............	July 15, 1940	32½to40	655,000	166,000c	25.3
Paper................	Sept.16, 1940	40	129,000	8,300	6.4

a No information on coverage in separate branches of industry. b Puerto Rico exempt.

c Does not include 10 branches of apparel industry, employing approximately 56,000 workers.

d See source for rates of the 26 apparel industries for which orders were issued; also for data on recommendations pending in four other industries, including leather, for which a 40-cent order was issued Aug. 14, 1940.

Source: "Two Years of the Fair Labor Standards Act," Mo. Lab. Rev., Sept. 1940, pp. 554, 555. (Col. 5 computed.)

27 Newsweek, Oct. 28, 1940, p. 36.

There have been but few well-documented charges of sub-stantial unemployment attributable to this law's operations; and there appears to be little doubt that, directly in step with the "escalator provisions," not less than 10% of the 12 million cov-ered workers have had normal-hours wages brought up to 30 cents or more, and all except professional and administrative employees have become eligible for time-and-a-half rates for work over 40 hours in a week.

In a later chapter (20) I shall comment further on the eco-nomic import of this great change (which was assisted, of course, by the 1939 recovery and the national defense activity of 1940); but a few points may be underlined at once. It will be observed that wage recommendations and orders usually call for single national minima, in each industry or sub-industry; mere sex and geographical differentiations, so common in the NRA codes, are frowned upon by the 1938 Act.[28] The result is that a large percentage of the wage raising attributable to the law occurs in the South and in small cities, where earnings below the minima named were most common.[29]

The comparative effects of the minimum-wage orders of 32½ cents and 36 cents respectively for cotton and woolen textiles depend, in part, on how the various blends and mixtures of these materials are interpreted. Cotton-textile mills have been rather rapidly developing fabrics containing small per-centages of wool; and if, as the full-fledged woolen manu-facturers desired, all workers employed on fabrics or yarns containing as low as (say) 10% of wool were paid not less than 36 cents an hour, it would become more difficult for the southern mills to produce these blends.[30]

---

[28] The latter law, however, permits (Sec. 8(c)) intra-industrial classifi-cations by reason of differences in matters such as "transportation, living, and production costs."

[29] See Ch. 20-B, below.

[30] Actually the Administrator, by an order dated May 22, 1939, rejected this plea of the woolen manufacturers, and decided that the woolen mini-mum-wage rate (36¢) should apply to the manufacture of yarn containing more than 45% of wool and to fabrics containing more than 25% of wool (the cotton minimum-wage rate applies to lower percentages of wool). He based this decision in part upon similar demarcations used by the NRA cotton and woolen codes. The woolen trade claimed that these low-wool blends have been developed, in the cotton mills, largely since NRA days.

The hosiery, hats, and apparel committees (as the above table shows), utilized the statute's authority to make classifications; and variable wage minima have been set for classifications or sub-industries within at least these three general industries. The highest minimum authorized by the statute (40 cents), for instance, was set for full-fashioned hosiery, much of which industry is located in the North, is well organized, and is characterized by comparatively high earnings. The seamless branch, which is much less organized and is much more prevalent in southern territory, received a "wage floor" of 32½ cents.

The reader will doubtless notice some anomalies in this structure of orders and recommendations, and in later wage orders. The differences in comparative effects of legal wage minima on competitive positions of various sections of industries, and in relation to substitutes for their products, are partly explicable by the requirement that separate industry committees must take the initiative in recommending rates between 30 and 40 cents, each for its own industry. The Federal Wage and Hour Administrator, however, has many means of coordination and reduction of anomalies throughout the entire national minimum-wage structure. Virtually all staff work, for example, is done under his direction; moreover, he has full power to reject any recommendation which he considers not based on sufficiently careful study, and he has wide latitude in appointment of members of the industry committees. In the course of time, therefore, it may be expected that the harsher discords within our minimum-wage family will be mitigated if not completely removed.

D. Enforcement of Legal Minimum Wage

A few words are now in order with reference to problems of enforcing a legal minimum wage. Obviously, enforcement difficulties vary directly with the height of the legal wage—if it is set low enough, there is no difficulty at all; but the higher it goes above the "free market" rate, the more does the official rate tend to be honored in the breach. The Massachusetts law relied entirely on the penalty of unfavorable publicity—the Commission was given powers of investigation and was directed to publish the names of firms found to violate the "directory" minimum-wage orders after they were set by the wage boards. A State Commission is not likely to secure very widespread distribution of such unfavorable publicity, yet some students have held that the Massachusetts law has been moderately effective. The tendency is now strongly toward "mandatory" wage orders, enforced by fines and compulsory restitution of wages due to the earners.

The Federal Fair Labor Standards Act initiates a compound method of enforcement. It not only provides (Sec. 16) that the Administrator shall set up inspection and enforcement machinery (in cooperation with State labor departments, so far as their standards are approved by him), and that violators may be fined up to $10,000 or imprisoned up to six months or both, but also that an employee (or ex-employee) or his agent, may bring civil suit against an employer for alleged violation of the Act, and, if successful, may recover twice the unpaid legal minimum wages, as well as attorney's fee and costs. This reference to the employee's agent, of course, brings trade unions into the picture, as they are naturally interested in enforcement; moreover, the labor representatives on each industry committee are nominated, so far as practicable, by the trade unions of the industry.

Although the problems of enforcement of the laws discussed above are less formidable than those of the NRA, they are still very great. Enforcement of the minimum-wage regulations alone is a huge task; and the Federal Wage-Hour Administrator is responsible also for implementation of the maximum-hour sections of the Fair Labor Standards Act. The latter, with its 50% penalty rate for overtime, affects nearly all the wage earners, as well as the more routine white-collar workers, of interstate industries subject to the law; and when maximum non-penalty hours came down to 40 in 1940, it meant a drastic change from the labor-cost situation of a few years before.[31]

[31] Cf. Ch. 11-D, above, on the nature of this law's flexibility as to hours of work in seasonal industries and under certain collective agreements.

Thus, thousands of complaints each year pour into the Federal Administrator's lap; and presumably as more states raise their standards to similar levels, they too will have to raise additional corps of inspectors. During the first two years the Federal Wage-Hour Division reported that it had built up a staff of some 2,000 persons, started nearly 1,000 civil and criminal suits, and collected over $4 million back wages for about 150,000 workers.

In appraising this record, naturally we should remember, not only how impossible the whole program would have seemed to most of our people as late as 1932, but also how violent had become the reaction from the NRA by 1935, and how rapidly the scope of Federal power over labor conditions has broadened under the New Deal. National labor inspection bureaucracies developed more gradually in such countries as Britain and her dominions, Germany, and Scandinavia; and so by 1938 all the latter were probably more efficient than ours. The French 40-hour week regulations under Premier Blum (1936-38) and our NRA, both of which required drastic rises in *hourly* wages, seem closer parallels.[32]

E. Summary

In this chapter, the first of several dealing with governmental regulation and pressure on private wages, we have outlined the development of legal minimum-wage rates, intended chiefly as protection for the lower-paid workers—and incidentally as protection for the employers already paying higher wages. Authoritative wage fixation was a commonplace of medieval and early modern Europe, but these early controls were in part designed to protect employers and consumers against *too-high* wages. After the comparatively laissez-faire policies of the nineteenth century, the modern legal minimum-wage movement was born in Australia and New Zealand— in rather close association with the authoritative determinations

---

[32] In Ch. 20-C, below, some notice will be taken of statistics of hourly earned wage rates, before and after the FLSA orders; also of the question: How high may legal wage minima be set without causing "substantial unemployment"?

of all manner of wages, as means toward settling and avoiding strikes, which will be studied in our next chapter.

The attempt has often been made, through legal minimum-wage agencies, to assure the workers a "living wage," to be determined statistically. Since the payment of such a wage, especially of one high enough to support properly the larger families, has been economically impracticable, minimum rates have nearly always represented compromises between the "living wage" and "wage capacity of the industry" principles. Our National Wage-Hour Law regulates hours and child labor as well as wages; it calls for a minimum rate of 40 cents an hour as rapidly as that can be achieved "without substantially curtailing employment." Official estimates indicate that the minima already ordered are higher than goodly percentages of workers were receiving when the Act took effect, in 1938.

CHAPTER 18

COMPREHENSIVE REGULATION OF WAGES
BY PUBLIC AUTHORITY

We now carry our study of wage controls beyond the confines set by legal basic-minimum rates, applying mainly to the low-paid work that is commonly done by women, children, and "unskilled" men, into provinces of more far-reaching regulation of wages by public authorities. Such controls of skilled workers' wages are ordinarily exercised as part of a larger program that includes basic minimum-wage determinations also. The more comprehensive schemes of regulation we are now proceeding to survey, however, do not in any case commit the governmental authorities concerned to *direct fixation of literally all wage rates;* and it will be part of our task (in Chs. 19 and 20, below) to inquire what are the *indirect* effects of authoritatively regulated wages upon wages controlled less directly, if at all. In the present chapter these matters are discussed through the following stages: First, in section A, a very brief, semi-historical, analysis of causes which have produced widespread State intervention in the determination of wage rates—including some beginnings in the United States; then, in section B, a more detailed account of wage regulation in Australia and New Zealand; and, finally, in section C, a short account of State wage controls in the three Western totalitarian nations.

A. Origins and Causes; American Analogues

Basic Wages; Industrial Peace.—What chief forces have produced this modern movement toward increasingly broad legal wage controls? Two influences are medieval and other pre-modern public fixing of wages for skilled as well as unskilled work, and the modern legal basic minimum-wage movement, both of which factors were sketched in the preceding chapter.

Let us consider several others, with special reference to democratic nations and between wartimes.[1] An outstanding source is State intervention into labor relations on behalf of industrial peace. This objective, especially in its phase of repression of monopolistic "conspiracies," is dimly apparent even in Elizabethan labor legislation; but of course the later vast industrial changes which produced larger firms, unions, employer associations, and greatly altered political and social status of wage earners, have correspondingly transformed public policy on actual and potential strikes and lockouts. While Europe and America continued the nineteenth-century struggle to deal with these problems by legal curbs on particular methods of industrial warfare and by voluntary conciliation and arbitration, New Zealand in 1894 took the first steps of the modern movement toward composing labor disputes, in part by authoritative determination of wages and other labor conditions.

Use of the State's Powers to Help Industrial Self-Government.—Several other nations, without setting up wage controls as comprehensive as those of the Antipodes, have developed one of the latter's methods, generally known as "extension of collective agreements."[2] Much the same "self-government" philosophy appears in several sorts of government regulation with which Americans are familiar—for instance, in the NRA (as noted below), in the influences of professional associations on procedures for granting and withdrawing licenses or certificates of practitioners (such as lawyers, doctors, teachers, plumbers), and of trade associations in framing and administering "fair trade" laws designed primarily to restrain various types of "unfair competition." And price cutting is very commonly thought to be a symptom if not a cause of wage cutting; hence, support for legal wage controls comes from many trade unionists, as well as from employers who regard the payment

[1] The acceleration of authoritative regulation of wages and prices, which occurs in any modern nation during periods when military defense dominates its life, is treated in Ch. 21, below.
[2] Discussed in next section of this chapter.

of wages lower than their own as unfair competition. Thus, private pressures for political support to organized employers, in their efforts to police the unorganized, constitute a major source of the trend toward wage regulation, along with other public controls of business. Though this sort of pressure took a very rapid and broad effect while our NRA lasted, it is more apt to be first accepted by the general public in industries whose continuous operation or rescue from chaos, is thought especially needful—as in the British cotton-textile controls and the American "Guffey" coal-industry laws.[3]

Wage Regulation Extends Itself.—When State control of wages is well begun, it is difficult to stop. A leading reason is one we have stressed many times above: interdependence throughout the total wage structure. Those public authorities who are called upon to guide the courses of minimum wages and/or others, in certain industries, very soon realize that they must assume some moral, economic, and political responsibility for repercussions upon many other labor incomes and costs beside those which are in their official provinces. A certain board may be directly charged with the regulation of only *minimum* wages in a single trade, such as cotton-textile manufacture; but if this board is realistic it will take account of this prospect (among others) : that raising minimum permissible wage rates throughout this industry will sooner or later exert a "bumping-up" or upward pressure on the wages of the more skilled people—who are apt to have rather firm ideas how their earnings should compare with those of the less skilled.

Several of the trends noticed above appear not to have been consciously directed toward a general system of public wage controls; on the contrary, in such nations as Britain and the

---

[3] The present Guffey-Vinson Act appears not directly to affect wages. Indirectly it does, in at least two ways: (1) it buttresses the Wagner Act, in repressing anti-union activities of employers, and (2) it invokes the Federal taxing power to support coal prices and restrain price cutting, thus removing one temptation or excuse for wage cutting. The "Guffey Act" of 1935 did provide that wage rates, determined in each district by producers of at least two-thirds of the tonnage and a majority of the employees, should be binding upon all code members in the district. (And non-code members would be prohibitively taxed.)

United States only piecemeal and indirect measures have hitherto been established. But the examples of Australia and New Zealand have recurrently provoked interest elsewhere in the idea of generalized regulation of labor conditions, to minimize strikes; and it is probable that recent discussions of the uncertain spiral movements of wages, prices, and employment, where uncoordinated yet large-scale wage adjustments are made by a number of private and public agencies, will become an increasingly important source of arguments for centralized national "planning," at least in the realm of wages.[4]

Government Regulation of Skilled Workers' Wages in U. S. A.—The very tentative steps taken by our own American government in the direction of direct control of higher as well as lower private wages can be reviewed in but few words. Since 1888, our statute books have contained laws designed to foster industrial peace in the railway industry. By the Railway Labor Act of 1926 (amended in 1934), we arrived at compulsory delay of strikes and lockouts—pending mediation and investigation; also in effect at compulsory arbitration (through National Railroad Adjustment Board machinery) of disputes over interpretation and application of collective agreements after they are voluntarily entered into. But even if we add the Adamson Act's favorable effects on trainmen's earnings, it would still be far-fetched to call all this *direct* public control of wages. The same may be said of nearly all other labor-relations legislation in the United States, including some state provisions for compulsory delay of strikes.

The short-lived Kansas Court of Industrial Relations (set up in 1920), on the other hand, was a real case in point. It was set up with an eye on the compulsory arbitration of Australia and New Zealand (but apparently with some anti-trade union bias); and, like these Dominions, Kansas undertook to settle labor troubles in part by authoritatively determining wages as well as other matters in dispute. The scope of the Kansas court, however, was restricted to four industries—transport, food, clothing, and fuel; and this extension of legal

---

[4] See Ch. 20-A-5, below.

doctrines concerning public-service industries was one rock on which the law foundered in the United States Supreme Court.[5]

The NRA of 1933-35, mentioned frequently above, was also invalidated by the Supreme Court, and little if any procedure easily recognizable as direct and comprehensive public wage control remains from it. But if the Supreme Court had been "liberalized" a few years earlier, our Federal power might now be enforcing wage rates for many grades of skill, in coal mines and building construction, in public utilities and apparel, and in hundreds of other "industries," through government-approved codes.[6] Soon after the NRA's collapse, the Court's outlook began to change; this was an important factor making feasible the state and Federal minimum-wage legislation surveyed in the preceding chapter. The present national Wage-Hour Act, as we saw, prescribes time-and-a-half for overtime for *all* wage and lower-salaried earners beyond 40 in a week, and thereby profoundly affects labor costs—directly, when employers must hire overtime work, and indirectly, by restricting the supply of labor which can be hired at normal wage rates. Such are the principal American ventures into what might be called unpremeditated public wage control.

B. Public Wage Controls in Britain, Australia, and New Zealand

What forms and effects has premeditated and more or less centralized wage regulation taken abroad? A tentative answer to this question will be afforded by a somewhat more detailed examination of several leading instances of public controls in other countries—beginning with Britain and her Australasian Dominions. Through these inquiries we can become better aware of how the public and semi-public authorities tend to evaluate

---

[5] Wolff Packing Co. vs. Kansas Court of Industrial Relations, 262 U.S. 522. Cf. H. Feis, "The Kansas Court of Industrial Relations, its Spokesmen, its Record," *Quar. Jour. of Econ.*, Aug. 1923, vol. 37, pp. 705-733. The law was repealed in 1925.

[6] See L. S. Lyon *et al., The National Recovery Administration,* Ch. 13, "Wages Above the Minimum" (Brookings, 1935).

living costs and other factors studied in our foregoing chapters, in their official wage determinations and awards.[7]

In the British Isles.—As has been intimated, during peace-times the general practice of British voluntary collective bargaining has been tempered by fixation of legal minimum-wage rates, mainly with reference to female and youthful rather than skilled adult male labor. Thus the general position was similar to that in such other lands as Sweden, Canada, and the United States.[8] By the outbreak of war in 1939, however, Great Britain had taken several further steps. More than three-fourths of the 49 wage boards[9] had fixed occupational differentials for skill, "in order that a reduction in the normal margin between the wages of unskilled and skilled should not take place";[10] also public or semi-public authorities had regulated wages in other industries than those of the trade boards, e.g., agriculture, mines, road haulage, and cotton manufacturing.[11]

---

[7] In Australia and New Zealand the distinctions among agreements, determinations, and awards are important. The first is voluntary; the latter two are generally authoritative. A wage "determination" in this context usually refers to a minimum rate (especially a "basic" wage for women or unskilled men) set without reference to any particular industry or to any actual or potential labor dispute. (In Victoria and Tasmania, however, this term is used for the decisions of wage boards in particular disputes.) An "award" is a decision of an Arbitration Court or similar tribunal in settlement of a dispute; it may, however, embody the results of a complete or partial agreement between the parties concerned on matters in dispute.

[8] Indirectly foreign, like American, "fair (prevailing) wage clauses" in legislation concerning public purchases and construction influence private wages. Such indirect controls are discussed in Ch. 19, below.

[9] Each board composed of representatives of employers, workers and the State.

[10] D. Sells, *British Wages Boards,* pp. 199-203.

[11] *Ibid.,* pp. 37, 66-69; and "In the cotton-textile industry, as described in appendix A, a special act of Parliament, passed in 1934 at the request of both the unions and the employers' organizations, authorizes the Minister of Labor by order to make legally binding on the weaving section of the industry, as minimum rates, the wage rates collectively agreed to by unions and employer organizations; and orders have been so issued. This legislation, the first of its kind in Great Britain, was occasioned by the break-downs in wage standards beginning in the unorganized portions of the industry and spreading to some of the organized employers. It is an exception to the preference for unenforceable agreements in only a very limited sense, for the whole collective agreements are not made legally enforceable, but only their wage provisions; and in another sense the legislation illustrates a further and complementary British attitude, namely, that where the collective-

These regulated wages applied, however, to but a minority of all skilled workers in the British Isles.

In Australia.—Much further-reaching has been the intervention of the British Dominions in the South Seas into private wages. The Australian Commonwealth [Federal government] Conciliation and Arbitration Court (set up in 1904), although its jurisdiction normally extends over only interstate cases, nevertheless exercises a preponderant influence on the decisions of the various Australian state tribunals and in effect sets the pace for private collective bargaining.[12] The Commonwealth Arbitration Court has full power to determine wage rates for workers under its jurisdiction, and to vary those rates periodically and simultaneously as it sees fit.[13] No explicit legislative mandate determines upon what principles the rates are to be fixed; but 35 years of continuous operation have developed a body of traditions and precedents, expressing rather definite principles.

---

bargaining process is not by itself able to maintain wage standards, and the conditions are sufficiently serious, Government sanction for standards should be sought, but only as a supplement and aid to collective bargaining and not in substitution for it."—U.S. Commission on Industrial Relations in Great Britain, *Report,* pp. 6, 7 (1938).

[12] Four of the six states have courts or commissions for compulsory arbitration of disputes; and the other two states have machinery of the minimum-wage board type. In the whole Commonwealth there were, at the end of 1936, no less than 660 industrial and wage boards authorized, and 1,452 awards and determinations by these authorities in force. Four states, moreover, fix certain minimum wages (in factories and retail shops) directly by statutes. Such statutory minima are often graded according to the worker's experience in his occupation. (International Labor Office, *The Minimum Wage, an international survey,* pp. 29, 32 (Geneva, 1939).

[13] Until recent extensions of its power and influence (see footnote 17, below), the Court's awards applied only to persons who were parties to disputes brought before it. Any employer could be made party to a dispute by a union's naming him so, however, whether he employed unionists or not; and the award applied to all the employer's workers, whether union members or not. There were several legal and practical limits on the extension of Court awards, nevertheless, one being the time and expense to unions of obtaining service on (as an extreme case) as many as 10,000 separate employers. (*Ibid.,* p. 9 and cf. O. deR. Foenander, *Towards Industrial Peace in Australia,* Melbourne Univ. Press, 1937, Ch. 11.)

Wage disputes concerning employees of the Commonwealth government itself are referred to the Public Service Arbitrator, whose office was created in 1920.

Australian Basic Wages.—We should first notice the chief types of wage determinations which the Commonwealth Arbitration Court makes. The most important of these is the "basic wage," which is the absolute minimum rate below which no full-time, non-handicapped, adult worker can be paid (in any establishment over which the Court holds jurisdiction).[14] In addition the Court establishes from time to time various single-industry minima, "loadings," and still other adjustments; so that the absolute legal minimum wage for unskilled workers in such an industry is sometimes higher than the current basic wage in the same territory. Further, there is added to the "total basic wage" a "secondary wage" or "margin" for each broad category of skilled workers. Finally, there are frequently added special differentials for particular groups, to recompense them for extreme disagreeableness or hazard of their employment.[15] The wage structure thus determined is subject to two types of automatic variation. In the first place, there is a *regional* adjustment to the cost of living—the basic wage is varied, accordingly, from city to city, as the official cost-of-living index is higher or lower. Secondly, the basic wage is *varied over time* (at quarterly intervals), according to changes in the currently used cost-of-living indexes.[16]

---

[14] Separate basic rates are determined for male and female workers, the latter being usually about 54% of the former.

[15] G. Anderson (*Fixation of Wages,* pp. 355-95) discusses eleven different kinds of disagreeable, dangerous, or laborious work for which extra payment has been claimed at one time or another, and for most of which it has occasionally been awarded. Following the precedent of Mr. Justice Higgins, however, the Court has been very reluctant to pay "dirt money," "heat money," "height money," etc., as it is frequently called. In regard to dangerous work, for instance, Higgins has said: "I cannot encourage the notion that by paying extra money an employer is justified in putting the employee under unnecessary risks of his life" [Seaman's case, 5 C.A.R. (Commonwealth Arbitration Reports) 147], and: "Nor is it well that employers should be encouraged to think that the Court sanctions the putting of human life in danger if certain extra rates be paid" (Gas Employees' case, 13 C.A.R. 437). This doctrine has been most strictly followed in regard to payment for hazard; but the corollary principles in regard to dirty or offensive work, work in confined or hot quarters, and in out-of-the-way places, have frequently been disregarded.

[16] As of Dec. 1, 1939, most of the Federal basic wages (in shillings per week) varied between 76 and 82 in the six capital cities; and in most provincial towns the corresponding rates were 3s. lower—*Labour Report,* 1938, p. 78. (Canberra: Commonwealth Bureau of Census and Statistics,

Thus the emphasis in Australia is placed upon the determination of the basic wages, to which all other wages are tied. The margins for skill and for disagreeableness, and the occasional other specific industry "loadings," are frequently a subject of contention when awards come up for review; but in normal times they tend to remain broadly stable and the whole wage structure usually varies in close sympathy with changes in the basic wage—which, as stated above, is pegged to official index numbers of living costs.[17]

Decline of Reliance on "Living-Wage Principle."—In an extraordinary degree, the Australian basic wages have exemplified the "living-wage principle" of wage determination. Even during the 1930's, after the Court proclaimed the national necessity of cutting all real-wage rates, it continued to assert that its own job was to fix living wages—and the government's job to provide sufficient tariff protection for such wages. In his famous "Harvester" judgment, Justice Higgins, presiding over the Commonwealth Court, had made an estimate of the necessary cost of satisfying "the normal needs of the average employee, regarded as a human being living in a civilized community."[18] This "Harvester wage," adjusted to an official index of cost of living in each city, remained the official specifi-

---

March 1940.) The automatic cost-of-living variations over time apply to the basic wage, and other wages fluctuate, not in proportion but by an arithmetically constant amount (i.e., the "margins" and "loadings" are left constant in shillings and pence, save for very infrequent overhaulings by the Court).

[17] The state tribunals employ similar, if not identical schemes of basic wages, which automatically vary directly and proportionately with some official living-cost index, and fixed margins above these basic rates for broad types of skill and for repulsive job features. In recent years the state wage awards and determinations have rather closely followed those of the Commonwealth Court; and a still closer approach to consistency throughout the national wage structure was produced by extension of the Commonwealth Court's jurisdiction to intrastate disputes and to workers not directly parties to any dispute, in Dec. 1940.

As will be noted below, authoritative real-wage changes of some importance have been made by shifting from one index of living costs to another.

[18] *Ex parte* H. V. McKay, Sunshine Harvester Works, 2 C.A.R. 1-19 (1907). This "average employee" was officially considered to have a wife and three children as dependents.

cation for the basic wage after 1907, except for the few changes to be noted below.

When the 1929 depression had reached catastrophic proportions, the first avowed departure was made from the "Harvester" sliding scale. (Earlier, there were minor modifications, as mentioned in the following paragraph.) After quarterly adjustments had carried the basic wage down some 12% from its 1929 peak, the Commonwealth Court in 1931 concluded that a general cut of about 10% in *real* wages was required by the economic position of the country.[19] Money-wage rates were therefore reduced at this time further than the amount required for automatic adjustment to current living-cost indexes. Another material departure from the constant, basic real-wage standard occurred (in the opposite direction) when, in 1937, rises in wages were awarded which were explicitly intended to raise real-wage rates above previous peaks.[20] These 1937 additions to the basic wage were called "prosperity loadings"; and they were awarded mainly on the ground that Australian industry had become able to bear higher real wages. An incidental reason was that these "real-wage" increases would check the boom which seemed to be getting under way.

A few bits of earlier history of "the living-wage principle" in Australia are also instructive. By the war's close in 1918, the general policy of basic and secondary wages had gone successfully through a decade of experience, but there was acute dissatisfaction with the current basic wage determinations, on two main grounds. One was the lag of wage rates behind living costs; automatic adjustment to a continuous price index

---

[19] In the Basic Wage Inquiry Case (1931), 30 C.A.R. 2. Subsequent automatic cost-of-living adjustments carried the wage structure further downward, until by the end of 1932 the basic money wage was more than 30% lower than in 1929. Since prices were falling so fast in these years, however, it is doubtful when and how far real-wage rates were cut—if at all. When, in 1934, the economic skies had cleared considerably, the Court shifted its quarterly wage adjustments from the "A" living-cost index (food and rent only) to the "C" index (including clothing and sundries), which change designedly improved the "real"-wage levels of the smaller states.

[20] By the Commonwealth Basic Wage Determination of June 23, 1937. This increase was 6s. in the larger states, 4s. in the smaller. Since the weighted average of basic (weekly) rates before this rise was about 70s., the increase was perhaps 7%.

was then in its infancy, and an *annual* index of living cost was used. This problem was tolerably solved by two measures: substituting *quarterly* adjustments, and Justice Powers' blanket addition of 3s. in 1921, as a rough coverage of the lag which remained.[21]

The other line of complaint, calling for a re-examination of the basis on which the real basic wage was officially determined, resulted in the 1920 report of the Commonwealth government's Royal Commission on the Basic Wage. This Commission was instructed to ascertain what weekly wages would be required to provide reasonable standards of comfort for a family of five (including three children)—in effect, to examine critically the "Harvester [real] Wage." The standards suggested by this Commission were nearly 50% above the existing legal basic wages, and were generally conceded to be above the ability of Australian industry to pay. The limited reforms mentioned in the preceding paragraph were soon made in the basic wage procedure; and discussion of the countervailing considerations of big-family needs and national wage capacity also led to some applications of the family-allowance philosophy, under the name of "child endowment."

Thus, although the claim could not be maintained that Australian wage regulation has attained the living-wage ideal in other respects, it is a striking fact that, since the "Harvester award" in 1907, the occasions when Australian basic money wages have been really wrenched loose from their automatic tie to the living-cost index have been few and far between. A few revisions in real-wage rates were, indeed, made under the guise of mere improved statistical procedure (in 1921 and 1934), and a couple of others (1931 and 1937) as explicit changes in real wages; but in each case the degree of change was less than 10%.

Wage Fixation in New Zealand.—Australia supplies our outstanding example of compulsory labor arbitration and other large-scale wage determination in a democratic *Federal* com-

---

21 The "Powers 3s." remained part of most Australian official wage determinations until 1934.

monwealth. The experience of New Zealand goes further back (to 1894), and concerns a single-state nation with a population much smaller (and rather less industrialized) than Australia's. The wage machineries of the two countries are sufficiently similar, however, so that we may treat New Zealand's more briefly, since we began with Australia's.

Before we proceed to examine some special points of her wage control through compulsory arbitration, we must pause to notice the other chief forms of *direct* public wage control in New Zealand. One is statutory wage setting, in whose realm the older instances (minimum rates in factories and shops) historically resemble the cases mentioned above in four Australian states, as well as a few of the older American minimum-wage statutes. Direct statutory wage control was recently used much more sweepingly by the Labor government[22] to restore all wage rates to their position before the wage cuts began in 1931, as told below. And in the same year (1936) was passed the Agricultural Workers Act, which amounts to a second type of wage control. It provided immediately for statutory minima for most dairy-farm workers, and for broadening the system to other agricultural types of work by Orders in Council.[23] The tripartite wage or trade board method of wage fixation, first developed in the Australian state Victoria and now much used in Australia, Britain, and the United States, never took root in New Zealand.

Wage Fixing by New Zealand's Arbitration Court.—This Court—our third type—has been until lately the sole and continuing public wage-fixing tribunal.[24] In many ways the functions and procedures of this agency are similar to those of the Australian labor arbitration courts treated above. All are arbitrators in a rather attenuated sense; in essence they are State courts with substantial compulsory powers. In all cases

---

[22] By the Finance Act of 1936.

[23] See I.L.O., *The Minimum Wage*, pp. 151-177; and E. J. Riches, "Agricultural Planning and Farm Wages in New Zealand," *Int. Lab. Rev.*, March 1937.

[24] As we shall see, its functions were severely restricted during the years 1932-36.

much of their wage fixing is incidental to safeguarding industrial peace.

Closer scrutiny, however, reveals many differences between
the two supreme labor tribunals, some of which are important
for our present purposes. We find the New Zealand Arbitration Court, for example, authorized only at its rejuvenation in
1936 to fix *basic* wage rates. It did promptly fix such rates
(at levels so low[25] that they were nearly ineffective at the
outset; and they have since become almost entirely nominal).
Most nearly corresponding (before 1932 and after 1936) to
the Australian Commonwealth Court's basic wage is the New
Zealand tribunal's *standard minimum rate for unskilled workers*
(see footnote 26, below). The latter Court, directed by the
statutes creating and recreating it to resolve labor disputes "in
such manner in all respects as in equity and good conscience
it thinks fit," developed its own tradition.

In several further respects New Zealand's wage-fixing procedure has differed rather substantially from Australia's,
notably in that:

1. The New Zealand Court has never made either a definite
   statistical estimate of "living wage," or used a living-
   cost index as the explicit and automatic basis of wage
   adjustment;

2. It has made wage awards running for fixed periods (usually one year or more), and only in exceptional times
   (1918-23, 1931-32, and 1940-) has it had power to
   change such awards during their lifetime;

3. It has issued "pronouncements," from time to time, as to
   the normal wage rates which would be reflected in new
   awards, by three grades of skill.[26]

---

[25] Adult male workers, 76s. per week; adult females, 36s.

[26] The "standard rates" thus "pronounced" on Sept. 7, 1937, for instance,
were (in pence per hour): skilled, 33; semi-skilled, 29 to 31½; unskilled,
28.—I.L.O., *The Minimum Wage*, p. 159. (In purchasing power the N. Z.
penny was then equivalent to 1½ to 2¢ of U.S.A. money.) In practice,
the awards during any short period provide much greater diversity of wage
rates than such pronouncements suggest, for in each case the Court recognizes a combination of criteria, especially "the rates actually being paid in
the district concerned and elsewhere for similar work," and "margins for

Thus, only in 1918-23, 1931-32, and 1940-, has this Court been empowered to change all wages within its jurisdiction simultaneously; and none of its wage awards have been based upon the living-cost index in any direct and automatic fashion. During 1932-36, moreover, a conservative government reduced the scope of this Court—for men's wages—virtually to *voluntary* arbitration.[27]

By contrast, Australian Federal compulsory arbitration has continued operating, from its inception, with less spasmodic and vital alterations in its scope; and, furthermore, for 20 years it has adjusted the dominant wages simultaneously and automatically to some official living-cost index (at quarterly intervals)—and at a few critical times it has made further wage changes, avowedly intended to alter *real*-wage rates. The Australian system, therefore, has operated in a more uniform and consistent fashion, and has made wages more quickly, directly, and proportionately responsive to changes in cost of living.

"Extension of Collective Agreements"; Compulsory Membership in Unions.—These two further peculiarities of New Zealand's industrial-peace program, developed earlier and more sweepingly than elsewhere, must now be noticed. An agreement between a registered trade union and a registered employers' association may be converted into an award of the Arbitration Court, and thus made a "common rule," legally binding upon *all* employers and workers in the industry and district concerned—if the Court finds that a majority of such workers were parties to the voluntary contract, and that the latter's terms are in the public interest. In Section A of this

skill and responsibility," "allowances for arduous, dangerous, or disagreeable work," "for irregularity of employment," as well as the "living wage" and "wage capacity principles."—See I. L. O., *The Minimum Wage,* pp. 170, 171, and articles by Riches cited there (cf. Ch. 5-B, above). Nevertheless, the Court's "standard rate for unskilled men" at any time is the practical men's wage "floor" for new agreements and awards.

[27] It retained compulsory arbitral power over women's rates during these four years, which gave it indirect power over men's wages in some industries. Notice that the Court's powers were *reduced,* partly in response to employer demands, in 1932; then restored and enlarged, by the *labor* government which came to power in 1935.

chapter we pointed out the similarity, in principle and motivation, between this practice and our American NRA and "fair trade" legislation; but now it must be observed that the Australasian policy of converting labor agreements into authoritative awards is not merely the resultant or sum of the achievements of more or less independent political pressure groups (each seeking government support), but is rather a logical development of the basic scheme of compulsory arbitration of labor *disputes*. Conversion of voluntary agreements into compulsory awards (when the agreements are acceptable to the Arbitration Courts) is an ounce of prevention—it fixes labor conditions before, instead of after, a dispute develops.

New Zealand's Industrial Conciliation and Arbitration Amendment Act of 1936 prescribed forward steps in the path of making membership in a trade union obligatory on workers. "Every award or agreement . . . must contain a provision making it unlawful to employ in the industry concerned any adult who is not a member of an industrial union bound by it or of a trade union registered before May 1936 and similarly bound."[28] Such unions, in turn, must admit any qualified worker, and must normally keep dues within one shilling per week. The Act in force before 1932 had allowed the Court to grant a measure of preference in hiring to trade unionists; the amendments of 1936 push such pressure for unionization further and also drive a bit deeper the nail of government regulation of union affairs.

Again be it stressed that by no means all wages in either of these Antipodean nations are directly regulated by law, nor are all strikes and lockouts illegal. In general, only registered unions are subject to compulsory arbitration; and unregistered unions there are. Yet the total of all such pressures as noted above has given the national Arbitration Courts of Australia and New Zealand unquestioned sway over the wage structures of their respective countries for a generation and more.

---

[28] Quotation is from summary by E. J. Riches, in "The Restoration of Compulsory Arbitration in New Zealand," *Int. Lab. Rev.*, Dec. 1936, vol. 34, p. 23 of article.

Criticisms of Compulsory Arbitration in Australia and New Zealand.—Although Australia and New Zealand are not Great Powers in any ordinary sense, their experience with compulsory arbitration, wage boards, and other public control of labor relations is extremely significant for the United States and other democracies. The latter nations, as will be shown in Chapter 21, turn as a matter of course to such regulation in wartimes; and after the present war it is by no means clear that a good deal of public wage regulation will not have to be continued and even extended. Although neither Australia nor New Zealand has lived up to the earlier publicity of "a country without strikes," their records for industrial peace are unusually good; and, as we shall see, these records have been obtained without advancing wage rates faster than other progressive countries.

The remainder of this section consists of a brief commentary on the wage regulation of Australia and New Zealand, in two parts. The first reviews some of the stock observations as to the difficulties and significance of compulsory arbitration; the second treats further the wage policies of these Dominions in prosperity and depression.

We may dispose quickly of what was for many years a very difficult problem in Australia—conflicting jurisdictions of state and Federal agencies. Several attempts to deal with this matter by legislation and by constitutional amendment were fruitless; but the problem has become much less acute in recent years (even before the wartime extension of the Commonwealth Court's jurisdiction), by reason of (1) a High Court decision invalidating conflicting state laws and awards, and (2) the tendency of state authorities voluntarily to use the Commonwealth basic wages and margins.

It is said, in both countries, that the wage-fixing and other public policies should be better coordinated; that (for example) suitable actions by other governmental authorities in 1930-31 would have made necessary lesser wage cuts, if any. Not infrequently the Arbitration Courts themselves call attention to such needs of actions beyond their own powers. But probably only in a totalitarian regime can there be maximum coordination of all public authorities; and to democrats one of the most attractive features of the Arbitration Courts of New Zealand and Australia is their judicial independence of the legislative and executive government of the day. Of course there should be—and usually there are—continuous informal consultations between wage authorities and others—as should occur between American regulators of (e.g.) railway rates and railway wages.

Several other problems pertaining to wage fixing as practiced in New Zealand and Australia have been considerably magnified by confusions and special pleading. Among these are the alleged tendency of legalistic procedures to promote contentiousness and class conflict, and to involve needless delays and expenses. These objections are most emphasized by people who underrate the real cleavage of economic interest between workers and employers, and who do not realize the value of time and money spent on open discussions of grounds for decisions in labor affairs. The Arbitration Courts in these Dominions were long ago wisely exempted from many or most rules of law court procedure; though no doubt many opportunities remain for economy of time and money. An associated charge is that the advocates who come before any labor tribunal tend to make exaggerated claims, which are apt to widen the breach between employer and employee. The present Prime Minister of Australia once expressed this point thus:

> When I [as a trade union official] get into Court, should I not fight like a tiger about everything, great and small, and regardless of industrial harmony, knowing full well that the weary-looking man at the end of the bench is taking down every word that I am saying, and that it will be read at the Union's mass meeting next Sunday afternoon, and that it will be accounted to me for virtue?[29]

One reason, it is said, why such far-fetched arguments are made by capital and labor advocates is that the Court is expected to compromise the contending claims. It has also been suggested that the Court sometimes feels obliged to bow to superior force and recognize a *fait accompli*. Justice Powers, for example, at one time dignified the latter idea by denying its

---

[29] *Studies in the Australian Constitution* (ed. by G. V. Portus), p. 63, quoted by W. R. MacLaurin, "Compulsory Arbitration in Australia," *Am. Econ. Rev.*, March 1938, p. 68.

validity with reference to his own Court—which, he said, "is not justified in buying industrial peace on such terms as any union or unions, or any body of employers, informs the Court are necessary to prevent strikes."[30]

The difficulties mentioned in the preceding paragraph are no doubt inherent in any democratic industrial-relations procedure. Not merely compulsory arbitration courts, but also voluntary arbitration proceedings and many other public and semi-public hearings are bound to be utilized as sounding boards or soap boxes by labor and employer spokesmen. Extreme claims, made for the benefit of rank-and-file constituents, do tend to fan the flames of class conflict; hence, measures consistent with fundamental democracy which restrain such distorted appeals are very much to be welcomed. Otherwise, they do not constitute a serious problem. At least the judges of the New Zealand and Australian Arbitration Courts have lengthy terms of office, and are otherwise well insulated against transient political unpopularity. Their experience, moreover, makes them hard to fool. It sometimes happens that a demagogic advocate fears that the Court has taken him too seriously; whereupon, he privately intimates as much to the judge.

Another set of difficulties consists of those connected with enforcing labor awards and determinations. (Incidentally, it should be remarked that our American method of settlement of railway labor controversies arising under collective agreements, which amounts to compulsory arbitration, has as yet given rise to no serious difficulties of enforcement of awards.) Considering the strong Anglo-Saxon traditions of personal freedom, and the strength of trade union organization in Australia and New Zealand, a remarkable degree of acceptance of Arbitration Court awards has prevailed. The inspections for enforcement against employers are mostly made, in Australia, by trade union officials, deputized by the Court.[31] Individual workers are not required to accept the awards as maximum wages, but are free to seek higher rates by individual bargaining. It is, of

---

[30] Foenander, *op. cit.*, p. 248, n. 11, citing 17 C.A.R. 184.
[31] In New Zealand, such officials have the right of entry but there are Inspectors of Awards on the staff of the Department of Labor.

course, not always a simple matter for the public authorities to secure conclusive evidence whether an individual employer has flouted an award by locking out his workers, or a given workman has illegally promoted a strike; nevertheless, penalties are actually imposed on enough persons to add these sanctions to the extremely powerful force of collective self-interest in the light of well-informed public opinion.

It is sometimes charged against these compulsory arbitration systems that they stand in the way of development of voluntary conciliation for the settlement of industrial disputes. Voluntary agreements filed with the Australian and New Zealand Arbitration Courts (somewhat as our railway labor agreements must be filed with the National Mediation Board) may usually be converted into awards, so that the Court serves (like our National Railroad Adjustment Board and the Swedish Labor Court) as an authoritative interpreter of such an agreement. The existence of this final arbitral authority may sometimes deter the parties from persevering with conciliatory action; on the other hand, it is also plain that these parties, as soon as they can predict what the Court's authoritative decision would.be, often if not usually prefer to save the time and expense of invoking its action. Which of these tendencies will be stronger in a particular case is apt to depend on the degree of novelty of the point in dispute. If the Court has already ruled upon a very closely related question, then the parties are apt to strive for a more suitable settlement than the Court could make for them. If, however, the matter has never been adjudicated, they are more apt to take it to the Court.

Economic-Statistical Information Needed by Wage Regulators.—Yet another line of criticism sometimes directed at the Australian and New Zealand Arbitration Courts is that the judges are not adequately informed about the industrial world whose fate rests so largely in their hands. This difficulty has been emphasized by scholarly employers' advocates;[32] and also

---

[32] E.g., by G. Anderson, counsel for employing printers: "We are forced to the conclusion that neither the Federal nor a State Arbitration Court is a proper tribunal to determine margins for skill . . ."—op. cit., Ch. 14.

by well-informed economists.[33] Less has been heard of the same point with reference to trade boards and other non-arbitral wage-fixing authorities, since each of these usually has jurisdiction over but one trade or a narrow group, and its employer and employee members are supposed to supply the needed technical and industrial information. This last assumption is only partially warranted, however. Specialized economic and legal assistance is needed, even by an individual-industry wage board; and it is indispensable for any sort of proper coordination of separate wage-regulating agencies. Such specialized research and legal divisions are doubtless more common in the United States (as in the national Wage-Hour Division) than elsewhere; hence, this feature will scarcely be overlooked in any further development of American public labor control.[34]

With reference to Australian and New Zealand Arbitration Courts, however, this line of criticism, like the others, is often ill-informed and exaggerated. The judges, as stated above, have secure tenure, give full time for many years to these labor courts (and, within the Court, individual judges specialize on particular industries) ; moreover, they are assisted by their arbitrating colleagues, who are drawn from employer and employee ranks. What does appear to be a somewhat serious limitation of these two Courts is that their judges have hitherto inadequately realized their own need of more research assistance; that they have been a little too content with the old-fashioned common-sense, not very precise or quantitative, methods—which, indeed, have enabled them to perform their functions with remarkable success. The rapidly growing mass of quantitative data relevant to wage policy is far beyond the powers of head policy-makers personally to assimilate; they need the assistance not only of part-time expert consultants but of full-time staffs of their own.

---

[33] See, for instance, the article "Australian Wage Policy, 1929-37," *Int. Lab. Rev.,* March 1938, vol. 37, pp. 314-337, by W. B. Reddaway, especially with reference to use of national productivity data; also E. J. Riches, "Conflicts of Principle in Wage Regulation in New Zealand," *Economica,* Aug. 1938, vol. 5 (N.S.), pp. 316-332.

[34] The recent Congressional abolition of the research division of the NLRB was a rather clumsy expedient of its critics to rebuke and reorganize the Board, more than a reaction against specialized research as such.

Adequate Skill Differentials? Job Analysis.—Of out-standing importance in public wage control are differentials or relations among wages, particularly what Australians call "secondary wages" or "margins for skill." Some employers, at least, are somewhat better satisfied with the public basic minimum-wage determinations than with the margins awarded for the various skills.[35] Here we touch upon the complaint, often made (in Australia, anyhow), that these differentials have not given enough incentive so that adequate supplies of skilled craftsmen could be developed.

Two rejoinders may be made to this last line of attack. The first is that the *percentage* wage margins of skilled workers were reduced in most countries during the World War of 1914-18, due to the combined effects of scarcities of "unskilled" workers and the rather common tendency to raise all wages by absolute cost-of-living increments.[36]

Another rejoinder often made in these Courts' behalf—that they have merely approved and enforced the customary differentials, appearing in common and reasonable voluntary collective bargains—must be accepted with more reserve. In these Dominions, for 35 years, legally determined wage rates have been the leaders of others; and in this situation we are reasoning in a circle when we say the public authorities are merely enforcing "prevailing wages." When such authorities prescribe the strategic wage rates which control most others, they should recognize that there are no longer spontaneously determined market or prevailing rates available as sufficient guides. The wage fixers are obliged to seek other fundamental principles. Particulars given elsewhere in this chapter tend to show that

---

[35] That is the point of G. Anderson's remark, quoted in footnote 32.

[36] "Since the war the normal differential—about 30% in terms of the average wage rate for the skilled worker—has been restored in the United States; but in a number of European countries, including Great Britain, Germany, and France, the difference is less now than it was in 1913."— W. S. Woytinsky, "Wages—History and Statistics," *Encyclopedia of the Social Sciences,* vol. 15, p. 315 (1935). It seems that in the building trades, the wages of unskilled labor rose much more, relatively to skilled, in Australia than in New Zealand, after 1914—see Int. Lab. Off., *Studies and Reports,* Series D, No. 16, p. 14; and E. J. Riches, "The Restoration of Compulsory Arbitration in New Zealand," *Int. Lab. Rev.,* Dec. 1936.

the Australian and New Zealand Courts have usually followed sound and realistic economic principles in their adjustments of *basic and general* wage levels. Apparently their facilities have as yet been inadequate for the application of modern methods of job evaluation to problems of *relative* wages.[37]

Wage History and Policy in Australia and New Zealand since 1918.—We now enter the second main phase of our commentary. What main principles and results can be discerned in the wage regulation we have just surveyed? As was shown above, in a limited sense the living-wage principle has prevailed, for the least skilled workers, and wages of skilled occupations have been attached to those of unskilled by comparatively fixed tethers. In the 1930's, the wage structures of both Dominions were regulated with much more reference to other factors than living costs—both in the earlier phase of real-wage cutting and in the later phase of restoration in greater measure than living costs alone would warrant. It seems worth while to scan numerous details of this history.

1. Labor Incomes, 1914-38.—It was remarked above that Australian wage rates, pegged to a comparatively new *annual* living-cost index, lagged well behind cost of living in the rising-price era of 1916-20. Thus, they became subject to less powerful downward pressure in the slump of 1921 than were the more inflated wage rates in some other nations. The change to quarterly automatic revisions, and the further compensation to labor of the "Powers 3s.," tided Australian wage regulation over; and after 1921 its automatic quarterly adjustments to the narrow "A" living-cost index (food and rent only) dominated all wage movements until 1930.

In New Zealand, too, wages were in effect made to vary almost directly and proportionately with living costs, 1918-23. From 1918 this Court could adjust wages simultaneously by means of war bonuses; in 1922 a special Act enabled it to

---

[37] See Ch. 10, above; also compare what is said in Ch. 3-D, above as to the need that collectors of fundamental wage statistics should utilize the job-analysis techniques now common in both public and private personnel management, to develop more significant occupational classifications.

modify existing awards and agreements; and in fact it did then cut wages in approximate measure with the decline in cost of living. From 1924 until 1931, the New Zealand tribunal had no power to alter wage rates during the year or more of life of each agreement or award.

And what happened in the boom-depression cycle of 1927-38? For a first approximation, let the reader turn to the table on page 119, above, which summarizes various attempts by the International Labor Office to arrange in comparable form the official over-all annual averages of money- and real-wage rates for Australia, New Zealand, and a number of other countries. The top series ("money wages") reflect the wage cuts of 1931-33—which were more early and more drastic in Australia and New Zealand than in several other nations.

Among numerous adjustments required to make international wage comparisons for these years more significant, the most important are those relating to hours of work. Weekly hours were changing at very different rates in the various lands; and in somewhat variable relationships to hourly wage rates. American hourly earnings were greatly boosted as early as 1933, to the accompaniment of extreme 40-hour-week compulsory work sharing; France followed suit in 1936; and the 40-hour week, with maintenance of weekly wage rates, was also introduced very generally throughout New Zealand industries in 1936-37. In Australia, on the other hand, up to the war's outbreak in 1939, weekly hours below 44 were quite exceptional. The result is that *weekly* wage rates and earnings in the 40-hour-week countries compare much less favorably with those of other nations than do their *hourly* rates. Since Australian hours also were rather materially reduced between 1929 and 1938, however, Australian average weekly earnings in 1938 were well below their own 1929 level; while the New Zealand average (as the table shows) was 6% above.

The lower half ("real wages") of my table, in which anomalies like those just cited are compounded by differences in methods of constructing and maintaining national living-cost indexes, purports to show that the total gain in real-wage rates, 1927-38 inclusive, was about 10% for Australia's *hourly* earned rates, and 15% for New Zealand's *weekly* minimum rates. A better comparison can be made, *1929*-38, of real hourly wages in these two Dominions. My table shows that, over this period, Australian real hourly wage rates rose 10%. It may also be calculated that average hourly real-wage rates in New Zealand rose 26% in the same years.[38]

The Australian wage changes thus noted are in the main accounted for by the actions of the Commonwealth Arbitration Court, mentioned above—automatic quarterly adjustments following a living-cost index, and a somewhat greater cut in 1930; restoration of the latter cut, in part by turning from the official "A" living-cost index to the broader "C" series; and the rise in real-wage rates ("prosperity loadings") awarded in mid-1937. In New Zealand, money-wage rates were also cut 10% by the Arbitration Court in 1931.[39] After this tribunal's power to fix men's wages was removed by the Act of 1932, wages declined further under spontaneous wage cutting of employers. In 1936 came statutory restoration of 1931 pay for all wage earners; and then the Court (under a new, Labor-appointed, judge) assisted the business upswing and the 40-hour-week legislation to push hourly money-wage rates to a level much above that of 1929.

Partly on account of the severity of the Australasian depression after 1929, the quarter-century trend of wage rates (1914-38) in New Zealand and Australia is less strongly upward than in some other lands, such as Britain and U. S. A. The official all-industries indexes of *weekly* wage rates, compared with those of living costs, indicate that, over this period 1914-38, real weekly wage rates rose about 15% in New Zealand and 27% in Australia.[40]

In Britain, on the other hand, "average [weekly money] earnings of the employed working class [including agriculture]

[38] See N. Z. Census and Statistics Dept., *Statistical Report on Prices, Wage Rates and Hours of Labor* . . . *for the year 1938*, pp. 8, 15 (Wellington, 1940). The rise in "standard" minimum hourly rates for unskilled workers, according to "pronouncements" of the N. Z. Arbitration Court, 1927-38, was also some 27%.

[39] By virtue of special enabling legislation of that year.

[40] *Ibid.*, pp. 8, 13; Australian *Labor Report*, 1938, pp. 69, 170-172.

approximately doubled between 1914 and 1937, while working hours have decreased more than 10%. In the same period retail prices have risen about 50%."[41] This calculation indicates a gain in British weekly real-wage rates of some 33%. No very nearly comparable set of indexes is available for the United States; but according to a recent estimate, our average real weekly *industrial* wage earnings increased, 1909-39, about 47%.[42]

2. Labor Costs.—Comparisons in terms of *hourly* wage rates or earnings, which would be more significant for labor costs, would of course show greater relative increases all around; but lesser gains in the public-wage-regulated Antipodes than in Britain and North America.[43]

The many important differences in national resources and history, as well as in official statistical practices and in occupations and sexes covered, make these comparisons rather superficial. Yet, together with other data cited herein, they do indicate that democratic-political wage regulation in the Pacific

---

[41] A. L. Bowley, *Wages and Income since 1860*, p. 19 (Cambridge, 1937). The discussion and tables in *ibid.*, Ch. 2, show that by "retail prices" in the above-quoted passage Bowley means "cost of living of wage earners."

[42] W. Bowden, "Wages, Hours, and Productivity of Industrial Labor, 1909 to 1939," *Mo. Lab. Rev.*, Sept. 1940. "Industrial" in this research means manufacturing, mining, and railroads. According to the same author (*ibid.*, July 1939), over the same 30-year period real annual earnings of agricultural wage earners in U.S.A. made only a very small gain, which was not true in the other three countries referred to above.

[43] The New Zealand official index of hourly money-wage rates (all industrial groups *except* farming) rose, 1914-38, some 103.6%; while retail prices were rising 51.4%—thus real hourly wage rates advanced some 35%. (*Op. cit.*, pp. 8, 15.) The Australian index of hourly money wages (adult males, all industry groups, *including* agricultural and pastoral) rose, over the same quarter-century, 83.2%, and the "C" living-cost index 30.5% (but the retail-price index 49%). Thus, by the "C" series the rise in Australian hourly real wages was 40.4%. (*Op. cit.*, pp. 64, 69.)

The following computations for Britain and U.S.A. are still more roughly comparable. Bowden's table 2 (*Mo. Lab. Rev.*, Sept. 1940, p. 524) shows a gain in average hourly earnings of *industrial* (manufacturing, mining, railway) workers in the United States from 23.7¢ in 1914 to 65.7¢ in 1938—177% increase; while living costs rose 40.5%. The implication is that real hourly earnings of employed American industrial workers nearly doubled—rose 97%. Bowley's statement (see preceding paragraph in text above) implies that real hourly wages of employed British wage earners, in agricultural as well as urban industries, rose more than 48%, 1914-37.

Dominions has by no means inflated wage rates—rather the contrary. By 1936, however, a "new era" was dawning; and at last appreciable gains in real-wage rates were being produced by supply and demand, as well as by newer labor political tactics.

But why did not Australian and New Zealand labor manage to maintain money-wage rates after 1929? Labor spokesmen did try to; they used vigorously the newer "increase purchasing power" arguments as well as older ones pointing toward wage maintenance. But these peoples have never long neglected the cost aspect of wages. One reason, in fact, why they were so long addicted to living cost as a wage regulator is that living cost is, very roughly, a business barometer. When workers need higher wages, by reason of rising retail prices, employers can generally afford to pay more; and vice versa. But more specifically, these countries were affected early in the 1930's depression by two tidal waves: catastrophic decline in the prices of their exportable produce, and abrupt cessation of large streams of loans and other investments from abroad. Add to these factors the many conservative elements in the national leaderships—including the Court judges, 1930-36—and you have the main conditions making feasible cost reductions by the route of scaling down nearly all wages and salaries almost simultaneously.[44]

Might this crisis of 1930-33 have been surmounted without wage cuts? Or with lesser cuts? Here a few points from the very able analysis by a young British economist who advised the Commonwealth Arbitration Court in 1937 will suffice to show what were the more realistic alternatives.[45] Actually most of the other expedients available were used, to unprecedented extents: scaling down of interest on outstanding as well as new debts, exchange depreciation, public works, subsidies to dis-

[44] The Commonwealth Arbitration Court adduced the disastrous rise of the percentage of unemployment (from 7-9% in the '20's—except 11.2% in 1921—to 19% in 1930, 27% in 1931, 29% in 1932) as an important ground for its action; and although this rate still seemed abnormally high (9.3%) in 1937, bullish business prospects appeared to warrant the real-wage increase awarded in the latter year.

[45] W. B. Reddaway, op. cit. My discussion at this point directly concerns Australia, but in most essentials the New Zealand picture is similar.

tressed industries, and expansive or "inflationary" banking policy. The Arbitration Court was among those who advocated all these measures; though its judicial status and traditions prevented its wage policy from responding directly and completely to the wishes of the government of the day. One reason why a larger degree of exchange depreciation was not attempted in 1930-31 was that this device was then in worse odor in world opinion than it soon became, as successive countries were obliged to adopt it. Thus, a strong case can still be made for the necessity of rather sharp money-wage rate cuts in Australia and New Zealand in the first couple of years of the Great Depression.[46]

Reddaway argues, to be sure, that more of the other emergency measures, and less of *money*-wage cuts (but perhaps the same measure of *real*-wage cutting, by achieving price rises) would have been better; and that the whole episode "lends no support to the thesis that a slump can be cured by such [money-cost-cutting] measures alone, even if their application is restricted to a single country. For the world as a whole, it is certainly easier and quicker to take expansionist measures to revive demand, whether or not it is theoretically possible to escape by cutting costs."[47] But surely exchange depreciation would not be a feasible "expansionist measure for the world as a whole"; and surely no dependable generalization is yet possible as to how far or long it will benefit any one country. Yet this evidence from the Antipodes does tend to confirm the arguments advanced above,[48] to the effect that general wage cutting, while it may sometimes become necessary, is far from an adequate means of combating almost any sort of severe business slump.

However the foregoing comparisons might have to be qualified in the light of more comprehensive evidence, we must remind ourselves at once that non-wage real incomes of wage earners may have risen further in these Dominions than else-

---

[46] Especially as centralized power over wages made it highly probable that the cut was definitive, not merely one step in a downward spiral. Compare Ch. 20-A-5, below.

[47] *Ibid.*, p. 334.

[48] Particularly in Ch. 13.

where—by such means as legally obligatory vacations and holidays with pay, social insurance, and other social services. This claim is freely made, however, in behalf of more than a few other nations;[49] and it would be very difficult to come by a convincing and unbiased international comparative evaluation of *all* elements in total wage-earner real incomes—taking account of both the employed and the unemployed.

C. Totalitarian Wage Controls

What have the dictatorships in Russia, Italy, and Germany done to the more "capitalist" wage structures which existed before they rose to power? That these regimes have extended their centralized controls over labor relations as well as over all others is universally known; and it is also a commonplace that, despite the socialistic wings of all three movements, their total policies have been oriented toward "guns not butter," and toward producer rather than consumer goods. This preoccupation has not been favorable to a continuous or considerable gain in per-capita real income. Let us delve a bit further, in search of mechanisms pertaining to labor costs and labor incomes, using present tense as of the 1930's. It will be a help to notice first some further important characteristics common to all three regimes; then to look for significant differences. The first of these inquiries leads to consideration of the rôle, in each dictatorship, of the Party-monopoly, with special reference to degrees of freedom of managers and workers; and of non-wage labor incomes. Even in the Soviet Union there has persisted a considerable variety of employing organizations—which include not only actual departments of conventional national and local governments and government-owned enterprises, but cooperatives and even one-man employments. These agencies have some freedom in bargaining about wages. They are subject, of course, to stringent controls from State authorities; but these latter controllers, as well as the controlled bodies, are permeated and coordinated by the Communist party, of which Stalin is the undisputed head.

---

[49] See, e.g., section C, below, in this chapter.

In the other totalitarian regimes, the centralized dictatorships are exercised likewise through the single parties which repress all others in their respective States. The Fascist and Nazi governments were much helped into power by their apparent willingness to allow most types of property owners to retain possession of their productive wealth, and many of these "private owners" still retain considerable economic power.

It would be erroneous to assume that the National Socialists, from the very beginning of their reign, attempted to centralize the economy. Their method of obtaining control over the economy was of a different kind. It was a political method. Supported by the powerful apparatus of the party, they penetrated into all economic units, from the single enterprise up to the large concerns and syndicates, everywhere replacing undesirable owners, managers, and personnel by their own followers.[50]

The processes by which Italian Fascists consolidated their economic powers may be described in very similar terms; and in both cases, as we shall see, the route led to a high degree of authoritarian control over "capital" as well as "labor." It will be recalled, too, that the Communist, Fascist, and Nazi parties have made free use of extra-legal methods of seizing power—both before and since they obtained control of their governments.

Another set of traits common to all three regimes concerns labor organization. All gave early attention to the task of replacing existing trade unions (if any) with labor organizations thoroughly permeated by party members, whose economic powers and activities are somewhat similar in the three regimes. In all cases the ruling factions obtained increasingly direct authoritarian control of all economic life.

This party domination of the labor organizations has had both negative and positive results. Together with other measures, it has almost completely obviated or repressed strikes (and lockouts). It has also made of the "unions" agencies for dis-

---

[50] Hans Staudinger and Fritz Lehmann, "Germany's Economic Mobilization for War," *Conference Board Economic Record,* July 24, 1940, vol. 2, p. 294.

pensing recreational and other services to the laboring population—and incidentally for propaganda inciting labor to greater productiveness.

These three totalitarian regimes are also similar among themselves, and like other countries, in that they continue to use wages as the main incomes of the working people.[51] To a much lesser extent than in "capitalism," of course, do totalitarian wage rates serve as important guides for economic activity. Within limits, as mentioned above, particular industries and enterprises still have some freedom in wage setting; wage rates are not minutely determined on a national scale, even in Germany and Russia.

Non-Wage Labor Incomes.—But the totalitarians claim to surpass other nations in the amount of labor income dispensed by other means than wages. Some of these benefits are in the nature of price controls and rationing privileges; some are of recreational and physical-culture natures, as in the Nazi "Strength Through Joy" and Fascist *Dopolavoro* movements; still others are more directly economic measures of social-security or relief work, like the Italian family allowances, the job-creating policies of the Soviet and Fascist States, and the paid vacations which are common in all three nations. These privileges are mainly financed, of course, by compulsory levies upon employers and employed, and partly by contributions which are nominally voluntary—to the Party-controlled associations. In 1934 the payroll taxes in Soviet industries for "wage extras"—in the nature of social insurance, worker housing, and the like—ran usually from one-fifth to one-fourth of the actual wage bill.[52] These non-wage benefits undoubtedly

---

[51] In Soviet Russian non-agricultural industry, by 1934, some 70% of all man-hours were reported paid for by piece rates (*Mo. Lab. Rev.*, Feb. 1936, p. 347) ; and payment by results is also very much used in Soviet agriculture. In Nazi Germany probably a greater fraction of civilian workers are paid by piece rates than in any other nation—except, perhaps, Russia.

[52] State Planning Commission ("Gosplan"), *Socialist Construction in the USSR, Statistical Abstract,* tables showing distributions of expenditures by industry groups (Moscow, 1936—in English). Many non-wage benefits, however—notably through low prices—have been cut when rationing was revised or abolished, as in 1935-36.

play an important rôle in the labor policies of the totalitarian States. The latter, however, were by no means pioneers in this matter and democratic countries, as was pointed out above, have been providing on an increasing scale the social-security types of service to their populations, through both taxes and voluntary contributions.[53] The total cost of such "social-wage" services to the working populations may, however, be higher in these three totalitarian nations (particularly in Russia), *relative to total wage payments,* than in other lands. If so, a probable reason is that these regimes have found that the total funds they could or would devote to the sustenance and indoctrination of all laboring families are most frugally dispensed by the combinations of wage and non-wage benefits they do provide. The comprehensive and compulsory Italian family-allowance system, for example, amounts to a tax on wages of individuals and small families for the benefit of large families containing at least one employed member. This scheme obviously drives toward three favorite totalitarian objectives: to relieve the worst poverty, to enable and force people to work, and to stimulate the birth rate.

Comparisons among Totalitarian Wage Policies.—While the dictatorships were developing other labor and social services as mentioned above, what were they doing about wages? And how and why? These are large questions, answered here only very sketchily. Our account still refers primarily to interwar years, say 1930-38. As actual warfare developed in 1939 the picture becomes much more confusing and "abnormal"; though one of the best single clues to the psychology of all of these regimes is that their policies from the outset have been dominated by haste to develop military power. It will be recalled that the Soviet government established itself in 1917, Italian Fascism in 1922, and German Nazism in January 1933. These seem very different lifetimes; yet in an important sense all three movements have achieved most of their development since 1921—which year ended the chaotic "period of war commun-

---

[53] See Ch. 4-A, above, on American employers' personnel costs, in relation to their actual wage bills.

ism," of civil wars, and of natural scourges in Russia, and was almost the eve of Hitler's first attempt to seize power.

Let us deal first with the query, *How* have the totalitarians regulated wages? The details differ greatly, of course, among the three Powers, and they change with time. The Soviet and Italian regimes, for instance, continued to use the *forms* of collective labor agreements between worker and employer organizations. But even this form runs too strongly counter to the Nazi gospel of identity of interest between employers and employed.

As an instrument for controlling wages the Nazis used wage determinations (*Tarifordnungen*) to cover entire trades or industries, by districts or by the whole Reich; from 1934 onwards these determinations replaced collective agreements freely concluded.[54]

In the matter of centralized legal controls of the wage structures, on the other hand, the Russian and German Five-Year and Four-Year "Plans" play rather similar rôles; and by comparison Fascist Italy was (on the eve of 1939) an "unplanned economy." In the Soviet Union,

The terms of the collective agreement which a union may make with any Trust or other state or cooperative organization must not depart from the limits upon wages and hours of labor which are specified in the [Gosplan annual] planned Control Figures for the given branch of industry and trade.[55]

And in June 1938 national legal control of Nazi wages had reached the point indicated by the following excerpt from the preamble of a decree giving ampler authority to Goering as Commissioner under the Four-Year Plan:

. . . the carrying out of plans for Reich defense and for the Four-Year Plan requires stability of prices and wages . . . the Labor

---

[54] L. Hamburger, *How Nazi Germany Has Mobilized and Controlled Labor*, p. 44 (Brookings, 1940).

[55] C. B. Hoover, *Economic Life of Soviet Russia*, p. 276 (Macmillan, 1932). (How effectively such regulations are administered, from time to time, is another story.) The first comprehensive Soviet Five-Year Plan began to operate in October 1928; but the general policy of approximately predetermining the total funds to be made available for wages is of longer standing.

Trustees and the Special Labor Trustees must supervise wages and conditions of work and must take all necessary measures to prevent an impairment of military preparations and the execution of the Four-Year Plan because of wage and labor conditions. In particular, they are empowered, with binding effect, to fix wages at higher or lower levels in branches of industry designated by the Minister of Labor, even though changes in shop ordinances and collective rules be necessary.[56]

In Italy (as in Russia), more of the form of independent and voluntary collective wage bargaining has been preserved. The Italian industries still in "private" hands are organized into "corporations" or guilds of representatives of both employers and employed—all officials being party members or acceptable to the party. The outstanding employer is the State, which (as told below) led the way when drastic wage cuts were judged necessary; and in March 1940, after living costs had risen 20% to 30% during the preceding year,

The Central Corporative Committee—Italy's supreme economic deliberative body—met with Premier Mussolini and decreed an increase of 10 to 15 percent in [wages and] salaries, effective March 25. It also ordered that prices of many basic commodities shall remain unchanged through July 31.[57]

Wage Trends and Apparent Reasons.—From our "how" question we turn to still more difficult ones: What have these regimes done with wages? Why? One clue is given by the excerpt quoted above from the mandate to Goering in 1938: "The carrying out of plans for Reich defense . . . requires stability of prices and wages." Objectives which could be similarly expressed have animated all three dictatorships throughout their existence—they wanted to raise real wages, but did not propose to allow wage costs to imperil their program of industrial and military preparedness.[58]

---

[56] Reichsgesetzblatt, vol. I, p. 691, quoted in H. J. Heneman, "German Labor Trustees," *Brooklyn Law Review,* Oct. 1940, vol. 10, p. 46.

[57] *New York Times,* March 10, 1940.

[58] The Fascist and Nazi leaders obtained power, in part, through public reactions against previous excessive "successes" of socialist-labor movements. The Bolsheviks had no such capitalist assistance in seizing power,

All three peoples, too, had suffered severely from currency inflations incidental to the War of 1914. Here, perhaps, is a master key to certain contrasts in their wage policies. The Soviet government has perhaps never failed in any year—at least since 1921—to advance money-wage rates, meanwhile claiming that living costs had, on the whole, advanced less and would soon turn downward.[59] This rather moderate rate of inflation was especially feasible in Russia, because all the rather slight economic intercourse with foreigners was monopolized by the Soviet government.

The Italian State, on the contrary, found itself between the horns of its people's dread of inflation and their desperate need of maintaining tourist and other foreign trade.

After 1927 the rigorous policy of deflation pursued by the regime in an attempt to defend the stability of the lira found expression, as we have noted, in repeated and drastic cuts in wages, rents, and prices. With the cooperation of the Fascist party and the Fascist syndical system, these government-decreed reductions were enforced everywhere with rapidity and thoroughness. After 1930, in fact, two major salary and wage reductions were put into effect. On November 18, 1930 the government decreed a 12% reduction of the wages and salaries of all persons in the employ of the state and of other public and semi-public bodies. Private employers soon followed suit, and after that date reductions of varying magnitude were applied everywhere. On April 14, 1934, a further reduction of government wages and salaries, ranging from 20% in the highest grades to 6% in the lowest, was decreed by the government.[60]

By 1938 came the further expedient of lira devaluation, in company with that of the French franc. By that time the

---

and of course their vocabulary and ideology were and are very different from those of the Fascists and Nazis; nevertheless, the similarities of behavior of the three regimes, as their dictatorships became more securely established, are very striking.

[59] Such increases in money wages have usually been accompanied, not only by rising prices, but also by lowering of ration privileges, increased work tasks, and (recently) by increased hours.

[60] W. G. Welk, *Fascist Economic Policy,* p. 233 (Harvard Univ. Press, 1938). Certain annual indexes of money- and real-wage rates in Italy are given in the I.L.O. table p. 119 above. Apparently the I.L.O. was unable to compile sufficiently comparable data on Soviet wages, at least for 1927-38.

average Italian hourly money wage had been twice increased, to slightly above the 1928 and 1929 levels; and unemployment had been combated, in part by an official 40-hour week. As stated above, the bitter pills of the earlier wage cuts were covered by the capsule of price and rent controls; yet, referring to the period 1934-38, the author just cited remarks:

> As is always the case during periods of rising prices, prices and the cost of living rose first (though they rose under the watchful eye and the restraining influence of special party price control committees), and wages were adjusted afterwards, a procedure which entails obvious drawbacks from the standpoint of the wage-earning and the salaried classes.[61]

Because the Nazi party achieved control of the State as late as 1933, when recovery from the 1929 depression was under way in most countries, and because a year or more was required to develop the centralized wage control alluded to above, this control has not yet been put to the test of a general wage cut, in peacetime. Hourly industrial wage rates, which for 1933 averaged about 24% below their peak in 1930, were held at the 1933 level. Living costs were not so well held down, with the result that real *hourly* earnings have declined, apparently throughout the Third Reich's history—though the virtual elimination of (male and non-political) unemployment signified a very substantial increase in total wage income.[62] Much of this reduction in unemployment is accounted for by the concurrent increases of military forces, of relief work, and of other military preparations. Expenditures along these lines are primary reasons why prices could not be kept down.

Very similar observations would apply to the Russian and Italian cases: the social burdens of military preparations and of forced industrialization tended to depress average real wages, whatever the policies followed as to money wages and currency expansion.

The most thoroughgoing central regulation of wages of our times, obviously, is found in the totalitarian States. Is the

---

[61] *Ibid.*, p. 241.
[62] V. Trivanovitch, *Economic Development of Germany under National Socialism*, Ch. 2 (Conference Board, 1937).

growth of State regulation in democratic societies a sort of Fifth Column, driving or leading such nations in the totalitarian direction? An affirmative answer to this question would mistake a symptom for the disease. The cases of Australia and New Zealand alone show that public wage controls do not necessarily lead to a totalitarian social order. These Dominions rather have demonstrated, for a half-century, their ability to hold their incipient socialisms within limits which are irritating to all doctrinaires, but which provide many of the most important foundations for wide diffusion of both material welfare and individual liberty.

D. Summary

In this chapter we have circumnavigated the globe in an abbreviated comparative and historical study of regulation of private industrial wage structures by public authorities. In our own country, as in most others, "minimum-wage laws" until rather recently affected only earnings of women and young people; and, up to the present time, legal fixation of American and British skilled men's wages has been very exceptional. But in several lands have occurred broad developments of legal minimum wages for both sexes and for all grades of skill. Such extension has occurred chiefly as one means toward minimizing labor disputes. Such is the main objective of the compulsory arbitration courts which have exercised leadership in Australasian terms of employment for more than a generation. Totalitarian wage controls, too, are in part by-products of legal and party repression of strikes and lockouts.

This survey has thrown some further light on principles invoked in wage settlements. Under centralized national wage regulation the mere making of wage surveys to determine prevailing rates is not significant for each new *general* change in wages—though some of such surveying is still needful to iron out discontents about certain margins for skill and other details of *relative* wages. These comprehensive systems tend to make general wage revisions mainly by reference to living costs (to equalize and maintain real-wage rates). Meanwhile, other so-cial-security programs have provided more adequate attacks on social problems of poverty than is possible by a mere living-wage approach; and this factor as well as growing prosperity led Australia and New Zealand, by 1936 and 1937, to adjust wage rates more largely by reference to national-prosperity indexes like exchange and unemployment rates. Real-wage rates were drastically cut in the 1930's—in these Dominions, temporarily because of unfavorable international economic relations; in totalitarian Europe, for the same reason and the added one of huge military costs.

CHAPTER 19

OTHER INFLUENCES OF GOVERNMENT ON PRIVATE WAGES

In addition to the direct and authoritative regulations of wages in private employments which were noticed in the preceding chapters, modern governments have exerted pressure on private wages in a great variety of other ways. By comparison the latter may be called indirect. Perhaps all governmental influences on truly private wages are negative, in that the employer is not required to hire any particular worker or amount of work—the activities of State agencies rather tend to prescribe many conditions which various employers must observe *if* they do hire this or that sort of labor.[1] In the present chapter, which does not attempt comprehensive treatment of these matters, we approach indirect State wage controls first through mention, in section A, of some principal sources of the political power necessary. Then we proceed to canvass outstanding wage effects, in section B of social legislation and social services, in section C of public wage and personnel practices, including, in section D, work-relief "wage" scales; and finally of legal "prevailing wage" requirements in section E.

A. Sources of Labor's Power; Sanctions

How is political support secured for minimum-wage and other labor legislation? As intimated in previous chapters, one method consists in attaching conditions desired by trade unions (and/or other organizations whose main interest is on the labor-welfare side) to legislation that is desired by business

---

[1] The above statement refers primarily, of course, to non-totalitarian States. Apparently the Nazi government, especially in its earlier years, required many employers to hire more labor than they would have taken on voluntarily.

interests. This aspect of the late NRA is universally recognized; and a great many other political advances for labor have been accomplished, in part through political concessions to employing interests. In European countries, for instance, high tariff protection for agriculture is very common nowadays, and such protection makes the farmers more willing than otherwise they would be to accept legislation in the interests of agricultural workers. In the United States, of course, such protective duties are of less benefit to farmers, who finally obtained a great system of cash subsidies; and these subsidies (combined with tariff protection) have enabled our national government to require some improvements in the conditions of farm labor, for example of labor occupied in growing and harvesting sugar beets. Subsidies to other industries in recent years, have been tied to wage requirements.[2]

As the rôle of government grows in importance, so do expenditures on public contracts, and this power of the purse has been utilized by labor organizations to secure and enforce the "prevailing wage" clauses discussed in the last section of this chapter.

B. Influences of Social Legislation on Private Wages

In what chief ways does social legislation tend to affect private wages? Restrictions of hours of labor, especially when these are accompanied by stipulations that daily or weekly wages shall not be reduced (or at least not reduced proportionately with the hours worked) furnish leading examples. Such influences may be traced in a widening circle, from many laws and regulations which have explicit and obvious connections with wages to a great fringe whose influence on supply of or demand for various types of labor is much less direct. As noted above, employers tend to reckon payroll taxes for unemployment and other social-security benefits, also the cost

---

[2] For instance, shipping subsidies under the Merchant Marine Act of 1936 require adoption of wages and other labor standards laid down by the U. S. Maritime Commission (given in *Mo. Lab. Rev.*, Jan. 1938); and somewhat less direct wage control is exercised by the Federal government in aviation, through the Civil Aeronautics Act of 1938.

of compulsory as well as voluntary compensations for accidents, diseases, vacations and sick leaves with pay and the like (these last are mandatory in several countries) as parts of their total labor costs.

Many laws and administrative regulations, moreover, which are ostensibly designed to protect employee and public health and safety may be plausibly attacked as restrictive "workmaking" devices of labor groups—e.g., requirements relative to size of crew and length of railway trains. Unquestionably the employer's self-interest, which generally operates powerfully toward making him content with older labor conditions, needs to be counteracted by an increasing mass of requirements for health and safety; yet it is frequently debatable how much safety we can afford or will tolerate. In general, people who are numerous and who therefore represent actual or potential political pressure groups, like farmers, domestic employers, and operators of private automobiles, are not likely to be held legally to such stringent and costly health and safety practices as are a few large employers.

Political Regulation of Labor Supplies.—Among the innumerable ways in which the State influences labor supplies— and thus, in the long run, wages—are various actions affecting population changes (births, deaths, and migrations). Control of immigration, on a national scale, has been an important factor in American wages for many decades; and especially since 1929 we have also had many difficulties about migrations of labor within the nation. Another indirect influence, which in the United States is of great historic importance, is education and training of young people at public expense. Many arts and skills, such as reading and writing and even stenography, which in various times and places have been sufficiently scarce to give the possessors high wages, have become common with us; and the endeavor is constantly made to adapt vocational education better to the current opportunities for employment. The general tendency of such public training, therefore, is to diffuse skills more widely and thus to reduce the differentials between skilled, semi-skilled, and common labor.

More controversial problems are presented by connections between social security (or the broader class, social services) and labor supply. The baffling volume of unemployment has accelerated the flow of proposals to curb the active labor supply by lopping off both its age ends—restraining younger people and (especially married) women from employment, and pensioning off the older at lower and lower ages, on condition that they should be withdrawn from the labor market.[3] It is readily apparent that, if fallacious and shortsighted views of this sort are widely entertained, these policies may be applied in such fashion as to reduce greatly the aggregate social productivity, however favorably they may affect job security and wage rates of some labor groups; yet many such projects do contain kernels of wise social policy. A great many types of voluntary and compulsory prolongation of the periods during which young people are educated and trained can be justified, for example, by reference to cultural or vocational values, or both; and the same may be said of numerous ways of dealing with the problems of old-age security. To an important extent both these periods of low or indirect productivity may be handled so that during the middle years the individual is much more valuable to society, as well as to himself, than he would be with less preliminary training and/or with less assurance of relative comfort in his later years.

But the argument that more young and old people should be kept out of competition with the middle group in the labor market states the problem in such fashion as to suggest "lump-of-labor" solutions which tend to freeze or aggravate the existing total of unemployment of human power, and merely to redistribute its burden. Some great pools of unemployment and poverty, as in decadent mining and lumbering regions, require special social services; but even in these cases care should be taken to prevent indefinite continuance of subsidies to property and labor in such localities and trades.

Finally, in a great many ways the State's power may make or break trade unions, and thereby indirectly influence wages.

---

[3] A condition of the latter sort was removed from the old-age annuity title of the U. S. Social Security Act in 1939.

This matter is sufficiently fresh in American minds so that a few illustrations will here suffice. The great growth of labor organization under our New Deal might well be studied in relation to an equally striking advance in France, under Blum's New Deal, and also by comparison with the marked increase in union membership in Britain since 1929, with little New Dealing. Part of all these gains was doubtless due to mere industrial revival after 1932. But the political makeups of the Roosevelt and Blum governments gave a much more favorable total legal status to labor organizations in these nations than they previously had.

In this connection one problem becomes better understood in the United States as its novelty recedes: I mean unemployment insurance and public "relief" or assistance in relation to labor disputes. During the sit-down strike era (1936-37), conservative opinion held that families of strikers should not be given relief, however destitute they became. The more moderate view is likely to prevail here, in the long run (as it has in other nations), that the minimum below which a family's income-per-person shall not be allowed to fall may not be qualified by any reference to the family's direct or indirect connection with labor disputes—if only because of the administrative difficulty of determining whether any member of a given family has directly or indirectly participated in a given "strike." This liberal or moderate policy, of course, would become the less practicable if and as the relief standard rose, in relation to the real wages earned by employed people, and as other deterrents to any family's acceptance of the status of "relief client" were reduced in force.

An analogous but distinct problem is presented by unemployment compensation, with reference to labor disputes. Not much objection is heard to the position commonly taken, that workmen directly affected by a dispute are not eligible for unemployment benefits, but that people are eligible who are unemployed by reason of "strikes" to which they are not parties. There are many degrees, however, which may be interpreted quite differently by public officials of differing preconceptions; moreover, trade unions can maneuver to utilize un-

employment compensation as far as possible. Thus, the pro-
longed dispute in General Motors plants in 1939 concerned
immediately only the highly skilled tool and die makers; yet
without their services the plants could not operate, and thus
many thousands of members of the same industrial union to
which the tool and die makers belonged were out of work.
A similar problem is raised in this industry, too, whenever
there is a labor dispute in either a car plant or a separately
owned body plant accustomed to supply the bodies for these
cars.[4]

Britain's several decades of unemployment benefits, moreover, have underlined another problem—what should constitute "suitable employment," under "reasonable standards" (of
wages, among other things), opportunity to secure which will
legally disqualify a person for unemployment insurance benefit? Democratic principles clearly forbid strike-breaking as
"suitable" working opportunity, from this standpoint; yet
labor's political power in several nations has secured many other
safeguards whose total effect appears to aggravate somewhat
the unemployment problem.[5]

C. Public Wages—How Do They Affect Private?

From these reactions of social legislation on private labor
costs (affecting available labor supplies, and requiring the employer to incur certain types of labor expense—if and as he
hires labor), we may now turn to the question: What influences
have the wages, salaries, and general employment conditions
of public employees upon those of corresponding private workers? Can public authorities, by acting as "model employers,"
pry upward all real wages, without injury to any social class?
Or, if the State is a "generous" employer, is such generosity
simply a form of political privilege, the favored people benefiting at the expense of others? This problem has been widely
recognized, and of course its importance has grown rapidly

---

[4] See Ch. 5-A, above.
[5] Cf. Ch. 13-B, above.

of late, with the great expansion of governmental payrolls, relative to private.[6]

In the present section, for simplicity, the discussion will be limited in two principal ways: (1) we shall deal but scantily with the interlocking question of inflation of public payrolls, through hiring *unnecessary amounts* of labor, and (2) we shall leave the important issue of payment scales for "work relief" for treatment in section D below.

Addressing ourselves to the incentive aspects of public personnel administration, and with reference to labor services really needed by public bodies, let us now consider the following questions: (1) How do *money* wages and salaries of government employees compare with those of similar workers in private employment? (2) How do their *real* wages compare? (3) What ideas, pressures, and principles do, and should, control these matters?

1. Money-Wage Rates in Government and Private Services; TVA Wages.—It is very difficult to arrive at significant comparisons of public and private wages, since there are innumerable variations and conditions within these two categories. We might find, for example, that state (or regional) and municipal governments tend to set wage rates more nearly in accord with local wages in private employment, than do the Federal (or central) government agencies—since the latter are under some pressure toward "equal pay for equal work," over the whole nation, and the rate for each occupation must be high enough to attract and hold employees in the location where the government needs such service and faces strongest private competition.

In some instances, however, Federal agencies do make efforts to adjust their labor remuneration to local prevailing

---

[6] Before 1914, the wages and salaries of all employees of American Federal, state, and local governmental bodies constituted some 9% of all employee compensation in the country. By 1929, this percentage had risen to about 10%. In 1932, the much greater relative shrinkage of private than of governmental expenditures drove the percentage up to 16, and in the more prosperous years, 1934-37, it averaged 14% (exclusive of work-relief expenditures). (National income estimates of National Bureau of Economic Research and of U. S. Department of Commerce.)

rates. An example is furnished by the Tennessee Valley Authority, which is required by law to pay wages prevailing in its area. From its inception, the TVA has maintained a capable personnel department, which has conducted wage and salary surveys, as well as collective-bargaining conferences with trade unions.[7] The wage rates thus established each year by the TVA are mimeographed and readily obtainable. In the scale effective January 1, 1940 for construction and temporary operating and maintenance work, for example (similar to those of the previous few years), the lowest rate was for laborers and probationary apprentices, 47½ cents per hour; and most of the skilled trades ran from $1.25 (e.g., blacksmith, boilermaker) to $1.50 (examples: bricklayer, crane operator). Other hourly rates for the commoner skilled crafts included carpenter (form and finish), $1.12½; cement finisher, $1.25; electrician, $1.25; machinist, $1.25; millwright, $1.25; painter, $1.12½; plasterer, $1.50; plumber, $1.37½; tile setter, $1.50. Truck operators received 62½ cents, for trucks under 3½ tons, and up to 85 cents for 7½ tons and over. All the TVA rates cited above refer to construction and temporary services; regular workers are paid, like most others in Federal service, annual salaries.[8]

Comparison of these sample rates with those for building trades elsewhere will show that in some cities the hourly rates are considerably higher than in the TVA scale. These markedly

---

[7] The Authority's pamphlet *Employee Relationship Policy,* states that collective bargaining is carried on through representatives of the workers' choice, and indicates there may be no "closed shop." Minimum-wage rate schedules are determined through collective bargaining for each calendar year, in accordance with the following, among other principles:

"19. In accordance with Section 3 of the Act creating the Authority not less than the rate of wages for work of a similar nature prevailing in the vicinity shall be paid to laborers and mechanics. In the event any question arises as to what are the prevailing rates of wages, which question cannot be settled by conference between the duly authorized representatives of the employees and the Authority, it shall be referred to the Secretary of Labor for determination, and the decision of the Secretary shall be final. In the determination of such prevailing rate or rates, due regard shall be given to those rates which have been secured through collective agreement by representatives of employers and employees." (P. 10 of pamphlet.) Cf. current *General Agreement between TVA and Tennessee Valley Trades and Labor Council* (mimeographed), which supplements the pamphlet.

[8] See Ch. 11-D above, as to relations between TVA hourly and annual rates.

higher rates, to be sure, are mostly, if not entirely, found in
the northern and largest cities; whereas the TVA operates in
southern territory and mainly in locations of rather light population density. Undoubtedly rates much lower than the TVA's
are paid in the South for similar labor, particularly in smaller
towns and to non-union workers. As mentioned above, the
TVA Act stipulates that "due regard" shall be given to local
trade union wage rates, and that the Secretary of Labor at
Washington is the final arbiter (if necessary) as to what are
"prevailing rates" for the TVA.

Personnel Classification Board Survey.—A much more
comprehensive comparison of the Federal government's rates
of payment with wages and salaries of similar occupations in
private industry was made by the Personnel Classification
Board in 1928.[9] These rates were all expressed in annual terms,
assuming full year-round employment of private, as well as
government, workers. This report, to be sure, is somewhat
discredited by its rather superficial treatment of "relation of
[private] wage rates to geographic area and density of population" (Chapter 6)—which topic is discussed only with
reference to stenographers, "since they comprise the largest
and most homogeneous group sampled [30,000]."[10]

Nevertheless, the survey of 1928 constituted a great step
forward, in that it was a serious attempt to apply the best
techniques of job analysis to both government and private employments, so that remunerations of fairly comparable jobs
might be compared. The report laid stress on the finding that,
whereas the less skilled grades of government employees (particularly office workers) were paid substantially more than
similar occupations in private services, the higher grades of
skilled and professional occupations were paid distinctly less
by the Federal government than by private employers (Chap-

---

[9] 70th Congress, 2d Session, House Doc. No. 602, *Report of Wage and
Personnel Survey* (Washington: 1929). The PCB is, or was, a coordinating
committee composed of representatives of the Civil Service Commission
and the Bureaus of Efficiency and the Budget.

[10] For stenographers in private employment the differences in pay among
regions and various sizes of city were found to be slight.

ter 4).[11] In general the comparison given for various grades of "custodial, mechanical, and institutional" service (which would include the more common manual occupations) purported to show lower annual pay to government, than to privately employed, workers. Grade CU-4, for instance, which includes the carpenter's helper, was said to receive, on the average, $1,422.59 per annum in the government's service and $1,537.43 in private; while grade CU-6, including "carpenter," was found to receive $1,785.47 in government service and $1,822 in private. In both these instances, therefore, the difference appeared to be in favor of private employment.

2. How Do Annual and Real Wages Compare?—It would be a very ambitious task to adjust such wage and salary comparisons, in order to bring out more clearly the comparative net advantages of public and private employments. We might, for example, follow the lead of the Personnel Classification Board in attempting to take account of all manner of perquisites in kind, and even try to ascertain degrees of pressure, discipline, fatigue, and pleasantness and unpleasantness of working conditions; but, like these investigators, we might well be so baffled as to make no attempt to sum up the net results of such inquiries. Some researches, too, have indicated that many public employments enjoy less prestige in American communities than similar private jobs—although the opposite might easily be supposed, particularly by foreigners.[12]

Several other comparisons, however, are more readily feasible and are of much greater importance. Two of these are the factors of time away from work without loss of pay, and continuity of employment—each contributing to security or assurance of income. How many carpenter's helpers, for example, in 1928 were really earning *more,* in a year's private employment, and how many in Federal service were earning *less,* than the $1,423 which was the average government salary

---

[11] Since 1929 the latter proposition has become much more doubtful—all net advantages considered.

[12] See, e.g., L. D. White, *The Prestige Value of Public Employment in Chicago* (Univ. of Chicago Press, 1929) ; and *Fortune* Magazine's Survey of Public Opinion, February, 1940.

in this grade? In this connection it is significant that rates of pay in public employment are not usually quoted on an hourly basis, more commonly in monthly or annual terms. The quoted unit of time by itself is not (of course) conclusive as to assurance of income, since (in private employment, at least) many hourly-paid workers have a high degree of steadiness of work, while others, engaged on the weekly or the monthly basis, may be laid off or discharged on short notice, for lack of work.[13]

But by and large, public employment is very much more stable than private; and such seasonality as the former displays is apt to be cushioned for the worker by relatively long vacations with pay. In the past, moreover, public employers have tended to be somewhat more generous than private with respect to sick leaves—at least for manual workers. Within limits, regular Federal employees are allowed, when they do not use all the vacation (4 weeks) and sick leave to which they are entitled in a given year, to carry forward credits, to be used later, and to receive forward pay on this basis if and when they leave the employer's service.

Of course many state, municipal, and other non-Federal public agencies offer less attractive conditions than these which we have just discussed;[14] but there is little doubt that public wage earners in general receive distinctly higher annual real wages than do the most nearly corresponding private employees. The former's *hourly* earnings appear usually to average about as high as, if not higher than, private workers in the same occupations and localities—and the public employees usu-

---

[13] When public authorities directly carry out building or construction or renovation programs, they may employ both skilled and common labor on the temporary and hourly basis; in fact most public, as well as private, employers, must have occasional requirements of very temporary service—though much progress can still be made in enterprises of both sorts toward employment stabilization. But to a considerable extent large employers, both public and private, contract-out new construction and other jobs—which practice tends to regularize their own direct employment but not the total work done on their account.

[14] Apparently New York City's weekly salary of $35 for "Sanitation Man Class A (laborer)" (for example) is generous (for year-round work), since early in 1940 some 85,000 men presented themselves for the Civil Service examination for the job, of whom not more than 10,000 could be hired over the next several years.

ally have a marked advantage with reference to continuity of
employment and sick leaves and vacations with pay.

In a fuller account, various complications would have to
be considered—such as the higher ratio of white-collar workers to all employees in the older governmental services (which
was doubtless a factor tending to establish monthly and annual
rates of pay), and perquisites like long vacations and early retirement on pension. As is well known, moreover, some government jobs, particularly those which have been recently
created and those of policy-determining officials, are insecure—
by reason particularly of turnovers with changing political administrations. And the job advantages cited above tend to make
for lower voluntary turnover in the public services—which
within limits makes for a relatively high average of capacity
in the public workers.[15] Investigatio.1 of these considerations,
however, I believe would not very substantially modify the
conclusion suggested in preceding paragraphs, to the effect that
public wage earners tend to receive higher real annual earnings
than private.

3. Pressures and Fallacies Encouraging Extravagant Public Wages.

—These high rates of annual real wages in
public service are due primarily, no doubt, to the power which
political patronage gives; it is unnecessary to dilate on this
well-known civic problem, which is by no means confined to
democracies. The mere purpose of patronage, however, would
appear to be better served by the expenditure of a "given"
amount of public funds to hire a larger number of employees
at genuinely competitive rates than to hire as many as possible
at unnecessarily high rates of pay. We need to look further,
therefore, to see what forces are at work tending to make
public authorities pay high wage rates.

It seems there are such forces, operating mainly through the
political influence of labor organizations. Some members of
these organizations, of course, like a great many other citizens,
are ambitious for public employment, and naturally on the

---

[15] Too great job security, of course, as well as favoritism in appoint-
ments, often leads to inefficient service by the jobholder.

best terms obtainable. But much more important than this factor is the tendency of labor leaders to secure from each employer the best wages and other conditions they can, hoping to bring other employers up to these marks as far and fast as possible. In the case of governmental employers (against whom the strike weapon may not be freely used), these leaders naturally invoke the power of their members' votes. And an outstanding factor making high public wages politically possible in our democracy is the popular theory that the terms of governmental employment *tend to be imitated* by private employers —and thus that the conditions of public employment ought always to be somewhat in advance of those prevailing in the labor market as a whole.

In a sense governmental agencies have historically led the advance in real wages, by such measures as shorter hours, annual salaries, and longer leaves with pay; and their examples have given encouragement to private employees to *demand* similar payments and privileges. But it is not at all clear that this force of example has (of itself) tended to *enable* other employers to grant better and better terms of employment— indeed, the opposite result is more probable. There is little opportunity or incentive for governmental authorities to demonstrate the "economy of high wages"—i.e., that their higher pay makes their workers more productive. On the other hand, the margin by which these governmental agencies pay more than really competitive rates clearly constitutes an unnecessary burden on taxpaying industries, which impairs the latter's ability to raise their own wages. This problem is of increasing importance, as the ratios of public to all employees, and of public to all payrolls, rise. Fortunately, an important branch of the profession of scientific management is now devoted to public personnel administration, thus to improving "civil service" rules and procedures. Even though the total sphere of public employment continues to grow in relation to private, there is reason to hope for some competition of public agencies among themselves and with private enterprises, with reference to labor and financial efficiency. This relative growth of public payrolls, too, will enforce more care in setting rates of pay commensurate with the general social productivity of the time, and with current actual and prospective unemployment.

D. "Wage" Scales for Public Relief Work

Beginning with the CWA in 1934, the United States for some years has wrestled with the great problems incident to the rapid development of new types of work, or semblance of work, for relief of the unemployed; and prominent among these problems are those of wage or stipend scales. The issues vary according to mixtures of such services and motives as training for youth and desire to promote "public investments," in the CCC, NYA, FSA, and still other alphabetical combinations. Let us concentrate attention on certain wage problems of the Works Progress (later, Projects) Administration (WPA), whose million and more workers on a Federal payroll of $1 billion to $2 billion a year bring the issues involved in remuneration of work relief into sharp focus. It will be useful also to seek sidelights from the concurrent national Public Works (PWA) program, which amounts to Federal subsidies to innumerable government agencies (central, regional, and local) for public constructions of the more durable types (e.g., pavements, bridges, dams, post offices), wrought usually by private contractors buying materials and labor in the open market. Obviously, WPA and PWA are two major attacks of the New Deal on the social menace presented by 10 million or so of "unemployed."

Prevailing-Wage Controversy in WPA.—WPA has had the commendable purpose (among others) of conserving and improving the morale and skills of its workers; and by comparison with some public-employment programs in other nations, WPA was a conservative venture: it was *labeled* work relief—no pretence was made that the work done was more than a useful by-product. The great difficulties incident to finding more useful and morale-conserving employment than "leaf raking" and "shovel leaning" appear to have been handled with fair success, so that reasonable objections to WPA on these scores seem to be markedly diminishing. The crucial problem is not to find employment which is generally conceded to be socially useful in *some* degree; it is to direct our *total productive resources into channels which give the practical optimum of productivity and freedom.*

An outstanding practical issue in any scheme of public relief work is that of "wage" rates, particularly for the more skilled relief workers. Such artisans, notably building tradesmen, constitute a very small minority among the multitude of WPA workers; but controversy has centered upon these, in large part because those trade unions which are especially concerned with their skills have exerted much political pressure to make WPA hourly rates sustain the wage scales of these unions.[16] Thus we had applied to this emergency work relief the political doctrine of "prevailing wages," which is further examined in the next section of this chapter.

WPA MONTHLY EARNINGS SCHEDULE
Effective September 1, 1939

1930 Population of Largest Municipality in County	WAGE CLASS				
	Unskilled "B"	Unskilled "A"	Intermediate	Skilled	Professional and Technical
Wage region I:[a]					
100,000 and over........	$52.00	$57.20	$68.90	$89.70	$94.90
25,000 to 100,000........	48.10	52.00	62.40	81.90	84.50
5,000 to 25,000.........	42.90	48.10	57.20	74.00	76.70
Under 5,000............	39.00	42.90	52.00	67.60	68.90
Wage region II:[b]					
100,000 and over........	52.00	57.20	68.90	89.70	94.90
25,000 to 100,000........	48.10	52.00	62.40	81.90	84.50
5,000 to 25,000.........	46.80	50.70	61.10	79.30	81.90
Under 5,000............	44.20	49.40	59.80	76.70	78.00
Wage region III:[c]					
100,000 and over........	46.80	50.70	61.10	79.30	81.90
25,000 to 100,000........	42.90	48.10	57.20	74.10	75.40
5,000 to 25,000.........	36.40	40.30	48.10	62.40	65.00
Under 5,000............	31.20	35.10	42.90	54.60	55.90

[a] Conn., Del., D.C., Ill., Ind., Ia., Me., Md., Kan., Mass., Mich., Minn., Mo., Neb., N. H., N. J., N. Y., N. D., Ohio, Pa., R. I., S. D., Vt., W. Va., Wis.
[b] Ariz., Cal., Colo., Idaho, Mont., Nev., N. M., Ore., Utah, Wash., Wyo.
[c] Ala., Ark., Fla., Ga., Ky., La., Miss., N. C., Okla., S. C., Tenn., Tex., Va.
Source: *Mo. Lab. Rev.*, Oct. 1939, p. 960.

[16] In any discussion of American trade unionism, it is difficult to avoid fallaciously attributing to all unions the characteristics which are so readily observed in the strategically situated building-trade group.

In general there was less dispute about *maximum monthly earnings* ("security wages"), whose structure has usually been rather similar to the table shown on page 535.

Before the legislation which led to this new schedule was passed,[17] the monthly "security wages" were divided by the officially determined "prevailing" hourly wage rates for the various skills and localities, and the quotient was the maximum number of hours which the worker was allowed to work within any month. In the vicinity of Washington, D. C. (e.g.), in the spring of 1938, WPA carpenters could earn a maximum of $73.50 a month by working 42 hours at $1.75 an hour.[18] The legislation of 1939 required that all WPA employees must work at least 130 hours a month (or 30 to 32½ hours a week), which stipulation, in conjunction with the above table, indicates that the maximum *hourly* earnings of professional and technical work under WPA became not much over 70 cents in September 1939. Of course, it is conducive to efficiency in the operation of nearly any project for workers of all degrees of skill to put in approximately the same daily and monthly hours.

Because of another feature of the 1939 Congressional mandate on which it was based, the WPA Monthly Earnings Schedule reproduced above brings out some further difficulties of government wage fixers, with reference to variable living costs. I refer now to the requirement that the national schedule of monthly earnings "must not vary for workers of the same type in different geographical areas to any greater extent than may be justified by differences in the cost of living." Study of the schedule on page 535 shows that, within each (column) skill classification, the wage variations for region and population density are substantial. The combined result is that the lowest figure in each column is about 60% of the highest. These variations, to be sure, are markedly less than those existing before this September 1939 schedule took effect. The leveling of sectional differences might have gone still further

---

[17] Pub. Res. 24, June 30, 1939—summarized in *Mo. Lab. Rev.*, Aug. 1939, p. 374.

[18] And many tradesmen were able to earn their monthly "security wages" over 12 or more consecutive months, before they left the WPA roll.

(under terms of another stipulation, that the national average labor cost per person should not be substantially modified), but for the increasing pressure, both from northern WPA employees against reduction in their rates, and from southern employers against heightening of the contrast in that section between public-political and private wage scales. The U. S. Bureau of Labor Statistics and WPA researches on costs of living have tended to show rather small differences between North and South, and between cities and villages; but apparently WPA administrators studied the matter afresh, with results shown in the table.[19]

These results produce the following anomaly (among others): The Federal Wage-Hour Administration and its industry committees, up to late in 1940, had established no regional or population differentials in legal minimum-wage rates—claiming that statistical data on living costs indicate that inter-sectional and population-density living-cost differences are not sufficient to call for lower legal minima in the South than in the North, or in small towns as compared with big cities. WPA, on the other hand, has confirmed, in part, the more general opinion that such living-cost differences are material and "justify" lower money wages in smaller and southern locations.

What "Wage" Scales Are Suitable for Work Relief?— In the midst of a profound depression in which millions of unemployed must be maintained, in great part at public expense, most of the new types of public employment will include some element of work relief. The 45% PWA grants in aid of public construction were given chiefly on the theory that the direct and induced ("multiplier") employment arising from them would tend to reduce public expenditures for direct relief of the unemployed.[20] For PWA projects, labor is hired in the open market, with no reference to the need of the individual worker. (But such grants are naturally made most freely to

---

[19] Compare Ch. 6-A, above, and pp. 553, 575, 576, below.
[20] This reasoning is sound, provided that the public funds to support such a program are drawn from idle reserves rather than taken away from already active uses; for in the latter case the contraction due to withdrawal of active funds would offset the gain produced by public spending.

communities where there is much unemployment.) However financed, public employment of this sort has no sound reason to pay other than wages really prevailing for the type of work hired—which will be, in general, the highest quality of labor unemployed. The products may be, in the long run, worth to taxpayers what they cost if not more—especially when alternative methods of dealing with unemployment (or being overwhelmed by it) are considered.

In WPA or outright work relief, it is generally recognized that such expenditure is much more largely an abnormal drain upon the taxpayers; and, however admirable may be many of its products, they are as a whole nevertheless in the nature of salvage and not in themselves economically self-sustaining. The corollary is also well recognized: that the conditions surrounding such work relief must not be allowed to set up vested interests, either in the sale of supplies or in making jobs. Thus, in fact, WPA workers are virtually always drawn only from needy people eligible for public assistance of some sort; and in theory they have earned low enough monthly wages so that they had adequate incentive constantly to seek normal employment.

The dilemma from which we can scarcely hope altogether to escape is this: On one hand, we cannot (if we would) find resources to assure all the "unemployed" public jobs at full wages of their occupations. On the other hand, we must keep the number of people requiring mere direct relief or dole as low as possible. Considerable progress can doubtless be made along the line of public works planning, from the depression-combating standpoint. For these jobs workers should be subject to normal tests of competence and industry, and paid according to their real competence. Also, during depression, it should be possible to expand adult-educational activities, to assist large numbers of the more promising then-unemployable people by measures, which, like WPA, use most of the money for labor stipends and confer the great boon of useful activity on the stipendiaries. But, unlike WPA, this latter program might well be framed explicitly as a vocational training and upgrading scheme, paying (in effect, as do many factory schools) normal *piece* rates for such real work as the trainees can do.[21]

E. Prevailing Wage Requirements in Public Contracts

Nature and Varieties.—The last type of indirect governmental pressures on private wages to be briefly surveyed in this chapter is supplied by "prevailing wage" or (in Britain) "fair wages" clauses in laws relating to public contracts. Such contracts are of two general sorts: (1) for construction of government buildings, roads, and the like; and (2) contracts for the purchase of commodities or supplies. The same principle is sometimes also applied with reference to ("conditional") grants-in-aid from central to local governments, whereby it is stipulated that the local agency must meet labor standards prescribed by the center. The latter case appears to be covered by the "model fair wages clause" of the Scottish Trades Union Congress, which in turn is an outgrowth of a resolution passed by the British House of Commons in 1909.[22]

In the United States, a long line of state and local enactments led up to the Davis-Bacon Act of March 3, 1931,[23] applying to public works construction; which was followed by the Walsh-Healey Act (June 30, 1936), applying to supplies or commodities purchased by agencies of the Federal government.[24] The prevailing-wage policy prescribed by law for the

---

[21] It is very important that lower "piece rates" should not be secured by public agencies, for public functions (clerical or what-not) which are, at the time, in their normal province, by substituting relief labor for regular staff. Each type of output should be remunerated at a reasonably uniform rate; and in depression government output should be expanded to the limit, in part by salary cuts if necessary. Yet much of this expansion of public-agency output should be done by staff which is temporary (in effect, composed of relief workers), and which is allowed to develop no vested interest or "security" comparable to that of the normal staff.

[22] In December 1934 this Scottish Congress published for its members a *Report on the Observance in Scotland of the Fair Wages Clause,* listing the municipalities making various types of labor requirements in connection with public contracts.

[23] Amended, lowering the minimum sum affected by the Act to $2,000, Aug. 30, 1935.

[24] A *Compilation of Laws Relating to the Payment of Wages on Public Works* was mimeographed by the USBLS as of Jan. 1, 1936, giving excerpts from laws of the various states. Particulars relating to administration of the Davis-Bacon and Walsh-Healey Acts are given from time to time in

TVA was noticed above; and still another galaxy of similar requirements appears in public activities relating to housing.[25]

Davis-Bacon Requirements and Administration.—The Davis-Bacon Act will serve as a leading example of the type of State action which we are now considering; very similar observations would apply to the prevailing-wage clauses in other legislation. What does it require? And how is it enforced? It requires of private contractors on public works, not only prevailing-wage rates but also other labor standards which were unusually high when this Act was passed. These standards included the eight-hour day, 40-hour week, time-and-one-half for overtime in excess of these daily and weekly limits, no employment of boys under 16 nor girls under 18, and no convict labor. All these are recognizable as directions in which trade unions have been pressing for many years.

The Secretary of Labor in the national cabinet is required to "predetermine" prevailing rates of wages for purposes of these requirements. His or her representatives may hold public hearings at which testimony and other evidences can be presented as to what is the prevailing wage of each occupation or craft affected in the area; and, on the basis of the information thus assembled, the Secretary announces the minimum-wage rates applying to all work done on the contracts concerned.

The evidence on which the Secretary relies for determining prevailing-wage rates, however, is by no means confined to testimony and documents improvised for such hearings. A very important basis is whatever official statistical data bear upon the occupations and locality in question. Thus, the Women's Bureau of the Department of Labor has made a number of special surveys of earnings and hours, with refer-

---

publications of the Bureau, e.g., in *Lab. Information Bull.*, May 1937, and *Mo. Lab. Rev.*, Oct. 1940.

[25] For example, in the U. S. Housing Act of 1937 (42 U. S. Code 1416), concerning subsidies and/or other government expenditures for residential construction, prevailing wages are required for architects and other white-collar workers. And the National Housing Act of 1938 makes the mortgage-insurance service of the FHA available in construction of apartment houses, only if prevailing wages are paid. Again it will be observed how prominent is the part played by building-trade unions in developing this political prevailing wage doctrine.

ence to the prevailing-wage requirements of the Walsh-Healey Act.[26]

Thus far the areas for which such wage determinations have been made are rather broad, in many cases including whole states and even larger sections; and apparently the determinations are made only on application by some interested party. But of course their influence is felt wherever the minimum amounts specified by these laws are expended by the government, since contractors and trade unions have precedents which afford some basis for estimating what wage rates would be officially determined for the localities concerned, if official proceedings were instituted.

Significance of Such Wage Determinations.—These are accomplished facts. What problems and potentialities may be discerned in the trend they establish? Naturally we can all find both favorable and unfavorable aspects.

Not too many complaints have been heard from employers with specific reference to the Acts cited and their administration, though these requirements do contribute no little force to the movement toward more complex and expensive "red tape" in labor management, and toward greater inertia and rigidity of wage rates. The principal difficulty thus far appears to concern the demarcation of the area to which the officially determined rates shall apply; a matter which has given rise to some litigation, for example, with reference to the iron and steel industry.[27]

---

[26] Examples: Women's Bureau Bulletins, No. 163, parts 1-4 (1938), reporting results of hours and earnings surveys in various men's wear industries, including shoes.

[27] Early in 1939 the Secretary of Labor undertook to determine prevailing minimum wages, under the Walsh-Healey Act, for governmental purchases of iron and steel. The decision established six geographical divisions, for one of which (the whole of Pennsylvania) the minimum wage was found to be 62½¢ per hour. Another was a southern area (including Birmingham, Alabama) where the prevailing minimum rate was found to be 45¢. This wage determination was suspended by Court actions resulting from protests of steel producers located in Eastern Pennsylvania, who claimed that their prevailing wages are lower than 62½¢; but the U. S. Supreme Court decided that would-be suppliers have no legal basis for attacking any wage determination the Secretary of Labor may make for public contracts. (F. Perkins *et al.* vs. Lukens Steel Co. *et al.,* decision April 29, 1940.)

One feature of the Walsh-Healey Act, however, which has encountered objections from business is significant for our study of wage problems: its disregard of the seasonal factor in hours and pay. As was mentioned in Chs. 11 and 17, above, under certain conditions our Federal Wage-Hour Act permits the working of hours longer than eight in a day and 40 a week, without the penalty rate of time-and-a-half; but the Walsh-Healey Act makes no such exceptions. One practical effect appears to be that Federal agencies cannot economically buy canned foods direct from the highly seasonal canning industry. It seems that the Walsh-Healey type of legislation should be made to correspond with the Wage-Hour law, as to overtime rates in relation to seasonal industries; and that both the Walsh-Healey and the Wage-Hour Acts should be amended to give employers more incentive toward annual-wage and other labor-income-stabilization plans.

The labor interests appear to have had little cause to complain about the determinations thus far made. The trade unions do find some details of the existing laws and of their administration unsatisfactory; but more publicity is given to their desire that the scope of these regulations should be extended. The principal extensions heretofore proposed are: amend the Walsh-Healey Act, (1) to lower the minimum value of contract to which it shall apply; and (2) to make ineligible for public contracts employers who are found by government agencies to be violating labor laws, particularly the Wagner and Wage-Hour Acts.[28] This latter demand suggests, to old-fashioned conservatives and liberals, impairment of constitutional rights of appeal to the courts from decisions of government administrative agencies. In any case it is clear that great public expenditures supply a very powerful lever with reference to labor standards. As the Federal machinery mentioned becomes broader and stronger, it will undoubtedly afford assistance and

---

[28] Conferences were also held between representatives of the National Labor Relations Board, Wage-Hour Administration, and Reconstruction Finance Corporation, looking toward withholding benefits of RFC from concerns charged with violating Federal labor regulations, according to testimony before the Smith Congressional Committee investigating the Wagner Act, 1939-40.

pressure to the states, municipalities, and other public authorities, tending toward universal prescription of high labor standards in connection with their expenditures.

Anti-social Possibilities.—Attempts to see the more dubious as well as the socially beneficial incidents in this trend are useful alike to radicals, liberals, and conservatives, since excesses in any direction are apt to lead to violent opposite reactions. It seems that this prevailing-wage philosophy, as applied in the United States to public construction and contracts, has not yet developed excessively bureaucratic control of private wages and other labor conditions. The movement, however, has potentialities of vast administrative police work and protracted litigation—even beyond that involved in our other labor legislation. Such regulation will doubtless grow under the existing statutes, as claims of violation are made; and the scope of such enforcement will be extended as the minimum sizes of contracts, mortgages, and whatever else can have wage strings attached, are lowered.

Another large social difficulty in this trend—and in public control of private wages generally—is the difficulty of representing adequately the general public and consumer interests in the processes of official wage determination. The parties most directly interested are sure to turn up at the hearings and submit voluminous evidence: in the procedures with reference to public construction and contracts these parties are firms wanting to submit bids, and trade union officials concerned. Other employers, taxpayers, and consumers are much less likely to avail themselves of the opportunity to be heard, since their material interest in each proceeding is very small in relation to the total range of their problems.

And the contractors submitting bids have less than the usual employer's motivation for keeping down labor costs, for all who receive public contracts will be equally affected by whatever wage rates are officially determined to be "prevailing," and it appears to many that the public purse is always adequate to pay generous wage bills. Most employers, on the other hand, must strongly defend their labor costs with reference to sales they want to make to private purchasers, in competition with other employers. These wage and allied labor regulations may, therefore, lead to a peculiar sort of "division of labor"—between high wage employers, subsisting chiefly on public contracts, and lower-wage firms supplying private buyers.[29]

Fortunately the representatives of the Secretary of Labor are able to interpret the testimony and hearings on prevailing wages in the light of labor statistics gathered by much more comprehensive, objective, and impartial methods; and thus far it would appear that most of the wage determinations have been but slightly, if at all, on the generous side. They do, no doubt, tend to give new protection to those firms whose geographical and other circumstances make their wages medium to high in relation to their whole industry.

F. Summary

In this chapter some principal ways in which public authorities *indirectly* affect private wage rates have been explored. Our illustrations were nearly all taken from United States national affairs within recent years. A fuller account would trace many similar phenomena, and a few back-pressures, in our state and local governments; while in a general way the record would be similar for most other industrial non-totalitarian nations.

After a few remarks on relevant political alignments, our story's first main stage was the support which "social legislation" gives to a national wage structure. In many ways this legislation affects labor supplies, e.g., by controls of migration and of ages of "entrance and exit" to gainful employment. These illustrations suggest mere quantity effects; but public education and training, as well as shorter-hours movements, also tend to improve the quality and intensity of work; hence the net over-all results on real-wage rates and annual earnings of the social services now common are not very clear. But there

---

[29] The great contrast noted in Ch. 11-B, above, between union longshore wages in southern ports in the 1920's—sustained by the U. S. Shipping Board—and non-union rates illustrates this point.

is little doubt that legal protection of trade unions (as by our Wagner Act) and rising standards of compensation and relief for the unemployed assist both organized and unorganized workers to raise and maintain wage scales.

In the last three sections we surveyed effects of as many types of publicly determined wage scales: for employees of government agencies, for public relief works, and for controlling labor standards of firms supplying commodities or services to government bodies. None of these types of public wage determination attempts actual positive and detailed regulation of the mass of private wages; but each directly affects millions of workers and gives opportunity for the political arms of the labor movement greatly to influence all wage scales.

The suggestion was made that public employments, at full prevailing wages according to the worker's competence, be further expanded in depression, contracted in prosperity; and that relief works be further transformed into by-products— paid for, in effect, at prevailing *piece* rates—of public training and upgrading programs.

CHAPTER 20

ECONOMIC EFFECTS OF STATE WAGE CONTROLS

Collective determinations of private wages, we have seen, are increasingly controlled by public authorities, in other as well as totalitarian lands. The social desirability, and the long-term practicability, of rising real annual wages per capita have long been manifest to most students of such matters (including a great many business men); and recently labor demands for "more, now" have been joined by other political forces (such as the increasing social menace of large strikes and lockouts) to generate increasing steam for the mills of legislation affecting wages.

In the present chapter, section A is devoted mainly to a review of arguments—qualitative and more or less deductive —as to economic effects of this trend. Section B then offers a few more "case studies," i.e., inductive or historical evidence, on problems, methods, and results of some of the plans hitherto tried.

A. Theory—Main Alleged Effects

Assumptions; Already-Treated Issues.—Several assumptions and collateral matters are not to be elaborated in this chapter. We assume without argument, for example, that various sorts of selfish pressure groups are constantly active with reference to all legislative, administrative, and even judicial actions; and that we are attempting impartially to understand and control these pressures in the general public interest. More specifically, let the goals of fullest, most continuous employment of labor, at the highest real incomes equitably distributed, be our chief criteria—and let us also try, as we proceed, to make more concrete these vague terms. And because we have seen that legal wage regulation is a world-wide response to modern industrial and social conditions, we need not consider laissez-faire as a *practical* alternative—though an idealized laissez-faire (or, if you like, of completely voluntary anarchist cooperation) serves well as a theoretical model.[1] The more or less crude and often biased authoritarian intervention which we are getting in labor relations at present undoubtedly is a lesser social evil than would be unrestricted enterprise of the various groups and individuals who now make up "capital," "labor," and "the public."

Brief mention will also suffice here for some aspects of wage regulation which, though important, are treated at some length in preceding chapters. One of these is wage control regarded as a means toward preventing or settling "strikes." This last objective, of course, is not absolutely controlling—most Americans would not want industrial peace secured by totalitarian methods. Yet Australasian experience is only part of that which shows that methods of carrying on labor controversies must be subjected to increasing public control; and as public authorities further abridge private rights to withhold work or employment, they will find it increasingly necessary to sanction terms of employment.

In several chapters above we have discussed wage-hour legislation as a "remedy" for unemployment. Various further interactions of wage-hour laws, employment, and labor incomes and costs, however, remain for analysis in the following sections. *General* increases in wage rates, for instance, like those of the NRA period, produce results very different from those of a single minimum-wage law of narrowly restricted scope. If wages are increased in only one industry or segment thereof, many buyers of its products will tend to resort to substitutes or to make their old supplies (including haircuts and dry cleanings) last longer; but if all the substitutes are likewise affected by higher wages, the first of these resorts cannot occur. It is clear, also, that any increase in total wage payments or purchasing power of wage earners will tend to stimulate most industries, probably beginning with those vending and produc-

---

[1] See Ch. 5-A, above.

ing the consumers' goods used by such workers. The repercussions on prices and employment, on the other hand, might nullify some (at least) attempts to stimulate general business activity and to improve all wage earners' welfare merely by "raising wages by law."

From these backward glances we turn to more systematic treatments of five complexes of problems in wage regulation— "exploitation," competitive labor standards, distribution and total of employment and real income, and wage flexibility.

1. Wage Boards and Collective Bargaining; Prevention of Exploitation.

—It will be recalled that determinations of legal minimum-wage rates for women, young people, and low-skilled men are most commonly made through wage or trade boards—one for each industry or industry-group so regulated. These workers are apt to be organized into trade unions but weakly, if at all. It is often suggested that wage-board regulation tends to stimulate trade unionism among these weaker workers—in fact, such boards are frequently represented as one form of collective bargaining. Officials of the most nearly relevant trade unions generally sit on them to provide at least part of the workers' representation; hence to some extent these boards do give experience in collective procedure in wage determination to wage earners who were previously unorganized.[2]

Trade unions, however, in the past have been rather lukewarm to a wide extension of legal minimum-wage regulation, in part because it seemed that such State regulation might become too popular as a substitute for trade union organization. This real or apparent conflict, of course, has had most import for unions organizing women and common labor—but little for unions of skilled men. And the difficulty diminishes even

---

[2] The setting of legal minimum wages through wage boards is more closely analogous to compulsory arbitration than to voluntary collective bargaining, however, since the former two procedures both involve representation of the public and assertion of State power to enforce the wage rate or rates arrived at through the boards' deliberations. But an outstanding difference, which has made wage boards much more acceptable to British and American employers and trade unions than compulsory arbitration, is that minimum-wage laws in the American and British Commonwealths do not attempt to prevent the employees from striking to secure better wages (or the employers from locking out).

with reference to unskilled workers, as trade unions extend their occupational frontiers and their political functions.

The foregoing notes suggest the theoretical basis for minimum-wage laws which is most significant, in the opinion of many economists. These proponents of such legislation claim that many low-paid workers are "exploited" in the sense of being paid less than the full local market value of their services. So far as this is the case, they are caught in a vicious circle, for their market value tends to be depressed still further by the poor physical and cultural nourishment which their low wages provide. These ideas are succinctly stated by an eminent British authority:

> If all relevant facts about the labor market were accessible to every workman, and if every workman was free to move on the instant and without cost from any one place to any other, . . . wage rates would be fixed by general market conditions and there would be no scope for individual bargaining. But in actual life there is usually a certain range of indeterminateness within which the wage rate may be moved up or down by such bargaining. Within this range the employers' superior strategic strength enables them, as against unorganised workpeople, to push rates below the real worth to them of the workpeople's services. If and in so far as they do this, they set in motion a train of actions and reactions that has very injurious social results. The workpeople, beaten in the first round of the bargaining contest, are by that very fact weakened for the second round. For, in consequence of lowered earnings, their efficiency as workpeople is diminished, so that, even if they obtained now the full worth of their work, that worth would be less than it used to be. This process is cumulative and threatens a progressive degradation of the standard and quality of the people subjected to it. When, therefore, they are not able, by organization, to protect themselves, there is a strong *prima facie* case for State intervention in their defence. Hence Trade Boards.[3]

It is very difficult to determine the practical limits within which this particular philosophy is valid; but we can at least observe that it obviously applies mainly if not solely to occupations in which wages are low *and* in which union organization

---

[3] A. C. Pigou, *Economics in Practice,* pp. 122-123 (London, 1935).

is weak or nonexistent.[4] This theory of exploitation, or "wages below the real worth of the workpeople," too, plainly suggests as guides for such wage setting: (a) current prevailing wages of workers better able to take care of themselves (allowance made for differences in important wage factors, such as skill, responsibility, hazards, continuity of employment), and (b) care that the legal wage be not set so high as to increase unemployment.

2. Legal Labor Standards and Employers' Competition.— A broader theoretical case has been developing over many years, in favor of legal control of wages as but one point in a wider program of "fair labor standards."[5] According to this view, business competition will take many markedly anti-social forms, in the absence of adequate legal restraints. Laws protecting property against theft and fraud, other laws enforcing contracts, are instances of authoritative prevention of certain modes of "competition" for private gain. These old legal standards are hallowed by usage; and now innumerable controversies rage over "trade practices" (e.g., misleading advertising, commercial bribery, and various forms of real or apparent price cutting) which groups of businessmen seek to have legally denied as methods of competition.

In analogous fashion, alliances spring up between employers who are actively interested in maintaining high labor standards[6] in their own concerns, and other labor-legislation leaders. These allies tend to argue that the more ethical employers have done the pioneering required to show that (for instance) a 40-hour week and a minimum wage of 40 cents an hour (only $16 a week) are feasible as national standards; and that there are many "chiseling" employers (even whole industries) who should be forced to conform to the labor standards sought. If the latter people are not thus coerced by law, they will "steal" business away from the "decent-standards" employers by price

---

[4] See Ch. 17-B, above.

[5] The "Fair Labor Standards Act of 1938," as its official brief title implies, was to a large extent advocated in terms of this philosophy.

[6] High relative to *all* their competitors; not necessarily high for the area(s) in which they hire most of their labor.

cutting based upon low wages, long hours, and still other skimp-
ings of labor cost.[7]

**Do Higher Labor Standards Call for Further Tariffs and
Other Employer Protection?**—The argument thus baldly
sketched on the theme of legal protection of the fair employer
is very widely accepted; but we all grope for light on the many
difficult questions involved in its practical application. Naturally, numerous employers seek to repeal or evade such laws,
whose adequate enforcement calls for some new taxation and
bureaucracy; but if the latter are kept within reasonable limits
the gains may far outweigh such costs.

Another political reaction speaks in behalf, or ostensibly in
behalf, of the *smaller* employers (among those covered). It was
remarked above[8] that income-tax statistics show that the larger
corporations tend to be more profitable than the smaller. If
higher wage-hour standards go into effect in a year of average
or declining prosperity (instead of upswings like 1933 and
1939), their initial costs may accelerate the disappearance of
smallish firms.

More clearly visible is the tendency of rising labor standards
to add to other pressures for higher protective tariffs. It has
long been a commonplace among economists that the amount of
tariff protection has no necessary relation to the level of the
nation's real wages;[9] real wages, for instance, were higher in
Britain than in most other nations while Great Britain's protective duties were negligible. Nevertheless, if we claim to raise
many American wage rates by law, we invite all employers who
face competition from imported goods to demand a compensating advance (at least) in customs duties. And in practice organized labor often gives political support to these demands.

---

[7] Naturally there are also further grounds for particular labor and
social standards, e.g., health and safety, workmen's compensation for injuries and occupational diseases, and withdrawing children from the labor
market by means of compulsory-school-attendance laws. Many items of
"social legislation," such as that providing *non-contributory* old-age assistance, however, have no direct reference to employment relations.

[8] See reference to W. L. Crum's researches, Ch. 9-C, above.

[9] See, e.g., J. Schoenhof, *The Economy of High Wages* (New York:
Putnam, 1892).

The result is higher prices to consumers, except so far as higher domestic wages are offset by lower profits or increased labor efficiency.[10]

Abroad, essentially this problem has been often discussed in terms of contrasts between "sheltered and unsheltered industries."[11] The former are "sheltered" by tariff protection or by some physical or technical barrier against foreign competition, or perhaps by a rapidly expanding demand. In such industries high wages can be passed on to all consumers, within practical limits of demand elasticity and possible dangers of competition from substitute services and/or from unemployed workers. The "unsheltered industries," contrariwise—notably those with big stakes in international exporting markets—find it more difficult to pass costs on to consumers; and their wage scales (for example, in British coal mining since 1920) often contrast painfully with wages of "sheltered" workers in the same nations.

What Wages Do Proper Labor Standards Require?—More immediately pressing problems are those of interpretation of "fair labor standards." Should the legal standards be in money- or real-wage terms? Is it reasonable to regulate by law only *minimum* wages? Or should rates be set authoritatively for all workers? How, in any case, is a fair standard wage to be determined? A short discussion of these topics will make clearer the significance and limits of the legal labor-standards theory.

The modern democratic peacetime idea of legal wage standards, of course, is a legal *minimum* wage for each occupation and plant covered. But other conceptions have also prevailed, and do prevail. Is not the exceptionally high wage-paying employer considered "unfair" by not a few other employers— somewhat as is the extra-strenuous-working laborer by *his* fellows? (In piece-working occupations, to be sure, the legal minimum hourly-earned rate necessarily must be suitable to

---

[10] In Australia, as mentioned in Ch. 18-B, above, the Commonwealth Arbitration Court has been among those calling for increasing tariff duties in the interest of higher wage rates.

[11] Cf. Ch. 12-C, above, and section B, below, in this chapter.

the lower range of abilities of non-handicapped employable workers, leaving the more competent people opportunity to make higher piece earnings per hour.)

Use of Living-Cost Indexes.—Our second question asks, in effect, what rôle (if any) should living-cost calculations play in legal wage fixing? Which query may well be stretched to include consideration of continuity of employment, or annual earnings. Here we encounter several clashes between abstract theory or equity and administrative realities. The earlier programs for legal assurance of a "living wage" aimed at the apparently limited objective of a statistically determined adequate real-wage rate, expressed as a "health and decency" (and so forth) commodities-and-services budget. If such a real wage were officially sanctioned, could we not collect appropriate local prices, add them up, and thus fix the local current "living wage" in money terms? But, as we have seen, this program has received decreasing support over the past couple of decades. A chief reason is that there is too low a probability that the budget prescribed by the "experts" of the day will be suitably within the ability of the industry to pay. This latter criterion (reflected, in part, by present and prospective unemployment) is usually dominant in any legal wage fixing. Official living-cost indexes, however, are increasingly utilized for calculations as to the course of real wages; and Australia (as we have seen) has attempted by means of her living-cost indexes to keep real-wage rates constant during most years. Many NRA codes contained geographic wage differentials, corresponding to supposed differences in living costs—minimum-wage rates were usually higher in the North than in the South, and they also tended to vary directly with population density. Our present national Wage-Hour law swings the pendulum away from such crude differentials, toward the extreme of administrative simplicity— in practice, we now have a single national minimum-money-wage rate for each industry (or *product* classification) covered. Undoubtedly, it is very difficult to measure comparative money costs of *equivalent* living standards in North and South, in metropolis and small mill town; yet these difficulties alone do not appear adequate to account for the small rôle which living cost plays in our present Federal wage controls.

Opportunity for Annual Earnings.—This factor in real wages is still more baffling from the administrative standpoint, but wage-hour laws certainly should offer employers inducements toward progressive stabilizing and increasing of annual labor incomes. We must not persuade ourselves that, if we regulate minimum hourly rates, including penalty rates of overtime, other wage problems will take care of themselves. As was shown above,[12] annual-wage plans and markedly seasonal industries are already receiving special treatment in Federal wage-hour control; and no doubt a good deal more can advantageously be done along these lines.

Occupational Differentials; "Bumping Up."—A few further reflections may now be added on our question whether legal determinations of wage standards, so far as they are intended to protect fair employers, can reasonably stop with a few minimum rates effective mainly for women and unskilled men. Again the claims of administrative economy and convenience are strong; to determine and enforce such lower-minimum rates seems clearly a much less ambitious task for government than comprehensive and detailed wage regulation. But does not this limitation leave both skilled workers and their "fair" employers unprotected? May not many employers, in fact, try to recoup the new expenditures they are forced to make on higher *minimum* wages by *reducing* wage rates which were formerly higher than the new legal minimum? Not a few minimum-wage systems have expressly combated such action or expected action. The British wage boards, for example, tend to prescribe wage rates for several areas, experience categories, and occupational classifications within each covered industry; and most of the NRA codes attempted in some fashion to preserve customary wage differentials.

Direct legal sanction of occupational wage differentials is unnecessary, however, if we may accept the "bumping-up"

---

[12] See Ch. 11-D.

theory which many employers and economists advance. The latter view is that, if the lowest wages are effectively raised, by law or otherwise, they will spontaneously push up all others, because the more skilled workers will insist on maintaining the old premiums.

There is considerable evidence,[13] (1) that such "bumping-up" does not occur *immediately* when minimum-wage rates are raised by law; and (2) that in the course of a year or so *some* "bumping-up" effect becomes apparent—how much, depending on such factors as how far and how generally the lower wages were actually boosted by legal control, and degrees of upward pressure put upon skilled workers' rates by trade unions and/or government. As we have seen,[14] world wage history, since 1914, shows many instances of *percentage* differentials in favor of skill remaining cut for long periods, after wage levels rose. Whatever may be the factors making for such lags, it seems that the "bumping-up" theory is within limits true; and, if so, the following implications (among others) may be inferred: (1) State control of only "basic" or lower minimum-wage rates drives toward the two objectives of protecting the weakest labor and the fair employers; and (2) the cost-raising effect of a minimum-wage law is by no means limited to its effects on the *lowest* wages alone.

3. **Distribution of Employment, Industries, Real Incomes.** —We have spoken above of "raising wages by law," without stopping to inquire to what extent such laws may be boomerangs which result in unemployment rather than higher wages. This set of issues must now be examined more systematically. The total problem may be more precisely indicated by such queries as these: what sorts of legal wage control (if any) are apt to cause undue unemployment? What sorts tend to improve the amount and distribution of total real-wage incomes—perhaps by making labor and/or management more efficient? What is to become of the displaced workers, if any? Is there real

---

[13] See, e.g., the chart of cotton-textile earnings before, during, and after NRA, p. 570, below, and accompanying comments.

[14] See Ch. 18-B, above.

danger that State wage regulation may affect unfavorably the national geographical and occupational distributions of industries, workers, and wage earnings?

Let us begin analysis of these matters, not with a question but with a cliché: "parasitic industries."[15] This phrase suggests that the lowest-wage employments should be abolished, and prevented from recurring. When our wage law (this argument continues) fixes a merely decent living minimum wage, any industry which cannot pay such a wage is parasitic—it is being subsidized by its workers' relatives and whoever else ekes out their too-low wages; and it should either be reorganized into such a position that it can pay proper wages, or be liquidated.[16] What would happen to the customers and workers of such firms? The "parasitic industries" theory calls attention to several favorable possibilities, such as: (1) both customers and employees will continuously be shunted toward the most capable employers, and (2) workers not competent to secure employment at the legal minimum rate (if they are not mothers who should be at home, or children who should be in school, or hopelessly handicapped people) can be trained into employability at public expense. This theoretical case, even more than the "exploitation" argument examined above, is confined in its relevance to State control of the *lower wages* (of children and the less skilled women and men).

Undoubtedly, as new social standards are initiated on any of a thousand fronts—e.g., in municipal zoning or traffic control—various marginal and sub-marginal businesses are harassed, and some unemployment may be caused. It is impossible, furthermore, in practice to determine accurately *how much* unemployment, if any, is due to any particular standard (such as a minimum-wage law) alone; unemployment and business losses result from many interacting causes. Thus our Federal Wage-Hour Act seems to be on the right track, as it reiterates that minimum wages are to be raised toward 40 cents an hour

---

[15] S. Webb, "Economic Theory of a Minimum Wage," *Jour. of Pol. Econ.*, Dec. 1912, pp. 977 ff.

[16] Compare remarks in this vein by the New Zealand and Australian Arbitration Courts, quoted in Ch. 9-A, above.

as rapidly as possible "without *substantially* curtailing employment." Acceptable evidences as to how much curtailing is caused by a given wage rate, and how the adjective "substantial" should be legally defined, must be worked out gradually and experimentally. Although under favorable conditions the application of an effective legal minimum wage may not significantly curtail employment (perhaps because the workers and/or employers thereby become more efficient), in practice political wage raising is not likely to be halted until sufficient reaction is generated, perhaps by widespread conviction that it has been an important contributor to unemployment. Hence, our administrative agencies and courts will be obliged to develop authoritative tests of "substantial curtailment of employment" attributable to too-high legal wage rates; and here is one reason (among others) why wage regulations should be kept somewhat flexible in both directions.

Coordination of Public Wage and Social-Security Policies.—As was remarked in an earlier chapter, the minimum-wage movement has outgrown its earlier attempts to serve as almost a complete program of social security. Now it needs careful integration with other social-security measures, especially those relating to very low family incomes and unemployment. As other attacks on family poverty go forward, we can perhaps become less hesitant in denying youths and others whose work has low value the right to earn pittances to supplement their meager family funds; and we can make such denial with better conscience, the better are the facilities we offer at public and philanthropic expense for vocational guidance, training, and placement. The more readily unemployed people can, in practice, find means of making their services valuable and salable, the higher may the legal minimum wage be reasonably set. So long, contrariwise, as the taxpayer is overburdened with the cost of a miserable dole to each of millions of hopelessly unemployed people, the more conservative should we be in pushing legal real minimum-wage rates upward.

Connections with Shortening Hours; Mechanization.— All measures, like shortening of hours, banning the labor of

children and married women, and early retirement, which tend
to restrict the supply of man-hours of labor, tend thereby to
enhance the unit price at which it can be sold. There are several
important analogies between restriction of effective supplies of
labor and of commodities, such as farm products; and the common danger is that what is mere shrewd business for a minority
may become wholesale scarcity and lowered living standards if
practiced assiduously by all. And, superficially at least, the
pressure of higher wages toward mechanization (and other
ways of economizing labor) seems an important avenue
through which State wage raising may aggravate unemployment—after the boom of machine-building promoted by higher-
wage prospects has worn itself down.[17] But it is also shrewdly
argued that, so long as the present accelerating tempo of technical change and progressive rate of obsolescence of equipment
continue, the "machine-building boom" may go forward indefinitely.

Geographic Distribution of Industries and Workers.—
One danger, then (to repeat), against which wage controls need
to be safeguarded is causing undue *new* unemployment. Another danger which is less obvious and less generally realized is
that wages should be raised by restrictive means which condemn
outsiders, if not to unemployment, then to employment in need-
lessly overcrowded occupations or territories. Most Americans
now agree to the national policy which attempts in part to protect American wages by restrictions on immigration; but *within*
our national boundaries it is not Utopian to allow and assist
labor to flow toward jobs, and jobs to gravitate toward labor
supplies. In our endeavors to assist the workers in already
industrialized regions, partly by protecting their high wage,
short-hour employers from "unfair competition in labor standards" in backward regions, we may unreasonably handicap the
efforts of agricultural areas to industrialize themselves. From
this standpoint (as well as others) there is an important objection to making the minimum money-wage rate which is high
enough to help the worker in large northern cities legally bind-

---

[17] See Ch. 13-B-3, above.

ing on the same industry in a southern or other village. Such a requirement may not cause unemployment in the village; but it may prevent the industry from locating in or near the village at all, so that people who could be employed at wages low according to northern standards have to continue working for still lower returns in their old-time rural jobs.[18] The recent catastrophic decline in our exports of farm produce such as wheat and cotton merely accentuates the need of hastening development of industries other than production of agricultural staples —for output of these per farmer steadily rises, and consumption per capita does not.[19]

In a similar way too-broad areas of inflexible labor standards (public or private) may stand in the way of rehabilitation of "stranded areas."

If we are to discuss a particular labor supply in a particular depressed area in relation, let us say, to its power to attract to itself the making of boots and shoes, what assumptions should we make as to the wage level that it will accept? That the labor will not work for less than a nationally agreed standard for all workers making boots and shoes? That it will not work for less than it might earn locally by making whatever else it can most profitably make?[20]

Continuing with this supposition, we may infer that both employers and workers in the existing shoe centers would strenu-

---

[18] In 1935-36, 50% of all our farm families had incomes below $1,000 a year (inclusive of farm value of produce consumed on farms), while the median for all wage-earning families was $1,259 (relief families excluded from both these classes).—Nat'l Resources Comm., *Consumer Incomes in the U.S.*, p. 26 (1938).

The farm-price dollar has high purchasing power, of course, for produce consumed on the farm where it is grown; on the other hand, farm families are bigger than city, so that income per capita is more unequally shared than the foregoing figures indicate. Thus, our rural population, comprising some 20% of all the nation's gainfully occupied and perhaps 25% of its total population, receives not over 12%—perhaps only 8%—of the national income. See also section B-3, below, in this chapter.

[19] It is sometimes suggested that farmers can be best helped by wage-hour laws for them, added to crop restrictions. Other nations, as we have seen, do regulate wages on farms, at least in the larger rural enterprises. But we should have to apply wage-hour limits to our millions of owning and tenant farmers to go far toward redressing the balance of outputs and real incomes per worker, between rural and industrial occupations.

[20] Austin Robinson, *Econ. Jour.*, June-Sept. 1940, vol. 50, p. 268.

ously oppose the development of a new, lower-wage shoe industry in the distressed region; and that if the latter did rise, loss of property and work would follow in the older centers. This is a hard choice for the legislator and mere citizen; yet much of the stranded population may be doomed to live indefinitely on doles if it can be hired only at high wage rates.

Thus, the total national interest demands attention to the practical earning opportunities of workers and would-be workers in all sections of the nation, and to the probability that standards high enough for the high-cost section would, if extended over all sections, serve as an intra-national, interregional barrier against free exchange of commodities and services.

4. Wage Regulation, Prices, and National Production.— When wage rates are "raised by law," what sort of a bill (if any) has the consumer to pay? Is an inflationary spiral begun or continued? The answer, of course, depends upon several circumstances, such as the percentage which the whole wage bill forms of the industry's total production costs, and the percentage by which the new wage law raises the total wage bill— making allowance for the "bumping-up" of other wages by the raised minimum rates. Combining estimates on these matters, the government's Wage-Hour economists are apt to figure that unit price to the consumer need not be appreciably affected.

But some other variables need to be reckoned with, too. An obvious one is the degree of competition among employers; for instance, the customers of an outright monopolist might not be affected at all by a moderate increase in his wage bill. Another factor is the number of industries whose wages are raised within a year or so. The more of these, the more probable and substantial is a spiral of wage and price rises—since the consumer-goods industries must try to recoup, *not merely their own wage increases,* but also the rises in material and service costs due to increased wages in other industries.

May not, however, the industry's productivity or efficiency increase enough to offset the wage rise? That is possible, especially if the increase in wages has been foreseen for many months. If we can get the social disease of unemployment (and the delusive short-hours prescription for it) under better control, the outlook is for a further gradual rise in real national productivity per capita; in which case all real wages can be *correspondingly* advanced without any inflationary spiral effect. In the lowest real-wage groups, undoubtedly, as Pigou remarked:

> If only an inefficient worker can be secured good payment for a little while, he or she may be so far improved in efficiency as to become worth the higher wage.[21]

As all real wages rise, this last point of Pigou's becomes increasingly academic; but the other factor mentioned in the present paragraph (secular upward trend of industry's real-wage capacity) appears to offer the probability that legal wage rates can be gradually but indefinitely advanced (spasms of war permitting).

5. Wage Controls and Economic Flexibility.—We have already dealt at some length with arguments which are very familiar nowadays, to the effect that wage rates have long been too "sticky" or rigid (especially against *downward* adjustments) and are becoming increasingly so.[22] Let us now suppose that *some* two-way wage flexibility is desirable (if only to permit correction of mistakes), and inquire for a moment how the trends in collective wage determination studied in this book affect the degree of such flexibility. We are now concerned with both private and public controls over wages in general, not merely over basic minimum rates. It will appear that, although the intermediate stage in which Americans now find themselves is one in which wage rates acquire increasing inertia, further centralization in collective bargaining and public wage control may well bring some return of flexibility.[23]

Some chief sorts of needed wage flexibility have been indi-

---

[21] *Economics of Welfare*, 1st ed., p. 555 (1920).

[22] Especially in Chs. 5-A, 13-B.

[23] And cuts in money-wage rates may also be decreasingly needed, if movements of the general price level become controllable. In many circumstances and ways, rising prices cut real-wage rates more equitably and promptly than do the types of wage-rate reductions that are feasible or are likely to be.

cated above; for instance, temporary plasticity for rising and declining industries, and more permanent readjustments of hourly wage rates and prices as part of a program for seasonal employment stabilization. And, apart from these types, it must be expected that either side of the wage bargain can better afford to make a concession if it has reason to believe that the ground thus lost can be later regained without too much effort and delay, when conditions change. One great merit of a sliding wage scale which is geared to some good indicator(s) of the industry's prosperity (especially if the workers help to enforce progressive policies in the pricing of products) is that total employment and total real wages tend to be maintained if not increased. This objective is also sought by clauses in collective agreements and in legal provisions, stating under what conditions wage rates may be changed. (Much more important than the words in such documents are the expectations, founded on past experience, as to how much time and strife will actually be required to correct a wage scale, in case future experience may prove it to be based on a mistaken forecast.) This last point suggests, moreover, that an important evil to be avoided in both private and public wage-fixing procedures is unnecessary delay in obtaining final action, after either party has exercised its right of asking for a wage change. Unless this need is widely realized, there is real danger that the increasing rôle of private arbitral machinery and public authorities in wage determination will of itself mean growing rigidity of money-wage rates—which may seriously pinch the workers in living standards (if prices are rising) or in unemployment (if prices and business activity are falling).

How Centralization May Bring Wage Stability or Plasticity.—The remaining group of data needed for the problem we are considering at this point is the varieties and degrees of centralized control over wage rates. The degree of centralization may be roughly measured by the percentage of all wage earners in the country whose rates are in effect fixed by a given leader or group (such as a national dictator, or the judges of the Australasian Arbitration Courts). Such centralization may, however, come about through private collective bargaining, if leaders on the labor or employer side (or both) manage approximately similar and concerted actions in many of the larger industries.

How do such factors affect the degree of wage plasticity? Most clearly in this way: Objection to wage cutting, so far as it rests upon the ground that such cutting may start or accentuate an uncontrollable downward spiral of wages, prices, and employment, may become doctrinaire or mere pleading if (1) the wage decrease is but an isolated case in a small industry, or if (2) for other reasons it is very unlikely to be part of a further downward sagging of the wage structure, which may go no one can guess how far. Thus, in wage bargaining through say a dozen or more large groups which are not centrally controlled or coordinated (this description fairly well fits modern "capitalist" nations with strong labor movements), the tendency is now to allow extreme degrees of unemployment to develop before resorting to wage cuts,[24] lest the advantage of labor-cost reduction should be outweighed by depressing spiral effects. And whole national economies, as those of Britain, France, and Germany, in not a few years since 1920, have suffered disastrous losses of foreign trade, in part because they had no means of making *definitive* reductions in labor and other costs. Here was an important source of the widening international circle of currency depreciations and other attempts to raise prices faster than wage rates.

But though wage bargaining and other collective determination thus tends to lose flexibility (or perhaps better, adaptability to the national economic outlook), as it concentrates into fewer and larger hands—if such concentration goes far enough, a measure of cost plasticity may be regained. Thus the private centralization of labor bargaining in Sweden appears to have cooperated with monetary and other government policies in maintaining wage rates, prices, and employment, and thus stable and widespread real incomes. In New Zealand and Australia, the trail of more rigidly stabilized minimum real wages

---

[24] Especially in the larger firms and industries.

was long followed, as cost of living led money wages uphill and downhill; then a drastic and general wage cut (combined with many other economic readjustments) was helpful toward business recovery—in part because these governments could give business reasonable assurance that the cuts in wages, prices, interest rates, and so on, were *definitive*—not steps downward in a nearly bottomless spiral.

B. Some Further Statistical Evidence

Thorough-going inductive testing of almost any proposition about wage controls would be a very ambitious task. It is not attempted here; in particular, no additional exhibits are offered in this section on the most comprehensive wage controls. But a few samples of the statistical evidence available on the operation of certain wage-hour regulations will make our problems clearer, and will moreover suggest some tentative conclusions. These samples relate to three "cases": the British trade boards, one of Ohio's wage orders, and recent Federal wage-hour control, with special reference to cotton manufacture.

1. British Trade Board Rates.[25]—Chart 11 shows the respective courses, since the base year (1914), of four categories of British wage rates, viz.: (a) and (b), legal minima for men and women respectively in "trade board" industries; (c) wage rates of male agricultural workers (legally fixed, 1917-21 and again from 1924); and (d) "general wage rates"—i.e., the official average of rates, mostly not legally controlled, in 32 industries. It will be observed that these curves show some important differences in the extent and timing of wage changes, 1914-22; also a high degree of stability after the latter year, by which time the State-regulated groups of wages stood markedly further above their own 1914 levels than did the "general" group. (The controlled rates also showed greatest inertia; in 1920 the "general wages" curve attained the highest peak of all groups shown here.) The full extent of the (employed) low-skilled workers' gain, moreover, is not reflected by this chart;

---

[25] See account of these boards in Ch. 18-B, above.

BRITISH MINIMUM AND GENERAL WAGE RATES

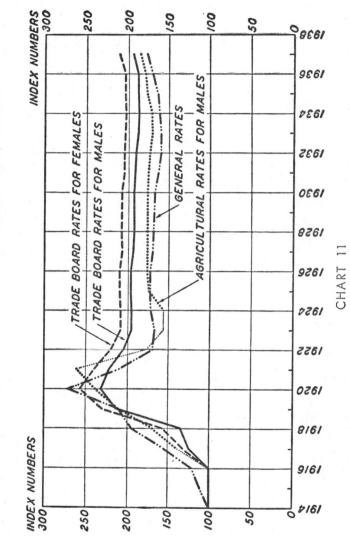

CHART 11

Source: Dorothy Sells, British Wages Boards, p. 275. Reproduced by courtesy of Brookings Institution.

for with extension of legal wage regulation during the period covered, new groups of low earned rates were being outlawed.[26]

The averages of these legal minima, however, are based in part upon the relatively high wages prevailing in local service and other "sheltered industries." In great "unsheltered" domains like coal mining and cotton manufacturing, the average earnings of all workers—skilled and unskilled—have run but little above average trade board rates applying mainly to workers of no or low skill in the regulated industries.[27]

2. Ohio and Indiana Dry Cleaning.—Our next specimen of evidence relates to an American state minimum-wage law. Chart 12 compares hourly earned rates in dry cleaning and dyeing establishments of Ohio and Indiana respectively, about one year before and two years after Ohio put into effect a mandatory minimum wage of 35 cents.[28] It shows that, in a sample period during the year before the Ohio wage order took effect (January 1935), nearly 50% of the workers in Ohio shops, and about 65% in Indiana, earned less than 35 cents; whereas two years after Ohio's wage order was issued, only 3.2% (presumably exempted as learners, etc.) were earning less than the legal minimum of 35 cents in Ohio, while 51.5% were still below 35 cents in Indiana. The Ohio data, it will be noticed, seemingly give some confirmation to the "bumping-up" theory; for in 1937 no less than 87% of the workers in this sample were earning *more* than the legal minimum. No significant

---

26 Only seven trade boards existed in 1914. Many new ones were set up in 1919-21; and the two established in 1938 made 49 in the latter year. (Sells, *op. cit.*, p. 353.)

27 *Ibid.*, p. 280. Miss Sells' Ch. 10 also gives many other significant data, and adduces statistical evidence tending to show that but little unemployment was caused by this British wage regulation. "With the establishment of each new trade board there has been a tendency toward elimination both of the least efficient workers and the least efficiently managed businesses ..." (p. 294). The system is also given high credit for the great reduction which has occurred in "sweating" of industrial homeworkers (p. 305).

28 The report cited as source of this chart gives many other particulars, including data for power laundries in New York state (with a legal minimum wage) and Pennsylvania (without). Strangely this report does not mention the NRA minimum of 27¢ to 33¢ (depending on population density) which affected both Ohio and Indiana cleaners in 1934.

Women were about 50% of all employees in Ohio cleaning and dyeing plants, 52% in Indiana.

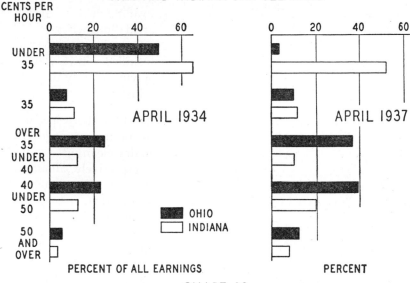

AVERAGE HOURLY EARNINGS OF WOMEN IN
OHIO AND INDIANA DRY CLEANING

CHART 12

Source: U. S. Dept. of Labor, Women's Bureau, Bull. 166, Table 3, p. 34 (identical establishments).

effect on employment was demonstrated; more workers were employed in 1937 than in 1934, which circumstance might be due to (a) the greater general prosperity of 1937, and/or (possibly) to (b) changes in price or service to consumers.[29]

Without lingering to extract further particulars from this official report or from my chart based upon it, we may infer that both the NRA and the Ohio wage order did accomplish

---

[29] ". . . in firms reporting sales that employed no members of the [proprietor's] family, the increase in sales was over 40% in both Ohio and Indiana."—*Ibid.*, p. 12.

Effects on *weekly* earnings were more complex. In 1934, both states seem to have been bound by NRA hours; about half the employees worked under 40 hours a week. Ohio's 1935 wage order prescribed time-and-a-half for work beyond 40 hours; nevertheless, in 1937 about one-third of the Ohio people were found working over 40 hours (an important cause of so many hourly-earned rates running above the legal 35¢ minimum). Average hours worked ran higher in Indiana than in Ohio in 1937; hence, weekly earnings differed less between the states than did hourly.

significant controls of wages and hours in this industry. In both cases, too, these laws were assisted by several other forces, notably: (a) an unusual rate of technical progress in the cleaning industry; (b) spontaneous general business recovery; and (c) the natural "shelter" which a service industry enjoys because its product cannot be transported in appreciable quantities over long distances in response to cost and price differentials. By 1935 these factors (also, very likely, a pronounced weakening of the NRA higher-price policy) enabled Ohio to push minimum-wage standards above the NRA mark, and to hold the high NRA hours standard (i.e., the 40-hour week). These regulations of hours undoubtedly tended to maintain or increase "employment," by wider sharing of the total work done; but how the Federal and state wage-hour controls affected *total man-hours of employment* remains obscure.[30]

3. U. S. Cotton Goods Manufactures.—For our third "case study" let us concentrate attention on this large industry's position in Federal wage-hour controls—making incidental references to the few other industries in which legal hourly wage minima set in 1939 were, for 25% or more of employees, higher than the earned rates of such employees just before this last set of wage orders.

Many significant contrasts would appear if we compared at length cotton-textile manufacturing with (for instance) dry cleaning and dyeing. The former, much the older and larger industry, employed some 472,000 wage earners in all states in its peak year 1923, and 422,000 in 1937 (but in recent years

---

[30] These data, in the report cited, bear upon the latter problem: national censuses of cleaners and dyers showed 278% increase in sales volume, 1919-29, also that employment and sales in 1935 were again at 1929 levels. As in other small concerns, there is high business mortality among cleaners-dyers. "Of the 388 Ohio firms visited [in 1937], 315 were in business in 1935 and only 298 were in business in 1934. Of the 290 visited in Indiana only 184 were operating in 1934. To what extent these 30% and 58% increases in numbers of firms over three years approximate the real increases in established firms cannot be ascertained, as there is no record of the number of firms that went out of business in any year considered. Consequently, the exact changes in employment within the industry will remain unknown." (*Ibid.*, pp. 11, 12.) A few scattering reports are given of liquidations and dismissals in marginal firms, more or less attributable to the Ohio wage order (p. 14).

usually below 400,000). Like dry cleaning, cotton manufacture employs many women—some 38% of all American cotton-textile wage earners are females, who are relatively most numerous in the northern section. Cotton mills in northern states are but little, if at all, "sheltered" from southern state competition, though our whole national industry has some effective tariff protection.[31]

The wage-hour structure of cotton manufacturing was subjected to greater stresses by the industry's Code (No. 1) of NRA than were most others. The minimum rate of 30 cents prescribed for southern *inside* workers was higher, as shown in Chart 13 (bottom), than some 90% of *all* southern workers earned in July 1933 (just before NRA took effect).[32] The 32½-cent minimum imposed by the NRA code upon the northern section was not quite so drastic a change for the North; and the new maximum work week of 40 hours may be compared with the just-pre-NRA national ,average of hours worked in cotton manufacturing, which was approximately 50 hours—but longer in the South than in the North.

Our chart gives us four later snapshots of percentage distributions of cotton mill hourly earnings. The one for August 1933 shows the immediate impact of NRA. There are very pronounced modes (statistical concentrations) at the respective sectional wage minima; furthermore, the curves' "tails" of above-minimum earnings have markedly shifted upward from their July 1933 positions. In August 1934, after one year of relative business recovery under NRA, some 96% of

---

[31] See chart, p. 330, above, and accompanying discussion; also cf. C. H. Chen, "Regional Differences in Costs and Productivity in the American Cotton Manufacturing Industry, 1880-1910," *Quar. Jour. of Econ.*, Aug. 1941.

[32] This chart is a composite of two appearing in A. F. Hinrichs, *Wages in Cotton-Goods Manufacturing,* pp. 117, 118 (USBLS Bull. 663), from which excellent report many of the data on earnings and other features of the cotton industry given in this chapter are taken. The "earnings" are earned rates per hour; piece work is much used in all the older textile industries. The earnings shown below legal minima while the NRA was in force presumably refer (in part, at least) to learners, handicapped, and outside laborers.

Reports of NRA's Research and Planning Division showed that NRA's immediate effect was to make a high percentage of workers in the shoe and leather industries, too, earn *just* the code minimum rates—another bit of evidence that "bumping-up" requires time.

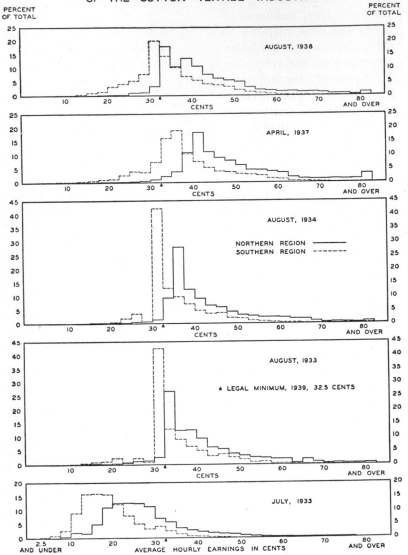

PERCENTAGE DISTRIBUTION OF AVERAGE HOURLY EARNINGS IN
THE NORTHERN AND SOUTHERN REGIONS
OF THE COTTON TEXTILE INDUSTRY

CHART 13

Source: U. S. Bureau of Labor Statistics, Bull. 663, pp. 117, 118.

northern hourly earnings are shown to be *above* the northern 32½-cent legal minimum.

By our next snapshot the NRA was already two years in the discard, and some relapse had occurred in labor standards. Nevertheless, the cotton wage-hour structure of April 1937 bears strongly the imprint of NRA, as well as of the current general business boom (employment was at a peak of 445,800). Only 2.2% of northern workers, and 20.7% of southern, were making less than 32½ cents per hour. By August 1938— just before the present national Wage-Hour law took effect— the business slump had dragged cotton manufacturing wages somewhat downward, and once more the NRA sectional minima have become the statistical modes—evidently these were made resistance points by some sort or sorts of private action.

We can now appreciate better the Wage-Hour Administration's task, synopsized by the table on p. 478, above. Reference to that table will show, for example, the official estimate that the 32½-cent minimum wage made mandatory for 668,000 cotton and other vegetable-fibre textile workers would "affect" some 27% of all such workers.[33] We see that the 32½-cent minimum is decidedly more difficult for the South than for the North; also that the whole industry approached much nearer to this goal, without benefit of legal wage control, in the boom-time of April 1937 than in the slump-time of August 1938.[34]

---

[33] All covered wage earners are affected by the "escalator" decreases of normal weekly hours and time-and-a-half for overtime; moreover in October 1938 25¢ an hour became the legal minimum wage for cotton textiles and all other industries covered by the Act (which general minimum was raised by the statute in October 1939 to 30¢). Thus the estimate cited implies that, according to reports for the year following Oct. 23, 1938, 26.9% of all these 668,000 textile workers were earning between 25¢ and 32½¢ an hour.

[34] In April 1937 the percentages of cotton mill workers' earnings below 32½¢ were: U.S. 16.3%; North, 2.2%; South, 20.7%. In Aug. 1938 the corresponding percentages (earning less than 32½¢) were: U.S., 34.7%; North, 6.1%; South, 44.2%.—Hinrichs, *op. cit.*, p. 119. (And in a slump, a larger percentage of lower-paid than of higher-paid people is usually laid off, so that average hourly-earned rates tend to rise.)

Other matters to be considered in appraising the 32½¢ legal minimum for these textile trades are (a) prospects based upon wage orders actual or expected in other industries, and (b) wage trends in all trades up to the summer of 1939 when the textile wage order was issued. For (a) the

Weekly Earnings, NRA and After.—We have viewed some landmarks of two periods of legal regulation of wages and hours in this industry. How have these spells of regulation affected *weekly* earnings? Employment and output by geographical section?

A large part of the answer to our question on weekly earnings is obvious: both NRA and FLSA reduced weekly hours as they advanced hourly earnings, hence spread work and in general raised weekly earnings proportionately much less than hourly-earned rates.[35]

Why do "average hours actually worked" (in this industry and most others) since 1933, almost always fall materially *below* 40?

One factor tending to make the actual average fall short of the nominal or normal working hours, of course, is numerous bits of part-time work due to employee absentism and starts and quits within the week. Another reason is intra-week layoffs, more or less due to slack business; in fact the "average hours worked per week" is an excellent barometer of the current prosperity of almost any industry.

But, apart from these older factors, working opportunity has been increasingly affected by legal and trade union penalty rates for overtime, which tend to overshoot their mark in spreading work. Why do they "overshoot"? Because the employer frequently is unable to provide just the normal work week for all hands; and often he will employ more people (for less than full weekly hours) rather than pay high penalty rates for overtime. Here is a too-little-appreciated reason why the im-

chief data are given in the table on p. 478, above (together with the rise in 1939 of the statutory rate for all covered employments to 30¢). (b) Reference to wage reports on most other industries will show no more than a slight rise in hourly-earned rates between Aug. 1938 and the summer of 1939.

35 The over-all national averages of the USBLS for cotton-goods manufacture show for 1934: average hours worked per week, 33.2; average hourly earnings, 37.8¢; average weekly earnings, $12.58. In 1936 (after invalidation of NRA and further industrial recovery), average hours actually worked lengthened to 37.5 and hourly earnings dropped to 36.8¢; but in 1937, 36.2 hours times 41.3¢ per hour gave average weekly earnings of $14.97—a point not later equaled until the new wage order carried average hourly and weekly earnings to 41¢ and $15.42 respectively, in Nov. 1939.

position of time-and-a-half for overtime tends both to raise labor costs and hourly earned rates, and to reduce working opportunity as measured by the general average of hours actually worked per week.

Effect of NRA on Employment and Payrolls.—Still more thorny is the path of him who undertakes to measure the effects of legal wage-hour regulations upon total real labor incomes and their distribution among employed, underemployed and unemployed—by regional, occupational, and other groupings. Let us consider briefly the *apparent* results of NRA and FLSA —in both cases using cotton manufacturing for concrete illustration, but attempting to avoid undue generalizations from problems peculiar to this industry.

The chart on p. 330, above, gives some sample materials: numbers of spindles (total and active) in New England and in the South, 1921-38, and indexes of hourly earnings and of total man-hours worked in the Conference Board's samples for "Cotton Manufacturing—North."[36] It will be noticed that the handicap of greater relative increase in wage rates in the South, imposed by the NRA code, helped to check the rate of decline of the New England section—though the southern section benefited too by the general rise in business activity and prices that may be attributed in part to the NRA. After the NRA's legal regulation of wages disappeared in 1935, indexes of northern total man-hours and active spindles dropped rapidly (except during the 1937 boom), notwithstanding that relative North-South wage-hour differentials did not resume their pre-NRA extent.[37] This persistence of narrowed wage spread (in percentage terms) between North and South seems traceable to such factors as: increased power of trade associations and trade unions to control the wage-hour structures, and the spontaneous tendency of the "migration" of the industry to pull down northern wage rates and push up southern.

---

[36] Some other figures were given above in this chapter on the total industry in all states—e.g., employment reached a peak in 1923 which had not been equaled at the end of the 1930's.

[37] See Ch. 12-D, above, for data on wages in relation to this sectional "migration" in the cotton-textile industry.

The familiar over-all indexes of factory employment and payrolls and of living costs show, too, that the NRA period was characterized by rising wage rates, rising prices, spreading of work, and also by somewhat more expansion of numbers of people employed and of total real-wage incomes than are accounted for merely by the NRA wage-hour changes and work spreading. This rise continued, too, for two years after the expiration of NRA.

Effects of FLSA.—The Fair Labor Standards Act, like NRA, came into effect in a general business slump, and at a time when national and world conditions were favorable for a recovery upswing. Total (all industries) factory employment and payrolls rose after mid-1938, and this gain in total wage payments (of some 35% to 40%) was not, by mid-1940 at least, in any appreciable measure nullified by rising living costs.

How have average hourly earnings, total man-hours worked, employment and payrolls behaved (meanwhile) in the particular large and low wage industries most sharply affected by the 1938 Federal Wage-Hour Act (FLSA)? Month by month these indexes become readily available, and I advise the reader to study the record as it stands when he is ready to look it up —especially with reference to the industries in which the legal minima which became effective October 24, 1939 or later were higher than 20% of the workers were previously earning.[38] Added to the usual difficulties of interpretation of events following 1938, of course, is the great abnormality of the war.

---

[38] See table, p. 478, above. Inquiry should also be made on collateral circumstances. The percentage of "hosiery" workers "affected" (given as 31.6), e.g., appears to be over-all for the whole industry; but actually the 32½¢ legal minimum is a much higher standard for the seamless branch (of which ⅔ of the plants are in the South) than is the 40¢ legal minimum set for the full-fashioned branch (⅔ in the North). In 1938, 48.8% of the former were earning under 32½¢ per hour; while only 19.4% of full-fashioned workers were making under 40¢.—*Mo. Lab. Rev.,* May and June 1939.

The successive monthly over-all average hourly earnings, too, should be read in the light of the corresponding monthly indexes of average hours worked per week and employment. The usual effect of even a very slight business recession is to raise the over-all average of hourly-earned rates, since the lower-paid wage earners tend to be laid off first.

Even so, the raw indexes give impressive demonstrations: first, that there was widespread and prompt compliance with these regulations,[39] and second, that rather substantial legal wage-rate advances were followed by little evidence of decreased employment and payrolls in the industries where they occurred.[40] As longer series of more finely sub-classified data are studied, we shall be better informed as to how such wage-hour laws affect different sections of particular industries.[41]

How Avoid Giving Competitive Advantage to a Section?

—What further significance can we discover in such bits of industrial history? Many important factors pertaining to cotton goods we have not discussed at all, for instance research and pricing and financing and non-wage costs in general.[42] And "each industry is different"—cotton manufacture is unusually large, old, spread over a wide area, employing many women, and so on.

Nevertheless, several points suggested by the foregoing recital can be tentatively generalized somewhat further. We can now better perceive, for example, the importance of the present Wage-Hour Law's mandate:

(c) The industry committee for any industry shall recommend such reasonable classifications within any industry as it determines to be necessary for the purpose of fixing for each classification within

---

[39] National cotton-goods average hourly earnings, e.g., rose from 38.4¢ to 41¢ from mid-Oct. to mid-Nov., 1939.

[40] The national indexes of employment and payrolls for cotton-goods continued, through Dec. 1939, the rise which had begun the preceding July; and through the first half of 1940 (at least) they held ground higher than in the first half of 1939.

[41] Apparently the northern section of cotton-goods manufacturing rebounded from the slump of 1938 at about the same rate as the whole national industry, at least through the first 9 months after the southern section was harder hit by the 32½¢ legal minimum wage imposed in Oct. 1939. The U.S. indexes of total cotton-goods payrolls (1923-25 = 100) rose from an average of 66.9 for 1938 to 78.0 for 1939 and to a high of 91.5 in Dec. 1939. The Conference Board's index of payrolls for the northern sector (1923 = 100) was 29.6 for 1938, 34.7 for 1939, and reached a high of 39.2 in Dec. 1939. (See various issues of the Board's *Economic Record*.)

[42] In Jan.-June 1936, according to a Federal Trade Commission survey, labor costs formed, on the average, 27.3% of total manufacturing costs in cotton spinning, and 29.2% in spinning and weaving.—Hinrichs, *op. cit.*, p. 34.

such industry the highest minimum-wage rate (not in excess of 40 cents an hour) which (1) will not substantially curtail employment in such classification and (2) will not give a competitive advantage to any group in the industry, and shall recommend for each classification in the industry the highest minimum-wage rate which the committee determines will not substantially curtail employment in such classification. In determining whether such classifications should be made in any industry, in making such classifications, and in determining the minimum-wage rates for such classifications, no classification shall be made, and no minimum wage rate shall be fixed, solely on a regional basis, but the industry committee and the Administrator shall consider among other relevant factors the following:

(1) competitive conditions as affected by transportation, living, and production costs; . . .[43]

In the first few years of this Act's administration, necessarily many somewhat rough approximations have to be adopted on such matters as measurement and significance of regional and local variations in living costs; but progressively their interpretation must be threshed out.

The question must be faced: "If the government can raise so many wages from 30 to 40 cents, why does it not go on to help the 40-cent or 50-cent man or woman who feels exploited?" If a single national legal minimum-wage rate is high enough to protect the 10% or 15% of lowest-paid workers in a whole industry, it seems likely also to confer a competitive advantage on the higher-wage section or sections; yet when we look for rationally as well as politically defensible bases for classifications, with differing wage minima, we are likely to be staggered by the difficulties.

Employers and workers in the higher-wage sectors of any industry, as was remarked above, tend to ally themselves with other high wage advocates—the former have a vested interest in handicapping their low wage competitors. In some cases the latter are perhaps really "chiselers," operating socially "parasitic industries."[44] In many cases, however, the low

---

[43] From Sec. 8 of Fair Labor Standards Act of 1938 (Pub. 718, 75th Cong.).

[44] But recall Thurman Arnold's quip, that "a chiseler is one who splits a frozen price."

money wages have higher purchasing power than is immediately apparent, because of low local living costs; and in most cases, if wage rates are sufficiently raised by law, the low wage workers will be kept or thrust into less favorable occupations (if any).[45]

C. Summary

In this chapter we have examined systematically some of the leading arguments as to economic tendencies of public regulation of wages, and have attempted to translate part of these rather abstract issues into concrete and statistical terms. The comprehensive controls reviewed in the two immediately preceding chapters were noticed only very incidentally in the present sketch, which was devoted mainly to wage-hour legislation now or recently prevailing in the United States, and to the British wage-board regulation which is perhaps the closest national parallel.

The bits of historical evidence thus examined lend support (as far as they go) to the view that legal wage-rate minima can be enforced at levels significantly higher than the lowest 10% or so of earned rates before such regulation, and without causing appreciable new unemployment.[46] Our own national experience with such regulation is still too short, and attendant circumstances too complex and unusual, to be confidently interpreted; but the total of world experience, including our own, points in the direction just noted. How far these results are due, respectively, to various factors, such as removal of "exploitation," stimulation or concurrence of cost reductions, and recouping higher wages by higher prices to consumers, are important problems on which little quantitative evidence is offered in this book.

---

[45] "Cotton-textile incomes in the South are low relative to northern wage standards and also in comparison with a number of other industries in the South, but they are substantially higher than farm incomes in that area."— Hinrichs, *op. cit.*, p. 73.

[46] By "new unemployment," I mean an increase over the amount reasonably attributable to the business mortality previously prevailing in the industry in question, and to the innumerable other factors in gross unemployment and part-time work.

World history shows too, that the economic effects of legal regulation which is nominally confined to wages of low-skilled labor are actually much further reaching. The "bumping-up" of higher wages by the latter controls, and the need of conserving industrial peace, combine to extend public regulation to skilled men's wages. And when either public or private wage control becomes nationally centralized, it becomes more feasible to stabilize wages and prices—even, in a crisis, to secure sweeping and definitive cuts of wages as well as prices and other business terms.

Before the Great Depression which began in 1929, public wage-fixing authorities, including those in "socialistic" Australia and New Zealand were usually conservative in estimating industry's wage-paying capacity; here was doubtless *one* reason why unemployment rates did not long remain excessively high. Since 1932, as was shown in Ch. 18, rather extreme work-sharing and wage-raising prescriptions for chronic depression have become almost universally popular. Unless we find better means of coping with the causes of unemployment, in the future we may expect stiffer doses of palliatives like work sharing, work relief, military employments—accompanied by higher wage rates. Although it is scarcely possible to give a rigorous quantitative demonstration of the parts which these prescriptions have played and can play in providing for *self-sustaining* increases in national production, few can doubt the possibility that they may be carried to the point where they will produce disastrous economic and political reactions.

CHAPTER 21

WAGE POLICY IN WAR AND PEACE[1]

In the preceding pages, we have referred rather frequently to changes in wages and other labor affairs associated with the first World War. Much less was said about the impact of the second World War, beginning in 1939. Many of the latter war's major effects are, of course, beyond prediction, yet it seems wise in this final chapter, first to survey the facts visible at the time of writing (section A, in other countries—section B, in the United States); and then (section C) to attempt a perspective view of the staple wage agencies and factors in their long-term peacetime relations.

A. Effects of World War II upon Foreign Labor Policies

Recent events abroad—especially in Britain and her Dominions and in Sweden—are discussed in this section, chiefly with reference to the great problems of production and distribution of goods, for which vast and speedy economic readjustments had to be made. We begin by noticing briefly how employment, public and private labor standards, and labor disputes were affected; then pass to wage policies in relation to inflation; and, finally, we consider how far price control and rationing appear to be alternatives to wage control in a war emergency.

1. Unemployment and Labor Standards.—As international conflicts reached great-war proportions in 1939, European belligerent and neutral nations alike promptly began a series of drastic cuts of their labor standards, notably hours of work.[2]

---

[1] Parts of this chapter were used in my *Labor Policy and National Defense* (Univ. of Mich., Bureau of Industrial Relations, Bull. 12, 1941).

[2] See *International Labor Review,* issues of the period, e.g., "Influence of the War and Mobilization on Hours of Work and Rest Periods," March, 1940, vol. 41, pp. 291-306.

In 1939, these nations had more slack of unemployment to take up than in 1914 (though relatively less than the United States in 1939-41); but outside of Germany, whose economy was already geared to war, there were many bottlenecks of supplies and of workers for key jobs and plants. Adequate supervisory and skilled forces had not been trained for this emergency in Britain and France; furthermore, owners and managers as well as wage earners were unwilling to shorten week-ends and holidays. The line of least resistance was to relax legal labor standards so as to give the war industries free hands; and one result was longer weeks, even for some occupations and areas in which capable unemployed workers were still available.

Penalty wage rates for overtime, however, were by no means discarded in the belligerent nations. In Belgium and Great Britain, for example, higher cash pay was continued (in some industries, at least) for work beyond normal hours. Other governments (like France) copied earlier totalitarian models in this matter and diverted part of the workman's overtime wage into social security or working-class welfare funds.

Again, as in 1914-15, a reaction followed within the war's first year. Probably in but few occupations and shop conditions, however, has it yet been rigorously demonstrated that the optimum work shift, from the standpoint of total wartime output, is below eight hours, or that the optimum rate of production per worker can be maintained by a week shorter than six eight-hour days.[3]

---

[3] The German reaction in December 1939 *shortened* the normal work shift to 10 hours in war industries. The circular of British Minister of Labor Bevin in July 1940, which called a halt on "the continuation of seven-day working, with an average working week of between 70 and 80 hours," recommended an average week in munitions production of some 60 hours (inclusive of short rest and refreshment pauses), until such time as recruiting and training of labor forces would permit "a reduction in the working week to the optimum hours, which experience in many manufacturing fields shows to be in the region of 55 or 56 hours. . . ." *International Labor Review,* October-November 1940, Vol. 42, pp. 267-271. (A year later, however, complaints were still heard that long-shift seven-day weeks were too often required.) When Mr. Bevin issued the circular just referred to there were still 763,000 or 5.3% of people *covered by unemployment insurance* unemployed.

2. Compulsory Arbitration and Suspension of Union Rules in Britain.—Labor abroad has been vitally affected by the second World War in many other ways, especially through authoritative measures for mobilizing labor supplies and avoiding disputes. The 1914-18 pattern is again easily recognizable, though with some important variations. The belligerents in 1939-41, e.g., resorted more promptly to industrial as well as military conscription and training, to the use of State employment offices and unemployment-insurance administration to minimize labor turnover and "labor piracy," to suspension of union work rules and practices, and (where it was not already in use) to compulsory arbitration. In Great Britain, for instance, the Minister of Labor received the significant additional title "and of National Service"; and in one of his numerous capacities, he became chairman of a Labor Supply Board which, with its local organs, secured emergency powers of conscription for civilian war service.[4]

One new instrument for this purpose was the following revision of administrative regulations in the British national unemployment compensation system:

The definition of "suitable employment" which must be accepted by an insured worker receiving benefit has been extended to include work certified to be of national importance. Such work, if on standard rates and conditions, is not deemed unsuitable merely because the worker has previously had better working conditions, or, if he has been unemployed for a fortnight or more, because the job is not in his usual occupation.[5]

As in 1914-15, British labor in 1939-40 gave up some of its cherished working rules for the war's duration, thereby again permitting such expedients as temporary "dilution" of union journeymen with unskilled and semi-skilled male and female labor. The Conditions of Employment and National Arbitration Order, effective July 25, 1940, provided incidentally for filing memoranda giving particulars of such departures from

---

[4] Particulars on these and other matters discussed in the above text are summarized in *International Labor Review*, October-November 1940, vol. 42, pp. 252-264.

[5] *Ibid.*, p. 262.

"established trade practices," which notations would serve as evidence if and when the unions ask for restoration of pre-war conditions.

The main effect of this Order, however, was to set up a top tribunal for final adjudication of any labor disputes not otherwise settled. In this function, at least, the new board was analogous to the Committee on Production of 1915 and following years; and like the old Committee, the later National Arbitration Tribunal became largely responsible for the main outlines of British wage policy. One way in which the 1940 compulsory arbitration system of Britain resembled those of World War I is that none of them was able actually to halt strikes.[6]

Another difference is this one: During World War II, British wage regulation approached somewhat more closely to the peacetime Australian model than to that of Britain itself in 1915-18. Many more British minimum-wage authorities, whose main business is protection of the lowest-paid workers, were operating in 1939 than in 1914. Apart from these latter wage boards and the new top arbitral tribunal, all with compulsory powers, numerous other agencies continued to assist in voluntary determinations of public and private wages and salaries.[7]

Many of the problems with which all these agencies have had to cope concern *relative* wages—comparisons and differentials among occupations and regions, and by age and sex. The Industrial Court, a distinguished full-time tribunal which has arranged voluntary settlements of labor disputes since it was created in 1919, has conserved a great deal of the experience and theory which was painfully wrought out in 1914-18. The large degree of independence among the innumerable British peacetime wage determiners, however, and the haste required

---

[6] Monthly statistics of labor disputes given in the Ministry of Labour Gazette show no marked trend upward or downward during the last several years. In March 1941 (latest figure I have seen), for instance, 121 labor disputes began. This was the first month in at least two years that the number had risen above the low 90's.

[7] Among these voluntary agencies are the Joint (Whitley) Industrial Councils.

to deal with wartime dislocations of employment, wages, and prices, made it needful after 1939 to deal roughly and swiftly with the anomalies and injustices which the new contest produced. Particularly menaced were and are the numerous low-paid, ill-organized or unorganized workers not yet under the jurisdiction of any minimum-wage board. Even if the lag of their earnings behind living costs leads to legislation committing them all to the care of new or old Trade Boards, the trend of their real wages is apt to depend much on the degree in which their work is deemed essential to the conduct of the war. In any desperate national struggle, the hard choice must often be made of sustaining best the producers and wielders of arms.

3. Wage Policy in Relation to Wartime Inflation.—Problems of relative wages in wartime are difficult enough at best; and their difficulties are multiplied when they are not handled with reference to a conscious national policy on general or average wages. What happens to wages is an important determiner as to how the great burdens of war shall be shared. The problems of war finance, of "paying for the war," are at bottom problems of distributing these great deprivations over the whole population, both during and after the war. The respective behaviors of the wage and price levels are key-factors in war finance.[8]

Where and Why Wartime Prices Are High.—Let us analyze a bit further the factors influencing prices in any war emergency and then notice the import of this analysis for wage policy.

Wartime price changes are by no means all upward, even where a government's policies or lack of policies in the long run spell inflation. For a time, lessened demand for specific

---

[8] Defense expenditures, which in modern total war may account for even more than half of the total national production, are not indeed quite a net social burden, for to some extent these defense activities (e.g., building ships, airplanes, and roads, preparing soldiers' food, clothing, shelter) replace normal peacetime industry. Nevertheless, it is broadly true that both the armed forces and the war industries divert a staggering amount of any belligerent's resources into destructive actions, leaving progressively less for civilian use.

products may cause rather widespread weaknesses, as in the prices of young men's civilian clothing when a large and unforeseen mobilization occurs. More sustained price weaknesses affect goods whose markets or transport facilities are reduced by the war—examples are the vast stocks of farm staples, oil and coffee soon dammed up in various spots on the American hemisphere. Retail price movements, moreover, tend to lag behind wholesale, notably because the "cost of goods sold" (at wholesale prices) is only part of the retailer's cost; other costs, for instance, are his own wages, rent, and taxes. In a neutral nation whose people are not making strenuous defense preparations and are not vitally dependent upon imports that are being riddled by a foreign war, the general price level is not greatly and immediately affected. Such a nation was the United States in 1939-40; and here are also clues to the much slower rise of living costs in the Dominions, as compared with Great Britain. By contrast, Sweden, though neutral, was immediately affected by sharp rises in cost of her imports and in her own defense taxation, as well as by decline in exporting opportunities; hence, in August 1940, her wholesale price index was some 32% above that of August 1939, and her living cost index about 12% higher.[9]

Many taxes occasioned by national defense, to be sure (especially income, inheritance, and expensive-luxury taxes), do not (at least directly) affect prices of the commodities and rents which are involved in the ordinary living-cost indexes. Yet when all people are required to pay vastly higher taxes, inevitably many of these levies do tend presently to help raise any broad index of prices.

As a war continues, each nation combats its own shortages by increasing production of the deficient goods and of substitutes for them—e.g., of agricultural as well as war goods in Europe, and of steel, aluminum, and optical instruments in the

[9] Skandinaviska Banken, *Quarterly Review* (Stockholm), October 1940, pp. 107, 110. In their article, "International Cost-of-Living Comparisons," *Conference Board Economic Record,* June 11, 1941, White and Mellon give indexes for the U. S. and 17 foreign countries for each of the years 1914-20 inclusive; also many data for the same countries in 1939-41.

United States. Such increases in production tend indeed to check price increases; yet even apart from the circumstances recited above, new wartime production encounters rising costs. Artificial rubber, for instance, will be very much more expensive than normally imported plantation rubber for some years to come. Extra-shift work, even in efficient plants, and use of marginal to obsolete fields, mines, furnaces, and factories (also of the less competent workers), generally signify high-cost productive capacities which are usable only when prices are high. Anticipating what will be said below, let us assume that the resources which *practically* can be secured by taking up industrial slacks such as unemployment are not adequate to provide the whole increase of defense effort required by modern war.

We arrive thus at the outstanding force in wartime price-wage spirals: competitive spending for scarce goods. The new taxation which appears politically possible soon becomes inadequate to enable the government to purchase requisite commodities and services; and the extent to which war loans actually induce consumers to restrict their purchases of consumer goods (including housing and other services) is insufficient to bridge the remaining gap. Then come several varieties of government borrowing through the banking system, by means of which the State outbids civilians for whatever supplies it requires (including those actually commandeered). Concurrent measures designed to protect the people with lowest incomes include: first, rationing the supplies of essential consumers' goods (at controlled—and perhaps subsidized—and relatively low prices); and second, advancing money wages on the heels of rising living costs. Such wage advances raise production costs and soon require further enhancement of prices.[10]

Among the numerous undesirable consequences of this inflationary war spiral are two which it shares with any peacetime boom: (1) it creates social unrest through "profiteering"

---

[10] The following estimates, referring to U. S. experience in World War I, will supply quantitative illustration of the above proposition. Taking 1912-14 as 100, our total factory wage payments or payrolls mounted sharply to about 220 in 1918, 290 in 1920. Our total output of consumer goods rose only to around 120 by 1916, and very slightly more in 1919. (Cleveland Trust Co., *Business Bulletin*, July 15, 1940.)

due to rising prices; and (2) it produces a great volume of debt (much of it the government's war debt) in the high-price period, which becomes doubly burdensome in the phase of deflation which in some degree is inevitable.

Both Price and Spending Controls Needed—Swedish Method.—Two lines of attack can be made upon this great problem. One is the tactic of governmental price and rent restrictions. In the absence of such controls, prices and rents rise much faster. But price and rent regulations require an obnoxious degree of bureaucratic rationing unless they are accompanied by suitable limitation of spending for current consumption. Thus, in the last few years, a second line of attack upon war inflation has been widely recommended—namely, a series of levies upon the spendable incomes of consumers. This tactic gives a negative answer to the question whether *all* wage rates should advance in full proportion with the cost of living. It remains urgently needful, to be sure, to shield those wage earners and others who receive *the very lowest incomes* from deterioration of their already abominably poor living standards; yet economists are largely agreed that defense costs are now so great, in relation to total national production, that even if all incomes above a modest level could be confiscated, the sum would not suffice for a major war's financing.

In neutral, Socialist-governed Sweden, which is now burdened by rising living costs as stated above, special protection was promptly provided to the poorer people by governmental subsidies to fuel and certain other necessaries of life; and, simultaneously, the trade unions agreed that during the war wage rates should be increased, not by the full rise expected in living costs, but by a distinctly lesser amount.[11]

---

[11] See *International Labor Review,* May 1941, vol. 43, pp. 564-568. Agreements made in 1939 advanced wage rates, on the average, to an extent estimated at 75% of the expected rise in living costs. A bad harvest in 1940 aggravated the difficulties, and agreements made in 1941 are said to bring wage rates up by little more than half the increase in living costs. (In many occupations, of course, weekly earnings have advanced as much as cost of living, if not more—by reason especially of steadier work and overtime.)

Compulsory War Loans in Britain.—A valuable perspective on the matters discussed above has been afforded by the "Keynes Plan" as to labor incomes in relation to war financing.[12] Doubtless its most novel feature is the one which Keynes called "deferred pay"—similar in effect to the deferred credits scheme adopted by the British government, as told below. To Keynes, however, "deferred pay" was but one cylinder of the war engine which he designed. Other cylinders were intended to improve the living standards of the poorest people, and to require progressive percentage contributions of both taxes and compulsory loans from incomes above the exempt level. Much of Keynes' argument was devoted to showing that it would be impossible to finance the war merely by current taxation (though everyone must pay enormously greater taxes), and that the practical alternative to compulsory loans would be concealed, inflationary taxation that would fall most heavily on small incomes. Hence, he said, "a demand on the part of the trade unions for an increase in money rates of wages to compensate for every increase in the cost of living is futile, and greatly to the disadvantage of the working class."

The principle of "deferred pay" or compulsory war loans was adopted by the British government in April 1941. The budget for 1941-42 undertook to raise a substantial part of the estimated $20 billion of war expenditure by many new types of taxes and loans. And

To mitigate to some extent the severity of these tax rates, the budget includes the innovation of a system of deferred credits to taxpayers. The essence of the plan is that the Government assumes an obligation to repay to both individuals and corporations a certain proportion of the taxes now levied upon them, and sets up for this purpose credits to their account in the Post Office Savings Bank, repayable after the war. Individual taxpayers will be credited with most of the increase in their taxes, up to £ 65 yearly, which results from the lowering of exemptions and the reduction of earned income allowance. As Sir

---

[12] J. M. Keynes, *How to Pay for the War* (London and New York: February 1940). For a digest and commentary on this plan, from the standpoint of labor problems, see article by E. J. Riches in *Studies in War Economics* (Montreal: International Labor Office, 1941).

Kingsley Wood explained in the Commons, a married man with two children who earns the equivalent of $1,400 will pay about $98 in income tax this year instead of about $22 which he paid last year; but some $69 will be credited to him in a post office savings account. Corporations are similarly to be credited with 20% of the 100% excess profits tax paid.[13]

Canadian Wartime Wage Policy.—Canadian labor problems have many elements in common with those of the United States—including the split between AF of L and CIO factions, and conflicts of federal-provincial government jurisdictions. The national war wage policy of this Dominion, however, goes beyond that of Great Britain, toward the compulsory arbitration systems of national wage regulation in the sister Dominions—Australia and New Zealand. It is less effective than the latter in that there is no central full-time personnel to administer the Canadian wage policy. Other Canadian war measures, which are not treated here but whose gears mesh more or less with those of the wage policy, are "anti-enticing of labor" orders, voluntary suspension of certain trade union rules, and the Wartime Prices and Trade Board.

The Canadian Industrial Disputes Investigation Act of 1907, together with later amendments and supplementary provincial actions, has accustomed the nation to compulsory "cooling-off" delays of strikes and lockouts, not only in the transportation industry (somewhat as in the United States), but in several others such as mining and public utilities. For each serious labor dispute a Board of Conciliation is appointed, which attempts to arrange a voluntary settlement; and if the dispute persists, the Board makes public its findings and recommendations. Then the disputants are legally free to strike or use certain other economic weapons. This "cooling-off" system has broken down in numerous instances;[14] but it was thought to offer the most suitable basis for democratic and non-bureaucratic labor regulation during World War II. Hence

---

[13] National City Bank Economic Letter, May 1941, p. 58.
[14] See, e.g., the Twentieth Century Fund's report, *Labor and National Defense,* p. 100 ff. (1941).

its application was extended to all Canadian industries in war work, also to the paper industry.

The new wage policy, given legal form by an Order in Council dated December 16, 1940,[15] laid down several principles to be observed by all Boards of Conciliation and by the Minister of Labour—who has powers of review over these boards and over the more important voluntary collective labor agreements. Among these principles are the following:

"(a) Except in certain special circumstances, the highest wage rates established between 1926 and December 16, 1940, are to be regarded as fair and reasonable; they may be restored, if necessary, and maintained but not increased.

"(b) Such wage rates may be supplemented by a separate cost of living bonus usually of $1.25 per week for each rise of 5% in the cost of living in order to safeguard the workers against increases in the cost of basic necessities of life."[16]

(No ceiling is placed, of course, on *weekly earnings*—which the war affects favorably in Canada, as elsewhere, via increased use of incentive payments, fuller employment, and overtime.)

This policy encountered many serious difficulties, not the least being the new current wave of wage rate advances in the United States—where increases of 10 cents an hour or more soon became commonplace.[17] Another problem arose from the

---

[15] P. C. No. 7440. One brief commentary is given in Bulletin No. 5 of the Industrial Relations Section of Queen's University, Kingston, Ont.; another in the address of Arthur J. Hills, Chairman of the Canadian National Labour Supply Council, on April 17, 1941—available mimeographed through University of Michigan Bureau of Industrial Relations. See also the Queen's bureau's report of its Industrial Relations conference of April 10-12, 1940, at which Professor Mackintosh's address foreshadowed most features of P. C. 7440.

[16] Supplement to *Labour Gazette*, July 1941, p. 1. This pamphlet reprints a declaration by the New Zealand labor movement recommending "that the Government be urged to provide for stabilization of present prices of essential commodities and services together with present rates of wages and salaries."

[17] The chief Canadian CIO organ, *The Canadian Unionist*, in its April 1941 issue gives the minority report (favoring the union side) of the Conciliation Board in the Peck steel dispute at Montreal, which was perhaps the first practical application of the new wage policy. The primary split in this board was on the question: was the basic minimum wage rate of 1926-29 in this plant (30.7¢ per hour) "fair and reasonable" in the sense of Order P. C. 7440?

attempt to coordinate actions of the *ad hoc* Conciliation Boards, and of those collective bargainers who avoid labor disputes, by mere part-time work of the Minister of Labor and his staff. National wage policy deserves the continuous attention of a top board, containing labor and employer representation, that is capable of securing and maintaining high prestige.

4. Price Control and Rationing Alternatives to Wage Control?—Thus, labor in the foreign democratic nations, on the whole, approved restraints upon rising wage rates in the war years beginning in 1939, realizing that great shortages in civilian goods were inevitable and that the attempt fully to maintain real-wage rates would enhance wartime inflation. Great differences in degrees of restraint appeared in the various countries, however, as well as in the many other forces affecting prices; hence, it is difficult to judge how far the 50% increase in British wholesale prices, August 1939 to December 1940 (for example), might have been stemmed by more adequate wage-rate controls. The wage and price controls of Germany (initiated before 1939, see Ch. 18-C) helped greatly to hold the Reich's indexes level.

In the latest, even more than in other great wars, though, price and wage indexes became more and more nominal. The steady indexes for Germany, of course, give little hint of the deterioration in quality and other resorts to substitute goods which occurred, as innumerable objects became dearer or entirely unobtainable; and, in some degree, similar figures for other nations must be accepted with the same reservations. Supplies of goods tended to be allocated, between military and civilian uses and among civilian families, less by supply-and-demand prices than in former wars—more by government commandeering, rationing, and subsidies, accompanied by price controls. In no country was the problem of civilian supply solved merely by voluntary or compulsory control of civilian incomes. Hence, increases in many wages and other incomes did not immediately and proportionately inflate prices.

Thus, some of the forebodings about rising wage rates, under war conditions, appeared not to be borne out by experience. Prices, however, obviously cannot be fixed independently of labor costs; and so, if wage rates rise, official prices tend to rise too; and many wage earners and others, whose money incomes lag, may become unable to buy the "ration" of necessaries which they are legally allowed to buy. Here is but one instance of the unbalance among wage rates, rents, and other prices which must be combatted during war, partly in order to minimize the problems of post-war reconstruction.

B. Wartime Trends in American Wage and Labor Policy[18]

The effects of World War II upon American labor show many parallels and many contrasts, as compared with its effects upon labor abroad, also with the impact of World War I upon ourselves—in both cases allowing for the time-lags during which the United States was less concerned than the belligerents. The import of these upheavals for American wages will become clearer as we notice, first, differences between our national emergency which began in 1939 and others; then, how this emergency was dealt with from the standpoints of production and distribution of goods, and of policies and agencies relating to wages and industrial peace.

1. **Differences Between American Emergency of 1939- and Others.**—Although the over-all pictures of wages, prices, and labor unrest were similar for all nations seriously affected by the World War of 1914-18, some major differences among countries and among years within this period are readily apparent. Until American entry into that war early in 1917, for example, our own cost of living was less affected by new taxation than were those of the belligerent nations; and but little of our labor supply had been drawn into national fighting forces. By contrast, these two factors had tended, in all the war-waging countries, to advance both cost of living and wages much faster.[19] By 1941 Americans saw trends very different

---

[18] On this topic see especially recent publications of Sumner H. Slichter, e.g., *Economic Factors Affecting Industrial Relations Policy in National Defense* (New York: Industrial Relations Counselors, 1941).

[19] For the year 1916, e.g., the British index of living costs averaged about 145, and of wage rates 115-120; while American indexes of both living costs and wage rates were in the neighborhood of 107 (1914 = 100).

from those we faced in 1916. Our rapid expansion of production of ships, planes, and other defense goods called forth vast increases in public expenditures, loans, and taxes.

Two other great differences are also obvious: in reserve of labor supply, on one hand, and in demand for armed personnel, on the other. The United States was more tightly squeezed from both these sides in 1917 than in 1940-41. We entered World War I with our labor force almost fully occupied, on account of the boom effects of our sales of war supplies to Europe; nevertheless, we proceeded quickly to raise armed forces aggregating several millions. The contrast, on both scores, of our positions in 1917 and 1941 is very striking. In 1941 we still had an unemployed labor reserve; and we were not planning to arm nearly so many men as we did in 1917-18.

Reversals of Emphasis in Wartimes as to Labor Standards.—Nearly everyone knows that a war, or a sustained rearmament program, has many boom effects, especially on total national employment. It is not so widely realized how far such conditions call for public labor policies contrary to those suitable to most of the 1930's. As one writer puts it,

. . . The national industrial problems of wartime, once initial difficulties of transition are overcome, are in many respects the reverse of those of a peace-time depression. The problem is not to find employment for labor, but to find labor to perform needed services. It is not to stimulate a more rapid flow of money, but to restrain the forces of inflation. Consequently, all policies designed to make work or spread work among a larger number of individuals than are needed, or to push incomes above competitive levels, must be reversed.[20]

Whereas in depression we properly appealed to employers to sustain wage rates to brake the *downward* spiral, in the armament or war boom we must appeal to labor to hold down basic wage rates, and thus to brake the *upward* spiral.[21] For achiev-

---

[20] C. O. Hardy, *Wartime Control of Prices*, p. 76. (Brookings, Sept. 1940.)

[21] Total payrolls, and hourly earned rates and weekly and family earnings, however, are quite properly boosted, by such means as fuller employment, night, holiday, and other overtime, intensive training to increase skills, and profit and living-cost bonuses.

ing full military strength we must train and ration our labor supplies, and ask labor organizations to forego full use of their power to strike and of their rules intended to safeguard job opportunities of their members. Large sacrifices, of course, must also be required of all other members of the community. Such sacrifices were not, indeed, required while our nation was initiating the defense program. During that period we could have both "guns and butter." But by mid-1941 most Americans realized that the military and naval production they wanted could not be merely superimposed upon normal peacetime production. Thus, our war emergency became increasingly like that of Britain, and more unlike our own depression emergency of the 1930's.

2. The Chief Objectives to be Sought.—Wartime labor policy is but part of the more general attempt to discover and mobilize national resources in such a manner as to get the needed efficiency in defense, with tolerably equitable sharing of the burden. By common consent great efforts are made to maintain, and if possible to increase, the consumption of the poorest families even in wartime—though very much remains to be done in this direction in every country. Public assistance and other social services are too apt to be unwisely curtailed; but at least subsidies of bread and rationing of scarce essentials is virtually universal war policy. Industrial slack, notably unemployment, should be taken up as fast and as far as possible; and neither wage earners nor other members of the community should be asked to make sacrifices unless and until the increase of war burden makes such sacrifice necessary.

The preceding paragraph is, in part, an application of "the living wage principle"—whose theoretical ground is modified by war's onset only in that, if war continues on a sufficient scale, it may degrade a rich into a poor nation and thus lower the standard of "living wage" which the country can guarantee as a minimum.

As to relative wages, or aifferentials for skill (and among industries and regions), the factors which are commonplaces in discussions of peacetime wage determination supply valuable hints for wage adjustments as they are multiplied and speeded up in wartime. Such wage changes should supplement the needful compulsory labor mobilization measures, to effect as rapidly as possible the many shifts among occupations and localities that war efficiency requires. Less careful and time-consuming comparisons among wages can be made than in peacetime; and governmental agencies should assume much responsibility for the wartime wage structure. Rapid job evaluation procedures are in order, to avoid glaring irrationalities of relative wages.

As to *general* wage adjustments, the arguments emphasized by Keynes show that, in a major war, prices, profits, and overall rates of physical output per man-hour lose much of their peacetime significance for wage fixing. The index of all hourly wage rates, which in peacetime normally advances faster than the living-cost index because of the upward trend in output per man-hour (all industries and all occupations considered), during a strenuous defense effort must lag behind. Even before the slack of unemployment is taken up as fully as ultimately it can be, the attempt completely to maintain real-wage rates becomes futile and inflationary. War effort, to be sure, supplies many plausible grounds for demanding wage rate increases, such as rising profits (in the earlier stages), rising living costs (in later stages), and the premiums necessary to recruit labor supplies for many defense operations. But unless this movement is restrained it leads to an unnecessary degree of price-wage inflation, whose handicap on the next post-war economic readjustments may be especially severe because wage rates since World War I have become more "sticky" or rigid against downward revisions.

To a very important extent the progress of inflation can be impeded, and the general public protected, by governmental price and rent controls and rationing. The last half of the title of Mr. Henderson's Office of Price Administration and Civilian Supply, too, symbolizes the obligation of governmental and private organizations to see that war industries do not unnecessarily encroach upon those ministering to our other wants. To prevent the regulative bureaucracies from becoming too inefficient and burdensome, however, it becomes needful, as the

war effort develops, to adjust individual spending downward
to match the restricted supplies of consumer goods.

What amounts of consumer incomes should be so diverted?
What part should be diverted by taxation, and what part by
war loans? And what sorts of taxes and loans should be used?
The first of these questions, though sufficiently difficult, is the
easiest. As the public authorities determine what supplies shall
be used for defense, the remainder available for consumption
can be estimated accurately enough to show approximately beyond what rate of consumer spending would lie price-wage
inflation or all-out rationing. The total of the prospective flow
of money incomes to consumers, and the portion of such flow
diverted by existing tax rates, can also be estimated. The difference between existing tax yields and the current value of all
supplies and services required by the government is the amount
of money income which, if diverted, will relieve the government
of the necessity of inflationary methods of "borrowing." How
much of this diversion can be accomplished by new taxes depends in part upon variable currents of social psychology and
balance of power among political-pressure groups; though beyond certain points this tax or that reduces the worker's or the
boss's efficiency.[22]

Nearly everyone, of course, would choose to have his inevitable contribution taken as a loan rather than as a tax; and
at first thought any of us will say: Let the individual decide
how much war loan, if any, he shall buy. But if too many people choose to spend too much of their current incomes on consumer goods, the resulting price advances tend to make it difficult for any wage earner to *lend*—each then tends to be taxed
through inflationary methods of war finance.[23] A program of

---

[22] Certain types of extremely high taxes on profits, for example, tend to
encourage lavish expenditures by employers for advertising and for labor
bonuses, as well as carelessness about costs in general; and to favor passive
as compared with active or venture investments. Low-paid workers may be
made still less vigorous by fresh burdens of war taxes.

[23] One very probable result of an increasing flow of consumer incomes,
not immediately and fully offset by higher prices, taxes, and war loans,
is a rapid advance of instalment buying, which expansion of instalment
credit may become inflationary in effect. More or less in keeping with
Fisher's "debt-deflation theory of business depressions," we may say that

compulsory war loans, along lines suggested by Keynes and the 1941-42 British budget, is surely better for consumers than great inflation. Still better, if feasible, is an adequate program of voluntary loans—supplementing, of course, rigorous war taxation. A chief social benefit of widely diffused holdings of war loans, too, is the cushion of consumer spending power thus provided for the transition at a later time from war to peace economy. In this way and many others, war policies and methods can be oriented in part toward means of developing optimum *economic* production—not merely relief employment, in and out of public works construction—after the war.

3. Taking up Industrial Slacks.—When we ask what happens to standards of living during wartime we are apt to confuse two problems. One is concerned with the direction and extent of changes in *real-wage rates per hour;* the other refers to changes in *annual real income per family.* It is still rather widely believed that American living standards in both these senses could be maintained or advanced despite the war emergency, mainly by putting the unemployed to work.

How unduly optimistic this view is, is revealed by a moment's thought. True, man-hours worked and payrolls do rise to new heights; but the goods bought by wage earners could be increased correspondingly (i.e., real earnings per hour could be maintained), only if the whole cost of defense preparations were borne by non-wage earners. That the latter class cannot bear the whole cost is indicated by the fact that it receives only one-third of the whole national income; the other two-thirds is received as wages and salaries by employees. Furthermore, among the non-wage earners are millions of recipients of modest incomes—farmers, shopkeepers, owners of small properties, professional people, and other self-employed persons. The sums needed to purchase the commodities and services necessary for the military and naval power we now require (including leaselend expenditures) are so huge that there must be some cutting

---

American experience in 1930-31 shows that, even if wage rates are not deflated, prices may be; whereupon deflation of debts incurred during the high-price era has a very inhibiting effect on economic activity.

of many real-wage incomes per hour—although, so far as the
levies upon such incomes are made in the form of *war loans,*
wage earners might, after their bonds were exchanged for
goods at some future time, have suffered no considerable reduction in the real hourly earnings for their wartime work.

The case as to annual real income per family, on the other
hand, is rather different. Many worker families will increase
their real annual incomes during the emergency—particularly
those engaged in defense industries. The men in such families,
on the average, will have fuller employment and more overtime
than usual, at rising wage rates; moreover, many members of
their families, not previously at work, will obtain employment.
Thus, through more persons employed in the family, and other
opportunities for more hours of well-paid work in the year, a
great many families will increase their money incomes more
than their living expenses and taxes. But these families will
doubtless be a minority of the whole population. The others,
if they escape an actual decline in money income, will not secure
enough advance in it to cover higher living costs and taxes.
The only way to minimize such deterioration of living standards is to take up all the industrial "slacks" we can. These
slacks are by no means all wastes, or even luxuries, in peacetime; but in wartime we cannot afford them, and must submit
(for example) to increasing standardization and simplification
of consumer goods, such as clothing.

Four potential resources or slacks which are of outstanding
importance will be discussed in the present section, namely:
reemployment; the basic work week; labor union rules and
practices; and labor disputes.

(a) **Reemployment of Idle Men.**—The president of an important firm told the National Association of Manufacturers'
Congress (in December 1940) : "Until we put back to work
those of the millions of unemployed who are able to work, I
cannot see that we should worry or complain about a 40-hour
week." Wartime demands for labor and wartime facilities for
training and placement do, indeed, offer unusual opportunities
for taking up the great peacetime slack of unemployment and

underemployment. Many complications appear, however, as one scratches below the surface of this set of problems.

It is very difficult to measure the extent of unemployment at any one time; and perhaps impossible to determine the minimum amount below which unemployment (including work relief) cannot be reduced. As was pointed out, the number of man-hours worked is one very important index of employment.[24] Here, however, it will suffice to review a few particulars on prevailing unemployment in the more popular sense of persons, able and willing to work, who are unable to find jobs. Most estimates of such unemployment are based upon statistics of *employment,* deducted from the estimated number of *employables.* Chief benchmarks as to size of this total labor force are the decennial Censuses of population and occupations, supplemented by estimates of the numbers of employables entering the labor market by way of immigration and other population increases.

For March 1940, the better-known current estimates of unemployment included the Conference Board's figure of 9.3 million and the CIO's 11.6 million. The decennial national Census, taken in that month, showed that all these private estimates were too high. Some 5.1 million persons were found actively seeking work, and in the same month about 2.9 million were on payrolls of public emergency work projects—chiefly WPA, CCC and NYA out-of-school programs. Thus we obtain a benchmark of some 8 million as unemployed in March 1940. The earlier estimates were inflated in both directions—the number of employables seeking work was increasing more slowly than was realized, and the extent of employment in new and rapidly developing industries was underrated.

Recent improvements in this important statistical field tend to correct both these sources of error. Employment, month by month, becomes more fully reported—especially in industries previously not well covered. Our social security and public employment office systems furnish increasingly comprehensive indications of extent of unemployment. And in mid-1941 the WPA

---

[24] *See esp.* Ch. 11-A, above.

initiated a monthly sampling survey, somewhat analogous to the
Gallup polls, of unemployment in the various industries and
regions throughout the nation.

What is the rock bottom of unemployment in a national-
defense emergency? No reliable answer can be given to this
question, but several factors can be pointed out. Whenever
labor demand is exceptionally strong in relation to available
supply, employers' hiring standards must be lowered; people then
become employable who are not so in a weaker market. In other
ways, too, the labor supplies show considerable elasticity. In
both war and peace booms, for example, many women and young
and old men, not normally statistically listed as employables, are
attracted into jobs. Of the 8 million of unemployed in March
1940, it is probable that at least one million (in and out of the
WPA) were so handicapped as to age, health, and personality
traits that they were, even in a sustained defense emergency,
unemployable.

In wartime, to be sure, there are added—to the strenuous
efforts of private persons toward reemployment—many new
powers of governmental authorities. The total result, we are
tempted to think, is soon to put all employables into jobs.

But, in addition to the minimum total of seasonal unemployment and voluntary labor turnover, serious defense efforts
produce innumerable industrial dislocations. Automobile production, for example, is spasmodically curtailed, as various shortages of materials develop; and masses of men are unemployed
before facilities can be developed for absorbing them into other
work—perhaps at distant places. As Americans felt the impact
of mounting "priority unemployment" in 1941, they became more
charitable toward the persistence of hundreds of thousands of
unemployed in Great Britain, in the face of her extreme national
peril. If a war lasts long enough, indeed, such unemployment
will decrease as the whole economy becomes readjusted. The
totalitarian regimes had relatively less unemployment than others
in World War II, because they went onto a war footing more
gradually long before 1939—and stayed there—while the rest
of the world carried on business-as-usual.

In short, the slack of unemployment which can practically be taken up in a war emergency is much less than the best-known estimates of unemployment have suggested. At times, more unemployment seems created by defense efforts than is being dissipated. Insensibly, too, many of the statistical groups change their significance. Employers, as mentioned, must lower their standards of employability; and many thousands of men and boys on NYA and CCC rolls become no longer unemployed work-relief "clients" but rather trainees for work of defense significance. Thus, a prosperous nation which, like the United States in 1940, enters a war emergency with an abnormally high rate of unemployment, can increase its output of war goods without *correspondingly* curtailing its total civilian supplies; but the net balance between reemployment and new "priority unemployment," during a period of strenuous arming, is unlikely to permit full maintenance of all *real-wage rates*.

(b) **Hours of Work for Machines and Men.**—There is no doubt that in under-employment due to layoffs and similar lost time we have a peacetime industrial slack which can be considerably taken up by intelligent wartime governmental and business management.

Is the 40-hour week itself a slack? If workers and plant facilities are available for longer weekly hours in war industries, where is the limit of weekly hours beyond which there is no slack to take up? An outstanding reason why flexibility of working hours is essential to wartime industrial efficiency is the immense premium which war puts upon *speedy* increase of many sorts of production. In most working organizations, with a work-day of eight hours or less, after the whole normal working force is employed, output can be accelerated much more effectively by working some of the already employed people longer hours (say, six days a week) than by securing and breaking in unemployed people, even if these are near at hand and, statistically speaking, have the requisite skills and experience. At least this is so up to the point when more shifts, and seven-day weeks, must be worked to secure the maximum production.

American legal labor standards, unlike the French 40-hour

week of 1936-38 (for example), contain but few absolute prohibitions of long hours of work for *men,* and virtually no
restrictions on the hours that *plants* may be operated. For the
most part our state regulations, as well as the federal wage-
hour and public contracts acts, rely on the comparatively new
idea of controlling working hours by penalty overtime wage
rates.

Does this method of regulation provide *adequate* flexibility
of hours of work, and of labor costs and incomes, in wartime?
If the hours of work per week which are compensable at
straight time were stretched out to (say) 48 during the war
emergency, no doubt this work-week would become more common and absorption of the unemployed slowed down somewhat.
Certainly labor cost would rise less rapidly; for in 1940-41
48 hours' work in a week usually required 52 hours' pay. In a
very few cases excessive fatigue and accidents might ensue from
making 48 hours the basic week; and some profits would be
raised, especially as many overhead costs are reduced as plants
are taken from five-day to six- or seven-day operation.

To these somewhat dubious consequences of weakening the
40-hour-week regulations should be added the important one
that, at the war's close, great unemployment might roll up, and
even then the pressure toward short hours afforded by high
overtime wage rates might not be restored. It was doubtful how
much effect a suspension of the legal wage-hour standards
would have on the rate of reemployment in the years 1940-41, or
on the rate of production of war goods (since the government
buyers of war goods commonly have little disposition to haggle
over costs and prices). But there could be little doubt that the
legal 40-hour week with 50% penalty overtime wage rates would
promote work-sharing in case of a post-war slump.[25] Laws and

---

[25] Monthly statistics of "average hours worked per week" in general
tended to show progressive increases, especially in war industries, after mid-
1940. In March 1941, e.g., the over-all average for durable-goods manufactures was 42.0, and higher averages were found in not a few industries,
such as machine tools (51.9), engines (46.0), and aircraft (45.2). Average
labor costs in such industries, even if wage rates remain constant, are
advanced more than 50% of the excess of the *average* hours worked above
40, for many workers are paid double time for holiday and other extreme
overtime, and many are paid premium rates for working unpopular shifts.

other public regulations concerning "prevailing wages" in public purchases and agencies in many cases set still higher standards for both straight and overtime pay. The Walsh-Healey Act, for instance, required most firms selling goods to the Federal government to pay their workers not less than 40 cents an hour straight time, and time-and-a-half in excess of 40 hours in any week *or in excess of eight hours in any day.* Here is no wage flexibility either for individual days within the 40-hour week or for seasonal employments; and of course in wartime the number of firms selling goods to the government becomes very large indeed.

Do all such wage-hour laws inflate wages and prices, under war-emergency conditions? Several grounds for a negative answer have been put forward; these became less convincing as time went by. One ground has already been considered above —the argument that, in the United States, supplies of consumer goods could be enormously and quickly increased (to keep pace with increasing consumer incomes), mainly by putting the unemployed to work.

Another argument is (or was) : If workers are allowed the full benefit of all the penalty overtime wage rates, they will not press so strongly for advance of base or straight-time rates; thus, in the post-emergency situation labor costs per unit of output will automatically fall as occasions to work overtime become rare. There remains some force in the last clause of this latter proposition; and when we notice that the average rate of hourly earnings of factory workers (for example), which in mid-1939 was some 63½ cents per hour, had risen by April 1941 to nearly 71 cents, we must remember that a significant part of this gain was due to application of penalty overtime rates. Such hourly earned rates will decline somewhat, as operations slacken.

Nevertheless, straight-time wage rates strongly tended to rise, after the latter part of 1940. The U. S. Bureau of Labor Statistics announced that, in one month alone (March to April 1941), "more workers were affected by wage-rate increases than during any month since April 1937; these increases averaged 9.6% and affected more than 800,000 (factory) wage earners."[26] A little later the railway unions initiated their demand for a general wage rise of 30%.[27]

Thus, although our wage-hour situation in 1941 contained several important elements of flexibility, and was an effective means of spreading work during depression, it did significantly reinforce the other inflationary forces then at work. The peacetime wage-hour controls of some other nations use sliding penalty rates—e.g., time-and-a-quarter for first four hours worked beyond 40, in any week; higher penalty for hours beyond 44. This type of scheme would appear to exert sufficient pressure toward work-sharing, in depression.

We had in this rising tide of both straight-time and overtime earnings an urgent reason for pushing sales of defense bonds to wage earners; and also for certain new taxes. The British plan of offsetting some new taxes on incomes by postal-savings credits available to the taxpayers after the emergency had to be very seriously considered. Another line of attack on the problem was also excellent in principle: higher rates of social security contributions. We were in a good position to raise the payroll tax for old-age benefits from 1%—and rather rapidly to the 3% or more which is required in the long run to maintain the present scale of benefit payments. Experimentation was in order, too, with dismissal compensation funds, which could provide another check on consumer expenditures in excess of the value, at existing prices, of the output of consumer goods during the war emergency, and a support to wage earners' consumption and reemployment efforts if and when a post-war slump came on.[28]

---

[26] At that time the U. S. national living-cost indexes were only 2½% above their (slightly depressed) positions in Aug. 1939; and the all-commodities wholesale price index was some 10% above its (distinctly depressed) level of Aug. 1939. In various defense centers, to be sure, living costs—notably rents—had risen more.

[27] The various combinations of legal requirements and voluntary agreements governing railway wages, however, in general permit weeks of longer than 40 hours before penalty overtime rates apply.

[28] See, e.g., J. Douglas Brown, "Dismissal Compensation in Defense Industries; a Proposal," *Proceedings of Academy of Political Science* (New York), vol. 19, No. 2, pp. 106-109 (Jan. 1941).

(c) Working Rules and Practices.—More than a little slack may also be found in private labor standards, including rules and practices concerning such matters as eligibility to work, methods of work and of payment, and standards of labor efficiency.[29] It will be recalled that "dilution" of skilled labor, together with other suspensions of trade union conditions, was a well-recognized contribution of British labor in 1914-18 and again in World War II; also that Canadian unions were co-operating with their government in this fashion. Here is implicit recognition of the principle enunciated above, that peacetime emphasis, as to many labor policies, must be reversed in a major defense effort. As long as the war emergency lasts, the great demand for labor which it creates makes old "job security" measures less needful than usual to trade unionists.

This aspect of wartime labor problems has been much less discussed in the United States than abroad. Although certain unions' restrictive practices were common knowledge in 1917-18, yet little if any attempt was made by the wartime public authorities—as they provided conditions favorable for union growth—to mitigate the zeal with which some unions pushed their old make-work rules into previously unorganized shops. So, also, in 1940-41, a few at least of our craft unions were resisting "dilution" of conventionally trained labor by recruits more quickly trained; some charged exorbitant fees for mere temporary working permits on closed-shop jobs; and among many unions there was still considerable resistance to any sort of wage incentive method. Apparently the Chicago hod-carriers still enforced their ban on ready-mixed concrete.[30]

Numerous enlightened American labor leaders, however, were dealing constructively with such matters. Especially did they discountenance exorbitant union fees. Toward influencing other leaders, however—particularly in local unions—progressive unionists needed the support of a better-informed public

---

[29] To a large extent the cause of the slack in public and private labor standards is the same: the fact and fear of unemployment and underemployment.

[30] The remarks on such matters by Thurman Arnold and others in *Fortune* Magazine's 9th Round Table (on Labor Policy and National Defense, published July 1941) are illuminating.

opinion. The Murray and Reuther plans, intended to utilize steel and automobile plants and labor more effectively, were welcome signs. President Murray's scheme seemed to utilize principles successfully applied in a number of the British (Whitley) industrial councils. Such joint councils might well explore ways and means, industry by industry, of accomplishing needed wartime productive readjustments; and one of their best services would be to keep impressed upon managements that the unions' private labor standards must be restored when peace comes, *unless other means, promising satisfactory job security, are then made effective.*

(d) **Labor Disputes.**—No extended argument is required to convince the reader that strikes are an important type of industrial slack. A wartime boom, like a peacetime boom, tends to make them more numerous by reason of brisk labor demand and rising prices; and probably the larger part of all wartime labor trouble is due to such factors as these.

Several special factors, however, were operative in the United States in 1940-41. One was the presence of Communists and other subversive elements in strategic union positions. The efforts of these people account for a sizable fraction of our working time lost in labor disputes, slow-downs, and other sabotage. Another source of strikes is the momentum of labor organizing campaigns; some unions grasp the opportunity to short-circuit the Wagner Act and establish themselves in hitherto unorganized plants by exercise of the strike weapon. And of perhaps greater significance than either of the above is the CIO-AFL rivalry. This leads to not a little "raiding"—to strikes and boycotts by unions which are not content with Labor Board elections, and it also spells weakened control by national unions over locals—since an AF of L local expelled from its national is often welcomed with open arms by a CIO national, or vice versa.

What is the *extent* of time lost by reason of labor disputes, especially in our defense industries? Over-all statistics of numbers of strikes, strikers, and striker-days idle lend themselves fairly well to optimistic interpretations; for instance, 1940's record was better than that of 1939, and vastly better than that of 1937. The strike rate ran higher in the earlier months of 1941 than in corresponding periods of 1940, but man-days lost by strikers were still only a small fraction of 1% of all man-days worked, and scarcely one-fourth as many as total man-days lost by industrial accidents.

Such optimistic calculations, however, disregard the unmeasurable amounts of man-days and efficiency lost, on account of strikes, by others than the strikers themselves. Partly due to the clever moves of subversive "labor leaders," defense industries have been especially plagued by strikes in strategic places. This point was thus expressed by R. W. Millar, President of Vultee Aircraft, Inc., in the *Fortune* Round Table:

> I am not quite receptive to these statistics about man-hours lost [through strikes] on percentage of the over-all. . . . In our contracts to make airplanes for this and the British government, we have six hundred subcontractors, suppliers of materials, parts, equipment and accessories. . . . The easiest thing for unprincipled strikers . . . to do to gum up the works is to pick one of those six hundred subcontractors. Now, if they pick off one of the six hundred, they probably are not only going to stop us, but a lot of other companies at the same fell swoop, and they can pick a relatively obscure company, a company that probably has very little chance of getting any public hearing or any public sympathy.

4. Toward More Rational Wage Policy and Practice.— These industrial slacks have been present in our own nation and others, as they reached for available sinews of war. There has also been evident determination among all classes to take up as much slack as possible. To be effective, this determination must be expressed through measures which give the various parties little reason to think their patriotism is being unfairly exploited. What wage policies conform best to these objectives? And how can such policies be implemented?

(a) Main Arguments on Policy Needed.—The foregoing parts of this chapter supply materials bearing upon the first of these questions. Our first task in this section is to summarize critically the views recently current as to what should be done about American wages during the war emergency; then we may ask how it is possible to make more rational policies effective in wartime.

The principal economic grounds upon which general wage advances are defended (in the earlier stages of rearmament) may be outlined somewhat as follows:[31]

ARGUMENTS FOR ENCOURAGING WAGE-RATE ADVANCES DURING WAR EMERGENCY

1. Living costs are rising, especially those of defense workers —who in many cases sustain special costs (such as moving and commuting to work) and uncertainties (as to how long job will last);

2. Most employers can afford to pay higher wages, because their profits have increased with fuller operation of plants;

3. Wage rises should not generally raise prices and cause inflation; for physical output per man-hour has been rising, year by year—causing unit wage costs to decline;

4. Sub-standard wage rates (particularly those below 40 cents an hour), however, should immediately be raised, even where such labor protection necessitates increase in prices of products;

5. Government should control prices, rents, profits—and see that outputs of civilian as well as war goods are increased;

6. The 40-hour week and 50% penalty rate for overtime should be retained, if only to assure work-sharing if a post-emergency slump develops; and

7. Industry-wide collective bargaining should develop much further, and should level up wage rates in each inter-regional industry.

---

[31] See, for example, files of *Labor's Monthly Survey* (AF of L) and of *Economic Outlook* (CIO); *Problems in Wage Adjustment* (Conference Board, 1941); and "Position on Wages"—leaflet of National Ass'n of Manufacturers, Dec. 1940.

Of course these economic points are buttressed by many other appeals, such as those based on the dismally poor livings still secured by millions of workers, and on the alleged fascist nature of any curtailment of labor weapons and tactics.

Facing about, we find the economic case for both voluntary and legal restraints upon wage-raising, during the war emergency, stated in some such terms as these:

Arguments for Discouraging Such Wage Advances

1. Rises in average weekly and hourly *earnings,* due to such factors as fuller employment, overtime rates, intensive training, more piece work, and the Walsh-Healey type of requirements meet but few reasonable objections, but increases of normal or straight-time wage *rates,* on jobs of given contents, should be conservative;

2. Recent profit rises are mostly out of sub-normal cellars, and are being rapidly cut off by special war taxes; and to adjust each company's wage rates to its own prosperity would mean too great diversity in rates between companies;

3. Output-per-man-hour statistics come more from the older, staple-commodity-producing industries than from newer and service-rendering industries; hence they exaggerate the rate of advance of total national production per man-hour—especially the rate in wartime (see 1917-20 data);

4. Minimum-wage rates of 40 cents or less (in 1940) should be advanced to keep pace with costs of such earners' living, including indirect defense taxation; but the attempt to advance *all* wage rates in full proportion to living costs, or faster, means inflation because it accentuates other tendencies for consumers' spending power to outrun the values (at present prices) of the supplies which can be made available for civilian consumption;

5. With labor costs left free to rise, price and rent controls are futile except as accompanied by sweeping bureaucratic rationing or drastic contributions in taxes and loans—or both;

6. The upward spiral tends to increase inequities among wage rates, thus to make more difficult the problems involved in demands for industry-wide wage determinations and leveling-up; and

7. After the war emergency, industry's operating rate will at best be considerably lower than now, and employment will be discouraged by inflexible high debts, taxes, and wage rates if price-wage inflation is allowed free rein.

Of the many issues thus suggested, the following seem most worthy of commentary here. The rapid climb of wage-earners' total incomes is symbolized by the advance of the USBLS index of factory payrolls, from slightly below 100 the first half of 1940 to 141.9 in May 1941. No satisfactory over-all measure of output of consumer goods and services is available, but comparisons of current and prospective rates of total national-income payments with rates of government expenditures for defense measure roughly the necessity for decreasing rather than increasing the output of civilian goods during the emergency.[32] To an important extent managements and workers can restrain inflation by supporting measures which divert increasing amounts of their rising money incomes into the government's hands for defense expenditures—for instance by buying bonds and arranging new contributions toward old-age annuities, dismissal wages, and extended unemployment benefits. Only by widespread voluntary restraints on consumption, prices, and costs, in addition to drastic new taxation, can the nation minimize obnoxious government rationing and allied regulations—and mounting demands for maximum-wage controls. Governmental price policies may also help to check this spiral, e.g., by restraint of monopolistic and other "profiteering,"

---

[32] For the calendar year 1940, our national income was officially estimated at $76 billion—which figure includes, probably, well under $5 billion of actual defense expenditures. By mid-1941, total "income payments" were running at the rate of about $85 billion a year; and prospects were that at the peak of war effort they would reach $100 billion or a little over (in dollars of 1940 purchasing power). But defense and lease-lend expenditures were rising still more rapidly. Indexes of production and trade of the Federal Reserve Bank of N. Y., July 1940 to July 1941, indicated a 56% increase in output of consumers' *durable* goods, but only a 19% gain in production of total consumers' goods.

and by giving employers no unnecessary margins for reckless wage advances.

(b) Implementing a National Labor Policy, by Mediation and Otherwise.—The foregoing paragraphs give an idea of the stuff from which wartime labor policy must be made. What sort of organization can best perform the tasks of framing and administering such policy? Naturally, we should take stock of the agencies already in being and of their respective activities; then attempt adaptation to wartime conditions. A summary report on such matters, made in mid-1941, for example, might read somewhat as follows:

Through their own military and civilian instrumentalities, the public authorities are becoming increasingly important employers; and ever more private concerns are made subject to Walsh-Healey and similar regulations, as they take government contracts. The federal and state wage-hour laws and commissions receive added responsibilities. The growing defense organizations, such as army, navy, and OPM continue to sprout labor-relations staffs and trouble-shooters; and the list of mediation and conciliation agencies tends to lengthen. The National Labor Relations Board combats employers' unfair practices, officially settles union representation disputes and in effect mediates some other disputes; several states operate somewhat similar boards. In the transportation labor field, we have the National Mediation Board, supervising a well-tried and generally satisfactory combination of what amounts to compulsory arbitration of disputes arising under voluntary agreements, and compulsory cooling-off of other disputes. The Conciliation Service of the U. S. Department of Labor is hitting on a lot of powerful cylinders. Uniform "stabilization" labor agreements have been secured among (e.g.) shipyards, providing for no strikes, standard wage scales to hold for six months, wage adjustments thereafter to material changes in living costs. The principal spotlight, however, now rests upon the National Defense Mediation Board.

As our labor, industrial, and political leaders cooperate for both study and action, the present machinery can be used much more effectively; yet some new organization and reorganization will also be expedient. The demand is now (1941) heard, especially from AF of L spokesmen, for more direct and responsible representation of *organizations* of both labor and capital on the chief policy-making board or boards.[33] Hitherto, *individuals* have been selected from these organizations—with more or less advice from their leaders; thus, John L. Lewis (for example) has felt free occasionally to denounce the Mediation Board as a strike-breaker. A national labor policies board, containing persons to be formally chosen for it by the principal labor and employer organizations (as well as public representation to be chosen by the President of the United States), it is reasonably argued, would not only better *reflect sentiments* of the people on the firing-line but—of more importance—it could make these organizations assume greater *responsibility for execution* of policies sponsored by the policy-making board. Feeling its way through vague commonplaces, it should strive to find workable solutions to such problems as what kinds of living-cost bonuses or wage advances are in the national interest —from both emergency and post-emergency points of view.

These functions can be performed by the National Defense Mediation Board, but less satisfactorily. That agency will continue to have its hands full of the most pressing issues involved in current *labor disputes*—many of these, at bottom, being controversies over wages. The Mediation Board, however, is the outstanding arm available for practical implementation of national labor policies. In its earlier months it made excellent progress, in the face of tremendous difficulties, notably the machinations of subversive labor elements and their momentary allies among American labor politicians. The Board has had to use whatever crude tools it could find, including use of military forces and rather generous wage increases. One of its worst handicaps, it would seem, is that each of the Board's distinguished members has too many other irons in the fire. Like the war or emergency industry boards, this agency's functions are of such vital importance that full-time personnel are needed

---

[33] This was an outstanding point in the Labor Policy Round Table, reported in *Fortune* Magazine, July 1941.

at the top. For a national labor *policies* board, on the other hand, part-time services of distinguished leaders like Messrs. Murray, Green, and Lewis are entirely appropriate.[34]

C. Suggestions on American Peacetime Wage Policy

In the peace succeeding the second World War, what recommendations on wage determination may be inferred from preceding pages of this book? Our burden of armaments seems unlikely soon to subside to pre-1939 levels; on the other hand, war is a great developer of technology and productive capacities. If our total resources are rationally used, the output should suffice for a resumption of steadily rising per capita real income. If this goal is to be achieved, we must avoid becoming too engrossed with either the income or the cost aspect of wages (and of various labor incomes, such as work-relief "wages," provided at public expense). Among the many significant trends noted above, let us choose these for recapitulation here: (1) public wage regulation; (2) determinants of relative earnings of individuals and (3) determinants of general real wages.

1. Future of Public Wage Regulation.—Within the first of these main trends, in turn, we may select four sub-trends, namely: wage-hour regulations, prevailing-wage laws, extensions of collective agreements, and public intervention on behalf of industrial peace. As with public actions generally, all these types have some undesirable tendencies on the score of increasing rigidity, red tape, the law's expense and delay, and numerous sorts of anti-social politics. We have here ample sphere for advice from a national labor policies board in peacetime. Thus far, however, the gains of labor incomes attributable to these four types of public wage control, even under peacetime condi-

---

[34] It is argued (e.g., by Hardy—*Wartime Control of Prices*, pp. 74 ff.), and apparently provided by the Canadian war labor policy, that wartime public control should be exercised over *all* large-scale collective bargaining, not merely over labor disputes. But the larger undertaking seems too difficult at the outset; moreover, a series of prompt and self-consistent settlements of disputes would soon exercise great influence over all voluntary agreements. See sec. C-1 below, on public supervision and enforcement of collective agreements, in peacetime.

tions, appear in each case to outweigh the strains they have imposed upon labor costs.

Authoritative determination of minimum-wage rates (for straight time and overtime) will long be experimental in many ways. The heritage of wartime inflation of prices, for instance, raises the question of automatic adjustment of minimum-wage rates to living costs. It is very desirable that workers in most intra-state industries should be covered by legal wage-hour standards; and by state acts, rather than by further legalistic stretching of the definition of interstate commerce. The 50% penalty wage, for the first hours over 40 in a week, represents an excessively simplified share-the-work philosophy. Sliding scales of penalty rates, rising as more hours over 40 are worked, would appear to exert sufficient pressure toward work-spreading during depression.

Prevailing-wage laws, with respect to public construction and contracts, have helped to sustain trade union power and wages of skilled workers in the past. Presumably they will continue to do so, despite the rise of other political agencies with the same tendencies, such as the Wagner Act and wage-hour legislation. Prevailing-wage and wage-hour laws should be coordinated, notably as to minimum rates and penalty schedules for overtime; and both types of legislation should afford more encouragement to plans to regularize employment and labor incomes in individual firms.

Public wage controls more novel to Americans are "extension of collective agreements" (i.e., legal enforcement of terms of work agreed to by unions and employers, if found in the public interest), and wage regulation incidental to regulation of labor disputes. The former is desired by many unions, and it can probably be best safeguarded from the standpoint of consumers and the general public if it is supervised by a continuing public tribunal which is occupied with problems of industrial peace.

By 1941 our public regulation of labor disputes in transportation industries was one promising germ of trends suggested in the preceding paragraph. Its extension to other important industries, with appropriate modifications, was often suggested for dealing with the numerous sources and types of labor warfare not adequately covered by the existing legislation. An alternative program was to broaden the scope of the Wagner Act, which already regulated many important phases of collective bargaining in all important industries save transportation, through the full-time National Labor Relations Board. By either of these routes comparatively comprehensive and consistent national policies might be developed and implemented—on wages and other labor affairs, such as "extension of collective agreements." But the NRA, the Guffey, and the Railway Labor Acts illustrate the persuasiveness of the argument: "Every industry is different" and needs independent machinery of its own. Here is an atmosphere in which pressure groups thrive with a minimum of effective representation of the consumer and general public interest. One great merit of both the NLRA and the national-labor-policies-board approaches is their common emphasis upon need of continuity and coordination of labor policies over all industries. Each new railway labor crisis, for example, should be handled by public authorities who have more assurance as to what is the long-term policy on wages and other bones of contention, not only in transport but in other industries.

In the peacetime before us, rights to strike and to lock out—even in various governmental agencies—will naturally be wider than during war; and crude anti-strike laws will be opposed by all sensible people. Nevertheless, these rights must be continuously modernized to keep pace with changing social conditions; new restraints must be put upon the economic powers of both labor and capital. Such restraints, to be effective, should not be predicated merely upon the public's need of continuity of operation of the industry. It should be based also—somewhat as in Australia and New Zealand—upon the availability of some competent and continuing as well as impartial agency to determine wage rates and other terms of employment.

2. Determinants of Relative Earnings of Individuals.— Resumption of peace allows more careful treatment of wage differentials, or comparisons of one person's earnings with another's. Such differences are innumerable; for instance, between the pay of men as compared with women, or between day and night shifts. But of outstanding importance are the two types of differences discussed briefly here : those connected with wage incentives and with degrees of skill. The first of these topics refers to piece work and other systems of payment by results, within the same occupation, while the second refers to occupational differentials. It may seem that these are quite distinct provinces ; also that people on "day work" are not concerned at all with wage incentives.

But progressive union leaders, as well as personnel specialists both public and private, realize that techniques of job analysis are fundamental to all these relations of work and pay. The day work man may, at any time, engage in a dispute with management over the reasonableness of the work load assigned to him or his group. Thus he, as well as the piece worker, needs a trusted representative who can audit the processes (time study, for example) used in the shop for determining standard labor efficiency. Such processes are often referred to as "job analysis," as are also those studies of occupational rates more commonly designated as "job evaluation." As management and labor become more familiar with uses and limitations of these job studies, it is nearly certain that the sphere of payment of individuals according to their merits will be greatly extended. Some steps in this expansion are these : When labor efficiency standards are based upon more careful research by management, audited by labor, the employer is more willing and able to pay in full proportion to the worker's efficiency, and less disposed to try to use some "bonus curve" which increases earnings (beyond standard achievement) at a lesser rate than the worker's output. Such research, moreover—accumulating records of "elemental times," merit ratings, and so forth—tends to make headway against the obstacles of increasing tempo of work and of technical change, as well as numerous other sources of variability in job conditions.

Union attitudes toward methods of industrial efficiency, of course, are greatly affected by their prevailing theories as to how they may best deal with the menaces of unemployment, underemployment, and skill displacement. Thus, employers may utilize measures for reducing these latter fears, to "sell" wage incentive methods. Unions can often bargain in the opposite direction.

Job evaluation amounts, in part, to continuous refinement of older methods of wage surveying. It tends to make wage quotations or statistics more meaningful, by stating more definitely in each case for what work each wage is paid, keeping occupational vocabularies abreast of changing methods of work, training, and types and degrees of skill. It is also, in part, applied economic theory on wage differences and reasons therefor. Thus, it supplements and makes more meaningful the confusing ranges of "prevailing rates" revealed in most wage surveys.

3. Determinants of General Real Wages.—The factors in *relative* earnings are also important for *general* trends of real wages. Incentive methods, for instance, obviously affect total labor efficiency, which sets one limit to total labor income. And, under individual competitive conditions, the efforts of practical people would be largely restricted to bargaining in terms of prevailing rates. If such competition were well-informed, moreover, and labor and capital sufficiently mobile, wage and price flexibility would doubtless prevent the rate of unemployment from reaching the levels we experienced in the 1930's. But as we move toward increasingly large-scale collective wage determination, the rates prevailing "outside" become less significant; other criteria more important. Among the latter, cost of living, industrial productivity and profits, and unemployment are outstanding.

In Australia and New Zealand, highly centralized public control of wages over many years has pegged weekly money-wage rates to living-cost indexes. Thus real wages per hour rose as the work week was shortened; moreover, non-wage labor incomes (social services) were advanced by taxation. Other nations displayed trends similar in type: rising real *hourly* earnings, shortening work week, and growing "social wages." It is doubtful whether labor efficiency per hour can be much further raised by shortening hours (below 40 per week); hence, we cannot count on indefinite continuance of the trends just mentioned. The living-cost index alone, anyhow, is clearly an inadequate guide for practical adjustment of wages or labor costs, however these are calculated.

Indexes of productivity and of wage-paying capacity promise to become increasingly valuable additional criteria. The trend of physical output per man-hour in a single industry, however, is not by itself a very significant guide. This trend is affected by many other factors besides wage labor; and it is in the interest of wage earners in general that each progressive industry should lower prices and increase employment, rather than keep for itself the chief benefits of its progress. Indexes of output of the various industrial fields, together with concurrent national-income estimates, supply much better indications of the total wage-paying capacity of the nation. Within each industry, too, empirical ratios based upon other operating and financial data, such as dollar-volume of sales, are likely to be useful but crude tests of the reasonableness of the firm's total wage payments.

In what chief ways may wage policy influence rates of unemployment, in the present world of imperfect competition? On this crucial question few widely-accepted conclusions emerge when economists are laid end to end; but the following inferences (among others) may reasonably be drawn. Adjustment of wages mainly by reference to the current rate of profit of the firm or of the industry may become anti-social for reasons cited above in connection with physical productivity—flourishing industries have a social obligation to reduce prices and increase employment, which they cannot do if too much of their prosperity is shared between the labor and other factors already employed in the firm or industry. Here is an important limit to the merit of the wage-paying-capacity principle—which, however, is acceptable in the form of moderate temporary variations of earnings (of labor and of capital) in accord with the current prosperity of any firm or industry, as means toward optimum employment in that industry. For this purpose the old type of sliding wage scales, geared merely to a few key prices, may be replaced by profit-sharing bonuses and scales based upon financial data published by leading firms in the industry. It should be recognized, however, that the firms publishing profit-and-loss data are, on the average, distinctly more prosperous than others; in many ways the trends shown by income-tax statistics relating to *all* corporations are more significant. As Professor Slichter argues, the prospect of pay-checks for capital is an important factor in rate of employment; and the number of companies operating in the red affords a rough index of this prospect.

The social obligation just mentioned implies one desirable type of downward price flexibility, yet flexibility of wage rates and prices is far from a panacea for unemployment. Apart from practical difficulties in thawing them out, stabilized costs and prices have (within limits) many merits; besides, the dangers of downward spirals in depression must be considered. Plausible arguments also are made to the effect that suitable money and banking policy could waft the price level slowly upward indefinitely, making nearly everyone optimistic because his money income is rising—even though his costs are sometimes rising more.

With due allowance for such limitations, there remain important reasons why a certain amount of wage flexibility—in the sense of practical possibility of *some downward* adjustments— is desirable. In certain seasonal employments, for example, reduction of hourly earnings may be necessary in order to effectuate increasing annual labor incomes by steadier employment. Reduction of this type of particular unemployment might make a considerable dent in cyclical and general unemployment. Another reason why labor should not insist too strongly that wage rates should never be reduced is that an employer is more likely to grant an advance, if he knows it will not be too difficult to secure a readjustment if sustained business adversity develops. Finally, "stabilized" prices and wages are rightly suspected as symptoms of monopolistic or other restrictive powers of the group. Restraint upon entry of capital or labor, and of "overproduction," may be profitable to monopolistic groups so long as they are few; but the multiplication of such groups is destructive of labor as of all other real incomes. As a long-term program, labor organizations will do well to submit gracefully to an increasing amount of public regulation of their activities, if only for the sake of insisting upon repression of monopolistic-restrictive tactics in other pressure groups.

Per capita public expenditures are likely to continue to increase—e.g., for social services, including the training and placing of the unemployed and old-age assistance, also for aids to distressed industries and areas, and for national defense. Unless the rate of unemployment can be cut considerably below the level of the 1930's, it is difficult to see how the productive industries can furnish taxes to sustain such public expenditures—and also can advance the level of real wages per annum.[35]

D. Summary

Attention was given above especially to the rôles played, in wartime policies affecting wages, by four matters: reemployment, public labor standards (notably on wages and hours), private standards (especially on working rules), and labor disputes. All these contain considerable amounts of industrial slack, and are thus potential resources for increased total production. But, since defense demands are so heavy, civilian goods supplies cannot be increased, at least in the measure of increasing payroll disbursements. Thus, average real earnings per hour must fall during a great war emergency, though annual real earnings per family may increase with fuller employment, upgrading, and overtime. To counteract the many forces tending to produce inflationary rise in prices, wages, and labor disputes, efforts are made both to increase civilian supplies and to divert civilian incomes, by war loans and by new taxes, some of which may later return to the payers in dismissal compensation or other credits and thus help to cushion the economic post-war disturbances.

As these post-war disturbances are overcome, prospects brighten for resumption of the upward trend of average real-

---

[35] Social security payments will constitute a great force tending to stabilize consumer spending in the future; and much, if not most, of this system can be financed without long-term excesses of public expenditure over tax income. Also, as a gradually increasing rôle of governmental agencies in the production and distribution of essentials such as transportation, power, insurance, and housing becomes accepted as normal, public works in these fields (as well as in the older fields symbolized by schools and other public buildings) can doubtless be planned to counteract business depression in such fashion as to arouse less fear of uncontrolled inflationary deficit financing than was aroused by the pump-priming and other works programs of the 1930's.

labor incomes—no small part of which may be through public social services rather than the pay envelope. Public wage regulation is likely to advance and become better coordinated, in part through an agency or agencies which regulate wages as a means of minimizing industrial disputes. If real incomes throughout the population are to be increased, it is also necessary that wages should be adjusted not merely with reference to cost of living or physical output in the particular industry. General productivity per capita must be pushed upward, in part by wage incentives and in part by wage policies which assist in minimizing unemployment.

INDEX

Ability of industry to pay (See "Profits," "Wage-paying capacity")
Acceleration principle, 343, 367n
Action, types of, in collective wage determination, 14-16
Adamson Act, 20, 471n
Age,
and sex groups, re labor supplies, 91-93
as wage factor, 51f
Agencies,
gathering wage-hour statistics, 57f
in collective wage determinations, 14-16
Agriculture,
in the gainful population, 3
incomes and opportunities in, compared with urban industries, 410, 411, 507, 508, 558-560
wage regulation in, 472, 495, 564-566
wages and salaries as per cent of income produced, 177-179
Aircraft industry, 306f
Alignment of wage rates (chart), 252
Amalgamated Clothing Workers, 380, 437, 449
American Federation of Labor (AFL), 203, 208, 220, 256, 276, 288, 378, 382, 396, 605, 611
American wage-hour structure,
distortion, by flat additions, 261
outline (statistical) of, 43f
real wage rates since 1890, 121
Amulree, Lord, 448n, 465n
Anderson, G., 491n
Annual earnings (See also "Wage rates and earnings")
in automotive industry, 47, 48
of families, in wartime, 596f
of government and private workers, 530f
of railroad workers, 42, 49-51
re wage-hour laws, 283f, 554
statistics of, general, 41f
Annual wage plans, 283f

Anthracite Board of Conciliation, 459
Apprenticeship, 386f
Arbitration, 18f, 441f
compulsory, 484f, 548n (wage boards), 581f (wartime)
essentials of, 442, 443
evaluation of methods, 452f
impartial chairman, 385 (hosiery), 451
in New York printing, 206
judicial vs. legislative applications, 449
note on American series, 459
types,
of arbitration, 445f
of machinery, 451f
Areas of wage rates, 407f
Arnold, Thurman, 94n, 576, 604n
Association of American Railroads, 383
Australia,
advancing wage rates to check boom, 140
annual indexes of money and real wages, 119
child endowment (family allowance), 467
compulsory arbitration and other public wage regulation, 22-24, 468, 488f, 496 (cf. with N. Z.)
Harvester case wage, 187, 188, 492f
historical correlations, wage and unemployment rates, 359, 363, 509n
production index considered as guide in wage fixing, 173
protective tariffs and wages, 552n
significance re wage flexibility, 563
variations in living costs among cities, 128
living wage vs. wage-paying capacity, 187, 188
stabilization of real wage rates, 135, 563, 564
wage history and policy since 1918, 505f

Clark, Colin, 164n
Classification,
of industry sections, under FLSA,
479n, 575f
of workers by competence, within
occupations,
re job evaluation, 243, 244, 257,
263
union attitudes on, 404f
Cleveland Trust Co., 203n, 585n
Closed shop, 386f
in N. Z., 497
Clothing industry, 328, 380, 449
unions and production standards,
437-439
Coal (See "Mining")
Cobb-Douglas function, 81f
Cole, G. D. E., 395n, 405n
Collective agreements (i. e., union
"contracts")
enforcement of, 386, 418, 421n,
455f
extension of, 15, 485, 497, 613, 614
general place in wage determination, 17, 18, 375f
Hart, Schaffner & Marx of 1916,
449
salient features of, 380f
wage terms, in relation to other
controversial matters, 25f
Collective bargaining, 269, 375f (See
also "Collective agreements,"
"Collective wage determination,"
"Unions")
areas of, 381
forms retained, in Italy and Russia, 515, 516
in wage theory, 101
present-day, re production methods
and standards, 425f
spread of, 4
types discussed, 15f
wage boards claimed form of, 548f
Collective wage determination (See
also "Arbitration," "Collective
bargaining," "Public wage regulation")
agencies and types of action, 14f,
443
and industrial peace, 22-24, 442f
aspects studied, 6-8
goals and criteria of, 108-110, 193,
546, 547
in totalitarian nations, 511f
relation to awards and agreements,
489n

Collective wage determination—
Continued
spread of, 4-6
tendencies re flexibility, 541, 561f
variables and patterns in (voluntary and authoritative), 15
Color, as wage factor, 51f
Common rule, 497 (See also "Standards, labor")
Commons, John R., 397n, 416n
Commonwealth (of Australia) Arbitration Court (and Reports),
490f
Communist Party, 511f, 605 (See
also "Russia")
Comparative wage trends, 232
Compensation of employees, in national income, 176f
Competition,
advantage of section of industry,
575
and custom, 32
from other industries, 282
imperfect, 31f, 93f, 98 (chart),
301f, 313 (railroads), 617
international and interregional,
293f, 318f, 411n, 575
perfect, and wage theory, 75f
"sets the payroll," 155 (printing)
Compulsory arbitration (See also
"Public wage regulation")
in Australia and New Zealand,
488f; criticisms of, 499f
Compulsory war loans, 587f
Conciliation, 18, 443f (See also
"Mediation," "Arbitration")
Congress of Industrial Organizations
(CIO), 207, 221, 256, 276, 378,
382, 588, 589, 605
Conscription, 581f
Consumer and general public interest, 171, 298f, 543 (See also
"Prices," "Restrictive policies")
Consumers' goods,
and cycles of employment, 344f
output of, in wartime, 584f
Contracts, union (See "Collective
agreements," "Collective bar-
gaining")
Cooke, Morris L., and Murray,
Philip, 328n, 329n, 436n
Cooperation (See also "Union-man-
agement cooperation")
hosiery shops, 211n
productive, in profit sharing movement, 219